THE WORLD HITLER NEVER MADE

What if the Nazis had triumphed in World War II? What if Adolf Hitler had escaped Berlin for the jungles of Latin America in 1945? What if Hitler had become a successful artist instead of a politician? Gavriel D. Rosenfeld's pioneering study explores why such counter-factual questions on the subject of Nazism have proliferated in recent years within Western popular culture. Examining a wide range of novels, short stories, films, television programs, plays, comic books, and scholarly essays that have appeared in Great Britain, the United States, and Germany since 1945, Rosenfeld shows how the portrayal of historical events that *never* happened reflects the evolving memory of the Third Reich's real historical legacy. He concludes that the shifting representation of Nazism in works of alternate history, as well as the popular reactions to them, highlights their subversive role in promoting the normalization of the Nazi past in Western memory.

GAVRIEL D. ROSENFELD is Associate Professor of History at Fairfield University (Connecticut). He is a specialist in the history and memory of the Third Reich and the Holocaust. His previous publications include *Munich and Memory: Architecture, Monuments, and the Legacy of the Third Reich* (2000).

THE WORLD HITLER NEVER MADE

Alternate History and the Memory of Nazism

GAVRIEL D. ROSENFELD

CAMBRIDGE
UNIVERSITY PRESS

CAMBRIDGE UNIVERSITY PRESS
Cambridge, New York, Melbourne, Madrid, Cape Town,
Singapore, São Paulo, Delhi, Tokyo, Mexico City

Cambridge University Press
The Edinburgh Building, Cambridge CB2 8RU, UK

Published in the United States of America by Cambridge University Press, New York

www.cambridge.org
Information on this title: www.cambridge.org/9781107402751

First published 2005
First paperback edition 2011

A catalogue record for this publication is available from the British Library

ISBN 978-0-521-84706-3 Hardback
ISBN 978-1-107-40275-1 Paperback

Contents

PART III HYPOTHETICAL HOLOCAUSTS

List of illustrations

Acknowledgments

One evening while nearing the completion of this study, I was finishing dinner at a Chinese restaurant in midtown Manhattan when I opened a fortune cookie and read the message: "It's not helpful to wonder what might have been." Had I taken such an admonition to heart, I never would have been able to finish this book. But I also never would have done so without the assistance of numerous persons and institutions.

I would like to thank Fairfield University for a third-year sabbatical grant, which provided me with a semester free of teaching that enabled me to complete an important portion of my research and writing. Special thanks go to my department chair, David McFadden, for steadfastly supporting my research proposals, to Harold Forsythe for passing along several tips on sources, and to Cecelia Bucki and Patricia Behre-Miskimin for patiently indulging my own speculations in the department hallway. I would also like to thank the students in my upper-level seminar on alternate history, all of whom contributed to my understanding of the subject. I owe a special debt of gratitude to John Cayer, the director of Fairfield's DiMenna-Nyselius Library's interlibrary loan office, who was unfailingly helpful in securing obscure source material and always a joy to chat with. And finally, I would like to thank Peter Sarawit at the media center for helping me to produce digital images from VHS tapes for many of the book's illustrations.

I am also grateful to scholars at other institutions. Particular thanks go to Alon Confino, Saul Friedländer, Paul Miller, and Eugene Sheppard, who read various portions of the manuscript and offered perceptive comments that helped me refine my thoughts. I would especially like to thank my father, Alvin Rosenfeld, for his careful copyediting and thoughtful stylistic suggestions. Thanks also go to Volker Berghahn, Noel Cary, Marion Deshmukh, Alexandra Garbarini, Jeffrey Herf, Wulf Kansteiner, Michael Rothberg, Kristin Semmens, and Denise Youngblood, for participating in conference panels at which selected chapters from the book were presented.

I am grateful to the American Historical Association, the German Studies Association, and the Association for Jewish Studies, for permitting me to present portions of my research at the organizations' annual conferences. Thanks also to Vicki Caron and Cornell University, as well as Jonathan Petropoulos, John Roth, and Claremont McKenna College for inviting me to speak on my research. I would also like to thank Peter Baldwin, Paula Hyman, Ned Lebow, Peter Mandler, Gary Kenneth Peatling, Dirk Rupnow, Jeffrey Weidlinger, and Jay Winter for providing answers to questions that arose during the course of research and writing, and for their general interest in my work.

In conducting the research for this book it was a real pleasure to come into contact and exchange ideas with the producers of the sources themselves. My most grateful thanks go to writers Jesse Bier, Michel Choquette, Christian v. Ditfurth, David Dvorkin, Al Franken, Gary Goss, Richard Grayson, Joseph Heywood, Brad Linaweaver, Arno Lubos, E. M. Nathanson, Kamran Pasha, Hans Pleschinski, Craig Raine, Arthur Rhodes, Leo Rutman, Norman Spinrad, Sabine Wedemeyer-Schwiersch, Len Wein, and Thomas Ziegler for offering personal insights into their own work. Thanks to playwright Robert Krakow for sending me both video and print copies of his play, *The False Witness*, and to scholars Adrian Gilbert, John Lukacs, Bruce Russett, Hugh Thomas, and Henry Turner for responding to various questions of mine.

Writing this book has also been a gratifying experience insofar as it has confirmed the old adage about the "comfort of strangers." In the course of my research I cast countless inquiries out into the heavily populated void of cyberspace like so many digitized messages in a bottle, hoping they would be found and answered. I was extremely gratified that numerous individuals, all unknown to me beforehand, responded with generosity and provided indispensable assistance by sending me copies of source material and answering tough questions. They include: Bill Black and Mark Heike of AC Comics for sending me a photocopy of the comic book *T-Man*, Issue Nr. 34 from 1956; Nick Cooper for sending me extremely rare tapes of *An Englishman's Castle*, as well as helpful information about Giles Cooper; Sean Delaney at the British Film Institute for sending me hard-to-find reviews of *The Other Man*, *An Englishman's Castle*, and *Night Conspirators*; Ida Heissenbüttel for faxing me reviews of her late husband's work; and Mark Squirek for generously sending me a scan of the 1950 *Strange Adventures* tale, "The Strange Fate of Adolph Hitler." I received other reviews from Frjthoff Müller of the *Süddeutsche Zeitung*, John Knowles of the Noël Coward Society, Matthias Seeberg at *Konkret* magazine, Beate

Volkenrath at the Institut für Zeitungsforschung in Dortmund, Monika Klein at the Innsbrücker Zeitungsarchiv, Esther-Beatrice von Bruchhausen at Eichborn Verlag, Friedel Wahren and Martina Geissler at the Lektorat Science Fiction/Fantasy, Sascha Mamczak at Heyne Verlag, Anne Zauner at the Dokumentationsstelle für neuere österreichische Literatur, Ray Russell at Tartarus Press, and the Science Fiction Versand Wolfgang Kratz. I am also grateful to Max Brooks for background information on *Saturday Night Live*. Finally, Anna Charin, Eli Eshed, Barton Hacker, Charles Mitchell, and Robert Schmunk were helpful in responding to various questions of mine.

I benefited not merely from helpful strangers, however, but also good friends who provided assistance at various stages of my research and writing. I would like to thank Melissa Clark for sending me a videotape of the *Twilight Zone* episode, "Cradle of Darkness"; Johannes Schmidt for sending me a copy of the hard-to-find film, *Conversation with the Beast*; and Felix Singer for providing technical help in producing additional digital images from VHS tapes for some of the book's illustrations. Thanks also go to Miranda Banks and Sidney Rosenfeld for assisting me with several thorny research questions. Finally, longtime colleagues Dani Eshet, Josh Goode, Ethan Kleinberg, Dave McBride, and Adam Rubin deserve mention for providing years of loyal friendship and intellectual camaraderie.

It is a pleasure to express my gratitude to the wonderful staff at Cambridge University Press for their assistance in bringing the present volume into existence. Michael Watson was unfailingly helpful in responding to my countless questions and in facilitating the editing and production process. Elizabeth Davey provided timely advice and was extremely resourceful in securing the rights to reproduce many of the book's images. Isabelle Dambricourt, likewise, was very helpful coordinating much of the publication process. Christopher Jackson deserves special thanks for his meticulous copy-editing. And I would also like to thank the two anonymous readers who offered many worthwhile suggestions and encouraged me with their enthusiasm for the manuscript.

For obvious reasons I cannot offer any personal thanks to the internet, but I owe it a substantial debt of gratitude for enabling me to conduct an enormous amount of the research for this project. Indeed, I sometimes wonder whether I would have been able to write this study at all without its existence. My family, in particular, is thankful that this wonderful research tool enabled me to conduct much of my work at home instead of having to take long trips out of town. That being said, I did make several research visits to various archives and libraries, where I completed research the old-fashioned way – by carefully reading through it. I would like to acknowledge the many helpful individuals at these institutions, in particular, Volker Kaukoreit and Peter Seda at the Österreichisches Literaturarchiv in Vienna, as well as the library staffs at the Academy of Motion Pictures' Center for Motion Picture Study in Beverly Hills, California, the University of California at Los Angeles's Young Research Library, Loyola Marymount University's Von der Ahe Library, Cornell University's Low Library, Columbia University's Butler Library, Yale University's Sterling Library, and Indiana University's Lilly Library.

Finally, I owe more than just a word of thanks to my family. My wife, Erika Banks, patiently listened to me expound upon my theories of alternate history in their roughest form and made the ultimate sacrifice by sitting through portions of the film *They Saved Hitler's Brain*. My children, Julia and Benjamin, meanwhile, were always eager to offer welcome respites from the long hours of research and writing. For providing the love and emotional support that only a family can, I dedicate this work to them.

Introduction

The streets on the way back into central Berlin seemed unnaturally quiet, and when [detective Xavier] March reached Werdescher-Markt, he discovered the reason. A large notice board in the foyer announced there would be a government statement at 4:30 ... He was just in time ...

How many of these events could March remember? ... In '38, he had been called out of his classroom to hear that ... Austria had returned to the Fatherland ...

He had been at sea for the next few broadcasts. Victory over Russia in the spring of '43 – a triumph for the Führer's strategic genius! ...

Peace with the British in '44 – a triumph for the Führer's counter-intelligence genius! ...

Peace with the Americans in '46 – a triumph for the Führer's scientific genius! When America had defeated Japan by detonating an atomic bomb, the Führer had sent a V-3 rocket to explode in the skies over New York to prove he could retaliate in kind if struck. After that, the war had dwindled to ... a nuclear stalemate the diplomats called the cold war.[1]

British novelist Robert Harris's description of a Nazi-dominated Europe after World War II in his international bestseller, *Fatherland* (1992), provides probably the best-known example of an unusual and increasingly prominent way in which the experience of Nazism has come to shape the Western imagination. Harris's novel is a work of "alternate history," a counterfactual mode of narrative representation that, in recent years, has been applied with striking frequency to the subject of the Third Reich. Since the end of World War II, and particularly in the last generation, numerous alternate histories of the Third Reich have appeared in Great Britain, the United States, Germany, and elsewhere in the form of novels, short stories, films, television broadcasts, plays, comic books, and historical essays. These diverse works have explored an equally diverse range of questions: What if the Nazis had won World War II? What if Adolf

I

Hitler had escaped from Nazi Germany in 1945 and gone into hiding in the jungles of South America? What if Hitler had been assassinated or had never been born? What if the Holocaust had been completed or could somehow be undone? Such counterfactual questions may initially strike us as absurd, even pointless. But they have been posed by an astonishingly varied range of people and appeared in a dizzying array of venues. Alternate histories on the subject of Nazism have been produced by high-brow writers like Philip Roth, prodigious mass-market novelists such as Harry Turtledove, playwrights like Noël Coward, politicians such as Newt Gingrich, filmmakers like Armin Mueller-Stahl, and historians such as John Lukacs. "What if?" scenarios involving the Third Reich have been featured in American television shows like *The Twilight Zone, Saturday Night Live*, and *Star Trek*, satirical journals like *National Lampoon* and *The Onion*, comic books like *Strange Adventures* and *The Justice League of America,* and innumerable internet web sites. The list is an eclectic one. But it demonstrates a clear trend: speculating about alternate outcomes to the Nazi era has become a notable phenomenon in Western popular culture.

What explains the growing tendency to wonder how the history of the Third Reich might have turned out differently? My interest in this question dates back over a decade to the year 1993 when I – like millions of readers around the same time – picked up a copy of Robert Harris's novel *Fatherland,* in my case to bring along for "light" reading on a research trip to Germany. I must confess that my encounter with *Fatherland* was hardly a transformative experience. Reading it was entertaining, but the novel hardly converted me into an avid fan of alternate history. In the early 1990s, as Europeans and Americans were fervently marking the fiftieth anniversary of the pivotal events of World War II, my attention was largely focused on how the Germans were coming to terms with the *real* historical legacy of the Third Reich half a century after its collapse. Nevertheless, in the ensuing years my interest in alternate history gradually, if imperceptibly, grew. Ironically enough, the reason was not so much my already strong interest in the past as my increasing fascination with the present. During the second half of the 1990s, the information revolution hit the mainstream and I, like so many others, became more and more intrigued with the internet and the new culture it was spawning. As I grappled with the concept of "cyberspace" and became aware of the blurring boundaries between the real and the imagined, I became reacquainted with the work of Philip K. Dick, a writer who was being celebrated for having anticipated the rise of a virtual world.[2] I had read Dick's classic novel depicting a Nazi victory in World War II, *The Man in the High Castle,* some years earlier, but only now began to see it from a new perspective. Soon enough, I recognized Dick's connection to Harris, and then to other counterfactual texts I had read long before by such disparate figures as William Shirer, Ralph Giordano, and George Steiner. Finally, thanks to the world wide web, I learned that my nascent object of interest was shared by others and that it had a name – alternate history.

As I immersed myself in the field of alternate history and learned of the surprisingly large number of counterfactual narratives that had been produced on the subject of Nazism, I became convinced that it represented a significant trend. I was especially encouraged in this belief after I realized that the phenomenon of alternate history was hardly new, but rather a relatively well-established genre. As far back as World War II, and then throughout the postwar era, a wide range of Europeans and Americans had been prompted to produce highly elaborate counterfactual narratives about the Third Reich. This compulsion had intensified in the last generation, I recognized, but it was hardly unprecedented. In reflecting upon these facts, I became curious about a variety of related questions: What set of motivations or concerns had led people over the years to wonder "what if?" with respect to the Nazi era? How had they imagined that the world might have been different? What explained the growth of such accounts in recent years? Finally, and most importantly, what did alternate histories reveal about the evolving place of the Nazi past in Western memory? My long-time interest in the shifting status of the Nazi legacy in postwar consciousness made this question the most intriguing of all. In setting out to write this study, therefore, I decided to focus on the various ways in which alternate history could help shed light upon the subject of historical memory.

In the process of researching and writing this book, however, I was surprised to encounter deep-seated resistance to alternate history as a genre worthy of serious study. Scholars of alternate history commonly lament the lack of respect for their subject. Yet the genre's growing prominence had led me to assume that such opposition had waned. Personal experience taught me otherwise. At conferences where I spoke about alternate history, more than a few prominent scholars raised epistemological, methodological, and even moral objections to it. Some argued that since history deals solely with the description and interpretation of events that really happened, exploring what *might have happened but never did* amounted to little more than idle speculation based on sheer fancy or wishful thinking. Others expressed skepticism about the value of examining works of popular culture, insisting that they were of inferior quality compared with works of high culture, that they were of marginal relevance, and that they were therefore unworthy of serious consideration. I suspect that the moralistic undertones to these objections, finally, were due to the fact that the particular alternate histories in question focused on the highly sensitive subject of the Third Reich. Several scholars expressed qualms about giving attention to narratives whose unconventional conclusions about the Nazi past they regarded as impious, at best, and dangerously revisionist, at worst. Such works, they insisted, should simply be ignored as the rantings of the lunatic fringe.

As I hope to show in the pages that follow, however, all of these objections fail to appreciate alternate history's significance as an important cultural phenomenon and overlook its unique ability to provide insights into the dynamics of remembrance. In writing *The World Hitler Never Made*, I hope to convince readers of alternate history's legitimacy as a subject of scholarly inquiry and persuade them that examining tales of what never happened can help us understand the memory of what did.

THE RISE OF ALTERNATE HISTORY

Understanding the appearance of alternate histories of Nazism requires understanding alternate history itself.[3] As a genre of narrative representation, alternate history resists easy classification. It transcends traditional cultural categories, being simultaneously a sub-field of history, a sub-genre of science fiction, and a mode of expression that can easily assume literary, cinematic, dramatic, or analytical forms.[4] At the most basic level, however, tales of alternate history – or what have been termed "allohistorical" or "uchronian" narratives – investigate the possible consequences of "what if" questions within specific historical contexts.[5] What if Jesus had escaped crucifixion? What if Columbus had never discovered the New World? What if the South had won the American Civil War? In posing and answering such questions, alternate histories assume a variety of different narrative forms. Those produced by historians and other scholars usually take the form of sober analytical essays, while those produced by novelists, filmmakers, and playwrights assume a more overtly fictional form through the use of such familiar narrative devices as plot development, setting, and character portrayal.[6] What links such "analytical" and "fictional" alternate histories is their exploration of how the alteration of some variable in the historical record would have changed the overall course of historical events. The inclusion of this element – often called a "point of divergence" – is what distinguishes alternate history from other related genres, such as historical fiction. Alternate history, to be sure, is far from monolithic and has various narrative cousins, some of which, such as "secret histories" and "future histories," I have included in this study.[7] Without getting bogged down by complex taxonomical distinctions, however, alternate histories are essentially defined by an "estranging" rather than a mimetic relationship to historical reality.[8]

As a genre of narrative representation, alternate history is an age-old phenomenon. Indeed, it traces its roots back to the origins of Western historiography itself. No less a figure than the Greek historian Herodotus speculated about the possible consequences of the Persians defeating the Greeks at Marathon in the year 490 B.C.E., while the Roman historian Livy wondered how the Roman empire would have fared against the armies of Alexander the Great.[9] Ever since antiquity, the posing of counterfactual questions has constituted an implicit, if underacknowledged, component of historical thought, helping historians establish causal connections and draw moral conclusions in interpreting the past.[10] Yet, with the rise of modern "scientific" historiography in the nineteenth century, allohistorical reasoning became stigmatized as empirically unverifiable and was banished to the realm of lighthearted cocktail party conversations and parlor games.[11] As a result, alternate history slowly migrated to the field of imaginative literature. It is no coincidence that the first allohistorical novels appeared in the mid-nineteenth century, most notably Charles Renouvier's *Uchronie* (1876), which lent the genre one of its defining terms.[12] Up through the first half of the early twentieth century, both fictional and analytical alternate histories appeared largely in scattered pulp science fiction magazines and scholarly anthologies.[13] On the whole, the genre remained fairly marginalized, known only to a handful of ardent practitioners.

Since the end of World War II, and especially since the 1960s, however, alternate history has gained both in popularity and respectability.[14] The mass media's recognition of alternate history as a contemporary phenomenon in the late 1990s is the most obvious indication of this trend.[15] But this new attention is itself the result of the even more notable increase in the publication of alternate history novels and short story collections.[16] Further evidence of alternate history's new status is provided by the fact that the writers of allohistorical novels no longer hail exclusively from science fiction circles but also from the cultural mainstream.[17] The proliferation of alternate history web sites, meanwhile, reflects the genre's popularity among the general public.[18] Overall, however, the best evidence for the increased acceptance of alternate history has been its embrace by the academic community, which has demonstrated a growing interest in the subject with a variety of recent publications.[19] Especially as the most skeptical academics of all – historians – have slowly begun to set aside their longtime reservations about the field, it is likely that alternate history will continue to gain in prominence and respectability.

It is, fittingly enough, still a matter of speculation why the fascination with alternate history has grown in recent years, but it seems to be the byproduct of broader political and cultural trends. To begin with, the new prominence of alternate history reflects the progressive discrediting of political ideologies in the West since 1945. In insisting that everything in the past could have been different, in stressing the role of contingency in history, and in emphasizing the open-endedness of historical change, alternate history is inherently anti-deterministic.[20] It is no coincidence that the upsurge in allohistorical thinking has taken place in an era where deterministic political ideologies have come under unprecedented attack from the political right, left, and center. The emergence of our post-ideological age began in the immediate aftermath of World War II, when rightwing intellectuals, eager to distance themselves from the failure of fascism, proclaimed the dawning of a new era of "posthistory."[21] By the late 1960s, leftwing intellectuals, chastened by the failure of socialist radicalism in Western Europe, helped further to erode the authority of political ideologies by establishing the foundation for the postmodern movement's rejection of all totalizing "metanarratives" in the 1970s.[22] Finally, the end of the cold war and the collapse of communism in the late 1980s prompted the belief among liberals that humankind had reached the end point of its ideological evolution and, indeed, had reached "the end of history" itself.[23]

The end of ideological struggle has promoted the rise of allohistorical thinking in diverse ways. Paradoxically, such thinking has been advanced by a simultaneous increase in both confidence and insecurity since the end of the cold war. On the one hand, by declaring liberalism victorious, the end of ideological struggle initially gave many in the West the security to reconsider whether our present-day world was indeed inevitable or whether other outcomes – once thought too frightening to consider – were ever possible. It is only since the threats of fascism and communism have been eliminated that historians have begun to reconsider whether liberalism's twentieth-century triumph over them had to occur as it did.[24] On the other hand, by opening up new ways for history to get "restarted" again, the end of ideological struggle has made us painfully aware of the open-ended nature of historical development. The end of the cold war has produced new worries in the West – about resurgent nationalism, religious fundamentalism, environmental destruction, and, most recently, global terrorism – that have contributed to an atmosphere of renewed insecurity. In our current transitional era, in which the future is less clear than ever, we recognize that nothing is inevitable at all.[25]

Closely tied to the death of political ideologies in promoting the upsurge of alternate history is the emergence of the cultural movement of postmodernism.[26] While alternate history clearly predates the rise of postmodernism, the latter movement has certainly enabled the former to move into the mainstream.[27] Postmodernism, of course, is a complex phenomenon that has shaped Western culture in a wide variety of ways. But it is in its distinct relationship to history in particular that it has helped to encourage the acceptance of allohistorical thinking. Postmodernism's playfully ironic relationship to history (seen most vividly in the simulated historical environments of postmodern architecture) has found expression in alternate history's playful rearranging of the narratives of real history.[28] Indeed, the blurring of fact and fiction so intrinsic to the field of alternate history mirrors postmodernism's tendency to blur the once-rigid boundaries that separated different realms of culture.[29] At the same time, the postmodern movement's general valorization of "the other" and its attempt to resurrect suppressed or alternate voices dovetails with alternate history's promotion of unconventional views of the past. Finally, postmodernism has encouraged the rise of a more subjective and relativistic variety of historical consciousness so necessary for allohistorical speculation.[30] If, as historians now recognize, history is not about discovering a single "truth" about the past but understanding how diverse contingent factors determine its varying representation, it is no wonder that accounts of the past that diverge from the accepted historical record have begun to proliferate as never before. All of these general trends have eroded the traditional dominance of an objectivist, scientific kind of historiography and have helped foster the acceptance of its alternate cousin.

Beyond the influence of postmodernism, recent scientific trends have further promoted allohistorical thinking. Ever since the appearance of Einstein's theory of relativity and Heisenberg's uncertainty principle, modern science has been moving away from determinism and towards a belief in indeterminacy. The notion of "complexity theory" or "chaos theory," which asserts that some universal laws are so complex that they appear to be chaotic or random in appearance, has lessened the appeal of determinstic explanations of history. Evolutionary biology has shed light

on the profound role of chance events – like meteor strikes – in negating
seemingly linear evolutionary patterns based on pre-existing genetic advan-
tages. Recent scientific theories regarding parallel or multiple universes can
also be seen as sustaining allohistorical speculation.[31] As a result of such
scientific theories, historians like Niall Ferguson have recommended that
the field of history grant new respect to counterfactual speculation and
embrace something known as "chaostory."[32] Such an amended notion of
history would aid our understanding of historical causation by considering
the probability of plausible alternatives to the real historical record. It
would make us realize that in order to understand "how it actually was"
we have to understand "how it actually wasn't."[33]

The new prominence of alternate history can also be seen as a byproduct
of technological trends, specifically the "information revolution." Through
the appearance of new, digitally based computer and communications
technologies, most notably the internet, we have witnessed the birth of
cyberspace, a realm of existence that has broken the restrictions of real time
and space and introduced us to an alternate or "virtual" reality. In a world
where the digital alteration of photographs has become commonplace on
magazine covers, where digitally altered (or generated) actors populate
movie screens, and where online chats replace face-to-face contact, we
have become increasingly separated from the real world. It is little wonder,
then, that in such a climate our imaginations have become separated from
the constraints of real history as well.[34] As the alternate realm of cyberspace
becomes the place where we live much of our daily lives in the present, so
too does our capacity – and perhaps inclination – to imagine an alternate
realm for the past.

The new interest in alternate history can further be explained by the
growing presence of what might be called a speculative sensibility within
contemporary popular culture. Instead of simply mirroring reality, recent
works of film and fiction have begun to explore alternatives to it. This
speculative sensibility has been most noticeable of late in major motion
pictures – among them, *Sliding Doors, Run Lola Run, Femme Fatale,* and
The Butterfly Effect – which have portrayed small points of divergence in
the lives of the central characters leading to dramatically different outcomes.[35] A similar embrace of speculation has further been visible in the
decision of directors to allow audiences to select alternate endings to
their films according to personal preference.[36] And the tendency to envision alternatives has found expression in the increasing popularity of
"fan fiction" – where amateur writers supply their own supplementary
narratives to established television shows and literary series. The growth of

this speculative impulse can be seen as part of a larger imaginative turn within popular culture in general. Over the course of the last generation, certain genres of narrative representation – especially science fiction and fantasy – have left their former location on the cultural periphery and assumed mainstream status. Beginning with the emergence of the "New Wave" of socially conscious science fiction literature in the late 1960s, through the Hollywood blockbuster space epics of Spielberg and Lucas in the 1970s and 1980s, all the way up to the current vogue for Philip K. Dick, science fiction has gained a sizable share of the pop culture market.[37] The same can be said about the genre of fantasy, as seen in the enduring popularity of J. R. R. Tolkien's epic novel (and Peter Jackson's recent Oscar-winning cinematic portrayal of) *The Lord of the Rings*, as well as the immense success of J. K. Rowling's *Harry Potter* series. Both genres, of course, are defined by their vivid imagination of alternate worlds far removed from contemporary reality – the world of science fiction typically set in a speculative future, that of fantasy situated in a magical, mythological past.[38] The popularity of both, however, seems to have facilitated the acceptance of that one related genre that focuses its imaginative gaze upon the *actual* past – alternate history. As allohistorical narratives rely on the same imaginative speculation as science fiction and fantasy narratives, it is no wonder that the first-named have ridden the coat-tails of the other two to new prominence.

Finally, the new prominence of alternate history is explained by the acceleration of what has been called the "Entertainment Revolution."[39] The emergence of entertainment as one of the primary standards of value in modern Western society is a complex phenomenon with distant origins, but it has become especially apparent in recent years.[40] If steady economic prosperity, an increase in leisure time, and growing opportunities for mass consumption explain the general public's insatiable appetite for pleasurable diversion, the fiercely competitive (but also immensely lucrative) forces of the capitalist free market explain why the television, film, newspaper, and book publishing industries – not to mention less overtly commercially minded fields like politics, religion, and education – have all attempted to lure viewers, readers, and supporters by entertaining them. Various observers have pointed out the worrisome consequences of this phenomenon: the shrinking attention span of a general public more interested in superficial images than complex analysis; the fascination with celebrity, scandal, and sensationalism; the dumbing-down of real news into "infotainment"; not to mention the encouragement of increasingly extreme behavior in the effort to satiate the craving for diversion.[41] Few fields have been spared this trend, not even the ivory tower world of academia, which has recently witnessed the rise of media-savvy, celebrity professors who can entertain with the same skill as television personalities. The discipline of history, too, has been affected by the entertainment revolution, as is demonstrated by the emergence of its own "media dons" like Simon Schama, Niall Ferguson, and Andrew Roberts, the success of the *History Channel,* and the increasing tendency of historical scholarship to focus on sensationalistic events like criminal trials, massacres, and other scandals (a genre recently dubbed "the new mystery history").[42] But the impact of entertainment on history is perhaps most obvious in the new popularity of alternate history itself. Unlike conventional history, which remains largely constrained by the serious imperatives of analysis and enlightenment, alternate history's penchant for the unconventional, the sensationalistic, and the irreverent caters to the general public's hunger for pleasurable diversion. Alternate history, in a word, is "fun." And in a culture increasingly oriented towards fun, it was probably only a matter of time before the genre's money-making potential was recognized and it established a firm niche for itself in the competitive publishing industry.

And yet, no matter how much alternate history's new prominence lies in recent cultural trends, the genre's appeal may ultimately be rooted in deeper human urges. It may well lie within our very nature as human beings, in fact, to engage in counterfactual speculation. Many of us at one point or another have doubtless asked the question "what if?" about pivotal moments in our personal lives: What if we had attended a different school, taken a different job, lived in a different place? What if we had never met certain individuals who became colleagues, friends, or spouses? In short, what if we had decided to go down Robert Frost's famous "Road Not Taken?" *Why* we ask such questions – and the issue of *when* we ask them – is far from simple, but at the risk of over-generalizing, it seems clear that when we speculate about what might have happened if certain events had or had not occurred in our past, we are really expressing our feelings about the present.[43] When we ask "what if?" we are either expressing gratitude that things worked out as they did or regret that they did not occur differently. The same concerns are manifest in the broader realm of alternate history.

Alternate history is inherently presentist.[44] It explores the past less for its own sake than to utilize it instrumentally to comment upon the state of the contemporary world. When the producers of alternate histories speculate on how the past might have been different, they invariably express their own highly subjective present-day hopes and fears.[45] It is no coincidence, therefore, that alternate histories typically come in the form of both fantasy and nightmare scenarios.[46] Fantasy scenarios envision the alternate past as superior to the real past and thereby typically express a sense of dissatisfaction with the way things are today. Nightmare scenarios, by contrast, depict the alternate past as inferior to the real past and thus usually articulate a sense of contentment with the contemporary status quo. Allohistorical fantasies and nightmares, moreover, each have different political implications. Fantasies tend to be liberal, for by imagining a better alternate past, they see the present as wanting and thus implicitly support changing it. Nightmares, by contrast, tend to be conservative, for by portraying the alternate past in negative terms, they ratify the present as the best of all possible worlds and thereby discourage the need for change. To be sure, these particular psychological and political implications do not stand in a necessary or deterministic relationship to the two scenarios. Indeed, it is fitting that both nightmare and fantasy narratives can reflect alternate psychological and political impulses. Nightmare scenarios, by showing how the past could have easily been worse, can function as liberal cautionary tales that challenge the conservative belief that the present-day world was inevitable, that it continues to be virtuous, and that it is destined to be permanent. Fantasy scenarios, meanwhile, can be used in conservative fashion to construct escapist alternatives to the present that evade the liberal injunction to confront its problems head-on. The implications of all allohistorical scenarios, in short, are complex. But, on the whole, they explore the past instrumentally with an eye towards larger, present-day agendas.

ALTERNATE HISTORY AND NAZISM

The presentist character of alternate history helps explain its special attraction to the subject of Nazism. Within the general field of alternate history, the Third Reich has been explored more often than any other historical theme.[47] The reason for the Nazi era's popularity is complicated, but it likely is due to its enduring ability to attract and repel the contemporary imagination. On the whole, alternate history as a genre tends to focus on pivotal events of world historical importance that have squarely left their mark on the world of today. These events, or "points of divergence," include the deaths of kings and politicians, decisive military victories or defeats, the rise of grand cultural or religious movements, and even demographic trends, such as migrations or plagues. The fact that the Third Reich is the most commonly explored subject in alternate history reflects Western society's enduring awareness of its creation as a pivotal event that has shaped the contemporary world like few other events have. It is no wonder, then, that it has become the most commonly explored topic in all of alternate history. In short, the many speculative narratives of the Third Reich reflect the enduring centrality of the Nazi past in Western memory.

What specifically, however, do alternate histories of the Nazi era reveal about how the Third Reich has been remembered? Despite the intrinsic interest of this question, there has up to now been little scholarly interest in allohistorical representations of Nazism.[48] This neglect is surprising for several reasons. For one thing, in recent years a great number of scholarly works have examined the memory of Nazism in a wide range of cultural fields – literature, film, architecture, art, theater, and photography, among others.[49] Scholars, indeed, seem to have examined nearly all aspects of Western culture *except* alternate history. It is possible that alternate history has been overlooked precisely because it spans many of these forms of cultural expression and belongs to none in particular. But whatever the reason, this omission is surprising, since alternate history possesses a unique ability to illuminate the workings of historical memory.[50] Oddly enough, alternate histories lend themselves very well to being studied as documents of memory for the same reason that most historians have dismissed them as useless for the study of history – their fundamental subjectivity.[51] Speculative accounts about the past are driven by many of the same psychological forces that determine how the past takes shape in remembrance. Biases, fears, wishes, the desire to avoid guilt, the quest for vindication – these and other related sentiments all influence the ways in which alternate histories represent how the past might have been, just as they influence the ways in which people remember how the past "really" was. The role of such forces in shaping the allohistorical reimagining of the past clearly shows that they are fundamentally rooted in subjective specu-lation. Yet while they are subjective, alternate histories hardly lack repre-sentative value. Since 1945, alternate histories of Nazism have rarely appeared in isolated fashion but usually have emerged in waves during specific eras. In a word, they have illustrated *collective* speculative trends that provide a revealing reflection of broader views of the past.

Of course, there exist numerous challenges to studying alternate his-tories of Nazism as documents of memory. The most apparent is the quantity and diversity of the narratives themselves. Well over one hundred allohistorical works have been produced on the Third Reich in the last half century.[52] They have appeared in a wide range of cultural forms: highbrow works of literature, pulp fiction novels, science fiction magazine short stories, independent and studio-based film productions, prime-time television broadcasts, theatrical plays, historiographical essays and anthologies, mass-market comic books, internet web sites, and role-playing video games. These narratives, moreover, have featured a wide range of allohistorical premises and outcomes. Understandably enough, the scope and diversity of alternate histories of the Third Reich make examining them a daunting task. After immersing myself in the field, however, I gradually came to see that analyzing them in comprehensive fashion provided the best means of gauging their overall significance. I became especially convinced of the merit of proceeding in this way once I recognized that among the many themes portrayed by counterfactual tales of the Nazi past, four recurred with striking frequency. These included tales in which: 1) the Nazis win World War II; 2) Hitler escapes death in 1945 and survives in hiding well into the postwar era; 3) Hitler is removed from the world historical stage either before or some time after becoming the Führer; 4) the Holocaust is completed, avenged, or undone altogether. The predominance of these four themes is significant, for it not only suggests their resonance within the Western imagination but enables us to impose some conceptual order on what otherwise would be a bewilderingly diverse range of works.

In structuring the present study, therefore, I have devoted separate chapters to the themes of a Nazi wartime victory, Hitler's survival, the world without the Führer, and the Holocaust. I examine each chapter's respective theme from a variety of analytical perspectives. First, I classify and analyze the various narratives either as nightmare or fantasy scenarios. Some scenarios, such as the Nazis winning World War II, are clear examples of the former. Others, such as Hitler's elimination from history, exemplify the latter. Certain themes, meanwhile, bridge both categories.[53] Exploring whether alternate histories have more commonly expressed fears or fantasies provides one index of Western views of Nazism. A second and more significant method is provided by analyzing how works of alternate history have actually answered their respective "what if" questions.[54] In changing the historical record – say, by having Hitler captured and placed on trial – have they projected alternate history turning out better or worse than (or no different from) real history? Examining this question, furthermore, illustrates the *function* of alternate histories: that is, whether their reimagining of the past has been intended to validate or criticize the present. Third, studying the identities of the authors of alternate histories and their motives for writing them clarifies their own relationship to the Nazi past. Such factors as an author's national origins, generational identity, and political affiliation can illuminate their motives for speculating about the past. Fourth, looking at how alternate histories of Nazism have been received by critics and general readers reveals the extent to which their depictions of the Nazi past reflect the views of the public at large.[55] Discovering whether a given narrative was a critical success or failure, whether it was a commercial hit or a flop, and whether it was ignored or caused controversy provides a sense of its larger resonance. Finally, examining how the conclusions and reception of allohistorical depictions of the Third Reich have changed *over time* reveals whether Western views of the Third Reich have remained static or have evolved. In short, a synchronic and diachronic method of analyzing alternate histories provides the most thorough means of understanding their significance as documents of memory.

ALTERNATE HISTORY, POPULAR CULTURE, AND MEMORY IN COMPARATIVE PERSPECTIVE

Looking at alternate histories of the Third Reich in this fashion can yield a variety of unique insights into how the Nazi era has been remembered in postwar Western society. First, analyzing alternate histories helps us better understand the role of popular culture in shaping the memory of Nazism.[56] While scholars have long explored the representation of the Third Reich in "high" culture, they have only recently begun to do the same thing in the more "lowbrow" realm of popular culture.[57] Alternate histories, whether appearing as novels, films, television broadcasts, or comic books, clearly belong to this latter category of cultural production. Like all works of popular culture, they have been intentionally made for a mass audience and thus have pursued commercial aims as much as artistic ones.[58] This fact is significant, for it alerts us to how commercial pressures can shape the content of a historical narrative and possibly distort the general public's broader understanding of history.[59] Arguably the most important thing to recognize about popular cultural representations of history, however, is their immense public reach. Given the millions of people who are exposed to historical films, television broadcasts, and novels, it is highly likely that mass-market historical narratives are shaping popular historical awareness to a much greater extent than the histories produced by professional historians.[60] Alternate histories of Nazism obey these same dynamics. Whether in the form of bestselling novels, feature films, or prime-time television programs, they have reached untold millions of readers and viewers. Analyzing their broader messages, together with their reception, provides an excellent means of extending our study of memory beyond the more limited realm of high culture and allows us to produce a more representative portrait of the views of society at large.

A focus on alternate histories of the Third Reich also allows us to examine memory in comparative fashion. While most scholars have examined the shifting consciousness of the Nazi era within individual national contexts, this book aims for a broader perspective.[61] Allohistorical accounts of the Third Reich have appeared in nations all over the world, spanning the continents of Europe, North America, South America, and Asia. The vast majority, however, have appeared in three countries: Great Britain, the United States, and Germany.[62] Of these three, Britain and the United States far and away have produced the most – 80 percent.[63] Explaining the significance of this trend is difficult, as we still lack comprehensive studies of the place of the Nazi past in postwar British and American historical consciousness.[64] At first glance, however, the Anglo-American origin of most alternate histories suggests that the impulse to produce them has been especially strong among those nations that were on the winning side of World War II. Similarly, the fact that alternate history is a variety of popular culture and thus a form of entertainment also helps to explain why the war's primary loser, Germany, has generated such a small number of accounts – around 15 percent. Audiences within World War II's victor nations have been able to read and enjoy alternate histories of Nazism as works of entertainment, but Germans have not been able to enjoy the luxury of embracing such a playful relationship to the past. Given that the Nazi era brought unprecedented misery to their country, Germans understandably have been reluctant to confront the Nazi experience through a genre of narrative representation whose chief characteristics and underlying motives may easily be dismissed as shallow and merely commercial. This is probably the same reason few alternate histories of Nazism have appeared in France and Russia, two nations that were ostensibly among the war's winners but that experienced the war's horrors much more directly than Britons and Americans. Whatever the case may be, the predominance of British, American, and German authors in producing alternate histories of Nazism allows us to compare and contrast how the three nations have remembered the years of the Third Reich and World War II.

THE NORMALIZATION OF MEMORY

Most importantly, examining alternate histories of Nazism in comparative fashion provides compelling evidence of the creeping "normalization" of the Nazi past in Western memory.[65] The concept of "normalization" has frequently been invoked by scholars, but it has rarely been systematically defined.[66] At the most basic level, however, normalization refers to the process by which a particular historical legacy (an era, an event, a figure, or a combination thereof) becomes viewed like any other. As a concept, normalization implies that a given historical legacy is somehow "abnormal" to begin with. It also presumes an ideal-typical condition of "normalcy" towards which all pasts teleologically proceed in consciousness. Such assumptions underlying the concept of normalization are problematic. But whatever one thinks of them, the fact remains that all pasts are not created equal: some are more "normal" than others.

What makes a particular era in history abnormal? What enables it to finally achieve the status of normalcy? Generally speaking, most periods of history are viewed with a relative degree of equanimity, if not apathy, by society at large. In current slang usage, they are "history" in the sense that they are "over" and no longer in need of special attention. By contrast, an abnormal past is one that occupies a disproportionate presence within a society's historical consciousness. Historical eras that tend to acquire such exceptional status are those that are associated with the occurrence of traumatic or otherwise controversial events, whether military defeats, civil strife, political crimes, or other major social or economic injustices. These are eras whose traumas remain vivid in the memories of the people directly affected by them – and, in many cases, among their descendants as well. The experience of trauma, loss, and injustice, in turn, directly shapes how the past is viewed, namely by leading it to be surveyed from a distinctly moralistic perspective. Indeed, a crucial identifying feature of a historical legacy that has not been normalized is the persistence of ethically informed calls to study it, learn its proper "lessons," and hold them in memory, lest the errors of the past be repeated one day in the future. In short, it is the continued aura of moralism surrounding a given historical era that helps to define its "abnormality."[67]

The waning of a moralistic perspective towards the past, by extension, is a crucial component of the larger process of normalization. Yet how and why this process occurs, is a complicated matter. It is important to recognize, first of all, that memory is not monolithic. There is never merely one single view of a specific historical legacy within a given society, but rather a multiplicity of diverse, competing views. Some can be seen as dominant, or "official," memories, in the sense that they enjoy widespread popular or state support, while others are better described as "counter-memories," owing to their dissenting perspective towards the past.[68] These competing memories, moreover, typically find expression in different forms. There exists the "communicative memory" of historical events, which refers to the oral transmission and preservation of original eye-witness recollections of the past. And there exists the "cultural memory" of historical events, which refers to the more objectified representations of the past in various cultural forms, whether monuments, holidays, films, novels, and the like.[69] Whatever their form, the dialectical relationship between official and counter-memories helps to define the overall character of a society's historical consciousness. A dominant memory in one era may be replaced later on by a countervailing memory – one which, in its own right, may be challenged by yet another dissenting set of views some time thereafter. With this dynamic in mind, the process of normalization may be understood to commence when a dominant moralistic view of the past begins to lose its privileged status within popular consciousness and is challenged by dissenting views that are less committed to perceiving it from an ethically grounded vantage point.

It is important to recognize, however, that the process of normalization can advance in multiple ways, all of which need to be understood in their own unique dimensions. To begin with, there exists what might be called the phenomenon of *organic normalization*, in which the passing of time, the gradual disappearance of older generations that personally experienced certain historical events, and the slow maturation of new generations bearing a less personal – and thus potentially more indifferent – relation-ship to those events bring about the emergence of a less morally driven, and thus more normalized, historical perspective.[70] In this sense of the word, "normalization" refers to a *descriptive* concept that denotes a natural, if not inevitable, process. At the same time, the concept of normalization also exists in a more *prescriptive* form, as a goal that can be deliberately pursued in aggressive fashion. Individuals and groups in society may seek to normalize the past for a variety of reasons, but they do so usually out of a sense of impatience with its continued abnormality. Advocates of this agenda may use different strategies to neutralize or redirect attention away from the past's resonant singularity. They may seek to *relativize* the past by deliberately minimizing its unique dimensions through compari-sons with other more or less comparable historical occurrences. They may also attempt to *universalize* the past by explaining it as less the result of particularistic trends distinct to the era in question than of broader, time-less, social, political, or economic forces that they hope to call attention to (and usually condemn). And they may try to *aestheticize* the past by representing it through various narrative techniques that neutralize its moral dimensions. These strategies all reflect a desire to make a given historical legacy no different from any other and can thus be seen as part of a larger attempt to reduce its prominence in current consciousness, if not to render it forgotten altogether.

The Third Reich is one historical era that has long resisted normalization. For many reasons, the Nazi period has been viewed as different from other periods of history. It has cast a long shadow not merely across German history but also across European history, Jewish history, and the history of modern Western civilization at large. The most obvious reason for the Nazi era's disproportionately prominent status in current consciousness is its notorious degree of criminality. In unleashing World War II and perpetrating the Holocaust, among many other misdeeds, the Nazis committed crimes that were so extreme as to be epochal in nature. Beyond being suffused with a unique degree of criminality, moreover, the Third Reich also lies in the very recent past. To a far greater degree than more distant historical eras, the Nazi experience survives within living "communicative" memory. For these reasons, historians and others have insisted for many years on seeing and assessing the Nazi era from a manifestly moral perspective. Non-fictional as well as fictional accounts of the Nazi period since 1945 have long been defined by a shared belief in Nazism's absolute evil.[71] They have been characterized by a commitment to judging the perpetrators for their crimes and granting appropriate respect and sympathy to the victims. The main reason for this practice has been the perceived necessity of transmitting moral lessons to posterity, chief among them George Santayana's oft-quoted admonition, "Those who do not remember the past are condemned to repeat it." This injunction has remained widely accepted up to our present day. The continuing effort to bring Nazi war criminals to justice, the ongoing attempts to financially compensate Holocaust victims, and the enduring vitality of the general culture of commemoration in Europe and the United States clearly demonstrate the enduring belief in the necessity of memory.

And yet, over the course of the last generation, the perceived obligation to depict the Third Reich in moral terms has been steadily challenged by the emergence of a more normalized counter-perspective. The normalization of the Nazi past has reflected different motives and assumed different forms. But their differences notwithstanding, the numerous varieties of normalization have all worked to break down the moral framework that has surrounded the history of the Third Reich since its collapse in 1945.

The normalizing trend first became noticed a generation ago with the increasing aestheticization of the Nazi era in European and American high and popular culture. Beginning in the early 1970s and lasting through the 1980s, a wide range of cultural works – Liliana Cavani's film *The Night Porter* (1973), D. M. Thomas's novel *The White Hotel* (1981), Leon Krier's rehabilitation of Nazi architecture in his 1985 treatise *Albert Speer: Architecture, 1932–1942*, and Anselm Kiefer's paintings of Hitler salutes and Nazi buildings (spanning the late 1960s to the early 1980s) – shifted their narrative focus away from the Nazi regime's barbarous crimes toward an aesthetic interest in its bombastic style and a prurient interest in its lurid projections of sex and violence.[72] For various scholars and cultural critics at the time, this "new discourse" on Nazism was of great concern. Coinciding as it did with the "Hitler Wave" of the 1970s – a period of intense attention to, and fascination with, the person of Adolf Hitler himself – the aestheticization of the Nazi era seemed to reflect a growing attraction to the world of the perpetrators and a diminished attentiveness to the suffering of the victims.[73] In the process, it seemed to signal a growing tendency to forget precisely those aspects of the past that most needed to be remembered in order to prevent their recurrence. This aestheticizing trend has continued in recent years, albeit in new form. Since the 1990s, narratives of the Nazi era have been defined less by prurience and aesthetic delight than humor. As seen in a wide range of films, plays, books, and television programs – Roberto Benigni's film *Life is Beautiful* (1997), Mel Brooks's theatrical revival of *The Producers* (2002), Achim Greser's book of satirical cartoons *Der Führer privat* (2000), and the recurring appearance of the character "gay Hitler" on *Saturday Night Live* – the Nazi era has ceased to serve the ends of titillation and begun to serve the ends of comic relief.[74] Whatever the manner of representation – gratuitous horror or offbeat humor – the abandonment of a moralistic emphasis has continued to define the ongoing aestheticization of the Third Reich.

The normalization of the Nazi era has also been pursued by efforts to relativize its criminal features. This strategy has been the most visible in Germany since the early 1980s, where politicians – mostly on the conservative end of the political spectrum – attempted to relativize Nazi crimes in order for Germans to regain a healthy or "normal" sense of national identity.[75] Following Chancellor Helmut Kohl's assumption of power in 1982, his conservative Christian Democratic Union (CDU) government actively strove to remove German history from the shadow of Nazism. Kohl's staging of the 1984 Bitburg "reconciliation" ceremonies and frequent comments by leading conservative politicians like Alfred Dregger and Franz Josef Strauss about the need for Germany finally to become a "normal" nation testified to an impatience with the enduring stigma left by the Nazi experience upon postwar German national identity. The

Historians' Debate of 1986, in which conservative historians such as Ernst Nolte attempted to diminish the uniqueness of Nazi crimes by comparing them to other twentieth-century atrocities, further reflected a German discomfort with the nation's exceptional historical legacy. The completion of reunification in 1989–90 has only further intensified the yearnings for normalcy. Although the negation of Germany's division should have satisfied conservatives by eliminating the chief source of Germany's abnormal postwar status, it actually did the opposite by leaving the past itself as the only impediment to full normalization. Thus, in the 1990s, calls to normalize German national identity have continued to appear – in large part from members of Germany's "New Right," but also from recently defected representatives of the old left as well. Thus, both conservative intellectuals belonging to the "generation of 1989," such as Rainer Zitelmann, and older left-liberals who lived through the Nazi years, like Martin Walser, have openly criticized the morally grounded view of German history established during the Bonn Republic by the radical "generation of 1968" and have called for a view of German history liberated from the burdens of Nazism.[76] It remains to be seen how the continuing focus on the Nazi era will shape German national identity. At present, the only thing that is certain is that every attempt to forcibly normalize the German past has ended up provoking fierce public debate and further emphasizing the nation's enduring exceptionality.[77]

The normalization of the Nazi era has also been advanced by the attempt to universalize its significance. This process has frequently (though by no means exclusively) been promoted by scholars – especially historians, political scientists, and sociologists – who have long been interested in the broader process of "historicizing" the Third Reich. At the most basic level, historicization refers to the scholarly attempt to explain the Nazi era by situating it in its larger historical context and subjecting it to rational analysis, often with the help of generalizing theories. This process commenced soon after the end of World War II and has since yielded many important insights into the origins of the Nazi regime. But the general explanatory frameworks that scholars have used to historicize the Nazi era have frequently contributed to its universalization. For example, the paradigms of "totalitarianism" and "fascism" which dominated academic scholarship from the late 1940s through the 1970s ended up portraying the Nazi period as merely the German variant of a broader European political and economic crisis.[78] This universalizing effect was one way in which the process of historicization promoted the larger phenomenon of normalization. But historicization promoted normalization in another way as well, namely by striving to explain the Nazi era from a distinctly non-judgmental perspective. In the 1980s, the German historian Martin Broszat famously argued that overtly moral analyses of the Third Reich suffered from their embrace of a "black-and-white" perspective that drew too rigid a dichotomy between perpetrators and victims, obscured the era's gray complexity, bracketed off the Third Reich from "normal" modes of historical analysis (such as an empathetic perspective towards the historical actors themselves), and prevented it from being integrated into the larger sweep of German history.[79] Significantly, when historians in the late 1980s and early 1990s heeded Broszat's call to assume a more objective perspective towards the Nazi era, they historicized it with yet another generalizing theory – that of "modernity" – that ended up universalizing it still further.[80] To be sure, the universalization of the Nazi era does not inevitably imply the absence of an ethical perspective. Indeed, many scholars have condemned Nazi crimes in the process of explaining them with generalizing theories. But by viewing the Third Reich as the result of larger universal forces, most scholars have de-emphasized its unique German dimensions and diminished its historic specificity.

Finally, beyond the deliberate strategies of aestheticization, relativization, and universalization, the normalization of the Nazi past has proceeded organically through the natural passage of time. Over the course of the postwar era, the social composition of the nations that were affected by the Nazi experience – especially Germany, Great Britain, and the United States – has dramatically changed, the eyewitnesses to the past getting older and gradually being replaced by members of younger generations who never experienced it personally. There is no automatic relationship, of course, between generational identity and memory, but it seems clear that for both Europeans and Americans, the passage of time has helped determine whether they have chosen to view the Nazi past from a moral perspective or have attempted to normalize it in one way or another. In Germany, for example, the generations that lived through the Third Reich were notoriously silent about it after 1945; twenty years later, however, the so-called 1968 generation born immediately after the war felt sufficiently unencumbered by personal ties to the Nazi era to confront it head on. The passage of time within German society, in this instance, essentially enabled a turn to moralism. The very same passage of time, however, ironically also promoted a kind of normalization, for as new postwar problems arose (such as the Vietnam War, economic recession, and so forth) they gradually began to overshadow the Nazi era in the minds of the ethically committed younger generation, which increasingly viewed it in universalized fashion as part of the continuing, transnational phenomenon of fascism. To cite a different example: the unpredictable dynamics of organic normalization manifested themselves in the 1980s, when conservative members of the aging German generation that had lived through the Nazi years impatiently declared that the time had finally come to normalize the German past, which they infamously attempted to do by relativizing the crimes of the Nazi era. In this case, the passage of time intensified a latent yearning for normalcy and helped bring it into the open. Finally, the passage of time has been involved in the aestheticization of the Nazi era, for it has helped dismantle the taboos that had existed throughout the West from the end of the war up through the 1970s against representing the Third Reich in anything but a morally conscientious fashion – an iconoclastic trend that has been advanced in particular by members of the younger postwar generations who have been less inhibited in their relationship to the Nazi era. These are but several examples of a complex trend. But the passage of time – or "organic normalization" – needs to be seen as an additional factor that has worked in tandem with the more deliberate strategies of aestheticization, relativization, and universalization to normalize the memory of the Nazi era.

Taken together, all of these dimensions of normalization reflect a broader tendency to view the Third Reich like any other historical period. At the same time, they reflect a growing willingness to challenge the virtues of memory itself. For by viewing the Nazi past as a past like any other, the injunction to remember its distinctive features has diminished in urgency. The long road of normalization, thus, may well point to indifference, if not amnesia, as its ultimate destination.

ALTERNATE HISTORY AND THE NORMALIZATION
OF MEMORY

Alternate histories of Nazism reveal clear signs of the intensifying pace of normalization. Since 1945, allohistorical works have slowly abandoned the traditional moralistic method of depicting the Nazi era in favor of a less judgmental approach that has considerably reduced its aura of evil. This trend has clearly been visible in the shifting portrayal of the four primary themes of postwar alternate histories mentioned earlier. A good example is provided by the subject treated in chapters 1–4, a Nazi victory in World War II. While early postwar narratives consistently portrayed a Nazi-ruled world as a dystopian place ruled by fanatical ideologues, later ones have depicted it as a tolerable place run by reasonable pragmatists. The same is true of the theme examined in chapter 5, Hitler's survival of the war and escape into hiding. Early postwar narratives portrayed Hitler as an unrepentant demon who is brought to justice for his crimes, but more recent works have portrayed him as a relatively normal human being who succeeds in evading humanity's judgment. The subject of chapter 6, the world without Hitler, demonstrates a similar trend. Early narratives fantasized that the world would have been better without the evil Nazi dictator, whereas most recent works have portrayed the world as being no better, if not worse, in his absence. Finally, alternate accounts of the Holocaust, the subject of chapter 7, confirm this same pattern. By focusing on perpetrators who are plagued by the memory of Nazi crimes and who fail in attempting to atone for them, these narratives have questioned the postwar faith in the utility of remembrance. Taken together, alternate histories of Nazism seem to indicate the emergence of an increasingly normalized view of the Nazi past within Western consciousness.

The reasons for this normalizing trend are complex. But they can be better understood by periodizing the appearance of alternate histories of Nazism into various eras and phases. Postwar alternate histories can generally be divided into two distinct eras: 1) an *era of moralism*, lasting from 1945 to the middle of the 1960s; and 2) an *era of normalization*, beginning in the middle of the 1960s and lasting up until the present day. There are several differences between the two eras. First, the accounts that appeared in the earlier era were consistently judgmental in their conclusions, while those that appeared in the latter era were far less so. Moreover, far fewer accounts appeared in the era of moralism (20 percent of the postwar total) than in the era of normalization (a weighty 80 percent). To be sure, the shift from moralistic to normalized alternate histories has not been absolute. Narratives situated in ethically informed frameworks have continued to appear since the 1960s. Moreover, alternate histories in Britain, the United States, and Germany have made the transition to normalized conclusions at different times: Britain was the earliest, exhibiting this shift in the mid-1960s; the United States was somewhat later, in the early 1970s; and Germany has been the last, only after the late 1980s. These distinctions notwithstanding, the broader trend remains clear: the progressively normalized conclusions of alternate histories have gone hand in hand with their increasing production.

What, then, explains why the decade of the 1960s represents a watershed in the West's broader views towards the Nazi era? This question can be answered by breaking down the eras of moralism and normalization into four smaller phases. During the era of moralism's initial *cold-war phase* in the years 1945–1958, Western fears of communism kept alternate histories of Nazism to a minimum. Nevertheless, the accounts that did appear consistently depicted the Nazi era in morally unambiguous terms as a symbol of absolute evil. This tendency intensified during a *rediscovery phase* that began around 1958 and lasted up through the middle of the 1960s, when renewed international attention to Germany's Nazi past at the time of the trial of Nazi SS official Adolf Eichmann caused a sudden upsurge in allohistorical works. During these years, the overtly ethical conclusions of alternate histories in Britain, the United States, and Germany served the self-congratulatory function of validating the Allied powers' real historical triumph over Nazism and affirming the positive features of the present-day world.

After the middle of the 1960s, however, the moral consensus of the early postwar years began to break down. During the era of normalization's initial *crisis phase,* from the mid-1960s until the early 1980s, new social, economic, and political crises began to eclipse the memory of Nazi crimes and place them in their shadow. At this time, Great Britain, the United States, and Germany entered periods of relative decline. The reasons were different: in Britain, it was the loss of empire and the onset of economic stagnation; in America, it was the upheavals of Vietnam, the civil rights movement, Watergate, and economic malaise; in Germany, it was the social upheavals caused by the rise of the 1968 generation and ensuing economic decline. With the emergence of a more pessimistic mood, alternate histories of Nazism largely changed their function. Instead of being used to validate the present, they increasingly became used as a means of criticizing it. Yet with the onset of a *post-cold-war phase*, beginning in the late 1980s and lasting up to the present, the tendency towards triumphalism returned, alongside the ongoing tendency towards self-critique. This dual phenomenon reflected the ambiguous character of the post-cold-war world. On the one hand, the cold war's end, the reunification of Germany, and the accelerating retreat of the Nazi era into the past produced a new climate of optimism that further eroded the horror of Nazism in certain works of alternate history. On the other hand, the emergence of new crises in the wake of the cold war's end produced a pessimistic environment that encouraged other alternate histories to preserve their self-critical streak.

The process of normalization visible in postwar works of alternate history has been promoted by diverse factors. In certain cases, it has resulted from the process of *organic normalization,* meaning the natural passing of time and the growing distance between the present and the increasingly remote past. In other cases, however, normalization has been the result of conscious intent. Some of the producers of alternate histories have deliberately *universalized* the significance of the Nazi era to make specific comments about contemporary problems on the world stage. Others consciously have *relativized* Nazi crimes in order to redirect attention to other historic crimes or contemporary dangers. Still others have *aestheticized* the Nazi era, whether for psychological or commercial motives. In the process, they have tended to undermine the injunction to preserve the memory of the Nazi era's crimes lest they be repeated in the future.

The normalization of the Nazi past in postwar alternate histories has not proceeded unopposed, however. For one thing, the ongoing appearance of morally principled accounts throughout the postwar world reflects an enduring commitment to remember the Third Reich's crimes in their historic specificity and to preserve their lessons in memory. But more importantly, the commitment to memory has also been illustrated by the strongly polarized reactions to many alternate histories of Nazism. Significantly enough, these reactions have shifted considerably over the course of the postwar period. During the era of moralism, a close correspondence existed between the production and reception of alternate histories. The ethically grounded conclusions of allohistorical narratives were consistently accepted and praised by audiences throughout the West. This confluence of views, however, ended with the onset of the era of normalization. For more often than not, the less judgmental conclusions of this period's alternate histories were rejected or otherwise attacked by critics and audiences. In short, the normalization of the Nazi past in works of alternate history has run up against the resistance of audiences unwilling to abandon the use of moralistic frameworks in representing the Nazi era. As a result, the memory of the Nazi past has become more pluralistic, contested, and divided.

We seem to have arrived, therefore, at a crossroads in the West's confrontation with the Nazi legacy. As the Third Reich fades ever more into the past, authors and audiences continue to disagree about the most appropriate way to represent and remember it. The producers of alternate history persist in extending the limit of what is permissible in portraying the Nazi years, but audiences and critics continue to insist on a narrow spectrum of representational boundaries. The consequences of these differences remain to be seen. But the broader trend is clear: allohistorical narratives of the Third Reich point to a growing normalizing trend in the Western memory of the Nazi era.

PART I

The Nazis win World War II

Comparative overview

We cut off the [Henry Hudson] Drive onto the Goethe Parkway ...
I still didn't know why we were heading out to Westchester, and to
tell the truth I didn't care much ...

'That's Croton-on-Hudson up ahead,' Kohler said. 'It's not far now.'

You could read the sign from 500 yards, a huge billboard draped
with swastika bunting and crested by an Imperial Eagle with the globe
clutched in its talons: 'Welcome to Croton-on-Hudson. Home of the
Final Solution. Visit the Frederick Barbarossa Death Camp, 1 mile
ahead, First Right. Admission 35 marks, children Free. No Dogs
Allowed. Picnic areas adjacent ...'

We drove along the road at fifteen or twenty miles an hour ... and
I looked out at the Barbarossa Camp without any great interest. There
wasn't really much to see, just a lot of old barracks and endless coils of
rusty barbed wire plus a string of road signs from the local Elks and
Rotarians greeting visitors: 'Croton-on-Hudson, where Four Million
Enemies of the Reich perished.' I remember reading that Croton was
second only to Auschwitz in its kill ratio, so I guess they had reason for
pride, but I didn't care for the commercialization. One big sign
was decorated with a blown-up color photograph of an emaciated
Jew ... [his] drowned eyes luminous with hunger. It was captioned
in huge red letters, 'If Bread and Water Isn't Enough For You, Visit
Schaumberger's Steak House, Rt. 1, 250 yards from the Wesley
Overpass.'[1]

New York City detective Bill Halder's blasé depiction of the Nazis'
extermination of American Jewry in Eric Norden's 1973 detective thriller
The Ultimate Solution provides a particularly chilling answer to the question that has dominated much of the allohistorical literature on the Third
Reich: what would have happened had the Nazis won World War II? This
nightmare scenario has been the dominant theme of all the alternate
histories on the Third Reich produced since 1945.[2] In Great Britain, the
United States, Germany, and scattered other nations, the premise of the
Nazis winning World War II has been explored time and again in a wide

range of novels, films, television programs, plays, comic books, and historical essays. These accounts have varied considerably in explaining the reasons for the Nazis' wartime triumph. But they have all focused squarely upon its consequences for the subsequent history of the world. Interestingly enough, the narratives that have appeared since World War II have diverged sharply in their approach to this question over time. For the first two decades of the postwar era, up until the mid-1960s, most narratives moralistically depicted a Nazi wartime victory as bringing about a terrifying hell on earth. Accounts since then, however, have diminished the scenario's sense of horror and portrayed it in far more nuanced terms as a relatively tolerable, if not benign, event.

This shift in the allohistorical representation of a Nazi wartime triumph points to the existence of a normalizing trend in the Western memory of the Nazi past. This trend has been visible in the particular ways in which British, American, and German narratives have depicted a Nazi victory. Overall, each nation's tales have focused on separate aspects of the scenario unique to its own wartime experience. British accounts have speculated as to whether the British people would have resisted or collaborated with the Germans after being conquered by them. American narratives have explored the extent to which a Nazi triumph depended on the United States' decision either to intervene or remain neutral in the war. Finally, German alternate histories have largely focused on how the Nazis' conquest of Europe would have affected Germany itself. Over time, the manner in which these themes have been depicted has changed considerably. Early postwar narratives in Britain, for example, portrayed the Nazis as demonic oppressors and the British as heroic resisters, but later accounts blurred the distinctions between the two by imagining the Germans as reasonable occupiers and the British as opportunistic collaborators. Similarly, early postwar tales in the United States depicted the Germans as ideological fanatics who needed to be stopped by military intervention, while later narratives projected the Nazis as much more moderate foes against whom America could safely remain neutral. Finally, most postwar German narratives consistently represented a victorious Third Reich as an unmitigated disaster for Germany, while more recent ones have portrayed it as not such a bad event after all.

The changing representation of a Nazi wartime victory reflects a broader shift in the scenario's allohistorical function. Initially, the vision of a Nazi triumph in World War II was conceived as a nightmare scenario. As such, it partly reflected the lingering trauma of the Nazi experience in popular consciousness after 1945. But it largely functioned – like many nightmare scenarios – as a negative foil that helped to validate the virtues of the present-day world. Early postwar narratives in Britain, for instance, depicted a Nazi victory in frightful terms in order to triumphalistically affirm the belief that the British people's real historical resistance against the Germans constituted what Winston Churchill called their "finest hour." American accounts from the same era portrayed a victory of the Nazis in similarly horrifying fashion in order to justify the United States government's decision to intervene in the war against them. German tales, by contrast, were somewhat more complex in motivation, depicting a Nazi triumph in bleak terms partly to condemn the bygone Third Reich, but also to celebrate the Federal Republic's superiority to it. Midway through the postwar era, however, the self-congratulatory purpose of alternate histories began to give way to a more self-critical orientation. This change was particularly apparent in British and American alternate histories. As Great Britain and the United States began to experience periods of crisis after the mid-1960s, the producers of alternate histories reduced the horror of a Nazi military victory in order to criticize their nations' progressive decline. This self-critical impulse began to fade somewhat with the ebbing of the era's crises and the restoration of stability by the late 1980s, but from this point on, alternate histories just as frequently functioned to criticize the present as to validate it. The exception to this rule was provided by German accounts, which moved in the opposite direction. While the dystopian narratives of the early postwar period had exhibited a self-critical dimension from the very beginning, the normalized accounts of more recent years have expressed a more triumphalistic sensibility, reflecting the new self-confidence produced by reunification.

In the end, the extent to which postwar allohistorical representations of a Nazi wartime triumph truly reflect a normalizing trend in the Western memory of the Third Reich is revealed by their popular reception. Not surprisingly, the postwar responses to alternate histories of a Nazi victory in World War II have varied by nation and era. But on the whole, as the narratives have become more normalized, the reactions to them have become more divided. British, American, and German audiences have hailed some accounts enthusiastically, while they have criticized others severely. These diverse responses are significant, for if the positive ones suggest the dawning of a less moralistic view of the Nazi era, the more critical ones indicate an enduring desire to preserve it intact.

A NAZI VICTORY IN ALTERNATE HISTORY

The allohistorical premise of a Nazi victory in World War II has a long history. Ever since the outbreak of war in 1939, but especially since the real historical collapse of the Third Reich in 1945, the idea that the Nazis might emerge victorious in the war has been a topic of enduring fascination. Professional historians have been especially interested in the scenario and have explored it in a variety of contexts. Some have investigated the premise of a Nazi wartime victory in the process of examining the Nazis' postwar plans for a new European order.[3] Others have explored it as part of their research into the controversial role of German scientists in developing the atomic bomb for Hitler.[4] Military historians have long ruminated about the multiple ways in which Hitler could have won the war (but did not).[5] And scholars of the Holocaust, in order to resolve the thorny question of the genocide's uniqueness, have pointed to Hitler's long-range plans for the racial "cleansing" of Eastern Europe in the expectation of a Nazi conquest.[6] The scholarly interest of historians in the premise of a Nazi victory, meanwhile, has been echoed by its strong presence in popular culture. Interactive video games have featured a Nazi military triumph as a prominent premise.[7] Broadway musicals have made reference to the Nazis winning the war.[8] Internet chatrooms have buzzed with discussions about what the world would have been like had the Nazis defeated the Allies.[9] And various academics, cultural critics, and political activists have polemically used the scenario of a Nazi wartime victory as a cudgel to wield against a wide range of cultural works and political trends.[10]

Of course, the premise of a Nazi military triumph has been most systematically addressed in the many works of alternate history that have appeared since 1945. Within the general field of alternate history, this counterfactual scenario has arguably been explored more frequently than any other historical theme.[11] Allohistorical accounts of a Nazi victory in World War II have appeared in a variety of national contexts over the entirety of the postwar era. But on the whole, these tales can be periodized in four separate phases: The first accounts appeared solely in Britain during the late 1940s and early 1950s, although in rather small numbers due to the era's preoccupation with the cold-war threat of communism. During the late 1950s and early 1960s, American narratives began to emerge for the first time, a trend that – together with the continued appearance of British works – reflected the increased attention to Germany's Nazi past at the time of the Eichmann trial. Up until this point, allohistorical accounts had been consistently situated within clear ethical parameters. Yet, beginning in the middle of the 1960s in Britain, the early 1970s in the United States, and the late 1970s in Germany (albeit to a lesser degree), tales of a Nazi wartime victory became more normalized. Finally, in the most recent period, from the end of the cold war in 1989 up through the present, alternate histories have resisted any single trend. British and German narratives have largely resisted judgmental conclusions, while American accounts have embraced them once more. In short, the changing allohistorical representation of a Nazi wartime victory over the course of the postwar era points to the slow emergence of a more normalized view of the Third Reich.

CHAPTER I

Great Britain defeated:
between resistance and collaboration

Some said there had not been even one clear week of sunshine since the cease-fire. It was easy to believe. Today the air was damp, and the colourless sun only just visible through the grey clouds, like an empty plate on a dirty tablecloth.

And yet even a born and bred Londoner, such as Douglas Archer, could walk down Curzon Street, and with eyes half-closed, see little or no change from the previous year. The Soldatenkino sign outside the Curzon cinema was small and discreet ... And if your eyes remained half-closed you missed the signs that said 'Jewish Undertaking' and effectively kept all but the boldest customers out. And in November of that year, 1941, Douglas Archer, in common with most of his compatriots, was keeping his eyes half-closed.[1]

The ambivalent attitude of detective superintendent Douglas Archer towards life in Nazi-occupied London in famed British writer Len Deighton's 1978 bestselling novel, *SS-GB*, offers a particularly pessimistic response to a question that has long dominated British alternate histories of the Nazi era: How would the British have behaved in the wake of a Nazi triumph in World War II? Britons have struggled to answer this question from the moment they first began to pose it. Counterfactual accounts of the Nazis emerging victorious in World War II date back in Great Britain to the time of the war itself. For obvious reasons, the British were the most prone of the major European powers to speculate about the possibility of a Nazi victory. Unlike the French, who no longer had any reason to speculate along these lines after their calamitous collapse in June 1940, and unlike the Americans, who never faced any immediate threat of German invasion, the British faced the grim possibility of a Nazi seaborne assault throughout the early stages of the war. Possessing the most pressing reasons to imagine the consequences of a Nazi military invasion, the British understandably produced the greatest number of wartime alternate histories depicting it.

Even after the war ended in 1945, however, British alternate histories continued to appear. These postwar narratives continued to focus on the likely severity of the Germans' occupation of Britain and the question of whether the British would have collaborated with them. Over time, though, their depiction of these themes, as well as their underlying motivations for doing so, changed significantly. Early postwar narratives uniformly depicted the Germans as brutal representatives of a criminal regime and portrayed the British as heroic resisters against it. In the process, they affirmed postwar Britain's foundational myth that the fight against Nazism represented the British people's "finest hour." Later narratives, by contrast, blurred the firm line between occupiers and occupied, between perpetrators and victims, by de-heroizing the British and de-demonizing the Germans. Their goal was to chip away at, if not to completely topple, the finest-hour myth and to redefine the nature of British national identity. Predictably, these accounts proved quite controversial, as was revealed by the fierce disagreements between their opponents and supporters. On the whole, however, the shifting representation of a Nazi wartime victory in British works of alternate history – together with their divided reception – reveals an increasing tendency of many Britons to view the Nazi era from a more normalized perspective.

PREWAR AND WARTIME ALTERNATE HISTORIES, 1937–45

British accounts of a Nazi wartime victory first appeared just prior to the outbreak of World War II and then proliferated during the war itself in the form of "future histories."[2] In imagining the Germans invading, defeating, and occupying Britain, these narratives clearly reflected acute British fears of Nazism. Not surprisingly, these tales painted a grim picture of life under German rule, depicting the Nazis as savage conquerors and the British as innocent victims. In so doing, they aimed to convince British readers of the need to defeat the Nazi regime in the present so as to prevent national catastrophe in the future.

The first British depiction of a Nazi wartime victory appeared in 1937, when author Katharine Burdekin, writing under the pseudonym Murray Constantine, published the short novel, *Swastika Night*.[3] Set in the distant future, 700 years after Hitler's triumphant victory in the so-called Twenty Years War, Burdekin's novel focuses on the struggle of its protagonist, an English airplane mechanic named Alfred, to understand, and if possible to resist, the Nazi-ruled world around him. This world is a highly frightful one. Not only have the Germans ruthlessly subjected the entire European continent to their brutal rule, they have replaced Christianity with the worship of Hitler, reduced all women to subhuman breeders of children, and systematically eradicated all forms of knowledge that "could remind Germans of old time."[4] Alfred is repelled by this world of violence and ignorance but only begins to comprehend its origins while on a pilgrimage to Nazism's "holy sites" in Germany, where he encounters one of Germany's few enlightened rulers, a member of the so-called "Knights of the Inner Ten," Friedrich von Hess. Enamored of Alfred's English individualism, Hess (a descendant of Rudolf Hess) reveals that he possesses what no other Nazi does – access to true knowledge, being in the possession of the only known work of history, painstakingly written down by one of his distant ancestors. This book not only describes the mundane truth of the real historical Hitler but also exposes how the Führer was posthumously shrouded in legends and myths by his hagiographers. Hess shares this knowledge with Alfred because he recognizes the longterm costs of Hitlerism for Germany (he expects a demographic catastrophe due to the system's discouraging of women to produce female offspring) and because he understands that spiritual renewal will only be possible by exposing the truth about the past. Hess thus bestows the book upon Alfred with the dual mission of disseminating its message throughout Britain and leading a spiritual rebellion against German rule. The novel concludes with Alfred being killed before he can accomplish his mission of spiritual rebellion. But, just before dying, he is able to pass Hess's book of history on to his son Fred who – the reader is led to believe – may eventually succeed where his father failed.

For British readers in the late 1930s, *Swastika Night* possessed an unmistakable political message. As was indicated both by its publishing house (the well-known Left Book Club, founded by the anti-Nazi publisher, Victor Gollancz) and by the publisher's note included in the 1940 edition, Nazism needed to be resisted lest "Hitler impose his will . . . upon [the world]."[5] *Swastika Night* was a cautionary tale that clearly reflected prewar British fears of Nazism. Yet the novel differed from subsequent wartime allohistorical works by preserving something of an optimistic message. Despite its dark narrative, *Swastika Night* remained hopeful in the possibility of resisting tyranny. This optimistic streak was partly visible in the bestowal of the mission of rebellion from Alfred to Fred. But it was epitomized by Burdekin's portrayal of Hess, who, as the proverbial "good German," represented the belief, still held by many Britons in 1937, that Germany might still rid itself of the Nazi disease without bloodshed.[6] No matter how well-developed Hess was as a character, however, the premise of a benevolent and cultured Nazi leader rebelling against the system reflected how Burdekin, like others at the time, naively misjudged the political realities of Nazi Germany. Burdekin's feminist agenda partly explains this oversight (in *Swastika Night*, Nazi evil stems from aggressive masculinity and it claims women as its primary victims), but it also reflected a certain degree of wishful thinking.[7] In the end, *Swastika Night* remained an exceptional account of a Nazi-ruled world. Before long, its hopeful message that catastrophe could be averted was soon crushed by the outbreak of war.

With the eruption of World War II in 1939, British alternate histories acquired a new sense of drama and urgency. Especially as fears of a Nazi invasion intensified during the summer of 1940 following the near-disaster at Dunkirk and the Battle of Britain, narratives portraying a Nazi attack began to appear in greater number. These accounts demonized the Germans and heroized the British, but they also introduced a subtle element of self-criticism by depicting the nation's collapse as largely the fault of a small number of treasonous Britons who supported appeasement. In highlighting the negative example of disloyalty, these wartime tales hoped to foster national unity in the fight against the Germans by graphically depicting the high costs of defeat.

The first wartime account to depict Great Britain's defeat and occupation by the Germans was a novel published in 1940 by British journalists Douglas Brown and Christopher Serpell entitled *Loss of Eden*.[8] With its title borrowed from Shakespeare's tragedy *Richard II*, *Loss of Eden* portrayed Britain's defeat through the eyes of a London-based New Zealand journalist, Charles Fenton, who witnesses it firsthand. As Fenton's account makes unmistakably clear, the nation's collapse is entirely due to the misguided policy of appeasement. In the novel, the Germans do not even have to invade Britain in order to defeat it. Instead, the British seal their own fate by swiftly signing a separate peace with Germany – the infamous "Peace of Nuremberg" – to bring World War II to an end. This treaty does not bring peace, however. For Germany reneges on its promises, threatens to bomb Britain from the air, and succeeds in compelling the nation's craven political leaders to sign a "Treaty of Friendship and Mutual Assistance" that paves the way for the outright German occupation of the island nation. From this point on in the novel, the Germans behave in bestial fashion, deporting political opponents to newly established concentration camps, enslaving British workers for forced labor in German factories, and attempting to germanize British culture by abolishing the English language. Yet, while *Loss of Eden* emphasized the victimization of the British, it did not portray them as wholly innocent. Indeed, Brown and Serpell's depiction of a small number of upper-crust Quisling politicians kowtowing to their German overlords clearly emphasized the role of internal betrayal as responsible for the nation's defeat.[9] Still, this self-critical impulse would be limited in scope. As would be true of many postwar alternate histories, *Loss of Eden* patriotically affirmed that collaboration was the fault of the few.

While *Loss of Eden* explored the reasons for Britain's defeat, other alternate histories concentrated on depicting its horrifying consequences. One of the most graphic was British writer H. V. Morton's 1942 novel, *I, James Blunt*.[10] Morton's novel was cast in the form of a diary, written by an elderly anti-Nazi tradesman named James Blunt, that chronicles the Nazis' occupation of Great Britain in the fall of 1944. As they extend their rule over the nation, the Nazis behave in extraordinarily barbaric fashion, destroying symbols of British culture (St. Paul's Cathedral is razed to make room for the Nazi party headquarters) and subjecting the population to a program of "complete Germanisation."[11] In order to dispel any doubts about the Germans' motives, Blunt affirms that the punitive character of their occupation reflects a special German hatred of the British. The Germans have come to Britain, he asserts, "to teach us that we are the one nation on earth that they hate, have always hated, have always longed to conquer, spit on, tear up by the roots, rape and humiliate !"[12] Blunt repeatedly drives this point home in his narrative, nowhere more explicitly than where he describes the Nazis' plans for Britain as representing the apex of their wartime savagery. As he recounts in his diary, "the revenge [the Germans] are now enjoying is more fiendish in its cruelty than anything they have done on the Continent" and is a clear sign that their ultimate goal is "the scientific extermination of British nationality."[13] The Germans are not the only villains in the novel, however. A former employee of James Blunt, a common criminal named Bill Grimes, reveals the British people's own potential for evil by turning in his old boss to the Gestapo as a means of settling a personal grudge.[14] Still, like *Loss of Eden*, Morton's novel portrayed collaboration as supported by the immoral few and thus exonerated the mass of "ordinary" Britons from any suspicion of wartime disloyalty.

Finally, if *Loss of Eden* and *I, James Blunt* expressed fears of Britain's German enemy, well-known writer Vita Sackville-West's 1942 novel, *Grand Canyon*, expressed British anxieties about fighting them alone.[15] Set not in occupied Britain but in the American southwest, Sackville-West's tale focused on a motley group of Americans and Europeans who, while staying at a fashionable hotel along the rim of the Grand Canyon, witness firsthand the Nazi invasion of the United States in 1945. The world in 1945 is one in which the United States government (led by an unnamed successor to the assassinated president, Franklin Delano Roosevelt) has made the questionable decision to ally with Nazi Germany, believing it to be the best remaining option in the wake of Britain and Russia's defeat in 1943. This decision soon proves disastrous, however, with the Nazis' treacherous invasion of the United States – an event that occurs when the manager of the Grand Canyon Hotel, an American Nazi sympathizer, sets it on fire to provide a beacon for Nazi bombers flying in to raid nearby American air-force bases. The hotel guests all die in attempting to escape the carnage, but they survive for the remainder of the novel in a surreal afterlife on the canyon floor sheltered from the catastrophic events shaking the outside world. Only by listening to crackling radio broadcasts do they learn of America's rapid devastation, a process that finds its apocalyptic climax with the destruction of New York City by a sudden act of nature, a violent earthquake that rips a vast rift down Fifth Avenue and topples the city's skyscrapers alongside it, creating, in effect, a macabre urban version of the Grand Canyon on the east coast. America, Sackville-West pointedly affirmed with this ending, was just as vulnerable to defeat as Britain.

In offering such grim conclusions, wartime alternate histories in Great Britain clearly revealed their larger didactic function as "cautionary tales." As H. V. Morton declared in the preface to *I, James Blunt*, his chief aim in depicting the terrors of an imaginary Nazi occupation was to convince "all [those] complacent optimists and wishful thinkers who ... cannot imagine what life would be like if we lost the war" that a Nazi victory would be catastrophic for the British nation.[16] This was especially necessary, according to Sackville-West, for the apparently apathetic Americans – a people who, her novel's protagonist, Lester Dale, explained, "had never known and scarcely imagined disaster" – and thus needed to be shown explicitly the catastrophic consequences of failing to confront the Nazi enemy.[17] Wartime writers, of course, tried to avoid being too pessimistic in their predictions. Brown and Serpell hoped their tale would not "cause despondency or alarm" and assured their readers that "No-one believes he would ever have the opportunity of telling this sad tale of Britain's ... fall."[18] Still, while the authors of alternate histories no doubt wanted to avoid charges of defeatism, their frequent embrace of dystopian scenarios reflected their broader conviction that exposing readers to the frightful consequences of defeat would help motivate them to prevent it from happening in the first place.

As the tide of the war turned in favor of the Allies after 1943, however, the character of alternate histories began to shift. Fears of the Germans continued to find expression, as in Humphrey Jennings's 1943 film *The Silent Village*, which used the Nazis' real historical destruction of the Czech village of Lidice in 1942 as inspiration for its tale of Nazi troops massacring the inhabitants of the Welsh village of Cwmgiedd.[19] But a new optimistic streak began to surface as well. Thus, Anthony Armstrong and Bruce Graeme's novel *When the Bells Rang* (1943) and Martin Hawkin's novel *When Adolf Came* (1943) depicted a Nazi invasion ending with the swift defeat of the enemy.[20] As British fears of defeat waned, wartime accounts ceased depicting the British as victims and began to portray them heroically as resisters. By the time the prospect of victory seemed certain in the last years of the war, alternate histories lost their original *raison d'être* and disappeared altogether.

RECEPTION

The positive reception of wartime narratives revealed the existence of widespread support for their broader goals. Brown and Serpell's *Loss of Eden* earned the most praise, being hailed by *The Times* of London in 1940 as "an outstanding ... work of fiction" that succeeded in powerfully "bring[ing] home ... all [that] we have to lose and what shall never happen."[21] More adulatory still was the *Times Literary Supplement* (*TLS*), which the same year called the book:

a cautionary tale with a ... frightful vengeance ... Here is the plain truth about the ... serfdom that once was the free garden of England if we were to temporize with the enemy. All those who would compromise with the forces of evil can surrender hope ... In view of the state of Europe to-day, there is no escape from the inexorable logic of this disquieting narrative.[22]

Other works received similar adulation. *I, James Blunt* was complimented by no less a reviewer than George Orwell, who described it as "a good flesh creeper, founded on the justified assumption that the mass of the English people haven't yet heard of fascism."[23] Martin Hawkin's *When Adolf Came* also met with general support.[24] Only Vita Sackville-West's *Grand Canyon* received mixed reviews, largely due to the novel's perceived literary weaknesses.[25] As shown by such positive responses, wartime alternate histories expressed a broader belief among Britons that the fight against Nazism was both urgently necessary and eminently just.

THE POSTWAR YEARS: ALTERNATE HISTORY AS VINDICATION,
1945–61

If British fears of the Germans helped spawn alternate histories during the war years, the disappearance of those fears after 1945 led such narratives to decline in number. In the first decade and a half after World War II, allohistorical accounts of a Nazi wartime victory remained relatively scarce.[26] In part, this trend reflected the ebbing of British interest in the subject of Nazism.[27] Having won the war, the British had no reason any longer to fear the Germans and so turned their attention to other pressing matters. The challenges of the postwar years were many, but Britons generally approached them with a strong sense of self-confidence that was rewarded with a variety of notable achievements. In domestic affairs, Great Britain successfully handled the tasks of restoring the nation's economic health and creating its modern social welfare system. By the mid-1950s, the nation had regained a solid economic footing and was widely admired for its social stability.[28] In the area of foreign policy, meanwhile, Britain continued to behave as a great power. The nation's leaders felt independent enough to develop their own nuclear arsenal by the early 1950s, confident enough to reject the invitation of European states to join in the European Economic Community (EEC) in 1955, and bold enough still to undertake foreign policy adventures, as at Suez in 1956. At the same time, the nation felt secure enough to begin to liquidate its colonial empire, beginning with its retreat from India and the Middle East in the late 1940s.[29] The psychological fallout of de-colonization would eventually manifest itself, and other worries remained acute, most notably the cold-war threat of communism, but on the whole during the 1950s most Britons were content with the postwar world. Overall, the first decade and a half after the end of World War II was more focused on the present than the past. In such a climate, few allohistorical accounts of a Nazi victory appeared.

Nevertheless, those that did revealed that the allohistorical premise of a Nazi wartime victory had acquired a new function. If wartime depictions of a Nazi triumph had aimed to warn ordinary Britons about what horrors might await them if the enemy were not defeated, their postwar function was to congratulate them for having ultimately prevailed. After 1945, alternate histories echoed the triumphalistic view, shared by many Britons, that the fight against Nazism had been their "finest hour."[30] Especially given the mundane, "postheroic" reality of Britain after the war, the patriotic myth that Britain had fought to save Western civilization from the evils of Nazism helped to reaffirm the nation's superior sense of moral virtue and enhance its sense of national identity.[31] Early postwar alternate histories of a Nazi victory directly supported this patriotic mission. By imagining history taking a turn for the worse, they ratified the present-day world as preferable to its nightmarish alternative. Early postwar alternate histories advanced this agenda in different ways. Some narratives portrayed the British people suffering under Nazi occupation but eventually overthrowing the enemy invaders. Others depicted the subjugation of the British people without offering any redemptive conclusion. In both cases, however, the narratives clearly celebrated Britain's real historical triumph over Nazi Germany.

The first alternate history of the postwar era appeared in July 1947 with the premiere of famed British playwright Noël Coward's play *Peace in Our Time*.[32] Set in Nazi-occupied London over a five-year period from November 1940 to May 1945, *Peace in Our Time* portrayed the diverse responses of ordinary Britons to German domination. Most of the play takes place in a pub called the *Shy Gazelle*, which is owned by the play's protagonist, Fred Shattock. As the play unfolds, Fred and his many patrons struggle to make sense of the nation's defeat. Some, like Fred's children, Stephen and Doris, enter into the resistance and try to repel the invader. Others, like the arrogant intellectual Chorley Bannister, decide to collaborate (see Figure 1). Overall, *Peace in Our Time* was a simple morality tale of loyalty and betrayal. While Stephen and Doris fight for Britain's freedom, Chorley betrays Doris to the Germans, whose primary local representative, the sinister Gestapo official Albrecht Richter, ends up torturing her to death. Doris's death, however, is given redemptive significance. For when the play ends in the spring of 1945, an uprising of the British resistance, together with a coordinated Allied naval landing, forces the Germans to retreat and holds out the promise of the nation's imminent liberation. Doris's sacrifice for her country, like that of thousands of other heroes, thus results in the enemy's defeat.[33]

In its overall narrative, *Peace in Our Time* emerged as a postwar critique of appeasement and a vindication of the British decision to fight against the Germans. This agenda was indicated, at the most basic level, by the play's title, a sarcastic reference to Neville Chamberlain's ill-fated claim to have brought "peace in our time" to Britain by appeasing Hitler at Munich in 1938. Coward further expressed his distaste for appeasement through the play's heroic main character, Fred, who laments early on that it was precisely the British people's fear of another world war and their resulting embrace of the ideas of that "silly old man," Chamberlain, during the 1930s

Figure 1 In this scene from the 1947 production of Noël Coward's play *Peace in Our Time* at London's Aldwych Theater, Nazi official Albrecht Richter (Ralph Michael) converses with British collaborator Chorley Bannister (Olaf Pooley), as Fred Shattock (Bernard Lee), Laura Shattock (Beatrice Varley), and Doris Shattock (Maureen Pryor) look on. Photograph by Angus McBean.

that made them unprepared for battle and vulnerable to defeat.[34] The play's main villains gave additional expression to Coward's opposition to appeasement. The ideological fanaticism of Richter – a man who believes it is Germany's "destiny to rule the world" – illustrated the folly of appeasing the Germans.[35] Meanwhile, those British supporters of appeasement, such as Chorley, end up betraying their homeland by collaborating with the enemy.[36]

In offering such an emphatic indictment of appeasement, Coward was driven by strong patriotic motives.[37] Having already personally promoted the nation's propaganda effort during the war by directing and starring in the acclaimed film *In Which We Serve* (1942), Coward not surprisingly affirmed the indestructibility of the British spirit under the imagined conditions of defeat and occupation.[38] Coward's patriotic tendencies were visible throughout the play, but nowhere so clearly as in an exchange between Richter and Fred. When the Gestapo official asks the pub owner how long it will take the British people to become "reconciled to the situation [of German rule]," Fred replies, "Never, Mr. Richter. Nor our children after us, nor their children's children."[39] Coward's proud defense of the British national character was further echoed by the play's heroic portrayal of the British people. Most Britons in *Peace in Our Time* either directly participate in, or covertly support, the resistance. Thus, when Royal Air Force (RAF) pilots Billy Grainger and Stephen Shattock return to the *Shy Gazelle* after escaping from German concentration camps, they are aided and sheltered by the broader community.[40] Such heroism, for Coward, would have been the rule (and collaboration the exception) under Nazi occupation. In the end, the British success in expelling the Germans confirmed the play's basic message that the fight against Nazism had been the nation's "finest hour."

Coward's upbeat narrative, however, would be exceptional in the first years after the war. No other allohistorical tales would echo his patriotic message in the same triumphalistic fashion. Instead, the next narrative to appear after *Peace in Our Time* would be much darker in tone – British writer John W. Wall's 1952 novel *The Sound of His Horn*.[41] Published under Wall's pen name, Sarban, *The Sound of His Horn* is set in the year 1949 and focuses on the figure of Alan Querdilion, a British naval officer who, in a late-night conversation with an unnamed friend, recalls the uncanny events that befell him while a German prisoner of war (POW) during World War II. Querdilion begins his tale by recalling his time in a German POW camp during the years 1941–43. One day, he decides to escape with a comrade, but after fleeing the camp he quickly loses his way in the surrounding forest and gradually succumbs to extreme fatigue. Dizzy with exhaustion, he stumbles into an electrified fence in the forest and loses consciousness. When he awakens, he finds himself convalescing in a hospital bed in an alternate world in which the Nazis have won what his doctor refers to as the "War of German Rights."[42] The year is no longer 1943 but 102 – as his doctor explains, "the hundred and second year of the First German Millennium as fixed by our First Fuehrer and Immortal Spirit of Germanism, Adolf Hitler."[43]

The Nazis, Querdilion learns, have ruled the entirety of Europe for over a century. They have done so, moreover, with the utmost cruelty. As the novel unfolds, Querdilion experiences the savagery of the Nazi-ruled world firsthand at the site of his imprisonment, the private forest reserve of the Reich Master Forester, Count Hans von Hackelnberg. The central villain of the novel, Hackelnberg epitomizes Nazi brutality through his sadistic brand of hunting. At his rustic estate, Hackelnberg entertains both himself and visiting dignitaries by organizing hunting excursions in which the game is not animal but human. He takes particular pleasure in hunting young women, bizarrely outfitted in bird costumes, with the aid of vicious dogs and genetically engineered, steel-clawed, human-cat hybrids. Yet it is not only women who are hunted, for Querdilion soon finds himself fleeing the sound of Hackelnberg's horn. By the novel's end, Querdilion escapes from the hellish forest reserve with the help of a female "bird," a fellow Briton named Kit, who, while fleeing the hunters, throws herself against the forest perimeter's electrified fence, thus disabling it and allowing Querdilion to regain his freedom. Even then, he does so only with the grudging permission of Hackelnberg, who vows to hunt him again.

As a work of alternate history, *The Sound of His Horn* was significant for its emphasis on Nazi brutality. Unlike most wartime accounts, which were set in occupied Britain and focused upon the suffering of British victims, Wall's tale distinguished itself by being set in Germany and focusing on the German perpetrators. Wall's motives in writing the tale are unknown. But as a career diplomat in the British foreign service, he most likely had strongly patriotic feelings about his homeland and correspondingly nega-tive feelings towards its erstwhile German enemies.[44] To a degree, Wall may have written the novel in order to comprehend the German roots of Nazism. If so, it is significant that, like Burdekin, he identified Nazism as a fundamentally antimodern movement.[45] Wall's focus on the cruelty of Nazism, however, also served to validate the postwar belief that the fight against Nazism was Britain's "finest hour." Wall chose a different method of doing this from Coward, preferring to demonize the Germans rather than heroize the British. Indeed, Wall depicted the scant "resistance [that] was still alive in England" as having failed to overthrow German rule for over a century.[46] Still, Wall's portrayal of German omnipotence and British impotence served a triumphalistic function. For by emphasizing British suffering in alternate history, Wall was able to accentuate the significance of his fellow citizens' real historical triumph over the Germans and make them grateful in the present for avoiding catastrophe in the recent past.

Following the tales of Coward and Sarban, allohistorical accounts of a Nazi victory disappeared in Britain for the remainder of the 1950s. At the beginning of the 1960s, however, they began to reappear in greater number. A variety of factors was involved in this trend. But one of the most important was the role of international events during the years 1958–61 in reviving British memories of the Third Reich. The unexpected appearance of neo-Nazi hooliganism in the Federal Republic in 1959 and the capture and subsequent trial of fugitive Nazi SS officer Adolf Eichmann in 1960–61 were instrumental in reminding many in the West about the Republic's Nazi past. The eruption of the Berlin crisis in 1958, culminating in the erection of the Berlin Wall in 1961, moreover, raised new concerns among Britons about the strength of the Anglo-American partnership with the Federal Republic.[47] This tense climate gave rise to new allohistorical accounts of a Nazi wartime victory that further confirmed the premise's early postwar role of validating Britain's real historical fight against the Germans.

The best example of this trend appeared in 1961 with British journalist Comer Clarke's book *England under Hitler*.[48] Unlike the works of Coward and Wall, *England under Hitler* was not a work of fiction but a non-fictional account of what Germany's occupation of Britain would have been like had the Germans won the war. Unlike such wartime narratives as *Loss of Eden* and *I, James Blunt*, which could only speculate on the likely treatment of the English under the Germans, Clarke combined personal interviews with surviving Nazi officials along with documentary support to paint a vivid picture of life as it would have been under Nazi rule.[49] Not surprisingly, Clarke's narrative was a bleak one. Following the successful defeat of the RAF in the skies and British defenders on the ground, the Germans proceed to institute a draconian occupation policy in accordance with German Field Marshal Walther von Brauchitsch's infamous "Orders Concerning the Organization and Function of Military Government in England" of September 9, 1940. This program of "bloody terror," according to Clarke, was intended to transform "the British [into] . . . the slave creatures of Hitler's Master Race."[50] In short order, the Germans would have used their infamous "Black List" of untrustworthy British elites to arrest thousands of Britain's leading political and intellectual figures, punished partisan actions disproportionately with mass executions, deported all adult males between the ages of seventeen and forty-five to the continent for forced labor, and promoted the twisted racial scheme of engineering a "new German-British race" through the compulsory mating of 2 million selected British girls with "virile young Nazis" on SS-run "stud farms."[51] Finally, through the leadership of SS official Franz Alfred Six (who was designated by Hermann Goering to be the chief of the Sicherheitsdienst (SD) in occupied England), "Britain's Jews . . . were destined to be sent to the gas chambers and incinerators of Auschwitz, Treblinka, and Birkenau."[52]

Having depicted the cruelty of the perpetrators, Clarke further emphasized the innocence of the victims. *England under Hitler* devoted considerable space to the creation of secret underground resistance movements – beyond the already extant Local Defence Volunteers and the Home Guard – that would inevitably have sprung into action in the event of Nazi occupation. Led by Colonel Colin Gubbins, this underground army would have avenged Nazi reprisals by assassinating Nazi officers, and thus would have served as a beacon of hope for ordinary Britons. Collaboration would have been unlikely. For, as Clarke noted in the concluding chapter of *England under Hitler*, even where the Germans actually did occupy British territory – namely, in the Channel Islands – they met with a general unwillingness to cooperate. Clarke cited numerous cases of Channel Islanders being deported to Europe for offenses against the Germans and concluded that "the story of the Channel Islands' occupation [was] ... overwhelmingly one of honor and bravery in the face of terror and fear."[53] In its black-and-white depiction of the victims and perpetrators, in short, *England under Hitler* adhered to the moralistic conventions of wartime tales.

Clarke's motives in writing *England under Hitler* were varied. A journalist who the previous year had published an impassioned mass-market book on the crimes of Adolf Eichmann, Clarke was clearly driven by moral considerations to preserve the memory of Nazi crimes.[54] At the same time, he maintained certain suspicions about the Germans. As he declared in a backhanded compliment in the preface to the book:

I have no wish to reopen any wounds that will hinder the growth of a new, democratic Germany ...
   I believe that the majority of Germans are now genuinely sorry that they were mesmerized and mentally twisted by Hitler ... Many of them agree that the ease with which they ... joined the march behind ... Hitler's crooked cross of evil is deplorable and shocking.[55]

Whatever Clarke's ultimate motives, *England under Hitler* clearly highlighted the important fact that, for some Britons, Nazism remained the epitome of evil. This view was driven home most powerfully in the book's last lines, where Clarke pooh-poohed cold-war fears of nuclear annihilation, noting, "However terrifying the advance of nuclear science has made the prospect of any future war, one thing is certain: the end would be quick. It will hardly be disputed that the victory of Hitler's hell on earth, permanent in its systematic organization of death ... slavery and horror ... would have been infinitely, terribly worse."[56] Even in a world plagued by cold-war fears of nuclear destruction, *England under Hitler* made clear that, for many Britons, Nazism's brutality remained seared in memory.

If the grim tone of *England under Hitler* resembled that of *The Sound of His Horn,* other works in the early 1960s revived the upbeat triumphalism of *Peace in Our Time.* A good example was provided by a long essay by the prominent British novelist C. S. Forester entitled, "If Hitler Had Invaded England."[57] Published originally in the conservative British newspaper the *Daily Mail* in 1960, Forester's three-part serialized essay was less a full-fledged alternate history of a Nazi wartime victory than a speculative military history of a German naval invasion of Britain. One of several studies of the planned Nazi sea invasion of Britain known as Operation Sea Lion that appeared around the same time, Forester's tale was the most speculative in chronicling the imaginary course of hostilities, beginning with the landing of a massive German flotilla of barges and motorboats at the port of Rye on June 30, 1940, and culminating in the Nazis' defeat by the Royal Navy and RAF several days later.[58] In keeping with the triumphalist British mindset of the period, Forester heroized the British, depicting the invading Germans being skillfully assaulted by snipers of the Local Defence Volunteer forces. Most notably, Forester's account reversed the wartime assumption that a Nazi invasion would have brought disaster to the British. In his view, the invasion of Britain actually leads history to turn out for the better. For as Forester concluded, "Hitler's decision to attempt the invasion [of England] was most important in shortening the war and hastening his own destruction."[59]

As was true of Coward's play, Forester's fantasy scenario reflected his own strong sense of British patriotism. Forester had been a strong supporter of the war against Germany, having been recruited to write propaganda on behalf of the Allied war effort for the British Ministry of Information in 1939 and later on in the 1940s in the United States.[60] Following the war, Forester clearly embraced the belief that the war had been the British people's "finest hour." This smug belief found ample expression in "If Hitler Had Invaded England," especially in some of the essay's more hyperbolic passages – for example, "that what was in the balance [in the battle between Germany and England] was the destiny of humanity."[61] This statement and others like it reflected the tendency to embellish allohistorically the importance of the *real* historical contribution of the British to the defeat of the Germans and, thus, provide the British nation one last starring role in an event of world historical importance. At the same time, Forester's tale reflected his strong moral commitment to preserving the memory of Nazi Germany's crimes. Forester was keenly aware of the potential horror of a Nazi wartime victory and was committed to preventing any such danger from recurring in the future. As he put it in the preface to his 1954 book of short stories *The Nightmare*:

[a] few more victories in Russia, or a moment of irresolution on the part of the British people, and [the Nazi] ... regime might be in existence to this day ... There is no purpose in studying history unless the lessons of the past are to influence present policy, and present policy can only have a basis in lessons of the past.[62]

It is unclear to what extent Forester was prompted by the resurgence of Western fears of the Germans in the early 1960s to write "If Hitler Had Invaded England." But his longtime moral revulsion towards Nazism leaves little doubt that his account of the Nazis' near-victory over the British served to reinforce the myth of the "finest hour."

Further reaffirming this point was the appearance in 1960 of an anonymously written novel entitled *The Occupation*.[63] This novel (which in all likelihood was written by well-known British historian Hugh Thomas) was the least distinguished work of the period, lacking both a compelling plot and well-defined characters.[64] In its overall contours, however, *The Occupation* reaffirmed the triumphalistic function of the period's alternate histories. Set in London in 1942, the novel portrays the struggle of the British resistance, led by the thinly drawn protagonist, Michael Arlen, to fight against the German occupiers. Predictably enough, the Germans are depicted as a brutal lot. The main German character, the Gestapo chief, Strichner, is a barbarous fiend with a sado-masochistic streak. The German rank and file, meanwhile, commit a wide range of atrocities against the British, whether interning intellectuals in concentration camps or massacring rowdy civilians at a cock-fighting contest.[65] By contrast, the British are depicted in much more favorable terms. Although the novel portrays some Britons collaborating (largely in the form of a Quisling government), it focuses on the efforts of the resistance to fight against the Germans. *The Occupation*, to be sure, does not romanticize the resistance like *Peace in Our Time*. Much of the novel, indeed, chronicles the internal divisions within the resistance – most particularly between the communists, who are under orders from Moscow to assert control over it, and other leftwing and rightwing factions.[66] Still, the novel's main message was ultimately triumphalistic. The resistance registers numerous victories over the Germans, assassinating their leaders, such as Strichner, as well as their British toadies. Ordinary Britons, moreover, also get the best of their conquerors.[67] Finally, as in the accounts of Coward and Forester, *The Occupation* ended with the Americans and British (led by Montgomery, playing the British role of de Gaulle) leading the liberation of the nation from German rule in 1945 and re-establishing the old political order.

RECEPTION

The desire of early postwar alternate histories to validate both the recent past and the present was itself validated by their positive postwar reception. The most prominent of the narratives, Noël Coward's play *Peace in Our Time*, received numerous favorable reviews. As the *Daily Telegraph* opined:

The play is one long thrill. Mr. Coward's account rings true. No less than his sincerity one admires his theatrical skill, which enables him to build up to a finish at once plausible and telling. This play cannot possibly fail. It is too moving, too exciting, too deft – and too timely. We need to be reminded, just now, that we are people of spirit.[68]

Wall's novel, *The Sound of His Horn*, also received special critical acclaim. Nearly all reviewers declared their admiration for the writer's vivid imagination and highlighted the novel's "queer power to horrify in an inexplicable way."[69] The most glowing praise came from noted writer Kingsley Amis, who hailed Wall for having written a narrative "in prose of greater energy and power than almost any science fiction writer can command."[70] Forester's speculative essay, meanwhile, was praised in *The Times* as "brilliant" and "highly plausible."[71] The weakest of the accounts, *The Occupation*, met with a more mixed response, but still received positive comments.[72] It is unclear how wide an audience the tales of the period reached. Still, the existence of support for them within the British public suggested a broad willingness to remember the Nazi past from an ethically informed perspective.

THE POSTWAR YEARS: ALTERNATE HISTORY AS SELF-CRITIQUE,
1964–78

Precisely at the time that this historical perspective seemed to be consolidated, however, an important shift in the allohistorical representation of Nazism began to occur. Beginning in the mid-1960s, the premise of a Nazi wartime victory ceased being depicted in black-and-white terms and instead became increasingly portrayed in a more nuanced fashion. British narratives now began to dissolve the once-clear divisions between heroic Britons and evil Germans by de-heroizing the former and de-demonizing the latter.

In many ways, the shifting representation of Nazism coincided with, and indeed reflected, the onset of a more pessimistic mood within postwar British society. By the early 1960s, most Britons had begun to recognize their nation's decline from great-power status. The humiliating foreign

policy setback in the Suez Crisis of 1956, along with the large-scale abandonment of overseas colonies in the Middle East and Africa during the late
1950s and throughout the 1960s, confirmed American Secretary of State
Dean Acheson's observation that "Britain has lost an empire and has not
yet found a role [in the world]."[73] The sense of a nation adrift was expressed
in British culture by the "Angry Young Men" of the late 1950s and early
1960s, who criticized the emptiness of contemporary British life.[74] This
sense of directionlessness intensified by the late 1960s, as Britain's economy
fell behind that of rival European nations (most notably Germany) in
productivity.[75] Meanwhile, Britain's entry into the EEC in 1974, after long
internal and external resistance, heralded a loss of sovereignty to growing
numbers of concerned Britons.[76] Finally, by the late 1970s, worsening
unemployment, inflation, and labor unrest, as well as new anxieties
about political "devolution" and the "break-up of Britain," sharpened the
overall sense of malaise.[77]

In this climate of growing self-doubt, British views of World War II and
the Germans slowly began to change. In the 1960s, British historians began
to challenge the reigning moralistic view of the war with a new wave of
historical revisionism, taking a more critical stance towards the British
government's share of blame for the conflict's eruption and a more charitable perspective towards the policy of appeasement.[78] This revisionist
trend (which found similar expression at the same time in France) was
largely advanced by representatives of the political left who were prompted
by the period's many crises to radically rethink inherited historical views.[79]
At the same time that Britons were assuming a more critical stance towards
themselves, moreover, they became more generous towards their former
enemies. With West Germany having re-established itself as a prosperous
democracy and a reliable member of NATO, it was no surprise that
growing numbers of Britons had begun to view the Germans in favorable
terms.[80] This trend was further echoed in British popular culture, where
films and novels portraying World War II – such as *The Battle of Britain*
(1969) and *The Eagle Has Landed* (1976) – increasingly distinguished
between "good" Germans and evil Nazis.[81]

Against the backdrop of these trends, the content and function of
alternate histories depicting a Nazi wartime victory changed dramatically.
Whereas the frightful portrayal of the scenario had originally helped to
vindicate the myth of the "finest hour," its more normalized depiction –
epitomized by the more frequent representation of British collaboration
with the Nazis – now became a means of questioning the myth's integrity.
It is probably not coincidental that these new alternate histories were

mostly produced by figures on the left wing of the political spectrum, who were eager to challenge reigning conceptions of British history, memory, and identity. By supposing that the British would have been capable of collaborating, these allohistorical counter-narratives expressed a declining belief in Britain's moral superiority to the rest of Europe. By depicting the British as behaving no better under Nazi rule in alternate history than other Europeans did under Nazi rule in real history, they reflected the existence of a more humble sense of national identity. In the process, however, they presented a more normalized portrait of the Nazi experience. For by humanizing the Germans and by showing that Nazism could take root anywhere – even in Britain – these accounts downplayed Nazism's specific German dimensions and universalized its overall historical significance.

The first self-critical allohistorical depiction of a Nazi wartime victory appeared in 1964 with well-known British playwright Giles Cooper's novel *The Other Man*.[82] An expanded version of Cooper's screenplay under the same name (which had been aired earlier in the year as a highly touted prime-time television drama on Britain's ITV network starring Michael Caine), *The Other Man* revolves around the figure of George Grant, a British brigadier-general who, as the novel opens in the "real" historical present, wonders how his life would have turned out had Britain made peace with Germany in 1940 and bowed out of the war (see Figure 2). As it dissolves into allohistorical speculation, *The Other Man* makes clear that such an event would have proved disastrous. Once the British government decides to make peace with Germany, those who decide to collaborate with it inevitably become corrupted. This is particularly true of George Grant himself. A simple, somewhat naive man who is devoted to the life of soldiering, George becomes the paragon of the collaborator, whose burning sense of ambition leads him to sell his soul in order to advance his career. As the novel opens, Grant is an officer in the famed Marlborough battalion as it is being re-staffed with German military advisers in accordance with the new Anglo-German alliance. In short order, George looks on silently as German brutalities begin to mount. He stifles vague feelings of indignation when he learns that German soldiers have massacred scores of innocent onlookers at a union demonstration in London, and he chooses not to protest when German commanders transfer several Jewish soldiers from his battalion to Dover to serve as forced laborers in a German scheme to build a tunnel under the English Channel.

By remaining silent and accommodating to the new order, however, George's career surges forward. After Hitler invades the Soviet Union with British support, George is transferred to northern India in 1948, where

Figure 2 Cover of the British television guide *TV Times*, profiling the broadcast of the film *The Other Man* (1964).

he eventually comes to be put in charge of a herculean German scheme to build a road several hundred miles long over the Hindu Kush mountains into Tajikistan to aid the German campaign against the Soviets. In this capacity, he willingly accepts the use of slave laborers, thousands of whom end up dying in the brutal environment.[83] Moreover, in order to further ingratiate himself with his German superiors, he betrays several of his fellow officers for making anti-German comments, and they end up being executed for treason.[84] As the novel nears its conclusion in the early 1960s, George's moral stature is as low as his rank is high. By the end, his moral collapse is complete. Just as he begins to recognize the immorality of his actions, he is wounded in a rebel attack and, after convalescing in Germany (where he is stitched together with body parts taken from captive "subhumans"), he accepts a promotion to the rank of general in exchange for agreeing to return to Britain and helping to shore up flagging British support for the Nazi cause.[85]

In portraying a Nazi wartime victory, *The Other Man* constituted something of a transitional work. On the one hand, it continued the wartime practice of demonizing the Germans. At their worst, the Germans are portrayed as fanatical racists – like the eugenicist doctor, Werner Klaus – while at their best they are still depicted as morally deviant, as with the anglophile officer, Karl Ritter, who turns out to be gay (and who ultimately kills himself).[86] Overall, the Germans emerge as an immoral people who live only to wage war. By the end of the novel, indeed, the year is 1964 and the Germans are still in the midst of fighting Russian partisans in Soviet Central Asia. Yet while *The Other Man* inherited the time-honored tradition of demonizing the Germans, it ceased depicting the British as heroic resisters and virtuous victims. Although earlier alternate histories had broached the sensitive topic of British collaboration, they had always depicted it as something exceptional. *The Other Man*, by contrast, made it more normative. While the British capacity to collaborate was epitomized by George Grant himself, it was echoed by the behavior of many other more minor characters. Most are depicted as accommodating themselves to the Nazi new order by identifying with their German superiors and displaying racist and antisemitic attitudes towards the slave laborers beneath them.[87] Even those British soldiers who have reservations about the new order continue to serve in it. In short, where earlier accounts drew a firm line between the British and the Germans, *The Other Man* blurred it.

In submitting a less idealized view of the recent past, Cooper largely criticized the present. His precise motives in writing *The Other Man* are unknown, but his personal background provides certain hints. Cooper's military service in World War II no doubt contributed to his critical view of the Germans.[88] His left-liberal political views, moreover, explained his tendency to look inward and criticize contemporary British social and political trends, whether the shallow bourgeois values of British society or the decline of the moribund British empire.[89] Significantly, this latter theme constituted a prominent subtext to *The Other Man*'s allohistorical plot. As a result of Britain's alliance with Nazi Germany, for example, Canada and Australia break free of British rule and join up with the United States in an alliance of free nations.[90] Britain's loss of empire is closely tied to its decline in other areas as well, such as the realm of technology, in which Britain is far outpaced by the Germans and Americans.[91] The main characters in the novel nervously try to laugh off comments that "Britain is a German colony," but they recognize their country's decline even as they pretend to ignore it.[92] Thus, George's estranged wife, Kate, complains to a mutual colleague, Henry, about the gap between Britain's former and current power, griping that, before the war, "we were the master-race . . . Now we know we're just pretending. Haven't you noticed the way we seem to take a step backward every year?"[93] Cooper's depiction of Britain's loss of national prestige in alternate history, in short, was likely intended to echo the same phenomenon occurring in real history. By all indications, Cooper himself welcomed de-colonization, given his novel's unsavory depiction of those characters who mourn the colonial era's passing. Rejecting any sense of nostalgia for empire, he portrayed its collapse as the inevitable demise of a corrupt institution. Any attempt to forestall Britain's decline from great-power status, he implied, would only lead to disaster. For as the novel makes clear, it is George's inability to accept Britain's decline and his feverish desire to demonstrate its continuing greatness that lead him to build the road to Russia, with all of its attendant horrors.[94]

In the end, then, *The Other Man* revised the function of the premise of a Nazi wartime victory to express new British concerns about the present. At the literal level, the novel's message was the same as prior alternate histories, such as Coward's *Peace in Our Time* – namely, that surrendering to, or otherwise appeasing, the Germans would have led to the nation's moral collapse. But the way in which Cooper drove home this message, as well as its purpose, was very different. Unlike Coward, Forester, and Clarke, he refused to heroize the behavior of the British under Nazi rule, depicting them as likely collaborators rather than resisters.[95] In the process, he chipped away at the reigning historical view that Britain's real historical resistance to the Nazis in 1940 constituted its "finest hour." The hostility to this view was made explicitly clear at the very outset of the novel, when the "real" historical George Grant begins to offer his reminiscences about his time in the British army and is interrupted by a colleague who groans, "Oh dear, now we're going to have it, our finest hour and all that."[96] It is no coincidence, moreover, that George himself notes the general ambivalence towards Britain's military heritage as a result of "this disillusioned age."[97]

Figure 3 Irish nurse Pauline (Pauline Murray) is inducted into the British fascist
organization, Immediate Action, and embarks upon a path of collaboration in this scene
from Kevin Brownlow and Andrew Mollo's 1964 film *It Happened Here*.

In short, Cooper's novel illustrated a new readiness of some Britons in the
mid-1960s to accept a less idealized version of their own recent history.

The same can be said about another important allohistorical depiction
of a Nazi wartime victory that appeared at exactly the same time: Kevin
Brownlow and Andrew Mollo's 1964 film *It Happened Here*. Like *The
Other Man*, *It Happened Here* also presented a more self-critical portrayal
of British collaboration. Set in occupied Britain in 1944, the film focuses
upon the struggle of an Irish nurse named Pauline (played by Pauline
Murray) to choose sides in the bitter battle between British partisans and
fascists belonging to a collaborationist group called the "Immediate Action
Organization" (IA). At the beginning of the film, the war drives Pauline
into the arms of the IA when a partisan ambush during the evacuation of
her village leads to the death of six of her friends and nearly her as well.
Fleeing to London, she finds work as a nurse with the IA, whose philosophy she resolves to familiarize herself with (see Figure 3). Pauline is
skeptical about much of the organization's program (especially its racial
hostility towards Jews and other "useless eaters," such as the handicapped),
but her pragmatic desire for normalcy, combined with a generally apolitical

mindset, prevents her from acting on her doubts. As she explains to her friend Dick Fletcher (an antifascist doctor, played by Sebastian Shaw, who harbors a wounded partisan in his apartment), "I know as much about politics as a lamp post. [But] . . . we fought a war and lost it . . . There's been a lot of suffering on both sides . . . The only way to get back to normal is to support law and order . . . and that's what I'm doing." Pauline is a muddle of contradictions, for while she bridles at being called a fascist, she willingly wears the IA uniform (complete with black lightning-bolt armband) about town. That is, until she is reprimanded for meeting with Dick and is transferred to work at a hospital in the countryside. On her first day at work, she is instructed to administer injections against contagious disease to Polish forced laborers suffering terminal cases of tuberculosis, only to learn with dismay the next morning that she has become complicit in the hospital's euthanasia program. Having been confronted firsthand with the true criminality of British fascism, Pauline quits and is arrested. Yet on her return to London, her train is ambushed and she is captured by partisans who provide her with the chance of once more switching her political allegiances by tending to their wounded. This move brings little comfort to Pauline, however. For as the film closes, her new protectors, the partisans, massacre English SS troops who have just surrendered following a victory in battle. Caught between varieties of brutality, Pauline finds no peace in the allohistorical world of Nazi-occupied Britain.

It Happened Here was highly significant for abandoning wartime clichés about the victims and perpetrators. Like Cooper, Brownlow and Mollo blurred the line between the British and the Germans, depicting both as mired in the same immoral world. While most Britons regarded the fight against fascism as one of good versus evil, the young directors hoped to show how fascism corrupted not only its adherents but also its opponents. Unlike previous allohistorical works, like Noël Coward's *Peace in Our Time*, which celebrated the anti-Nazi resistance, Brownlow and Mollo de-glamorized it. This iconoclastic impulse was vividly illustrated in the film by the partisans' killing of civilians and captured prisoners. But the de-heroization of the resistance was epitomized by the claim of Pauline's friend Dick, who midway through the film declares, "The appalling thing about fascism is that you've got to use fascist methods to get rid of it." In making this point, Brownlow universalized fascism into a force latent within all human beings. As Dick says to Pauline, "We've all got a bit within us and it doesn't take much to bring it to the surface. It stays with us. Probably always will." Moreover, by showing that fascism could, in fact, "happen here" – in Britain, just as easily as in Germany – the film challenged the triumphalist belief, central to the myth of the "finest hour," that Britain possessed a certain moral status above that of other European nations. At the same time, the film universalized the significance of the Nazi experience by conceiving it as part of a broader fascist era instead of as the specific byproduct of German historical forces.[98] In a radical departure from prior British alternate histories, *It Happened Here* drove this point home by providing the Germans with a more sympathetic image. Brownlow in particular was driven by what he called a humanistic desire to "depict the German soldier as a human being, [rather than as] a melodramatic monster" and thus presented the Germans not solely as perpetrators but as victims as well.[99] Indeed, by ending the film with the massacre of defenseless German soldiers by agitated partisans, he went so far as to ask for his audience's identification with their hypothetical occupiers.

Brownlow's own motives in presenting such a nuanced depiction of a Nazi wartime victory largely stemmed from his relative youth. Unlike Coward, Forester, and Wall, he belonged to a generation that had little personal memory of the war. Born in 1938, Brownlow began work on *It Happened Here* as a mere eighteen-year-old in 1956, at a time when, as he put it, "the Nazi era was as forbidden a subject . . . as pornography [was] to the Victorians."[100] At this early stage of his life, Brownlow's interest in Nazism came as much from an aesthetic fascination with Nazi uniforms and regalia as from any moral-political interest in Nazism itself. This sense of aesthetic fascination gradually changed as he matured, but throughout the making of the film Brownlow embraced a value-neutral approach to his subject. Rather than preach to his viewers, Brownlow wanted to "simply . . . present the facts in the film and allow the audience to make up its own mind [about fascism]."[101] Brownlow extended his even-handedness so far as to employ real British Nazi sympathizers to "act" out a key scene involving an antisemitic diatribe. This value-neutral approach reflected the new political realities of postwar Britain. In an era in which the nation had declined to a second-rate power and was dependent upon the Western alliance for its defense against communism, British youth, like their continental counterparts, were strongly concerned with nuclear destruction and largely forswore the use of force to settle disputes.[102] Brownlow himself was an ardent pacifist, believing in the pointlessness of all wars.[103] As these remarks make clear, it was the concerns of the new postwar generation that largely explained why *It Happened Here* abandoned a moralistic, in favor of a more universalistic, depiction of a Nazi victory.

A similar perspective underpinned another work that appeared around the same time, British journalist and writer Ewan Butler's 1968 novel,

Without Apology.[104] As indicated by the novel's subtitle, *Without Apology* was the (fictional) *Autobiography of Sir George Maudesley, Bart.*, a Conservative member of parliament who, in Butler's alternate history, has the historically dubious honor of more or less functioning as the Philippe Laval of Britain after its defeat by the Nazis. *Without Apology* is written by Maudesley while in an American psychiatric hospital in 1943 in the effort to "'set the record straight'" about the historical circumstances that led him to become reviled as Britain's most notorious wartime collaborator.[105] As he retraces his life, Maudesley emerges as an upper-crust Briton whose frustration with his nation's interwar political aimlessness leads him to admire the vigorous sense of national mission projected by Hitler's Germany.[106] Impressed by Germany, Maudesley tries to foster a comparable revival of national strength at home, urging national rearmament, but is dismissed as a witless fascist.[107] In reality, Maudesley distrusts Hitler's Third Reich by the late 1930s because of its territorial rapaciousness. But when the time comes to go to war with Germany over Poland in 1939, he votes against Churchill's decision to fight, highlighting both the moral and practical problems of doing so.[108] Moreover, when Germany finally invades Britain in September 1940, he refuses to support Churchill's rejection of Hitler's peace terms and is thrown in jail. After the Germans defeat the British, however, they free Maudesley and get him to agree to serve as the head of the puppet organization known as the "British Union," whose task is to get Britain up and running again.[109] Maudesley willingly serves in this capacity until the Germans begin to deport Britain's Jews to Europe, at which point he joins his superior, Lord William Lambourn (Britain's equivalent of Marshal Philippe Pétain), in protesting the action to Britain's de facto ruler, Hermann Goering. Finally, Maudesley follows Lambourn's lead in quitting his position altogether and is smuggled out of the country to the United States by his wealthy American sister and brother-in-law. Once in America, however, Maudesley finds little sympathy. Widely reviled as a traitor (Churchill, in Canada, demands his extradition for treason), he pleads his case to the American government, but to no avail. In the end, after depression leads his wife to commit suicide, he suffers a nervous breakdown and is placed in a mental institution, where he remains until his death in 1949.

Compared with *The Other Man* and *It Happened Here*, *Without Apology* was somewhat less emphatic in blurring the line between the Germans and the British. Butler, like Cooper, offered a demonic portrait of the Germans, depicting them executing innocent villagers in retaliation for partisan activity, establishing concentration camps for political prisoners, and deporting British men to Europe as forced laborers. As Maudesley notes, "The Germans have been much tougher here than they were in France or anywhere else in the West. We're getting the Polish treatment ... because Hitler thinks that we've let him down by refusing to make peace."[110] The novel, indeed, offered a heroic portrait of the British people, depicting the majority as engaged in fierce resistance against the Nazis. No less a figure than Maudesley's own seventy-year-old father is portrayed as being killed by the Germans defending the homeland. By showing such heroic resistance as normative, *Without Apology* seemed to ratify the early postwar belief that collaboration was the exception to the rule.

And yet the novel's portrayal of collaboration was less morally judgmental than that of other works. *Without Apology* notably depicted collaboration from the perspective of the collaborator himself, a narrative strategy that forced readers to empathize with the novel's protagonist and prevented them from making snap decisions about the morality of his actions. Butler rejected Noël Coward's portrayal of collaboration as driven by treasonous opportunism and instead represented it as fully compatible with a patriotic sensibility.[111] Throughout his autobiography, Maudesley insists that his decision to cooperate with the Germans was driven by the desire to "give the people of England a chance to survive."[112] Even though Butler raises the possibility that Maudesley's political actions are driven by careerism, this point is ultimately muted by countervailing evidence.[113] Especially when Maudesley resigns his position in protest at the deportation of British Jews, he gains a degree of moral credibility that Giles Cooper's much more corrupt, careerist protagonist, George Grant, never earns. Moreover, Butler never demonizes Maudesley, preferring to highlight the moral ambiguities of collaboration rather than preaching about its evils. Indeed, when Maudesley and his Amercan psychiatrist discuss the reasons for his actions late in the novel, the latter rejects the claim it was "vulgar careerism" that was at work, concluding, "I'd say you'd just be a human being, like the rest of us."[114] Collaboration, *Without Apology* seems to say, is not the product of evildoers but ordinary people. Having said this, Butler was hardly a rightwing apologist for fascism. By the end of the novel, the protagonist's bitter end leaves no doubt that the failure to fight the Germans is a mistake. In this sense, *Without Apology* resembled *The Other Man* in validating the real historical British decision to stand up to the threat posed by Nazism in 1940. Still, in offering a considerable degree of understanding for the pressures that led people to collaborate, *Without Apology* followed the lead of *It Happened Here* in embracing a less judgmental approach to the past.

In abandoning the ethically informed perspective of wartime and early postwar narratives, *Without Apology* challenged the reassuring belief that the fight against Nazism was Britain's "finest hour." Butler's precise motives in drawing such a self-critical portrait of Britain under Nazi rule were varied. As a Berlin-based correspondent for *The Times* during the 1930s, and as an officer who served in the British Expeditionary Forces during the war, Butler had few sympathies for the Germans.[115] As was true of Cooper, his demonic portrait of the Germans was likely meant to accentuate the misguidedness of those Britons who collaborated with them. Yet, unlike Cooper (and also Brownlow), whose self-critical stance came from the left, Butler's pessimism seemed to reflect a more conservative concern about Britain's future status as a great power.[116] In particular, Butler seemed to chafe at Britain's postwar decline with respect to the United States. It is significant that *Without Apology* depicted America in highly critical terms – as a self-righteous nation that fails to live up to its democratic principles and fight against Nazi evil.[117] Instead, the isolationist American government remains neutral and thus is to blame for the terrible fact (outlined in a postscript to Maudesley's autobiography) that the Soviets win the war against the Germans and occupy the entire European continent.[118] In attacking America's foreign policy in alternate history, Butler may have been also criticizing contemporary American foreign policy, which at the point of the novel's publication (1968) was widely being condemned because of the war in Vietnam, and which British conservatives had resented ever since the United States forced Britain to back down over Suez in 1956.[119] Further still, Butler may have been criticizing the British government's close postwar partnership with the United States.[120] The fact that the novel ends with Britain's liberation *not* by joint American-British forces (as in Coward's *Peace in Our Time*) but by troops exclusively from the British Commonwealth suggests a recommendation for Britain to wean itself away from its unreliable American ally and become more self-reliant. In the end, *Without Apology*'s sympathetic portrayal of a man acting on behalf of the national interest may have been intended to possess the same message for Britain at large – to arrest postwar decline by unilaterally focusing once more on the nation's own priorities.

With the dawn of the 1970s, allohistorical accounts of a Nazi victory continued to express an increasingly normalized view of the Nazi era. Early in the decade, works such as British science fiction writer Keith Roberts's 1972 short story "Weihnachtsabend" and the 1972 BBC documentary film *If Britain Had Fallen* (which later appeared as an identically titled book, written by Norman Longmate) explored the capacity of the British to collaborate.[121] But the best expressions of this continuing trend appeared several years later with two high-profile alternate histories that appeared in 1978: the dramatic, three-part, BBC2 television mini-series *An Englishman's Castle* and Len Deighton's novel *SS-GB: Nazi-occupied Britain, 1941*.

Based on a play written by well-known British playwright Philip Mackie and broadcast in three installments as the "play of the week" from June 5 to June 19, 1978, *An Englishman's Castle* portrays the struggle of a successful British television writer, Peter Ingram (played by the veteran British actor and star of many war films, Kenneth More) to recognize the sordid reality of life in Nazi-ruled Britain. In clever fashion, Mackie crafted *An Englishman's Castle* as a television show within a television show. As the first episode opens, the viewer sees the credits for the series superimposed upon a scene of employees in a modern television studio, at which point the camera zooms in towards a television set as it begins to broadcast the image of a medieval castle and additional credits announcing the broadcast of a show called *An Englishman's Castle*. This show-within-a-show is a historical soap opera featuring a family of middle-class Britons in 1940 on the eve of the German invasion of Britain. After a bit of melodramatic banter, the scene shifts back to two executives discussing the show's taping for the day, and it is then that viewers realize that *An Englishman's Castle* is being filmed in a world in which the British have actually lost the war to the Germans. The show's creator, Peter Ingram, is initially depicted as proud of his creation (which portrays the failure of the British resistance against the Germans), satisfied at its high ratings in "German Europe." But as *An Englishman's Castle* progresses, his pride gradually fades. Ingram is a conservative man, at peace with the reality of life in Nazi-ruled Britain, until he begins an extramarital affair with one of the show's leading female stars, Jill, who confesses to him while in bed that she is Jewish and a member of the British underground. Jill is highly critical of Ingram's show, arguing that its message of "calm, decentness, docility, peacefulness, order-liness, obedience to authority ... and making the best of things" serves to defuse potential opposition to the German-controlled British puppet government. As the show progresses, Ingram is faced with the dilemma of whether to remain a tacit supporter of the system or to enter into more active resistance. He soon decides in favor of the latter, however, after he begins to experience the brutality of the state firsthand (both of his sons are killed due to anti- and pro-government activity respectively, while he himself is interrogated by the secret police). In the end, Ingram fulfills a heroic role by broadcasting a code word issued by the resistance – "Britons strike home!" – in the final episode of *An Englishman's Castle,* which serves as a signal to launch the long-hoped-for nationwide rising against the fascist British government. As the series concludes, explosions erupt outside his office window while bullets tear away at his locked office door. Ingram, the viewer is led to believe, has finally sacrificed himself to a greater cause.

In its overall narrative, *An Englishman's Castle* normalized the scenario of a Nazi wartime victory through its critical portrait of British collaboration. Unlike Cooper and Butler, Mackie diminished the demonic character of the Germans. Even though the show reveals that the Germans have completed the final solution of the Jewish question and have since moved on to persecuting other minorities, these crimes are portrayed as lying thirty years in the past. The Germans of the late 1970s are largely invisible, preferring to exert power discreetly from afar through such subtle means as economic inducements and media censorship. Instead, the most brutal characters are the British collaborators themselves. In *An Englishman's Castle,* most Britons have prospered in the German-ruled New Order and have come to accept its legitimacy. None do so more heartily than Ingram's crafty boss, the station censor, Mr. Harmer. Early on in the show, Harmer discusses Britain's defeat by the Germans with Ingram and notes, "I look back on it now as a victory, for common sense, and decency, and humanity – a triumph for peace-loving people everywhere." Harmer's Orwellian view of defeat as victory, and his callousness towards the extermination of the Jews, symbolizes the decision of most Britons to just get on with their lives and ignore its brutal foundations. Supplementing Mackie's critical portrayal of British collaboration was his de-heroization of the resistance. Britain's postwar recovery is depicted as succeeding thanks to the decision of the resistance after the war to accept the Germans' offer of a general amnesty and give up the struggle to liberate their country, pragmatically preferring, as Ingram (a resistance member himself) notes, to "get on with the business of living." Mackie's critical depiction of the resistance extends to the present, where Jill and Ingram's own son, Mark, exhibit a callous acceptance of ruthless tactics (such as killing suspected informers without decisive proof) to preserve their movement.

Still, despite drawing a skeptical portrait of British society under Nazi rule, Mackie ends *An Englishman's Castle* by sneaking in a degree of heroism through the back door. Ingram's own decision to join the resistance ends up redeeming his prior collaboration with the regime. But further still, Mackie undercuts the critical portrayal of British collaboration by revealing most Britons to be closet resistance figures. Since, as Jill tells Ingram, the motto of the resistance is to appear to cooperate with the German authorities, even Britons who seem to be enthusiastic supporters of the regime are eventually unearthed as members of the underground. The best example is the seemingly pro-Nazi television executive, Mr. Harmer, who ends up being arrested by the secret police after being accidentally betrayed by Ingram. Thus, the collaborators are partly vindicated by their anti-governmental activities. Moreover, since Mackie concludes *An Englishman's Castle* by portraying the British rising up to fight the oppressor (however doomed the effort may turn out to be), the writer supplies a more redemptive ending than the accounts of Cooper and Brownlow. Even so, Mackie's portrayal of the British people as all engaged in some degree of collaboration was far removed from the heroized accounts of writers such as Noël Coward.

Mackie's aims in writing *An Englishman's Castle* are uncertain. At one level, he clearly intended it to be a critique of the hubris and self-importance of the modern television industry.[122] But Mackie doubtless intended his trilogy to be viewed on the historical level as well. As a man of moderate leftwing political sympathies, he possessed the capacity to take a more self-critical look at the nation's past. Writing at a low point in Britain's postwar history, at a time of economic malaise and political discontent, he no doubt had little incentive to sustain the simplistic patriotic nostrums associated with the myth of the "finest hour." Thus, his portrayal of allohistorical British enervation was likely intended as a comment on the real historical present. At the same time, as a war veteran (born in 1918) who fought for six years in World War II, he no doubt maintained some degree of allegiance to the concept of heroism.[123] One might surmise, therefore, that by combining a self-critical portrait of British life under Nazi rule with a partly redemptive ending, Mackie intended *An Englishman's Castle* to inspire British viewers to rally their strength in order to meet the difficult challenges of the present.

Strikingly similar to *An Englishman's Castle* in combining cynicism with hope was the most prominent alternate history to appear in the 1970s – famed British writer Len Deighton's bestselling novel from 1978, *SS-GB*.[124] Set in German-occupied Britain in the year 1941, *SS-GB* is a fast-paced thriller that focuses on a pair of British detectives – a young, ambitious technocrat named Douglas Archer and a grizzled World War I veteran named Harry Woods – who are called to investigate a seemingly ordinary murder of an antique dealer. As their investigation progresses, Archer and Woods learn that the victim, William Spode, was really an atomic scientist tied to the British resistance who has struggled (but failed) to prevent his research from falling into the hands of the Wehrmacht, which has begun a secret program of atomic research on the English coast. At the same time that the detectives uncover these disturbing facts, Archer and Woods become involved in a convoluted scheme, hatched by a cabal of British politicians and military men, led by one Colonel Mayhew, to free the King of England (who is being held by the SS in the Tower of London) with the help of the Wehrmacht, which is hoping to embarrass the SS and thus attain sole control over occupied Britain. The rescue mission goes horribly awry, however, when the detectives and a team of American special forces hired by the cabal are ambushed by the SS, which the cabal itself has secretly informed of the mission. The deliberate sabotaging of the mission (in which the King is killed), however, is soon revealed to have served a greater patriotic end, for it diverts the SS's attention away from the simultaneous landing of American marines sent by Mayhew's group to seize the documents necessary to make the atomic bomb from the Wehrmacht's nuclear research station, which they thereafter destroy. Most important of all, the sabotaging of the rescue mission helps Mayhew realize his primary goal of embroiling the Americans and Germans in mutual hostilities and ensuring American assistance in liberating Britain from German rule. In the end, although it is through deception and murder (Spode, it turns out, is killed by the cabal to prevent him from giving the Americans the atomic research), Britain's wily leaders safeguard their nation's future.

Like the alternate histories that preceded it, *SS-GB* was most significant for its nuanced depiction of collaboration. Of all the works of the 1960s and 1970s, Deighton's novel went the furthest in narrowing the distance between the British and Germans. While the works of Cooper and Butler continued to demonize the Germans to varying degrees, *SS-GB* considerably humanized them. Deighton's novel featured well-developed German characters – such as the genial but scheming SS-Gruppenführer Fritz Kellermann and the icy but brilliant SS-Standartenführer Oskar Huth – who compete with each other as much as they cooperate in implementing German policy. Indeed, while the novel did not feature any "good" Germans per se (as in *Swastika Night*), its focus on the intense Wehrmacht–SS rivalry, as well as its mentioning of a plot against Hitler led by Admiral Wilhelm Canaris, showed the Germans in a more complex light than previous works had done. Unlike other narratives that depicted the German occupation as a ruthlessly efficient program of brutal domination, Deighton rendered it as plagued with prosaic internal bureaucratic

turmoil. Similarly, *SS-GB* painted a more complicated picture of collaboration by stressing its moral ambiguity. Nowhere did it do so more
clearly than with the novel's protagonist, Douglas Archer. A man described
as "keeping his eyes half-closed" to the Nazis' brutal policies in occupied
London, Archer is caught between his careerist desires to cooperate with his
SD bosses and his yearning to preserve his own self-respect and the respect
of his young son.[125] For much of the novel, Archer's ambiguous behavior is
contrasted with Harry Woods's steadfast opposition to the regime; yet by
the novel's end, Woods too is revealed to be a collaborator, having agreed
to act as an informant for Kellermann on Archer's independent investigation of the Spode murder. Significantly, the motives of both detectives are
highly complex and ambiguous in their morality. Finally, Deighton's
depiction of the resistance to Nazi rule was equally nuanced. Colonel
Mayhew's callous willingness to sacrifice the King for the greater good of
the nation shows the resistance to be capable of amoral pragmatism, like
their German occupiers. For Deighton, in short, occupation and collaboration resisted easy judgment.

Deighton's motives in presenting such a nuanced image of Britain under
Nazi occupation in *SS-GB* were complex. Given his membership in the
generation that experienced World War II firsthand (Deighton was born in
1929), as well as his postwar military service in the RAF, one might have
expected him to adopt a traditional, patriotic view of the recent past.[126]
However, other aspects of his background predisposed him to more
contrarian views. As a man who came from a working-class milieu and
received little formal education, Deighton's profile as a writer was anything
but traditional.[127] This was reflected in his writerly style and sensibility,
which critics have described as marked by a "tongue-in-cheek attitude" and
a tendency towards "subtle ridicule ... picaresque satire, [and] parody."[128]
Deighton has insisted upon the apolitical nature of his written work.[129] But
he has strongly affirmed that "a writer should destroy clichés and make
people rethink assumptions."[130] More than anything else, this iconoclastic
proclivity seemed to lead him towards dispelling myths about the British
past, which he has done in many of his novels, as well as in his non-fictional
works.[131] This attitude, in conjunction with his abiding fascination with
Germany's Nazi past, led him to the overall universalistic conclusion –
expressed in *SS-GB* – that fascism was not unique to Germany and "could
happen here."[132] In challenging any notion of British moral exceptionality,
in short, Deighton chipped away at Britain's myth of the "finest hour."

Overall, the alternate histories that appeared between the mid-1960s and
late 1970s painted an increasingly normalized portrait of Nazism. While

certain accounts, such as those of Cooper, Butler, and Mackie, continued to portray the Germans as evil villains, they reduced the heroic stature of the British by showing them collaborating with their occupiers. Moreover, the narratives of Brownlow and Deighton moved to humanize the Germans themselves, depicting them in a far more empathetic fashion than earlier accounts. The dissolving line between the Germans and British helped to undermine the early postwar belief – so crucial to the myth of the "finest hour" – in Britain's moral superiority to the rest of Europe and reflected a willingness to accept the universalistic conclusion that Nazism was hardly only a German phenomenon and could have easily taken root in Britain as well.[133] This sober, self-critical realization reflected Britain's postwar decline from great-power status and the emergence of a more humble sense of national identity.

RECEPTION

And yet, if the alternate histories of the 1960s and 1970s slowly abandoned the belief that World War II had been Britain's "finest hour," their highly divided reception indicated a lingering desire of the British public to maintain that belief. Kevin Brownlow and Andrew Mollo's film *It Happened Here* met with a strongly polarized response. When the film was first screened in London in the late fall of 1964, critics praised it as "remarkable," "uncannily brilliant," and "one of the most interesting British films ... for a very long time."[134] In 1966, indeed, *It Happened Here* won the award for best original screenplay from the Writers' Guild of Great Britain.[135] Many ordinary movie-goers, however, were appalled by it. The film met with widespread condemnation on several grounds. Some firmly rejected its assertion that ordinary Britons could have collaborated with the Germans, being of the mind that, as one critic put it, "No one will believe for a moment in the sheeplike acceptance of Hitlerian rule by the British people."[136] Others regarded Brownlow's value-neutral depiction of the Nazis as recklessly irresponsible. The most controversial section of the film was where Brownlow employed real British Nazi sympathizers to "act" out a key scene involving an antisemitic diatribe, without overtly repudiating it in the film.[137] Brownlow's reluctance to do so was rooted in his perhaps naive trust in the ability of audiences to make up their own minds about the film's "correct" political message without directorial guidance. But following vociferous complaints from Jewish groups fearing that the film might incite acts of antisemitism, the film's American distributor, United Artists, insisted that the director cut the offending sections.[138] British supporters of the film protested this decision as an act of "censorship" that "gravely damage[d] . . . its integrity."[139] Brownlow and Mollo, for their part, put up a fight that ended up delaying the film's general distribution until 1966. But, in the end, they obliged and deleted the contested scenes (which were only reinserted in 1996). For an era still wedded to the wartime pattern of depicting the fight against Nazism as a war of good versus evil, the more nuanced approach ran afoul of prevailing perspectives and was roundly rejected.

Giles Cooper's *The Other Man* also met with a mixed response. When first aired on Britain's Independent Television Network (ITV) in September 1964, *The Other Man* represented a milestone of sorts for British television. Billed at the time as "a major television event," *The Other Man* was pathbreaking both in its budget (it was produced with a cast of 200, including 60 speaking roles) and length (at two-and-a-half hours it was the "longest play ever run on one night" on ITV).[140] For these reasons, as well as ITV's shrewd decision to keep the subject of the broadcast secret prior to its airing, the British media devoted considerable attention to it. Yet the reviews were highly mixed. Although some called the film "brilliant," others found its subject overly "gloomy" and resented being reminded of so many "dated horrors."[141] More significantly, there was palpable resistance to its universalistic message that "within us all exists 'the other man.'" While the *Daily Mail* conceded that some men would have succumbed to the lure of collaboration, it found the broadcast "implausible" for its portrayal of "the speed and final acceptance of the British collapse."[142] As *The Times* astutely concluded, "[The film] asks questions about the value of professional duty and personal ambition which are still too close for comfort."[143] In short, British reviewers exhibited discomfort in facing the possibility of collaboration.

This same resistance was still vigorous more than a decade later. Reactions to *An Englishman's Castle* were just as divided as they were to *The Other Man.* Many reviewers hailed the three-part series as "absorbing," "compulsively entertaining," and "the most original drama on the screen" to air in a "fortnight."[144] Many of the show's fans noted with approval that Mackie was less interested in making Britons confront a past that never was than in pointedly challenging them to take stock of their present. As one reviewer put it, "Mackie . . . is clearly asking questions about the complacency of Britain in the comfortable 'seventies . . . Have we grown so soft that we are no longer prepared to fight for what we believe in?"[145] Others, however, objected to Mackie's pessimistic assessment of the British people's behavior in adversity. While one noted that "the Germans would have had a hell of a time subduing Britain," another described Mackie's contention that "we live in a restrictive, semi-Fascist society controlled by cynical villains [today]" as "puerile."[146] As one last reviewer summed it up, "To persuade an audience that Britain has lost the war is almost an impossible feat. But it is asking too much to propose that in 1978 all is ticking over very much as it is now, and that, for example, all the Jews in Britain have been done away with without making too many ripples on the surface."[147]

Interestingly, British reviewers seemed somewhat more comfortable with the depiction of collaboration in Len Deighton's *SS-GB*. By all accounts, Deighton's novel was a critical and commercial success. One of the leading bestsellers of the year 1978, *SS-GB* was widely praised by British reviewers.[148] Calling the novel one of Deighton's "best," Anthony Burgess wrote, "The occupying Nazis are human beings, vulnerable, men with problems. The occupied Britons are not ... particularly heroic ... One can hardly doubt that London in the early winter of 1941 ... would have been pretty much as Deighton presents it."[149] Or as another reviewer wrote of the novel's narrative, "All this is presented convincingly. There can be little doubt that this is much the way things would have turned out if the Germans had won the war in 1940."[150] Many other reviews made similar claims about the book's plausibility.[151] In the process, such remarks testified to a growing British willingness to countenance the possibility that they would not have behaved heroically had the Nazis won the war. Still, the appearance of criticism towards *SS-GB* revealed an ongoing British reluctance to accept the normalization of the Nazi past. One reviewer protested the book's lack of moral outrage towards its subject. Noting that Deighton was probably on the mark in portraying the misery of life under Nazi rule, James Cameron nevertheless concluded that the novelist ultimately "doesn't really *mind*. Action is all, and spendidly done in the slightly down-market John Le Carré style. The really implicit wretchedness you have to bring yourself."[152] In depicting a Nazi victory, in other words, Deighton left out the horror. Indeed, the portrayal of Nazi-occupied Britain served as a mere backdrop to a conventional spy thriller. As Cameron noted, "[The] political background of defeat and occupation seems somehow not integral to the plot; the mystery could almost as well have happened anywhere at any time."[153] In short, Deighton's novel treated the scenario of a Nazi victory like a scenario from any other historical era. Finally, some other reviewers doubted that Deighton even wrote the novel to expose Nazism's criminality. Wondering "what ... the point of this kind of historical 'might have been'" even was, Paul Ableman concluded that "[the] purpose behind *SS-GB* ... is not to ... expand consciousness, generate beauty, or reveal truth but to keep the paying customers happy."[154] Instead of probing the Nazi experience for moral lessons, in short, Deighton according to Ableman had exploited it for commercial purposes.

Overall, the production and reception of allohistorical portrayals of a Nazi victory in the 1960s and 1970s revealed the slow transition of British memory away from a self-congratulatory to a more self-critical view of the past. Although the narratives met with a mixed reception, enough Britons found their speculations about the likelihood of British collaboration to be plausible as to reveal a growing willingness to question the myth of the "finest hour." Significantly, as would be revealed in the 1990s, Britons remained highly divided about the nature of their recent past.

ALTERNATE HISTORY BETWEEN SELF-CRITIQUE AND SELF-AFFIRMATION, 1990–PRESENT

Following the efforts of the 1960s and 1970s, allohistorical depictions of British behavior under Nazi rule disappeared for most of the 1980s. There is no clear explanation for this trend. But given the proliferation of self-critical alternate histories during the period of national decline in the 1960s and 1970s, it is possible that their disappearance resulted from a general improvement in the national mood. Margaret Thatcher's tenure in office during the 1980s was highly controversial, but in many respects she ushered in a more upbeat period in Britain's postwar national existence. Her role in improving the nation's economy was important, but it was her feisty determination to boost its self-esteem that was decisive.[155] Whether in the form of military adventures such as the Falklands conflict with Argentina in 1982 or her campaign on behalf of "Victorian values," Thatcher beat the drum of British patriotism quite effectively. As she put it after the Falklands triumph in 1982, "We have ceased to be a nation in retreat. We have instead a new-found confidence – born in the economic battles at home and tested and found true 8,000 miles away."[156] To be sure, not all Britons shared these views, but Thatcher's political dominance over the remainder of the decade suggested that a great many did.[157] As the national mood improved, the impulse to self-criticism waned, and so too did the need for self-critical alternate histories.

The connection between the British national mood and the production of alternate histories is further supported by their reappearance during the era of renewed uncertainty following Thatcher's departure from office. After 1990, Great Britain once more suffered from a crisis of confidence.

Thatcher's replacement by the bland John Major and the return of economic recession were significant factors in this trend. But perhaps the most decisive event was the end of the cold war. The fall of communism provided a reason for many Britons to celebrate, but it paradoxically augmented British fears of national decline. The cold war's end brought about major changes in the European balance of power, most notably the emergence of a powerful unified Germany eager to accelerate the pace of European integration. Especially in the period surrounding the much ballyhooed year of European unity, 1992, British fears of being absorbed into a German-dominated Europe (a phenomenon that came to be called "euroskepticism") became quite pronounced. British perceptions of the Germans were unavoidably affected by these trends, though no consensual view of them seems to have emerged within the British public. While politicians like Margaret Thatcher and her Secretary of Trade and Industry, Nicholas Ridley, sparked controversy with their skeptical comments about the German people's aggressive national character, and while the British press nurtured stereotypical images of the Germans as closet Nazis, a strong majority of ordinary Britons nevertheless voiced their support for German reunification.[158]

In this ambiguous climate of optimism and anxiety, it was fitting that Britons once more began to reassess – and disagree about – the legacy of World War II. During the first half of the 1990s, British interest in the war increased dramatically due to the fiftieth anniversary commemorations of its pivotal events. Much of this attention was nostalgic and celebratory. But in a notable dissenting trend, a significant number of British historians on both the left and right began to pick apart the myth that the fight against Nazism had, in fact, been the nation's "finest hour." This revisionist trend had clear political dimensions. Some historians on the left, such as Clive Ponting, assailed Britain's patriotic myths as a means of criticizing the departed Thatcher government.[159] Other British leftists believed that the myth of the "finest hour" had kept the nation insular and prevented it from participating in the broader project of European integration. As the leftwing journal *New Statesman and Society* opined in the fall of 1989, the "pretension of national greatness, reproduced by the myth [of the finest hour has] ... contributed to keeping this country out of the European community" and sustained a mindset of "childish regression" that has left the nation ill-prepared to face future challenges.[160] Significantly, fears of national decline also drove certain renegade conservatives to assail the myth of the finest hour, most notably historian John Charmley, who, as is discussed below, declared that British intervention in World War II had caused the nation's postwar decline. At the same time, however, more traditional British conservatives strenuously defended the finest hour against such leftwing and rightwing challenges, arguing that it was crucial for preserving British national identity.[161] By the middle of the decade, in short, the subject of World War II had became divisive as never before in Britain.

The allohistorical accounts of a Nazi wartime victory that appeared in the 1990s reflected the new polarized climate. As in the 1960s, the revived sense of decline lent a self-critical tone to the decade's alternate histories that surfaced in the continued assault on the finest-hour myth. Both leftwing and rightwing writers participated in this trend, though they utilized different strategies. Left–liberal accounts, like those of the 1960s and 1970s, tended to promote this goal by continuing to portray the British unheroically as likely collaborators with the Germans. Yet unlike the earlier tales, which had mostly continued to depict the Nazis as the incarnation of evil (in order to emphasize the criminality of those Britons who collaborated with them), the accounts of the 1990s began to de-demonize them to an unprecedented degree, portraying the victorious Third Reich as a much more vulnerable and far less fearsome entity than in earlier narratives. Significantly, certain maverick conservative accounts did the same thing, portraying Nazi Germany as posing no real threat to Great Britain as a means of challenging the finest hour's basic belief that British intervention against Nazi Germany had been in the national interest. Albeit for different reasons, these leftwing and rightwing alternate histories honed in on the same target – the myth of the finest hour. At this same time, however, the myth had its supporters, especially among more traditional British conservatives, who vocally condemned the self-critical alternate histories of the early 1990s and, later in the decade, went on to produce their own accounts defending the nation's conduct in the war. This clash of counter-factual narratives revealed a nation strongly at odds on the significance of its past and its relevance for the future.

ALTERNATE HISTORY AND LEFT–LIBERAL SELF-CRITIQUE IN THE EARLY 1990S

The first allohistorical work to appear in the 1990s was British military historian Adrian Gilbert's 1990 book *Britain Invaded: Hitler's Plans for Britain: A Documentary Reconstruction.*[162] A quirky work, *Britain Invaded* was a pseudo-documentary picture book, replete with creatively recaptioned historical photographs, that claimed to chronicle the "real" Nazi

BRITAIN UNDER THE NAZI YOKE·113

<u>Below</u> Under police supervision Jews are directed onto waiting trains as part of a deportation order. The involvement of the British in the persecution of the Jews remains a controversial question. Besides the direct involvement of fascist and other anti-semitic groups, elements of Local Government, the Civil Service and the police all played their part in the shipment of Jews to the death camps.

Figure 4 A sample page from Adrian Gilbert's book *Britain Invaded* (1990).

invasion, defeat, and occupation of Great Britain in World War II (see Figure 4). After opening with a description of the landing of 200,000 German soldiers on English soil on July 23, 1940 (the infamous "S-Day" of Operation Sea Lion) and the resulting armistice on August 7, Gilbert's narrative largely followed that of Comer Clarke thirty years earlier in depicting how the Germans go about implementing the directives contained in Walther von Brauchitsch's "Orders Concerning the Organization and Function of Military Government in England" of September 9, 1940. Unlike Clarke, however, who had strongly demonized the Germans, Gilbert humanized them, writing that "once the strangeness of the Germans had been overcome, people found to their surprise that they could be human too."[163] Gilbert further diverged from Clarke in downgrading the heroism of the British. As he noted, "At the end of the war . . . [the] story of the dogged fight against a hated oppressor . . . became the new national mythology . . . [But] . . . the truth was that until 1945, the resistance never exceeded one or two percent of the population."[164] At the same time, Gilbert portrayed the British as more than open to collaboration with the Germans, as is made clear by the remark that "the Gestapo and SD . . . received aid from certain sections of British intelligence which were only too keen to throw in their lot with the Germans, [believing] . . . Britain's future lay in the Europe of the New Order."[165] Finally, Gilbert critiqued the British with respect to the Jewish question, remarking that the British "were not impermeable to the antisemitism of the war years and some Jews were sent to their deaths as a direct result of action by the indigenous population – perhaps the biggest scar on Britain's postwar conscience."[166] Finally, when liberation comes, it comes from outside. Following the Anglo-American landing in the south of France in September 1944 (and the nuclear destruction of Hamburg and Nuremberg in December), the British resistance rises up, but it cannot "liberate the country on its own."[167] In short, *Britain Invaded* offered a far from heroic portrait of a Nazi invasion of the island nation.

In writing *Britain Invaded*, Gilbert expressed a decidedly normalized perspective towards the war years and the legend of the finest hour. Gilbert did not conceive his pseudo-documentary text for any overt political reasons. As he has noted, he came up with the idea for *Britain Invaded* as a result of his work as an editor in illustrated military book publishing, a job that brought him into contact with photographs of the Germans' occupation of the Channel Islands and prompted him to develop his "what if" scenario in mock-documentary form.[168] From that point on, Gilbert used the analytical tools of his trade as a military historian to speculate how Britain might have behaved under occupation. In doing so, Gilbert compared Britain to other European nations under Nazi rule, such as Denmark and Norway – a decision which was significant, for it implicitly abandoned the notion (central to the myth of the finest hour) that the British were morally superior to the rest of Europe. In part, Gilbert's readiness to abandon this view was a byproduct of his generational identity. Born

in 1954, he belonged to a cohort that had no personal experience of the war
and thus little emotional investment in portraying it in any particular
manner, whether heroically or self-critically. At the same time, however,
his narrative had political implications. By placing Britain on the same plane
as other European nations, Gilbert expressed his center–left distaste for any
notions of British exceptionalism and thus evinced a more inclusive view of
British national identity, marked by an acceptance of Britain's involvement
in Europe.[169] At the same time, this view entailed, as a corollary, a diminished fear of present-day Germany, which may have subtly influenced his
humanized depiction of the Germans in his narrative.

Following *Britain Invaded*, the next major alternate history portraying a
Nazi wartime victory was a play by celebrated British poet Craig Raine,
'*1953*.'[170] Commissioned by the prestigious Old Vic Theater in London in
1988, published in 1990, and staged at various theaters in Britain between
1992 and 1995, '*1953*' was – as its subtitle indicated *A Version of Racine's
Andromaque* – transferred from its original context of seventeenth-
century France to the allohistorical context of Axis-ruled Europe in the
early 1950s.[171] Where Racine's original play focused on the relations
between the respective losers and winners of the Trojan war, Troy and
Athens, Raine's adaptation transposed these roles to Britain and the Axis
powers of Germany and Italy. '*1953*' is a story of intrigue and betrayal
among characters fated to meet a tragic end. Set in Rome, the play revolves
around the figure of Vittorio Mussolini, the son of the Duce and King of
Italy, who, having destroyed London, holds as hostages the Jewish widow
of the King of England, Annette LeSkye, and her young son and the heir to
the British throne, Angus. Vittorio is desperate to win the love of Annette,
even though he is pledged to marry the German Hohenzollern Princess Ira
as part of a broader plan to strengthen German–Italian relations. Not surprisingly, Hitler perceives Vittorio's lust for Annette as a serious political threat
and he therefore sends a special envoy, Klaus Maria von Orestes, to Rome
to kill Angus and restore the health of Axis relations. Orestes' mission is
complicated, however, by his own lust for Princess Ira, his former lover,
who, for her part, lusts only for Vittorio. Ira's plan to marry Vittorio,
however, collapses when Annette reluctantly agrees to marry him in order
to protect her son. Enraged, Ira cajoles Orestes into murdering the Italian
leader, which he does by stabbing him immediately after his wedding to
Annette. Vittorio's murder, Ira's ensuing suicide, and Orestes' arrest bring
the play to a climax, leaving as the sole survivors the last symbols of the
British monarchy, Annette and Angus.

Although historically unrealistic in its plot, *'1953'* was significant for its nuanced representation of a Nazi wartime victory.[172] Raine's depiction of Italy as an equal power to Germany was historically implausible, given the dramatic imbalance of power between the two Axis partners in real history. Nevertheless, this portrait was significant for its implicit downgrading of German might. *'1953'* showed Germany as much less of a fearsome threat than previous allohistorical works. Indeed, the play portrayed Italy, not Germany, as the power that has brutally destroyed London. Mussolini, not Hitler, is the innovator in brutality. As Orestes recounts to the Italian king:

Your majesty, why did London surrender?
Because you changed the face of war,
With gas, carpet bombing, mass reprisals,
Phosphorus, the anthrax spore.
Your father was famous for military deeds.
You were his son. You killed a city.
Realizing that warfare, modern warfare,
No longer had a place for pity . . . [173]

As the dictator who left "London . . . without a single landmark," Vittorio, not Hitler, is represented as the arch war criminal.[174] By comparison, the Nazis are relatively weak. They remain in difficult military straits, being bogged down on the Eastern front against the unvanquished Soviet armies. Moreover, their economy is in a shambles. Precisely these weaknesses are what embolden Vittorio to resist Hitler's threat to invade Italy if he does not surrender Angus to the Germans. As Princess Ira puts it to one of her servants:

You think the King is terrified?
Of what? Germany's economic miracle?
The currency in cigarettes?
Food coupons? Clothes coupons? Petrol coupons?
Our powdered eggs? Our foreign debts?
The haemorrhage on the Russian front. Forget it.
We can't afford another war.
And anyhow, Vittorio would probably win.[175]

By describing Italy as the likely victor in a battle against the Germans, Raine further contributed to the dismantling of the well-established image of Nazi omnipotence. Finally, Raine's nuanced rendering of the perpetrators was echoed by his far from heroic portrait of the victims. Like many authors before him, Raine refrained from representing the British resistance in heroic terms. Indeed, by depicting the main British character,

Queen Annette LeSkye, agreeing to marry Vittorio in order to protect her son, the heir to the throne, Raine showed the British embracing collaboration in order to ensure national survival.

Like Gilbert, Raine did not have overt political intentions in drawing his complex portrait of the Nazis.[176] Instead, literary concerns seem to have been of paramount importance for him. Raine's initial decision to transfer Racine's *Andromaque* to a fascist-ruled world reflected a desire to accommodate the general tradition at London's Old Vic Theater of updating classical productions by placing them in modern contexts.[177] Moreover, many of the characters and plot twists of '*1953*' were dictated by the need to retain the contours of Racine's original play.[178] Still, Raine's predominantly literary concerns, in and of themselves, reflected a deeper, normalized view towards the Nazi past. One of Raine's most important considerations in drafting '*1953*' was what he called a "writer's belief that historical caricatures, those noble simplicities, make for bad drama because they're ideological in conception."[179] Raine was uninterested in adhering to wartime and early postwar stereotypes of evil Nazis and virtuous Britons, in part because they made for poor literature. But his willingness to abandon these stereotypes also reflected their diminished functionality by the late 1980s. If British writers in the 1950s and early 1960s saw a need to preserve the memory of Nazi brutality in moralistic terms, Raine felt no such obligation. As was true of Gilbert, this attitude may have been due to his relative youth. Born in 1944, he differed from the writers of the previous generation in lacking any direct experience of the war and a personal stake in maintaining the myth of the finest hour. Befitting the times, he was much more interested in inserting a degree of "complication back into 'history.'"[180] In depicting Hitler's Reich as vulnerable, Raine expressed his belief that the Nazis could be "incompetent as well as vicious" as well as his conviction that "all tyrannies are riddled with loopholes."[181] Even if this portrait was not consciously drawn as a reflection of the changing political map of Europe in the aftermath of the cold war, it nevertheless reflected a largely aesthetically oriented mindset unconcerned with preserving the ethically grounded traditions of representing the Nazi past.

After Raine's '*1953*,' the flurry of alternate histories in the early 1990s reached a milestone with the publication in 1992 of Robert Harris's international bestseller, *Fatherland* (see Figure 5).[182] Like *SS-GB*, *Fatherland* was a swift-moving detective thriller. But in important respects, Harris's novel explored the scenario of a Nazi victory in World War II in a radically innovative fashion. Whereas most British allohistorical works on the subject had focused on British collaboration with the Germans, *Fatherland*

Figure 5 Cover of the first American edition of Robert Harris's novel *Fatherland* (1992).

was the first work since Sarban's *The Sound of His Horn* to focus primarily on the Germans themselves. Rather than setting his tale in Nazi-occupied Britain, Harris placed it in Berlin in the year 1964. More provocatively, in contrast to most prior works that had featured English protagonists (with German characters sprinkled in as background), *Fatherland* featured a protagonist, Xavier March, who was not only German but a member of the SS. Finally, unlike most earlier works which portrayed the victorious Reich as the omnipotent epitome of evil, *Fatherland* represented Nazi Germany as a vulnerable empire threatened with decline.

As the novel opens, Xavier March, a detective for the Kriminalpolizei (or Kripo) is called to investigate the mysterious death of a man by the side of a suburban west Berlin lake who turns out to be a high-ranking member of the Nazi party, Josef Buhler. What begins as a routine murder investigation, however, soon becomes a crusade to discover the truth about the Third Reich. For in the course of investigating Buhler's identity, March, together with a female American journalist, Charlotte "Charlie" Maguire, discovers the man's links to twelve other high-ranking Nazis who have also experienced sudden deaths in recent years. What connects them all, March soon learns, is their presence twenty-two years earlier at the infamous Wannsee Conference to coordinate the Final Solution. March recognizes that Buhler's death is merely part of a larger government conspiracy, led by the SS, to cover up all signs of the Holocaust by eliminating those responsible for ordering it in the first place. This anxious plan reflects the Nazi government's larger desire to avoid any potential embarrassment on the eve of the visit of United States President Joseph Kennedy to Berlin to discuss improving relations between the two hostile superpowers. Exposing the knowledge of the Holocaust thus becomes March's chief goal, and he enters into a de facto state of resistance against the state by trying, together with Charlie's assistance, to help the sole surviving attender of the Wannsee Conference, Martin Luther, gain asylum in the United States in exchange for his turning over sensitive documents pertaining to the genocide. March, however, is betrayed by those closest to him (by his partner, Jaeger, and his ardent Nazi son, Pili), and he not only fails to save Luther, who is assassinated by the Gestapo, but himself as well. In attempting to escape to Switzerland, he is cornered by the Gestapo and (in an ambiguous dénouement) either takes his own life or is killed. Only the chance that Charlie has successfully fled to Switzerland with Luther's inflammatory documents preserves the possibility of the world learning the truth about the Holocaust.

In its overall narrative, *Fatherland* offered a strikingly normalized portrait of a Nazi wartime victory. The image of an omnipotent Nazi dictatorship portrayed in most prior allohistorical novels had begun to wane already in *SS-GB*, but *Fatherland* revised it more dramatically still. Nazi Germany, in Harris's novel, is beset by many troubles. Ruled by an aging and increasingly remote Hitler, the Third Reich in 1964 suffers from severe external threats in the form of an American-supported guerrilla rebellion in Nazi-occupied Russia. More ominously, Nazi Germany is also experiencing internal social problems, including a high murder rate, the emergence of a counter-culture fascinated by the underground novels of Günter Grass, and the appearance of anti-Nazi graffiti throughout the nation's cities. These problems stem directly from the very postwar prosperity produced by the Nazis' wartime victories. Having defeated the Soviets in 1943, the English in 1944, and fought America to a stalemate in 1946, the Germans quickly turn soft. As March begins to realize, once the "Germans tasted the comforts of peace, they . . . lost their taste for war."[183] This de-demonized depiction of Nazi Germany was echoed by Harris's sympathetic portrait of Xavier March. In many ways, March was the first sympathetic German character portrayed in British allohistorical literature since *Swastika Night*'s Friedrich von Hess. By asking the reader to identify with March's struggle to unmask the truth of the regime's crimes, Harris crossed an important line by positing the existence of a "good" Nazi. In doing so, Harris by no means aimed to rehabilitate Nazism; indeed, by killing off March at the novel's end, he showed an unwillingness to elevate him to heroic stature. Still, by presenting March as a tragic character, caught between his inclinations towards good and his career service of evil, Harris moved well beyond wartime and postwar stereotyping.

In drafting his portrait of a Nazi victory in World War II, Harris was strongly influenced by the end of the cold war. A well-respected liberal journalist who had long been interested in the subject of Nazism, Harris started writing *Fatherland* at the precise time that Mikhail Gorbachev's reforms in the Soviet Union had begun to trigger the revolutionary events that culminated in the collapse of communism.[184] As he noted in a 1992 interview, "I wrote the book when communism was crumbling and I was struck by the parallels between Nazism and any totalitarian state."[185] The Soviet Union's collapse led him to imagine an analogous process of German decline. As he put it:

Nazism, after Hitler's death, would have collapsed for much the same reasons that Soviet communism did after Stalin's. The need for security would have bred yet more authoritarianism, which would in turn have bred a sullen and unresponsive population, an inefficient economy, ruinous wars, a corrupt bureaucracy, a dissident intelligentsia, a society unable to keep pace with the dynamic of American capitalism.[186]

Yet while the end of the cold war was responsible for *Fatherland*'s optimistic depiction of the Nazi regime, it also contributed to its strong pessimistic subtext. Although Harris portrayed the victorious Reich as a vulnerable empire, he still showed it to be an evil regime enjoying total political and economic dominance over Western Europe. In doing so, Harris drew a not-so-subtle analogy to reunified Germany and its support for European integration.[187] This seemingly polemical comparison between Nazi Germany and the Federal Republic led many euroskeptical Britons (as well as many offended Germans) to interpret *Fatherland* as primarily driven by a fear of Germany and the European Union.

In reality, though, Harris's primary agenda lay elsewhere. The novelist feared neither a reunified Germany nor European integration.[188] For him, the fact of German reunification was significant primarily for further underscoring the reality of Britain's postwar decline. That Harris was influenced by the heightened sense of British decline was suggested by the fact that he followed the pattern established by the writers of alternate histories in the 1960s and 1970s in using the scenario of a Nazi wartime victory to engage in self-critique. Although overlooked by many readers, *Fatherland*'s critical gaze was not directed outward so much as inward. It did not so much condemn the evil of the victorious Nazi empire as the willingness of the British and Americans to collaborate with it. Harris's depiction of the allohistorical losers of World War II – the British and the Americans – was far from flattering. Instead of resisting the victorious Reich, both the British and Americans are inclined to collaborate with it. In Britain, the germanophile Edward VIII and Queen Wallis occupy the throne, while more reputable British leaders like Churchill have fled to Canada. Worse still is the behavior of the United States, which, under the pro-German president, Joseph Kennedy, is willing to put aside moral reservations about the Reich and, in the spirit of realpolitik, improve relations with it. By portraying the Allies in such cynical fashion, *Fatherland* directly questioned traditional notions of Anglo-American moral superiority and thereby further challenged the myth of the "finest hour."[189] Ultimately, then, the cold war's end was crucial for normalizing the Nazi past in two ways: by generating the optimism necessary to de-demonize the Germans and the pessimism required to de-heroize the British.

After *Fatherland*, the final narrative of the decade to assail the myth of the "finest hour" was journalist Madeleine Bunting's 1995 book *The Model Occupation: The Channel Islands under German Rule*.[190] Although a traditional work of history, *The Model Occupation* contained a clear allohistorical subtext. Bunting's primary agenda in writing her study of the German occupation of Britain's Channel Islands was to take aim against the smug view that the British people had "'an unblemished record'" in the wartime fight against Nazism. Throughout *The Model Occupation*, Bunting identified numerous instances of shameful behavior under the Nazis. These included fraternization between British women and German soldiers, the betrayal of fellow Islanders to the occupiers, the absence of active resistance, indifference towards the deportation of Jews, and unresponsiveness towards the sufferings of forced slave laborers. All of these things, Bunting concluded, amounted to outright collaboration. More important still was the allohistorical implication of this conclusion: namely, that "what happened on the Channel Islands ... could have happened in the rest of Britain."[191] In making this claim, Bunting challenged the notion, central to the myth of the finest hour, of British moral exceptionalism. As she put it, "[under] occupation, the British behaved exactly like the French, the Dutch or the Danish."[192] If this hypothesis put forth a less than heroic view of the British, its attendant effect was to humanize the Germans. For as Bunting demonstrated in her book, an important, if understated, reason why the Islanders amicably cooperated with the Germans was because of the occupation's mildness.[193] Rather than showing the Germans to be sadistic psychopaths, Bunting portrayed them in all of their human complexity. In blurring the lines between occupiers and occupied, then, Bunting further muddied the once black-and-white British view of the war.

Bunting's goal in offering this revisionist historical account was largely political in nature. Like Gilbert, Raine, and Harris, she stood on the liberal wing of the political spectrum, being a longtime journalist for the leftwing newspaper, the *Guardian*. She also belonged to the same postwar generation that lacked personal experience of the war years and thus was inclined towards a less dogmatic and more flexible view of the past.[194] For her, debunking the finest-hour myth was part of a broader process of reconceptualizing British national identity for the twenty-first century. As she put it, it was necessary to challenge the "stock of legends" surrounding World War II in order to help "Britain's national identity ... adjust to the development of European integration." By showing the nation's capacity for collaboration, Bunting aimed to debunk the myth of British moral exceptionalism and overcome the "separation caused by twenty miles of water which has shaped Britain's destiny."[195] Getting the British to realize that they were not "inherently different from the rest of Europe," in short, would have the salutary function of merging their destinies towards the common goal of future cooperation.[196]

In short, the allohistorical works of Gilbert, Raine, Harris, and Bunting reflected the waning hold of the finest-hour myth among left–liberal Britons. These writers used the scenario of a Nazi wartime victory to question the nation's self-congratulatory myths and create a new sense of national identity, less aloof from, and better able to meet the challenges of, a united Europe. In so doing, they normalized the portrayal of a Nazi victory, depicting the Germans in human rather than demonic terms. Appearing as Britain was facing the question of its national future in the wake of the cold war, these tales reflected a diminished fear of the Germans in the present and a willingness to involve Britain in the broader, German-led project of European integration.

ALTERNATE HISTORY AND CONSERVATIVE SELF-CRITIQUE IN THE EARLY 1990S

At the same time as the self-critical works of left–liberal writers like Gilbert, Raine, Harris, and Bunting there appeared self-critical allohistorical speculations coming from British conservatives. Beginning in early 1993 and lasting for several years thereafter, a major controversy erupted in Britain over the allohistorical conclusions offered by maverick conservative historian John Charmley and controversial ex-junior defense minister, MP, and military historian Alan Clark. In a series of historical monographs, essays, and television documentaries that appeared between 1993 and 1995, Charmley and Clark challenged the reigning postwar belief that the fight against Nazism had been Britain's "finest hour" by providing alternate visions for how history could have turned out.

The revisionist assault began in January 1993 with the appearance of Charmley's book *Churchill: The End of Glory: A Political Biography.*[197] In this massive monograph, the historian iconoclastically challenged the orthodox belief that Churchill's wise leadership had saved Britain from disaster during World War II. Instead, Charmley insisted that the prime minister's decision to fight Nazi Germany lay at the root of the nation's precipitous postwar decline.[198] By committing Britain to a six-year struggle against the Nazis, Charmley argued, Churchill succeeded in toppling Hitler, but at the price of bankrupting the nation, stripping it of its empire, and demoting it to a minor satellite of the United States. Most regrettable, according to Charmley, was that all of this could have been avoided. In his book's boldest speculations, Charmley highlighted alternatives to the real course of history, implying that British leaders could have extricated the nation from a ruinous war by showing more receptivity to peace feelers issued by Hitler in the spring and summer of 1940 or by seeking out a similar deal following the Nazi invasion of the Soviet Union in 1941.[199] As it turned out, according to Charmley, Churchill was so obsessed with defeating Hitler in order to save his own political career that he passed up such opportunities and led the nation to ruin. In the end, Britain's involvement in World War II was a total failure. Fought in order to protect the world from totalitarianism and to maintain Britain's role as a world power, the war resulted in Soviet domination over eastern Europe and Britain's dependence upon the United States.[200] "Surveying the situation in July 1945," Charmley concluded, "it was hard to argue that Britain had won [the war] in any sense save that of avoiding defeat."[201]

At precisely the same time that *Churchill: The End of Glory* appeared, Alan Clark amplified and extended Charmley's conclusions in an extremely laudatory and widely read book review in *The Times*.[202] In this piece, Clark provided further allohistorical support for the notion of a separate peace with Hitler. Like Charmley, Clark argued that Churchill's "reckless radicalism, bombast, [and] posturing" ill served the nation when it had the chance to end the war on favorable terms. Insisting that "there were several occasions when a rational leader could have got, first reasonable, then excellent, terms from Germany," Clark argued that a separate peace with Hitler in 1940 would have allowed Britain to preserve its vast empire and remain a great power.[203] As he asserted, "It is incontestable that had the war stopped in 1941 Britain would have been richer, stronger and more of her people would have been alive than was the case in 1945."[204] In short, whereas most British writers of alternate history had depicted the British accommodation with the Nazis as leading to disaster, Charmley and Clark perceived it as a missed opportunity.

In arriving at this revisionist conclusion, both Charmley and Clark directly challenged the reigning myth that the fight against Nazism had been the British people's "finest hour." Neither scholar had much tolerance for the heroization of the British people entailed in the myth and worked hard to debunk it. Charmley and Clark opposed the self-congratulatory belief that Britain's fight against Nazism was motivated by moral considerations. Rejecting the claim that Nazi crimes against the Jews provided moral vindication for Britain's campaign against the Germans, they pointed out that the Holocaust had not yet commenced in 1940 and 1941 when the issue of peace with Hitler was being weighed. As such, the Nazi genocide was irrelevant for judging the wisdom of Britain's decision to stay in the war; to claim otherwise, they argued, was to fall prey to the historical sin of retrospective vision.[205] Moreover, Clark pointed out how the British government's conduct of the war proceeded with no particular regard for the fate of the Jews or other persecuted groups.[206] Charmley, finally, attempted to puncture any British sense of moral superiority by reminding readers about their nation's complicity in the crimes of Churchill's ally, Stalin, arguing, "and while we're on moral high ground, what about the people in Stalin's concentration camps? Were they not worth dying for?"[207] "The Soviets were just as morally bad as the Germans," he concluded, "and nobody argued against Britain's alliance with the Soviet Union."[208] For Charmley and Clark, in short, the British had little reason for moral smugness after 1945.

Challenging the myth of the "finest hour" further entailed overturning the traditional belief that a compromise peace with the Nazis would have helped the Germans win World War II. Charmley and Clark demonstrated a strong degree of faith that the Germans would have granted favorable peace terms to the British and would actually have adhered to them thereafter.[209] Both dismissed the idea, moreover, that a resulting Nazi attack upon the Soviet Union – launched without British interference, if not with British support – would have brought the Germans to the brink of victory in the European conflict. Indeed, Charmley insisted that British non-involvement would have best served the nation's interests in the long run. As he put it in a 1993 interview, "If we hadn't got in the way by getting into the war . . . both the Germans and the Russians would have been so exhausted that they would have presented no threat to anyone."[210] By remaining on the sidelines and letting the two dictatorships do battle "like two dinosaurs badly wounding each other," he suggested, Britain would have ensured the defeat of Nazism *as well as* Soviet communism.[211]

Charmley and Clark's revisionist assault on the myth of the "finest hour" had clear political dimensions. As representatives of the conservative Tory establishment, they were highly nostalgic for Britain's empire and obsessed with discovering the reasons for its demise. Writing at a time in which the Tory party was seeking to redefine itself in the wake of Thatcher's departure, moreover, they participated in the conservative movement's broader process of self-examination. A crucial dimension of this process entailed critically re-evaluating the party's view of the recent British past. The wave of historical revisionism that emerged from this process in the 1990s addressed a variety of themes and did so from diverse perspectives. But the most common target for reassessment was the person and policies of conservative icon, Winston Churchill. Charmley and Clark concluded that Churchill's obsession with foreign affairs led him to neglect domestic matters to such an extent that he essentially paved the way for the rise of the Labour party after 1945.[212] For his part, Charmley hardly stopped with Churchill. Given his belief that an interventionist foreign policy was the root of Britain's postwar decline, it was no surprise to him rehabilitate the reputations of arch-appeasers Neville Chamberlain and Lord Halifax, and even blame Britain's postwar problems on its decision to intervene in World War I in 1914.[213] In short, by criticizing the globalist, interventionist, and idealistic character of twentieth-century British foreign policy as lying at the root of the nation's decline, revisionists like Charmley and Clark hoped to clear a path for the embrace of a nationalistic, neo-isolationist, real-political program of pursuing the national self-interest.

Whatever its political motives, this revisionist assault reflected the ongoing normalization of the Nazi past in the consciousness of certain conservative Britons. To a degree, of course, Charmley's de-demonization of the Nazis arose inevitably from his re-evaluation of British policies. In order to criticize Britain's intervention in World War II, he had to de-emphasize the threat posed to Britain by Nazi Germany. This was the direct reverse of the practice of early postwar alternate histories, which vindicated Britain's decision to intervene in World War II by emphasizing the Third Reich's evil. Yet the rehabilitation of the Germans was no mere means to an end. It also reflected a less judgmental view of the Nazi past. In a sense, Charmley was able to take a more critical approach to the nation's postwar myths precisely *because* British fears of the Germans had considerably faded. It was no coincidence that Charmley (born in 1955) belonged to a generation far removed from the war years and lacked the same visceral feelings about the horrors that almost were. In the end, this distanced relationship to the past was what linked his conclusions to the accounts of Gilbert, Raine, Harris, and Bunting. Although driven by different motives, their narratives reflected the interdependence between the decreasing belief in the myth of the "finest hour" and the increasingly normalized perception of the Nazi past.

RECEPTION

Yet if the shifting portrayal of the Germans and the British in the alternate histories of the early 1990s expressed a readiness to accept a less idealized image of the national past, their polarized reception revealed a desire to abide by traditional views. The British response to the allohistorical narratives of the 1990s was the most divisive of the postwar period. While some accounts were received favorably, others were subjected to fierce criticism. The dual nature of the public response revealed that the British people remained split on how to remember the past.

The reception of Robert Harris's blockbuster novel, *Fatherland*, reflected some of the ambiguities of British memory. *Fatherland* was a phenomenal commercial success, rising to the top of the British bestseller list in 1992 and selling some 3 million copies worldwide.[214] As is true of any bestseller, of course, readers flocked to the book for diverse reasons. Judging by the numerous reviews praising its dramatic plot, many enjoyed *Fatherland* simply as entertainment.[215] Yet deeper factors were also at work. In part, *Fatherland*'s commercial success in Britain reflected the novel's ability to exploit British uncertainty about a reunified Germany and the desirability of European integration.[216] Yet the book's success also suggested the emergence of support for a more nuanced view of the Nazi era. In snapping up millions of copies of *Fatherland*, British readers implicitly endorsed the novel's daring decision to feature a "good German," Xavier March, as its protagonist. It is notable that no reviewers rejected Harris's characterization of March as a sympathetic figure.[217] This response suggested a willingness of readers to accept a humanized portrait of the Germans. Similarly, the many reviewers who praised *Fatherland* as a believable work tacitly accepted Harris's depiction of a victorious Nazi regime.[218] At a time in which dictatorships were being toppled throughout Europe, the premise of a threatened Third Reich was highly plausible indeed. The popularity of *Fatherland* thus reflected an increased British readiness to accept a more nuanced view of the Third Reich.

Suggestive, if partial, evidence of shifting British views of the Nazi past was also provided by the positive reception of Craig Raine's play '*1953*'and Adrian Gilbert's book *Britain Invaded*. Raine's play was widely praised by reviewers, who hailed it with a wide range of compliments, ranging from "intriguing" and "remarkable" to "exciting."[219] Most, though, focused on the play's literary qualities and did not address its allohistorical dimensions. When they alluded to its depiction of the victorious Nazi Reich, moreover, they offered conflicting views. While some called '*1953*'"alarmingly real," others declared that the play's "details seem much less plausible than they do in [Robert] Harris['s novel *Fatherland*]."[220] Still, on balance, the absence of objections to Raine's portrayal of Nazi Germany suggested a readiness of the public to accept a less morally informed view of the recent past. The same can be said of Adrian Gilbert's *Britain Invaded*.

Although the response to the book was limited, it was praised by certain scholars who admired its hypothetical depiction of English behavior under occupation.[221] Meanwhile, the response in the British regional press was largely positive and exhibited little criticism of Gilbert's allohistorical contentions.[222]

Madeline Bunting's *The Model Occupation*, by contrast, met with a much more divided response. Significantly, many reviewers supported Bunting's controversial conclusions about the British capacity for collaboration. Speaking for a great many, the distinguished historian Hugh Trevor-Roper called the book "objective," while others described it as "scrupulously fair."[223] Still others affirmed the book's conclusion that most Britons behaved "no better or worse than other Europeans in similar circumstances."[224] Finally, one reviewer tellingly noted that the book's chief lesson was that "we are no different from the Europe we affect so vociferously to despise."[225] As these comments reveal, plenty of British reviewers were willing to abandon a belief in British moral superiority and, in the process, eliminate one of the foundational beliefs underpinning the myth of the finest hour. Bunting's book, however, also had its share of conservative critics eager to maintain the myth of British exceptionalism. John Keegan, for example, argued that Bunting had misunderstood "the nature of the British people" in making her "indefensible" claim that they "would have been ready to collaborate" with Hitler, concluding that it was "fallacious" to hypothesize that military defeat would have eroded the nation's sense of pride in its traditions of democracy and law.[226] Linda Holt, meanwhile, scorned Bunting's "shallow" and "defamatory" book as an effort to reduce the occupation to a "beguiling morality tale" that justified her "disenchantment with the myths of Britishness which [her] ... parents' generation helped to create."[227] As this split reception indicates, Britons were divided along political lines about the hypothetical behavior of Britain under Nazi occupation.

The most dramatic evidence signalling a British desire to maintain the myth of the finest hour, however, was the stormy reaction to the revisionist theses of John Charmley and Alan Clark. Immediately on the heels of the publication of *Churchill: The End of Glory*, a firestorm of condemnation erupted in the British press. Predictably enough, the criticism touched on a wide range of themes. Some criticized Charmley and Clark's political agenda.[228] Others criticized their allohistorical method of analysis.[229] But most focused their attention on Charmley's claim that Britain should have made peace with Hitler in 1940 in order to save its empire. Ironically, these critics (most of whom were conservatives) did so by making use of the same allohistorical reasoning that informed Charmley's own interpretations, concluding that a compromise peace would have led to a Nazi victory in Europe. Norman Stone, for example, wrote that "[a] British pact with Hitler would have made him master of Eurasia . . . and it would have made Britain a huge Guernsey, ruled in the manner of Vichy."[230] John Keegan agreed, arguing that "[a] negotiated peace would not have deterred [Hitler] . . . from the wickedness he planned against Russia and the objects of his racial hatred."[231] Alan Bullock similarly insisted that any peace with Germany would have been followed by a "final clash . . . when Hitler dominated Europe and had the wealth and resources of Russia. Then would have come the reckoning with the Anglo-Saxon powers, Britain and America. Britain would then have been brushed aside, so I don't think the British Empire would exactly have lasted."[232] Perhaps the most strident critic was the most predictable – Winston Churchill's eponymous grandson, who insisted that:

[a] negotiated settlement would have allowed Hitler to concentrate all his force on the Eastern Front and defeat Russia. That done, he would have turned his attentions to Britain, with demands that became ever more unacceptable, until a quisling government was established at Westminster and the Gestapo were in effective control of Britain.

Hundreds of thousands would have been deported from their homes, death-camps established and the full panoply of Nazi terror instituted in England's green and pleasant land. A London Ghetto would have been created and, no doubt, even a London Ghetto Uprising would have ensued.

Worst of all, the surrender of Britain would have represented the extinction of all hope for those living under the Nazi jackboot in Europe, for without Britain as a springboard from which to launch the D-Day invasion, the liberation of Europe – impossible to mount from the far side of the Atlantic – would have been indefinitely postponed. It is no exaggeration to say that the Nazi swastika might be flying over the capital cities of Europe to this day.[233]

As seen by these comments, moral considerations largely motivated the rejection of Charmley's thesis. Coming largely from conservative critics, moreover, these comments reflected an enduring desire to keep intact the foundation of the nation's positive self-image. All in all, the condemnation of Charmley's thesis revealed two significant facts: first, it reflected the enduring centrality of the finest-hour myth to postwar British identity; and second, it illustrated a continuing belief in the ideological ferocity of Nazism. In short, the stormy reaction to Charmley and Clark's revisionist theses revealed that many Britons refused to countenance the normalization of the Nazi past.

ALTERNATE HISTORY AND BRITISH MEMORY AT THE TURN OF
THE MILLENNIUM

The alternate histories that have appeared most recently in Great Britain reveal that the British have remained highly divided about how to remember the Nazi past. By the end of the 1990s, the self-criticial alternate histories that had flourished at the beginning of the decade, had largely disappeared. This trend was bolstered by the improvement in the national mood following the return of economic prosperity after the middle of the decade, as well as the rise to power of a Labour government under Tony Blair in 1997. In their place, there now appeared a spate of self-congratulatory narratives that once more reaffirmed the "finest hour." Penned by some of the same conservatives who attacked the self-critical alternate histories of the early 1990s, these accounts valorized the nation's heroic wartime accomplishments against Nazi Germany in order to reinforce a sense of British particularism and challenge the perceived need for Britain to pursue any further moves towards European integration.[234] At the same time, however, the continued appearance of narratives debunking the finest-hour myth reveal that the broader normalization of memory has persisted.

The best examples of the return to allohistorical triumphalism were provided by the young, conservative British historians Andrew Roberts and Niall Ferguson. In their jointly written essay, "Hitler's England," which was published in Ferguson's edited volume *Virtual History* in 1997, Roberts and Ferguson once more drew clear lines between the demonic Germans and heroic British.[235] Both scholars took explicit aim at both liberal and conservative opponents of the finest hour. In exploring the question how the British would have responded to a Nazi invasion, the two historians rejected Madeleine Bunting's claims in *The Model Occupation*, arguing that it was impossible to extrapolate from the *actual* experience of the Channel Islands to the *likely* experience of mainland Great Britain, and insisting that a variety of factors – such as the stronger faith in democracy in Britain compared with other nations that collaborated with the Nazis, such as France – would have inclined the British to offer fierce resistance against the Germans.[236] Yet they also explicitly rejected John Charmley's benign view of the German wartime threat to Britain by pointing out how Hitler had always planned on a final reckoning with the island nation and could never have been trusted to let it live in peace after a cessation of hostilities.[237]

The insistence upon Nazism's evil also informed Roberts's allohistorical essay from 2001, "Prime Minister Halifax."[238] Published in Robert Cowley's *What If? 2: Eminent Historians Imagine What Might Have Been,*

Roberts's essay was based on the premise that Lord Halifax in May 1940 accepted the post of prime minister instead of Churchill and approved the secret negotiations between R. A. B. Butler and Mussolini's government to engineer an end of hostilities between Britain and Germany. Significantly, Roberts painted a bleak portrait of the consequences of such a separate peace. With Britain sitting on the sidelines and America preoccupied with Japan in the Pacific, Nazi Germany would have faced better odds in its invasion of the Soviet Union. Yet, in the end, Roberts concluded, the Soviets' vast resources would have let them defeat the Germans eventually anyway. The results would have been terrible. Without the presence of British and American forces on the continent, the Soviets would have succeeded in asserting their control over all of Europe and thereby threatened the entire free world. The clear message of "Prime Minister Halifax," as with "Hitler's England," was to vindicate Churchill's decision in 1940 to fight against Nazi Germany as correct .

In reaffirming the myth of the finest hour, Roberts and Ferguson were driven by political motives. As openly conservative historians, they reaffirmed the myth of the finest hour as part of a larger campaign to reinforce a positive sense of Britain's national identity. Both were outspoken opponents of Britain's surrender of sovereignty to the European Union and adhered to a notion of British autonomy and independence from European affairs.[239] Like their conservative colleague John Charmley, they too were nostalgic for the nation's lost empire.[240] And indeed, both men entertained multiple allohistorical fantasies of ways in which Britain could have preserved its imperial holdings – most notably Ferguson's claim, articulated in his 1997 speculative essay "The Kaiser's European Union," as well as in his larger monograph, *The Pity of War*, that Britain's decision to remain neutral in World War I and let Imperial Germany win and reign over the continent would have allowed Britain to remain an imperial power.[241] Still, both men drew the line at appeasing Nazi Germany. The decision to stand up and fight against Hitler was too much a part of the nation's historic identity for them to follow Charmley.[242] In the end, they adhered to a conservative mixture of germanophobia and euroskepticism, reminding everyone that Britain's triumph over Nazi barbarism was the source of the nation's superiority.[243] At a time in which the foundations of British national identity were being challenged by left and right, in short, Roberts and Ferguson firmly used allohistorical speculation to sustain it.

That this battle will remain a difficult one was demonstrated by the publication of celebrated British writer Christopher Priest's prize-winning novel *The Separation* in 2002.[244] A carefully crafted, intricately plotted, and extremely engrossing novel *The Separation* is a genre-defying work of "slipstream" fiction whose haunting blurring of the boundaries between hallucination and reality makes it extremely difficult to summarize. In its essential contours, however, the novel portrays the different impact that two identical twin brothers in Great Britain, Jack and Joe Sawyer, have on the course of British and world history during World War II. Among the novel's multiple story lines, the main narrative is set in a world in which Joe Sawyer, a pacifist conscientious objector working for the International Red Cross, succeeds in persuading Winston Churchill to sign a separate peace with Nazi Germany on May 13, 1941. Many factors help to precipitate this event – among them, Rudolf Hess's successful flight to England to cement the agreement. But the main significance of the story is its upbeat view of the peace treaty's allohistorical consequences. As a result of the treaty, Nazi Germany is able to defeat the Soviet Union (thanks to the assistance of the United States, which invades it from the east after having first defeated Japan) and goes on to win World War II in Europe. Yet unlike the many postwar alternate histories that portrayed a Nazi triumph as bringing about a disaster for the civilized world, Priest's tale represented the outcome as a relatively positive event. With the collapse and disappearance of the Soviet Union, for one thing, the world is spared the cold war. Moreover, as a result of the ensuing "Third War" between Nazi Germany and the United States – a conflict which bankrupts both nations and turns the latter into "a shaky ... [and] authoritarian republic, run ... by capitalist adventurers and armed militias" – Britain is able to emerge as the "dominant political and economic power in world affairs."[245] In short, Britain's separate peace with the Third Reich helps ensure its postwar prosperity.

Needless to say, in portraying this rosy vision of a world in which the Nazis win World War II, Priest expressed a comparatively non-judgmental view of the Nazi era. Rather than showing the Nazis intensifying their fanaticism after their military victory, Priest imagined them launching a program of pragmatic internal reform. Thus, after the Nazis and British conclude their separate peace, Churchill goes on the radio to report the unexpected news that "in a sudden access of good sense, the German people have [just] removed Adolf Hitler from office," and the new Chancellor, Rudolf Hess (who, in reality, has engineered the coup), guarantees that the peace agreement will stand.[246] The Nazis' lack of ideological fervor is further visible in their decision in the treaty to let the British "assume responsibility for the Jewish question," which the British do by launching "Operation Maccabeus, the ... sea- and air-evacuation of European Jews to Madagascar" (which eventually comes to be known as the Republic of Masada).[247] Thanks to this historic effort, the Holocaust does not transpire as it does in real history. Finally, by the year 1999, Germany has largely recovered from the Nazi experience thanks to a "denazification programme" sponsored by the European Union.[248] In short, as a result of the separate peace between Nazi Germany and Great Britain, alternate history turns out much better than real history.

Priest's aims in painting this de-demonized image of the Nazis were varied. His membership of the generation that did not experience the horrors of Nazism firsthand (he was born in 1943) helps explain why he did not share the same sense of Nazism's absolute evil as did Britons of an earlier generation. Like many other Britons who came of age after 1945, present-day events were more at the forefront of his concerns. And if his portrait of the alternate past as superior to the real past is any indication, he seems to have viewed the present with a certain degree of dissatisfaction. Some of this feeling may well have been political in nature. At first glance, his position resembles the conservative stance of John Charmley and Alan Clark in implicitly blaming Britain's decision to fight against Nazi Germany as the root of the country's postwar decline. In defending the viability of a separate peace, Priest seemed to place himself in the conservative camp of those Britons seeking to defend the policy of appeasing the Germans in the 1930s. Indeed, the writer has admitted as much, confessing that "maybe there was, after all, something to appeasement."[249] At the same time, however, Priest's support for appeasement was due less to any conservative nostalgia for the British empire than what he has termed his "general anti-war sentiments." It was largely due to his pacifist principles, then, that he challenged the myth of the finest hour – going so far as to describe the real historical figure of Churchill as a "warmonger" instead of as the nation's savior.[250] Ultimately, Priest's motives for producing his vision of the Nazi era may be idiosyncratic. But the considerable success reaped by *The Separation* – which was effusively praised by critics and won both the Arthur C. Clarke Award and the British SF Award in 2003 – suggests that its views of Nazi Germany are perfectly acceptable for many Britons.[251]

CONCLUSION

From the outbreak of World War II up to the present, British interest in the allohistorical premise of Britain's invasion, defeat, and occupation by the Germans has remained consistently strong. Not only have the British continued to produce a steady stream of new alternate histories, they have begun to rediscover older ones as well. Just in the last few years, Britons have witnessed the restaging of Noël Coward's *Peace in Our Time* in 1995 for the first time in nearly fifty years, the re-release of the film *It Happened Here* in 1996 for the first time in its uncensored version, and the first-time publication of the notorious secret SS handbook for the invasion of Britain, *Invasion: 1940*, in 2000.[252] In view of these milestones, the British penchant for wondering "what if?" has clearly continued unabated up through the present day.

Yet in speculating about the consequences of Britain's defeat by Nazi Germany, Britons have seldom drawn consistent lessons. If early postwar alternate histories painted a black-and-white portrait of German barbarism and British heroism, later accounts offered a much grayer picture. This shift in the depiction of a Nazi wartime victory reflects a larger shift in British views of the nation's "finest hour" and its postwar identity. While the myth's affirmation in early postwar accounts revealed a self-confident view of Britain's superior status in the world, the myth's progressive erosion in later narratives reflected an awareness of Britain's relative decline. As the British people's sense of moral superiority began to fade, their readiness to acknowledge their own moral shortcomings and recognize the humanity of their erstwhile enemies increased.[253] Allohistorical accounts of a Nazi victory thus provide suggestive evidence of the progressive normalization of the Nazi past in British memory. At the same time, however, the divided reception of postwar alternate histories reveals that British views of the war years are far from monolithic. While positive responses to these accounts certainly imply a willingness to accept a more nuanced perspective on the past, the frequent criticism of them reflects a desire to maintain the nation's foundational postwar myth that the real historical triumph against Hitler was its finest hour.

In the end, it is hard to say whether the normalized image of the Nazi past in British alternate histories or the moralistic response to them is more representative of British historical consciousness. Today, conventional wisdom holds that most Britons continue to view World War II from a nostalgic and highly moralistic perspective. As has been repeatedly demonstrated in British popular culture, the tabloid press, and political discourse in recent years, Britons remain eager to trumpet their nation's wartime achievements and remind the Germans of their wartime crimes.[254] Yet while such trends suggest that the myth of the finest hour is alive and well, postwar alternate histories of a Nazi victory over Great Britain reveal the existence of a more self-critical counter-memory within British society. In short, British alternate histories of a Nazi triumph in World War II underscore the genre's provocative ability to subvert traditional views of the past.

CHAPTER 2

The United States and the dilemmas of military intervention

'You're damn lucky, young man, that you're not speaking German today!' The speaker was an elderly man ...

Alan Whittmore was used to this sort of abuse ... As editor of the ... *American Mercury*, it was par for the course ...

'Do I know you?' asked Whittmore, affecting a smile.

'I'm Dr. Evans. Why don't you ever publish my letters to the editor?'

So that was it! Whittmore's memory was suitably jogged ... 'You know I'm sticking with the majority view on this issue. I still believe it was for the best that Roosevelt was impeached ...'

Evans was having none of it: ... 'This business of [the United States] normalizing relations with the Greater Reich is not going over. The American people won't stand for it.'

There was no levity in Whittmore's voice as he said, 'I agree that the Nazis are evil, but no more so than the Communists [whom] they tried and executed at the war crimes trials ...'

'Well, no matter what you say, isolationism will destroy us in the end. There is no neutrality in this world.'

'Non-intervention opens doors that an empire would close.'

And so forth ...'

American novelist Brad Linaweaver's description in his 1982 novella *Moon of Ice* of a lunch-counter argument between isolationist New York newspaper editor Alan Whittmore and an interventionist war veteran raises one of the central questions lying at the heart of all American alternate histories of a Nazi triumph in World War II: should the United States have intervened in the conflict against Nazi Germany or remained neutral? As in the case of Great Britain, American writers and audiences have argued over this question from the moment it first surfaced. The first American alternate histories on the subject of a Nazi military victory appeared at the time of the war itself. In contrast to the situation in Britain, however, they appeared less frequently and in smaller numbers. Since Americans had less reason than Britons to fear an imminent German invasion of their country, they may have had less incentive to explore its imaginary consequences and thus produced fewer counterfactual accounts during the war years. Whatever the case may be, this trend persisted during the first decade and a half of the postwar era. In a period in which cold-war anxieties about the Soviet Union overshadowed any lingering concerns with the bygone Third Reich, it was predictable perhaps that no alternate histories on the subject of a Nazi wartime victory appeared whatsoever.

Only in the late 1950s and early 1960s, with the renewal of international attention towards Germany's Nazi past, did allohistorical explorations of an imaginary German defeat and occupation of the United States begin to emerge in significant numbers. These early narratives uniformly depicted a Nazi wartime victory as having horrific consequences. In so doing, they pursued a dual agenda of preserving the Nazis' crimes in memory and vindicating the United States' decision to intervene in World War II against the Germans. By the late 1970s, however, both the content and function of narratives portraying a Nazi wartime victory began to change. If early postwar accounts depicted a Nazi-ruled world in dystopian terms, subsequent narratives rendered it in far less frightening fashion. Moreover, if the function of early postwar allohistorical depictions of a Nazi triumph was to justify the recent past, the function of later accounts was to critique it. This shift reflected the dawning of a more pessimistic mood in the United States during the 1970s. In the years since 1989, by contrast, the end of the cold war and the restoration of American optimism have led alternate histories to return to their traditional self-congratulatory function of vindicating both the past and present. At the same time, though, these narratives' relatively mild depiction of the victorious Reich provided further signs that the Nazi era's horror has continued to fade in memory. In short, over the course of the postwar era, the shifting character of American alternate histories of a Nazi triumph points to the emergence of a more normalized view of the Nazi past.

WARTIME ALTERNATE HISTORIES

Wartime alternate histories were fewer in number in the United States than in Britain.[2] Those that did appear, however, resembled their British counterparts in depicting Nazism as the epitome of evil. These "future histories" aimed to convince Americans of the dangers posed by the Nazis and of the need to intervene in World War II in order to defeat them. At the time that these accounts appeared, not all Americans were convinced of the wisdom of getting involved in the war. Unlike the case of Britain, whose population was largely in favor of fighting Germany by 1939, Americans at the time were deeply divided into separate interventionist and isolationist camps. While President Franklin D. Roosevelt was firmly convinced that Nazi Germany posed a serious threat to American interests, isolationist politicians like Burton Wheeler, Robert Taft, and Gerald Nye, along with openly "revisionist" intellectuals like Charles Beard and Harry Elmer Barnes, argued that a Nazi victory in Europe was preferable to the detrimental impact that intervention in a European war might have upon American democracy.[3] Over the course of the 1930s, public opinion gradually swung over to the interventionist camp, but Roosevelt remained constrained by isolationist demands all the way up to the Japanese attack on Pearl Harbor on December 7, 1941. The alternate histories of the war years reflected these larger tensions within American society. Significantly, however, they all clearly supported the interventionist cause.

Wartime depictions of a Nazi victory were motivated by the desire to dramatize the dangers posed by Germany to the United States. The two most important accounts of the war years appeared in 1940: Hendrik Willem van Loon's novel *Invasion* and Fred Allhoff's serialized novel *Lightning in the Night*.[4] Although the novels were set in different times (van Loon's in 1940 and Allhoff's in 1945–46), they resembled each other in providing highly detailed chronicles of a German military invasion of the United States. *Invasion* was the more upbeat of the two tales. While it featured the Nazis' bombing of New York City, Galveston, and New Orleans, the novel concluded by having the combined forces of the American air force and navy repel the German assault in forty-eight hours. *Lightning in the Night*, by contrast, painted a gloomier picture, depicting the Nazis bombing such cities as Rochester, Cleveland, and Indianapolis before conquering Washington D.C. and blowing up the White House (see Figure 6). Yet while *Lightning in the Night* imagined a dire future for the United States, it too ended on a positive note. For when the American president dramatically informs Hitler that the United States possess an atomic bomb and will use it unless Germany agrees to peace on American terms, the Nazi dictator refuses and is summarily killed by his own generals, who are desperate to avert the Reich's atomic destruction. Like *Invasion*, therefore, *Lightning in the Night* ultimately provided readers with a happy ending.

In their overall function, *Invasion* and *Lightning in the Night* resembled British wartime alternate histories in their attempt to warn readers about the serious threats posed by Nazism to the United States. Both writers' motives in writing their tales were to encourage popular support for interventionism.

Figure 6 Adolf Hitler visits the Lincoln Memorial after the Nazi invasion of
Washington D.C. in Fred Allhoff's serialized novel, *Lightning in the Night*, which appeared
over several issues in the American magazine *Liberty* in 1940.

Van Loon, a naturalized Dutch-American writer who was active in the propaganda war against the Germans, warned his readers against complacently believing "it can never happen here" by reminding them that the inhabitants of the Netherlands and Norway had naively said the very same thing before being occupied by the German Wehrmacht.[5] Instead, he urged readers to recognize the need for intervention against the Germans, underscoring this point by depicting them in the novel as fanatically committed to a racist vision of world dominance.[6] Allhoff, meanwhile, was equally committed to intervention, even soliciting the advice of military officials in writing his novel.[7] In their depiction of German fanaticism, in short, both *Invasion* and *Lightning in the Night* rejected any prospect of America remaining neutral in the European conflict.

Once the United States entered the war against Nazi Germany in late 1941, however, the goal of intervention was fulfilled and wartime alternate histories largely disappeared. Of course, Americans remained aware of the need for national unity in the fight against Nazism. Thus, the only other allohistorical narrative to appear during the war – Marion White's 1942 novel *If We Should Fail* – graphically depicted the Nazis committing vicious atrocities in occupied America in the hope of overcoming the worrisome fact that Americans had still not yet "united sufficiently to pursue this greatest of all wars."[8] This work remained exceptional, however. Although the Nazi threat remained a fixture in American popular culture throughout the war – especially in films and comic books – it largely ceased to inspire works of alternate history.[9] By the time the war ended, indeed, they had entirely vanished.[10]

RECEPTION

Significantly, the positive reception of wartime alternate histories testified to a public willingness to accept their underlying interventionist messages. *Invasion* was praised in many American journals and newspapers as "no hoax" and as a book that succeeded in "[making] the blood run cold."[11] *Lightning in the Night*, meanwhile, was an even greater success, boosting the sales of the magazine in which it was serialized, *Liberty*, to an all-time high. So successful was the tale that it was condemned by the German government in 1940 as an "outlandish exaggeration."[12] Finally, Marion White's tales of German brutality in *If We Should Fail* were hailed as "pack[ing] a propaganda punch" even though "the warning they convey is no longer questioned."[13] In short, the public approval of wartime alternate histories revealed a nation united about the need to defeat Nazi Germany.

THE POSTWAR YEARS: ALTERNATE HISTORY
AS VINDICATION, 1945–73

With the collapse of the Third Reich in 1945, however, allohistorical accounts of a Nazi victory became scarce. Indeed, none appeared whatsoever for the first decade and a half after the war. This absence was largely due to growing cold-war fears of Soviet communism, which gradually began to overshadow the importance of World War II and the Third Reich in the American consciousness.[14] To be sure, Americans had hardly forgotten about the conflict, which they continued to view largely from a moralistic perspective as a "good war" fought against evil enemies.[15] The war, after all, had benefited the United States more than any other nation, making it the world's pre-eminent economic, political, and military superpower.[16] And as was demonstrated by the representation of the war in postwar popular culture – especially films – Americans continued to regard the Germans according to old stereotypes as formidable adversaries who needed to be defeated lest they impose their rule on the world.[17] In short, in the early years after the war's end Americans had every reason to follow the lead of the British and produce their own self-congratulatory alternate histories on the Nazi era. Yet for the first decade and a half after 1945, Americans were too preoccupied with leading the fight against communism in the present to smugly dwell on the recent successes of the past. If it surfaced at all in these years, the impulse towards counterfactual speculation in the United States addressed such themes as a Soviet invasion of America and superpower nuclear showdown.[18] This trend changed in the late 1950s and early 1960s, however, when the same international events that sparked new interest in the Third Reich in Britain provided a hospitable climate for new works of alternate history to appear in the United States.[19] As in Britain, these narratives revived the wartime image of Nazism as the epitome of evil. Yet their function was new. Instead of motivating Americans to fight against the Germans, these accounts served the didactic function of preserving the Germans' crimes in memory and of vindicating America's historic decision to intervene in World War II against them.

The first work to revive the demonic wartime image of the Germans was a short story by the well-known science fiction writer, Cyril M. Kornbluth, entitled "Two Dooms."[20] Published in July 1958, Kornbluth's tale focuses on an American nuclear scientist named Edward Royland who is busily engaged in the effort to develop the atomic bomb at the American research facility at Los Alamos during World War II. As the story opens, Royland is highly ambivalent about the moral dimensions of the project – so much so, that he keeps secret a recent breakthrough that promises to clinch the bomb's creation. That is, until he visits a Native American colleague who provides him with some hallucinogenic Mexican mushrooms that send him off into (or at least prompt him to hallucinate the existence of) a world, 150 years in the future, in which the Nazis have won World War II. In this alternate world, the Nazis have won because of the failure of the United States to develop the atomic bomb. For without it, the United States is forced to launch a sea-borne invasion of the Japanese islands that leads to the decimation of American troops and allows the German army time to regroup and eventually conquer all of Europe and America.

However implausible, Kornbluth's vision of a Nazi wartime victory was notable for its nightmarish quality. In the tale, Royland first witnesses the horrors of life in the Japanese-occupied American southwest, a brutal place ruled by feudal samurai overlords who have enserfed the native population and forced them to live impoverished, ignorant lives in small-scale, collective farming villages. More horrific still is German-occupied America, which Royland comes to know firsthand after being deported to an extermination camp outside of Chicago. There he witnesses the selection of sick prisoners for immediate death and is himself selected as a candidate for live vivisection by a quack camp doctor. Only once Royland ingratiates himself with the doctor by telling him a fantastic story about having been sent into the future by a satanic Jewish magician is he able to discover, and quickly ingest, a hidden cache of the same hallucinogenic mushrooms that sent him into the alternate world in the first place. By the time he groggily regains consciousness in the real present, Royland recognizes the implications of his otherworldly experience and resolves to notify his boss, Rotschmidt, that he has figured out how to make the atomic bomb a reality. As the tale's narrator recounts:

He wouldn't wait until morning; a meteorite might kill him ... He would go directly to Rotschmidt ... [and] tell him we have the Bomb.
    We have a symbol to offer the Japanese now, something to which they ... will surrender.
    Rotschmidt would be philosophical. He would probably sigh about the Bomb: 'Ah, do we ever act responsibly? Do we ever know what the consequences of our decisions will be?'
    And Royland would have to try to avoid answering him very sharply: 'Yes. This once we damn well do.'[21]

With this ending, "Two Dooms" revealed its chief allohistorical function – to justify the United States' conduct in World War II. By depicting Royland

and his fellow atomic research scientists overcoming their pacifist reservations about developing and using the bomb, the tale vindicated the United States' decision in 1941 to reject isolationism and intervene in the war against the Germans. Kornbluth likely had several motives in promoting this message. On the one hand, he may have been hoping to justify the reality of the postwar world. Indeed, "Two Dooms" provided a certain sense of solace to readers during the cold war by reminding them that the main source of their present-day worries – the atomic bomb – had helped avert terrors that might have become reality without it. At the same time, however, "Two Dooms" aimed to remind readers about the real, historical crimes of the Nazis. As a World War II veteran who had fought the Germans as an infantryman in the Battle of the Bulge, Kornbluth, after 1945, was a fierce opponent of fascism who was personally committed to preserving the memory of Nazi crimes.[22] Kornbluth, indeed, seemed eager to counteract the era's forgive-and-forget attitude by re-demonizing the Germans. Throughout the tale, he depicted the Germans as worse villains than the Japanese, thereby inverting racist wartime stereotypes of America's Asian foes and debunking any belief in the existence of moral or cultural affinities between Germans and Americans. Kornbluth advanced this agenda through his critical depiction of Royland's own cultural biases. After witnessing the brutality of life in the Japanese zone, Royland initially greets the first Germans he meets with relief, assuming that, in contrast to the primitively violent Japanese, they are at least "human" and "members of Western Industrial Culture like him."[23] So confident is Royland of the Germans' basic rationality, indeed, that he offers the Germans his services in building them a bomb. Yet his faith in the Germans is quickly exposed as misplaced. Before long, he is deported to an extermination camp, at which point he regrets having dismissed as mere rumor-mongering the lamentations of a Jewish fellow scientist at Los Alamos about Holocaust atrocities. By the end of the tale, Royland's exposure to Nazi barbarism convinces him of the fundamental irrationality of the German mind. It is unclear to what extent the political events of the late 1950s influenced Kornbluth's tale. Yet at a time in which Germany's Nazi past was coming to dominate the headlines, "Two Dooms" could not help but remind Americans about the pitfalls of viewing the present without a full awareness of the recent past.

If Kornbluth inaugurated the new allohistorical attention towards Nazism, no one did more to spread it into the American mainstream than famed journalist William L. Shirer. Having sparked international controversy with his blockbuster work of history, *The Rise and Fall of the Third Reich*, in 1960, Shirer abandoned non-fiction for fantasy one year later in a widely read essay, published in the December 1961 issue of *Look* magazine, entitled "If Hitler Had Won World War II."[24] This essay was largely an empirically documented discussion of what the Nazis *did* do in occupied Europe as a method of debating what they might have done in the United States had they succeeded in defeating it. Indeed, Shirer stressed that his essay was not merely a product of the imagination, writing, "One has only to consult the captured German secret documents dealing with Hitler's confidential plans for the subjugation of the conquered peoples and then observe how he began to carry them out in the lands he occupied."[25] Using this method, Shirer proceeded to describe the brutal occupation that never happened.

In "If Hitler Had Won World War II," the defeat of the United States comes about as the result of a joint German and Japanese invasion in 1944. While the Japanese march ashore on the Pacific coast and proceed to occupy the western third of the nation up to the Rocky Mountains, the Nazis seize the remaining two-thirds of the country. In short order, both nations subject the United States to a policy of brutal occupation. Like Kornbluth, Shirer imagined the Japanese approach as much more lenient than that of the Nazis. The Japanese exploit their territory for its "oil, minerals, lumber, and food," but otherwise leave the Americans "pretty much to themselves."[26] In contrast, the Nazis follow up their invasion of the east coast by dissolving the nation's main political institutions and arresting its political and intellectual leaders. After suppressing the mass media, outlawing trade unions, closing churches, and destroying synagogues, they move on to more dramatic criminal acts, such as razing Washington D.C. as a symbol of what Hitler calls "'decadent Western democracy.'" Nazi criminality reaches its apex, however, with the extension of the Final Solution to American Jewry. According to Shirer:

Under Hitler's specific orders, occupied North America has been made *Judenfrei* (free of Jews). The figures for those gassed at the great extermination camp in New Jersey have never been published. Eichmann, who was in charge of the grisly business, recently boasted ... that they amounted to nearly five million. More than a million Jews have [escaped] ... to the Japanese-occupied West ... [while] some quarter of a million have escaped to Mexico, many going from there to South America.[27]

Jews are not the only ones persecuted, however. So are other Americans, such as the "Negroes," who suffer "complete segregation," as well as the majority white population, which is subjected to severe economic exploitation as part of the Nazis' program of turning them into "Americans slaves for the ... Master German Race."²⁸ Ultimately, for Shirer, the Nazi occupation of the United States, like the Nazis' real occupation of much of Europe, inaugurates a "truly dreadful era" of unmitigated, unimaginable horror.²⁹

In writing "If Hitler Had Won World War II," Shirer aimed to revive the American memory of Germany's real historical crimes. The tone of moral outrage that framed his allohistorical discussion of a Nazi victory mirrored the tone used in his bestselling historical study of the Third Reich's rise and fall. Both were rooted in Shirer's own left-liberal, anti-Nazi political leanings, but they also reflected the resurgence of American concerns about Germany's Nazi past in the late 1950s and early 1960s. Despite official US–German friendship and cooperation in the NATO alliance, Shirer did not want the American public's forgetfulness towards the Germans' not-so-recent Nazi past to lull it into a false sense of security. It was most likely for this reason that Shirer's alternate history, like Kornbluth's, emphasized that nothing – not even the putative racial similarities between the Germans and the "Germanic" Americans – would have spared them the same savage treatment meted out by the Nazis to the Slavic peoples of Eastern Europe. It was thus a political lesson that Shirer hoped his allohistorical essay could provide: not to place America's future security in the hands of former enemies (no matter how officially embraced in NATO) but to preserve the nation's long tradition of self-reliance. As he declared in his concluding description of American resistance activity against the Nazis: "The spirit of the American people has not been broken. They may not have fully appreciated their freedoms when they had them. Perhaps they took them for granted – until it was too late. But they are determined to win them back."³⁰ In short, like Kornbluth, Shirer used the grim scenario of a defeated America to highlight the wisdom of the United States' real historical decision to fight against, and finally defeat, Nazi Germany.

Shirer's moralistic writing on the subject of Nazism, in turn, was echoed by the early postwar era's most important allohistorical narrative about a Nazi victory in World War II, legendary science fiction writer Philip K. Dick's 1962 novel *The Man in the High Castle* (see Figure 7).³¹ Like the tales of Kornbluth and Shirer, Dick's narrative was also set in an America that had been defeated and occupied by the Germans and Japanese. Unlike them, however, *The Man in the High Castle* was distinguished by an extremely intricate and multilayered plot. Dick's novel resists simple summary, but in its broadest contours it chronicles how the lives of various American and Japanese characters in San Francisco are disrupted by the erratic policies of the hegemonic Nazi regime. The central character, a

Figure 7 Cover of the first American edition of Philip K. Dick's 1962 novel
The Man in the High Castle.

benevolent Japanese diplomat named Mr. Tagomi, spends most of the novel attempting to gather intelligence from a suspected Swedish spy, named Mr. Baynes, about Germany's internal political turmoil and its implications for the nation's geopolitical behavior in the near future. Nazi Germany, at this point in its history, is in the midst of a fierce power struggle between competing party factions following the death of Chancellor Martin Bormann (the successor to the senile Führer, Adolf Hitler, who has been placed in a sanitarium). Agitated by this news, Tagomi is alarmed to learn from Baynes (who turns out to be a well-meaning German Abwehr agent named Rudolf Wegener) that the new chancellor, Josef Goebbels, is preparing an apocalyptic plan called "Operation Dandelion" to destroy Japan with nuclear weapons, seize its colonies, and extend German domination across the entire globe. Tagomi works tirelessly to avert this scenario, helping Wegener arrange a meeting with a high-ranking Japanese military official, General Tedeki, in order to warn him of Operation Dandelion, and ultimately plays the hero by shooting dead several German SD agents who try to assassinate the general. Tagomi and Wegener's modest efforts, however, fail to bring the novel to a happy conclusion. Although their disclosure of Goebbels' doomsday plan helps avert immediate disaster by boosting the fortunes of the chancellor's chief rival, Reinhard Heydrich (who opposes the plan), the world remains a highly unstable place, poised on the brink of a nuclear holocaust. As Wegener pessimistically concludes after arriving back in Germany, "The terrible dilemma of our lives. Whatever happens, it is evil beyond compare."[32]

The Man in the High Castle's plot was far more nuanced than is suggested by the preceding synopsis, but it was deceptively simple in its depiction of the allohistorical origins and consequences of a Nazi wartime victory. Like Kornbluth and Shirer, Dick shared the interventionist belief that the United States had been correct in fighting Nazi Germany. This assessment was apparent in the novel's pointing to isolationism as responsible for America's defeat by the Nazis. For it is the assassination of President Roosevelt in 1932 and the resulting rise to power of his isolationist successor, President Bricker, that prevents the United States from re-arming and being able to resist the eventual Nazi attack.[33] Dick's support for interventionism was furthermore visible in the novel's horrific portrait of the United States under Nazi occupation. Like Kornbluth and Shirer, Dick juxtaposed Japanese and German occupation policies in order to accentuate the severity of the latter. The Japanese, for their part, treat occupied America in traditional imperialistic fashion, exploiting it economically but refraining from overt acts of terror or violence. Tagomi, in particular, is a tolerant and humanitarian figure, who firmly rejects the lure of antisemitism and recoils at the uncouth barbarity of the Nazi leadership.[34] Tagomi's moral stature, indeed, stands in sharp contrast to the barbarism of the Nazis, whose fanatical excesses Dick outlines in fleeting, but nevertheless graphic, terms. Not only have the Nazis murdered most of American Jewry, they have exterminated much of Europe's Slavic population, and embarked upon horrific genetic experiments on the continent of Africa, where they have transformed the few surviving natives into cannibalistic slaves. There is no limit to the Nazis' craving for power, as is demonstrated by their completion of such herculean, if demented, schemes as using nuclear energy to drain and transform the Mediterranean Sea into farmland and using rocket technology to colonize Mars. The omnipotence of Nazi rule, finally, is underscored by the lack of resistance to it. Not only have the Nazis conquered America physically, they have done so mentally as well. Many of the characters in *The Man in the High Castle* embrace Nazi values, especially antisemitism, and are inclined to collaboration, the worst being the antiques dealer, Robert Childan, who so admires the Germans that he proclaims that the world would have been much worse had they lost the war.[35] More than anything else, the articulation of such a defeatist remark by an American underscores the totality of the Nazis' victory.

In the end, though, *The Man in the High Castle* was at its bleakest in actually raising doubts about the reality of the Nazis' triumph. As a writer who consistently questioned the nature of reality in his literary work, Dick appropriately concluded *The Man in the High Castle* by provocatively undermining its essential allohistorical narrative.[36] One of the most important subplots in the novel revolves around the publication of a work of alternate history entitled *The Grasshopper Lies Heavy*, written by a man named Hawthorne Abendsen who is rumored to live in a fortified mountain retreat (the "high castle" that gives the novel its name) near Cheyenne, Wyoming. This controversial book, though banned throughout North America and Europe, engrosses all of the novel's central characters with its "fictional" account of the Nazis' defeat in the war. All of them are highly entertained by the novel, although they all dismiss it as far-fetched. By the end of *The Man in the High Castle*, however, it becomes clear (thanks to the services of the ancient Taoist oracle known as the *I Ching*, or *The Book of Changes*) that the novel's counterfactual premise is actually true. The Nazis really *have* lost the war, but no one knows it.[37] In a conclusion typical of Dick's writing, fiction is exposed as reality and reality as fiction. At first glance, this ontologically disruptive sci-fi twist might be seen as diminishing the frightful quality of *The Man in the High Castle*. For it could be taken to mean that the reality of Nazi rule is nothing but an illusion. Yet the bleakness of the novel's conclusion remains. For the reality of a Nazi victory only becomes an illusion for those who are capable of recognizing the fictionality of their own existence. And, as is implied by Abendsen's ultimate reluctance to face the truth penned by his own hand, most human beings are innately unable to deny their own reality.[38] Dick concluded *The Man in the High Castle*, then, on a pessimistic note by casting doubt upon the likelihood of any escape from political oppression.[39]

In painting such a gloomy portrait of life under Nazi rule, Dick was prompted by a passionate moral commitment to preserving the memory of Nazi barbarism. The writer's interest in the history of the Third Reich was longstanding and dated back to the early 1950s. Dick, indeed, spent seven years conducting research for *The Man in the High Castle*, even reading captured Nazi war documents housed at the University of California, Berkeley, research library. This period of immersion in the primary sources of the Nazi era turned the writer into a fierce anti-Nazi. As he put it, "I thought I hated those guys before I did the research. After I did the research ... I had created for myself an enemy that I would hate for the rest of my life. Fascism. Wherever it appears ... it is the enemy."[40] Like Shirer, then (whose work he admired), Dick was driven by moral reasons to expose the evils of Nazism.[41] It is unclear whether the growing attention to Germany's Nazi past in the late 1950s and early 1960s provided Dick with extra motivation to write his novel, but it may well have made a contribution, given his conviction that fascism had not died with the Third Reich but lived on in the present.[42] Ultimately, his longstanding commitment to exposing the historical evils of Nazism and to fighting its contemporary manifestations in the present provided enough passion to make *The Man in the High Castle* the era's most eloquent portrayal of the horrific character of a Nazi-ruled world.

Following the influential accounts by Kornbluth, Shirer, and Dick, allohistorical depictions of a Nazi wartime victory ebbed during the remainder of the 1960s. Still, the final such account of the decade – episode number 28 of the fledgling science fiction television series, *Star Trek*, entitled "The City on the Edge of Forever" – further demonstrated the scenario's enduring appeal. Regarded as one of the series' most famous episodes, "The City on the Edge of Forever" was based on a screenplay by the well-known writer Harlan Ellison, and was first aired on April 6, 1967.[43] While the episode controversially diverged from the screenplay in certain respects, it generally followed Ellison's dramatic account of the consequences of a Nazi wartime victory.[44] The basic premise of the television episode is that the Starship Enterprise's doctor, Leonard McCoy, in a state of drug-induced insanity, beams down to a mysterious planet and accidentally enters into a time portal that transports him back to the Earth of the 1930s. As a consequence of his actions, the course of history is drastically altered. (When the Enterprise's chief communications officer, Uhura, tries to get in touch with the Starship, for example, she finds that it no longer exists.) To try to undo McCoy's calamitous actions, Captain Kirk and Mr. Spock follow him back in time to discover the cause of history's radical transformation. As it turns out, McCoy has accidentally changed the course of history by preventing a young woman named Edith Keeler (played by Joan Collins) from meeting her intended fate of being killed by a speeding car while crossing the street. A strongly humanitarian woman who runs a homeless shelter and preaches a philosophy of pacifism, Keeler, as a result, is now able to pursue her dream (cut short in "real history") of spreading her pacifist movement across the nation. This achievement, however, ends up having unforeseen consequences, as is made clear by an exchange between Spock and Kirk. Looking into recorded images of the 1930s stored in a makeshift version of Spock's tricorder, the two men note the results of McCoy's interference with the past:

SPOCK: This is how history went after McCoy changed it. Here in the 1930s a growing pacifist movement delayed the United States' entry into the Second World War. While peace negotiations dragged on, Germany had time to complete its heavy water experiments.

KIRK: Germany ... Fascism ... Hitler ... – won [the] Second World War ...

SPOCK: Because all this lets them develop the A-bomb first ... With the bomb and with the V-2 rockets to carry them, Germany captured the world.[45]

Following this pivotal interchange, "The City on the Edge of Forever" does not go into any further detail regarding the horrors of Nazi rule. Yet, as with other more detailed accounts, its chief lesson was clear. All history in the wake of a Nazi victory – in this case, all interplanetary history – is changed for the worse.

In its overall allohistorical narrative, "The City on the Edge of Forever" served to vindicate real history. Like Kornbluth's tale, "Two Dooms," it justified the American decision to intervene against the Germans in World War II by pointing to the horrific consequences that a platform of isolationism – driven by pacifism – would have wrought. In the process, it found redemption in tragedy.[46] Just as Kornbluth's tale viewed the horrific atomic devastation of Hiroshima as necessary for later peace, "The City on the Edge of Forever" depicted Edith Keeler's death (and, symbolically, the death of pacifism itself) as necessary for averting allohistorical catastrophe. Both Spock and Kirk demonstrate a clear recognition of this fact in meditating over the painful ironies of Edith Keeler's historical fate. When Kirk exclaims, "But she was right. Peace *was* the way," Spock responds sagely, "She was right – but at the wrong time." Finally, in the episode's emotional climax, Kirk overcomes his deep feelings of love for Edith Keeler and allows her to be killed by a speeding truck, knowing that it is for the sake of humankind's future. In the end, history has to be allowed to unfold as it really occurred, in all of its tragic dimensions.

Interestingly, the didactic message behind "The City on the Edge of Forever" was multifaceted. Ellison's original screenplay and the eventual televised version diverged in their goals. Harlan Ellison's specific views on the subject of Nazism are unknown. But as a writer of Jewish background who felt the pain of antisemitism directly as a youth growing up in the midwest, he no doubt viewed it with disfavor.[47] His apocalyptic description of a Nazi wartime victory thus most likely expressed personal views in addition to confirming the reigning view of Nazism as the epitome of evil. Significantly, however, the intended message of the televised version of "The City on the Edge of Forever" was much more presentist in orientation. In portraying Edith Keeler's death as necessary for the progress of history, the producers of the *Star Trek* television series expressed their opposition to the growing pacifist movement protesting the war in Vietnam.[48] This explains why the producers transformed Edith Keeler's profession from a well-meaning social worker in Ellison's original draft to a more overtly political leader of a pacifist movement in the television broadcast. This shift was not to the liking of Ellison, who himself was opposed to the Vietnam war, and who went apoplectic upon learning of the changes made to his script. Yet he had no authority over the final version. Whether or not audiences in 1967 America perceived the pro-Vietnam war subtext, the final version of "The City on the Edge of Forever" ended up subtly universalizing Ellison's historically rooted screenplay to offer a political message about the present.

Following the ultra sci-fi account of a Nazi wartime victory in "The City on the Edge of Forever," the portrayal of the scenario assumed still another literary form with journalist Eric Norden's 1973 novella *The Ultimate Solution*.[49] Written as a detective thriller, *The Ultimate Solution* anticipated later British works like *SS-GB* and *Fatherland,* which also borrowed from the genre's conventions. Yet where Deighton and Harris's novels featured protagonists who were generally sympathetic despite their moral short-comings, Norden's featured a central character, New York City detective Bill Halder, who was thoroughly loathsome. *The Ultimate Solution* takes place in 1974 in an America that has been under Nazi rule since 1946, the year that the Nazis succeed in compelling the United States government to accept German rule or suffer total nuclear destruction (the Nazis nuke Chicago and Pittsburgh as a demonstration of their seriousness). As the novel opens, a routine police investigation into the assault of a New York City antiques dealer quickly snowballs into a larger political crisis. The assailant, Lieutenant Halder learns, was in all likelihood a Jew – indeed, "the last Jew on earth," as the irate German official sent to investigate the case, the former German Einsatzgruppen death-squad chief, Johann von Leeb, ominously declares.[50] By 1964, the Nazis have murdered all of the world's Jews, having killed some four million in the United States and raided the globe's other continents for the remainder, even threatening Japan (which controls one-third of the non-Nazi-ruled part of the globe) with nuclear destruction unless it hands over its few Jewish inhabitants. Halder, chosen by Leeb to lead the search for the last Jew on earth, earnestly pursues his mission but comes up empty. Having failed to locate him, the best Halder can do is to theorize that he is somehow being sought by the Japanese, who are eager to embarrass the Germans and register a diplo-matic coup. Through further investigation, however, during which he tortures to death one of the Jew's acquaintances, Halder learns that a colleague in the Gestapo, Beck, has captured him on his own. In the novel's climactic, if implausible, end, Beck discloses that the Jew, Felix Hirsch, has mysteriously arrived in New York City from an alternate world in which the Nazis actually *lost* the war in 1945. While Halder scoffs at this explanation, Beck confesses that he has kept Hirsch hidden in order to fight the Nazi regime, hoping that Hirsch can be used as a "gateway to another world ... that isn't drenched in blood."[51] Halder, a good Nazi collabora-tor, will have none of it, however, and kills both Beck and Hirsch with his Schmeisser submachine gun. With this deed, *The Ultimate Solution* abruptly ends, the last Jew from an alternate past as dead as all remaining hope for an alternate future.

Although weaker than Shirer and Dick's creative efforts, *The Ultimate Solution* effectively articulated its interventionist agenda in depicting the allohistorical origins and consequences of the Nazi victory over the United States. Like Dick, Norden explicitly blamed isolationism for America's defeat. As in *The Man in the High Castle*, *The Ultimate Solution* portrayed the removal of Franklin D. Roosevelt as president (once more through assassination) as bringing about the more isolationist successor, Huey Long, who keeps America out of World War II and thereby seals its fate. Just as Norden's explanation of the reasons for America's defeat served to justify America's real historical entry into the war, so too did his unsparing depiction of the brutality of life in America under Nazi rule. Like Sarban's *The Sound of His Horn*, Norden's tale emphasized the brutal, sadistic, and perverted dimensions of Nazism. The Nazis conquer America with the utmost savagery, punishing the home-grown resistance for sheltering Jews by destroying entire towns – *à la* Lidice – such as Mount Kisco, New York, and executing hundreds of thousands of non-Jewish Americans for defying German orders. After consolidating their rule, moreover, the Nazis elevate sadism to a social norm, breeding blacks as domestic animals, using Slavs for savage blood sports, and rendering all racially "inferior" peoples defenseless by giving them tracheotomies at birth to prevent them from speaking or screaming. This inversion of conventional values is epitomized by the commonly heard view that the Final Solution was "the greatest single achievement of recorded history."[52]

No less brutal than the situation in the United States is that in Germany itself, which continues to be ruled by ideological fanatics well into the 1970s. Although Hitler by this time has retreated into the background with dementia (a double appears at all state occasions), the Reich's leaders, most prominently Reinhard Heydrich, continue to lust after total power, plotting a final nuclear reckoning with Japan to achieve complete world domination. Indeed, by the end of the novel, the Nazi government has given the Japanese a final ultimatum to surrender or face nuclear destruction. On the whole, the vast majority of the German and American characters in *The Ultimate Solution* are either wholly depraved or pragmatically immoral, suggesting that a Nazi victory in World War II would have been nightmarish both for the victors and the vanquished.

Norden's precise aims in painting such a horrific portrait of a Nazi victory are unclear, but they most likely grew out of a deep moral commitment to preserving the memory of Nazi criminality.[53] The journalist's interest in the subject of the Third Reich reflected the surging fascination in Hitler and the Nazi past during the early 1970s known as the "Hitler Wave." This growth of interest in Nazism (discussed in greater depth in chapter 2) had partly been unleashed by the publication of former Nazi armaments minister Albert Speer's bestselling memoir, *Inside the Third Reich*, in 1970. Significantly, Norden conducted a marathon ten-day-long interview with Speer which was published in the June 1971 issue of *Playboy* magazine.[54] Speer's comment to Norden that "If the Nazis had won, [people] . . . would be living in a nightmare" no doubt inspired the writer to imagine some of the very scenarios that he described in *The Ultimate Solution*.[55] In this sense, Norden's novel can be seen as a morally informed critique of the Hitler Wave. During an era in which many Americans seemed to be losing sight of Nazism's criminality, Norden redirected readers' attention to it – in the process, vindicating the real historical decision of the United States to intervene in World War II. At the same time, however, even Norden's tale, by graphically depicting Nazism's criminal tendencies, betrayed certain signs of a lurid fascination with his topic. His artistic inventiveness in conjuring up unimaginable future horrors leaves the suspicion that it was done not only to condemn Nazism but out of a calculated desire to appeal to the lowest instincts of a pulp-fiction audience and sell books. Although he would hardly be the first, Norden, too, seemed to fall victim to the Hitler Wave's tendency to aestheticize Nazi evil.

The same year as Norden's novel, the final portrayal during this period of a Nazi victory in World War II appeared in the form of a two-part story in the popular DC comic book the *Justice League of America* (see Figure 8).[56] Entitled "Crisis on Earth-X," and written by prolific comic book writer Len Wein, the story describes the attempt of the superheroes of the Justice League of America or JLA (including Superman, Batman, Green Arrow, and others) to help their superhero colleagues, the Freedom Fighters (including the Human Bomb, the Ray, and Uncle Sam), escape from an alternate earth where the Nazis have somehow won World War II.[57] Although the plot is highly convoluted (with a predictable amount of high-octane comic book fisticuffs), it confirmed the reigning bleak image of a Nazi-ruled world.[58] Not only do the Nazis assume total control over the United States (they carve Hitler's face into Mount Rushmore for effect), they create an interstellar system of mind-control satellites that maintain their global hegemony. So demonic are the Nazis, indeed, that they end up being overwhelmed by their own twisted ideas. In the story's climactic – if far-fetched – conclusion, the superhero Red Tornado succeeds in penetrating the main Nazi mind-control satellite and appears to encounter Adolf Hitler himself, only to punch off his head and discover that he and the entire Nazi leadership on earth are androids who have been installed in power by the very mind-control machines they have invented to implement their rule. The resolution of the plot is not particularly significant (the superheroes succeed in their mission to liberate

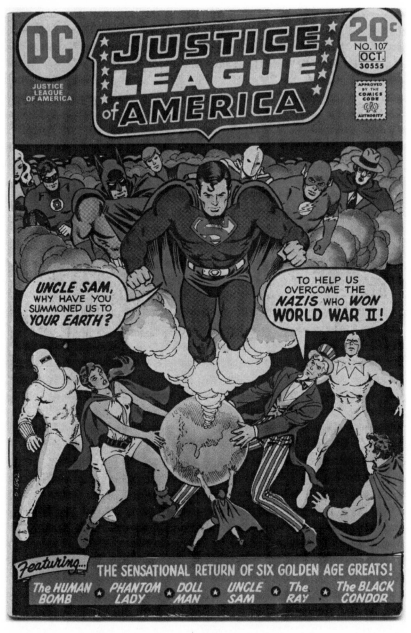

Figure 8 Cover of the comic book story, "Crisis on Earth-X," in the *Justice League of America*, Nr. 107, October, 1973.

Earth-X from the Nazi menace). The story's writer, Len Wein, moreover, did not intend it to convey any particular political message.[59] In general, then, the story was largely significant for confirming the reigning allohistorical view that a Nazi-ruled world would have been hell on earth.

All in all, up through the early 1970s, American alternate histories were united in their depiction of a Nazi victory in World War II. By representing Nazi rule as fanatical, evil, and omnipotent, these accounts expressed a clear sense of moral revulsion against it. This is not particularly surprising given that many of the authors of these tales belonged to the generation that had experienced the traumas of the Nazi era firsthand.[60] More importantly, these narratives served to vindicate America's real historical decision to intervene in World War II against Germany. After 1945, the ominous scenario of a Nazi wartime victory gave Americans a sense that (like the British) their real, historical triumph over the Germans constituted a "finest hour" for them as well. Especially in a cold-war era of renewed tensions and worries, the function of this scenario was particularly welcome. For even if the present constituted a source of anxiety, the nightmare premise of a Nazi victory served to remind Americans that it could have easily been much worse.

RECEPTION

Significantly, the positive response of American readers to these narratives demonstrated the existence of a considerable degree of support for their broader conclusions. The tales of Kornbluth, Dick, Ellison, and Norden largely met with a positive reception during the first postwar decades. *The Man in the High Castle*, for example, won the prestigious Hugo award for best science fiction novel of 1962 at the World Science Fiction Convention.[61] Ellison's screenplay for "The City on the Edge of Forever" won the Writers Guild award for best dramatic teleplay for the 1967–68 season. Meanwhile, the episode itself was a phenomenal hit, having earned the reputation not only of being one of the most beloved of the original *Star Trek* series, but one of the most memorable broadcasts in American television history.[62] Reviews of the era's literary works were also effusive. The most acclaimed was Dick's novel, which, originally hailed as "one of the finest works in [the] . . . field [of science fiction] in a long time," has since come to be recognized as the classic expression of the allohistorical scenario of a Nazi victory in World War II.[63] Positive reviews were also received by Eric Norden for his "bone-chilling novel," *The Ultimate*

Solution, which one reviewer termed a "marvelous read."[64] Kornbluth's short story was less widely reviewed but today is acknowledged as a classic pioneering work in the field of alternate history.[65]

The one major exception to the otherwise uniformly positive reception of early postwar narratives was William Shirer's essay in *Look* magazine, "If Hitler Had Won World War II." Shirer's essay had a mixed reception, largely due to readers' diverging views on the essay's political implications. As was the case with Shirer's magnum opus, *The Rise and Fall of the Third Reich*, his *Look* piece also sparked international controversy. The furor erupted in 1961 when the German news magazine *Stern* blasted it in a cover story entitled "Swastika over New York."[66] In criticizing the piece, *Stern*'s reporters cited the same reasons mentioned by most German critics of *The Rise and Fall of the Third Reich* – namely, it was the work of an alleged German-hater who was "poisoning ... public opinion in the United States" towards Germany at a sensitive moment in the cold war.[67] *Stern* sniped at Shirer's speculative description of the Nazi defeat and occupation of the United States, retorting that "neither Shirer nor any other qualified historian has ever discovered a single serious reference to plans for the occupation of America."[68] Certain American readers agreed with this assessment. Among the letters sent by readers to *Look*, one stated that the essay was "nothing but hair-raising madness," while another insisted that "Shirer is just as dangerous to the peace of the free world as Hitler or Goebbels was. He is the typical propaganda man: half-truths mixed with imagination."[69] At the same time, other American readers praised the piece for preserving the memory of Nazi crimes despite cold-war pressures to ignore them. Thus, one called the story "tremendous" and concluded that it would "awaken the American public to the fact that we face a menace today, as great as the one that faced the free world in those dark days of World War II."[70]

The reason Shirer's piece sparked more of a mixed reaction than the era's other equally critical accounts of a Nazi victory likely had to do with exposure. "If Hitler Had Won World War II" was published in a magazine with a circulation of seven million readers and probably reached many more.[71] Its ability to shape American views of the Germans was thus substantial. In contrast, many of the other allohistorical narratives of the era were comparatively obscure, reached far fewer readers, and thus did not possess the same capacity to shock. Whatever the case may be, the polarized reaction to Shirer's piece was highly exceptional in the early postwar period. On the whole, the moralistic, interventionist depiction of a Nazi-ruled world conformed to the horizon of expectations of most readers and was largely accepted.

THE POSTWAR YEARS: ALTERNATE HISTORY AS
SELF-CRITIQUE, 1972–89

As the 1970s progressed, however, allohistorical accounts of a Nazi victory in World War II began to portray the scenario in markedly less frightening terms. Many of these accounts ceased depicting the Nazis as fanatical demons and instead portrayed them as rational pragmatists. Some of these tales even portrayed a Nazi victory as not such a bad thing after all. Other accounts went further still in abandoning the ethically informed narrative approach of the past, adopting the mode of satire and portraying the victorious Nazis in humorous terms. To be sure, certain works continued to view a Nazi victory in negative fashion; but they were now in the minority. These shifting allohistorical depictions of a Nazi wartime victory reflected the onset of a normalizing trend in the American memory of the Nazi past.

By the 1970s, the fears of Nazism that had survived World War II and that had been revived during the late 1950s and 1960s were beginning to fade. Contributing to this trend were both generational and political factors. By the 1970s, the passing of time had enabled the emergence of a generation of Americans who lacked any personal memories of the war. Unlike the producers of early postwar narratives, such as Shirer and Kornbluth, who had witnessed Nazism's evils firsthand in Europe, many of the writers in this later period viewed the scenario of a Nazi victory from a more detached perspective. At the same time, this generation – and society at large – was confronted with new, present-day concerns that helped to displace traumatic memories of the Nazi era. As was true in Britain after the mid-1960s, the flurry of new alternate histories that appeared in the United States in the 1970s coincided with, and strongly reflected, the emergence of a pessimistic national mood. In domestic affairs, the scandal of Watergate and the oil-crisis-driven stagflation in the early 1970s spawned an atmosphere of acute crisis that persisted through the economic malaise of the Carter years. In foreign affairs, the trauma of the Vietnam War continued to cast its shadow over the nation well after its conclusion in 1975, while escalating cold-war tensions between the United States and the Soviet Union following the Soviet invasion of Afghanistan in 1979 led to renewed fears of nuclear conflict. Out of such events, finally, emerged a broader skepticism towards government and a general opposition to war, both of which found ample expression in the popular culture of the period.[72] It was hardly surprising, therefore, that increasing numbers of Americans began to reconsider how good the "good war" against the Axis powers had really been.

In this climate of crisis, alternate histories now assumed a new function. As in Britain, the scenario of a Nazi wartime victory in the United States ceased to be used for the purpose of self-congratulation and was instead now used for self-critique. In contrast to the situation in Britain, however, where the central themes were collaboration and resistance, the American counter-narratives of this period generally focused on the question of whether the United States should have intervened in, or stayed out of, World War II. Significantly, these accounts offered highly divergent answers to this question. A good number of them voiced support for the isolationist position that the United States should have remained on the sidelines and allowed the Germans to defeat the Soviets, even if it enabled them to become the masters of the European continent. These anti-interventionist accounts, whether rightwing or leftwing in origin, clearly reflected how the cold war elevated the Soviets above the Nazis as objects of fear in the American consciousness and relativized the Third Reich's historical evil. Other allohistorical tales, by contrast, continued to defend the traditional interventionist position that fighting the Germans was in the nation's best interests. Yet in doing so, they adopted a more self-critical stance, abandoning the triumphalism of early postwar accounts in favor of a more polemical tone. Even if they continued to depict the Nazis as an evil enemy, they did so less to vindicate the real historical decision to fight against them than to criticize present-day American decline. In short, even though the narratives of this period differed widely in content, they strongly resembled each other in function. Instead of validating the present by depicting its superiority to a horrific past that never was, they criticized the present by implying its inferiority to a better past that could have been.

THE REHABILITATION OF ISOLATIONISM

The first example of the new normalizing trend was provided by distinguished American political scientist Bruce M. Russett's 1972 book *No Clear and Present Danger: A Skeptical View of the U.S. Entry into World War II.*[73] Although not specifically a work of alternate history, Russett's study liberally used counterfactual reasoning to criticize the previously sacrosanct cause of American intervention in the war. Calling his book a "retrospective analysis of 'might-have-beens,'" Russett right from the outset presented its bold thesis – namely, that "most Americans probably would have been no worse off, and possibly a little better, if the United States had never become a belligerent [in World War II]."[74] The reason for Russett's upbeat conclusion was his contention that even if American neutrality had allowed Germany to remain undefeated in the war, the Nazis would never have been able to deliver a knockout blow that would have defeated the Soviet Union for good.[75] Indeed, the result would have been "a mutually exhausting war that would have left the Russians even more battered than they were from their victory in 1945, and the Germans hardly better."[76] Even if in control of Eastern Europe, Germany would have suffered from the divisive forces of nationalism, as well as from the heavy burdens of reconstruction, and would not have been able to threaten the continent for some time to come.[77] More important still for Russett was the fact that Nazi Germany never posed a serious threat to the United States. Not only did Hitler have no intentions of invading America, he lacked the means to do so, having failed to develop the atomic bomb. For these reasons, American intervention ended up being an enormous mistake. President Roosevelt had failed to anticipate that, by defeating Germany, "American intervention ... would bring Russia into Central Europe to fill the vacuum."[78] As history turned out, "American participation in World War II brought the country few gains" and made it "no more secure ... than it could have been if it had stayed out."[79]

In arriving at his revisionist conclusions, Russett openly cited the traumatic experience of the Vietnam War. As a member of the generation that came of age after the end of World War II (he was born in 1935), he was less concerned with the war's legacy after 1945 than with the contemporary crises of the postwar world. Russett's leftwing political tendencies further reinforced this orientation. A scholar writing in the isolationist tradition of Charles Beard, Russett saw the debacle of Vietnam (like American involvement in the cold war more broadly) as directly attributable to the interventionist legacy spawned by the decision to become engaged in World War II.[80] Russett thus declared his intent to "reconsider my old myths" about America "fighting for its very existence" in World War II and to question whether it was necessary at all.[81] In so doing, of course, he clearly revealed how the trauma of Vietnam diminished the horror of Nazism in American consciousness. While early postwar alternate histories emphasized Nazism's inherent evil, Russett's study relativized it, insisting that "Nazism as an ideology was almost certainly less dangerous to the United States than ... Communism."[82] Moreover, throughout his analysis, Russett de-emphasized moral factors in arriving at his real-political conclusions. Thus, while he recognized that separating "ethics from an objective assessment of the threat Germany ... actually posed to American national security" might get him labeled "a first cousin of the Beast of Belsen," he reminded readers that moral considerations were not involved in the American decision to fight against Germany in the first place (news of the atrocities emerging only late in the war) and that the United States sided with the equally unethical dicator, Stalin, to defeat the Germans in the end anyway.[83] In short, *No Clear and Present Danger* directly challenged the moral-mnemonic consensus of the early postwar years.

A similar set of concerns animated the next allohistorical discussion of a Nazi wartime victory, well-known conservative historian John Lukacs's speculative essay "What if Hitler Had Won the Second World War?"[84] Published in 1978 in the runaway bestseller, *The People's Almanac*, Lukacs's essay was based upon the premise that Hitler won the war by immediately invading Britain following his victory at Dunkirk in 1940.[85] From this point, Lukacs's "plausible tale" outlined an allohistorical vision that was surprisingly upbeat. Although "What if Hitler Had Won the Second World War?" fleetingly sketched a brutal scenario for German-occupied Eastern Europe – epitomized by the "killing [of] large numbers of Russians and even larger numbers of Jews" – its overall assessment of the Nazis' European empire was relatively rosy. "Things were not as unbearable as had been expected," Lukacs wrote, for, after their victory, the Germans declined to remain in a perpetual state of war and instead devoted most of their energies to economic expansion, building "gigantic superhighways" and "Volkswagen factories." Indeed, despite the aging Hitler's exhortations for continued brutality, his rhetoric fails to appeal to most Germans, who "after 10 years of relative peace ... were no longer at arms" and preferred to enjoy the soulless consumerism and pop culture enabled by postwar prosperity. With Hitler's death in 1952, it is the defenders of this materialistic and technocratic order, such as Albert Speer, Claus von Stauffenberg, and Wilhelm Canaris, who triumph over the ideologues, led by Himmler and Goebbels, and who "proclaim ... that the destiny of the German people ... [is] to uphold law and order in Europe instead of ruling over other peoples by force alone." This pragmatic Nazi government, in fact, succeeds in "laying the ground plan for the eventual unification of Europe" and enables "an era of peace and prosperity [to] ... dawn ... upon the world." So peaceful is Europe by the mid-1960s that a non-German for the first time is elected president of the European Union, and former Field Marshal Erwin Rommel feels no qualms about describing World War II as "all a big mistake."

In its overall conclusions, Lukacs's essay offered a strikingly benign view of a Nazi wartime victory. This was most clearly visible in his marginalization of the Holocaust from his broader narrative. Unlike the tales of the late 1950s and early 1960s, which focused on the Nazis' genocide to underscore the regime's brutality, Lukacs largely ignored it. Even though his essay essentially implied that the Nazis end up completing the Final Solution of the Jewish question throughout Europe (Hitler, after all, lives through the end of the war), this horrific fact does not prevent Lukacs from concluding that everything in the end works out fairly well. Lukacs's rather cavalier attitude towards the Final Solution was echoed in his essay's intermittently lighthearted tone. At certain points in "What if Hitler Had Won the Second World War?" Lukacs found room for humor, liberally peppering his description of German hegemony with such satirical flourishes as the Germans "forcing the French to consume huge quantities of inferior German beer" and Himmler's English SS recruits "establish[ing] themselves in Liverpool, where they eventually turned their savage energies to making music."[86] By virtue of the inclusion of such comical asides, Lukacs's essay lent a degree of humor to a scenario that had once been viewed solely with horror.

Lukacs's reasons for submitting such an uncritical depiction of a Nazi victory are difficult to discern. He has noted that he wrote "What if Hitler Had Won the Second World War?" as "a *jeu d'esprit*" – that is, a lighthearted or witty intellectual game with no broader political significance.[87] Yet the essay contained a clear political message. In fairly unambiguous fashion, "What if Hitler Had Won the Second World War?" defended the lost cause of isolationism and thereby criticized the interventionist character of American foreign policy in World War II. In Lukacs's essay, the Germans end up winning the war in Europe because America (respectively governed from 1940 to 1944 by a much more hesitant Roosevelt, and from 1944 to 1952, by the strongly isolationistic presidents Charles A. Lindbergh and Robert A. Taft) declines to fight against them. Yet, defying conventional wisdom, Lukacs characterized this decision in positive terms. Although American isolationism allows Germany to dominate Europe, the victorious Reich brings about the same processes of European reconstruction and integration that occurred in real history. Moreover, thanks to America's refusal to fight the Germans, the world is spared the cold war, for, after the Nazi invasion of the Soviet Union, Stalin flees to the Siberian city of Omsk, where he has little ability to threaten world peace. The Nazi victory in World War II thus ends up for the best.

It is difficult to know whether the isolationist political message contained in "What if Hitler Had Won the Second World War?" was intentional. Although Lukacs's own political views defy easy categorization, he has long stood firmly on the conservative wing of the political spectrum.[88] His conservative views manifested themselves in various ways, but they included a strong opposition to the Soviet Union's domination of Eastern Europe – a stance that reflected his personal background as a native Hungarian who fled his homeland as a twenty-three-year-old in 1946.[89] Lukacs was not only opposed to Soviet communism, of course, but was critical of Nazism as well. Yet his views of the Third Reich have long been regarded as highly idiosyncratic.[90] The possibility thus exists that as cold-war tensions were intensifying in the late 1970s, Lukacs's opposition to Soviet communism overshadowed his distaste for Nazism and found its way into his broader allohistorical narrative. Whether intentionally or not, "What if Hitler Had Won the Second World War?" can plausibly be seen as reflecting how heightened American fears of communism during the late 1970s could contribute to the waning memory of Nazism's historical evil. In relativizing the horrors of Nazi rule – indeed, in affirming that a Nazi victory in World War II would not have been that bad for Europe, despite the completion of the Final Solution of the Jewish question – Lukacs's essay attested to the role of the cold war in hastening the normalization of the Nazi past.

This political instrumentalization of the premise of a Nazi wartime victory continued in the next major work to appear, well-known science fiction writer Brad Linaweaver's 1982 novella *Moon of Ice*.[91] Set in America in the 1980s, *Moon of Ice* tells the story of the Third Reich's turbulent evolution after its wartime victory through the eyes of Hilda Goebbels, the estranged daughter of the Nazi propaganda minister. As the novel opens, Hilda has arrived in New York City to meet with an American newspaper editor named Alan Whittmore in the hope of securing a book deal to publish the final postwar section of her recently deceased father's diaries, as well as her own autobiography. As Whittmore settles down in a hotel room to review Hilda's manuscripts, he learns much unsettling information about recent events in Nazi Germany. The most sensational revelations concern a major power struggle that erupts after Hitler's death in April 1965. The Nazi empire of the mid-1960s is a powerful but threatened entity. The Nazis dominate Europe, having successfully used atomic weapons to defeat the Soviets and the British, and to force a nuclear stalemate with the United States. But in the wake of his titanic victory, Hitler has become "indolent" and permitted his underlings to run the affairs of state.[92] Germany has thereafter begun to suffer from imperial overstretch and has fallen behind the Americans in economic strength.[93]

In this climate of uncertainty, civil strife emerges in the Nazi empire with an attempted *coup d'état* led by fanatical SS men from Burgundy, an independent state (created after the Nazi victory) whose SS rulers are eager to pursue an antimodern, occultist, and mystical agenda of world domination. The Burgundians believe that postwar Germany has become weak owing to the abandonment of its holy racial mission in favor of pragmatic, technocratic policies.[94] The Burgundians thus decide to kidnap Goebbels (whom they regard as a traitor to the Nazi religion) with the intent of ritually sacrificing him alongside Hitler's stolen corpse in order to redeem the nation and send the Führer to Valhalla. Meanwhile, the Burgundians are busily preparing a final, mystical *Götterdämmerung* with the help of a brilliant but deranged geneticist, Richard Dietrich, whom they have entrusted with developing a final plague virus to kill all human beings on earth except for blue-eyed, blond men and women. The conclusion of this confrontation occurs with the Burgundians' defeat (and Goebbels' inadvertent rescue) by a ragtag coalition of anarchist, Marxist, and Zionist guerrilla groups led by his daughter Hilda. At this point, the manuscript comes to an end, and Whittmore, breathless from its astounding revelations, realizes that the woman in front of him, Hilda Goebbels, may well in fact have prevented World War III.

Despite its sensationalistic dimensions, *Moon of Ice* concludes by asserting that a Nazi victory in World War II would not have been the nightmare so feared by previous generations. As in Robert Harris's *Fatherland*, the Nazi empire after its wartime victory is far from being an omnipotent force, being plagued by worrisome economic and political problems. Linaweaver went beyond merely debunking the image of Nazi omnipotence, however, by asserting, like Lukacs, that the Nazi regime's postwar policies actually end up promoting the general European good. This outcome is made explicit at the conclusion of the novel when Hilda, in a postscript written to Whittmore in the year 2000, provocatively declares that "Adolf Hitler achieved the opposite of all his long-term goals ... by winning World War II." As she explains, "economic reality subverted National Socialism," for as the Nazis united Europe under German rule, their New Order "knock[ed] down the barriers of ethnic and national separation" and thus worked to dampen their racialist ideology. Over the long term, she notes:

Nazi Germany was becoming less National Socialist with every passing decade. For all the talk of Race Destiny, it was the technical mind of Albert Speer and his successors at the controls of the German Empire. Ideology would surface long enough to slow down the machine ... but in the end technical management would reassert itself.

According to Hilda, the victory of the pragmatists in Nazi Germany enables a remarkable thaw to occur. "Historical revisionists" have popped up within Germany and have begun to criticize Hitler's policies, while in the sphere of international relations, German and American scientists are cooperating in the development of space colonies. The capstone to the defeat of the ideologues is the founding of a Jewish state in space, an event which happily confirms that "*Der Jude* could not be stopped by a mere *Führer*." These events, for the hopeful Hilda, signal the emergence of a "sane new world" recovered from the disasters of the recent past.[95]

Moon of Ice's optimistic portrayal of a Nazi victory in World War II largely stemmed from its author's background. Born in 1952, Linaweaver belonged to the generation that did not experience the Nazi era firsthand and thus easily adopted a more detached perspective in portraying it. More important still were Linaweaver's conservative political beliefs. Like many science fiction writers, Linaweaver was a committed libertarian whose faith in the principles of limited government and free-market economics was on clear display throughout the novel.[96] This political stance manifested itself most obviously in his narrative's juxtaposition of the present-day United States and Nazi Germany. *Moon of Ice* depicted the United States as a libertarian paradise, having reduced the power of the Federal Government dramatically since the impeachment of President Roosevelt (for covering up his foreknowledge of the Japanese attack on Pearl Harbor) and having liberated private corporations from state restrictions.[97] By contrast, the Third Reich remains stagnant, unable to complete mammoth state construction projects due to its slavish adherence to the Nazi collectivist ideal.[98] As Josef Goebbels himself notes in his diary, "The American Republic was thriving, even as our economy was badly suffering."[99] The most important key to America's postwar success, however, is its libertarian hostility towards using the power of the state to promote an interventionist foreign policy. This view is made clear through the character of Whittmore (described as a "professional advocate of limited government"), who defends the American government's isolationist stance (inaugurated by Presidents Dewey and Taft) of remaining disengaged from German affairs.[100] As he says, "Nonintervention opens doors that an empire would close."[101] By the end of the novel, the reform of the Nazi state is not brought about by any state power but by libertarian forces. Thus, the anarchist philosophy of Hilda Goebbels and her various comrades is credited with defeating the Third Reich's ideological fanatics, while free-market economic forces ultimately bring about the reform of the Third Reich from within.

The libertarian message of *Moon of Ice* reflected Linaweaver's own comparatively value-neutral view of Nazism. Overall, Linaweaver imagined a

Nazi wartime victory in relatively upbeat fashion. Like Lukacs, he represented America's isolationist decision not to fight against Nazism as well conceived. For one thing, Linaweaver seemed to share the common isolationist belief that the Third Reich never posed a serious threat to American interests. As Josef Goebbels notes in his diary at one point, "We never intended to subjugate decadent America anyway. Ours was a European vision."[102] Moreover, by remaining distant from Europe's conflict, the United States profits handsomely. Even if American isolationism enables the Germans to achieve European hegemony, it nevertheless enables the nation to prosper economically and avoid the cold war. In the end, the United States merely has to sit back and wait while Germany, racked by internal division, eventually reforms itself from within. This optimistic conclusion reflected how cold-war fears could displace the memory of Nazism's horror. To be sure, Linaweaver recognized the evil character of Nazism, but he finally considered communism to be a far more threatening political movement. Linaweaver came to this position less as a result of any precise political events in the late 1970s than out of a general turn towards conservative politics, which itself was rooted in the broader tensions of the cold-war years, specifically his disagreement with American leftists over the conflict in Vietnam.[103] As a result of his conservative political turn, he came to the conclusion that Nazism hardly had a monopoly on evil. As Whittmore says at one juncture, "The Nazis are evil but no more so than the Communists."[104] In the end, however, *Moon of Ice* did not so much place Nazism and communism on a comparable footing as evil ideologies as relativize the horror of the former.

INTERVENTIONISM AS SELF-CRITICISM

While the neo-isolationist works of Russett, Lukacs, and Linaweaver constituted one type of self-critical response to the cold war, other accounts combined self-critique with support for interventionism. The first such narrative to appear was famed American science fiction writer Ward Moore's 1975 short story "A Class with Dr. Chang."[105] This bleak tale portrays the difficulties faced by a Chinese-American professor of history named Chang Liango-ho as he attempts to deliver a lecture on recent (allo)historical events to the surly students in his introductory history class at the University of California at Monterey. In Professor Chang's world, Nazi Germany has won World War II because of its shrewd decision to ally with China instead of Japan. Thanks to the "Berlin-Peiping Axis's" successful attack against, and conquest of, Japan, the bombing of

Pearl Harbor never takes place and the United States ends up sitting out the war as a neutral power. America's isolationist stance, however, has the adverse effect of leading the country down the path towards fascism. This outcome is made clear in the story by the angry reaction of Professor Chang's students to his sober historical survey. When he describes the Germans as "a people moved by their ... mystical yearnings" and "fascinated ... with the celebration of heroic death," students wearing "ALL" buttons (designating the "American Loyal League") drown him out with the cry "America First!" and respond that the Germans' success was due to their single-minded commitment to getting "rid of all the foreign elements – the Jews, Gypsies, Slavs and such who were corrupting ... the racial will with their foreign philosophies."[106] Their fervor building, the students go on to vent their disgust at America's failure to enter the war, exclaiming, "We should have fought. Fought for the glory of fighting. Bled, sacrificed, gotten rid of all ... the tainted blood, and come through as one people, totally united ... so that every American felt and thought like every other American – 'ALL' for one and one for 'ALL.'"[107] At the tale's grim conclusion, the students' hatred boils over and they seize Dr. Chang and lynch him – together with a Jewish professor and a black teaching assistant – on an improvised gallows.

In writing his short story, Moore most likely intended to offer a critical commentary on what he believed to be worrisome social and political trends in the United States in the wake of the Vietnam War. A lifetime supporter of leftwing politics, Moore provided hints of a broader political agenda in his story by having the racist 'ALL' students use the same rhetorical phrases employed by conservative supporters of American involvement in Vietnam to attack leftwing members of the antiwar movement in the 1960s and early 1970s.[108] For example, one student decries "pink draft dodgers and flag haters" for their refusal to purge America of "foreign elements," while later on, a large group of students call for "an all-American university for all Americans" and begin rhythmically chanting, "Love it or leave!" "Love it or leave!"[109] By showing such phrases being used in racist fashion in alternate history, Moore clearly implied that their real historical usage during the Vietnam years was equally politically suspect, if not outright fascist. Moore's approach to the allohistorical scenario of a Nazi victory in World War II was thus quite novel. By showing America's failure to intervene in the war as having calamitous domestic political consequences, he sided with earlier writers like Kornbluth, Dick, and Shirer in defending American interventionism. Unlike them, however, he did so not to ratify the reality of the postwar world, but rather to condemn it.

A similar example of this trend, but from the opposite political camp, was provided several years later by a satirical piece that appeared in the October 1980 issue of the humor magazine *National Lampoon* entitled "If World War II Had Been Fought Like the War in Vietnam."[110] Written by well-known humorist P. J. O'Rourke, along with Tod Carroll, and illustrated by Rick Geary, "If World War II Had Been Fought Like the War in Vietnam" was a comic-strip critique of what the authors perceived as the insufficiently vigorous American military campaign in Vietnam. In a series of fifteen illustrated panels, O'Rourke and Carroll expressed their primary contention that if the half-hearted policies in Vietnam had been used during World War II, the Nazis would have won the war. Beginning with the inadequate response of the United States to the Japanese attack on Pearl Harbor (American military advisers are merely sent to Midway Island "to assist natives in strengthening their defense against possible Japanese aggression"), American involvement in World War II steadily grows. Troop morale remains low, however, especially following such events as the court-martial of an American bomber pilot for "murdering civilians in ... Dresden," the visit to Germany of a high-profile "delegation of prominent peace activists," including Charles Lindbergh and Ezra Pound, to inspect bomb damage, and the eruption of antiwar protests at the 1944 Democratic National Convention. Before long, the United States pulls out of World War II with its tail between its legs, attempting to evacuate its diplomats from London as it would from Saigon in 1975. (At this point, the strip notes, "Unfortunately, helicopters have not been invented yet," and the diplomats are depicted waiting on the embassy roof for nothing.)[111] The tale sarcastically concludes by commenting, "German occupation of most territories was peaceful, although some people who were identified as having 'democratic tendencies' were temporarily placed in re-education centers" (here, a Jewish family is being directed to an extermination camp). And the last panel concludes, "Today, 36 years after the end of American involvement in the controversial Second World War, the country finds itself at peace, once again a unified nation" (depicted above this line is a Washington D.C. street scene full of advertisements for German-made products).

Like "A Class with Dr. Chang," "If World War II Had Been Fought Like the War in Vietnam" supported interventionism not to validate the past but to critique the present. The comic's grim depiction of a Nazi victory was intended less to remind readers of the evils of the 1940s than the mistakes of the 1960s and 1970s. This agenda is suggested by the staunch conservative reputation of the tale's best-known author, P. J. O'Rourke, who clearly used the narrative to advance his belief that the American government had not been resolute enough in prosecuting the battle against communism in Vietnam.[112] For if the nation had fought in the cold war as decisively as it had in World War II, the United States would never have let the communist Vietcong emerge victorious. Overall, "If World War II Had Been Fought Like the War in Vietnam" illustrated the role of the cold war in normalizing the memory of Nazism. By drawing a parallel between the Vietcong and the Nazis, the piece dramatically effaced the considerable differences between them. Indeed, it universalized the significance of Nazism, shifting attention away from it for its own sake in order to direct it towards an unrelated cause. O'Rourke and Carroll's comparison of the two eras, in short, illustrated the declining specificity of World War II in the consciousness of some Americans at a time of new worries and concerns.

Another work that used the premise of a Nazi wartime victory for self-critical purposes was American writer William Overgard's 1980 novel *The Divide*.[113] In many ways, *The Divide* was the last of its kind – a novel that followed in the tradition of Kornbluth, Shirer, Dick, and Norden by depicting the United States losing World War II to, and being brutally occupied by, the Germans and Japanese. Overgard, however, did not merely restate the premise of America under Nazi rule but used it in order to explore new concerns. Set in the year 1976, the novel's plot focuses on the emergence of a homegrown American resistance movement thirty years after the United States' humiliating defeat in World War II. A rough-and-tumble group, the resistance is led by the aged but crafty American, Wayne Kenneth Stubbs, and his adopted son, Cooper, both of whom spend the majority of the novel planning to sabotage a high-level political summit in the middle of the country (known as "the Divide") between the dottering Führer, Adolf Hitler, and the more gracefully aging Japanese premier, Hideki Tojo. Stubbs and Cooper attempt to enlist the cooperation of the last official representatives of the United States military who have hidden out for the last thirty years in the "National Redoubt" deep within a mine shaft in the Rocky Mountains. After decades stuck underground, the aged generals have lost the will to fight, but they permit the resisters to take with them the sole prototype of the American Manhattan project, a nuclear weapon created by the Jewish scientist, Isaac Blum, together with his daughter, Lisa. Stubbs and Cooper devise a bold plan to load the bomb onto an aging freight train and ram it into the armored railroad car carrying Hitler's entourage to meet Tojo on the Great Plains of Kansas. Yet the Nazis foil the plan, discover the bomb, and seem poised to force a terrified Lisa to divulge the secrets of its creation. At the novel's conclusion, however, Stubbs and Cooper succeed in assassinating Tojo at the festivities (though not Hitler, who escapes) and sparking a general revolt of the crowd against the assembled Nazi dignitaries. This revolt culminates when Lisa, still in captivity, detonates the atom bomb in the presence of Hitler's designated successor, Rausch, killing him and everyone else for miles around.

The overall plot of *The Divide* superficially resembled the classic interventionist narratives of the early postwar years. Like these works, Overgard's novel supported interventionism in rendering the allohistorical origins and consequences of the Nazi triumph in World War II. *The Divide* directly blamed isolationism for the United States' defeat, portraying President Burton K. Wheeler (who defeats Roosevelt in the election of 1940) as having failed to prepare the nation for foreign invasion.[114] The novel further supported the cause of interventionism by depicting the Nazis' occupation of the United States as inordinately brutal. Unlike the Japanese, who defeat the United States using relatively conventional means, the Germans use powerful new weapons – such as ME-262 fighter planes and deadly V-4 missiles – to devastate Washington D.C. and Kansas City (the seat of Wheeler's government in exile). After dividing up the country along the Rocky Mountains into two occupation zones, the Nazis complete the Final Solution of the Jewish question and proceed to exterminate other undesirables, especially Native Americans, who are targeted in the "Great Herding" and turned into soap and dog food at a massive 1,000-acre extermination facility at Cedar Bluff, Kansas.[115] Only a certain percentage of minorities are permitted to survive: several thousand sterilized blacks who labor at the Cedar Bluff facility and even fewer Native Americans, for the purpose of anthropological study.[116]

Despite resembling earlier alternate histories in its forbidding portrayal of Nazi-occupied America, however, *The Divide* differed in significant ways. The most notable was its avoidance of black-and-white depictions of evil German perpetrators and virtuous American victims. The novel painted an extremely unflattering portrait of the American people under Nazi occupation. Instead of resisting the Nazis, the American people largely collaborate. At their worst, the Americans are depicted as inveterate racists who support the Nazis' agenda of ethnic cleansing. As the novel's protagonist, Cooper, recalls at one point, "In the beginning, the racial purification program had been resisted, but ... the great mass of surviving Americans were glad that the country had been cleansed of minorities and misfits ... How many times had he heard the phrase *Hitler was right about one thing ... "*[117] Moreover, most Americans tolerate the Nazis' crimes in exchange for the unseemly motive of economic gain. The Nazis' decision to "create a showcase of National Socialism" by pumping billions of marks into reconstructing the economy of the eastern zone largely succeeds in earning them the political quiescence of the American public.[118] Commenting upon the political apathy of the American masses, Cooper exclaims:

They're fat and happy down there, they got jobs and Volkswagens. Shoot! They've even convinced themselves that it was all for the best – they've accepted the elimination of other races, 'dangerous' minorities, political 'criminals' – anything that don't include them – euthanasia, sterilization ... all that stuff – as long as it ain't used on them – they've forgot the Constitution and the rights of man and the U.S. way of life. It ain't the enemy we got to instruct in freedom ... it's our own people.[119]

The Divide's self-critical portrait of the American people under Nazi occupation was most likely intended to serve as a pessimistic commentary on the American malaise of the late 1970s. Overgard's personal background suggests that he would have been especially disaffected by the nation's postwar decline. A longtime novelist, cartoonist, and screenwriter, Overgard belonged to the generation that lived through World War II – in his case, serving as a sailor in the United States navy during the years 1944–45.[120] Having witnessed the United States' heroic achievements in the past, Overgard may have projected its allohistorical moral and political collapse under Nazism in order to criticize the nation's decline in his real, historical present.

At the same time, the novel also expressed its author's hope for national recovery. Overgard exhibited an unambiguous patriotic streak in his writing that placed him on the conservative – if not libertarian – wing of the political spectrum. In many ways, his novel was a traditional celebration of American individualism. Overgard's depiction of most Americans as self-interested collaborators was meant as a foil to highlight the efforts of those few patriotic Americans who intended to "relight the torch of liberty."[121] *The Divide*'s valorization of ordinary Americans went hand in hand, moreover, with a strong distrust of the official representatives of the state. It was revealing that the established military brass continue to hide out impotently in their mountain bunker, while the more virile average citizens undertake the heroic struggle against the enemy. Finally, Overgard's patriotism was obvious at the novel's end when Stubbs, having just witnessed the detonation of the atomic bomb, enthusiastically exclaims,

"We got 'em! We got the damn Germans and Japs! Hell, we got 'em all! . . . We built it! Made in America! The good old U.S. of A!"[122] Just as this passage clearly expressed the desire of the novel's protagonist to restore the nation's wounded pride, so too did it likely express a similar wish on the part of its author. In the end, to be sure, Overgard offered no panaceas, only a sober message of the necessity of tireless struggle. Even though *The Divide* concludes with the American resistance dealing a severe blow to the Nazi occupation, the Germans remain strong. Not only does Hitler survive the attempt to assassinate him, his successors are lined up and ready to go. In the novel's last lines, Germany's most highly decorated war veteran, Hans Loftner, is shown stroking the pregnant belly of his wife – Hitler's daughter, Ilse – who, the reader is led to assume, will shortly give birth to the future Führer. In short, the struggle against the Germans – like the struggle to revive the spirit of America – has only just begun.

Overgard's critical portrayal of America in the wake of a Nazi victory in World War II was echoed several years later by another biting tale, science fiction writer David Dvorkin's 1987 novel *Budspy*.[123] Yet where Overgard criticized American decline during the cold war from the political right, Dvorkin did so from the political left. Set in the year 1988, *Budspy* was a spy thriller that focused on the cloak-and-dagger exploits of its protagonist, Chic Western. Chic is a high-ranking employee in the so-called Ombudsman Commission, an agency founded by American President Joseph McCarthy in 1957 to root out corruption within the Federal Government. It is in the capacity as a "budspy," or "budman," that Western is sent to Nazi Germany to investigate the leak of sensitive military secrets from the United States embassy in Berlin to the Soviet Union. Although Chic is of Jewish descent and has negative feelings about Germany (his parents were Polish Jews named Weintraub who survived the war), his concerns are quickly dispelled soon after his arrival in Berlin, for Nazi Germany in the year 1988 is the world's pre-eminent superpower. In strolling through the nation's capital, Chic is awestruck by the monumentality of its architecture, the healthy appearance of its blonde-haired, blue-eyed citizens, and the general atmosphere of orderliness. As he learns from his German acquaintances, the nation's success is largely due to the efforts of Germany's ruler of forty years, Kurt Nebel. The onetime secretary to Martin Bormann, Nebel succeeds Hitler after the Führer's death on the eastern front near Stalingrad in 1943 thanks to his skillful negotiation of a separate peace with the British and Americans that enables the Nazis to defeat the Soviets and win the war in Europe. In the wake of the Nazis' victory, the Reich under Nebel's leadership undergoes a radical metamorphosis, abandoning "the more extreme and distasteful ideas of the older generation" and adopting "the milder, technocratic, cosmopolitan world-view of . . . Albert Speer."[124] The most significant development in this broader process is the Nazis' turn away from antisemitism. Not only has Nebel's government officially stated its regret about the extermination of 10–12 million Jews during the war, it has backed the creation of the state of Israel as a refuge for Holocaust survivors and a strategic base to protect German oil interests in the Middle East. Impressed by these achievements, Chic's initial caution about Germany gradually yields to moderate enthusiasm. Tolerant, prosperous, and powerful, the nation of 300 million people, he begins to think to himself, may well in fact be "the Master Race."[125]

Yet, as *Budspy*'s narrative unfolds, Chic slowly begins to recognize that the brilliant appearance of the Reich hides a more sordid reality. As a result of his burgeoning relationship with his anti-Nazi American girlfriend, Judy, Chic comes to learn of the existence of an underground resistance movement known as the "Yellow Rose," whose members are involved in agitating against the regime. Through Judy, Chic personally comes to know some of the German dissidents, who alert him to the cruel exploitation of Slavic forced laborers in Germany and the continued resistance of Soviet partisans in German-occupied Eastern Europe. Meanwhile, through his own sleuthing in the American embassy, Chic discovers a hidden letter in his office suggesting that Hitler's death in 1943 was in fact part of a larger assassination plot engineered by Nebel. Yet despite unearthing the lies that underpin the Nazi regime, Western does not stray from his mission to expose the leak at the embassy, which turns out to be the work of his on-and-off-again girlfriend Judy and her co-conspirators in the Yellow Rose, whom he promptly betrays to the secret police. Although he effectively sends Judy and her colleagues to their deaths, Chic displays minimal regret for the consequences of his actions, convinced, as he is, that his work is helping to purify America. Only at the end of *Budspy* does he realize that his cooperation with evil has corrupted him, and he resolves to atone for his sins. At the novel's jarring climax, set twenty-four years later, in the year 2012, a television broadcast of the sixty-ninth anniversary celebrations of Hitler's death from the Adolf-Hitler-Platz in Berlin reveals that the man presiding over the festivities, the Führer of the Reich, is none other than Chic Western himself. Having symbolically changed his name to Karl Busse (a name denoting repentance), Chic has taken control of Germany in order "to systematically destroy . . . [it]" by deliberately undermining the continuing war against the Soviets. Through these actions, the onetime budspy and now Führer of Nazi Germany, Chic Western, hopes to vindicate his life's work by proving that cooperating with evil can ultimately lead to good.

In its imaginative rendering of a Nazi wartime victory, *Budspy* submitted a leftwing critique of contemporary America. At first glance, this agenda could easily be missed, owing to the novel's resemblance to the more isolationist accounts of Lukacs and Linaweaver. *Budspy*, after all, also showed the victorious Third Reich to be a relatively moderate place ruled by rational technocrats instead of fanatical ideologues. Yet Dvorkin did not present a positive image of Nazi Germany to vindicate America's allohistorical neutrality in the war but to condemn it. *Budpsy*, indeed, portrayed the American government's decision not to fight the Germans as calamitous. In the text, the reason the United States and Britain make a separate peace with the Nazis is their fear of communism (which becomes acute when the Soviets nearly defeat the Germans at Stalingrad in 1943).[126] But giving in to fears of communism has far-reaching consequences, for it soon brings Joseph McCarthy to the presidency, whose policy of cozying up to the Nazi regime gradually ushers in a period of steep national decline. Under the rule of McCarthy and later conservative administrations (the current president in 1988 is named Helms – presumably Jesse), the United States succumbs to the ills of poverty, homelessness, and race riots.[127] America's economic health lags behind that of Germany as well.[128] The root of the problem is suggested at one point by Chic's girlfried, Judy, who proclaims, "We are corrupted by our accommodation with evil."[129] This accommodation, Dvorkin suggests, represents a betrayal of fundamental American values. As Judy tells Chic, "Remember what America was supposed to be? . . . The land of freedom, the place where people went to escape Old-World oppression? Look at it nowadays. We're just a minor-league version of the Reich."[130] Compared with the ills of contemporary America, Nazi Germany actually looks quite good. Chic's admiration for the Nazi Reich, in fact, largely stems from his disgust with America's social problems; it is partly due to his frustration with the poverty, filth, homelessness, and drug abuse of the American capital, Washington D.C., that Western so admires Berlin.[131] Overall, Chic envies the Germans' adherence to the ideals of National Socialism precisely because America seems to be drifting away from "the ideals of her founders."[132] By the time he is back in the States he is so distraught by the sight of its forlorn cities that he is moved to exclaim, "What went wrong with America?"[133]

In writing *Budspy*, Dvorkin was partly inspired by political goals. A self-described liberal, Dvorkin portrayed the victorious Reich as superior to the

United States in order to criticize the adverse impact of the cold war on American society.[134] Having written *Budspy* during the Reagan era, Dvorkin was partly targeting some of the worrisome social and political developments of the 1980s. But more broadly, he was taking aim at the many political and moral compromises made in accordance with cold-war anticommunism. As Dvorkin has noted, "I was using ... alternate history ... to comment on the America of the time, but ... it's a more longterm, general problem. Even before Viet Nam ... thrust itself on our awareness ... [I was] upset by the general American pattern of supporting evil regimes because we thought they were better than the alternative."[135] Dvorkin's present-day political concerns obviously shaped the plot of his alternate history. Just as anticommunism led the United States to under-take questionable alliances in the cold war, so too does America's anti-communist-based alliance of convenience with Nazi Germany lead to its allohistorical decline. In the end, the Nazis emerge as victorious not so much through military successes (though they achieve those as well) as "by infecting the world and making the West into an etiolated copy of the Reich."[136]

In utilizing the scenario of a victorious Nazi Reich to criticize American political trends in the 1980s, however, Dvorkin ended up producing a strikingly non-judgmental portrait of Nazism. His unfavorable compari-son of America with Nazi Germany was intended to critique the former, but it inevitably worked to relativize the evil of the latter. To be sure, this result was far from Dvorkin's primary intention. The writer's Jewish background gave him little reason to be sympathetic to, let alone serve as an apologist for, Nazism.[137] Yet his portrait of the Third Reich did partly reflect a deliberate attempt to provoke. As a writer who has openly declared his ambivalent sense of Jewish identity, Dvorkin was particularly eager to challenge what he viewed as the undue centrality of the Holocaust in American Jewish consciousness.[138] Dvorkin rejected the widespread notion among many American Jews that the Holocaust was unique (he insisted that "there were other[s]" as well) and declared that "it's past time for Jews to forget."[139] His representation of the Nazis as less than absolute evil (epitomized by the regime's apology for the Holocaust and its establish-ment of a Jewish state in Israel), therefore, can be seen as part of his desire to challenge the postwar view among Jews that barbarism was predomin-antly a German (as opposed to a universal human) trait. Dvorkin's render-ing of the victorious Reich, however, did not merely reflect his iconoclastic tendencies. It also reflected a more personal attempt to work through what he has described as his "fascination" with its aesthetic allure.[140] In confessing to this fascination, of course, Dvorkin was hardly alone, for his exploration of the Reich's aura of power mirrored the same psychological dynamics that underpinned the Hitler Wave of the 1970s and 1980s. While it is impossible to determine whether it was Dvorkin's desire to universalize or aestheticize the Nazi era that was more influential in the making of his novel, it is clear that both were involved in making *Budspy* one of the most normalized tales of the period.

Yet even *Budspy* was trumped by the most anomalous, and yet perhaps the most telling, allohistorical account of the period – a brief comedy sketch aired on the NBC television show *Saturday Night Live* entitled "What If: Überman."[141] Unlike the other narratives of the era, the sketch took no stand on the issue of interventionism or isolationism. Instead, it was most significant for reducing the premise of a Nazi wartime victory to the stuff of humor. Originally broadcast on January 27, 1979, "What If: Überman" portrays a television talk show called "What If?" that is devoted to the weekly exploration of what its host, Joan Face (played by Jane Curtin), describes as "a hypothetical question about a specific historical event." As the sketch opens, the host introduces her panel of experts, Brigadier-General Kevin Temple (played by Garrett Morris) and Wellesley College history professor Eileen Houton (played by Gilda Radner) and invites them to address the question of the evening: "What If Superman grew up in Germany instead of America?" In short order, the show answers the question by staging a dramatic re-enactment of Nazi Germany winning World War II. The re-enactment commences in Hitler's Berlin Chancellery, where a young clerk in the Ministry of Propaganda by the name of Klaus Kent (played by Dan Aykroyd), together with his colleagues Lois Lanehoff (played by Laraine Newman) and Jimmy Olsteyn (played by Al Franken), is ushered in to meet the Führer (played by guest host, Michael Palin) who has just concluded a meeting with his top generals. After some humorous banter, Kent uses his X-ray vision to notice the presence of a bomb inside a suitcase left in the room by one of the generals in the attempt to assassinate the Führer. At this moment, Kent ducks into a nearby closet, strips off his clothes and leaps out into the room again proclaiming, "I am Überman! I ... fight for untruth, injustice, and the Nazi way!" (see Figure 9). Thereafter, he shields Hitler by jumping onto the bomb, exposes Jimmy Olsteyn as a Jew by using his X-ray vision to look through his pants, and motivates the amazed Führer to declare, "What an amazing stroke of luck. We might win this war after all!" Within a brief span of time, indeed, Überman helps the Nazis win World War II, as is revealed by a series of newspaper headlines from the Nazi newspaper *Der*

Figure 9 Überman (Dan Aykroyd) and Adolf Hitler (Michael Palin) in the Berlin Reich Chancellery in the *Saturday Night Live* skit "What If: Überman," originally broadcast on January 27, 1979.

Daily Planet, superimposed over documentary newsreel footage, which read: "Überman Takes Stalingrad in 5 Minutes: Diverts Volga," "Überman Rounds Up Two Million Jews: Total Past 6 Million," and "Überman Kills Every Person in England, U.S. Next."

The significance of the *Saturday Night Live* episode had less to do with its schematic plot than with its transformation of a Nazi wartime victory into the subject of comedy. The skit's writer, Al Franken, has noted that he wrote it primarily to entertain.[142] But the very ability to poke fun at a scenario long regarded as a nightmare attested to the increasingly relaxed perspective towards the Nazi era in American consciousness. Indeed, "What If: Überman" proved that the scenario of a Nazi-ruled world no longer had to serve moral or didactic purposes, but could be used for pure entertainment. Viewing the Nazis as funny, of course, was more imaginable during an era in which they had been displaced as the epitome of evil by the Soviet Union. Such a sketch would have been impossible twenty years earlier, when current events revived Western fears of the Germans. In short, then, while the comedy sketch made no references whatsoever to the cold war, its presence can nevertheless be sensed in the blithe manner in which the old avatar of evil, namely Nazism, was reduced to an off-color joke. The *Saturday Night Live* sketch was an exception in its era. Most allohistorical depictions of a Nazi-ruled world would not be devoted to entertainment but rather to political critique. Both, however, illustrated the role of the cold war in fostering a less morally judgmental view of the Nazi era.

RECEPTION

The generally positive response of readers and critics to the alternate histories that appeared after the 1970s demonstrated a willingness to accept their normalized depictions of a Nazi wartime victory. Of all the works of this period, the most widely praised was David Dvorkin's *Budspy*. Hailed by one reviewer for its "subtlety" and "insight," *Budspy* received the most glowing review from famed American science fiction writer Norman Spinrad, who, in 1988, called it a "masterful novel" that was "superior to just about everything short of *The Man in the High Castle* itself."[143] Tellingly, much of the praise singled out the novel's nuanced depiction of the Nazi regime. Thus one critic commended the novel for depicting "a successful Third Reich … more evenhandedly," while another declared that "through [the protagonist] … we come to admire the new Reich."[144] But it was Spinrad who, more than any other reviewer, analyzed the significance of the novel's unconventional approach to its subject. As he wrote:

Dvorkin's Nazi Germany is *alluring* … to the reader … He subtly gives us a perhaps somewhat uncomfortable understanding of its attractions as well as its horrors which raises our understanding of the real Nazi Germany to a new level. For after all, the central enigma of the Third Reich is not why we find its memory repellent, but how a whole nation could have been seduced by its charms.

Dvorkin's evolved Nazi Germany has genuine virtues. The most monstrous abuses are long past. It is the highest civilization on earth in terms of science, technology … [and] art …

Dvorkin gives … us an evolved Nazi Germany that, like all evolved societies, is a mixture of vice and virtue, visionary impulse and decay, national pride and national guilt, good and evil. Making the trenchant point thereby that *no* culture is really a black-and-white cartoon reality.[145]

Such favorable comments indicated a wider willingness after the mid-1970s to depart from the early postwar era's understanding of Nazism.

The response to the period's other works was more mixed, but they too earned enough critical support to further illustrate this trend. Brad

Linaweaver's novel, *Moon of Ice,* received favorable blurbs from science fiction legends Robert Heinlein and Isaac Asimov and was hailed as a "fine" novel that provided a "complex, credible look into ... the Nazi era."[146] Bruce Russett's *No Clear and Present Danger* was praised as "a model of logic and clarity" as well as a work of analytical "sophistication" that contained "relevant lessons."[147] Both works, it should be noted, also earned skeptical responses. One reviewer of *Moon of Ice* criticized its libertarian subtext as heavy-handed, and a reviewer of *No Clear and Present Danger* found its central proposition to be "repellent."[148] Such comments revealed that readers at the time were hardly unanimous in accepting a less morally judgmental view of the Third Reich. Yet, aside from the works of Dvorkin, Linaweaver, and Russett, few of the other works of the 1970s and 1980s generated any negative response. The lone exception was the *Saturday Night Live* sketch "What If: Überman," which received isolated expressions of complaint.[149] On the whole, the relatively scant criticism of the era's works suggests a growing receptivity of audiences to their normalized representation of a Nazi wartime victory.

ALTERNATE HISTORIES SINCE THE END OF THE COLD WAR, 1989–PRESENT

After the end of the cold war in 1989, alternate histories of a Nazi triumph in World War II changed still further. The works of this period reflected the complex realities of the post-cold-war world. The fall of communism was a joyous event that, in much of the West, encouraged the optimistic belief that liberalism had triumphed and ideological struggle – if not history itself – had come to an end. This sense of triumphalism was bolstered in the 1990s by the patriotic surge in attention towards World War II, which was occasioned by the arrival of the fiftieth anniversary of its central events and marked by the appearance of such bestselling books as Stephen Ambrose's *Band of Brothers* (1992) and Tom Brokaw's *The Greatest Generation* (New York, 1998), blockbuster films like Steven Spielberg's *Saving Private Ryan* (1998), and the commissioning of the national World War II memorial on the Mall in Washington D.C. in 1995.[150] Yet however much Americans in these years embraced a nostalgic view of the recent past, they simultaneously displayed growing concerns about the present. In foreign affairs, the eruption of the Persian Gulf War and the Yugoslav Civil War revealed that the end of superpower tensions by no means heralded a new era of peace. Within the United States, meanwhile, the disappearance of the traditional external enemy of the Soviet Union allowed internal problems to assume greater visibility and intensity. During the first half of the 1990s, as the nation was buffeted by economic recession, urban riots, and fierce debates over multiculturalism, many began to speak worriedly about the "disuniting of America."[151] The end of the cold war, in short, ushered in an ambiguous era poised between optimism and pessimism.

The alternate histories of a Nazi wartime victory that appeared in the years after 1989 directly reflected this ambiguous atmosphere. Most accounts during this period exhibited a return to moralism. In contrast to the works of the 1970s, whose value-neutral depiction of a Nazi victory in World War II reflected a self-critical view of American interventionism, most of the narratives after 1989 vindicated American intervention by portraying a Nazi triumph as a calamity. The new triumphalistic streak of these accounts largely reflected the euphoria produced by the victory over communism and expressed the conviction that history had ultimately worked out for the best. Yet the optimistic post-cold-war climate para-doxically contributed to the broader process of normalization as well. For while most accounts portrayed the Nazis' wartime triumph as a disaster, they broke new ground by depicting the victorious Reich eventually becoming a weakened and highly vulnerable entity. Some, indeed, went so far as to show Nazi rule being challenged, if not overthrown, by anti-Nazi resistance movements. This new tendency of American accounts to embrace happy endings reflected the obvious influence of the Soviet dictatorship's collapse – an epochal event that provided writers with a model for what might have happened eventually to the Nazi empire after its military triumph. At the same time, the fact that these narratives painted a comparatively mild portrait of the victorious Nazi regime reflected the fading memory of the Third Reich's historical evil.

Not all works of alternate history in this period, however, portrayed a Nazi triumph in World War II in self-congratulatory fashion. Indeed, alternate histories of a more self-critical variety continued to appear, as they had in the 1970s. The majority of these accounts used the occasion of the cold war's end to once more question America's decision to intervene against the Nazis in World War II. These neo-isolationist tales insisted that the Third Reich had never constituted a threat to American interests and that the United States should never have fought against it in the first place. Had the United States only refrained from doing so, the terrible course of postwar history – most notably, the long struggle against Soviet communism – could have been avoided. In making this claim, these narratives expressed some of the pessimism of the post-cold-war era. At the same time, they illustrated the fading horror of the Nazi era in the consciousness of some

Americans. Not all self-critical accounts in this period, however, reflected feelings about the cold war. One major work in particular used the scenario of a Nazi wartime victory to criticize domestic trends in the post-9/11 world. In so doing, it highlighted new ways in which the scenario may evolve in the future.

THE RETURN OF TRIUMPHALISM

One of the first works that illustrated the era's return to triumphalism was Leo Rutman's 1990 novel *Clash of Eagles*.[152] In many ways, *Clash of Eagles* was a throwback to the accounts of the war years. Like *Invasion* or *Lightning in the Night*, it described the Nazis' conquest of the east coast and midwest along with a lengthy account of life under occupation. Set in Nazi-ruled New York City, the novel's 530-page plot portrays the new Nazi order in familiar bleak terms, featuring American civilians being executed in Central Park, tortured by the Gestapo, and subjected to all manner of sexual degradation by assorted Nazi sadists. At the same time, though, most of the novel chronicles the successful mobilization of resistance to Nazi rule. Although Rutman hardly idealizes the resisters – portraying them as composed of rough-and-tumble Irish nationalists, two-bit American crooks, assorted mafia dons, and average working-class joes – he portrays their rebellion against the Nazis as quite effective. The novel was notable for being the first postwar account since C. M. Kornbluth's "Two Dooms" to conclude with a happy ending. *Clash of Eagles* offers numerous scenes of Americans avenging themselves against their German oppressors before finally concluding with the lines, "The city ran riot. All its children and its people. They were surging from Harlem to the Bronx, from Coney Island to Washington Heights . . . Torches burned brightly in the night . . . held proudly by the people of New York. The Americans had taken their city back."[153]

In closing with this upbeat ending, Rutman's novel exhibited many of the ambiguities of the post-cold-war era. Its portrayal of the brutal Nazi occupation of America clearly vindicated the United States' real historical decision to intervene in the war against Hitler's Germany in 1941. Yet Rutman's depiction of Nazi vulnerability suggested the possible influence of the Soviet Empire's collapse. The author has denied that his novel was in any way "ideological" and noted that it was mostly intended to be an entertaining drama. Whatever the case may be, *Clash of Eagles* was notable for its comparatively de-demonized portrayal of the Nazis. Unlike previous writers such as Dick and Shirer, who emphasized the significant danger

Figure 10 The Nazi regime's nuclear-bomb-equipped stealth bomber in Stephen Cornwell's 1993 film *The Philadelphia Experiment II*.

posed by the Germans to the United States in World War II, Rutman confidently insisted that "Hitler could not have conquered the East Coast, much less America."[154] Of course, Rutman was writing at a time in the late 1980s in which most Americans viewed Germany as a reliable ally, in contrast to the situation in the early 1960s, when such confidence was in shorter supply. While Rutman still portrayed the scenario of a Nazi victory in World War II in moralistic terms, therefore, his depiction of the Germans as eventually succumbing to American counter-attacks reflected how the passage of time had diminished the sense of Nazism's horror.

The same upbeat tone seen in *Clash of Eagles* was visible in another work that appeared three years later, Stephen Cornwell's 1993 film *The Philadelphia Experiment II*. In this film (a sequel to the 1984 film *The Philadelphia Experiment*), a super-secret experiment of the United States military to test newly developed teleportation technology goes horribly wrong when it accidentally sends a stealth bomber equipped with nuclear weapons back in time to Nazi Germany in the year 1943 (see Figure 10). The result of this snafu is the catastrophic alteration of history, for the

Nazis use the bomber to nuke Washington D.C. (killing some 15 million people) and defeat the United States in World War II. Most of *The Philadelphia Experiment II* is set fifty years later, in Nazi-occupied Southern California, and focuses on the attempt of its protagonist, an unfortunate naval officer named David Herdeg (played by Brad Johnson), to extricate himself from the alternate world into which he has somehow been propelled. Compared with *Clash of Eagles*, the film is less heavy-handed in depicting the brutality of life under the victorious Nazi regime. The worst that Americans experience under Nazi rule is forced labor and a steady barrage of propaganda messages ("health, hygiene, happiness") administered by the state. Little of the outright terror seen in prior decades' accounts is visible in the film. Ultimately, indeed, the film's priorities lay elsewhere. Like *Clash of Eagles*, *The Philadelphia Experiment II* was mostly concerned with offering viewers a redemptive ending. Thus, at the film's conclusion, Herdeg plays the hero when he outwits his opponents, tele-ports himself back to Nazi Germany, and destroys the stealth bomber before it can take off and attack the United States. Having dramatically corrected the course of (alternate) history, Herdeg is quickly sucked back through time to his own world and is reunited with his overjoyed son, a Little League baseball player who, in the film's final scene, provides the hokey redemptive gesture by hitting a home run.

With this happy ending, *The Philadelphia Experiment II* resembled *Clash of Eagles* in ratifying the real historical record of American interventionism in World War II. In many ways, *The Philadelphia Experiment II* clearly expressed the buoyant climate of the early 1990s. Produced after the United States' victory in the cold war catapulted it to unrivalled global pre-eminence, the film differed from the triumphalistic tales of the early postwar years, whose proximity to the Nazi era and lingering concerns about the Germans lent them a bleaker character. At the same time, however, the film can also be seen as responding to, and providing consolation for, those domestic problems in the United States that persisted in the wake of communism's collapse. Herdeg expresses this presentist subtext explicitly when he attempts to convince one of the government officials responsible for altering history to correct his mistake by saying, "There's a different world ... with a different history. I was just there yesterday. It's better than it is here ... It's not perfect, it's got its problems, but not like this. It's a nightmare here." For a nation that was just emerging out of economic recession, race riots, and culture wars, this message was no doubt appealing. The film's portrayal of an alternate world inferior to that of contemporary reality clearly vindicated the latter as the preferable alternative.

Figure 11 The aging Führer, Adolf Hitler (Rudolf Fleischer), looks on in grim resignation as American President Joseph Kennedy's motorcade bypasses his Berlin reviewing stand in Christopher Menaul's 1994 film *Fatherland*.

The American penchant for happy endings continued with the release of Christopher Menaul's 1994 cinematic adaptation of Robert Harris's novel *Fatherland*. First broadcast on the American cable network HBO, the film was notable for adding a much more redemptive ending than the book. Harris had originally concluded his novel on a grim note by critically portraying isolationist President Joseph Kennedy visiting Berlin to improve relations with Hitler. By contrast, the television version portrays the protagonist, Charlie MacGuire (played by Miranda Richardson), interrupting Kennedy's imminent meeting with Hitler by rushing up to his limousine and providing him with incontrovertible photographic evidence about the Nazis' genocidal crimes against the Jews. An aghast Kennedy then motions the limousine driver to continue driving past the waiting Führer, who ends up getting snubbed by the head of the world's other superpower (see Figure 11). While the reasons for this change in plot can only be guessed at, the fact that other Hollywood studios had found *Fatherland*'s original ending too depressing (and had insisted that it be made more upbeat in order for it to get produced) no doubt was involved.[155] The ending also dovetailed with the broader tendency in the wake of the cold war's conclusion for Americans to view their own past from a more triumphalistic and less self-critical perspective. Released at a time of great commemorative attention to the fiftieth anniversary of the events of World War II, the film expressed the abundant patriotism that existed within the nation about its role in helping to keep the world safe for democracy. By portraying the Third Reich as an evil empire (and under-playing the likelihood that any American government would have collab-orated with it), *Fatherland* provided a self-congratulatory vindication of America's intervention in the war.

Following *Fatherland*, the most prominent work of alternate history to partake of the renewed patriotic trend appeared one year later with the publication of then Speaker of the United States House of Representatives Newt Gingrich's novel *1945*.[156] Co-written with science fiction writer William Forstchen, *1945* portrays a world in which Hitler's temporary elimination from power (due to serious injuries suffered in a plane crash on December 6, 1941) keeps the Germans from declaring war on the United States and, in turn, enables them to concentrate all their attention on defeating the Soviet Union, which they do in 1943. Given that the United States defeat the Japanese in the same span of time, a showdown between the world's two superpowers becomes merely a matter of time. Finally, in 1945 the treacherous Nazis decide to defeat their last remaining enemy once and for all. Aware that the Germans are considerably lagging behind the Americans in atomic weapons research and development, a recovered Hitler orders a pre-emptive strike against the American research facility at Oak Ridge, Tennessee (as well as against the facility at Los Alamos, New Mexico) to decisively render the enemy powerless to defend itself against the vastly superior conventional weapons of the Nazis. Led by the reliable villain, the malicious Austrian SS killer, Otto Skorzeny, an elite team of Nazi assassins, supported by a fleet of long-range German bomb-ers, penetrates deep into American territory and destroys the Oak Ridge facility in a fiery inferno. Only due to the heroic efforts of the novel's protagonist, an American naval intelligence officer named Jim Martel, are the Americans able to learn of the attack soon enough to organize a semblance of resistance that prevents the assault from being a total fiasco. The novel's final outcome, however, is highly ambiguous – on its final page appear the words: "to be continued." Still, while the ending is never spelled out, *1945* implies that the Americans face a dire situation in the wake of the German attack. Not only do they now trail the Germans in the race to develop the bomb, but they lag far behind in conventional weapons capacity and have no capable allies to help them face the Nazi menace.

In its ominous description of the Nazi threat to the United States, *1945* emphatically endorsed the United States' real historical decision to fight Nazi Germany. Throughout the novel, Gingrich and Forstchen criticized isolationism. The main supporter of isolationism – the chief of staff to President Andrew Harrison, John Mayhew – is depicted as morally corrupt and treasonous. Meanwhile, the President himself muses at one point, "Were it not for Hitler ... isolationism would look pretty good. As things were, he had to run with the internationalist crowd."[157] In the end, the evil of Nazism makes intervention an obvious choice. As Winston Churchill puts it to a vacillating President Harrison at one point in the novel, "There is no clearer enemy than Hitler."[158] At the same time, the authors justified interventionism by underscoring Nazi brutality. The American hero, Jim, proclaims that "Hitler and his scum ... [are] evil incarnate," and the American General George Marshall adds, "We are in a de facto state of war with a power that makes the Japanese Empire at its height look like a Gilbert and Sullivan threat."[159]

Gingrich and Forstchen's motives in defending the historical struggle against Nazism spanned a range of political and personal concerns.[160] As was true of the Anglo-American accounts of the 1960s, portraying the Nazis as the incarnation of evil helped accentuate the heroic quality of America's struggle against them. It was significant that *1945* valorized the American resistance. When the Germans invade Oak Ridge, local World War I veterans, led by none other than war hero Alvin York, help repel the German assault, rescue Oak Ridge's atomic scientists, and preserve the nation's hopes of restarting the Manhattan project in time to defend the homeland against future German attacks. The desire to glorify America's struggle against the Nazis was further suggested by the fact that *1945* denied the Soviets a role in defeating them. By having the Soviet Union conclude an armistice with Germany and bow out of the conflict in 1943, Gingrich and Forstchen spared the Americans the obligation of having to share the credit for defeating Nazism with its real historical communist ally and instead give it the exclusive glory of doing so alone.[161] As Jim says at one point, "We [Americans] are all that stands between the world and Hitler."[162] This fantasy scenario partly reflected a smug sense of satisfaction about the demise of the Soviet Union and the end of the cold war.

This sense of triumphalism, to be sure, was not unalloyed. Written in a period of the early 1990s in which conservatives were bemoaning the threat to American values by big government, multiculturalism, and other "liberal" dangers, *1945* partly expressed the era's conservative cultural pessimism. At one juncture, the authors charge the federal government under

Roosevelt with incompetence due to its misguided decision to pass gun-control legislation in Oak Ridge, thus making its citizens more vulnerable to Nazi attack.[163] Still, *1945* was less of a libertarian rant against big government than a patriotic celebration of the American character. As shown by the vigorous defense against the Germans mounted by the local inhabitants of Oak Ridge, *1945* seemed to say that, even when challenged, ordinary Americans exhibited a strong capacity for valor. Furthermore, at the end of the novel, the authors affirmed the important role of the central government in choosing the best and brightest to devise new ways of defending the nation from external attack.[164] On the whole, *1945* was an affirmative rather than a self-critical tale. It expressed a sense of nostalgia for a simpler time where there was a unity of nation and state. Epitomizing this was Gingrich and Forstchen's dedication of *1945* to "the generation that fought the Nazis in the real world, especially our parents" – a gesture that allows the book to be placed within the broader wave of attention to the "greatest generation" of Americans that began to surge in the mid-1990s.[165] Given his underlying faith in the virtues of the American people, there is little doubt that Gingrich would have carried the narrative of *1945* through to its logical conclusion – namely, an American triumph over the Nazis – had he ever produced the promised sequel to it. But even in its abridged version, *1945* implied this happy ending in clear enough terms.

Since the turn of the millennium, this upbeat view has continued to find confirmation in other novels. Two that provided further evidence of the decreasing frightfulness of a Nazi wartime victory were Arthur Rhodes's 2001 novel *The Last Reich: America Strikes Back*, and J. N. Stroyar's 2001 novel *The Children's War*. Both books portrayed Nazi rule in familiar fashion as defined by great brutality, but their focus was directed less towards the crimes of the perpetrators than to the heroic resistance marshaled by the victims. For its part, Rhodes's novel resembled Rutman's *Clash of Eagles* by portraying the Nazi occupation of the United States as ultimately being overthrown by American resistance forces in the 1960s.[166] Stroyar's mammoth 1,149-page novel was far more intricate in its characters and plot; its portrayal of Nazi barbarism, in particular, was extremely vivid and bordered on the gratuitous. Yet it too ended on a redemptive note. After spending hundreds of pages describing the Nazi persecution of the Poles, Stroyar finally portrays the Polish resistance as successfully infiltrating one of its members, a man by the name of Richard Traugutt, into the highest circles of the Nazi leadership. By the end of the novel, Traugutt seems poised to become Germany's next Führer and inaugurate a reformist course in the Nazi state.[167] While *The Children's War* never gives the reader the satisfaction of the happy ending, it clearly points in that direction.

Finally, the same can be said of eminent alternate history author Harry Turtledove's 2003 novel *In the Presence of Mine Enemies*.[168] Set in 2009 in a world in which Nazi Germany has conquered Europe and occupied the United States, the novel focuses on the daily life of Heinrich Gimpel, a German bureaucrat employed by the military (the Oberkommando der Wehrmacht, or OKW) who turns out to be one of a handful of Jews who have escaped the Holocaust and survived in Berlin by hiding their true identities. Much of the novel focuses on the great lengths to which Gimpel and his family must go in order to remain undetected as Jews. But the significance of *In the Presence of Mine Enemies* lies less in the details of this suspenseful subplot about Jewish survival than in its portrayal of how German society evolves in the wake of a Nazi victory. While the beginning of the novel paints a familiarly grim portrait of Nazi omnipotence and barbarism – Germany rules over the entire globe (except for Japan) and has completed the Final Solution – it quickly shifts gear to portray the Nazi Reich undergoing a major internal crisis that culminates in revolution.

Great changes begin to occur in the Reich following the death of its third Führer, the ninety-year-old Kurt Haldweim (a not-so-thinly-veiled dig at the former Austrian President and Wehrmacht officer, Kurt Waldheim), who is succeeded by a dynamic young technocrat by the name of Heinz Buckliger. Having served as the Minister of Heavy Industry, Buckliger is well aware that the Reich has become a bloated and inefficient state, and he vows to usher in a long overdue process of economic and political reform. In attempting to advance this goal, Buckliger delivers a secret speech to the party at Nuremberg and thereafter goes on national television to admit a wide range of historical mistakes, declaring that "for far too long, this state has been founded on ... terror." He thereupon vows to cease the racially grounded "exploitation" of subject peoples, such as the British and Dutch, who have increasingly been voicing a desire for greater autonomy.[169] Moreover, by promising real political reforms, such as free elections for the Reichstag, Buckliger launches a thaw within Nazi society that quickly assumes its own dynamic. Before long, the Gauleiter of Berlin, a populist radical by the name of Rolf Stolle, demands further democratizing reforms and directly challenges the SS establishment at a mass demonstration by declaring, "We're going to show the world where the bodies are buried – and we all know there are lots of them."[170] With ordinary Germans encouraged by this trend – many enthusiastically embrace the slogan

"We are the *Volk*"– the worried SS tries to suppress the fledgling democracy movement by kidnapping Buckliger and seizing power in a brazen *coup d'état*. But in the end, Stolle comes to the rescue with the help of the Wehrmacht, which joins the broader revolutionary cause and overthrows the SS conspirators by force of arms. At the novel's conclusion, Buckliger and Stolle speak before the German people and promise not only to respect their will in the upcoming elections but also to "give democratic rights back to some other Aryan peoples too." As a television reporter concludes, "Where the *Volk* ... comes out into the streets ... how can things possibly remain the same after that?"[171]

In arriving at this happy ending, *In the Presence of Mine Enemies* reflected the ambiguities of the post-cold-war era. Turtledove's moralistic depiction of Nazi evil, and his triumphalistic validation of American intervention in World War II, revealed that he shared the era's optimistic mood. He clearly partook of the broader celebration of the "greatest generation" of war veterans, for example, as was made clear by his dedication of the book to family members who served in the war and who "helped ensure that this [the novel's story] is alternate history." He was also strongly influenced by the dramatic events surrounding the dissolution of the Soviet Union in 1990. Indeed, his heroic characters of Buckliger and Stolle were clear stand-ins for Mikhail Gorbachev and Boris Yeltsin, who provided the obvious inspiration for them. At the same time, though, the optimistic mood fostered by the events of the early 1990s led Turtledove to paint a comparatively normalized portrait of the Nazi era. As was true of Robert Harris's *Fatherland*, Turtledove's belief that the dissolution of the USSR provided a model for what would have eventually happened had the Nazis won World War II indicates how the end of the cold war contributed to the fading memory of Nazi barbarism. *In the Presence of Mine Enemies*, indeed, offered a much milder depiction of the Nazis than other accounts. While the tales of Harris, Rutman, and Gingrich, for example, diminished the horror of a victorious Reich by representing it as being successfully challenged by external resistance movements (whether Soviet or American), Turtledove portrayed the Reich's internal collapse from within. Instead of heroizing the Nazis' opponents, Turtledove heroized – or at least dramatically humanized – the Nazis themselves. He departed from most previous accounts, which depicted the Nazis as uniformly evil, by portraying them as a diverse group, ranging from ideological fanatics to reasonable pragmatists.[172] As one Jewish character named Esther concedes near the novel's end, "There were Nazis ... and then there were Nazis."[173] Turtledove, of course, was no apologist for Nazism. But this highly relativistic statement – which would have been unimaginable in earlier eras that viewed the Third Reich as the incarnation of evil – epitomized the further waning of a moral perspective towards the Nazi experience.

THE PERSISTENCE OF SELF-CRITIQUE

The triumphalistic trend of the 1990s, however, did not stand unopposed. The most vociferous dissent was provided by conservative pundit and three-time Reform party presidential candidate Pat Buchanan's controversial 1999 book *A Republic, Not an Empire*.[174] Although not a work of alternate history, Buchanan's book liberally utilized counterfactual reasoning in critiquing the interventionist character of twentieth-century American foreign policy.[175] In advancing his argument, Buchanan echoed Bruce Russett's conclusions from a generation earlier that the United States should have stayed out of World War II. Not only were vital American interests not at stake in this conflict, Buchanan argued, but the United States was not under any threat from the Nazi regime. Buchanan sharply downplayed the likelihood that Hitler would have sought war with, let alone invaded, the United States, arguing that he was primarily interested in expanding Germany's borders to the east by defeating the Soviet Union. As he put it, "If Hitler could not put a soldier into England in the fall of 1940, the notion that he could invade the Western Hemisphere . . . was preposterous."[176] It was therefore doubly tragic, he went on to note, that Britain and France declared war on Nazi Germany after its invasion of Poland. For this decision led Hitler to invade Western Europe (in which he allegedly had no prior interest) and also prevented him from throwing all of his forces against the Russians, thus ensuring that the Soviet Union would survive the Nazi onslaught and remain communist.[177] The main thrust of Buchanan's counterfactual analysis culminated with his provocative claim that "Had Britain and France not given the war guarantees to Poland, there might have been no Dunkirk, no blitz, no Vichy, [and] no destruction of the Jewish populations of Western Europe."[178] In this view, the wrong-headed decision of the British and French to declare war on the Germans, and the dishonest means through which Roosevelt brought the United States into the fray on their side, ended up having tragically paradoxical effects. As Buchanan concluded, "In 1941, Roosevelt had gone to war to make Europe . . . safe for democracy, and had made Europe safe for Stalinism."[179]

In drawing this pessimistic conclusion, Buchanan expressed a highly normalized view of the Nazi past. To be sure, Buchanan's primary motives for questioning American intervention against the Nazis in World War II were political. The presidential candidate's political platform of economic nationalism and diplomatic isolationism logically required him to rehabilitate the beliefs of American isolationists that staying out of the European conflict would have allowed Hitler to crush Bolshevism.[180] Still, regardless of this argument's political utility, Buchanan's embrace of it was significant in illustrating the fading fears of Nazism. Like John Lukacs in "What if Hitler Had Won the Second World War?" Buchanan relativized Nazism's evil by comparing it to that of Soviet communism. By 1939, he noted, "Stalin had amassed a record of murder and enslavement that dwarfed Hitler's." "Estimates of the dead at the hands of the Great Terrorist before September 1939," he added, "run to twenty-two million, one thousand times the number that could then be charged to Hitler. Stalin's concentration camps also held one thousand times as many souls as did Hitler's."[181] Moreover, Buchanan observed, even after two years of war, on the eve of Germany's invasion of the Soviet Union in 1941, "the body count of those murdered by Stalin still exceeded Hitler's by the millions." It was no wonder, he concluded, that "many Americans [viewed] Stalin's Russia . . . [as] a far greater long-term threat than Hitler's Germany."[182]

Yet no matter how much Americans might have endorsed this view during the 1940s, Buchanan's support for it ten years after the fall of communism seems puzzling. Given the dramatic events of 1989, conservative attention to the evils of communism might have been expected to disappear. But in fact the opposite was true. Throughout the West, there appeared new attention to the historical evils of communism, epitomized by the publication of Stéphane Courtois's mammoth compendium of communist crimes *The Black Book of Communism.*[183] Such works proliferated in the 1990s as part of a triumphalistic desecration of communism's corpse and also as an effort to vindicate the cold-war crusade against the Soviet Union. In order for this campaign for vindication to be effective, however, it needed to relativize the crimes of Nazism, against which communist crimes were usually deemed less horrific. Buchanan's allohistorical downplaying of the Nazi threat to the United States in *A Republic, Not an Empire* was part of a broader attempt to justify the cold-war struggle against communism. So important was this mission to him that, in the book's final section, he abandoned his allegedly principled stance of isolationism and defended the United States' intervention in the cold war.[184] In doing so, while simultaneously rejecting American intervention in World War II against Nazi Germany, of course, Buchanan exposed a fundamental inconsistency of principle that dramatically weakened the overall argument of *A Republic, Not an Empire*. At the same time, though, he provided further confirmation of the enduring role of cold-war anticommunism in attenuating Western fears of Nazism.

The same can be said for A. Edward Cooper's 1999 novel *Triumph of the Third Reich*.[185] Written with a less overt political agenda than Buchanan's book, Cooper's text nonetheless exhibited a mixture of neo-isolationist and anticommunist leanings in his depiction of a Nazi victory in World War II. In the novel (which is largely an extended timeline with little character development), Hitler wins the war in 1944 by developing superior weapons (V-1 and V-2 rockets, Me-262 fighters, and the atomic bomb), which he uses to defeat the Allied landing at Normandy and thereafter compel the British and Americans to accept an armistice and separate peace agreements. Significantly, Cooper describes the decision to bow out of the war by isolationist President Joseph Kennedy (who becomes commander-in-chief after the death of Roosevelt and the assassination of successor President Henry Wallace in 1944) as a prudent one. With the United States out of the conflict, Hitler re-invades the the Soviet Union, thus fulfilling Kennedy's fantasy of having the Nazis and Bolsheviks fight to the death. But an even better outcome ensues, for the continued fight against Bolshevism and the continued occupation of Western Europe ruin the German economy and earn Hitler the opposition of a powerful cabal of generals and civilian resistance figures which eventually succeeds in assassinating him in early 1949.[186] Under the new chancellor, Erwin Rommel, Nazi Germany abandons ideological fanaticism in favor of pragmatism, holding war crimes trials of leading Nazi figures, closing down the concentration camps, ending the atomic weapons program, and generally reforming the nation's political system in a more progressive democratic direction. In the end, the way seems to be paved for the forging of a German–American alliance in the ongoing fight against Soviet communism. In short, by sketching out the fantasy scenario of Nazi Germany reforming itself from above after a wartime victory, Cooper – like Brad Linaweaver almost twenty years earlier – challenged the persistent belief that American intervention against Nazi Germany in World War II was historically necessary.[187]

Unlike Linaweaver – and certainly unlike Buchanan – however, Cooper does not seem to have written his novel with a partisan political agenda in mind. As a retired aerospace engineer and part-time novelist writing for the religiously oriented, Utah-based publishing house, Agreka Books, he portrayed the ultimate result of a Nazi victory in World War II in optimistic fashion most likely as a way of celebrating the universal human desire for freedom.[188] It is possible, moreover, that the end of the cold war and the liberation of Eastern Europe from the communist yoke inspired Cooper to portray the Nazis ultimately reforming their regime from above in order to avert later collapse. Just as Robert Harris was influenced by the collapse of the Soviet Union in portraying the victorious Nazi empire as progressively more vulnerable due to the longterm costs of victory, Cooper portrayed President Kennedy confidently predicting that "an empire as evil as Hitler's cannot possibly exist for long, [for] once ... the day-to-day realities of running such an empire sets in, the German people themselves will grow weary of it."[189] Whatever Cooper's specific motives may have been in arriving at this upbeat conclusion, it was implicitly founded on the belief that America would have been better off remaining neutral in World War II. As such it reflected the tendency of some Americans after the cold war to rethink older moralistic views of the Nazi past.

THE TRANSFORMATION OF SELF-CRITIQUE SINCE 9/11

If the scattered self-critical works of the 1990s expressed a fading sense of the Third Reich's horror, the opposite is true of the most recent work of alternate history to address the theme of a Nazi victory – Philip Roth's much-publicized 2004 novel *The Plot against America* (see Figure 12).[190] Although Roth's book only flirts with, and never fully develops, the scenario of the Nazis winning World War II, it is significant for several reasons. The fact that Roth, one of America's most celebrated and accomplished writers, chose to write a work of alternate history to begin with affirms the genre's arrival into the American cultural mainstream. Beyond constituting something of a milestone in that respect, the book is notable for inaugurating what may be a new phase in the representation of the Nazi era in American works of alternate history.

The Plot against America portrays the struggle of its protagonist, a nine-year-old boy named Philip Roth, to adapt to the new world that results from the novel's main allohistorical point of divergence, Charles Lindbergh's defeat of Franklin Delano Roosevelt in the American presidential election of 1940. Having campaigned on a platform of isolationism – "Vote for Lindbergh or Vote for War" is his slogan – Lindbergh moves as president to relax relations with Hitler's Germany, going so far as to forge a neutrality pact with the Reich in the fall of 1940 known as the "Iceland Understanding" that, together with the signing of a similar agreement, the "Hawaii Understanding," with Japan, essentially makes the United States a member of the Axis alliance. This turn of events is understandably

Figure 12 Cover of Philip Roth's novel *The Plot against America* (2004).

worrisome for American Jews like Philip and his family, and their fears of worse to come are soon realized as Lindbergh goes on to enact fascist-inspired policies – like the newly established Office of American Absorption's "Homestead 42" program to forcibly resettle inner-city Jewish families in the rural midwest – that are meant to hasten their Americanization and dilute their ethnic cohesion. Events deteriorate still further in the fall of 1942, when ongoing American Jewish criticism of the president's warm relations with Nazi Germany – Foreign Minister von Ribbentrop receives a state dinner at the White House – sparks antisemitic riots in midwestern cities like Detroit, Cleveland, Cincinnati, Indianapolis, and St. Louis, in which hundreds of Jewish synagogues and businesses are burned and hundreds of Jews murdered. This American version of Kristallnacht quickly brings young Philip and his family to despair, and before similar anti-Jewish violence arrives in their own Newark, New Jersey neighborhood, they resolve to flee into exile in Canada.

Up until this point in the novel, Roth essentially echoed the bleak conclusions of such earlier writers as Philip K. Dick, Eric Norden, William Overgard, and David Dvorkin. Like them, Roth asserted that the United States government's decision to remain isolationist and refrain from fighting Nazi Germany in World War II would have led the nation to turn towards fascism and collaboration. Furthermore, he implicitly endorsed the idea that American isolationism would have ultimately permitted Germany to win the war. By the fall of 1942, indeed, Roth writes that Lindbergh's policies had "provided the German army with additional time to quell the continuing . . . resistance from the Soviet Union" and had "furnished German industry and the German scientific establishment – already secretly developing a bomb . . . powered by atomic fission, as well as a rocket engine capable of conveying this weapon across the Atlantic – with a further two years in which to complete preparation for the apocalyptic struggle with the United States."[191]

Yet, before this bleak outcome can occur, Roth radically alters his novel's counterfactual trajectory by introducing a *deus ex machina* twist that restores historical events to their rightful course. The twist begins when President Lindbergh's private plane disappears without a trace on his return flight from Louisville, Kentucky to Washington D.C. in the fall of 1942. Soon thereafter, Vice-President Burton Wheeler declares martial law, citing FBI reports from Nazi sources that the president has allegedly been kidnapped by "Jewish interests" who are holding him captive in Canada. As calls emerge for the United States to invade Canada, as German troops set out to occupy Mexico (ostensibly to "protect" America's southern border), and as FBI agents arrest various liberal and Jewish members of Roosevelt's former administration for their suspected roles in the kidnapping scheme, Lindbergh's wife, Anne Morrow Lindbergh, goes on the radio to drop the bombshell that she has just escaped from Walter Reed Medical Hospital, where she has been been confined by agents of the Wheeler administration involved in a broader plot against the United States government. As the novel goes on to reveal in highly convoluted fashion, Lindbergh's disappearance was part of a decade-old Nazi conspiracy, in which Hitler used the president's young son (who had been famously kidnapped and thought dead, but actually had been smuggled into Germany in the early 1930s) to blackmail Lindbergh into becoming a Nazi fifth-columnist who would do the Reich's bidding once he rose to power. Lindbergh's failure to heed Heinrich Himmler's demands for more ruthless action against the American Jewish community, however, ultimately leads the Nazi government to oust Lindbergh, whom they covertly bring back to Germany after staging his disappearance. In the wake of these events, Anne Morrow Lindbergh invokes the American constitution to call for new elections in 1942, and in short order, Roosevelt sweeps back into power, the Japanese bomb Pearl Harbor, and the United States enter the war against its former German and Japanese allies, finally defeating them in 1945. Although America has suffered a serious crisis, it ultimately triumphs, just like in real history.

The upbeat conclusion of *The Plot against America* is significant for a variety of reasons. To a degree, the novel resembles many other American accounts from the 1990s, such as *Clash of Eagles* and the *Philadelphia Experiment II*, which also culminated with happy endings. Unlike these works, however, Roth's novel hardly diminishes the horror of the Third Reich and makes no attempt to normalize its legacy. Instead, by depicting the Nazis as fearsome enemies who come dangerously close to realizing their demonic goals in the United States, *The Plot against America* expresses an enduring sense of their evil. Still, by refraining from portraying the Nazis as emerging victorious, Roth somewhat undercuts the effectiveness of his tale's underlying cautionary lesson. *The Plot against America* thus represents something of a return to the future histories of the early 1940s, such as *Invasion* and *Lightning in the Night*, which also tempered their cautionary lessons about the Nazi menace with happy endings so as not to demoralize the reading public. Yet while Roth's novel partakes of an older tradition, his specific goals in writing it are quite new. Most likely, Roth wanted his novel to serve as a warning about the contemporary dangers facing America in the wake of the terrorist attacks of 9/11 and the war in

Iraq. In portraying the United States becoming a fascist-like state under the administration of an ill-qualified, naive, and incompetent president, Roth offers a not-so-thinly veiled critique of the United States under the administration of President George W. Bush.[192] Roth's use of the nightmare scenario of the Nazis (almost) winning World War II to criticize present-day problems, of course, has ample precedent – most notably, in the practice of American writers during the crisis-ridden 1970s, who were the first to abandon the scenario's original self-congratulatory function in favor of one that was more self-critical. Whether or not the premise of a Nazi victory in World War II continues to be used in such self-critical fashion in future works of alternate history remains to be seen. But in commenting on post-9/11 events, *The Plot against America* clearly confirms the tendency of alternate histories to adapt to changing times and may thus eventually be seen as inaugurating a new phase of the scenario's evolution.

RECEPTION

On balance, the narratives that have appeared since the 1990s reflected a growing tendency to view the Nazi past from a less judgmental perspective, yet the strongly negative reaction to them illustrated a desire of American audiences to preserve traditional, moralistic views. In contrast to the largely positive reception of the normalized works of the 1970s and 1980s, the response to the accounts of the 1990s was predominantly negative. This was particularly true of the higher-profile works of the period.[193] HBO's television version of *Fatherland*, for example, was accorded a wide reception but was generally regarded as a "disappointment."[194] Reviewers cited a variety of reasons in making this assessment, but most found the film inferior to the original novel, with more than a few specifically criticizing the film's "depressingly hokey and stupid climax."[195] It may well be that such complaints reflected a reluctance of critics to accept the nakedly patriotic happy ending forced upon the film by network executives and, thus, a willingness to embrace a less self-congratulatory view of the American past. Yet it is easy to exaggerate such a point. Other reviewers, after all, found the film not patriotic enough. One reviewer seemed motivated by conservative anticommunism when he called *Fatherland*'s basic premise – that "the United States bowed out of the war while the Soviets fought valiantly on" – "unacceptable."[196] It is impossible to know with certainty what political implications viewers perceived the film as containing. But politics aside, perhaps the most significant complaint was that *Fatherland* made the premise of a Nazi victory boring. One reviewer polemically branded the film a "thrill-free thriller," concluding "Zey haff vays of making you yawn in *Fatherland*."[197]

Such complaints are significant, for they were echoed in the responses to the film *The Philadelphia Experiment II*. To an even greater degree than *Fatherland*, *The Philadelphia Experiment II* received low marks across the board, being called a "contrived" film that did not exceed "grade-C science fiction." Notably, certain reviewers alluded to the film's mild portrayal of a Nazi-ruled world, arguing that it merely portrayed "the new Nazi nation ... as a bummer" and did not succeed in leaving viewers with anything more than a "few jitters."[198] It is significant that the two major films of the decade were both faulted for failing to inject the appropriate degree of terror into the premise of a Nazi victory in World War II, for it suggests that while the horror of a Nazi-ruled world had perhaps faded in the minds of the creators of alternate history, it persisted in the minds of audiences.

Yet while *Fatherland* and *The Philadelphia Experiment II* received negative marks, they did not fare so poorly as the two forays into alternate history produced by the nation's two most visible conservative politicians: Newt Gingrich and Pat Buchanan. Gingrich's novel, *1945*, met with the most savage reception of any work of alternate history in the postwar era. Called a "dud" by one of the more charitable reviewers, the novel was described as outright "torture" by another, who proclaimed he would rather "spend a year in solitary confinement with nothing to read except Danielle Steel than [spend] another nanosecond with the prose of Gingrich."[199] Critics lambasted everything, from the novel's literary ineptitude to its conservative political subtext.[200] One reviewer described it as "muddled, military mishmash: part Rambo, part Tom Clancy, with *Pulp Fiction*-esque gore tossed in," and another criticized it for its eroticization of military hardware.[201] So bad were the reviews of *1945* that the majority of the unsold copies ended up being pulped.[202] Yet, in surveying the reviews, it is notable that most criticized the Speaker of the House for temporarily ignoring politics to make a profit in the publishing world.[203] Few objected to the novel's allohistorical function of validating the United States' real historical intervention in World War II to fight Nazi Germany.[204] Indeed, the only reviewers to object to the novel's triumphalistic message were British critics who resented *1945* for denying the British and Soviets any role in defeating the Nazis and selfishly reserving all the credit for the United States.[205] For this reason, the book's negative reception does not necessarily mean that its interventionist message was repudiated by American readers.

Significantly, the opposite was true of the critical response to Pat Buchanan's *A Republic, Not an Empire*, which was explicitly condemned *because* of its revisionist view of Nazism. Some, like John Judis in the *New York Times Book Review*, criticized Buchanan for harboring an overly "benign view of Hitler" and for glossing over "the fate of ... German and East European Jews and Poles" under Nazism.[206] Others criticized Buchanan for underestimating the Nazis' aggressive intentions towards the West.[207] Various scholars, for example, cited Hitler's commissioning of the ME-264 (known as the Amerika-Bomber) and a fleet of super battleships as evidence of a long-range plan to engage the United States in military confrontation in the future.[208] Had the Nazis actually been able to gain dominance over Europe, critics added, they would have been a major threat to the United States. As journalist Michael Lind concluded, a "Third Reich that had consolidated its power would have been far more technologically advanced and perhaps more aggressive than the Soviet Union ever was."[209] Buchanan's claims actually caused a major controversy within the Reform party in 1999 when Donald Trump (who was challenging Buchanan for the party's presidential nomination) accused him of "denigrating the memory of Americans who died fighting in an unavoidable war," noting, "Pat says Hitler had no malicious intent toward the United States ... Well, Hitler killed six million Jews and millions of others. Don't you think it was only a question of time before he got to us?"[210] Despite such criticism, however, other observers defended Buchanan's thesis. Conservative stalwart William F. Buckley supported Buchanan, noting, "Would things have been better if Hitler had conquered Moscow? They could hardly have been worse."[211] Moreover, Buchanan's book enjoyed considerable commercial success and was a hit with many readers.[212] On the whole, though, mainstream opinion looked unfavorably upon Buchanan's argument.

    The strongest indication of the enduring desire of American audiences to view the Nazi era from a morally informed perspective was provided by the negative reaction to Harry Turtledove's *In the Presence of Mine Enemies*. This reaction was particularly significant, given Turtledove's status as the most skilled and acclaimed writer working in the field of alternate history today. His distinguished reputation notwithstanding, Turtledove earned widespread criticism for what was largely viewed as a disappointing work of fiction. While many reviewers complained about the book's "tepid characterization and clumsy plot devices," a good number focused upon his mild portrait of the victorious Reich.[213] One reviewer, for example, described Turtledove's representation of the Nazi regime's "political thaw" as "unlikely" and "unconvincing"; another found it "disconcerting" that "unrepentant Nazis" were among the novel's "unlikely heroes."[214] Even average readers posted reviews declaring that "Turtledove thinks a little too highly of Nazi civilization."[215] In short, by rejecting Turtledove's vision of the Third Reich's internal reform as both implausible and unbelievable, readers expressed a basic commitment to remembering the Nazi regime as the embodiment of evil.

CONCLUSION

On balance, the conclusions of, and responses to, alternate histories of a Nazi victory in World War II suggest that the memory of the Nazi past in the United States has slowly become more normalized over the course of the postwar era. From 1945 up until the early 1970s, works of alternate history uniformly portrayed a Nazi victory in horrifying terms, thereby affirming the wisdom of the United States government's decision to intervene against the Germans in World War II. With the period of national decline that peaked during the era of crisis in the late 1970s and early 1980s, however, alternate histories became more self-critical. Some challenged the prevailing interventionist consensus by depicting a Nazi triumph as a relatively benign event; others affirmed the interventionist belief in Nazism's evil, but less to validate the past than to criticize the present. These tales reflected the existence of a counter-memory opposed to the dominant memory established during the early postwar period. The accounts that have appeared since 1989, by contrast, have reflected the post-cold-war return of national self-confidence by once more validating interventionism and portraying a Nazi victory as a terrible event. At the same time, these accounts have portrayed a Nazi victory in much less horrific terms than those of the 1950s and 1960s. Indeed, in providing audiences with happy endings, these narratives suggested the fading horror of the Nazi era in the minds of many Americans. How many, though, is difficult to gauge. The continued desire of audiences to see the Nazis portrayed as the epitome of evil, and their disapproval of works that have failed to offer such portraits, reflect an enduring moralistic perspective on the Nazi era in the popular consciousness.

Especially compared with the case of Great Britain, therefore, the degree of normalization in the United States seems to be less pronounced. If in Britain the challenge to (and defense of) the myth of the finest hour has been both prolonged and vehement, the limited number and cool reception of works criticizing interventionism in the United States suggests that it represents more of a marginal phenomenon. The reluctance of Americans to criticize one of their nation's postwar foundational myths as stridently as Britons have criticized theirs suggests that Americans have maintained a greater degree of self-confidence than Britons about the status of their nation in the postwar world. Without having to face the reality of decline in as pressing a manner as the British, Americans have had less occasion to question inherited views of the past. They have largely continued to believe that the fight against Nazism was both strategically necessary and morally just. Nevertheless, the Nazi past has gradually shed some of its horrific dimensions in American consciousness over time. The decreasingly grim portrayal of a Nazi victory, its increasing use for comedic entertainment, and the growing desire for happy endings all reflect the decline of moralism and the growth of normalization.

CHAPTER 3

Germany's wartime triumph: from dystopia to normalcy

November 9 was a Saturday. A wet and cold wind swept sluggishly through the streets of Heydrich ... and stripped the last leaves from the trees ...

The mail would come soon. Höllriegl quickly glanced through his appointment calendar ...

The local party headquarters held the customary weekend courses for officials ... at ten that morning ...

A light rain began to fall as he drove down Hindenburg Avenue, and it soon turned into a steady drizzle ...

The lecture about the Tschandal areas ... stirred him mightily ... The northern and middle regions of the old Soviet Union, settled by the German-blooded armed peasants, were surrounded by a garland of states dependent on the Reich ... Where once extermination camps had stood, the fortresses of the SS ... rose atop artificial hills which, legend had it, were really heaps of skulls ... Scattered across the vast Slavic land were thousands of racial breeding stables, in which the future elite of the master race was growing up. Right after the final victory, blond Germans and blond Slavs ... had been crossed with some success, and these bastards ... had marched out into the steppes, the forests, and icy deserts in order to crush ... the Tschandal worms, and to clear the depopulated areas for future pure-bred colonies. All this had only been started, but the results ... already took your breath away. Heil to the Führer who had created such greatness![1]

Austrian writer Otto Basil's bleak depiction of a Nazi-ruled world in his 1966 novel *Wenn das der Führer wüsste* (*If Only the Führer Knew*) offers a disturbing answer to a question that few Germans during the postwar period felt courageous enough to confront: what would have happened had Nazi Germany actually won World War II? Unlike the case in Britain and the United States, few alternate histories portraying a Nazi triumph in World War II have appeared in Germany since 1945.[2] Those that have, moreover, have only partly followed the pattern established by their

Anglo-American counterparts. German accounts have mirrored those in Great Britain and the United States in their content: early postwar tales in the Federal Republic depicted the scenario of a Nazi victory in moralistic fashion, while later ones portrayed it in much more normalized terms. Yet German alternate histories have differed from British and American narratives in their function. If early accounts mostly aimed to affirm West Germany's postwar rehabilitation by showing how much worse history could have been had the Nazis won the war, they also enabled Germans to express regret for the disastrous course of their recent history. This self-critical function has disappeared, however, from the alternate histories that have appeared in Germany since the country's reunification in 1990. In contrast to British and American narratives, which normalized the premise of a Nazi military triumph for the purpose of self-critique, recent German tales have done so for the triumphalistic purpose of re-establishing a normal sense of national identity.

ALTERNATE HISTORY AS DYSTOPIA

The first German alternate histories of a Nazi victory in World War II appeared much later than British and American accounts. Indeed, they only began to emerge after the mid-1960s, nearly twenty years after the first narratives in Britain.[3] These early German alternate histories followed the pattern of Anglo-American tales by being situated in clearly defined ethical frameworks. Yet, appearing in a period when early postwar views were being abandoned, they too exhibited subtle signs of a normalized mindset, primarily in their tendency to universalize the Nazi experience into a larger metaphor of evil.

The earliest and most nightmarish representation of a Nazi victory in World War II was Austrian writer Otto Basil's 1966 novel *Wenn das der Führer wüsste* (*If Only the Führer Knew*). In its overall narrative, Basil's novel chronicles the disastrous course taken by history after the death of Hitler in an undisclosed year sometime in the 1960s. Like Anglo-American accounts of these same years, *Wenn das der Führer wüsste* depicted a Nazi victory as bringing about an unprecedented catastrophe. Unlike them, however, it did not focus on the catastrophic consequences for the victims of German aggression, but for the Germans themselves. The image of German domination sketched by Basil was a wholly frightful one. By the early 1960s, German rule stretches from the United Vassal States of America (which is ruled by a KKK-led puppet government) to the furthest reaches of Eastern Europe. Hitler's new order is unimaginably brutal.

Having already exterminated world Jewry and eradicated London with nuclear weapons, the Nazis maintain their new order through a strict system of racial segregation and genetic domination. The KKK government reintroduces slavery in the United States., and Nazi rule in Eastern Europe is sustained by the forced labor of genetically altered sub-humans.

This new order is fully to the liking of the novel's central character, Albin Totila Höllriegl, a committed Nazi and quack medical healer, known as a "gyromant," who travels through Germany's newly renamed cities, such as Eichmannstadt and Goeringstadt, utilizing pendulums and other oscillating devices to probe clients' homes for unhealthy "earth radiation." Höllriegl is a wholly unsympathetic character, a sexual deviant strongly committed to the hierarchical racial ideology of the regime. Yet he demonstrates human traits – if distasteful ones – in his struggle to master his recurring, sado-masochistically inflected feelings of inferiority (feelings that the state has labeled a capital crime). The central theme of the novel involves Höllriegl's attempt to maintain his faith in Nazism as Hitler's world empire begins to crumble after the Führer's death. Hitler's demise quickly unleashes a dis-astrous series of events: a power struggle within the party – won by Werewolf leader Ivo Köpfler (who, it soon emerges, has actually murdered Hitler to gain power) – followed by a sneak Japanese attack on Germany that quickly escalates into World War III. Within a short span of time, Germany experiences the eruption of civil war, suffers widespread nuclear devastation, and swiftly descends into an apocalyptic "war of everybody against every-body else."[4] In satirical fashion, Basil depicts Höllriegl only slowly grasping the looming signs of the coming disaster. As the signs of degeneracy, corruption, and unrest within the German Reich begin to mount, however, he begins to abandon his smug confidence in the regime's outward signs of triumph and realizes that "the evil now in the open had been in the making for a long time."[5] In the end, the apocalyptic collapse of Germany forces a despairing Höllriegl to accept the bankruptcy of Nazism.

The past day, which he had called the 'Last Judgment,' had opened his eyes – finally ... Nothing existed that had any value. The Führer was dead and with that Höllriegl's world had lost all meaning ... [The] war ... carelessly and criminally begun ... had been utter madness from the first moment, a completely senseless, instinctive battle of all against all ... A war of life against itself.

And ... his belief in a holy salvation embodied on earth in the person of the Führer? It was all deceit ...

This life was one great shit and vomit.[6]

In depicting the nightmarish vision of a Nazi victory in World War II, Basil expressed the traumatic memory of the *real* historical disaster brought about by the Third Reich. Like many Germans of his generation, Basil was deeply affected by the Nazi experience. Born in 1901, he had worked actively in Austria in the 1930s as a politically engaged, avant-garde writer composing antifascist literature for the journal PLAN.[7] After the war, he also maintained an interest in Germany's Nazi past, one which intensified as international attention refocused upon it after the late 1950s. Indeed, in conceiving of the premise for *Wenn das der Führer wüsste*, Basil seems to have been influenced by the full publication of the Nuremberg trial transcripts, which, among other revelations, exposed the full scope of the Nazis' barbaric plans for Europe.[8] In short, Basil was strongly driven by moral considerations to write his novel. Yet signs of a normalized perspective were also visible. After 1945 Basil remained a broad-ranging intellectual, concerned with major issues facing postwar Western society, such as the cold war and the nuclear arms race.[9] These universalistic concerns also inspired him to write *Wenn das der Führer wüsste*. Although Basil has claimed that "in writing the novel, I did not pursue any ... didactic goals," he added that "it was ... intended to demonstrate the potential bestialization (*Bestifikation*) of human beings ... as we are currently seeing everywhere on a daily ... basis (for example, the Americans in Vietnam)."[10] In short, Basil used the particular German case of the Third Reich to arrive at general conclusions about the human condition.

Basil's universalistic agenda was next to invisible in the body of the novel itself, but other signs of his particular moral stance were sensed by certain Germans and proved controversial. After completing *Wenn das der Führer wüsste*, Basil had great difficulties finding a publisher for it. According to the writer, the reluctance of publishers to accept the novel stemmed from their inability to accept a work of fiction that featured a fanatical Nazi protagonist without a more explicit moral framework.[11] Publishers seem to have been most suspicious about the novel's underlying premise; when one asked Basil to append a preface clarifying his motives for writing it, he refused, saying he did not want "to function demiurgically as a critical authority, a moral woof-woof, or a judging super-ego."[12] Like Kevin Brownlow in Britain, Basil possessed a fierce artistic preference for his characters to condemn themselves by their very actions without "being bothered by a caressing or punishing [authorial] hand."[13] Still, in the end, Basil partly surrendered by adding a cryptic prefatory note to the novel that read:

In a completely mundane world
such as described here,
through which, however,
the outlines of today's real world can be glanced,

the author cannot pardon anyone,
only negative characters can occur.
The author considers himself to be
one of them.[14]

However opaque, this note signalled Basil's admission of the immorality of
his novel's characters, while facetiously identifying himself with them.
That such a note was necessary, of course, was significant, as it testified
to German fears that readers might misunderstand the very depiction of a
Nazi victory as an endorsement of it. Although by Anglo-American standards the book assumed a clear ethical stance, the hesitant German reaction
revealed a greater sensitivity to the slightest signs of representing the Nazi
past in unconventional fashion.

Still, Basil's literary stubbornness did not prevent *Wenn das der Führer
wüsste* from being a surprise critical and commercial success. Despite a few
tepid reviews that criticized the book's overt sexual content, most were
highly congratulatory.[15] While one praised the novel as an "interesting
satire," another gushed that Basil's "eminent ... accomplishment ... [was]
tormentingly valuable" in painting a "convincing depiction of the possibilities of a world after Hitler's victory."[16] Judging by the book's impressive
sales figures, moreover, the popular reception was equally positive.
Published with an initial print run of 25,000 copies, *Wenn das der Führer
wüsste* was widely regarded as a bestseller in both Germany and Austria.[17]
The reasons for this enthusiastic response are complex. The apparent
willingness of Germans to embrace Basil's narrative testified to the existence of a profound moral consensus in Germany about Nazism's inherent
evil. This consensus on the Nazi past was regularly invoked to counter
worrisome trends in the present. Aware of the upsurge in rightwing politics
at the time, one journalist wrote that Basil's book "should be distributed
free of charge to young NPD voters" (i.e. the far rightwing National
Democratic Party) – thereby, presumably, showing them the logical endpoint of their misguided beliefs.[18] But like all nightmare scenarios, the
success of Basil's novel also served to vindicate real historical developments
since 1945. Especially for Germans eager to recover from the disasters of the
recent past, confronting a fictional image of how much worse things would
have been had the Nazis won threw into even sharper relief how much
progress they had made since the end of the war. "So monstrous" were the
implications of a Nazi victory, one reviewer put it, "that they would even
lead [one] ... to reconcile one's self with the not-so-wonderful reality of
the 1960s."[19] In short, whatever Germans' views were of the postwar
present, Basil's novel allowed them to feel grateful it was not far worse.

Following Basil's novel, the next German alternate history to appear was Helmut Heissenbüttel's short story from 1979 "Wenn Adolf Hitler den Krieg nicht gewonnen hätte"(see Figure 13).[20] As was indicated by the story's title – "If Adolf Hitler Had *Not* Won the War" (emphasis added) – Heissenbüttel's tale unfolds in a world in which the Nazis have, in fact, triumphed in World War II. Set in Germany in the year 2006, Heissenbüttel's story centers on an unnamed elderly resident of Hamburg who reflects on the reasons more and more Germans in his era are posing the question, "What would have happened if Adolf Hitler had not won the war?" Especially given the fact that Germany is a prosperous, politically stable, and peaceful state, the narrator is puzzled by the posing of this question and thus proceeds to recount Nazi Germany's postwar path to success as a means of answering it.

In his brief summation of recent history, the narrator describes how Hitler wins World War II after being convinced by the Russian officers, Leonid Brezhnev and Nikita Khruschev (who are POWs in the Führerbunker in Berlin), to join up with Stalin and fight together against the Western Allies. In the wake of his victory, Hitler establishes Nazi Germany as one of several socialist "people's republics" linked to the Soviet Union and proceeds to implement his ambitious social-engineering program for German society. Significantly, the Führer does not appear to achieve his vision through racial fanaticism or violence but by the completely rational implementation of a technocratic plan to reduce the population to a level dictated by the state's overall economic program. Although certain delays hamper the implementation of this system, it is finally stabilized by the 1970s. The resulting system is a highly ordered one, in which the inhabitants – known as the "obliging ones" (*die Gutwilligen*) – live in a state of permanent surveillance by the state, being required at all times to carry portable microcomputers called "Cokrs" (short for *Computerkränze*) whose contents are readily accessible by the state via satellite. Keeping the system stable comes at a price (the population level is regulated by the random elimination of people once their numbers increase beyond a certain state-approved threshold), but it generally enables great liberties. As the narrator declares near the end of his tale, "We are more free than anybody else."[21]

Compared with Basil's overtly critical novel, Heissenbüttel's short story was a more subtle, but no less sharp, critique of Nazism. In many ways, its complex structure anticipated Hayden White's hypothetical description of a comedic emplotment of a Nazi victory whose ironic tone clearly identified it as a metacritical commentary on the past.[22] "Wenn Adolf Hitler den Krieg

Figure 13 Cover of Helmut Heissenbüttel's book *Wenn Adolf Hitler den Krieg nicht gewonnen hätte* (1979).

nicht gewonnen hätte" affirmed the legitimacy of the Nazi triumph at one level only to subvert it at another. Throughout the story, the narrator paints a rosy picture of life in the triumphant Reich, noting, "Things are going well for us ... The economy is stable ... Politics follows the principles of reason ... Peace is secured."[23] At a deeper level, of course, Heissenbüttel intended this description to be read ironically as a symptom of the funda-mental amorality of the Nazi system's inhabitants. Thus, the narrator's laconic description of the human costs entailed in the implementation of Hitler's postwar dystopia – the "SS rebellion ... epidemics, and famines of the rebuilding years of the 1950s ... [the] regional rebellions, religious paroxysms, alcohol and drug excesses ... and the nearly ineradicable suicide epidemic ... [of] the 1960s" – exposes both the criminality of the Nazi system as well as the complicity of ordinary Germans in it.

Lest this subtle criticism be missed by readers, however, Heissenbüttel went further in expressing his own disapproval of the Nazi system by having the narrator exhibit signs of dissatisfaction with the regime. Although he enjoys the fruits of Nazi prosperity, the narrator longs for an undefinable something that is missing from his life and admits to having periodic "yearnings" to join the roving groups of men and women known as the "slow wanderers" who "gave up participating [in the system]" around the time of the millennium in favor of pursuing a more simple, peripatetic existence. It is precisely the increasing appearance of such "longings for anarchy" that, the narrator ultimately speculates, lies behind the rigidly structured society's interest in what life would be like "if Adolf Hitler had not won the war." In the end, the posing of this question suggests a criticism of the status quo. For as the narrator concludes:

If Adolf Hitler had not won the war ... things would be lousy for some of us, some would have to struggle to keep their heads above water, some would be in for it, etc. There would be differences between societies, cultures, classes, and people. Violence, revolt, wars, crime. Also, the striving for justice. Democracy. Upturns, despair, shocks, defeats, collapses, and triumphs ... The attempt to survive on one's own. Humanity. Much-too-human humanity. Happiness. Perhaps.[24]

Had Hitler lost the war, in short, Germany would have had to endure the turbulent forces characteristic of liberal democratic societies. Yet while the narrator initially notes this with some degree of aversion, he ends on a note of cautious wistfulness that reflects an underlying yearning for a humanistic world, open to the play of chance and struggle. In the end, the act of reflecting on the possibility of Hitler having lost the war preserves visions of an alternate order and thus perhaps prevents the Führer's victory from being a final one.

Heissenbüttel's tale demonstrated the enduring moral consensus surrounding the Nazi past. At the personal level, Heissenbüttel had many reasons for preserving this consensus. Like Basil, he was a well-known poet, writer, and critic who belonged to the generation of Germans who experienced the horrors of Nazism firsthand – in his case, as a soldier who was severely injured during the war.[25] After the war, he became active in the German literary world, distinguishing himself with his "experimental literature" and his long-running radio shows on *Südwestrundfunk*.[26] What drove him to produce his tale of a victorious Nazi regime is unclear. Yet, like Basil, Heissenbüttel was hardly only interested in the Nazi past, but in the many political and social problems of the present. Whether overpopulation, growing bureaucratization, or the authoritarian suppression of individual freedom in East Germany, these problems weighed heavily on his mind at the time he wrote "Wenn Adolf Hitler den Krieg nicht gewonnen hätte" and may well have influenced its narrative.[27] Moreover, the emergence of a more conservative political climate in the Federal Republic in the late 1970s (epitomized by economic downturn, radical leftwing terrorism, and intensifying state repression) may have influenced Heissenbüttel as well. Therefore in writing about a Nazi wartime victory, he, like Basil, may have been intending to universalize the Nazi experience to comment upon the state of the present.

This supposition is supported by some of the positive reviews of his book, which saw in it the presence of a critical political agenda.[28] While one left-leaning critic called *Wenn Adolf Hitler den Krieg nicht gewonnen hätte* "an extremely important book, especially in these years of lachrymose old sixty-eighters," another more provocatively asserted:

Heissenbüttel ... counterfactually speculates how the much-desired Greater Germany would be structured today. To be sure technological progress (*zivilisatorische Fortschritte*) would be at least as considerable as ours. The rulers, who would have replaced the Führer's old guard, would be modern technocrats. And the surveillance and direction of every citizen would be somewhat more perfect. But we would presumably be just as accustomed to this state as we are to the current Federal Republic ... This small volume will prevent us – and perhaps a few government politicians – from sleeping.[29]

Whether or not Heissenbüttel intended readers to draw such polemical comparisons between the democratic Federal Republic and the authoritarian Third Reich, it is significant that such a universalized message was read into his tale. Such comparisons were not untypical of the German left, which, in its pessimism about the development of the West German state in the late 1970s, tended to exaggerate its repressive character. At the same

time, of course, such comparisons minimized the far greater repressiveness
of the Nazi police state and reflected the subtle normalization of its legacy
in the consciousness of some Germans. Whatever Heissenbüttel's views of
such comparisons might have been, his tale had the opposite function of
Basil's. While *The Twilight Men* reminded readers of the superiority of the
present over the past, "Wenn Adolf Hitler den Krieg nicht gewonnen
hätte" served to awaken discomforting similarities between them.

Several years after the publication of Heissenbüttel's short story there
appeared the most substantial German alternate history of the postwar
period, literary critic and writer Arno Lubos's massive 616-page novel from
1980 *Schwiebus*.[30] Set in Breslau in the year 1979, *Schwiebus* resembles
the tales of Basil and Heissenbüttel by focusing on the struggle of a single
man – an obscure, middle-aged German radio journalist named Joseph
Schwiebus – to maintain his faith in the Nazi state. Like Basil and
Heissenbüttel's protagonists, Schwiebus is a self-proclaimed "convinced
National Socialist."[31] Yet he is also a man who suffers from a growing sense
of disaffection about his place in Nazi society. Although he possesses a
burning sense of ambition and a Nietzschean will to exert power over
others, he recognizes his limited talents and refrains from attempting to rise
above his middling position as the director of regional affairs at the Breslau
radio station. One day, however, after covering a military parade on the
occasion of the Führer's birthday, Schiwebus impulsively resolves to
become more "logically consistent" and make something of himself.[32]
After becoming infatuated with an attractive German war widow named
Frau Parsche, whom he notices sitting on the reviewing stand, he decides to
produce a special series of radio broadcasts, which he hopes will bring him
the favor of his bosses. The first broadcast, which covers a discussion led by
Frau Parsche in her high school civics class on the German Reich's
economic interests, is in fact warmly received by his superiors, who call it
"brilliant." Gratified at his unlikely success, Schwiebus grandiosely begins
to muse that "this must have been the way it happened when Hitler came to
power," and he resolves to continue his ascent within his profession.[33]

Yet, before long, Schwiebus's growing sense of ambition brings him into
conflict with the conformist values of the Nazi state. After completing the
first radio broadcast, Schwiebus goes on vacation in the mountains of the
Sudetenland, where he plans on relaxing his frayed nerves and looking up a
local writer, Andreas Zenglass, who has sent him a series of fictional tales in
the hope of having them aired on the radio. When he encounters the
writer, however, he meets a man whose written work is critical of the Nazi
regime. Zenglass's stories incorporate local myths that tell of people living a

hidden existence in the mountains: forced laborers, soldiers, and other so-called "vagrants" who escaped in the last months of the war and have never been seen since.[34] Schwiebus is skeptical about such legends, but he is sufficiently curious about them to inquire among local residents in an effort to learn more. In doing so, however, he eventually runs foul of the secret police, who are aware of Zenglass and suspicious of Schwiebus's relationship with him. At the same time, once he returns to work in Breslau, Schwiebus becomes embroiled in an intensifying political feud between representatives of liberal and conservative movements within the Nazi state, both of which want to recruit him for their cause. Schwiebus, however, remains stubbornly committed to his independent course and continues to plan further radio broadcasts on subjects (such as Polish laborers in Germany) that his superiors deem unsuitable. He then quickly loses all support at the radio station and is eventually betrayed to the Gestapo by his colleagues, who fabricate evidence in order finally to be rid of him. Although innocent of any wrongdoing, Schwiebus faces total exclusion from German society. As the novel ends, Schwiebus flees from the Gestapo, which is planning to do away with him, into the Sudeten mountains in the hope of joining the legendary hidden men who have long sought refuge and freedom there.

In chronicling how the victorious Nazi regime consumes even its most loyal children, Lubos's novel offered a critical portrait of a world in which the Nazis won World War II. More than anything else, Lubos effectively showed how the Nazi system completely stifles all individuality and humanity. Schiwebus's own sense of alienation stems from the very ideology he ostensibly remains committed to. As he gradually realizes through his long discussions with Zenglass, Schwiebus suffers from a profound crisis of identity. "I don't have any character," he tells Zenglass, "I don't know who I am."[35] Schwiebus's Nazi education and its collectivist ideals have driven out any sense of who he is as an individual. "Besides the Jungvolk and Hitler Youth," he notes, "I could name a series of institutions in which every trait and belief was … methodically exterminated."[36] The Nazi educational system has also impeded his capacity to engage with other human beings. Schwiebus is incapable of intimate relationships, whether romantic or platonic. He is largely friendless, unmarried, and satisfies his sexual urges by meeting up with prostitutes in hotel bars. "I have become … desensitized," he notes; and "unlearned the ability to empathize."[37] The only thing that remains for him is a goal-oriented desire for achievement. "I can explain the guiding principle of my life in a few sentences," he concludes. "I do not expect any human congeniality, no affection, no love, no sympathy, no fussing over me (*Betulichkeit*). I only expect compensation for an accomplished task."[38]

Yet while Schwiebus's sense of alienation reflects the powerful thrust of collectivist Nazi ideology, it ironically also reflects the progressive impoverishment of that ideology in the wake of the regime's victory. Having won the war (by defeating the British at Dunkirk and the Soviets in Eastern Europe), Nazi Germany gradually evolves from a militantly ideological society to a prosperous leisure society. Thanks to the efforts of the German Labor Front (the DAF), the standard of living for German workers has increased, as has their preference for entertainment over indoctrination. It follows that few bother believing in Nazi ideology any longer. Schwiebus himself demonstrates this trend, noting that while the roots of Nazi ideology may remain sound, it has become "insane," "dumb," and "sick."[39] As he eventually asserts, "I believe in nothing."[40] Like many average Germans, he mostly yearns for "success" and a share of the growing economic pie. Yet the conflict between the new materialistic ethos and Schwiebus's ideological upbringing creates new disappointments. As Schwiebus notes:

The drama of the old era is no more. There are no more persons who behave heroically and spark meaningful conflicts ... There are only people who find themselves in a stagnant situation (*in einem Brei befinden*) ... It is no different for the elite leadership. They have to cooperate, the ideas are already established, the ideology is set; even the highest leaders can only complete what has already been decreed and programmed.[41]

The prosaic reality of daily life is profoundly unsatisfying, especially as few alternatives to it seem to exist. As Schwiebus muses to Zenglass at one point, "One yearns today for a utopia, even if it is merely an existence on some island or other refuge. But one thing remains certain: whoever goes there will not be able to accomplish anything. Nothing decisive can take place, no political revolution, no historical turn, not even an episode that garners any attention."[42] Schwiebus, in short, exhibits all the disappointments of a man who realizes that history has come to an end.

Yet history is far from being at an end, as the remainder of the novel makes clear. For the ideological stagnation of Nazi society after its wartime triumph dialectically brings about the reinvigoration of Nazi ideology. Midway through the novel, Schwiebus learns of growing opposition to the consumerist excesses of Nazi society on the part of a secretive organization known as "the movement," whose representatives aim to halt the DAF's liberalizing tendencies and return to the Nazi ideology's founding principles. Many of

Schwiebus's co-workers, including his boss, Körner, support this reactionary trend. For Körner, the labor organizations have helped create "a nasty sort of person, a type of unimaginative, politically ignorant, physically incapable, and completely apathetic cripple," who has contributed to the growing "lack of consideration towards ... the national community," as well as to a "destructive individualism."[43] Schwiebus rejects Körner's assessment of the situation and, as a man of working-class background, believes that the workers will triumph in their conflict with conservative representatives of "the movement."[44] Yet, as he slowly falls into the hands of the state police, Schwiebus is forced to concede the enduring power of ideological fanaticism. As one of his SD (*Sicherheitsdienst* or security service) interrogators, Kurbiun, convincingly tells him:

A radical change is in the works; we find ourselves in a phase of renewal ... We are once more heading forward ... with reawakened strength ...

Our National Socialist worldview is in total accordance with the laws of nature. Not only does the worldview require war, but so too do ... human beings.

Most of the people demand a war, even if they do not admit it ... The era of mourning and the memory of the terrible experiences [of the past] are over. The young men view the last war as a fascinating adventure and are steadily advancing ...

Even the people ... who participated in the last war [believe] that ... peace, lethargy, prosperity, and daily life have lasted too long. Have you ever observed how an accident on the street is ogled, how hundreds rush over to see a dying or bloodied person ... or a destroyed automobile? Or with what eagerness the public follows the depiction of a murder on film?

We call this excitement ... Excitement is the law of nature. The era of peace was much too long.[45]

In the end, Lubos makes clear that the ideological fanaticism of Nazism will once more reassert itself and neutralize the more "progressive" features of the postwar era. Although he does not proceed to depict the renewed outbreak of war, Lubos clearly agreed with Basil that Nazism inherently tends towards apocalyptic destruction.

In writing *Schwiebus*, Lubos resembled Basil and Heissenbüttel in using alternate history to condemn the real, historical phenomenon of Nazism. Born in 1928 in Upper Silesia, Lubos was younger than both Basil and Heissenbüttel, yet he also experienced the war firsthand, having been called to serve as a young Luftwaffe assistant (*Luftwaffenhelfer*) and a member of the Reich Labor Service (*Reichsarbeitsdienst*) before being taken prisoner by the Americans in 1945. After his family was displaced from their home in Upper Silesia, Lubos eventually settled in Coburg, where he became a literary scholar who published widely on Silesian regional literature.[46] As a result of his disruptive historical experiences and humanistic sensibility, he developed a sharply critical view of the Nazi past that found ample expression in the novel. To a degree, Lubos drew upon his own personal experiences in the war – most profoundly, his own desire in early 1945 to desert from his *Reichsarbeitsdienst* unit and flee into the woods – in developing the characters and plot of *Schwiebus*. Lubos refrained from deserting in large part because of his own personal uncertainty about whether anyone could be relied upon to help him.[47] This uncertainty carried over to his description of Schwiebus's own helplessness and reflected a more broadly pessimistic view of German society's behavior under the Nazi dictatorship. Having written the novel out of a longstanding sense of curiosity about what his acquaintances who had "played a role in the Nazi era [would have done] . . . if Germany had won the war?", Lubos's answer – that they would have become "representatives of the leadership" – reflected his own critical stance towards the past.[48] Like Basil and Heissenbüttel, Lubos ultimately wanted readers of the novel to take away the fundamentally moral lesson – that it would have been impossible "after a [Nazi] victory and the extermination of minorities and alleged opponents, for people to be able to live in peace."[49]

Yet while *Schwiebus* seemed to impart a pessimistic message about German society under Nazism, its reception expressed something quite different. Uniformly praised in the German press, the novel was hailed for its realistically bleak portrayal of a Nazi-ruled world; the main point emphasized by reviewers, however, was the novel's depiction of the helplessness of the individual to challenge a powerful dictatorship.[50] Many reviewers favorably quoted the novel's central passages concerning the option of simply retreating and disappearing from Nazi society. Conservative historian Hellmut Diwald identified such an act as "the resistance of unconditional refusal," while Horst Köpke believed it signified that "the individual still has a chance even under a dictatorship."[51] This frequent emphasis on what one reviewer called "retreat, because resistance is no longer possible" was significant because of its self-exculpatory function.[52] By highlighting retreat as the only possible response to the totalitarian Nazi terror state, reviewers exonerated the German people for failing to mount heroic resistance against the regime in real history. Such reviews relativized German guilt for the Third Reich. Others, meanwhile, universalized the novel's significance by comparing it to Franz Kafka's *The Trial* and interpreting it as a "modern fairy tale" or "parable" that illustrated the "singularly modern" conflict between the individual and the modern state.[53] Both kinds of review reflected a tendency to overlook Lubos's intention to have the novel read as a historically specific portrayal of German behavior under the victorious Reich. As a result, while the novel maintained a moralistic perspective towards the Nazi past, the reviews expressed a desire to normalize it.

Following *Schwiebus,* the most thorough German exploration of the consequences of a Nazi victory in World War II was journalist and writer Ralph Giordano's 1989 book *Wenn Hitler den Krieg gewonnen hätte (If Hitler Had Won the War).*[54] In contrast to the works of Basil, Heissenbüttel, and Lubos, which were cast in fictional form, Giordano's book explored the subject of a postwar Nazi empire from a more scholarly perspective. As a journalist and popular historian, Giordano drew upon a wealth of secondary and primary sources to clarify the precise nature of the Nazis' plans for a "new order" following their expected wartime victory. Ominously, Giordano emphasized, these plans did not focus merely upon Europe but upon the entire world. Drawing upon speeches and quotations by Hitler and other leading Nazi officials, Giordano argued that the Nazi regime aimed to achieve world domination through a three-step program. Beginning with the establishment of hegemony over the entire European continent between the Atlantic ocean and the Ural mountains, the Nazis would have attempted to impose colonial rule over the entirety of Africa, after which they would have embarked upon a final climactic battle with the United States. Frightening as a mere possibility, Nazi global hegemony would have been even more horrific in practice. From the conquered lands of Western and Eastern Europe the Nazis would have forcibly seized millions of slave laborers to assist them in a wide range of labor-intensive projects, whether the monumental redesign of German cities (which would have sorely taxed the continent's supply of both labor and building materials) or the expansion of German agriculture and industry into the nation's newly won territories in the east.[55] Many would have died from this de facto policy of "extermination through work," but even more would have perished in what Giordano called "the other Holocaust" – the genocide of the Slavs.[56] In a lengthy chapter on the infamous *Generalplan Ost,* Giordano described the plan, devised by various Nazi planning agencies in the early 1940s, to transfer some 31 million Poles and Russians beyond the Urals and enslave 14 million others as part of a broader program of germanizing Eastern Europe. Importantly, Giordano noted that such a plan, which would have entailed many deaths, was not the "unrealizable fantasy of Nazi horror-theoreticians" but would have been fully implemented had the Nazis won the war.[57] To heighten the horror of a Nazi wartime victory, Giordano pointed out the awful consequences not merely for the Germans' victims but for the Germans themselves. After a victory, Hitler would have tried to radically remake German society by abolishing Christianity and introducing polygamy to promote the Nazis' racial goals. For the Germans themselves, like their defeated enemies, a Nazi victory would have amounted to a disaster.

In arriving at his pessimistic conclusions, Giordano expressed a highly personal distaste towards Nazism. Like Basil, Heissenbüttel, and Lubos, Giordano belonged to a generation that had experienced the horrors of Nazism directly. Born in 1923 in Hamburg of a mixed Jewish-Christian marriage, he was in danger of being deported as part-Jew, or *Mischling*, throughout the war. As a journalist after 1945, he devoted much of his literary career to chronicling the crimes of the Nazis and the postwar failure of the Germans to own up to them.[58] Giordano's main motive in embracing allohistorical speculation in writing *Wenn Hitler den Krieg gewonnen hätte* was his belief in the moral need to preserve the lessons of the Nazi past. As he asserted, "There can be no full description of National Socialism without knowing its end-historical (*schlussgeschichtlichen*) vision of German world domination and without having viewed the plans that were to lead to the final victory and be implemented in its wake."[59] While this moral outlook provides a general motive for his book, a more specific catalyst may have been the attempts of conservatives in the late 1980s to normalize the Nazi past. Such controversies as the Bitburg Affair and the Historians' Debate provided great motivation for Giordano to remind readers of the unique savagery of Nazi terror.

Significantly, the reception of *Wenn Hitler den Krieg gewonnen hätte* was strongly positive. Giordano's book, in fact, became a bestseller in Germany.[60] While certain reviewers criticized the book for heavily relying upon and popularizing the primary research of previous scholars, most affirmed the book's overall conclusions about the global nature of Hitler's war aims.[61] Volker Ullrich praised it for offering a "precise picture of the unleashed criminality of a regime which, had it not been halted, surely would have brought about the end of the civilized world."[62] And Arno Weckenbecker lauded it as "an excellent and depressing book that one should not put down until the last line."[63] It is impossible to know what factors explain the book's commercial and critical success. But it is possible that its appearance at the same time as the epochal events of 1989 played a role. With the specter of German unification looming in the distance, many readers may well have gravitated to the book as a cautionary lesson regarding the hubris that comes with the quest for power. As it would turn out, however, reunification would bring an end to such cautionary lessons in German alternate histories.

ALTERNATE HISTORY AND NORMALCY

If German allohistorical depictions of a Nazi wartime victory remained rooted within a strong moral framework in the years leading up to reunification, the years since have witnessed a more normalized approach to the subject. This trend was first demonstrated by German historian Alexander Demandt's iconoclastic essay from 1995 "Wenn Hitler gewonnen hätte?" ("If Hitler Had Won?").[64] Published in the magazine *Tango* to coincide with the fiftieth anniversary of the end of the war in Europe, Demandt's piece dramatically departed from those of his predecessors in offering a much more optimistic account of what would have happened had Hitler won World War II. "Wenn Hitler gewonnen hätte?" was divided into two parts, the first of which discussed the short-term, the second the long-term, reality of what a victorious Reich would have been like. Significantly, in both Demandt was able to locate more than a token silver lining to redeem an otherwise cloudy picture.

In the short run, Demandt argued, the Nazis would have followed up their victory by transforming German society along racial-biological lines, continuing their real historical policies of sterilizing the hereditarily ill, banning abortion, criminalizing homosexuality, and more broadly ensuring conformity through the Gestapo. Personal liberties would have been limited, the rights of the sexes would have been unequal, and antisemitism would have been normative.[65] At the same time, however, more positive social consequences would have emerged as well. As he observed:

the idea of the people (*Volksgedanke*) would have been realized in comprehensive health care and an extensive sports culture (*Sportwesen*) ... Child allowances and kindergartens would have supported the younger generation ... The death penalty would still exist. Street crime, drug addiction, and vagrancy would hardly have been able to spread ... Non-smokers, vegetarians, and opponents of alcohol would have been in the ascendant. Order and cleanliness, environmental protection, and historic preservation [would have been seen as] the commandments of patriotism.[66]

Even if the Nazi regime had persisted in many of its older authoritarian features, many of its more "progressive" features would have come to the fore.

In the long run, moreover, a Nazi victory would have brought about even more positive changes. Explicitly dismissing the grim scenarios of earlier writers, Demandt insisted that even in the event of a total Nazi victory (entailing the unconditional surrender of the Allies), the "darkest fantasies" of a "brown hell" imagined by other writers of alternate history would not have come to pass.[67] As he argued:

Colonial empires were already anachronistic since the First World War ... Who was supposed to implement the 'Generalplan Ost'? An extensive occupation of eastern Europe would have considerably thinned out German forces. The creation of a sufficiently loyal and large soldier caste ... would not have been [possible] ... Hitler ... dramatically overestimated the number of people who could have been Nazified.[68]

Rather than intensifying the regime's ideological ferocity, a Nazi victory would have encouraged a pattern of moderation. Nazism could not have survived in the long term, Demandt argued, unless it followed the pattern of "Turkey after Ataturk, Italy after Mussolini, and Spain after Franco." In order to survive, Nazism would have had to allow itself to be "watered down" as an ideology and acquire a "human face."[69]

The process of humanizing Nazism, while difficult, would have been possible, Demandt optimistically argued, thanks to the efforts of the German people themselves. Declaring that "[every] people has its limit of corruptibility," Demandt affirmed that the Germans would have reached a pivotal moral crossroads following the eventual (and inevitable) revelation of the genocidal crimes of the Holocaust.[70] Once news of the "mass murder" became known, the German people would have eventually reacted "with horror" and embarked upon an "internal ... reckoning with the [Nazi] thugs."[71] As he contended, "a prolonged Third Reich would have experienced its own 1968 generation, and I doubt that these rigorous young people would have allowed themselves to be intimidated."[72] Even if some of them had suffered martyrdom in protesting Nazi atrocities, the "domestic political explosiveness" of their act would have quickly been exploited by certain Nazi officials (even perhaps Hitler himself, who had obscured any personal involvement in the genocide) in order to "eliminate the demonic figure of Himmler and his accomplices."[73] Demandt's conclusion was that it was perfectly realistic to expect that "if Hitler had won, National Socialism would have [either] suffocated on its own radicalism" or – as he clearly believed was more likely – "it would have become civilized (*verbürgerlicht*)."[74] Where most other accounts had affirmed Nazism's ideological fanaticism, Demandt insisted it possessed the capacity to evolve in a more pragmatic direction.

In arriving at this upbeat conclusion, Demandt dramatically departed from the judgmental tone of prior depictions of a Nazi victory. To be sure, Demandt paid lip service to the need for ethical judgment, declaring that, in speculating about a Nazi victory, "the demand for a 'value-free approach' exceeds the degree of neutrality that could be expected [toward the subject]."[75] Yet many of his comments reflected a clear awareness that his conclusions deliberately violated prevailing moral perspectives. Thus he acknowledged that his suggestion that Nazism might have been humanized would probably be considered "political heresy" and he asserted that his belief that the German people would have reacted with horror to news of the Holocaust would "find little agreement."[76] It was in his final conclusions about the ultimate consequences of a Nazi victory for history at large, however, that Demandt overturned the moral framework of earlier narratives. While the latter had consistently affirmed that a Nazi victory would have brought disaster to Germany, Demandt reasoned that it would not have been such a bad thing after all. Had the Nazis won, many of the negative results of their real historical defeat would have been undone, including "the loss of the eastern territories, the division of Germany ... the cold war, and ... the [destruction] of ... German cities."[77] "A victory over Stalin," he added, "would have reduced the lifespan of the Soviet Union by fifty years."[78] Eastern Europe would then have been spared "fifty years of socialism" and the world at large would never have known the "the danger of nuclear war (*atomaren Overkills*)."[79] In general, a victory in the war would have brought about a world better than the one created by real history.

In drafting this upbeat fantasy, Demandt was largely driven by political motives. A well-known professor of ancient history at the Free University of Berlin, he had long embraced a conservative brand of politics, ardently supporting the cause of German reunification prior to 1989 and urging the creation of a "normal" sense of national identity in the years thereafter.[80] Demandt's nationalistic feelings permeated his essay, but nowhere more clearly than in his confident belief that the German people would have been able to reform the Nazi system in the wake of a wartime victory. This fantasy scenario served to redeem the Germans for having supported the Nazi regime (and for having failed to overthrow it) in real history. Like many conservatives, Demandt was uncomfortable with the fact that the Nazis' defeat and the nation's postwar democratization had come from without rather than within. Thus he explicitly noted in his essay that his expectation of an inner German reckoning with the Nazi thugs would have been due especially "if we do not merely want to attribute our [contemporary] political conscience to [the Allied program of] re-education."[81] Convinced that "we would have possessed the capacity to de-Nazify ourselves," Demandt embraced a fantasy of self-reform in order to boost the nation's self-esteem by freeing it of any dependence upon Allied assistance.[82] In the process, Demandt implicitly rejected the prevailing view among most Germans that they had been liberated by the Allies in

May 1945. Like other conservatives who were rethinking the significance of May 8, 1945 at the time of its fiftieth anniversary – epitomized by the controversial nationwide manifesto circulated by the New Right entitled "Against Forgetting" – he too wanted to distance Germany from owing any debt of gratitude to the Allies.[83] Instead, he reminded readers of German suffering and Allied crimes, criticizing in his essay how most dystopian allohistorical accounts of a Nazi victory served to legitimize such crimes as the bombing of Dresden and Hiroshima.[84] By depicting a Nazi victory in positive terms as leading to domestic self-reform and a glorious victory over Stalinism, Demandt allowed the Germans to have their cake and eat it too, permitting them victory *and* democracy.

In submitting such an optimistic account of a Nazi wartime victory, however, Demandt distorted much of the real historical record. In many ways, "Wenn Hitler gewonnen hätte?" allohistorically rehabilitated the German people by relativizing the singularity of the Third Reich's crimes. First, Demandt dramatically downplayed the role of German antisemitism in causing the Holocaust. One way in which he did this was by speculating that the Holocaust would not even have taken place had Hitler won an early victory in World War II. Arguing that, in real history, "the mass exterminations were ultimately forced by fear of a military defeat," Demandt concluded that in the "event of an early peace, a deportation [of the Jews] would have been conceivable," most likely to somewhere like "Madagascar."[85] This hypothetical statement obscured the fact, generally agreed upon by most historians today, that the Final Solution had its roots in ideological hatred rather than circumstantial contingency and thus can only be seen as an act of premeditated mass murder. Moreover, Demandt diminished the culpability of the German people for the Holocaust. In speculating that the Germans would have reacted to news of the Holocaust after a Nazi victory "with horror," he stipulated that they would have done so "just as they did after ... [their real historical] defeat" – an overcharitable observation that elided the fact that most Germans after 1945 reacted with churlish resentment. Moreover, he attempted to minimize their degree of culpability by arguing that antisemitism "was a worldwide phenomenon" and hardly only "popular" in Germany. Finally, his prediction that "a normalization of relations to the Jews and the Americans would have been conceivable" following the revelations of the Holocaust represented the height of wishful thinking.[86]

Demandt further relativized the Nazi regime's crimes by comparing the allohistorical Third Reich to the real historical German Democratic Republic. Ever since 1989, comparisons between the two have been made by conservatives attempting to demonize the latter and normalize the former.[87] Demandt used this strategy throughout his essay. In discussing the likely trajectory of Nazi domestic policies, for example, he argued that "we can perceive it . . . in looking at daily life in the GDR, which in many ways continued the policies of the Hitler regime."[88] Many of the ensuing comparisons, however, blurred the substantial differences between the two regimes. Thus, in predicting that a victorious Reich would have been ruled by the Gestapo, "modernized in the form of the Stasi," Demandt helped diminish the far more ample crimes of the former by comparing it to the comparatively benign latter.[89] Moreover, by claiming that "foreign workers" in a victorious Reich "would have been placed in barracks and controlled just like the Vietnamese in the DDR," Demandt minimized the far harsher experiences of workers in wartime Nazi Germany, many of whom suffered slave labor conditions and outright death.[90] Finally, in noting that one positive consequence of a Nazi victory would have been the embrace of environmental protection, which would have ensured "there never would have been Bitterfeld" – East Germany's most polluted city – he distracted attention away from the exponentially more extensive environmental and human destruction caused by the Nazis' unleashing of World War II.

In its conservative rejection of prior German allohistorical depictions of a Nazi wartime victory, Demandt's essay predictably met with a divided reception. While "Wenn Hitler gewonnen hätte?" was not reviewed extensively, it was attacked by liberal German critics for its rightwing political subtext. The most vociferous was Joachim Rohloff who, in a long review of the essay in the leftwing magazine *Konkret*, called Demandt to task for his many attempts to relativize the crimes of the Nazi era.[91] Dismissing the essay as composed of "questions that no reasonable person asks himself," Rohloff nevertheless viewed it as significant for its political agenda. He pegged Demandt as a proponent of "national rebirth" who, like his conservative Free University colleague, Ernst Nolte, was engaged in the "renovation of German history" through dubious means. For Rohloff, Demandt's speculative usage of alternate history degenerated into "falsifying history when it serves the exculpation of Germany" and placed him in the ranks of such figures as Holocaust denier David Irving.[92] More conservative Germans, in contrast, welcomed Demandt's essay. Indeed, as Rohloff himself reported, Demandt expressed satisfaction at having received many letters of support for his essay from "rightwing" readers. The numbers of such readers are unclear, but their endorsement of Demandt's essay, like the essay itself, revealed a notable desire for a normal national identity cleansed of the stain of the Nazi experience.

If Demandt's essay served as a strident example of the German desire for normalcy, a more subtle example was provided by a brief allohistorical depiction of a Nazi victory in World War II written by German historian Michael Salewski in 1999. Entitled "N.N: *Der großgermanische Seekrieg gegen Japan und die USA im Jahre 1949. The Near Miss. Eine Buchbesprechung*" (N.N.: *The Great German Naval War against Japan and the USA in 1949. The Near Miss. A Book Review*"), Salewski's piece assumed the form of a review essay written by an allohistorical version of himself in the year 2048.[93] The review's subject is a newly published historical monograph recounting the near-eruption of naval hostilities in 1949 between Nazi Germany and the unlikely maritime allies of the United States and Japan. As (the allohistorical) Salewski recounts, this close call was the result of Nazi Germany's surprising defeat of the Soviet Union in 1941. With Hitler having secured his dominance over the European continent and enlisted the assistance of fence-sitting neutrals like Spain (which now joins the Axis), the Führer proceeds to establish an effective naval blockade against Britain, and begins to plot a final naval campaign against the United States and Japan, who now forge an alliance out of mutual self-interest. In the years 1941–48, the Pacific powers and the Nazis' newly established European Race and Defense Organization (ERVG) engage in a grueling arms race (building up both conventional and nuclear arms) in expectation of the inevitable showdown. But before this "Great German Naval War" can become historical reality, Salewski reminds his readers of the intervention of other significant events – the economic strains placed on the Nazi system by the arms race, the death of Hitler in 1948, and the emergence of a new Führer, Admiral Karl Doenitz, who is far less fanatical than his predecessor – all of which help to pull the great powers back from the precipice of World War III. In the end, the allohistorical Salewski makes the profoundly allohistorical point that, while the Great German Naval War was "thank God only [a] virtual [one]," it reveals that "history, even racial and national history, is not always a history of success, but can turn out quite differently."[94] As he concludes, there are many works that depict "England, France, China and the USA winning [World War II] instead of the Hitler coalition."[95]

The most interesting and significant aspect of (the real) Salewski's fictional essay is the allohistorical context in which it is situated. As (the allohistorical) Salewski notes at the outset of his book review, the time in which he is writing – the year 2048 – is "the longest period of peace in European history, [one] which has only occasionally been interrupted in the past sixty years ... by civil war-type conflicts in narrowly bounded regions."[96] In other words, like Demandt, Salewski portrays the Nazis' victory in World War II as having an overall positive effect upon history at large. Although he notes that there have been periods of crisis – especially the "near miss" year of 1949 – peace has generally reigned throughout Europe since World War II. The Nazis have succeeded in fostering European unity in both the economic and political spheres, thanks to the "conscious suppression of Nazi ideology among the ranks of the younger technocratic brown elites" whose resulting pragmatism has met with a positive reaction from neighboring satellite states. Like Demandt, Salewski portrayed a victorious Third Reich as a largely normal nation that has abandoned ideological fanaticism for the sake of traditional power politics.

Salewski's upbeat portrayal of a Nazi victory could easily be regarded as part of a rightwing agenda to normalize the German past. This interpretation of his essay is especially plausible given the fact that the allohistorical Salewski neglects to mention any of Hitler's war crimes, such as the Holocaust (which has presumably occurred in tandem with the German military triumph in Europe). That the essay expressed a larger conservative agenda, moreover, is supported by the fact that the real Salewski, like Demandt, belongs to the conservative wing of the German political spectrum, having served as the longtime head of the conservative *Ranke Gesellschaft*, along with being an active contributor to the conservative *Frankfurter Allgemeine Zeitung*.[97] And yet it is possible that the real Salewski deliberately intended his narrative to possess rightwing political implications in order to make the point that had the Nazis won the war, German historians (like his allohistorical self) would have written precisely the kind of rightwing triumphalist history that would have omitted the Holocaust and other crimes from the historical record. In such a world, Saul Friedlander's prediction that the Nazis would have written about the Holocaust in narrative modes other than tragedy would have become reality.

It is difficult to know which meaning Salewski intended. Although his review lacks the same moral framework of prior narratives, it is notable that his allohistorical counterpart does not abjure making moral judgments in his review. Thus he blames "Nazi ideology" for having plunged ahead towards an unwinnable World War III and concludes that the "admonishing lesson" of the "near miss" of 1949 is the need to "defend against the budding signs" (*den Anfängen zu wehren*) of excessive militarism and ideological fanaticism. This final remark – an adaptation of the antifascist Left's slogan of the 1990s (*"Wehret den Anfängen!"*) to be on vigilant guard against the resurgence of neo-Nazism – suggests, in fact, that the allohistorical Salewski is hardly an uncritical Nazi hack. Still, in the end, by refusing to address the Holocaust, he reveals himself to be complicit in glossing over the regime's crimes. It is unclear whether the real historical Salewski shares this perspective. Overall, his text resists an unambiguous reading because the historian never reveals how much he identifies or sympathizes with his allohistorical counterpart. Where Otto Basil and Helmut Heissenbüttel, for example, used ironic distancing to separate themselves from their tales' protagonists, Salewski refrained from clarifying his own stance. His relatively upbeat description of a Nazi victory thus seemed to endorse it more than condemn it.

CONCLUSION

The shifting trajectory of German allohistorical depictions of a Nazi wartime victory since 1945 points to a normalizing trend in the German memory of the Nazi past. Up until the late 1980s, German narratives regularly affirmed the horrific character of a Nazi-ruled world. Even if a certain tendency to universalize the lessons of Nazism was visible in both the intentions behind, and reactions to, the tales of Basil, Heissenbüttel, and Lubos, the overall conclusions and reception of these early works reflected a general commitment to preserving a moralistic view of the Third Reich. By contrast, the arrival of reunification has brought about a notable abandonment of this black-and-white perspective. Whereas the Germans who produced alternate histories prior to 1989 were largely liberals eager to condemn the Nazi era, those who have done so since reunification have been conservatives eager to relativize it in order to help fashion a more positive sense of national identity. This tendency has not stood unopposed, as was demonstrated by scattered hostile reactions to it by reviewers. But on the whole, it is clear that since reunification, German alternate histories of a Nazi wartime victory have shifted both in content and function.

To be sure, the representativeness of this trend can easily be seen as minimal. Germans have never distinguished themselves as large-scale producers of alternate histories, having created only a small fraction of the accounts produced by Britons and Americans.[98] This fact is in itself significant, for it suggests that a far less normalized view of the Nazi past exists in Germany than in Britain or America. Germans have been more inhibited than their Anglo-American neighbors in crafting counterfactual tales of the Nazi era. In part, political considerations explain this trend. It would be quite easy for a German rendering of a Nazi wartime victory to be misinterpreted as a rightwing or neo-Nazi fantasy. This was illustrated not so long ago when the (now-deceased) neo-Nazi leader Michael Kuehnen spoke of his desire to have been able to live in a world in which Hitler had won World War II.[99] The same was revealed by a 1994 poll that showed 63 percent of rightwing *Republikaner* voters eager to live in such a world.[100] But the reluctance is also rooted in the fact that alternate history – as a form of entertainment – has been seen as too lighthearted a genre for representing such a serious subject as Nazism. The relative absence of German tales of a Nazi triumph in World War II, in short, reflects the desire to view the past from an ethically grounded perspective.

And yet the German reluctance to produce alternate histories is partly deceiving, for they have distinguished themselves as avid consumers of them. Many Anglo-American accounts of Hitler winning World War II – in addition to other related themes – have appeared in German translation and been snapped up by German readers.[101] Some, such as Robert Harris's *Fatherland*, have become bestsellers. The persistent demand for such narratives, together with a reluctance to bear the authorial responsibility for them, may reflect a larger sense of uncertainty among Germans about how to deal with their nation's Nazi past. While the reluctance to produce such accounts reflects ongoing reservations about violating a morally informed stance towards the Nazi era, the large audience for them suggests a desire to be liberated from the burdens of remembrance and adopt a more carefree attitude towards it.

These contradictory impulses were perfectly illustrated by the diverging German reactions to *Fatherland*. When the novel first appeared in 1992, *Fatherland* caused a storm of controversy in Germany. Some critics attacked it as an "anti-German" work that provocatively refocused attention on Germany's Nazi past in order to exploit and resurrect Western fears of a reunified Germany.[102] As with the controversy over William Shirer's 1961 *Look* magazine essay, "If Hitler Had Won World War II," a German sense of political vulnerability at a transitional moment of history, as well as an abiding desire for normalcy, accounted for some of the criticism of the book. Other critics attacked *Fatherland* as a "tasteless work of frivolity" that "minimized the Third Reich" by depicting it through a genre of narrative representation that was unserious and exploitative.[103] Such comments expressed the underlying belief that Harris had somehow violated the need to represent the Nazi era in clear moralistic fashion. This was the same view that explains why more than twenty-five German publishers refused to publish the book and why the Hamburg police confiscated thousands of Swiss copies of it for violating a law prohibiting public display of the swastika to boost sales.[104] No matter how well-intentioned these responses may have been, however, they reflected a misunderstanding of the book's anti-Nazi message – the same kind of misunderstanding that drove numerous neo-Nazi skinheads to buy the book thinking it was an endorsement of a Nazi-ruled world.[105] Whatever the responses, German readers clearly saw Harris's novel as embracing a new method of representing the Nazi era.

Yet many Germans welcomed Harris's portrayal of a Nazi wartime victory. For one thing, the German public bought the German-language edition of *Fatherland* in large numbers.[106] Moreover, in 2000, the well-known German theater director Frank Castorf produced a mammoth four-hour dramatic adaptation of the novel for the German stage, which received considerable attention.[107] As is to be expected, the ongoing interest of Germans in *Fatherland* stemmed from a variety of motives. But in light of some readers' remarks that only a non-German writer could have gotten away with producing a novel featuring an SS man living in a Nazi-ruled world, one reason may have been a sense of envy at the ability of non-Germans to depict the Nazi era from a non-judgmental perspective.[108] The German reaction to *Fatherland* demonstrates in microcosm what many have long realized about Germany at large – that it is a nation caught between the simultaneous desire to preserve the lessons of the Nazi past and escape from its oppressive shadow.

CHAPTER 4

Other nations: a dissenting view

The scandalous signs of arbitrary rule on the part of the victors . . .
and the slavish subservience shown by everyone to the new lords of
the world . . . fill me with deepest disgust.

It is completely impossible to serve such a regime any longer . . .
The only reason I have remained at my post this long has been to serve
my Sycambrian fatherland, which needs help surviving these grim
years. But now I can do so no longer . . . The official party has
become mistrustful of me . . . Friends from Sycambria have
informed me that secret reports exist about my true feelings . . .

At night I have been suffering from insomnia and nervousness . . .

Because I felt the need to find a way to offset my unhappiness . . . I
began to imagine how the world would have turned out had the Allies
won the war.

What would have happened if the Anglo-Americans had invented
the atomic bomb? If fate had given the Allies a unique chance to
fashion a better world and a definitive peace?[1]

The wistful musings of the anonymous Sycambrian narrator in Randolph
Robban's 1950 novel *Si l'Allemagne avait vaincu* (*If Germany Had Won*) are
significant for having appeared in one of the few substantive alternate
histories of a Nazi wartime victory to be published outside of Britain, the
United States, and Germany after 1945. To be sure, alternate histories on
the premise of the Nazis triumphing in World War II have appeared in a
variety of other countries during the postwar period, including France,
Russia, Poland, the Czech Republic, Norway, and Israel.[2] Yet, their relative
scarcity means that they have never assumed the necessary critical mass for
drawing larger conclusions about the historical consciousness of the
nations in which they have appeared. Still, while these works may be
quite exceptional in character, examining a few of the more prominent
examples provides an intriguing perspective on the content and function of

the narratives examined in the three preceding chapters. Like British, American, and German alternate histories, the tales of other nations depicted a Nazi victory in strongly dystopian terms. Yet they did so not for reasons of triumphalism but to criticize the Western Allies – especially the United States – for postwar misdeeds. Produced in countries that did not benefit from World War II like the other three nations, these narratives expressed a more pessimistic view of the war's real historical significance.

One of the most interesting of these alternate histories was *Si l'Allemagne avait vaincu*.[3] Published in 1950 by an anonymous Hungarian author writing under the pseudonym Randolph Robban, the novel is narrated from the perspective of an anonymous diplomat from the fictional Eastern European nation of Sycambria, who is posted in France when World War II comes to an abrupt end. In the novel's point of divergence, Germany ends up snatching victory from the jaws of defeat at the last minute in January 1945 when it uses its newly developed atomic bombs to obliterate London and Chicago and force unconditional surrender. From this point on, Germany imposes a postwar order upon Europe and the United States that is the mirror image of the real historical order imposed upon Germany by the Allies. After occupying the United States, Germany enforces a strict policy of re-education upon the defeated nation in order to nazify its population and make it compliant with its new masters. The Germans further decide to punish their wartime foes by fashioning the new legal principle of "crimes against humanity," which they employ at the high-profile war crimes trials held in Nuremberg. Before long, however, Germany adopts a more lenient course of action towards the United States. Growing tensions between Germany and Japan over the nature of the postwar order lead Hitler to rearm the United States, with the intention of using the country as a potential bulwark against the Japanese. By the novel's end, a conflict over Korea sparks a new war between the former Axis partners, which leads to their mutual nuclear devastation. In the book's last lines, the narrator personally experiences the nuking of Berlin and concludes with the grim observation, "I will never again have the strength nor inclination to imagine what would have become of the world if the victors had somehow been transformed into the vanquished and the vanquished transformed into the victors."[4]

Si l'Allemagne avait vaincu was exceptional as an early postwar work of alternate history that criticized rather than vindicated the recent past. While at first glance Robban's novel resembled contemporaneous Anglo-American works by painting a grim portrait of a Nazi military victory, its thinly veiled ironic tone revealed that its true target was not the vanquished

Germans but the victorious Allies.[5] By positing that the Nazis would have behaved more or less like the Allies had they won the war, Robban critiqued the real historical postwar order imposed by the Allies upon Europe. When the Sycambrian narrator condemns the Nazis' war crimes trials of the Allies at Nuremberg for their retroactive legal character as well as for the Nazi government's hypocritical failure to regard its own wartime conduct as criminal, he clearly voiced Robban's own disapproval of the Allied Nuremberg trials.[6] And when the narrator condemns the Nazis' postwar exploitation of Sycambrian and other nations' prisoners of war as forced laborers, he expressed Robban's own criticism of Stalin's similar behavior after 1945.[7] Finally, the narrator's depiction of the American people's willingness to accommodate themselves to the new totalitarian order imposed upon them by the Germans reflected Robban's cynical belief in the shallowness of American democracy and expressed his opposition to the central role that the United States was playing in the reconstruction of postwar Europe.[8]

In essence, the anonymous narrator in *Si l'Allemagne avait vaincu* was a fictional version of Robban's own pseudonymous self. This becomes clear towards the end of the novel, when the narrator reveals his decision, in the midst of a Nazi-ruled world, to write an alternate history novel entitled *And If They Had Won?*, outlining what would have happened if the Allies had triumphed in World War II. In undertaking this project, the narrator takes the advice of colleagues who advise him not to use his own name, for fear he will suffer recriminations from the victorious authorities who will perceive his fictional scenario as a bitter satire on the present.[9] In summarizing what he believed would have happened, the narrator in his novel essentially outlines a utopian vision of what Robban believed the Allies *should have done* (but did not do) in setting up the real historical European postwar order. This vision included refraining from exacting revenge on the Germans, abstaining from a principle of collective guilt, embracing swift economic reconstruction, and fostering reconciliation between collaborators and resisters through a blanket policy of amnesty and forgiveness.[10] In short, both the narrator's utopian vision of an Allied victory and his dystopian description of a Nazi triumph expressed Robban's pessimistic view towards the recent past.

In writing *Si l'Allemagne avait vaincu*, Robban expressed the perspective of a Hungarian writer (and a former diplomat) whose nation did not benefit in the same way as the Allied nations did from the outcome of World War II.[11] The defeat of Nazism in 1945, after all, allowed Hungary to become swallowed up by Stalin's bloc of Eastern European communist

satellite states. From a Hungarian perspective, the Allied victory constituted a disaster. In writing his novel, Robban wanted to alert his largely
Western audience to the fact that Nazism's real historical defeat had
brought about terrible unanticipated consequences for Eastern Europe:
rather than bringing about liberation, it brought about a new form of
oppression. To be sure, by likening the real historical postwar behavior of
the Allies to the allohistorical postwar behavior of the Nazis, Robban
stretched the bounds of both plausibility and taste to make his broader
political point. Most likely for this reason his book received little attention
in the Anglo-American world. It did, however, receive praise in Germany,
where reviewers eagerly supported its relativistic conclusions.[12] Despite
largely being ignored, however, the novel fulfilled a significant task. For
in using the premise of a Nazi victory to criticize the recent past, *Si
l'Allemagne avait vaincu* served as a foil that further underscored the
dominant early postwar trend of Anglo-American writers using alternate
history to vindicate the course of real history.

Another work that also sheds interesting light on the function of postwar
alternate histories was famed Dutch novelist Harry Mulisch's 1972 novel,
De toekomst van gisteren (*The Future of Yesterday*).[13] Hardly a conventional
work of alternate history, *De toekomst van gisteren* is really a confessional
book about Mulisch's *failure* to complete an allohistorical novel about the
Nazis winning World War II. The author first came up with the idea of
writing such a novel in the wake of the Eichmann trial, which he covered as
a reporter for the Dutch press in 1961.[14] Yet after beginning to write it in
1962, he struggled for ten years before abandoning the project in 1972. In
De toekomst van gisteren, Mulisch reflects on many themes in attempting to
reconstruct the reasons for his failure, discussing his own personal biography,
and his thoughts on literature and on contemporary affairs, before finally
arriving at a description of the novel that never was. At this juncture, which
comes more than midway through the book, Mulisch provides a thirty-
page chronicle of the origins and the consequences of the Nazi victory.

In this account, the Nazis win World War II as a result of Hitler's
assassination by Claus von Stauffenberg on July 20, 1944. In the wake of
this pivotal event, Hitler is succeeded by Ludwig Beck, who forges a
separate peace with the Western Allies and thereafter moves to invade the
Soviet Union, which he defeats. Beck is then overthrown in a coup by
Heinrich Himmler and Reinhard Heydrich, who move to reconquer all of
Western Europe, including Britain, whose fleet they then use to invade and
conquer the United States. The consequences of this event, as Mulisch
describes them, are grim. In the wake of their victory, the Nazis let their

ideological fanaticism run wild. Under the leadership of the new Führer, Heydrich, they pursue the extermination of all undesirable social groups, including all of world Jewry, the handicapped, the aged, criminals, Arabs, and Blacks. Nazi barbarism further manifests itself in the destruction of the holy sites of the Middle East (Jewish and Muslim alike). But the epitome of Nazi fanaticism appears when Heydrich's successor, the new Führer, Konrad Bayer, proclaims a radical new racial policy of abolishing all medicines and hospitals so that the racially weak – even Germans – will be eliminated through natural selection. The Nazis even declare the abolition of all science except for "racial science" and pledge that no means will be spared, including human experimentation, in the effort to achieve a perfect "racial purity."[15]

These bleak events provide the backdrop for the dramatic narrative of Mulisch's projected novel. Set in early 1967 in the ruins of Nazi-occupied Warsaw (which has been re-named "Amsterdam" and repopulated with hundreds of thousands of deported Dutch refugees), the novel's outline describes the events that befall its protagonist, Otto Textor – a journalist from the only extant Amsterdam newspaper, *De Telegraaf* – after he is sent to the monumentally rebuilt capital of Germania to cover the trial of the recently captured fugitive nuclear scientist, J. Robert Oppenheimer, for war crimes. Oppenheimer's alleged crimes include his role in the wartime nuclear destruction of Berlin, but more broadly, they focus on his role in inventing the most destructive weapon in the history of mankind, the atomic bomb. Before long, Oppenheimer is found guilty and hanged, and Textor, having just witnessed the event, retires to his hotel, where he comes into conversation with two other Dutchmen, one of whom, while drunk, makes the observation that "If Germany had lost the war, World War III would probably already be over and our planet would be flying through space thoroughly depopulated."[16] This off-the-cuff observation startles Textor and shakes him profoundly – so much so, that he resolves to write a novel on the subject.

In portraying how Textor depicts a Nazi defeat in World War II, Mulisch provocatively complicates his otherwise frightful portrayal of a Nazi-ruled world. Unlike Philip K. Dick's *The Man in the High Castle*, whose interior allohistorical novel-within-a-novel, *The Grasshopper Lies Heavy*, portrayed a Nazi loss in upbeat terms (in keeping with the fantasies of the defeated Americans), Mulisch depicts Textor envisioning a Nazi loss as a nightmare. As Textor muses to himself:

If Germany had lost the war ... What would have happened? ... Would ... the Jews have been able to pursue their machinations unhindered, so that humanity today would in fact have been exterminated – not decimated, as today, but completely expunged? The Jews would have remained alive! ... That is completely unimaginable. The Dutch would then probably not have been deported, but completely sucked dry in a grisly manner by the Jewish-plutocratic leeches ... and it is questionable whether [the Dutch] ... would not have been better off than today in the General Government ... And while the west would have been plundered by the world-hydra of international financial Jewry, the east would have been trampled by the boots of the Jewish-Bolshevistic beasts.[17]

As these musings make clear, Textor shares the antisemitic prejudices of the master race and largely identifies with them. Despite his Dutch background, he briefly fantasizes about publishing his novel in Germany and winning the right to become germanized.[18] Yet his optimism is shattered when he arrives back in Amsterdam/Warsaw and learns that his wife is pregnant. Realizing that the child will be seized by the Germans and used for medical experiments, he resolves to write a more critical alternate history of a Nazi defeat and spread it throughout occupied Poland, like a work of *samizdat* literature. Before he can do so, however, he is captured by the secret police and sent to Auschwitz for liquidation. Upon arriving and witnessing children being ripped from their parents' arms, he recognizes with horror that his allohistorical imagination has completely "failed in light of the reality" of Nazi barbarism, and he jumps in despair into the next transport for the gas chambers.[19]

With this bleak ending, Mulisch signaled the existence of a critical agenda behind his grim portrayal of a Nazi victory. At the most obvious level, Mulisch used the character of Textor to condemn the misguidedness of his fellow Dutch countrymen for collaborating with the Nazis in real history. Mulisch was particularly sensitive to this issue, given his own background as the son of a Dutch Catholic father (and Jewish mother) who served the Germans as a banker during the war.[20] Yet Mulisch further used Textor's attraction to Nazism in order to make larger polemical points about a variety of contemporary political concerns. Chief among them was Mulisch's opposition to cold-war nuclear proliferation. In *De toekomst van gisteren*, Mulisch provocatively points out the merits of the Nazis' claim that their successful defense of the world from nuclear annihilation justifies their totalitarian rule. In fact, thanks to the Nazi wartime victory and their subsequent banning of nuclear research, the world knows no nuclear arms race or threat of nuclear devastation. Provocatively, Mulisch seems to flirt with the notion that such a world might have been superior to our own, portraying Textor's friend Ramaker soberly telling him that a world in which the Nazis lost would not have been so much "better" as "different."[21]

Although Mulisch ultimately shrinks back from endorsing such an implication, by broaching it at all, he revealed his highly pessimistic view of his own present. At the time that he was writing, in the late 1960s, Mulisch was highly alienated by world events, largely as a result of the intensifying cold-war struggle in Vietnam. As a radical writer on the far left, Mulisch was hostile to the United States, comparing its postwar behavior to that of the Third Reich.[22] Indeed, in numerous sections of *De toekomst van gisteren*, Mulisch likened the war crime of Hiroshima to that of Auschwitz, suggesting that the former was merely a more modern, faceless version of the latter, neither being morally worse than the other.[23] What most irritated Mulisch, however, was the fact that, in his own world, the horrors of the Holocaust trumped those of Hiroshima and blinded people to the West's perpetration of new atrocities – such as the "American genocide in Vietnam."[24] It was for this reason that Mulisch depicted the reverse being true in a Nazi-ruled world – with Auschwitz valorized and nuclear weapons demonized, and with Textor speculating counterfactually about a nightmare world in which "the gassings would have probably been surrounded by the same taboo that currently surrounds the atomic bomb."[25] In the end, Mulisch affirmed the misery of a Nazi-ruled world, but by depicting the Nazis' sly attempts to distract attention from their allohistorical crimes by trumpeting their opposition to nuclear weapons, he polemically highlighted the Allies' comparable dwelling on the Nazi past to redirect attention away from their own real historical misdeeds. In the end, Mulisch's disaffection with the ways the Nazi past was being used to distract from the crimes of the present was an important reason he decided to give up writing the novel.[26] Believing Nazism to be merely a symptom of universal evil, he no longer wanted to be a part of a project that sustained viewing it as sui generis.

Although written in two different eras by writers from very different nations, the novels of Robban and Mulisch resembled each other by offering horrifying portrayals of a Nazi victory for critical rather than triumphalistic purposes. Both men used alternate history to cast doubt upon the self-congratulatory postwar truths adhered to in England and America – namely, that the real historical victory of the Allies over Nazi Germany had produced the best of all possible worlds. For Robban, the outcome of World War II had led to the subjugation of Eastern Europe, while for Mulisch it had produced the enduring threat of nuclear destruction. Such critical novels can be seen as representing the views of countries that were not involved in decisively shaping the course of the war, but that nevertheless were dramatically shaped by it. A sense of frustration and powerlessness emerges from the texts, one which expressed the widespread suffering experienced by many in wartime Hungary and the Netherlands. Of course, Robban's novel, being written quite early after the war, was more self-pitying compared with Mulisch's, which, as a product of the self-reflexive 1960s, also tackled the issue of his compatriots' collaboration. In the end, though, both novels showed how alternate histories could challenge the dominant trends of the era.

Comparative conclusions

The alternate histories of a Nazi triumph in World War II that have appeared in Britain, the United States, Germany, and other countries since 1945 point to significant transformations in the Western memory of the Nazi past over the course of the last generation. To begin with, the conclusions of all narratives have shifted over time. While early postwar alternate histories mostly portrayed a Nazi victory in bleak terms, later ones depicted its consequences in far more nuanced, and frequently upbeat, fashion. Moreover, the function of all the narratives has shifted, if not exactly in the same manner or for the same reasons. British and American texts have become less triumphalistic and more self-critical over time, whereas German narratives have largely abandoned their early tendency towards self-critique in favor of a more value-neutral stance. These shifts in the content and function of alternate histories have been closely tied to the changing fortunes of the countries in which they have appeared. If the Anglo-American triumph in World War II initially brought about self-congratulatory British and American narratives that vindicated both the recent past and the contemporary present, the growing sense of decline within Great Britain and the United States after the 1960s and 1970s respectively brought about more critical narratives that questioned whether the course of real history was so positive after all. These pessimistic British and American accounts have differed, however, insofar as the former have exceeded the latter both in quantity and quality. Indeed, whereas self-critical alternate histories have continued to appear in Great Britain in the last two decades, they have declined in number in the United States. This trend reveals that Britons have shown a greater readiness than Americans to reassess their past and view it from a less idealized perspective. In the process, they have given voice to a greater sense of dissatisfaction with the postwar world caused by their nation's comparatively dramatic decline. Finally, Germany's postwar development proves this trend in reverse. The Federal Republic's insecure early postwar history helped generate self-critical narratives, but its growing sense of self-confidence since reunification explains the appearance of less critical accounts in recent years. In all of these nations, it becomes obvious that the scenario of a Nazi victory in World War II has been represented in increasingly normalized fashion.

The reception of these tales, by contrast, offers a much more complicated picture. To a significant degree, audiences in Great Britain, the United States, and Germany have exhibited a growing willingness to accept a more normalized perspective towards the Nazi era. Yet this response has hardly been unanimous, as audiences have frequently demonstrated an enduring commitment to viewing the Nazi past from an ethically informed perspective. Not surprisingly, the responses have varied by nation. The greatest acceptance has been visible in Great Britain, where increasing numbers of Britons have embraced the less judgmental view of Nazi Germany that has accompanied the dismantling of the finest-hour myth. Americans have been somewhat less willing to regard the Third Reich as anything less than the epitome of evil, having accepted this view firmly in the 1950s and 1960s, strayed from it in the 1970s, and returned to it in the 1990s. The greatest refusal to perceive the Nazi era from a value-neutral perspective has been evident in Germany, where readers supported the black-and-white accounts of the pre-1989 years and condemned the less critical narratives that emerged thereafter. Such expressions of criticism are significant. But compared with the unanimously favorable response of audiences to the moralistic portrayals of a Nazi victory in the early decades after 1945, the mixed reactions of audiences to the more recent accounts of the last generation suggest that – from the broader perspective of the entire postwar period – the memory of the Nazi past has become increasingly affected by the powerful forces of normalization.

PART 2

Alternate Hitlers

CHAPTER 5

The fugitive Führer and the search for justice

Kronhausen ... picked up the corpse of Adolf Hitler. He laid it down gently and once more straightened the arms and legs and began to cover them.

'Stop ...'

The single word, though weakly uttered, carried with it the command Kronhausen recognized so well.... He watched as Adolf Hitler's eyes fluttered open and the cold gaze rose up directly at him.

'Stop ...'

'My Führer!'

Adolf Hitler ... groaned in pain and rolled over, exposing the wound on his temple. Kronhausen immediately lifted him forward, and Hitler vomited...

... 'I will tell you what happened,' he said ... [to Kronhausen] ...

'My wife took poison. When she bit into the capsule she fell against me. At that moment I had the gun to my head. Her movement jostled my arm, and when the gun went off the bullet grazed my flesh, nothing more. I reached for the remaining capsules and swallowed four, chewing on them. I lost consciousness, but knew I was not dead ... You see what happened? The poison did not kill me. Destiny decreed that I should not die – not here; that there was still work to be done and my role in history had not yet ended. In spite of the defeat brought upon me by traitors, I should continue to live.''[1]

Canadian writer Philippe van Rjndt's account of Hitler's failed suicide attempt in his novel *The Trial of Adolf Hitler* (New York, 1978) provides a classic example of one of the more commonly explored questions of postwar alternate history: What would have happened had Adolf Hitler survived World War II? In the years since Hitler's death by his own hand on April 30, 1945, a substantial number of short stories, novels, films, plays, and comic books have appeared in the United States and, to a lesser extent, other nations on the subject of the Führer's survival.[2] These narratives have all imagined that Hitler did not commit suicide in the Führerbunker but, rather, fled into hiding – whether to the countryside of southern Bavaria, the steamy jungles of South America, or the dank sewers of Berlin. Whatever the location of Hitler's ultimate refuge, these works have largely focused on the consequences of his survival for the subsequent course of history. In doing so, however, they have arrived at very different conclusions. From 1945 to the early 1960s, most tales of this kind depicted the fugitive Führer as an unrepentant demon who, in one way or another, ends up being brought to justice for his crimes.[3] After the early 1970s, however, alternate histories began to represent Hitler in surprisingly humanized terms as an unthreatening figure who succeeds in evading justice. Throughout the postwar years, both kinds of narrative have coexisted. Yet, on the whole, since 1945 accounts of Hitler's evading justice have exceeded both in quantity and quality narratives of his being held accountable for his crimes.[4]

The shifting portrayal of Hitler's survival reveals clear signs of a normalizing trend in the Western memory of the Nazi past. In its original conception, the theme of the fugitive Führer constituted an unusual hybrid type of counterfactual premise that combined both nightmare and fantasy components. If the scenario expressed the nightmarish possibility that Hitler's escape might worsen the course of history, it also indulged in the fantasy of improving history by capturing the ex-dictator and bringing him to justice. In both of its dimensions, significantly, the theme reflected a certain sense of disaffection with the postwar present. As a nightmare, the idea that Hitler had survived World War II reflected Nazism's enduring traumatic historical legacy, as well as lingering anxieties about the possibility of its future resurgence; as a fantasy, it reflected the present-day frustration that Hitler had escaped humanity's judgment by committing suicide.[5] In the first two and a half decades after 1945, the enduring power of these nightmares and fantasies was clearly expressed in alternate histories that depicted Hitler being brought to justice. The recent upsurge in narratives showing Hitler's evasion of justice since the 1970s, however, suggests that both the nightmare of his survival, as well as the fantasy of judging him for his crimes, have dramatically faded in intensity.

This trend reflects the gradual recovery of Western society from the traumas of the Nazi era. As the Third Reich has retreated further into the past, the process of organic normalization – rooted in the passing of time and the turnover of generations – has helped to reduce the horror of the past in memory. At the same time, new postwar concerns have displaced the Nazi experience in the minds of many and promoted its universalization. Recent alternate histories depicting Hitler's evasion of justice confirm both of these trends. They also suggest a growing apathy towards preserving the memory of the Nazi past for its own sake. Whereas narratives portraying Hitler being brought to justice described this desirable allohistorical outcome as the result of the enduring commitment to remembering and avenging his crimes, accounts representing Hitler's evasion of justice have criticized the concern with memory as an unhealthy obsession. More than anything else, this declining commitment to remembrance testifies to the broader phenomenon of normalization. Still, this trend has not stood unopposed. The many critical reactions to accounts of Hitler eluding justice demonstrate an enduring commitment to preserving the lessons of the past. In short, the production and reception of accounts of the fugitive Führer reflect the increasingly divisive nature of the memory of Nazism in the West.

THE FUGITIVE FÜHRER IN ALTERNATE HISTORY

The premise of the fugitive Führer traces its origins back to the emergence of the so-called "survival myth."[6] The fear that Hitler somehow had survived World War II and escaped to an unknown destination emerged immediately after his suicide in the spring of 1945. Given the absence of Hitler's corpse and the Soviet Union's politically motivated reluctance to clarify the dictator's fate, many in the West were left with the uneasy suspicion that the architect of the twentieth century's worst crimes might have evaded his own conflagration.[7] During the early 1950s and into the 1960s, these fears were stoked by a flood of sensationalistic articles on the Führer's alleged whereabouts by a wide range of journalists, self-proclaimed Hitler-hunters, and eccentric cranks in the European and American tabloid press.[8] Over time, however, the aura of fear surrounding the possibility of Hitler's survival began to wane. In more recent years, the survival myth has acquired a more lighthearted character, as has been demonstrated by its incorporation into popular television programs like *The Simpsons*, comic books like *Howard the Duck*, and rock music lyrics by such bands as The Clash.[9] Continuing reports of Hitler's survival in tabloids like the *Weekly World News*, popular satirical journals like the *Onion*, and internet web sites, moreover, testify to the resilience of the survival myth.[10] While its symbolic significance has changed over time, the legend of Hitler's survival, like Elvis's, has lost none of its staying power as a dominant myth of postwar Western popular culture.[11]

The allure of the survival myth is confirmed by the many allohistorical depictions of the fugitive Führer that have appeared since 1945. These narratives have differed from most expressions of the survival myth by exploring its fictional potential to the fullest possible extent. Unwilling merely to utilize the premise of Hitler's postwar escape for a sensationalistic headline or a cheap gag, they have speculated at length about its possible consequences for world history. In so doing, these narratives have distinguished themselves as unusual works of alternate history, since they have seldom represented Hitler's survival as leading to any substantial historical change. As such, they are most accurately described as "secret histories."[12] Whatever one calls them, these narratives are extremely valuable documents of the Western imagination.

Alternate histories portraying the theme of the fugitive Führer have appeared in various national contexts throughout the postwar era. They have done so, moreover, in four distinct phases. The first narratives emerged in the early 1950s along with the growing popularity of the "survival myth," but they remained somewhat limited in number as a result of the era's reduced concern with Nazism. Beginning in the early 1960s, however, new versions began to appear, in large part owing to the reawakening interest in Germany's Nazi past at the time of the Eichmann trial. After 1970, the growing number of narratives increased still further, thanks to the "Hitler Wave"'s stoking of public fascination with the life of the Führer.[13] Finally, the most recent flurry of alternate histories has appeared since the late 1980s, a period that witnessed a notable increase in German language accounts. In comparing and contrasting the changing allohistorical representation of Hitler's survival in these four eras, as well as by examining how the many narratives have been critically received, a better sense can be gained of the shifting status of the Nazi past in Western consciousness.

BRINGING THE FÜHRER TO JUSTICE IN THE 1950S

The first postwar depictions of the fugitive Führer were strikingly consistent in their portrayal of Hitler as an evil figure who is ultimately held accountable for his crimes. In their quest for justice, these accounts continued in the tradition of such wartime "future histories" as Max Radin's 1943 novel, *The Day of Reckoning* and Michael Young's 1944 novel, *The Trial of Adolf Hitler*, both of which described Hitler being captured, tried for his misdeeds, and suitably punished.[14] Postwar accounts differed fundamentally in plot, however, due to their embrace of the survival myth. All of them expressed the nightmare that Hitler remained alive following the war's end and continued to pose a threat to the world; all of them, at the same time, indulged in the fantasy of capturing the

Führer and bringing him to justice. In the process, these early accounts expressed a strong belief in the necessity of remembrance.

The earliest postwar depictions of the fugitive Führer appeared in comic books. Given the frequent presence of Hitler in American comic books during the war years, his continued appearance after 1945 was perhaps a natural extension of a prior trend. Now, however, instead of focusing on the wartime struggle to defeat Hitler, comic book tales concentrated on capturing and judging him. The first such account was published in 1950 in issue Nr. 3 of the classic DC comic book series *Strange Adventures*, entitled "The Strange Fate of Adolph Hitler."[5] In this tale, Hitler fakes his own suicide by murdering a double (along with an unsuspecting Eva Braun) and is about to embark upon a daring escape from Berlin under the assumed identity of a carpenter named Hans Brecht when the unexpected happens. Just as the Führer is in the process of shaving off his signature moustache, he is interrupted by a group of visitors who announce that they have come from Mars to arrest him and bring him back to their planet to stand trial for his "vicious crimes against humanity." As one of the Martian judges subsequently proclaims in the courtroom, "Mars had to be interested in Adolph Hitler and his Nazi empire! . . . If the Nazis had won, they would have sent expeditions into space . . . and Mars would have been overrun by gangsters and murderers!" As the trial proceeds, Martian prosecutors chronicle Hitler's multiple crimes (among others, his bombing of Rotterdam), and, in short order, the trial ends with Hitler's defense attorney requesting the merciful punishment of the death penalty. Initially, the uncomprehending Führer objects, but then the judge explains that he will reject this particular punishment in any case, explaining, "Death is too good for a monster like you. Our punishment will be much more suitable!" Hitler, at this point, is apprehensive, but when the court announces that the punishment is "perpetual exile," he silently exults within himself, thinking, "Martians are even bigger fools than the Democrats. As long as I'm alive I can always return to earth . . . and power!" In the end, however, the joke is on Hitler, for the Martians reveal that he will be placed in a spaceship that will orbit the universe forever, all the while being kept alive by special "nutritive rays" that will sustain "him indefinitely . . . to the end of his long tormented life (see Figure 14)." In arriving at this conclusion, "The Strange Fate of Adolph Hitler" clearly illustrated an abiding desire for justice. The tale's writer, legendary science fiction author and editor, H. L. Gold, no doubt intended this message to be the dominant one taken away by readers. As a writer of Jewish background who had served in World War II (in the Pacific theater), Gold had plenty of personal reasons to

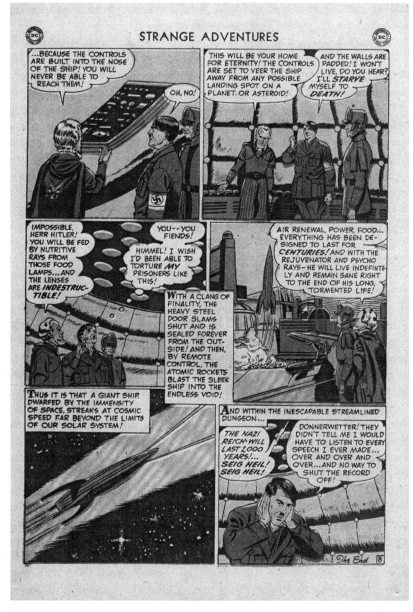

Figure 14 Adolf Hitler is brought to justice for his crimes in the 1950 story "The Strange
Fate of Adolph Hitler" in the comic book *Strange Adventures*.

preserve the memory of Hitler's criminality in the postwar period. As someone who had long been conscious of antisemitism within American society, he, like many other postwar comic book writers, most probably hoped that the story would provide a morally instructive lesson about the dangers of political extremism in the past as well as the present.[16] Whatever Gold's specific aims, the overall plot of his story explicitly confirmed the appeal of the fantasy of allohistorically judging Hitler for his crimes in the early postwar era.

The same can be said of the next account to appear: a 1954 tale entitled "The Man Who Could Be Hitler," which was published in issue Nr. 6 of the classic Quality Comics series *T-Man: World Wide Trouble-Shooter* (see Figure 15).[17] In this issue, the protagonist, Pete Trask, a dapper investigator in the U.S. Treasury Department, travels to Egypt to investigate the death of a well-known American Egyptologist, Professor Sandweg. Once in Cairo, Trask sneaks into one of the great pyramids of Giza and is startled by a "clang" that resounds behind suspiciously modern steel doors. Before he can act, however, he is overpowered by guards and soon learns the terrifying secret of the pyramids: Nazis have fled from Germany and resettled in Egypt as part of a broader plan to wage a new assault against their former wartime enemies with newly developed germ warfare. As told to him by one General Oberdorfer, "Despite der temporary victory of der inferior races, ve continue our vork! Mitt der cooperation of Egyptian sympathizers, ve prepare vunce again to restore to power our great leader!" At this point in the tale, Trask's identity as an American government official is discovered, and he is confronted by another Nazi, an elderly bald man, who (in the best style of wartime Hollywood propaganda classics) declares, "Ve haff vays to make you talk, American spy!" Trask reacts by thinking, "There was something nauseatingly familiar about the little guy's shrill hysterical voice! And that pasty face haunted me in some other nightmare!" Soon, after making his daring escape from his captors, he stumbles upon a photograph of the man, quickly doodles a moustache and black lock of hair across his forehead, and exclaims, "Holy smokes! No wonder I thought I'd seen him before!" The picture, predictably enough, is that of Adolf Hitler. As the tale climaxes, Trask chases the fugitive Führer up the side of the great pyramid, exclaiming, "Stop running, guy! The whole world has some old business to settle with you!" But before Trask can capture him, the ex-dictator falls to his death. At the end, Trask learns that the badly battered corpse cannot be positively identified and concedes, "We'll never really know [who he was]." But in the comic's final line, he declares confidently to a colleague, "if anybody ever asks you ... tell 'em you know the guy who killed Hitler!"

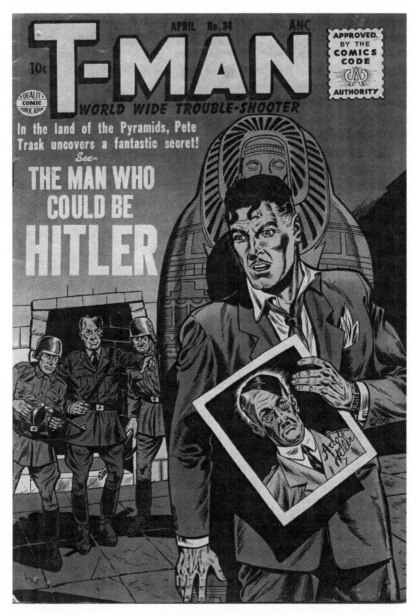

Figure 15 The fugitive Führer is tracked down in Egypt by U.S. Treasury agent Pete Trask
in the 1954 story "The Man Who Could Be Hitler" in the comic book *T-Man*
(reprint version from 1956).

By killing off the dictator at the tale's conclusion, "The Man Who Could Be Hitler" subjected the Führer to a more punitive form of justice than "The Strange Fate of Adolph Hitler" did. Why this was the case is open to question. But it is possible that news stories of ex-Nazi security officials and rocket scientists aiding the Egyptian military under King Farouk and his successor, the saber-rattling nationalist leader Gamal Abdel Nasser, in the early 1950s influenced the increasing concern about the existence of a revived Nazi "threat" at the time.[18] Whatever the case may be, the emphasis on killing the fugitive Führer in "The Man Who Could Be Hitler" reflected a deeper tendency to remember the Nazi era from an ethically informed perspective.

The theme of Hitler's postwar survival was hardly confined to comic books but also appeared in works of literature.[19] One of the most notable was a 1954 short story by the well-known British-American writer, C. S. Forester, entitled "The Wandering Gentile."[20] Originally published in a volume of short stories on the Third Reich entitled *The Nightmare*, this tale featured an unidentified narrator recounting his experience of picking up two elderly hitchhikers while driving to San Francisco on Highway 101. In attempting to make conversation with the couple, the narrator overhears scattered German words coming from the back seat and concludes that they are probably German immigrants, perhaps even concentration camp survivors. Yet his suspicions increase after hearing the old man muttering under his breath about the treachery of "international Jewry" and talking about his dog "Blondi" to his companion, whom he addresses as "Eva." Especially after overhearing Eva refer to her companion as "Adolf" and reassure him that they will soon be arriving in Washington D.C. (where he imagines he will seize power), the narrator concludes that his passengers are none other than Adolf Hitler and Eva Braun. At this moment of realization, the narrator's car suddenly suffers a flat tire, and he is forced to ask his two hitchhiking passengers to stand by the side of the road and flag down a new ride for themselves. In relating his tale to a passing highway patrolman, however, the narrator is taken for crazy, and he finally concludes that his experience may have been more supernatural than real. As he puts it, "Perhaps that was not a man to whom I gave a hitch. It may have been a spirit, a wraith, doomed to eternal wandering."[21]

In its overall conclusions, "The Wandering Gentile" distinguished itself by taking a clear stance in support of justice. Insofar as it depicted Hitler as fated to wander America eternally as a hitchhiker, with no real hope of regaining political power, the story more or less condemned the dictator to a hellish existence of vagrancy, isolation, and anonymity. In one sense, this brand of justice was an ironic one. For, by being subjected to a life of permanent roaming, the world's greatest anti-Semite suffers the same fate as the mythological "wandering Jew"– only now, he is condemned to travel by car instead of on foot. In another sense, however, Hitler's fate represented a form of divine justice. It is not humanity, after all, that has compelled him to wander, but an otherworldly power, possibly God himself. Unlike later narratives, in which Hitler would be charged by the entire civilized world with crimes against humanity, Hitler in Forester's tale remains unrecognized by postwar society. In the end, then, it is up to the divine to do what society cannot – namely, hold the dictator accountable for his crimes.

This conclusion was, in some sense, a reflection of its times. By assuming a quasi-mythological form, Forester's story subjected Hitler to a comparatively mild form of justice. Without having to fear being recognized and judged for his crimes in a conventional legal manner, Hitler essentially escapes the more severe variety of allohistorical punishment seen in later narratives. The reluctance of Forester to judge Hitler more severely may well have reflected the diminished attention to the Nazi era in the 1950s. During this period, the cold war, not the Third Reich, was at the forefront of most people's concerns. Indeed, the fact that the narrator initially assumes that Hitler's mutterings about wanting to overthrow the government mean he is "presumably . . . a Communist" demonstrates how even Forester himself may have been influenced by the climate of the times.[22] This remark, however, also permits an alternate interpretation. In a sense, "The Wandering Gentile" can be seen as a critique of the West's lack of interest in the Third Reich during the 1950s. By depicting society as oblivious to Hitler's survival (epitomized by the misinterpretation of his fascist political rantings as signs of "communist" sympathies), Forester may well have been satirizing the era's political obsessions and historical blinders. Fear of communism had led people to forget the horrors of Nazism. The metaphysical origins of Hitler's judgment, thus, perhaps expressed Forester's belief that a society that forgets the past is incapable of pursuing justice in the present. For his part, Forester was committed to fighting against amnesia: he explicitly intended his tale, as well as the volume of stories of which it was a part, to preserve the memory of Nazi criminality.[23] In this sense, it strongly resembled the aims of the era's comic book tales.

Beyond its inclusion in comic books and short stories, the premise of the fugitive Führer was also portrayed on television, as was demonstrated in 1956 with the airing of an episode of the American television series *The Adventures of Dr. Fu Manchu* entitled "The Master Plan of Dr. Fu Manchu."

Originally broadcast on June 2, 1956, the episode begins with the evil doctor, Fu Manchu (played by Glen Gordon), watching a documentary film about Adolf Hitler and commenting to his shapely female assistant, Karameneh, that it was "catastrophic that time ran out on him." Before long, however, Fu declares that "There is a man living who awaits my command to put the plan into action again," and then motions towards a man lying on a surgical table awaiting plastic surgery – the fugitive Führer himself. After this abrupt beginning, "The Master Plan" goes on to show Fu Manchu forcing a kidnapped plastic surgeon, Harlow Henderson, to alter Hitler's appearance (the doctor gasps "It can't be!" when he first sees the dictator) and then ordering one of his henchman to kill the doctor with one of the most feared weapons featured in 1950s B-movies – a poisonous tarantula. Soon thereafter, one of Henderson's colleagues, Dr. John Petrie, goes to Fu Manchu's apartment to investigate his friend's disappearance and is himself kidnapped after stumbling upon the by-now physically altered Hitler (who he thinks looks familiar but does not recognize). Also joining the chase is Petrie's colleague and Fu Manchu's sworn adversary, the British agent Sir Dennis Nayland-Smith, who, after arriving at Fu Manchu's abandoned apartment, finds clues – including a copy of *Mein Kampf* – that lead him to the unthinkable conclusion that Adolf Hitler is indeed alive and "planning another attempt to conquer the world." As the episode culminates, however, Nayland-Smith and soldiers of the World Council of Nations track down Hitler at his secret hideout on an uncharted island in the South Pacific, where they end up cornering him and shooting him dead (see Figure 16). As the episode concludes, one soldier mutters, "[Do you] think he was the man who was supposed to have died in Berlin years ago?" Dr. Petrie replies, "Whoever it was, another enemy of civilization is gone now." In arriving at this ending, "The Master Plan of Dr. Fu Manchu" largely confirmed the moralistic trend established by the earlier works of the period. As crafted by the episode's creator, veteran Hollywood screenwriter Arthur Orloff, the program clearly expressed a deep-seated belief in Hitler's evil and a desire to hold him accountable for his crimes.[24] At the same time, like Forester's tale, "The Master Plan of Dr. Fu Manchu" reflected the cold-war environment in which it was written. It is notable that the episode portrays Hitler plotting his comeback with a new secret device that can detonate any nuclear weapon within one mile of it. This device, Hitler gloats late in the episode, will leave the United States "virtually defenseless," adding "without atom bombs, America will be attacked by its most powerful enemy and conquered of course." Fu Manchu jumps in at this point to add, "Then the same process will be

Figure 16 Adolf Hitler, having undergone plastic surgery, looks to his Nazi henchmen to help fight off invading agents from the World Council of Nations in his South Pacific hideout in a 1956 episode of *The Adventures of Dr. Fu Manchu* entitled "The Master Plan of Dr. Fu Manchu."

followed until the greater powers of the world are exhausted. Then we will step in, subdue the little countries with our fifth columns that are ready to march." Finally, Hitler passionately concludes, "And the world will be ours!" Needless to say, by showing Hitler targeting the United States' nuclear umbrella, "The Master Plan of Dr. Fu Manchu" expressed cold-war fears of Soviet nuclear attack and affirmed that America's nuclear arsenal was the best deterrent against it. In this sense, the episode resembled C. M. Kornbluth's tale "Two Dooms." For, by portraying the fugitive Führer menacing the United States in an alternate present, it triumphalistically ratified the course of real history as a preferable one.

On the whole, the allohistorical accounts of the 1950s reflected the era's complex views of the Nazi past. All of the narratives confirmed a general readiness to view the Nazi era from an ethically principled perspective. At the same time, however, many accounts betrayed signs of new postwar concerns, most notably an increased fear of Soviet communism. This fact was illustrated, finally, in one of the era's more unconventional, but telling, works to feature the fugitive Führer – the 1951 RKO film *The Man He Found*. Directed by William Cameron Menzies (the famed production designer of *Gone with the Wind* and many other films), the film originally depicted a demonic Führer hiding out with an assortment of neo-Nazis in the backwoods of Wisconsin, biding his time until he can unleash a deadly germ assault on the United States. This premise confirmed the dominant view of the Nazi dictator as the archetypal symbol of evil. *The Man He Found*, however, was never released in this form. After the film flopped in test marketing, its producer, RKO chief Howard Hughes, had it re-edited so that all the scenes with Nazis were deleted and replaced with newly shot scenes featuring communists as the film's villains. When the film was ultimately released under its new title, *The Whip Hand*, all signs of Hitler and the Nazis had been completely expunged.[25] Motivated by Hughes's politically driven desire to accommodate and exploit American fears of communism during the early years of the "red scare," the decision to radically alter the film's plot reflected how new cold-war political realities shaped American views towards the subject of Nazism. The film revealed a basic truth of the time: although Americans were more than willing to condemn Nazism, it was hardly the only subject on their minds. Following the flurry of accounts of the fugitive Führer in the early 1950s, their total disappearance after the middle of the decade suggests that Americans' interest in this allohistorical theme may ultimately have been somewhat shallow.

RECEPTION

Gauging the reception of the tales of the 1950s is difficult. Few reviews appeared, and those that did were of mixed quality. C. S. Forester's short story "The Wandering Gentile" was the only work to receive meaningful attention, earning praise from several reviewers who admired the writer's goal of preserving the memory of Hitler's crimes in an era oriented towards other concerns.[26] Yet few reviewers considered the tale to be a successful piece of literature – the consensus view being that it was "a somewhat strained excursion into fantasy."[27] There is no record of any response either to the comic book tales of the time or to the television broadcast of "The Master Plan of Dr. Fu Manchu." It is likely, though, that all of these narratives reached untold millions of readers and viewers, given the mass reach of comic books – and, increasingly, television – in the 1950s.[28] There is no way to know how readers responded to their portrayals of Hitler's survival. But given their formulaic, morally judgmental tone, they probably confirmed the prevailing conceptions of the Nazi era in the minds of most Americans at the time.

Beginning in the early 1960s, however, this moralistic trend began to undergo something of a subtle transformation. Following the sharp fall-off in narratives depicting Hitler's survival in the second half of the 1950s, their rapid return after the turn of the decade signaled a new phase in the scenario's existence. As was true of the many alternate histories of a Nazi triumph in World War II at the same time, the growing attention to Germany's Nazi past during the period of the Eichmann trial helped stimulate this broader trend. As Western society became more committed to hunting down Nazi war criminals and putting them on trial for their crimes, a reawakened concern with justice began to inform allohistorical portrayals of Hitler's survival. This interest was most visible in those tales in the 1960s that depicted the fugitive Führer paying for his misdeeds and meeting with a just end. But it was also evident in new narratives that represented the ex-dictator evading justice and surviving into the present as an enduring menace.

The enduring fantasy of bringing Hitler to justice was expressed in three strikingly similar motion pictures that appeared in the middle of the decade: David Bradley's 1963 film *They Saved Hitler's Brain*, Brad F. Ginter's 1967 horror film *Flesh Feast*, and Joseph Kane's 1967 thriller *He Lives*. Like the accounts of the early 1950s, these three films all presented the fugitive Führer as an enduring demon who ultimately pays for his sins with his life. The most famous of the films, *They Saved Hitler's Brain*, has Hitler escaping from Berlin after radical surgery that transforms him into a disembodied head submerged in a water-filled tank mounted on what looks like an oversized radio transmitter. Having fled to his South American hideout of Mandoras, Hitler proceeds to conceive of a bold plan to take over the world by raining a new form of nerve gas upon it.[29] His plan is soon uncovered, however, and he meets with a grisly death when an enemy hand grenade explodes in his car, setting his head on fire and melting it into a general state of black goo. Similarly, *Flesh Feast* portrays Hitler meeting a just end, showing him conspiring with shadowy Latin American Nazis to mount a political comeback, only to suffer a gory demise when the female plastic surgeon in charge of altering his appearance cons him into undergoing a procedure that entails having flesh-eating maggots devour his face.[30] Finally, *He Lives* represents the Nazi dictator lurking in a South American hideout together with Martin Bormann and planning the establishment of a Fourth Reich – until they are discovered by a team of Israeli secret agents who kill them with a barrage of mortar rounds.[31]

The strikingly similar representation of the fugitive Führer in *They Saved Hitler's Brain*, *Flesh Feast*, and *He Lives* is significant for several reasons. By depicting Hitler as irredeemably evil and ultimately punished for his crimes, the films suggested a heightened desire for justice. The precise aims of the films' directors are unknown, but it is likely that the Eichmann trial in the early part of the decade had an influence. To be sure, the three films were hardly meant as political statements and largely served the goal of low-brow entertainment. All of them were rather unconcerned with Hitler as a figure of historical significance and instead used him as a convenient stock-in-trade villain to anchor their sensationalistic narratives. The three films were also low-budget affairs of minimal quality. This assessment is confirmed by the uniformly negative reviews of the films. Heading the list was *They Saved Hitler's Brain* which, when originally released, was panned as "a melodramatic fiasco" and an "incoherent rumpus," and has since earned the reputation among cinema aficionados as one of the worst motion pictures ever made in the history of American film.[32] Most critics did not even bother to waste the effort condemning *Flesh Feast* and *He Lives*, which were largely ignored and have since been acknowledged only by scattered connoisseurs of bad taste. Overall, the schlocky nature of the films makes it tempting to dismiss them as entirely insignificant. Still, it would be a mistake to ignore them altogether. All of them, for one thing, attracted major studio talent. The director of *They Saved Hitler's Brain*, David Bradley, had directed a number of major films, such as *Peer Gynt* (1941) and *Julius Caesar* (1950) – both starring Charlton Heston – and later became a distinguished film historian.[33] *Flesh Feast* featured the one-time major Hollywood starlet Veronica Lake in her last starring role (she also was the film's producer). And *He Lives* was directed by Joseph Kane, a longtime director of Hollywood westerns featuring such legends as Roy Rogers and John Wayne.[34] These figures' distinguished careers did not prevent their films from failing as works of cinema, but they were nevertheless important for confirming the dominant view of Hitler as the embodiment of evil.

The same can be said of the era's narratives that, for the first time, depicted Hitler *evading* justice. The first example of this new trend appeared in Great Britain on May 6, 1962 with the airing of British playwright Robert Muller's major television drama (and later stage play)

"Night Conspirators."[35] Broadcast as part of the BBC's prominent *Armchair Theatre* series, this political thriller is set in contemporary Germany and portrays a group of leading German figures from the realms of industry, politics, the army, and media, who meet in clandestine fashion at a foreign embassy in order to hatch a plot that will enable them to seize power. As they conduct their discussions, the cabal is taken aback when an "old visitor," swathed in bandages, is suddenly wheeled into the room by a young male attendant. The "old visitor," of course, is Adolf Hitler, who after seventeen years of exile in Iceland has returned to Germany accompanied by his blond-haired teenage son. In the drama, Hitler is initially shown as a broken-down and feeble individual who remains mute as the conspirators decide what to do with him. But as the drama unfolds, and as the conspirators gradually decide to seize power by enlisting the Führer's name and reputation for their cause, Hitler recovers his past oratorical powers and, in demonic fashion, predicts renewed greatness for Germany. The drama thus ends on an ominous note of expected political upheaval in West Germany.[36]

Less than a year after the broadcast of "Night Conspirators" in Britain, the popular American television show *The Twilight Zone* aired a very similar episode entitled "He's Alive!"[37] Written by the show's creator, Rod Serling, and aired on January 24, 1963, the episode portrays the struggle of an aspiring neo-Nazi agitator named Peter Vollmer (played by a young Dennis Hopper) to reinvigorate his moribund movement in the United States. After delivering a clumsy speech on a street corner in front of a hostile crowd about the dangers posed to America by minorities, communists, and the Vatican, Vollmer is pelted with rotten tomatoes and roughed up. In despair, he seeks refuge in the apartment of a longtime friend and father-figure – an elderly concentration camp survivor, named Ernst – and begins to drift off to sleep. Before doing so, however, he senses the presence of a mysterious stranger on the street below. The stranger, hidden in shadows, voices his support for Vollmer's ideals, but gives him some stern advice about how better to enlist the support of the masses. Vollmer listens intently, and before long he is speaking far more convincingly in front of larger and larger crowds. The stranger, however, forces Vollmer to make increasingly difficult choices, such as killing his loyal but oafish supporter, Nick, in order to create a "martyr" who can further galvanize the movement. Vollmer struggles internally to put aside his sentimentality and, when upbraided by the stranger, angrily demands that he identify himself, only to learn to his astonishment that he is none other than Adolf Hitler (see Figure 17). After recovering from his initial

Figure 17 American fascist Peter Vollmer (Dennis Hopper) returns to his deserted party headquarters to find Adolf Hitler waiting to give him political advice in the 1963 *Twilight Zone* episode "He's Alive!"

shock, Vollmer resolves to become as "hard as steel" and ends up following Hitler's advice to kill his longtime friend, Ernst, who is critical of his neo-Nazi activism. Just as he seems to have turned the corner into becoming a ruthless demagogue, however, Vollmer is confronted by the police, who kill him in a shootout before he can escape. In the episode's ominous conclusion, Hitler's shadow is seen against a brick wall walking slowly forward towards a new destination, while the narrator's voice intones:

Where will he go next, this phantom from another time, this resurrected ghost of a previous nightmare – Chicago; Los Angeles; Miami, Florida; Vincennes, Indiana; Syracuse, New York? Anyplace, everyplace, where there's hate, where there's prejudice, where there's bigotry. He's Alive. He's alive so long as these evils exist. Remember that when he comes to *your* town. Remember it when you hear his voice speaking out through others. Remember it when you hear a name called, a minority attacked, any blind, unreasoning assault on a people or any human being. He's alive because through these things we keep him alive.

Like "Night Conspirators," "He's Alive!" was significant for portraying Hitler's evasion of justice. While both episodes depicted Hitler in the same demonic terms as the accounts of the early 1950s, they resisted indulging in the fantasy that he could be held accountable for his crimes. In all probability, both shows avoided this rather predictable plot device and instead adopted the novel – and far more disturbing – premise of Hitler eluding capture in order to express renewed Western fears of the Germans in the early 1960s. The author of "Night Conspirators," Robert Muller (himself a German refugee who fled to England in 1938), imagined the fugitive Führer conspiring with postwar German elites to create a Fourth Reich as a means of casting doubt on the political reliability of the Federal Republic.[38] Serling's portrayal of Hitler's survival, meanwhile, spanned a wider range of concerns. As an American Jew who had fought in World War II, he was understandably sensitive to the history of the Third Reich and intent on preserving its lessons in memory.[39] He too was likely caught up in the upsurge of attention towards Germany's Nazi past in the early 1960s. But Serling had broader goals in writing the episode as well. By allowing Hitler to roam free, Serling utilized him as a symbol of the enduring threat of rightwing ideas to American society. Indeed, evidence exists that by setting "He's Alive!" in the United States he was obliquely referring to the persistence of American racism at the time of the civil rights movement.[40] In a sense, then, "He's Alive!" universalized the significance of Nazism in order to expose the persistence of contemporary injustice. On balance, though, even if "Night Conspirators" and "He's Alive!" abandoned the allohistorical fantasy of judging Hitler for his crimes, they did so to serve the ethical aim of reminding audiences about the enduring dangers of political extremism.

Both "Night Conspirators" and "He's Alive!" were significant, finally, for the considerable attention they attracted. In Britain, "Night Conspirators" met with a largely positive reception. Muller's pessimism about postwar Germany's structural continuities with the Nazi past resonated with British reviewers, many of whom agreed with the drama's skeptical assessment of the nation. One praised Muller for pointing out the "danger" represented by the fact that "the same men, with the same aims, are back in power in West Germany," while another wrote that his work provided "a terrifying and ... all too likely glimpse of the future."[41] Conversely, but not surprisingly, "Night Conspirators" met with an angry response from the Germans. Indeed, the West German ambassador to Britain went so far as to protest the airing of the television drama and declared his hope "that a play like this will never again be shown on British television."[42] In the United States, meanwhile, "He's Alive!" generated a comparable response. The episode was one of the most controversial in the entire history of *The Twilight Zone*, receiving more than 4,000 letters of complaint. Some letters expressed extreme rightwing sentiments typical of the anti-civil rights activists, attacking Serling and his staff as "kike lovers" and "nigger lovers." Most, however, came from conservatives who were irate that Serling had been overly soft on communism. In a January 31, 1963 editorial, the *Indianapolis Star* complained that by portraying the fascist leader Vollmer as an anticommunist, Serling's program had left "the impression ... that people who warn against Communism and people who talk about getting back our freedom are probably secret Nazis." This conclusion was particularly inappropriate, the editorial opined, at a time in which the world continued to be "strangled by Communism."[43] Given the intense anxieties caused by the Cuban missile crisis the year before, it was no surprise that many Americans continued to be preoccupied with the present-day threat of communism and preferred to forget about the past horrors of Nazism. This fact notwithstanding, it is clear that while some Americans resented being reminded of the legacy of Nazism – and rejected comparing it to communism – they continued to view it as a symbol of evil. Thus, even if the American reception of "He's Alive!" was more negative than the British response to "Night Conspirators," both television dramas revealed that American as well as British audiences had continued to remember the Nazi era within ethically informed parameters.

THE HITLER WAVE AND THE NARRATIVES OF THE 1970S AND 1980S

This mnemonic consensus began to break down in the early 1970s, however, just as the number of alternate histories portraying Hitler's survival began to explode in number. The intensifying allohistorical attention to the fugitive Führer was largely the result of the so-called "Hitler Wave."[44] Beginning in the late 1960s and lasting until the mid-1980s in West Germany as well as the United States, a seemingly unending series of historical biographies, films, novels, and scandals signaled the resurgence of interest in the deceased Führer.[45] Originally, the Hitler Wave was a reaction against the simplistic early postwar depiction of the Führer as a demonic figure, whose monstrous powers had thrown the world into turmoil.[46] By the late 1960s and early 1970s, many Germans of the interwar generation (those born in the 1920s) were reaching maturity and seeking to understand why their parents' generation had supported the dictator.[47] This desire for understanding necessitated viewing Hitler less as a demon – that is, someone removed from the sphere of rational explanation – and more as a human being. Attention towards Hitler thus began to move beyond his political policies to the ins and outs of his private life – including his early education, friendships, romantic relationships, artistic interests, habits, hobbies, and pets. While understandable, this new tendency to humanize Hitler soon sparked concerns among various observers. Some argued that the quest to understand Hitler in all of his human dimensions had become debased by the entertainment industry, which was eager to exploit the growing popular interest in the deceased dictator for commercial gain.[48] Others expressed concerns about what they identified as a deeper "fascination" with Hitler, rooted in the alluring contrast between his personal banality and his maniacal capacity for destruction.[49] For all, however, the most worrisome thing was the Hitler Wave's tendency to aestheticize the Nazi era by focusing on its peculiar allure instead of its evil crimes.[50] This general attraction to the world of the perpetrators instead of the suffering of the victims seemed to provide the best evidence of all that the place of Nazism in contemporary memory was becoming steadily normalized.

The Hitler Wave directly influenced the new allohistorical depictions of the fugitive Führer that began to appear in the 1970s. Like some of the accounts of the early 1960s, most of these tales portrayed Hitler evading justice. But they were markedly different in their representation of the ex-Führer. Rather than demonizing Hitler as monolithically evil, these accounts elevated him into a more complex historical figure who displayed a wide range of human traits – including creativity, sentimentality, kindness, weakness, and humor. This humanized and aestheticized portrait of Hitler was one indication of the encroaching normalization of the Nazi past. Another indication of this trend can be found in the motives that drove the writers of these tales to portray Hitler's evasion of justice. While they varied, one of the most common reasons underlying the depiction of the Führer's evading justice was the left-leaning desire to universalize the lessons of the Nazi past in order to comment on the persistence of injustice in the contemporary world. This trend reflected the deepening pessimism of an era that, in the late 1960s and early 1970s, was suffering through such traumatic crises as the war in Vietnam, domestic social unrest, political turmoil, and economic stagnation. Writers who instrumentally utilized the premise of Hitler's survival to criticize present-day events were clearly driven by ethical principles, but in so doing, they diverted attention away from Nazism's historical singularity.

Alternate histories depicting Hitler's evasion of justice in this period were not alone, however. By the late 1970s and early 1980s, accounts of the

Führer's being brought to justice began to reappear. These tales echoed those of the early 1950s in their conclusions, but their function was new. By re-demonizing Hitler and portraying his meeting a just end, these narratives resisted the Hitler Wave's normalization of the Führer and expressed an enduring commitment to preserving the memory of the Nazi past for its own sake. On balance, however, the relative scarcity of these narratives reflected the uphill struggle of their cause.[51]

FOREVER A FUGITIVE: THE FÜHRER ELUDES JUSTICE

The first work to express doubts about judging Hitler was famed British science fiction writer Brian W. Aldiss's 1970 short story, "Swastika!"[52] In Aldiss's tale, Hitler has unaccountably survived World War II and ended up living in Ostend, Belgium, under the assumed name of Geoffrey Bunglevester. As the story opens, Hitler is paid a visit by the narrator, a fictional version of Aldiss himself, who is attempting to secure the rights to create a musical based on his life story, entitled "Swastika!" In the dialogue that follows, Hitler emerges as an alert and multifaceted individual, "amazingly spry for his age," who takes an interest in contemporary politics, writes poetry, and muses regretfully, "I wish I'd done more with my painting."[53] The real focus of the story, however, is Hitler's upbeat view of his historical legacy. In response to the narrator's query, "Looking back... do you ever have any regrets?" Hitler insists that his legacy has been one of success. "I've not been defeated," he argues.

'What happened in 1945 is neither here nor there! It just happens to be the year when I chose to step back and let others take over the arduous role of waging war ...

... 1945 ... was the year the Americans dropped the first A-bomb and started the nuclear arms race which shows no signs of slackening yet ...

[The cold war] ... is still part of World War II, just like the Korean War and Vietnam and the Middle East hot-pot. They are all conflagrations lit from the torch I started burning in Europe ...

My war, as I pardonably regard it, is still being waged, is breaking out afresh, and may soon even return to its fatherland. What does it mean if not victory for me and my ideals?'[54]

Despite Hitler's positive assessment of his career, however, he remains bitter. When the narrator inquires "Do you ever wish things had worked out differently ... for you personally?" Hitler responds that he never got credit for engineering the chaos of the postwar world. As he tells Aldiss, "I've had emissaries come to me over the years ... Soviet and

American – and British too ... in secret ... They've all begged me to take charge of their war aims, clarify them, implement them ... Always it was me they wanted ... [But though] the imbeciles asked me to rule them [they] ... wouldn't give me full power! ... They wanted me and yet they were afraid of me!"[55] With this frustrated remark, Hitler bids the narrator farewell, agrees to his planned musical, and goes back to his apartment to spend time with his "concierge," Martin Bormann.

In writing "Swastika!", Aldiss used the theme of Hitler's survival in order to condemn the political realities of the postwar world. Aldiss's humanized portrait of Hitler directly served this end. Although Hitler in the tale is still a loathsome figure, he is no longer dangerous, as his capacity for mischief has been surpassed by new evils, such as cold-war superpower rivalry and nuclear proliferation. Aldiss's motives for focusing on these contemporary problems were varied, but they reflected his background as a British World War II veteran who became a leading member of the left-leaning "new wave" movement of science fiction in the turbulent 1960s.[56] Aldiss's leftist sentiments were clearly reflected in "Swastika!"'s critical references to the United States during the upheavals of the civil rights movement and the Vietnam War. Aldiss condemned American racism by having Hitler muse, at one point, that the extermination of the Jews was merely a "warming-up exercise" for the "extermination of the Negro races" – a plan he should have pursued more vigorously, for, as he insisted, then "the Americans would have been sympathetic and stayed out of the war."[57] Further, Aldiss diagnosed the rise of an American version of proto-fascism by having Hitler tell the narrator:

Let's be fair to the Americans. I know as well as you do that their whole continent is overrun by a rabble of Slavs and Jews and Mexicans ... but just recently a more upright no-nonsense element is coming to the fore and triumphing over the flabby democratic processes. I'm extremely encouraged to see the vigorous uncompromising attitudes of American leaders like Reagan and Governor Wallace. President Nixon also has his better side ...

Yes, a more realistic spirit is growing in America. They failed ... by hesitating to use thermonuclear weapons in Vietnam but that obscurantist attitude is altering and soon I expect to see them employing such solutions to restore discipline within their own frontiers.

The most damning evidence of America's resemblance to the Third Reich is Hitler's revelation of a secret meeting with American President Lyndon B. Johnson, in which the latter, desperate for help against "the communists abroad and the Negroes at home," nearly enlists Hitler's help in using nuclear weapons to "conquer ... the world" before suffering an attack of "namby-pamby ... yellow liberal[ism]" and backing out.[58] In the end, Aldiss used Hitler's evasion of justice as a means to condemn the world's continuing toleration of evil. The fact that the tale ends with the narrator bidding farewell to Hitler in full public view, yet without anyone noticing the ex-Führer despite his obvious gray trenchcoat with swastika armband, clearly signifies the world's indifference to Hitler's legacy. Yet, while Aldiss's story was morally grounded, it also expressed a normalized view of the Third Reich, for by comparing the crimes of the Nazi past to the deficiencies of the American present, he diminished the uniqueness of the former in order to direct attention to the latter.

The same year that Aldiss's short story appeared, a full-length novel by American writer and journalist Edwin Fadiman Jr., *Who Will Watch the Watchers?*, also portrayed Hitler's evasion of justice (see Figure 18). In this pulpy tale, a CIA employee named Jeff Whitson is sent to Paraguay on a routine mission, only to discover through a series of chance encounters that Adolf Hitler has survived World War II and is being kept alive by a vicious neo-Nazi organization known as the Sons of Liberty, which is plotting to establish a "Fourth Reich" in the near future. As in Aldiss's story, Hitler in Fadiman's novel is a comparatively humanized figure, having become completely physically debilitated by numerous health ailments and confined to a small, boarded-up room where he "eats baby food ... and moans."[59] Hitler has only a minimal presence in the novel, the plot of which does not merit extended discussion, being overly padded with unnecessary narrative twists, flashbacks to Word War II, and obligatory scenes of sex and violence. It is most significant at its conclusion, where Jeff Whitson arrives back in the United States and, encouraged by his Jewish girlfriend, Debbie Bernstein, tries to prove Hitler's survival to his skeptical superiors at the CIA. To their shock and dismay, Jeff and Debbie learn from a CIA official that the American, British, French, and Soviet governments have all been aware of Hitler's survival since 1945 and have simply abandoned the attempt to bring him to justice following the failure of early postwar attempts to get the Paraguayan government to extradite him. As the CIA official explains, "[None of the Allied leaders] felt that Hitler's life or death ... was of any prime importance. He was dead politically, Germany was dead as a world power. The information was labeled top secret, and the reports were filed away."[60] Hearing this, Debbie makes an eloquent plea for justice, condemning the Allies' tacit willingness to "keep ... [Hitler] ... alive" as "the most profoundly evil thing I have ever heard."[61] But the CIA officials believe otherwise, once more insisting on the suitability of their policies, noting, "What does it matter if a blind,

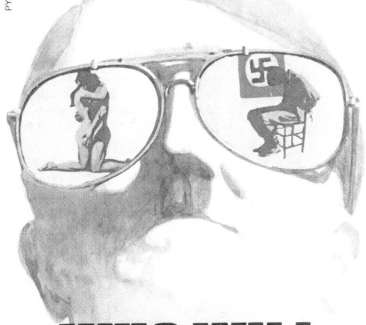

PYRAMID ★ V2499 ★ $1.25

THE SMASHING SUSPENSE OF
"A SMALL TOWN IN GERMANY"
A STRANGE TRAIL LED FROM A FLAMING
BERLIN BUNKER, TO A SOUTH AMERICAN
VILLA, TO THE SECRET CHAMBERS OF
WASHINGTON, D.C. **BY EDWIN FADIMAN JR.**

WHO WILL
WATCH THE
WATCHERS

Figure 18 Cover of Edwin Fadiman Jr.'s novel *Who Will Watch the Watchers?* (1970).

paralytic, diseased hulk who sits all day in his own ordure ... continues to exist a little longer? Do you want to rescue him from his hell, resuscitate his name, profoundly disturb the peoples of the world for no reason? ... His punishment has been long and terrible. We could not have done as well. And you want to take him out of his misery?"[62] As the novel concludes, Jeff and Debbie's crusade for justice goes unfulfilled, as they are forced to turn over the only proof of Hitler's survival – an edition of *Mein Kampf* signed by the Führer in 1946 – to the CIA for destruction.

In portraying Hitler's evasion of justice, Fadiman, like Aldiss, seems to have been eager to make a larger political point. The pivotal event in the novel is less Hitler's survival than the Allied governments' complicity in it. Fadiman was especially critical of the United States government, presenting it as engaging in various immoral schemes to protect the secret of Hitler's survival – most notably supporting the Paraguayan secret police's decision to murder one of its own security operatives (the novel's other main character, Jeff Whitson's friend, Ricardo), who has stumbled upon it. Overall, though, the main critique of the American government is leveled by Debbie, who vehemently criticizes its paternalistic style of making decisions for the citizenry without its consent. Responding to a CIA official who maintains, "We must decide these things. We watch over the people. That is our sworn responsibility," Debbie retorts:

It's wrong ... First one decision, and then another, and another, and all the time, ordinary people, what happens to them? How many decisions will you make for them? Until there are no decisions left to be made. You say it is your job to watch out for us? But who will watch the watchers? ...

You're murdering America. I don't know what we'll have in the future. Whatever it will be, if this continues – and it's getting worse – you won't have an America. Not the America I want for my children. Or for myself ... Or, for that matter, for you. I'm sorry for all of us.[63]

This concluding lament – evoking the novel's title – expressed much of Fadiman's underlying political purpose for writing the book. As in Aldiss's short story, Fadiman's goal in portraying Hitler's evasion of justice was less the particularistic one of wrestling with the Nazi legacy than the more universalistic one of criticizing what he believed was the American government's increasingly dictatorial behavior at a time of war and internal unrest. The background of the Vietnam War was likely quite important for Fadiman, who, as a World War II veteran, no doubt saw the conflict as corroding the nation's democratic traditions.[64] By universalizing Hitler into a broader symbol of evil, Fadiman, like Aldiss, expressed how contemporary political concerns were gradually normalizing the memory of the Nazi experience.

Following the works of Aldiss and Fadiman, another work that used the subject of Hitler's survival to direct attention to contemporary problems was American writer Gary Goss's 1973 novel, *Hitler's Daughter.*[65] Goss's clever novel is actually a book within a book. From the first page, the reader encounters not a novel by Goss but an unpolished, Spanish-language manuscript, entitled *Hitler's Daughter,* written by a leftwing Mexican professor of history, Reyes Tejedor, and translated into English by an American professor of comparative history and literature, J. Hillis Fillmore. Tejedor's manuscript is a semi-autobiographical work in which he explains his scholarly interest in rediscovering the "histories of forgotten men." In so doing, he reveals his discovery in the 1950s of several obscure and puzzling references to the existence of one Cynthia Hitler. While leafing through the autobiography of a long-forgotten film actress in the course of his research, Tejedor runs across what seems to be an account of Adolf Hitler's survival in the jungles of South America. According to the actress's testimony, following the crash of her private plane in the Brazilian rain forest, she encountered the ex-Führer, who, lured by her calls for help, assaulted and raped her. The account of the actress's rape, together with other obscure news clippings on Cynthia Hitler collected by Tejedor, lead him to suspect that the former dictator of the Third Reich has survived the war and produced an illegitimately conceived child.

While this hypothesis unsettles Tejedor's understanding of history, it is shaken even more dramatically by his discovery of another elusive figure linked to Cynthia Hitler, a shadowy forger of historical documents by the name of Otto Tumiel. Through a university colleague named Harold Sundowne, Tejedor learns that Tumiel has been forging new endings to classical works of literature (for example, adding 300 pages to Charles Dickens's unfinished novel, *Edwin Drood*) and slipping fraudulent journal articles into library collections worldwide. Tejedor links Tumiel to Cynthia Hitler after discovering a newspaper clipping describing him as the publicity man for her new rock group. His interest in Tumiel aroused, Tejedor is shocked to learn, in the course of conducting further research, of a listing for him in the *Encylopedia of Knowledge* describing him as an eighteenth-century Austrian scientist (1716–67) known for his alchemical experiments. Convinced that Tumiel has embarked upon a dangerous plan to rewrite history, Tejedor resolves to stop him, fearing he "might prove more barbarous than Alexander the Great, who burned the complete works of Zarathustra, some two billion verses."[66] In this effort, he prepares a full exposé, documented by microfilm evidence, and sends it to a variety of literary journals. To his shock, however, the journals call Tejedor's own sources into question and reject his exposé as factually "in error." The drama escalates still further when Tejedor learns of Professor Sundowne's disappearance and is informed of a new article by Tumiel referring to him as "the late Reyes Tejedor." As his health precipitously starts to take a turn for the worse, Tejedor fears Tumiel is able to "bend reality to his will."[67]

Before long, however, Tejedor learns the surprising truth about Cynthia Hitler and Otto Tumiel. Through connections at the CIA, Tejedor traces both Cynthia and Otto to a radical anarchist squatter's house in Buffalo, New York. It is there that he confronts Cynthia – an ordinary hippie college student – who leads him to Tumiel's vast underground storehouse of vintage printing presses which he has used over the years to fabricate his fraudulent stories. Among these stories are many pertaining directly to Cynthia's true identity. By this point, Tejedor has realized that Cynthia – as far as he knows her through "documented" newspaper and magazine articles – is entirely the product of Tumiel's imaginative forgeries. Having put various clues together, Tejedor informs Cynthia that, far from being the daughter of Hitler, she is in fact an orphan adopted by her actress mother, who invented the story of being raped by Hitler in order to revive her sagging career.[68] Tumiel, he explains to Cynthia, learned of her existence shortly after her adoption and further embellished her identity by concocting various press releases. In the process, Tejedor recognizes that the "forgotten" woman he so desperately wanted to find was the product of allohistorical manipulation.

Goss underscores this theme of deception, finally, by concluding his novel with the following tour de force ending. In the book's afterword, the translator J. Hillis Fillmore notifies the reader that, after completing the final draft of *Hitler's Daughter*, Tejedor disappeared in mysterious circumstances. Worried about his well-being, Fillmore attempts to track him down in Mexico but is shocked to discover no records of him – no birth certificates, addresses, or university affiliation – or of anyone else mentioned in the manuscript anywhere in Mexico. Has Otto Tumiel, Fillmore wonders, succeeded in erasing Tejedor from the historical record after all? The answer to this fantastic possibility is provided by an even greater surprise revealed in a publisher's note at the very end of the novel. In it, the publishers report Fillmore's own disappearance and hint that the translated manuscript was, all along, a "mock biography" written by none other than Fillmore himself.

In crafting his novel's playful narrative, Goss was influenced by the Hitler Wave, even if – as he has noted – he meant to satirize it.[69] Like many writers of the period, Goss refused to depict Hitler in traditional demonic fashion. In the few places where he described the fugitive Führer in hiding, his portrayal was highly unorthodox, even farcical. For example, Goss describes Hitler's alleged rape of Cynthia's mother as follows: "Hitler burst out of the cover, his plug dangling, all naked and hairy like a bear, and threw her down on her butt, ripped off her pants, jumped into the saddle, shrieked, jumped back to his feet, farted, and raced off into the forest pursued by a swarm of gnats."[70] Such comical descriptions of Hitler were further echoed by Goss's wholly conventional rendering of the ex-dictator's "daughter," Cynthia. Unlike certain postwar novels and films that described Hitler's children as evil chips off the old demonic block, Goss's novel represented Cynthia as a sympathetic, left-leaning woman, whose alleged family background does not prevent Tejedor from falling in love with, and eventually marrying, her.[71] Late in the novel, Tejedor replies to Cynthia's fearful query, "And my being Hitler's daughter doesn't turn you off?" by remarking, "Not at all," and thinking to himself, "Hitler no longer horrified me. He did to men what we've done to the land. We are most of us Hitlers and incestuous to boot."[72]

This passage, coming from the mouth of the left-leaning, former anarchist, Tejedor, is one of the most revealing in the novel, for it suggests the possible existence of political reasons for Goss's particular treatment of Hitler. A longtime professor of creative writing, Goss possessed leftist political allegiances, as was suggested by the publisher's description of Fillmore (clearly the author's alter ego) as "that familiar campus type, the anarchist socialist pacifist conservative eccentric."[73] Writing at a time of political ferment in the late 1960s and early 1970s, Goss believed present-day concerns deserved more attention than Hitler and the Nazi past. By describing environmental destruction as just as bad as Hitler's historical crimes, for example, Goss hoped to shift attention away from the intensifying fascination with the Third Reich's legacy towards a more fruitful focus on the problems of the present.[74] In the process, he exhibited a universalized view of Nazism's significance.

By the same token, Goss resented the fascination with the Nazi past for its role in overshadowing the many unsavory aspects of America's own past. This point clearly emerged in the novel's final passage, in which Tejedor reflects upon the reasons Cynthia has saved a motel-restaurant placemat from a previous summer hitchhiking trip in Wyoming. Printed on the placemat, Tejedor relates, was:

a photograph of Big Nose George Parroti . . . taken by Theodore Tifferau. A short biography had been printed under it. Parroti had been a murderer and a robber of the Western mail. At 7:30 p.m., March 22, 1881, he had been lynched in Rawlings, Wyoming . . . In the Rawlings museum are a number of articles made from parts of Parroti's tanned skin: razor strops, a coin purse, a medical instrument bag, and a pair of lady's shoes. One can still find them on display.

Hence this book and my hope that every school child in America learns the name of George Parroti and that presidents are elected in his memory to make the most powerful state the world has ever known humble, humane, and free from canting self-righteousness, which seems unlikely.[75]

By citing the real historical atrocities committed against George Parroti in American history (especially the tanning of his skin), Goss drew a parallel to the atrocities committed in Nazi concentration camps, thereby further highlighting the larger universalistic point that *all* human beings possessed the potential for Hitlerian violence. Although believing the Nazi genocide to be horrible, Goss did not believe it to be unique, and he was equally, if not more, concerned with other, less-noticed genocides, whether past or present.[76] Dismayed over the lack of attention to other injustices, Goss saw little reason to bring Hitler to justice in his own tale. For this reason, Tejedor's descriptive comment, "Hitler no longer horrified me," can be read as a *prescriptive* recommendation to diminish public attention towards the Nazi era. One of Tejedor's final remarks to Cynthia – "Each is forgotten in turn . . . Even Hitler someday" – suggested a degree of support for the cause of amnesia itself.[77]

Significantly, Goss's skeptical attitude towards remembrance was echoed by the period's most pessimistic account of Hitler's survival, British writer and literary critic George Steiner's 1981 novel, *The Portage to San Cristóbal of A.H.* (see Figure 19).[78] Although it resists simple explication, Steiner's novel essentially focuses upon the struggles of a team of Israeli Nazi-hunters to capture Hitler and bring him back to Israel to stand trial for his crimes. As the novel opens, the searchers have penetrated deep into the Brazilian rain forest where Hitler is rumored to be living. After much strenuous effort, they eventually discover Hitler eking out a primitive existence in a small hut and undertake the grueling process of transporting him back to civilization. The trek is an arduous one. Not only do the searchers face physical hardships, they also face the need to maintain the secrecy of their accomplishment and avoid the prying eyes of the world, which threaten to turn the event into a media circus. As the British, French, Germans, Russians, and Americans close in on their elusive quarry, the Israeli team finally decides to bow to the mounting pressure and conducts a hastily prepared trial in the middle of the jungle in which Hitler takes the stand in his own defense.

Figure 19 Cover of George Steiner's 1981 novel *The Portage to San Cristóbal of A.H.*

At this climactic point in the novel, Steiner depicts the ex-Führer as an obstinate and unrepentant, but still eloquent, figure. In a long monologue, Hitler defends himself by accusing the Jews of the same crimes with which he is charged. The Nazi idea of the master race, he claims, was merely "a parody ... a hungry imitation" of the Biblical notion of the Jews being the "chosen people."[79] The Jews' invention of monotheism, Christianity, and Marxism, he continues, was a worse punishment than anything that happened in "our camps," for it imposed upon man the "enslavement" of a "bad conscience."[80] His own alleged crimes, Hitler asserts, moreover, pale in comparison with the many other evil deeds of the century. As he declares:

I was not the worst. Far from it. How many wretched little men of the forests did your Belgian friends murder outright or leave to starvation ... when they raped the Congo? ... Some *twenty* million ... What was Rotterdam or Coventry compared with Dresden and Hiroshima? ... Did I invent the camps? Ask the Boers. I was a man of a murderous time, but a small man compared with ... Stalin, [who] slaughtered *thirty* million ... In a world that has tortured political prisoners and poured napalm on naked villagers, that has stripped the earth of plant and animal. That ... continues to do [these things] ... without my help and long after I ... was thought to have been extinct.[81]

Finally, Hitler asserts that he should be declared the "true Messiah" for having enabled the creation of the State of Israel and providing the Jews "with the courage of injustice ... [to] drive the Arab out of his home."[82] In resting his impassioned defense, Hitler proves himself once again to be the dangerous demagogue he always was.

Significantly, *The Portage to San Cristóbal of A.H.* portrays Hitler's self-defense as highly convincing. The ex-dictator is given the last word in the novel, for immediately after he rests his defense, the arrival of helicopters prevents any rebuttal from the prosecution. Steiner thereby effectively grants Hitler a final victory. So rhetorically powerful is his self-defense that it rings true at a pre-linguistic, emotional, level. This response is suggested by the exclamation of an Indian native present at the trial, a man named Teku, who, despite not speaking Hitler's language, is so viscerally moved by his words that he begins to exclaim "Proved!" before being drowned out by the approaching helicopters. By declaring Hitler the de facto victor, Steiner suggested that humanity's attempt to bring Hitler to justice is destined to fail.

In making this point, Steiner also sounded a cautionary note about the perils of memory. This theme, which loomed large in much of the writer's other work, is pervasive in *The Passage to San Cristóbal of A.H.*[83]

For Steiner, the act of unearthing Hitler from his jungle refuge is far more dangerous than allowing him to survive hidden away and forgotten. This point is best illustrated by the heavy toll that the quest for Hitler takes on the members of the Israeli search party. Over the course of the difficult journey, all the members of the Israeli team suffer physical ailments in the jungle. Some even die. In describing the searchers' sufferings, Steiner underscored the high costs of remembrance. The search for Hitler is driven by the memory of his victims, the Jews, who are unable to forget the wrongs done to them and crave justice. Epitomizing this drive is the figure of Emmanuel Lieber, the search party's commander in Israel, who remains in radio contact with the group throughout its mission. Lieber is personally consumed by a fanatical hatred of Hitler, a fact suggested by the ironic name given him by Steiner (*Emmanuel* comes from the Hebrew term for "God is with us," while *Lieber* contains the German root for "love"). Yet while Lieber hates Hitler, he recognizes that the search-party members, belonging to the younger generation of Israelis born after the Holocaust, lack the same emotional feelings rooted in the traumatic past. Aware that the searchers will likely discover a debilitated, elderly man, Lieber admonishes them to look past his "human mask," to remember his crimes, and to beware of his enduring demonic powers. Informed of the searchers' success, Lieber instructs them to handle their quarry like the snake in the Garden of Eden, declaring:

You must not let him speak ... Gag him if necessary ... If he is allowed speech he will trick you and escape ... You will hear the crack of age in his voice. He is old ... Let him speak to you and you will think of him as a man. With sores on his skin and need in his bowels, sweating and hungering like yourselves, short of sleep ... Do not listen to his sleep ... If you think of him as a man ... you will grow uncertain ... You will think him a man and no longer believe what he did.[84]

Despite Lieber's encouragement, however, certain members of the search party begin to recognize the paradoxical consequences of memory. One of these consequences, Steiner seems to suggest, is that the obsessive search for Hitler actually serves Hitler's own aims. As one Israeli searcher named Gideon provocatively exclaims in a fever-induced tirade, "Without Lieber there would be no Hitler," adding, "To be a Jew is to keep Hitler alive."[85] Hitler's survival, in a sense, is dependent upon his persistence in Jewish memory. A better strategy, Steiner seems to say, is to turn one's back on the past. Only by forgetting Hitler can his evil truly be consigned to oblivion. To dwell on the past enables Hitler to have his final revenge on the Jews by keeping them from more productive tasks. As another searcher, Simeon, declares in the midst of the jungle, "So what? Even if he is alive. Why drag the aged swine out of this stretch of hell? Who cares, now, thirty years after, or is it more? We're doing his bidding here, emptying our lives in this stinking jungle when we could be building ... and forgetting."[86] In the end, as the quest to bring Hitler to justice only leads to suffering, Steiner, like Goss, appeared to recommend a healthy dose of amnesia.

It is hard to tell whether or not Steiner intended this conclusion to be read programmatically, especially since he claimed in a 1982 interview that his book was "not a sermon."[87] His powerful portrayal of Hitler's triumph at the novel's end, however, likely stemmed – as many observers noted at the time – from his own fascination with the dictator's dynamic personality at the time of the Hitler Wave.[88] Steiner, of course, did not seek to normalize Hitler and, in fact, stressed his enduring capacity for evil. But by failing to bring Hitler to justice for his crimes – indeed, by leaving the impression that he had successfully exonerated himself – Steiner made Hitler's evil less than absolute. In all likelihood, this decision was part of a broader objective of universalizing Hitler's significance. Although *The Portage to San Cristóbal of A.H.* would be interpreted by most readers as a novel about the Holocaust, Steiner openly declared in the 1982 interview that "the novel is also about Cambodia, and Vietnam, El Salvador and Burundi, and so on."[89] Like Aldiss and Goss, then, Steiner was less concerned with Nazism as a specific historical phenomenon than with the continued existence of other sources of evil in the contemporary world. It was most likely for this reason that Steiner universalized the historical significance of Hitler's crimes and ultimately declined to bring him to justice. For just as insisting upon the uniqueness of the Holocaust would shift attention away from other contemporary atrocities, finding Hitler guilty of his crimes would provide a false sense of security that absolute evil had been banished for good.[90]

If the tales of Aldiss, Fadiman, Goss, and Steiner normalized Hitler by universalizing him into a symbol of contemporary evil, other narratives did so by using diverse literary and visual means to transform him into a relatively average individual seemingly indistinct from other human beings. One example of this burgeoning pattern of aestheticization appeared in 1971 with the publication of a short story by the well-known French writer Pierre Boulle entitled "His Last Battle."[91] In Boulle's tale, Hitler has fled Berlin for the mountains of Peru, where he enjoys a happy, peaceful life together with Eva Braun and an adopted "half-caste" boy named Pedro. In his Edenic mountain retreat, Hitler (who lives under the assumed name of "Herr Wallj") spends most of his time outdoors,

gardening, painting, and tending his beehives. Like other retired gentlemen, he relishes the good things in life. Indeed, in his twilight years, he has
developed impressive culinary skills, which he has used to produce what he
proudly describes as "the finest ham in the country," "delicious pastries,"
and even his own wine.[92] Only when visited one day by Martin Bormann
(who also has somehow escaped Berlin) does he confess to having recently
developed heart trouble, which he believes is related to "importunate,
nauseating memories" of the Jews.[93] Bormann, surprised, takes Hitler's
candidness as a sign of contrition and of his readiness to do penance for his
crimes and perhaps even "give himself up to the law."[94] So inspired is
Bormann by his Führer's example that he decides to give in to his own
recurring nightmares (he constantly hears the refrain in his ears "Six
million Jews, six million Jews ...") by resolving, "I will give myself up
to justice."[95] The next morning, after an extremely fitful sleep, Hitler
reports to Bormann that he will now be able to "die at peace with myself,"
concluding, "It took me a long time to make my decision, but it is final. I
have driven all hatred out of my heart ... The Jews, Bormann, the Jews –
I have forgiven them."[96] With this surprise ending, Boulle undermines the
broader portrait of Hitler developed over the course of the tale. The same
humanized Hitler who claims he has "built a new soul" in exile reveals
himself to be as unrepentant as ever for his crimes. Indeed, the reader is left
to conclude that he will be able to go laughing into his grave, thoroughly
content with his successful evasion of justice.

The short story's surprise ending notwithstanding, Boulle's tale left as its
dominant impression a distinctly normalized portrayal of Hitler as a
human being. The numerous pages chronicling the hum-drum reality of
the Führer's daily routine reflected the Hitler Wave's deeper fascination
with the dictator's personal life. Boulle's aestheticization of Hitler, however, was hardly an end in itself but a method of pursuing a larger goal – not
a political one, as in the tales of Aldiss, Fadiman, Goss, and Steiner, but a
psychological one. In all likelihood, "His Last Battle" expressed Boulle's
deeper desire to explore what one of his biographers has described as the
dominant theme in his literary work – namely, "the human capacity for
self-delusion."[97] Boulle's interest in this theme reflected his own life
experiences, especially his service in the French army during World War II.
Having been a prisoner of war in French Indochina from 1942–44, Boulle
had firsthand experience of absurd and futile situations (which, as a writer,
he addressed in such famous works as *The Bridge over the River Kwai* and
Planet of the Apes). In "His Last Battle," Boulle explored the human
capacity for self-delusion by raising the reader's hopes that Hitler was

prepared to repent and submit to justice, only to dash them in the end. In offering this conclusion, however, Boulle revealed that he was less interested in Nazism as a topic in and of itself than in broader patterns of human psychology.

If Boulle broke new ground in humanizing Hitler, another narrative that appeared shortly thereafter went even further. In March 1972, the American humor magazine *National Lampoon* published a satirical photoessay by its editor, Canadian writer Michel Choquette, entitled "Stranger in Paradise." The essay's theme is symbolically presented on the magazine's front cover – a photograph of a scowling Hitler (played by Hitler impersonator Billy Frick) sitting in a wicker chair holding a tropical drink with a parrot on his shoulder beneath the headline "Escape!"[98] After this clever double-reference to vacation getaways and Hitler's postwar survival, the actual essay, "Stranger in Paradise," opens with a photograph of a tropical sunset and the lines, "All of us dream of a return to paradise . . . But few of us are fortunate to find [it] . . . Here is one man who has." From this point on, Choquette's piece offers an extremely banal description of Hitler's daily life in exile, supplemented by numerous photographs. The "modern-day Robinson Crusoe," as the article calls the Führer, lives a life of "simple pleasures," such as taking "a refreshing dip in the ocean each day" and "cultivating his garden" in the company of his "native companion . . . Freitag." Hitler lives simply as a "gentle recluse," a man who is at home with the local natives, to whom he "delights in recounting tales of his faraway homeland." To be sure, Hitler continues to display subtle signs of his old ways, being "a stickler for neatness" and an opponent of "indolence." But there are no signs of the Führer's evil personality. "The fervent idealism of youth has mellowed with the passing years," the article concludes. "He has stopped trying to save the world. Occasionally he looks up at the migratory birds flying overhead. But he finds in himself no longing to leave with them . . . [This] stranger in paradise is, by now, very much at home."[99]

"Stranger in Paradise" was significant for being the first tale to portray Hitler's evasion of justice strictly for laughs. For the most part, Choquette's piece achieved its degree of humor through the jarring contrast between its text and images. From the text alone, one would have no idea that the man featured in the photographs is in fact Hitler; nowhere, indeed, is Hitler even mentioned by name (not even in the photo credit).[100] The photographs, by contrast, offer obvious images of the Führer, depicting him as engaged in such incongruous activities as skinny dipping and clearing brush. The resulting effect was an absurd one and admittedly humorous.

But what was most notable about Choquette's narrative technique was its representation of Hitler from an entirely value-neutral perspective. By failing to explicitly identify Hitler in the text as the ex-Führer of Nazi Germany, Choquette made it the responsibility of the readers themselves to provide the essay with the intended degree of irony. Only readers aware of Hitler's real historical crimes, after all, would catch the discordant note of his living an exotic life of leisure; those ignorant of Hitler's identity would miss the point of the piece entirely.

Choquette's photoessay was distinguished by its rejection of authorial moralism. Whereas Boulle's tale concluded by reminding readers of Hitler's enduring evil, Choquette provided no such reminder and produced the most humanized image of Hitler to date. Choquette, of course, was hardly interested in rehabilitating Hitler and had no political motives in producing the photoessay. Rather, he was largely moved by aesthetic and satirical concerns. A longtime photographer, he has noted that it "was really the visual possibilities ... offered" by photographing Hitler impersonator Billy Frick in the incongruous setting of a tropical beach – together with his desire to satirize the tabloid notion that "Hitler is still alive and living in South America" – that were pivotal in leading him to produce it.[101] Yet, no matter how benign and lighthearted his intentions, his aestheticization of Hitler, in its own way, both reflected and contributed to the waning moralistic perspective towards the Third Reich.

Several years later, Choquette's tale was itself surpassed by the most normalized of all the decade's narratives – American writer Richard Grayson's 1979 short story "With Hitler in New York."[102] Set in an indeterminate year, Grayson's work recounts an unnamed narrator's several days of socializing, partying, and walking the streets of New York with Adolf Hitler. The Hitler described by the narrator is a contemporary Everyman, indistinguishable from others of his generation. A tall, dark, and handsome individual who wears a leather jacket, Hitler is quick-witted, gregarious, and popular. Nothing of much importance happens in the story, which is more a loose chronicle of banal events than a sustained plot. Its most intriguing aspect, indeed, is its vagueness regarding whether the Hitler of the story is in fact the "real" Hitler or simply another man coincidentally possessing the same name. By the end of the tale, it is clear that the man in question is, indeed, the (allo)historical Hitler. The hostile reactions towards him by other characters in the story show that he continues to suffer from a sullied reputation due to unspecified historical misdeeds. The mother of Hitler's girlfriend, Ellen, dislikes him and will not speak to him; a patron in a coffee house "recognizes Hitler, [but] everything is too mellow for him to make a scene."[103] Yet Hitler's negative image is complicated by the fact that his girlfriend is Jewish and he enjoys strolling around Brighton Beach listening to elderly Jews sing old Yiddish folk songs. The historical significance of this allohistorical Hitler remains ambiguous. The narrator's drunken observation at a party that Hitler deserves to win the Nobel Peace prize is as cryptic as his concluding question to him whether he "ever feels bitter." Hitler's laconic response – that he feels "useless" – suggests some kind of a grand past that has given way to a banal present, but nothing more.[104]

Grayson's portrayal of Hitler's survival in an alternate New York City, like Choquette's, was notable for its complete abandonment of a morally grounded narrative framework. Unlike the tales of Aldiss, Steiner, and Boulle, which still depicted him as unrepentant for his crimes, Grayson's story left unspecified which historical misdeeds he may have committed – or whether he had committed any at all. Without a clear criminal background to be held accountable for, Grayson's Führer is no fugitive but merely another human being who blends into the crowd in New York City. And yet it would be a mistake to see Grayson's humanization of Hitler as an act of rehabilitation. Rather, Grayson's tale imagines an alternate world that has largely forgiven Hitler for his crimes and forgotten them. Such a world – in which the story's narrator can ignore his grandfather's own death in order to get stoned with Hitler and can muse, "I wonder if I am beginning to fall in love with him" – is a callous, unfeeling one, in which historical consciousness has either atrophied completely or become irrelevant to most human beings.[105] In short, it is a nightmarish world of total amnesia. In all probability, this is the primary point Grayson was looking to make. Evidence for this reading is provided at the very end of his autobiographical introduction to *With Hitler in New York* (which immediately precedes the short story by the same name), where he describes his adolescent withdrawal from his family and concludes "I just lay in my bed trying to sleep. When I slept I had nightmares."[106] Given this de facto preface to the short story, "With Hitler in New York," Grayson's account of a world in which Hitler hardly differed from anyone else was meant to be seen as a bad dream.

In offering this conclusion, Grayson's story can be taken as a complex response to the Hitler Wave. Like Boulle and Choquette, Grayson was strongly influenced by the Hitler Wave's de-demonization of the Führer and drafted the most humanized portrait of him yet to appear in postwar alternate history. Yet Grayson was also concerned about, and tried to counteract, the Hitler Wave's progressive normalization of the deceased dictator.[107] As a writer of Jewish background who grew up around Holocaust survivors in Brooklyn, Grayson was concerned by the increasing fascination with Hitler and aimed to show, in *reductio ad absurdum* fashion, its dangerous endpoint – a Hitler who was regarded as no different from any other human being.[108] The author's decision not to bring Hitler to justice in "With Hitler in New York," then, was animated by different aims from those that shaped the tales of Aldiss, Goss, Steiner, Boulle, and Choquette. For while these narratives were less overtly committed to the need to remember the Nazi past for its own sake, Grayson's story was intended as a plea not to forget its historically specific horrors. Still, in effect, "With Hitler in New York" did not differ substantially from these other tales insofar as it, too, dramatically challenged the limits of representing Hitler and offered a radically altered portrait of him as a "regular guy."

Taken together, the tales of Aldiss, Fadiman, Goss, Steiner, Boulle, Choquette, and Grayson all reflected the broader phenomenon of normalization. This was most obvious in their de-demonization and attendant humanization of Hitler as a character. The fact that, in nearly all of the narratives, Hitler's enduring capacity for evil was overshadowed by his average human traits reflected an increasing willingness, in the wake of the Hitler Wave, to view the Führer in non-judgmental terms. The motives underlying many of these narratives also reflected an increasingly normalized view of the Nazi past. These writers showed Hitler evading justice in order to offer universal conclusions about the human condition – most of them pointing to the continued existence of contemporary political crises. For all of their moral emphasis on left-liberal politics, however, the effect of their tales was to divert popular attention from Nazism as a specific historical phenomenon.

THE CONTINUING QUEST FOR JUSTICE: HITLER ON TRIAL

At the same time that many alternate histories in the 1970s permitted Hitler to elude the judgment of humanity, others held him accountable for his crimes. The best example of this enduring trend appeared in 1978 with Canadian writer Philippe van Rjndt's novel *The Trial of Adolf Hitler*.[109] This work traces the course of the Führer's life after his failed suicide attempt in the Berlin Führerbunker in the spring of 1945. Having failed to kill himself by pistol and poison, Hitler flees in the last days of the war to the Bavarian village of Emmaus under the name of a van driver named Werner Busse – a man whom Hitler's SS bodyguard, Kronhausen, has murdered in the process of aiding the Führer's escape. After Kronhausen is

fortuitously killed by the villagers in a fit of anti-SS anger, Hitler proceeds
to blend into the local population, who accept him as a displaced war
refugee. Hitler remains in Emmaus for the next twenty-five years working –
ironically enough for a life-long anti-Semite – as a money-lender who
finances his loans to the local citizenry with smuggled gold bars which he
has deposited in a Swiss bank. Through this activity, Busse becomes a
much-admired pillar of the community and is credited with supporting its
postwar recovery. In an ironic inversion of the village's symbolic name
(Emmaus is the place in the New Testament where several disciples of Jesus
initially fail to recognize him after his resurrection), Hitler is, for all intents
and purposes, its unrecognized messiah.

For all the good and generous acts he performs, however, Busse betrays
his surname (meaning "repentance" in German) by failing to contritely
turn his back on his former career as the leader of Nazi Germany. Indeed,
he gradually becomes re-intoxicated by his influential role as a village leader
and eventually resolves to re-ignite the dormant fires of German nationalism. Busse provocatively pursues his mission of resurrecting National
Socialism by deliberately re-emerging from hiding. In the fateful year
1970, he reveals his true identity as Hitler to Germany's leading war crimes
prosecutor, Hans Kleeman, and demands to be put on trial. In explaining
his reasons for resurfacing, Hitler declares, "For twenty-five years my name
has been blasphemed . . . [A]ll manner of lies have been propagated about
me. I am no longer in the best of health and fear that there isn't much time
left to me. Therefore I wish to reveal myself and be given the chance to
prove my innocence before my death."[110] In short, Hitler's demand for a
trial is part of a larger attempt to perpetuate his legacy.

From this point on, the novel explores the important question of whether
placing Hitler on trial can possibly bring justice. Van Rjndt's discussion of
this complicated issue is appropriately nuanced. The chief agent of justice,
prosecutor Kleeman, believes that trying Hitler before an international
tribunal will serve a didactic purpose for the German people and the world
at large. Yet his colleague, Dieter Wolff, a jurist in the German Federal
Constitutional Court, objects that a trial may well backfire, insisting:

You know better than to think that one more act of castigation will help us. The
Germans are inured to it. They have had too much of the past shoved into their
mouths for too long. By giving them Hitler you will be giving them a demon they
would like to believe has been exorcised. But if they see he is not, they will again
plunge into their pathetic act of breast-beating, navel examining and pathos. They
will resent having Hitler thrust upon them like that. And this resentment could
well cause them to embrace him again.[111]

Wolff's reservations resonate with Kleeman, for they echo Hitler's own words to him in his office: "A new spirit is passing over this age. We Germans have had enough of groveling, of having the past spat back at our faces."[112] Nevertheless, despite his worries about the trial, Kleeman finds support for his position among other prospective members of the tribunal. The Soviet jurist Ivan Morozov affirms the importance of confronting the past by declaring, "Only by bringing this evil forth can we banish it forever."[113] Moreover, American prosecutor Thomas Worthington's admission "that no one will really care" about the trial in the United States reinforces Kleeman's belief in the need to push forward.[114]

As *The Trial of Adolf Hitler* unfolds, however, the perils of memory are clearly revealed. Following Hitler's reappearance on the world stage, the reluctance of the Germans to face their Nazi past and their continued susceptibility to Hitler's message become glaringly apparent. The announcement of Hitler's surrender unleashes a wave of rightwing activism in Germany. Contributions to the Führer's legal defense fund pour in from the citizens of Emmaus, Wehrmacht veterans, and others, while mobs of his supporters cheer his arrival at Munich's Palace of Justice for his official indictment. Behind the scenes, meanwhile, a cabal of media barons, industrialists, and politicians – all secret National Socialists – collaborate with Hitler's attorney, Helmut Toller, in crafting Hitler's defense. Toller is an aspiring rightwinger himself, convinced that if "Hitler is vindicated ... so much of our past history will have to be rewritten ... and ... [the] years of shame can be put behind us."[115] To Toller's shock, however, the cabal informs him that he must be prepared to "engineer the martyrdom of the Führer" by ensuring a guilty verdict. According to the architects of the incipient Fourth Reich, the Nazi movement has outgrown its creator and can only take root in Germany once more if it takes advantage of the younger generation's growing "wonder and curiosity" about National Socialism by adapting itself to new postwar conditions.[116] Hitler "must die," Toller is instructed, "yet he must do so a hero."[117]

As the trial unfolds, the picture of Hitler that emerges is a contradictory one. Images of the demonic Hitler and the human Hitler clash repeatedly. Throughout the proceedings, the Führer is unrepentant about his criminal misdeeds. After prosecutor Kleeman recounts his numerous crimes against the Jews, Hitler responds, "How sick your preaching makes me! ... If Jews were such a precious commodity, why didn't anyone take them from me? Answer that! I did not want Jews in Germany ... but which country opened its arms to them? Not one!"[118] The Führer furthermore attempts to relativize the Nazis' crimes, arguing, "You know it was not the Germans who invented the modern-day concentration camps but the British in the Boer War; it was not the Germans but the Russians ... who brought a new meaning to the word 'genocide' in our age."[119] Outside of the trial, too, Hitler's penchant for stirring up trouble is on full display, as is evidenced by the eruption of street violence on his behalf in Germany and the appearance of offers of asylum for him in Latin America. As his defense attorney Toller realizes, Hitler, although over eighty years of age, still possesses the abilities of "a tribal sorcerer of the Dark Ages ... [who] had only to put his hand here and pestilence would erupt; lay his eyes there, and blood would flow."[120] Yet, while Hitler's demonic powers clearly emerge in the course of the trial, so too does his humanity. Hitler's lawyer, Toller, reminds the jury that Hitler is "a human being of flesh and blood" who, after 1945, lived an honorable life for twenty-five years.[121] One defense witness, a citizen of Emmaus and a longtime acquaintance of Hitler, testifies, "In Emmaus, he is regarded as a human being of rare courage and compassion. I cannot believe that in 1945 all these qualities were suddenly bestowed upon him; they must have been there before ... Too much has been made of Adolf Hitler as a symbol; no one has spoken for the man."[122] As Toller sums up his case, "Whatever Adolf Hitler's oversights may have been in the war years, they pale before his achievements of the last quarter century."[123]

The course of the trial finally illustrates the ambiguities of justice. In deliberating on Hitler's fate, the four tribunal members argue about the inadequacy of finding the Führer guilty and sentencing him to death. The American jurist Thomas Worthington thus asserts, "It is ironic that the most severe penalty ... death ... is still not enough to expiate ... the enormity of the crime committed ... I desire something more. I want our sentence to reflect the fact that we have come to terms with this man; that we understand his nature, what he represents."[124] In response, another jurist, Sir Adrian Potter, responds, "It is my belief that no one ... can even begin to approach, in justice, the feat Hitler created through crime ... The lesson ... is found not in the nature of the sentence, but in the fact that this trial ever took place ... *The fact that justice endures* as a living entity in the minds of men ... is our victory."[125] In the end, a degree of justice, however imperfect, is achieved as Hitler is found guilty of the charges leveled against him and is executed by an Israeli paratrooper at a secret island location in the Indian Ocean. Up until the bitter end, Hitler is unrepentant, berating his executioner with antisemitic slurs and vowing, "I shall have vengeance for this!"[126] Meanwhile, halfway around the world, his words resonate chillingly, as the neo-Nazi cabal, together with Helmut

Toller, drink a champagne toast to their martyr – "The Führer is dead; long live the Führer!" – and vow to revive the movement under the leadership of Hitler's personally designated heir, Toller himself.[127]

Despite this ominous conclusion, *The Trial of Adolf Hitler* still affirmed the virtues of striving for justice by directly confronting the past. Even though van Rjndt implied that the survival, discovery, and trial of the dictator could lead history to take a turn for the worse, he ultimately asserted its legitimacy. It is difficult to know what van Rjndt's precise aims were in arriving at this conclusion, given his notorious penchant for privacy and his apparent retirement from writing after a productive early career.[128] But his personal background as a child of Ukrainian immigrant parents (he was born in 1950) leaves open the possibility that he inherited suspicions of the Germans that ended up being expressed in his novel.[129] The book's suggestion that Nazi sentiment lay dormant within postwar West Germany may have reflected personal fears of neo-Nazism and suspicions about the depth of the nation's commitment to democracy. It is possible, finally, that van Rjndt's affirmation of the need to remember the criminal legacy of Nazism was intended as a corrective to the normalizing tendencies of the Hitler Wave. Whatever his intentions may have been, *The Trial of Adolf Hitler* clearly affirmed the virtues of remembrance as the only true path to justice.

A similar conclusion was offered by another novel written around the same time, American writer James Marino's 1983 cloak-and-dagger thriller *The Asgard Solution*.[130] Set in 1973, Marino's novel opens with the aging Israeli Holocaust survivor and Nazi hunter, Viktor Trauberg, attempting to uncover the reasons for the murder of his cousin, Jakob, by fanatical PLO terrorists. The key to his investigation is an unfinished book manuscript on fugitive Nazi war criminals left by Jakob (also a Holocaust survivor and Nazi hunter), as well as cryptic handwritten notes alluding to the possible discovery of Martin Bormann and his Latin American hideaway known as "Asgard." As Viktor tries to decipher the particularities of Jakob's coded message, brutal assassination attempts against him and his family by various Arab and Nazi operatives convince him of the urgency of his task. Through sheer determination, Viktor makes great strides towards solving the puzzle, but he ultimately comes up empty. Only once he is kidnapped and taken to Buenos Aires is he presented face to face with the awful truth: Hitler himself has survived World War II and escaped to Argentina. Worse still, the ex-Führer is behind a reckless plan (Operation Thorstrike) to supply Yasir Arafat with nuclear weapons to aid the Palestinians against Israel during the 1973 Yom Kippur war. Predictably enough, however, Viktor possesses the wily skills necessary both to outwit Hitler and save the world from nuclear warfare. Left alone in his holding cell, he fashions a bludgeon out of Jakob's manuscript and uses it to knock out his Nazi guard as well as Hitler himself. Viktor then strangles the unconscious Führer, thereby preventing a conflagration in the Middle East.

Although it did so in much more pulpy fashion, *The Asgard Solution* echoed *The Trial of Adolf Hitler* in its overall affirmation of the virtues of memory and the possibility of justice. The novel's support for these values is demonstrated by Viktor's own personal reconversion to the cause of remembrance. Initially, Viktor is portrayed as someone exhausted from his links to the Nazi past. Having retired from his job at Yad Vashem, he has arrived at the conclusion that "enough was enough ... it was time to forget."[131] Yet the death of his cousin – an original member of Al Tishkakh ("We Will Never Forget"), an organization committed to bringing Nazi war criminals to justice – renews his faded sense of mission. From this point on, Viktor works tirelessly to discover the truth about the past in order to prevent present-day disaster. Only through this herculean commitment to memory is he able to put himself in the position of securing justice.

This opportunity arises when his powers of deduction allow him to come face to face with Hitler himself. At this climactic point in the novel, Marino, like van Rjndt before him, underscored the urgency of justice by portraying the aged Führer as the enduring epitome of evil. Although the feeble, graying dictator was "no bodily threat to anyone," his eyes – "storming with half-crazed vindications, brooding with poisons"– revealed his continuing commitment to criminality.[132] As long as Hitler was "still alive, still functioning, [he was] still capable of planning and implementing a murderous scheme like Thorstrike."[133] It is this fact, finally, that transforms Viktor's vigilante-style murder of Hitler into a socially acceptable form of rough justice:

Viktor ... stood in front of Hitler. He had meant to simply overpower him ... but he was unable to control himself. As he looked down into those yellowish fearful eyes, he saw too much.

He saw Jakob [murdered] on the bus ... He saw Thorstrike and nuclear devastation.

Maybe, if he had shut his eyes, he could have held back ...

He shuddered. He lost control. His fingers went deep into the flesh, pressed deep into Hitler's neck so that he could feel the neckbones.

'Die, you monster! Die!'

One feeble kick, and it was over. Asgard was done.[134]

Although unimaginatively written, this scene articulated the fantasy of holding Hitler responsible for his crimes. Not only does it depict Hitler's death as preventing a historical calamity (nuclear war in the Middle East) but it provides a cathartic release for the long-suffering victims of Nazi aggression. In the last line of the book, Viktor's recitation of the Jewish prayer for the dead, or Kaddish, for his cousin Jakob, indicates that only the exorcism of Hitler's ghost can bring relief to those suffering from the burdens of memory.

The final work to express the yearning for justice and remembrance was American writer Joseph Heywood's 1987 novel, *The Berkut.*[135] Like the works of van Rjndt and Marino, Heywood's novel featured Hitler surviving World War II and being spirited away by fanatical Nazis to a postwar refuge – this time, a chilly cave in the Harz mountains, which serves as a temporary waystation to his ultimate destination of Latin America. In a new twist, however, *The Berkut* featured the hunt for Hitler being led by the Soviets. Leading the pursuit is a team of Russian special agents headed by the novel's protagonist, Vasily Petrov, a man whom Stalin has given the nickname "the Berkut," a term which denotes a fierce Russian wolf-hunting eagle. In the novel, Stalin is depicted as thirsting for revenge against Hitler for the latter's duplicity in invading the Soviet Union. Hitler, meanwhile, is portrayed in predictably demonic terms as an unrepentant villain who continues to rail against the Jews and exhibit delusions of grandeur.[136] For the most part, the novel describes Hitler's escape from Berlin and the extended manhunt that climaxes with his capture by the Russians on a Greek-owned merchant ship outside the port of Genoa. In potboiler fashion, the novel is also saturated with numerous gratuitous acts of sex and violence involving sadistic SS-men and voluptuous Valkyries. But the novel's most significant feature becomes visible with its lurid ending. Whereas van Rjndt and Marino brought Hitler to justice through relatively conventional (if violent) means, Heywood imagined a particularly fiendish denouement. The novel's last chapter is set in the year 1953 and describes Petrov receiving a request from a dying Stalin to carry out a final order. At this point, Petrov enters the basement of the Kremlin, goes down a long corridor to an elevator that brings him far down into the earth to a steel door, which opens into a white tiled room. In it:

suspended from the ceiling, was a cage of stainless steel bars [containing] . . . a living thing that looked vaguely human . . . There was not enough room for it either to stand or to lie down. Stalin had designed the cage and personally oversaw its construction . . . Over the years it had become increasingly difficult to keep the beast alive. Sores had formed on its legs and induced gangrene causing an amputation first of the left leg ... and later of the right leg ... Technically the beast lived, but it was no longer a man.[137]

The man, of course, is Hitler, and after several pages of nauseating prose describing his degraded state of existence, Heywood finishes him off by having Petrov strangle the ex-Führer so that Stalin can die in peace, knowing he outlived his longtime rival.

In writing the novel, Heywood was mostly driven by a personal fascination with the survival myth and the many possibilities it offered as a literary premise.[138] But he was driven by a clear moral agenda as well. By allowing the Soviets to be the ones who capture Hitler and bring him to justice, Heywood showed a substantial degree of sympathy for their real historical suffering at the hands of the Nazis. It is no coincidence that the lone American character in the novel, upon learning that the Soviets have captured Hitler, exclaims, "[It's] poetic justice. Of all of us, [the Soviets] ... had the best reasons for wanting him. For us it's more a matter of principle ... For the Russians it's necessity; they want their vengeance."[139] Heywood has noted that making the Soviets into the novel's main heroes was mostly intended to lend its plot greater plausibility, but his decision to do so also can be seen as symbolically reflecting the waning of cold-war tensions between the United States and the USSR.[140] In a sense, *The Berkut*'s sympathetic representation of the Soviet hunt for Hitler revealed how the shared fantasy of bringing Hitler to justice could help bridge longstanding superpower antagonisms.

RECEPTION

However much the allohistorical accounts of the 1970s and 1980s demonstrated a growing tendency to normalize the Nazi past, their mixed reception revealed an enduring desire to view it from a moralistic perspective. Many of the tales portraying Hitler's evasion of justice received positive reviews. Pierre Boulle's work, for instance, was praised in the *New Yorker* as "witty and amusing."[141] Richard Grayson's *With Hitler in New York* received positive marks from the *Los Angeles Times*, which hailed the writer as possessing a "special ... gift for dreaming up outrageous premises."[142] Gary Goss's novel, *Hitler's Daughter*, was commended in the *New York Times* as a "funny" and "elegant satire."[143] Edwin Fadiman's novel, *Who Will Watch the Watchers?*, was described as "engrossing."[144] And Michel Choquette's photoessay, "Stranger in Paradise," was widely reprinted in the European media and admired by avant-garde artists like Andy Warhol and Salvador Dalí.[145]

At the same time, however, some of these same tales were viewed more critically. Richard Grayson was taken to task for having "de-Nazified Hitler, pacified him, and projected him as normative."[146] Pierre Boulle was criticized for "having develop[ed] ... an image of Hitler that ... largely de-demonizes him" and for having made him "more or less like one of us."[147] The most controversy of all, however, was sparked by George Steiner's novel, *The Portage to San Cristóbal of A.H.* When published in 1981, Steiner's novel quickly achieved impressive commercial and critical success. A bestseller in England and France, it was critically hailed in the United States, where it received high-profile attention in such major publications as *Time* and *Newsweek*. Many critics were effusive in their praise, calling the novel "extraordinary," "stunning," "a scintillating ... tour de force," a work of "extraordinary power and thoughtfulness," and "a philosophic fantasy of remarkable intensity."[148] Linking these positive comments was a belief that Steiner, in choosing the genre of alternate history, had devised an innovative method of exploring the nature of Hitler's evil. Otto Friedrich in *Time* said it avoided "both the satisfactions of the traditional novel and the horrifying details of Holocaust literature."[149] Peter S. Prescott in *Newsweek* noted that Steiner's abandonment of "conventional narrative" enabled him to fulfill the primary role of fiction, which was "to provoke an audience to thought."[150] Still other reviewers found him "brave" in writing the book, given the certainty that "literal-minded Jewish readers ... [would] find it objectionable."[151]

Yet soon after its publication in Europe, *The Portage to San Cristóbal of A.H.* was swamped by an avalanche of condemnation. Many reviewers criticized Steiner for having succumbed to the Hitler Wave and exploited the contemporary fascination with Hitler.[152] As Peter Conrad wrote, "The moral license of fiction allows [Steiner] ... to explore his own imaginative infatuation with the historical dementia he elsewhere reviles."[153] Similarly, Morris Dickstein described Steiner's work as "a misconceived and badly executed novel, a sideshow distraction from the serious business of thinking through the unspeakable horrors of the Nazi era."[154] Some reviewers went so far as to suggest that Steiner had justified the actions of the Führer. Martin Gilbert scolded Steiner for allowing Hitler the "last word" and permitting his "self-defense [to go] ... unanswered."[155] This accusation surfaced especially frequently after the novel was dramatized on the London stage in the spring of 1982. Many critics were aghast at the impact of Hitler's final speech (performed in impassioned fashion by actor Alec McCowen) on British audiences. As the reviewer for the *Observer* wrote, "Instead of a horrified silence, there was an immediate storm of applause and shouts of 'Bravo.' I think these were in some measure for Hitler as much as for McCowen."[156] In light of such views, it was not surprising for one reviewer to conclude that Steiner was guilty of "collaborationist prose" in depicting Hitler, while another called the novel "an upsetting and misleading piece of anti-Jewish propaganda ... which may prove to be of aid and comfort to anti-Semites for some years to come."[157] Finally, some described the very allohistorical premise of Hitler's survival as immoral. Having slammed Steiner's story as "worthless," "phoney," "nonsense," and "kitsch," Hans Keller observed that "any reinvention [of Hitler] blurs, weakens, and even hides," and concluded that, "in the face of this still little understood catastrophe [of the Holocaust], poetic license is license to lie, to commit the ultimate offence against art and morality alike."[158] In short, for readers used to seeing Hitler represented from an ethically principled vantage point, Steiner's blithe dismantling of that perspective was profoundly disturbing and sparked resistance.

By contrast, readers of the 1970s seemed to be much more comfortable with depictions of Hitler being brought to justice. This preference was demonstrated most vividly by the commercial and critical success of the novels *The Berkut, The Trial of Adolf Hitler,* and *The Asgard Solution.* For its part, *The Berkut* became a national bestseller and was widely praised in the mass media, which called it a "first-rate," "sizzling," and "compellingly readable thriller."[159] More significantly, the novel was praised for "not trivializ[ing] ... Hitler" and for ending on a note of "poetic justice."[160] Philippe van Rjndt's novel, *The Trial of Adolf Hitler,* was also widely applauded, being praised in the United States by the *Washington Post* as "powerful and thought-provoking," and in the UK by the *Observer* as "serious, well researched, and ... good reading."[161] Equally significant was the positive response to James Marino's *The Asgard Solution,* which the *Los Angeles Times* commended for doing "a chilling job [of] leaving you with a sinking thought: Is that despot [Hitler] still alive?"[162] These narratives' general success revealed the receptivity of readers to accounts that held the Führer accountable for his crimes.

Overall, the reception of the alternate histories of the 1970s revealed a general unwillingness of readers to accept the burgeoning normalization of the Nazi past. The substantial criticism of *The Portage to San Cristóbal of A.H.* and the praise directed towards *The Berkut* and *The Trial of Adolf Hitler* typified the desire to maintain traditional, moralistic views of the Nazi era. Significantly, however, this position would stiffen as the pace of normalization itself accelerated in the accounts of the 1990s.

THE END OF THE COLD WAR AND THE NARRATIVES
OF THE 1990S

Following the explosion of alternate histories depicting Hitler's survival in the 1970s, the next major wave appeared after 1989. As was true of the period that preceded it, far more tales represented Hitler evading justice than being held accountable for his crimes.[163] The reason for this trend is unclear, but it may have to do with the pivotal events of 1989–90. With the end of the cold war and the completion of German reunification, the postwar era came to a symbolic end. Many in the West, particularly in the United States, optimistically celebrated this event as heralding an end to ideological conflict – indeed, perhaps even to the end of history itself. In this climate of peace, one of the major purposes of portraying Hitler evading justice – namely, to highlight the continued existence of evil in the world – declined in importance. In the tales of the 1990s, Hitler's survival acquired a very different function, as was indicated by the new ways in which he was depicted. The alternate histories of the 1990s went far beyond those of the 1970s in diminishing Hitler's evil, representing him as increasingly aged, incapacitated, or mentally unhinged. The major thrust of some – though not all – of these narratives was that the passage of time had rendered the quest for justice illusory and futile. This focus on the issue of time also reflected the new realities of the post-cold-war world. With the problem of German national division solved thanks to reunification, with the fiftieth anniversary of the events of World War II approaching, and with the growing awareness that the eyewitnesses to the past would soon be gone, there emerged a growing sense that the Nazi years were fading into history. An increasing satisfaction with the present thus diminished the appeal of judging Hitler for his crimes. This sentiment also sheds light on the appearance, for the first time, of German language accounts of Hitler evading justice. In Germany, the turn of the decade brought not only German unity but also the call to restore a "normal" sense of identity to the nation by ending the ceaseless focus on the Nazi years.[164] The German depictions of Hitler evading justice in this period can be seen as expressing this desire for normalcy.

And yet not all allohistorical narratives of Hitler's survival after 1989 represented him evading justice. Some placed him on trial for his crimes. These tales continued the tradition of emphasizing Hitler's evil, of striving to bring him to justice, and supporting the cause of memory. Yet they were also noticeably of lower quality than earlier efforts, being largely derivative and formulaic in character. Ironically, then, the uninspired depiction of the quest to bring Hitler to justice reflected the fading fantasy of doing so.

The first major work of this period to depict evasion of justice was well-known American writer Steve Erickson's novel *Tours of the Black Clock*.[165] Published in 1989, *Tours of the Black Clock* is an ambitious work of fiction whose interweaving of the real and the imagined, of historical time and allohistorical time, resists simple explication. In brief, however, *Tours of the Black Clock* explores Hitler's life in a world in which the Nazis do not lose World War II. The novel's allohistorical point of divergence from the real historical record occurs by way of an unlikely relationship between the Führer and an American pulp fiction writer named Banning Jainlight. Born in Pennsylvania in 1917 as the illegitimate child of a Native American rape victim, Banning is a tragic character of dubious morals, who murders one of his two sadistic half-brothers after nearly being tricked by them into losing his virginity with his own mother. After fleeing to New York City, Banning wrestles with his sexual demons by becoming a writer of pornography. Although he initially pursues this trade to appease his own psychological demons, he soon begins to make a living at it. Through his Austrian distributor, a man named Kronehelm, he begins to reach an elite audience, which, he soon learns, includes a very high-ranking political figure in Germany – "client X," the Nazi Minister of Propaganda, Josef Goebbels. Shortly thereafter, in 1937, Banning decides to move to Kronehelm's home town, Vienna, in order to be closer to his primary literary patron and escape the police, who have learned of his whereabouts in New York. It is in Vienna that the course of history is profoundly altered. For it is there that Banning, who has grown bored of his prior sexual muses, glimpses from an upper-level apartment window a fifteen-year-old Russian girl named Dania, who becomes his new object of sexual obsession. Soon, his pornographic writing takes on renewed vigor and attracts the attention of a new patron, "client Z," the Führer himself. Unbeknownst to Banning, Hitler has been transfixed by the literary character of Dania, imagining her to be his own lost object of love and sexual desire, Geli Raubal. So distracted does Hitler become with Banning's literary creation that (to the relief of other German officials) he calls off Operation Barbarossa against the Soviet Union. Instead, in August of 1942, he invades and quickly defeats England, after which he occupies Mexico's Yucatan peninsula as a jumping-off point for a full-scale invasion of the United States.

In Erickson's narrative, this course of events hardly constitutes a success for the Nazis. While they avoid defeat in the Soviet Union (with whom they form an alliance) and eventually come to dominate Europe, the Nazis do not defeat the United States, with whom they continue to battle into the early 1970s. As the war drags on, the Germans suffer many battle casualties and are confronted with frequent guerrilla insurrections. Banning, in Vienna, observes that "the black and red twisted cross [on] the banners that hang on every building . . . are worn, shredding. The empire becomes dilapidated."[166] By this point, Hitler has long faded from the scene. Already by 1948, the German army has seized control of the Reich, shunting aside the Führer, who is left to dwell in his increasingly delusional world of sexual obsession. Banning, for his part, has taken refuge in his imagination as well. Having lost his wife and young daughter, whom the Nazis murder in 1942, he lives in a near daze, without memory. For years, he is kept as a prisoner in a small basement room in Nazi-occupied Venice, blankly writing stories for the Führer who, for his part, clings to life only through Banning's literary imagination.

Gradually, however, Banning becomes animated by the spirit of revenge. By the year 1967, he realizes that the man for whom he has continued to write shares his prison with him. "It's you," Banning says to the nearly eighty-year-old Führer, as he meets him in his cell for the first time. Banning's initial impulse is to kill Hitler and thus rid the world once and for all of pure evil. But he soon realizes the futility of doing so:

I knew that even if I could kill the old man . . . even if I could kill him long enough to speak the names of the six million, or ten or twelve, or however many flesh markers he lay down in the pages of time to gauge his evil, in the end there'd only be one little old throttled life to pay for it. That wasn't revenge enough. If I could find my way into this room every night for another thirty years and kill him little by little each night, it was still just the small miserable life of an old senile memoryless man to whom his own evil no longer meant anything even if I snarled the name of every victim into his wrinkled little face. What's the revenge of killing a man who's forgotten his own evil?[167]

Instead, Banning comes up with a more imaginative plan of revenge. Aware that Hitler is kept alive only by his burning desire to read the latest installment in the writer's ongoing literary saga, Banning decides to introduce a significant plot twist by having the Führer's love, Geli, unexpectedly bear him a child. Yet it is no ordinary child that Banning helps Geli conceive. Drawing upon his hatred of Hitler, of history, and of himself, Banning imagines Hitler's son as a monster:

I find a fertile plain on the banks of [Geli's] womb and begin to work. I ... transform the whole belly of her into a cauldron. There I make the very ooze of the thing that's to be born. I concoct it from a hundred things. I concoct it from the hush of those who vanished into the fog on his orders ... I concoct it from the mealy red ice left beneath those shot face down in the snow. I concoct it from the terrified squeal of children transformed abruptly into gunfire ... I concoct it from the gypsies in the ghettos and the Jews naked in the pits ... I concoct the garbage of evil ... which he's fathered without the passion and sex of a man ... I ... do this ... for that moment when the old face of the god gazes on what his godseed has spawned, not something grown from an embryo or fetus or even, godlike, from a star, but rather from larva.[168]

Banning inexplicably yields to mercy, however, as he finds himself permitting Geli to give birth to a normal baby boy whom, after struggling with further murderous inclinations, he decides not to kill after all. Instead, he decides to deal with Hitler in non-literary fashion, spiriting him away from his cell on a long journey from Venice, through southern Europe, across the Mediterranean Sea, to the Yucatan, and through the southern United States up to New York City, which they reach in 1970. It is there, in Banning's old apartment, where the 81-year-old Führer dies from sheer exhaustion.

In submitting this ending, *Tours of the Black Clock* illustrated the adverse effect that the passage of time has on the possibility of justice. Despite Banning's great hatred for Hitler, and despite his own history of murdering people with relative ease, he never is able to bring himself to kill the dictator personally. This is primarily because the Hitler of Erickson's novel, unlike the Hitlers of other allohistorical tales, is a faint shadow of the man who has long enjoyed the reputation of being the incarnation of absolute evil. *Tours of the Black Clock* suggests, in Nietzschean fashion, that absolute values such as evil simply do not exist. Time takes its toll on all. In his advanced and delusional stage, Hitler is no longer evil, but merely pathetic. As Banning remarks:

What came to repulse me the most was how time made the client's evil so feeble and therefore shredded the illusion that his evil was inhuman. It was utterly human ... In the way time and age broke him down, it broke down his vicious godliness, his distinct monstrousness.[169]

Significantly, it is not only in the eyes of Banning that Hitler becomes humanized (after all, we are led to doubt Banning's capacity for moral judgment), but in the eyes of others as well. Throughout Banning

and Hitler's arduous trek to New York City, many of the people they
meet – even the anti-German resistance fighters in Mexico – take pity on
the ex-dictator, whom they regard simply as a weak old man. Banning, in
contrast, is the recipient of scornful stares for seemingly subjecting his
elderly companion to such a strenuous journey. Ultimately, Banning's
recognition that time has humanized Hitler is what convinces him to
keep the Führer's survival a secret. Although he is tempted to reveal the
identity of his prisoner, he realizes that if Western society comes face to face
with the "humanity of Hitler's evil," it will lose "the pure righteous wrath
of . . . [its] fight" against the Nazi regime and thereby lose its best chance
of defeating it.[170] It is for the sake of a greater good, then, that Banning
allows Hitler to elude accountability for his crimes.

   In its skeptical depiction of the quest for justice, *Tours of the Black
Clock* provocatively questioned the utility of memory. By all accounts,
Erickson wrote *Tours of the Black Clock* in part to reveal the ordinary
human roots of Hitler's evil. As the writer put it in an interview, "I meant
to present Hitler in human terms . . . because morally it's too easy to
dismiss him as an aberration. The horror of Hitler is that his monstrousness was human."[171] Whatever Erickson's overall intentions may have
been, the way in which he emphasized Hitler's humanity in the novel
clearly implied the perils of remembrance. By showing how the passage of
time humanizes the Führer, Erickson exposed the futility both of striving
for justice and preserving the memory of Nazi crimes. Erickson, indeed,
rejected the notion, central to many allohistorical portrayals of Hitler's
survival, that the refusal to forget the past is the indispensable precondition for justice. Instead, like George Steiner in *The Portage to San
Cristóbal of A.H.*, he implied that the obsessive preoccupation with
remembrance and the unending pursuit of justice could potentially backfire with calamitous consequences. The only alternative, thus, was to
surrender to the corrosive forces of time and accept the inevitability of
amnesia. In so doing, Erickson's novel expressed the declining fantasy
of justice as the Nazi era faded increasingly into the past.

   The same can be said of another novel published several years later by
bestselling American writer E. M. Nathanson, together with first-time
writer, Aaron Bank, entitled *Knight's Cross*.[172] Published in 1993, *Knight's
Cross* is set in the waning days of World War II and describes a secret
mission of a special team of American OSS (Office of Strategic Services)
forces to capture high-ranking Nazis suspected of fleeing Berlin to the
so-called "Alpine Redoubt" in the Tyrolean region of Austria. Little does
the team or its leader, a hard-nosed American agent named Dan Brooks,

know that among the Nazi fugitives is none other than the Führer, Adolf Hitler, himself. Having faked his own suicide and undergone reconstructive facial surgery, Hitler is flown from Berlin to Austria, swathed in mummy-like bandages, posing as a Nazi rocket scientist named Siegfried Schmidt. Before long, Brooks learns of Hitler's arrival and captures him along with his SS escort, Obersturmbannführer Dietrich Reiter. Brooks, however, shrewdly refuses to alert Hitler to his knowledge and strings him along, promising him his freedom in exchange for the passwords to secret Swiss bank accounts containing billions of dollars in plundered funds. As the novel nears its climax, Brooks succeeds in transferring most of the ill-gotten money to the OSS. But before he can conclude his operation, Soviet agents who have been tracking the drama ambush Brooks and Hitler on Lake Geneva, and in the process of attempting to capture the Führer (whose real identity they still do not know) inadvertently shoot him to death.

With this ending, *Knight's Cross* affirmed the difficulty of bringing Hitler to justice. To be sure, Hitler's death at the end of the novel could easily be seen as constituting a just fate. After all, unlike the works of Boulle, Goss, or Steiner, Hitler fails to escape Europe and to live to a ripe old age. Yet *Knight's Cross* pessimistically rejected the premise that Hitler could be placed on trial for his crimes.[173] Brooks himself is determined to hide the fact of Hitler's survival, thinking to himself at one point, "It was much too late in the game to even think of revealing that Adolf Hitler was alive and then to turn him over to ... the international tribunal being planned to try war criminals."[174] Brooks's skepticism about the possibility of justice is rooted in multiple factors, but the main reason is due to cold-war politics.[175] Brooks realizes that American–Soviet relations will be poisoned if the news leaks out "that Adolf Hitler was alive, that he had been in his custody for almost three months, that billions of dollars in Nazi plunder were being coerced out of him, and that the ... United States government did not want to share any of it with its allies."[176] But more importantly, Brooks does not trust his own government enough to reveal he has captured Hitler. Significantly, *Knight's Cross* emphasized the cold war's role in corrupting American political and moral values by depicting the OSS being involved in the cynical attempt to recruit ex-Nazis in the effort to gather intelligence against their soon-to-be mutual Soviet enemies. Brooks is morally outraged by this change of strategy and notes that if his superiors "were making deals with useful Nazis to ... abet their plans against the Russian bugaboo ... why wouldn't they make a deal with Hitler too?"[177] To forestall this possibility, Brooks decides "to kill Adolf Hitler in secret and make him vanish without a trace."[178] Yet Hitler evades

Brooks's own brand of rough justice and, when accidentally killed by the Russians, ends up taking to his grave the secret password for the final Swiss bank account. Ultimately, then, even though Hitler dies, he succeeds in denying the world the brand of justice it craves.

In presenting such a pessimistic portrait of the quest to capture Hitler, Nathanson and Bank revealed the influence of several factors. Their overarching desire in writing the novel was a literary one, namely to tell a good story.[179] But the political atmosphere of the late 1980s and early 1990s also played a subtle role. Although it did not directly inspire the novel's narrative, the end of the cold war provided a climate of security for the authors to give vent to their critical views of American foreign policy. For his part, Bank (whose real-life identity – as an ex-OSS captain who had been placed in charge of capturing Hitler in 1944 – provided the premise of the novel) had witnessed and disapproved of the shifting alliances of the United States in the early cold-war years after 1945. Nathanson, meanwhile, was strongly inclined to revisionist views of American foreign policy, having made his mark as a writer who, during the Vietnam era, de-glamorized war in such bestselling works as *The Dirty Dozen* (1965) by exposing the capacity of all soldiers to commit atrocities.[180] In *Knight's Cross*, Nathanson did the same thing. By utilizing his trademark "Machiavellian" approach in fictionalizing his co-author's experiences, he de-heroized the Americans and thereby lent a greater sense of moral ambiguity to a war that had traditionally been seen in morally simplistic terms as a fight of good against evil.[181] This subtle process of normalization, finally, was epitomized by Nathanson and Bank's humanized portrait of Hitler himself. Like other writers, Nathanson was largely guided by the literary desire to make Hitler "a more believable character" and to avoid producing "a stiff, comic book caricature."[182] As a result, he rendered him less as evil than pathetic – as a drug-addicted maniac whose dream of reviving the Nazi movement in exile is no longer believed even by his most fanatical follower, Reiter.[183] By exposing Hitler's spell as broken, Nathanson and Bank differed from van Rjndt, whose *The Trial of Adolf Hitler* in the late 1970s worriedly depicted Hitler finding a receptive audience among postwar Germans. By the early 1990s, of course, Germany's peaceful reunification had helped allay traditional Western fears of resurgent German nationalism. While this momentous event played no direct role in influencing the narrative of *Knight's Cross*, the novel nonetheless confirmed the era's declining sense of the Third Reich's horror.[184]

Echoing *Knight's Cross*'s skepticism about judging Hitler was American playwright Robert M. Krakow's 1995 play, *The False Witness: The Trial of Adolf Hitler*. Performed throughout the late 1990s in theaters along the east coast of America, the play is more a work of surreal fantasy than a work of alternate history, but it merits discussion for reviving the scenario of the Führer on trial for his crimes. At the beginning of the play, Hitler stands before the "Gate of Purgatory" and is asked to defend himself for his deeds before the "Criminal Court of the High Tribunal."[185] As the play unfolds, the parade of witnesses called to Hitler's defense quickly reveals Krakow's agenda: to shift the entire blame for the Holocaust away from Hitler and onto Western civilization's long tradition of antisemitism.[186] The testimony of such figures as Martin Luther, William Shakespeare, Richard Wagner, and Henry Ford all demonstrate that the Führer's antisemitic views were hardly unique and indeed emanated from a deep anti-Jewish tradition in the West. This testimony supports Hitler's own contention, when he finally takes the stand himself, that he has been scapegoated for a deed – the Holocaust – that all of humanity wanted. This point emerges most dramatically when Hitler responds to the query of his defense attorney, Martin Luther, about the attempt of the 1938 Evian conference to raise immigration quotas for German Jews:

LUTHER: What was the result of the conference?
HITLER: That no country was prepared to increase their quotas to accept these refugees.
LUTHER: And when no country took them?
HITLER: Their fate was sealed. The world made its judgment and I carried it out. (*angrily*) Where do you think we got our ideas? What do you think was the foundation of our policy [?] The forces of history converged in the 20th century to do what the civilized world wanted us to do for centuries. We carried out that judgment.[187]

In short, Krakow's Hitler, like George Steiner's, is unrepentant for his deeds and demands that culpability be placed elsewhere. As the play's title suggests, he is the false witness. The witnesses who precede Hitler in the play are the true witnesses who need to be interrogated, for their complicity in the Holocaust has been ignored too long.

In advancing this line of argumentation, *The False Witness* continued the recent trend of questioning the possibility of bringing Hitler to justice for his crimes. It is because the guilt for the Holocaust is so widespread that the play deems judging Hitler insufficient. "You can't hold one entity solely responsible for what happened," Krakow said in a 1996 interview.[188]

Indeed, as the concluding remarks of the chief prosecutor in the trial, Joan of Arc, make clear, the net of guilt is cast far and wide:

These proceedings demonstrate beyond doubt that death factories of the Nazi regime were conceived many centuries ago. That these assembly line murders were the ultimate embodiment of evil myths that were transmitted through the millennia, finding their perfection in the modern era of man.
Or is it possible that mankind has never really left the dark ages?[189]

In the end, the question of justice is left suspended. Like the ending of Steiner's novel, which never answers the question whether any international trial of Hitler will ever take place, Krakow's play defers providing any clear answer about the possibility of justice. Rather than preach a message of guilt, like Philippe van Rjndt, *The False Witness* concludes by turning the audience into the jury and asking its members to make up their minds for themselves. Krakow's play is hardly "soft" on Hitler.[190] Yet, in refusing to take a clear stance on his guilt, *The False Witness* abandoned earlier moralistic methods of portraying the Führer and subtly contributed to his further de-demonization.

This skeptical attitude towards justice was amplified in a somewhat different sense by American director Barry J. Hershey's 1996 film *The Empty Mirror*. Set in an undefined time in a dank bunker presumably in Berlin, the film opens by depicting Hitler as somehow having survived the war (the exact circumstances go unexplained) along with Eva Braun, Josef Goebbels, and others.[191] There the Führer spends all of his waking moments reliving his past, watching old documentary film clips of himself, and practicing his famous salute (see Figure 20). Proclaiming "nothing is more important to me than the preservation of these images," Hitler begins the film firmly committed to justifying his past actions. Initially he is supported in this endeavor by his sycophantic sidekicks. In studying his never-to-be-built architectural fantasies together with a gimpy Josef Goebbels, for example, the latter whispers fawningly to his master, "Compared to you, Wagner was a minimalist." Similarly, while adoring Hitler Youth children listen to Hitler in awe, an unnamed SS secretary dutifully sits at his typewriter as the Führer dictates his memoirs, spouting pompous proclamations like "History is an error to be rewritten by a visionary playwright." As the film progresses, however, Hitler's confident sense of his overall place in history is gradually undermined. Signs of dissension first emerge from his secretary who, displaying visible signs of growing skepticism, asks him why Germany ended up losing the war. More importantly, Hitler himself begins to succumb to internal self-doubt.

Figure 20 Adolf Hitler (Norman Rodway) practices his traditional salute in his
underground bunker in Barry Hershey's 1996 film *The Empty Mirror*.

In one significant allohistorical rumination, he laments, "If I had stopped
with the conquest of France, I would have built the greatest sustained
empire since Caesar Augustus." As these feelings intensify, other disturbing
images – ranging from hazy scenes of wartime carnage to the recurring
vision of a menacing female dominatrix – gradually unnerve Hitler to
breaking point. By the end, face drawn, hair gray, and soaked with sweat,
the Führer is reduced to a shadow of his former self.

Like many previous portrayals of the fugitive Führer, *The Empty Mirror*
revolved around the question of justice. But, diverging from them, it
resisted the temptation to import judgment from the outside in the form
of, say, obsessed Nazi-hunters. Instead it explored Hitler's own personal
attempts at self-judgment. As a preview for the film described it:

'The Empty Mirror' defies the Hitler taboo and explores what might have
happened inside Adolf Hitler's mind if, after World War II, he had been cut off
from his role as Führer and left to contemplate his deeds, the myths he created, and
the man he really was.

Remembering, analyzing and regretting, this Hitler begins to break down, to
open up and let loose the fantasies and illusions to which he so stubbornly clung
and which he foisted upon the world.[192]

The Empty Mirror suggests that Hitler achieves some sort of self-realization about his historical crimes through a dual process of introspection and dialogue with others.

By orally recounting his achievements and failures to the other inhabitants of the bunker (all of whom are imagined figures, as is clearly indicated by the presence of the famed psychoanalyst, Sigmund Freud, among them), Hitler gradually attains a disturbing sense of clarity about the truth of his past actions. Symbolically, this enlightenment comes about through the visual act of self-perception. In an imagined conversation with Freud, Hitler becomes agitated and violently strikes out at the psychoanalyst, only to smash a mirror into which he has actually been gazing. By attempting to strike Freud – the dictator's superego in battle with his id – Hitler lashes out at himself. What he discovers, in the process, is a crushing sense of nothingness, an empty mirror. This realization – made explicit in the film's title – finally leads him to despair.

As with much of the film, *The Empty Mirror*'s ending was highly ambiguous as a commentary about the possibility of bringing Hitler to justice. The fact that Hitler's "survival" (metaphysical as it is) is never discovered by the outside world indicated that Hershey lacked faith in the conventional modes of justice (such as trials) utilized by writers such as Philippe van Rjndt. Yet if he denied the possibility of society passing judgment on the dictator, Hershey allowed for the possibility of his passing judgment on himself at the level of psychological self-exploration. By suggesting that only Hitler himself was capable of a kind of self-judgment, the film implied that justice is only possible at the private or individual level or (as indicated by Hitler's hallucinatory encounters with Sigmund Freud in the bunker) at least with the help of a psychoanalyst. In the process, Hershey's film further humanized Hitler by showing him capable of a kind of repentance. Although his crimes are amply recounted in the film, they do not tar him as irredeemably evil, for in the end, Hitler too can face his sins. Even if the act of repentance is a wrenching one, even if he is ultimately fully spent, Hitler is no different from other human beings in being able to face up to his past.

This process of humanizing Hitler culminated with the appearance of alternate histories in Germany. In 1996, well-known German actor Armin Mueller-Stahl released his directorial debut, *Conversation with the Beast*. Unlike *The Empty Mirror*, Mueller-Stahl's film imagines Hitler surviving the war into an advanced state of old age. The setting of *Conversation with the Beast* is contemporary Berlin, where the now 103-year-old ex-Führer (played by Mueller-Stahl) has lived a rat-like existence in a subterranean bunker-apartment since 1945. The elderly Hitler is discovered by a Jewish historian, Arnold Webster (played by Bob Balaban), who, following up on various rumors, descends into the bunker to interview a man who he initially believes cannot possibly be the dictator. Over the course of ten separate visits to the bunker, Webster has many conversations with the elderly man and his nurse, Hortense, that do little to disabuse him of his skepticism. Hitler insists, for example, that the corpse discovered in the Reich Chancellery courtyard was really a double – a man named Andreas Kronstaedt – who was one of six look-alikes created for the Führer during the war. Yet for Webster, the likelihood of the real Hitler having passed himself off as his double ever since is just as remote as Hitler's claim that he has been married to his youthful-looking wife, Hortense, since 1945 (by Webster's reckoning, she would now be sixty-three). These and other facts seem to undermine the possibility of Hitler's authenticity. Yet Webster's sense of confidence is gradually whittled away by the ex-Führer's eagerness to be recognized for who he is. Eventually, Webster comes to believe that the man is in fact Hitler. This leads to a somewhat anticlimactic conclusion. At the end of the film, Webster takes vengeance upon the man responsible for his people's unprecedented suffering by shooting him dead with a pistol.

It is questionable, however, whether Mueller-Stahl considers Hitler's death to constitute an act of justice. For one thing, Mueller-Stahl's Hitler is a relatively harmless fellow. Although he displays flashes of his old demonic self (for example, claiming "I didn't want the war"), he more often shades into the laughable.[193] Mueller-Stahl mostly depicts Hitler as a petulant old man who grumbles at Hortense's stern admonitions to take his pills and curses her as an "old goat" when she takes away his matches. At his worst behavior in the film, he plays childish practical jokes on Webster, such as sawing off the leg of his chair so that he falls down when he sits on it.[194] By humanizing Hitler, Mueller-Stahl, like Erickson, suggested that the opportunity for justice has long since passed. Indeed, although near the film's end Webster tells a colleague in a phone conversation that his plans for Hitler involve "bringing him to justice," Hitler himself is closer to the truth in telling Webster at the film's climax that "You will announce to the world that the opportunity to bring me to justice has been missed."

Ultimately, *Conversation with the Beast* defers answering the question of whether killing a relatively harmless man can constitute any meaningful measure of justice. A complicating factor is that we never know for sure whether the man killed by Webster is truly Hitler. Signs throughout the film point in both directions. Flashbacks to the early postwar era (including one in which a colleague of Hitler laughs at the fact that he is mistaken for his double, Kronstaedt) seem to suggest his authenticity; yet, since these flashbacks are communicated orally by Hitler/Kronstaedt to Webster, their veracity depends upon the truthfulness of the teller, who may be an imposter inventing them out of nothing. Mueller-Stahl, for his part, helped little in sorting out the question. When asked by a journalist whether "the protagonist is merely imagining himself to be Hitler," he responded: "Is he or is he not? I only raise questions. I do not have an answer."[195] The question of truth aside, the most significant point regarding Hitler's authenticity is that Webster believes it. Whether or not he is right in his conviction, in turn, bears heavily on the question of justice. If Webster is correct in his belief, then the killing of Hitler may well represent a just act. For despite his advanced age, Hitler's lack of repentance for his past implies he is deserving of his punishment. Mueller-Stahl's statement "I have always wanted to grant a Jew the right to shoot Hitler" in fact suggests he intended to have Hitler's murder constitute a moral deed.[196] But if the old man killed by Webster is merely a deluded double, then the act of murder is patently unjust. By never clearly answering this question, *Conversation with the Beast* abstained from offering any clear statement on the possibility of justice.

In the process, however, the film offered a cautionary message about the perils of memory. As with George Steiner's *The Portage to San Cristóbal of A.H.*, Mueller-Stahl's film can be interpreted as depicting the obsession with the past as leading to regrettable consequences. If, in fact, Webster actually kills one of Hitler's innocent doubles, then the ultimate responsibility lies in Webster's obsessive search for the Führer. Although a historian, Webster decides that Hitler is authentic without ever discovering incontrovertible, empirical proof of it. His conclusion is based upon faith, perhaps even desire. Webster's belief in Hitler's authenticity is a function of his own identity as a Jew obsessed with his people's tragic history. His emotional desire for justice clouds his capacity for reason. Thus, while Webster hesitates before shooting Hitler (sweating and in tears, he misses several times before hitting his target), he shoots anyway. The desperation for justice, rooted in a stubborn commitment to remembrance, ultimately leads to death. Moreover, Mueller-Stahl suggests, this death is largely pointless. For, until being sought out by Webster, Hitler was essentially dead to the world already. Like George Steiner, who made the same point in *The Portage to San Cristóbal of A.H.*, Mueller-Stahl suggested that only in memory – especially Jewish memory – does Hitler live. As Hitler remarks to Webster at one point, "My enemies don't let me die." Insofar as the film asserts that Hitler lives only as long as he continues to be viewed with fascination by society, therefore, *Conversation with the Beast* seemed to advocate the cause of forgetting.[197]

In its broader conclusions, Mueller-Stahl's film expressed an exhaustion with, and desire to normalize, the memory of the Nazi past. Mueller-Stahl's goals in making the film illustrated these broader tendencies. Having declared in interviews that the film represented "my desperate attempt to finally be rid of the guy" (and having reportedly considered naming the film *Goodbye Adolf*), Mueller-Stahl evidently made *Conversation with the Beast* as a means of exorcising him from German memory.[198] This aim was partly reflected in the director's choice of a comic mode of representation for the film. Mueller-Stahl's decision to follow in the tradition of Chaplin's classic, *The Great Dictator*, and to make Hitler "funny" was prompted by the need "to keep him at a distance."[199] This need for comedy, in turn, may well explain why the director deliberately chose the genre of alternate history for his film in the first place. For, as he put it, the answer to the film's basic allohistorical premise – "What kind of person would [Hitler] be without power?" – was "He ... is not dangerous any more ... The man who destroyed almost the whole world, without power – it makes him funny."[200] Mueller-Stahl's comic depiction of Hitler may be seen as satirical in intent, yet his stated need for distance bespoke more escapist motives. Indeed, insofar as a comic representation of Hitler humanized him by directing attention away from his evil crimes, it reflected a desire for normalcy, if not outright amnesia.

The declining German belief in the power of memory and the possibility of justice, finally, found its fullest expression in bestselling German comic book author Walter Moers's ribald two-part comic, *Adolf die Nazi-Sau* (*Adolf the Nazi Pig*).[201] Appearing in 1998 and 1999 respectively, the two volumes of the *Adolf* series quickly dispensed with the two major premises of the allohistorical literature on the fugitive Führer: namely, the enduring nature of Hitler's guilt and the enduring desire of society to bring him to justice. Moers abandoned these two premises right from the outset of the first volume of *Adolf*. In the opening installment of the strip, Moers presents a reductionalistically rendered image of Hitler crouching in an abandoned sewer as follows (see Figure 21): "Let us remember: Adolf had unfortunately lost the Second World War and had to go into hiding. For years he lived in the sewers and was allowed to reflect upon his mistakes." (Hitler is portrayed deep in thought reflecting, "I should have attacked Russia more skillfully across its flank.") In the next panel, the narrator continues, "Finally one day his guilt elapses." At this point, Hitler emerges

Figure 21 Opening page of the first volume of Walter Moers's 1998–99 comic book
Adolf die Nazi-Sau.

from under a manhole cover, thinking to himself, "Ahhh … fresh air."
The final panel in the strip raises the overarching question for the entire
series, "And yet, can Adolf overcome … the shadows from the past …!?
Now begins his struggle for a new life – 'His Struggle' (*Sein Kampf*) so to
speak."[202] Unlike all prior allohistorical treatments of the theme, Moers
permitted Hitler to re-emerge from hiding by declaring the statute of
limitations on his guilt to have expired. Thus liberated from the fear of
being brought to justice, Hitler proceeds to a new struggle – the struggle for
a normal life.

And yet from this point on Hitler's life in the contemporary world is
anything but normal. Both volumes of *Adolf* chronicle a series of

misadventures of alternating quality: some are quite funny, others fall flat. Nearly all are obscene in one way or another – often gratuitously so. Profanity, awkward sexual situations, and politically incorrect scenarios abound in the individual strips. (To name merely one in passing: when Hitler re-emerges from the sewer he consults a quack physician – Dr. Furunkel – to explain his lingering sense of malaise. When the doctor prescribes "a good old-fashioned fuck," Hitler proceeds to Hamburg's red-light Reeperbahn district, where he ends up having sex with his long-lost colleague, the renamed "Hermine" Goering, who, also having survived death, has undergone a sex change operation and become a dishevelled crack addict.) From this point on, Moers in successive installments repeatedly rams home his central allohistorical premise: that if Adolf Hitler had in fact survived World War II, gone into hiding, and re-emerged at some point in the future, he would have continued to cause mayhem. The trouble begins when Hitler, in Paris on Dr. Furunkel's orders, answers a job advertisement for a chauffeur and finds himself driving a romantically entwined Princess Diana and Dodi Al-Fayed in a limousine, which he promptly crashes, killing both lovers.[203] In despair, he attempts to commit suicide by leaping off the Eiffel Tower but is kidnapped by space aliens who drop him off the coast of Japan. There, Hitler experiences a fit of xenophobic anger against the "fish eaters" which, thanks to genetic alterations performed by the aliens, triggers his mutation to Godzilla-like size, and he proceeds to lay the city of Hiroshima to waste.[204] Finally, while eating sushi, Hitler is poisoned and kidnapped by Dr. Furunkel (in reality, a misanthropic, militant Princess Diana in disguise), who, having hijacked Air Force One, wants to compel him to launch a nuclear strike against Russia. Hitler averts sparking World War III, however, by pushing Princess Diana/Dr. Furunkel out of the plane and parachuting into Latin America.

Vol. II of the *Adolf* series picks up where the first left off. Having settled in Asunción, Paraguay, Hitler has married Hermine Goering and opened up a "Sushi and Black Bread Bar," patronized by aged Gauleiters and other assorted Nazis. Instead of receiving the respect of his fellow Alte Kämpfer, however, Hitler is the object of constant ridicule (racing to deliver a sushi order to his Nazi customers, the frazzled Führer has to put up with impatient comments like, "So, Adolf no longer the quickest, eh?" "Yeah, it's taking nearly one thousand years! Ha ha!"). More demoralizing for Hitler are the snide comments of his three children who, when told by their father to stop smoking marijuana, respond, "Scram, you old Nazi pig!" "Jew-murderer!" "Book-burner!" "Fascist pig!"[205] Finally, when he seeks out the comfort of Josef Mengele at his bar, "The Black Hole," and complains

that his wife, Hermine, thinks him a failure, the former Auschwitz doctor
replies:

'Oh come now! Just because you lost the world war? Because you senselessly
transformed half of our planet into rubble? Because you failed as an artist, statesman, strategist, and father? Simply because you are the statistically most hated
man in human history? Nonsense, Adolf – you're just imagining things!'[206]

Hitler's woes continue when Mengele drugs Hitler in a bid to seize world
power for himself and his envisioned race of super-Nazis. Waking up from
his drug-induced stupor, Hitler finds himself in a world destroyed by
World War III. Fearing he is responsible, he seeks help from a mad
scientist, Professor Pickel, who gives him a time-travel helmet in order to
find out what his role has possibly been in history's recent disastrous
course. In a series of highly satirical episodes, Hitler travels back in time
and ends up, in rapid succession, accidentally killing Franz Ferdinand to
spark World War I, assassinating President John F. Kennedy in Dallas,
sinking the Titanic, killing rock star Kurt Cobain, (nearly) crucifying Jesus,
and altering the course of human evolution by aiding a fish struggling to
climb onto dry land. Finally, although he discovers that it is, in fact,
Mengele who (having infiltrated the White House as Monica Lewinsky)
has pushed the button to launch World War III, Hitler finds himself forced
by the mad Professor Pickel in the year 2525 to launch World War IV and
cause total planetary destruction. This notwithstanding, however, Hitler is
able to travel back to his own time, where he dispenses with Mengele, frees
his captive wife Hermine, and walks off with her into the sunset against the
backdrop of his world's ruins, dreaming of grand future plans.

In permitting Hitler to evade justice in his two *Adolf* volumes, Moers
was not motivated by any larger "didactic intentions," but he clearly did
not feel any obligation to present its theme from a moralistic perspective.[207] Born in 1957, he belonged to a generation with no personal
entanglements with the Nazi era and thus viewed it in a rather detached
fashion.[208] Moers's initial attraction to the topic, indeed, had less to do
with its historical resonance than its potential to turn a profit. Inspired by a
Japanese comic book on Hitler and in desperate need of money, Moers
realized that he "could achieve high sales figures with 'this crazy (*verblödet*)
fascist [Hitler]" and thus set out to exploit him for commercial purposes.[209]
Yet while Moers may not have originally set out to normalize Hitler, the
comic means he employed in writing *Adolf* did so nonetheless. Like Mueller-
Stahl, Moers humanized Hitler through satire. This makeover was visible on
the book's cover, where a goofy-looking and good-natured Hitler greets the

reader with the cheery, Austrian-accented words, "Äch bin wieder da!" ("I'm baaack"). This is not to imply that Moers glamorizes Hitler. He demeans him consistently in Three-Stooges-like fashion, subjecting him to such indignities as prostituting himself for crack and forcing him to have sex with the reanimated corpse of Mother Theresa. Yet in showing Hitler suffering his many unfortunate turns of fate, Moers shrinks him down to the status of a buffoonish shlemiel, whose bumblings and misadventures the reader can readily empathize with. Moreover, with its triumphant ending, the first volume of *Adolf* reversed many of the primary features of the allohistorical representations of Hitler, for instead of nearly unleashing World War III (as he does in many allohistorical tales), this version of Hitler ends up *preventing* it and thus performs an essentially heroic – if clumsy – function in the text. Vol. II, as noted above, restores some of Hitler's evil, but on the whole Moers's Hitler was the most humanized of the postwar era.

In sum, the allohistorical portrayals of Hitler evading justice that appeared throughout the West in the 1990s clearly expressed an increasingly normalized view of the Nazi past. By humanizing Hitler and skeptically rejecting the possibility of holding him accountable for his crimes, they cast doubt upon the utility of remembrance. At the same time, they illustrated how the passage of time and the growing distance of the postwar world from the Nazi era diminished the intensity of the fantasy of justice. The end of the cold war provides the general background that explains this shift. By directly benefiting the nations from which all the narratives appeared – namely, the United States and Germany – the end of the cold war illustrated how the relative contentment of American and German writers with the real historical present led them to normalize the scenario of Hitler's survival in an alternate past.

THE FADING FAITH IN JUSTICE: HITLER RETRIED

Alternate histories in the 1990s, however, did not merely depict Hitler evading justice but also placed him on trial for his crimes. The first such tale in this period to do so was prominent American science fiction writer Barry Malzberg's short story from 1994, "Hitler at Nuremberg."[210] In this competent if unimaginative tale, Malzberg followed the lead of van Rjndt and portrayed Hitler surviving his own suicide attempt – this time through duplicity rather than chance. Malzberg, indeed, drew a familiar demonic portrait of Hitler by having him betray an understandably furious Eva Braun by refusing, at the last minute, to also take poison. After describing

Hitler's capture by the Allies, the tale proceeds to explore his thoughts while on trial for his crimes at Nuremberg. Malzberg, however, did not display the skill of van Rjndt in describing Hitler's own view of his criminal deeds. Whereas van Rjndt's Hitler attempted to justify his crimes, Malzberg's Führer simply denies them outright, claiming "[The] camps, the exterminations ... the crematoria working frantically ... I knew nothing of this."[211] It was disloyal underlings like Eichmann and Himmler, Hitler insists, who disobeyed his orders merely to "intern" the Jews and who ordered them killed. After further rantings about his innocence – "They have the wrong man," he claims – Hitler ends up on the gallows, a rope around his neck, muttering the story's final line: "[It] could have been any of you, any of you." With this ambiguous and rather anticlimactic ending, Malzberg added little to the already extant image of Hitler on trial in van Rjndt's novel. While "Hitler at Nuremberg" echoed previous portrayals of the dictator as unrepentant and irredeemably evil, it finally succeeded only in doing something once thought unthinkable – making Hitler uninteresting.

The same can be said of a work that stands at the other end of the spectrum from Malzberg's short story – David Charnay's seemingly endless 954-page novel, *Operation Lucifer: The Chase, Capture, and Trial of Adolf Hitler* (2001).[212] Readers with the stamina to plow through this three-inch-thick tome by the octogenarian American television producer, public relations manager, and writer will find the same scenario explored more elegantly and concisely by van Rjndt twenty years earlier. Charnay added some new creative flourishes to his account of the fugitive Führer, depicting Hitler acquiring a new identity by undergoing plastic surgery, transforming his trademark moustache into a 1990s-style goatee, and perversely passing himself off as a Jewish financier named Frederick Nordheim. Otherwise, the plot of *Operation Lucifer* is derivative, interminable, and does not merit detailed exposition.[213] The most notable insight to glean from the book is its unrelenting portrayal of Hitler as a demonic figure bent on bringing about a Nazi revival (this time, by exploiting tensions in the Middle East in the early 1950s). When he is finally captured and placed on trial, the Führer, as in prior accounts, offers a predictably defiant defense of his past actions. Not surprisingly, he is quickly found guilty. When the verdict is read, there is no doubt of Hitler's enduring evil. Judge Chester Nimitz's final statement to Hitler at his sentencing is unambiguous: "You are found guilty of all charges. You have committed every war crime. You are responsible for millions of murders. You are not human. You are ... the devil incarnate. You are to be hanged by your neck until you are pronounced dead and returned to your abode in hell."[214] After this melodramatic statement, the only surprise left in the novel is the perfunctory fashion in which Hitler is finally hanged on the gallows.[215]

In the end, *Operation Lucifer* was distinguished by few literary merits, but it was strongly marked by its unambiguous portrayal of Hitler's evil and its deep moral commitment to remembrance. Charnay's background as an American who, born in 1912, belonged to the "greatest generation" and personally experienced World War II (in his case, actually, as a member of the OSS) no doubt explains his stated desire to prevent hatred and intolerance in the present by producing an ethically informed account of Hitler's survival and ultimate demise.[216] Thus, at the outset of the book Charnay cited the contemporary persistence of antisemitism, drive-by shootings, and the massacre of high-school students in Littleton, Colorado, before concluding bleakly, "More than five decades have flitted by and students, parents, educators and the media still know little of the Nazi carnage during 1933–1945." "Dear God," he concludes, "let the *world remember* . . . for *what is past is prologue.*"[217]

Not all accounts of the Führer on trial, however, have been driven by such a clear emotional thrust. American historian Roger Spiller's 2001 essay "The Führer in the Dock: A Speculation on the Banality of Evil" was surprisingly dispassionate in outlining the likely course of Hitler's capture, trial, and execution.[218] In developing his scenario, Spiller argued that Hitler, after being captured by the Soviets, would most probably have been placed on trial for his crimes in Moscow, where he quickly would have been found guilty and executed. While plausible, Spiller's account was distinguished by its unemotional character. Unlike other writers who have depicted the trial of Hitler as a climactic clash of good versus evil, Spiller characterized it as an anticlimax. He argued that Hitler in the dock would have hardly resembled a demon but rather a defeated human being. His health having declined precipitously by the war's end, Hitler most likely would have sat on the witness stand, like his co-defendants at Nuremberg, dressed in shabby civilian clothes and been exposed as the mediocrity he always was. As Spiller put it, Hitler's aura of power and authority "would have faded to blandness" until, like Eichmann in Jerusalem, he "personified the banality of evil."[219] Spiller may be right in his sober analysis, but the conclusion of his essay was less significant than its sobriety. For by abstaining from emphasizing Hitler's evil, he declined to take pleasure in his punishment, thereby offering further evidence of the fading fantasy of justice.

All in all, the tales that have appeared in the 1990s imagining Hitler being convicted for his crimes have ambiguous significance. While they ostensibly reflect the enduring fantasy of justice, their small number and mediocre quality suggest that the fantasy has diminished in intensity.

RECEPTION

The reception of the tales of Hitler's survival further complicates our understanding of the dynamics of normalization. The narratives of the 1990s suggest an increasingly non-judgmental view of the Nazi era, yet their mixed reception demonstrates a persisting reluctance of readers to abandon traditional moralistic modes of representing it. Certain works portraying Hitler evading justice earned significant acclaim. The most widely celebrated narrative was Steve Erickson's *Tours of the Black Clock*, which was hailed as "remarkable" and compared to the work of such major writers as Thomas Pynchon, Vladimir Nabokov, and Don DeLillo.[220] Such praise partly implied support for its normalized portrait of Hitler. Thus, the *New York Times* commended Erickson for "[showing] his readers the humanity of evil."[221] Likewise, E. M. Nathanson and Aaron Bank's novel, *Knight's Cross*, was not only lauded as "entertaining" but commended for its "believably realistic" ending.[222] Both novels, though, also met with considerable criticism. A great many other reviewers found *Tours of the Black Clock* opaque and inaccessible, some even calling its plot "preposterous."[223] Similarly, other critics disparaged *Knight's Cross* as "disappointingly unimaginative."[224]

    If the mixed reviews of these works suggested a limited receptivity to normalization, the much stronger criticism directed towards other works expressed it in explicit terms. No narrative was as roundly condemned for its treatment of Hitler as Barry Hershey's film, *The Empty Mirror*. By all accounts, Hershey's film was regarded as a flop.[225] Assailed as "insufferable," "a colossal bore," and "kitsch on a wild roll," reviewers skewered the stylish film for its inability to add any substantial insights (psychological or otherwise) into the Nazi dictator.[226] More notably, some focused on its problematic ending. Fulfilling Hershey's prediction that "his movie may offend ... because it doesn't depict Hitler as evil incarnate," the film critic of the *Chicago Sun-Times* noted that:

[to] suggest that even Hitler couldn't escape conscience and doubt is the equivalent of tacking on a happy ending to a Hollywood tearjerker; it's bogus, artificially comforting and not what occurs in real life. A more interesting filmmaker would have shown what we don't want to see, a Hitler so submerged in his sickness and so devoid of conscience as to appear entirely healthy and ethical. That Hitler would never have viewed films of himself in a bunker because that Hitler, the real Hitler, still would have been scheming how to kill 6 million.[227]

Or as the *Los Angeles Times* film critic observed, the film was "offensive," since in it the "remarkably . . . introspective Hitler becomes more and more Lear-like . . . a tragic figure. Hitler may have been complex, but he was above all evil and hardly deserving of the stature that tragedy confers."[228]

Finally, the two German works, Armin Mueller-Stahl's *Conversation with the Beast* and Walter Moers's *Adolf die Nazi-Sau* met with a largely divided reception for their comic depictions of Hitler. Like Barry Hershey's *The Empty Mirror*, Mueller-Stahl's film fell short of expectations.[229] Many reviewers found the film "strange" and faulted it for shortcomings of casting and direction.[230] The majority, though, simply found Mueller-Stahl's comic portrayal of Hitler to be unconvincing.[231] Most notable was the response of Germany's national film evaluation agency (the Filmbewertungsstelle Wiesbaden), which refused to award its much sought-after endorsement to the film, noting that Mueller-Stahl had "defiantly" disregarded "possible moral scruples" about showing Hitler as anything but a "stigmatized" figure and had instead transformed him into a "crazy clown."[232] Only isolated reviewers welcomed Mueller-Stahl's comic portrayal of the dictator.[233]

Walter Moers's *Adolf die Nazi-Sau*, meanwhile, also met with negative reactions, yet reaped impressive commercial success as well. The two-volume series was a hit, selling over 400,000 copies in two years.[234] The widespread popularity of the controversial book, in turn, quickly generated intense reactions. Predictably, many groups were offended by the *Adolf* series. Neo-Nazis sent threatening e-mails to the publishers, Eichborn-Verlag, protesting Moers's "desecrating the memory of Hitler." German Jews, meanwhile, were also upset, as was indicated by the observation of one of the leading representatives of the Zentralrat der Juden in Deutschland, Michel Friedman, that in reading Moers's strip the "smile that *should* freeze in one's throat [emphasis added] does not freeze sufficiently. The reader should shudder about the fact that he has smiled."[235] On balance, the chief question raised by Moers's book was whether it was permissible to laugh at Hitler (and, by extension, the Nazi past). For its part, the Eichborn-Verlag loudly answered in the affirmative, declaring in a prominent blurb, "Should one be allowed to make fun of the Nazis? No – One has to!" More negatively disposed critics disagreed. Beyond Jewish critics, older Germans who had lived through the Nazi years also objected. Joachim Fest noted, "It is not the time yet for the Germans [to be joking about Hitler]."[236] Moers and his publisher did not originally intend for the *Adolf* series to "constitute an act of mastering the past," but, in sparking a debate about the limits of representing Hitler, *Adolf die Nazi-Sau* became precisely that.[237]

Overall, Moers's comic can be viewed as providing unique insights into the evolving German memory of the Nazi era. *Adolf die Nazi-Sau*, of course, was hardly the first work to encourage audiences to laugh at Hitler. After all, from the propagandistic comic books of the 1940s in the United States (where Hitler was regularly bashed by such superheroes as Captain America, Daredevil, and Superman) to the films of Charlie Chaplin and Ernst Lubitsch, Hitler has long been made fun of.[238] But Moers's comic book did raise the novel question of whether the *Germans* could laugh at him.[239] Especially since laughing at Hitler had been a traditional method of coping with the past for Hitler's victims (for Jews in particular), allowing this privilege to the descendants of the perpetrators was more controversial. Of course, whether or not it was permissible was in the end a moot point, since a growing willingness to laugh at the Nazi past was already evident in German culture, as has been demonstrated by the popularity of *Hogan's Heroes* reruns, the broadcast of Kai Wessel's 2000 film *Goebbels und Geduldig*, and the appearance of comic books like Achim Greser's *Der Führer privat*.[240] The significance of this trend is difficult to evaluate, but it seems to bespeak an increasing yearning for normalcy. One German reader of Moers's book notably explained his enthusiasm for the comic by declaring that "Laughter liberates the inhibited soul and eases every cramp."[241] For Germans who have long felt the immense psychological burdens of the Nazi past, laughter no doubt provides welcome relief. Moers's commercial success in creating a humanized Hitler whom Germans can laugh at indicates that he more than satisfied these yearnings.

CONCLUSION

Ever since their initial appearance after 1945, postwar alternate histories portraying Hitler's survival have expressed a deep yearning for justice. The counterfactual premise at the heart of these tales has long possessed a strong psychological appeal, a fact supported by Donald McKale's observation that "[Our] imaginations insist on bringing ... [Hitler] back to life so that we may condemn and kill him again and again, the pleasure he so fiendishly denied the world in 1945."[242] Notwithstanding this comment's plausibility, however, postwar allohistorical depictions of the fugitive Führer reveal a progressive decline in the fantasy of bringing Hitler to justice. While the earliest postwar accounts clearly illustrated this fantasy's potency, and while they have continued to appear to the present day, they have been exceeded both in quantity and quality by narratives portraying

Hitler escaping accountability for his crimes. This increasing apathy towards justice suggests a declining tendency to view the Nazi era from an ethically grounded perspective and the growing emergence of a more normalized historical mindset.

There are several reasons for this trend. Beginning in the late 1960s, intensified concerns about contemporary political problems began to over-shadow the memory of the Nazi era and led writers to shift their moral energies towards the former by universalizing the significance of the latter. In addition, the Hitler Wave weakened the reigning ethical perspective by portraying the Führer in more humanized and aestheticized fashion. Finally, the perceived need for moralism declined still further after the end of the cold war, when the victory over communism and the ending of Germany's national division seemed to reduce the Nazi era's present-day relevance and accelerate its retreat into the past. In short, the forces of universalization, aestheticization, and organic normalization were all involved in the diminishing tendency to remember the Third Reich in a morally conscientious fashion.

This increasingly normalized view of the Nazi era, however, has not stood unopposed. Even as more alternate histories have represented Hitler in humanized terms, they have been frequently assailed by critics outraged at their cavalier approach to a topic of such historical seriousness. These hostile responses attest to the enduring desire to see the Third Reich through a prism of ethical judgment. Yet there have also been many instances where alternate histories on the theme of the fugitive Führer have earned critical accolades, a fact that indicates a growing degree of receptivity to non-judgmental ways of viewing the Nazi past. The divided public response to these works reveals that the struggle to shape the memory of the Third Reich is an ongoing one. But the growing popularity of such alternate histories suggests that a tradition of moralism is slowly giving way to one of normalcy.

Whether or not this trend ultimately should be seen as worrisome remains unclear. Some observers have provocatively argued that a perpetu-ally moralistic – that is, a perpetually demonic – portrayal of Hitler is actually counterproductive, as it perpetuates his mythic aura and preserves him as an object of fascination. "Only if Hitler is anchored in human reality," Robert Hughes has noted, "will he stay dead. If not, he will continue as he has been since 1945: a nightmare of history from which we cannot wake."[243] Only Hitler's de-mythologization via his humanization, according to this argument, promises to end the grip of Nazism on Western consciousness. Yet, while this supposition may be true, it is questionable whether it is desirable. Humanizing Hitler may in fact eliminate him from our nightmares, but it may also diminish his place in popular awareness altogether. In the end, only as long as the dictator continues to haunt us are we likely to continue studying, reflecting upon, and drawing historical lessons from, the Third Reich's destructive legacy.

CHAPTER 6

The world without Hitler:
better or worse?

I talked ... about America, feeling a strange ability, for the first time
in years, to speak frankly ... America, this strange power, moving
inexorably in the twilight of the European Empires, but filled with a
people vain, childish, unpredictable, and mongrelised. Slav sentimentality, Jewish venality, Nigger barbarisation. I was aware of this from
the first, from that terrible year we first arrived here ... refugees ... mingling with the Jews, the Poles, the starved illiterate
Russkis, the Latin-American half-castes. Adolf, one must admit,
kept us alive, with the power of ... his vision. In Germany those
visions might have become all-powerful. But in America they were
misaligned. It fell to me then to guide him, to mould him and
ourselves into a political force here. No easy job. So many organisa-
tions about that seemed to serve our purpose, but riddled with
delusions, wishful thinking, and above all, corruption, sexual and
financial. The Klan, the White Leagues, the Knights of this and that.
Religion was their main curse. Protestant fundamentalism. A sort of
smudged romanticism ... So Adolf lost his place in History. But I,
on the other hand ...¹

The melancholy ruminations of Josef Gable (né Goebbels) about his
longtime colleague, the retired United States Senator from Illinois, Adolf
Hitler, in Simon Louvish's 1994 novel, *The Resurrections*, point to yet
another frequently explored allohistorical scenario on the subject of
Nazism: How would history have been different without Hitler as the
Führer of Nazi Germany? Since 1945, a wide range of alternate histories
have examined this provocative theme. Some have depicted Hitler emigrating from Germany to the United States after World War I and
becoming a politician or a science fiction writer. Some have imagined
a world in which he is killed as an infant or never born at all. Still
others have depicted him being assassinated – some before 1933, others
in 1938, still others in 1944. Whatever the time and means imagined, all
of these narratives have examined what eliminating Hitler at some point

in his life would have meant for the subsequent course of history. In doing so, however, these accounts have arrived at very different conclusions. Some narratives have depicted history in Hitler's absence as much improved, but many more have portrayed it as no better, if not actually worse.[2]

The inconsistent depiction of the world without Hitler provides further evidence that the memory of the Nazi past has become increasingly normalized in recent years. Since its inception, the counterfactual scenario of the absent Führer has been based upon the alluring and commonsensical fantasy that the direction of history could be improved by eliminating the man widely regarded as one of its most notorious villains. The reluctance of most narratives to depict Hitler's removal as actually producing a better world, however, reflects this fantasy's declining appeal. In their overall conclusions, these accounts illustrate a growing sense of contentment with the postwar present and express the fading horror of the Third Reich in Western consciousness. By portraying how the world would not have been any better in Hitler's absence, these alternate histories reflect a decreasing tendency to view him as the symbol of absolute evil.

This de-demonization of Hitler, however, should not be seen solely as a sign of normalization. At a deeper level, the inconsistent depiction of the world without Hitler also reflects a disagreement about whether individual agency or structural constants are more decisive in shaping historical events. Alternate histories that have portrayed Hitler's absence as improving history express a belief in the primacy of individual decisions and actions. By contrast, the tales that have shown his elimination as failing to improve the course of historical events reflect a belief in the greater power of structural forces. This disagreement about historical causality is notable in its own right, but it is especially important for highlighting the existence of national differences in the memory of the Nazi past. It is significant that most structuralist accounts have been Anglo-American in origin, while narratives emphasizing the pivotal role of individuals have tended to be German. British and American alternate histories have pessimistically argued that even with Hitler's elimination, the nationalistic or authoritarian tendencies of the German people would have led to some other kind of disastrous historical outcome. German accounts, meanwhile, have optimistically claimed that in Hitler's absence, the German people would have been able to successfully prevent their nation's turn to dictatorship. As these diverging explanations demonstrate, the scenario of the world without Hitler has largely revolved around the issue of assigning historical guilt for the origins of the Third Reich.

CHANGE FOR THE BETTER: THE WORLD WITHOUT HITLER
IN ALTERNATE HISTORY

The belief that the world would have been better without Hitler is a longstanding one. The earliest evidence testifying to this belief is provided by the multiple assassination attempts directed at the Führer during the Nazi years. Whether Claus Graf Schenk von Stauffenberg's bombing of Hitler's East Prussian headquarters, the "Wolf's Lair" (*Wolfsschanze*), on July 20, 1944, or the British government's cloak-and-dagger plan, "Operation Foxley," to kill the dictator with anthrax-infested clothing, the numerous attempts to kill Hitler were linked by a basic conviction that doing so would improve the subsequent course of history.[3] Ever since these assassination attempts, the allohistorical premise of eliminating Hitler has become a common theme in Western historical discourse. As early as the 1930s and 1940s, various works of fiction and film featured the premise of assassinating the German dictator: Ralph Milne Farley's 1941 short story "I Killed Hitler" depicted a time traveler murdering the young Führer-to-be in 1899; an anonymously written novel, *The Man Who Killed Hitler* (1939), featured the Führer getting bludgeoned to death in his office with a bust of German chancellor Paul von Hindenburg; and the Hollywood film *Hitler: Dead or Alive* (1942) envisioned a trio of American gangsters attempting to kill him in order to collect a million-dollar bounty.[4] Since the end of World War II, professional historians – particularly those who have written on the German resistance against the Nazis – have frequently implied that eliminating Hitler would have improved history.[5] And in recent years, non-specialists have echoed this belief as well. Indeed, the notion that the world would have been better without Hitler has been voiced by celebrities, such as lawyers Marcia Clark and Alan Dershowitz, alluded to in works of historical fiction, such as Kris Rusch's 1998 novel *Hitler's Angel*, addressed in Hollywood movies, like Stacy Title's 1995 film *The Last Supper*, and heatedly debated in internet chat rooms.[6] It has even apparently led certain deranged individuals to go on murder sprees.[7] All of these cases testify to the broad allure of the basic allohistorical premise that eliminating Hitler from history would have improved its overall course.

Given the deep roots of such speculative reasoning, it is surprising that full-fledged allohistorical narratives portraying Hitler's death as changing things for the better are of relatively recent origin. Dating back to the early 1980s, these accounts have been few in number. But they have all been united by a shared emphasis on Hitler's evil, a belief in the power of individual agency to shape historical events, and by the conviction that eliminating Hitler from history would have dramatically improved its course. In the process, these narratives have expressed a certain degree of discontent with the present that, more often than not, has reflected the Third Reich's enduring traumatic legacy.

The first major account to portray Hitler's elimination as improving the course of history appeared in 1984 with American writer Jerry Yulsman's novel *Elleander Morning* (see Figure 22).[8] Yulsman's story opens in Vienna in 1913 with a nervous but well-dressed young woman entering a café, ordering a cup of coffee, pulling out a revolver, and shooting to death the man sitting across from her – a young, impoverished art student named Adolf Hitler. Seventy years later, in 1983, a young woman named Lesley Bauman travels to England to visit her estranged father, Harry Morning, who dies before her arrival, leaving a generous inheritance and a mysterious letter. In the letter, Harry reveals his illegitimate origins (born in 1911, he never knew his father) and expresses his lifelong attempt to understand why his mother, Elleander, killed an art student in Vienna as a young woman. His interest in this matter is understandable, given that it led directly to his mother's arrest and execution in 1915 – an event that left Harry, then four years of age, an orphan. The mystery deepens, however, with the final bequest of Harry Morning to his daughter: an illustrated coffee-table book entitled *The Time-Life History of the Second World War*. In leafing through the volume (which is a real historical account of World War II), Lesley glimpses a photograph from 1942 of the French passenger ship, the *SS Normandie*, burned out at its berth in New York's Hudson River. Realizing that she has just arrived in Britain on the very same ship, she asks an acquaintance, Fred Hayworth, to explain the striking coincidence. Befuddled himself, Hayworth testily responds, "What in the bloody hell is the Second World War?"[9]

Elleander Morning takes place in a world that knows nothing of World War II, thanks to the premature death of a man destined to remain an obscure figure in history, Adolf Hitler. Before long, however, this world learns more than it would like to know both about the war and the man responsible for it. The novel's protagonist, Lesley, is the first to become aware of the terrifying alternate historical reality. Although at first she is convinced that the *Time-Life* book is a highly skilled forgery, she begins to believe in its authenticity after learning in a June 20, 1913 news clipping from the *Illustrated London News* that the identity of the murdered art student, Adolf Hitler, matches that of the dictator of Germany depicted in the *Time-Life* book. It is at this point that Lesley realizes the historical significance of her grandmother's violent deed, exclaiming, "My

Figure 22 Cover of Jerry Yulsman's 1984 novel *Elleander Morning*.

grandmother prevented [the war] and so it never occurred."[10] How
Elleander Morning knew to kill Hitler, however, is a question that resists
Lesley's attempts to answer for much of the novel. Initially, she believes
that her grandmother murdered Hitler in 1913 out of some clairvoyant
awareness of his role in the coming apocalypse. But she comes nearer to the
truth after making the shocking discovery of two burial plots for Elleander
at the local cemetery, which, after being exhumed, contain two identical
skeletons, one of an approximately thirty-year-old woman and one of a
woman approximately eighty years old.[11] What Lesley never deduces (but
what Yulsman discloses in a parallel narrative) is that her grandmother has
willingly died *twice* for the sake of broader personal and historical goals.
Elleander Morning is a woman whose tragic personal experiences in real
history – she loses her son in World War II, her best friends on the *Titanic*,
and her husband in a car crash – lead her on her deathbed in 1970 to wish
herself successfully back in time to 1907 to eliminate the origins of her
sufferings at their source. Killing Hitler is merely one of several ways in
which she rearranges the course of history to her own personal advantage.
But it is by far the most significant. While her successful assassination of
Hitler entails a high cost – the sacrifice of her own life at an early age – it
permits her (and the rest of the world) to avoid a lifetime of suffering. For
the elimination of the never-to-be dictator of Nazi Germany erases World
War II from the historical record for the benefit of all humanity.

Yet, while *Elleander Morning* expresses the commonsensical notion that
Hitler's early death would have vastly improved the course of history, it
does so only in a qualified sense. Yulsman complicates his narrative by
questioning whether history would have repeated itself even *without* Hitler
on the scene. Here, the competition between human agency and structural
constraints to shape the course of history finds clear allohistorical expression. The absence of Hitler can be seen as having a positive effect on world
history by sparing it the horrors of World War II, the Holocaust, and
Hiroshima. Most significantly, it is beneficial for the development of
Germany, which, without Hitler, grows into a democratic, prosperous,
and technologically advanced society. By 1984, indeed, Germany has
become the sole nation to have developed nuclear capability and explored
outer space.[12] Despite the nation's successful historical development without Hitler, however, Yulsman suggests that Germany may well have
developed in an equally threatening manner owing to the enduring force
of German nationalism.

What triggers the resurgence of German nationalism in the 1980s in
Elleander Morning is the furor that erupts following the revelation of the

existence of the mysterious *Time-Life History of the Second World War.*
After Lesley discloses the book's existence to a small international panel of
experts convened to determine its authenticity, one of the invited guests,
the retired German Field Marshal, Rudolph von Seydlitz, takes offense at
the book's account of Nazi atrocities and declares that it "is [a] malignant
fiction ... a damnable insult to the German nation!"[13] Convinced that the
book is a product of a Jewish "conspiracy," driven by envy towards their
nation's "hard-won ... superiority in science ... art, technology, and
commerce," Seydlitz resolves to defend Germany's besmirched reputation
by mobilizing the nation against its imagined enemies.[14] In this effort,
Seydlitz shrewdly uses the same *Time-Life* book that causes his rage as a
guide for his broader agenda of revenge and begins to see in the history
that never was a blueprint for how it might still be. Modeling himself
after Hitler, Seydlitz, together with a small group of fellow conspirators,
plots the overthrow of Germany's democratic government as part of a
larger plan to threaten the Western Allied powers with nuclear destruction unless they agree to return Germany's lost territories. To this end,
Seydlitz skillfully exploits the anger of the German people that erupts
with *Time-Life*'s decision to (re)publish the book to an international
audience. With Seydlitz's encouragement, German protesters picket the
nation's bookstores, chanting "[the] Second World War Insults German
Honor," and begin to assault Jews in the streets. (In an amusing side-
note, an odd assortment of retirees, including an ex-insurance salesman
named Martin Bormann, a department store owner named Rudolf Hess,
and an ex-magazine publisher named Josef Goebbels, file lawsuits
against *Time-Life* for libel.) Soon thereafter, Seydlitz takes power and
begins plotting his strategy for the fateful military confrontation to
follow.[15]

In sketching this turn of events, Yulsman clearly points to the importance of structural (in this case, cultural) constants in shaping the course of
history. Even without Hitler, the Germans – even after living in a free
democratic state for more than half a century – remain an essentially
intolerant, racist, and authoritarian people. As Seydlitz's liberal nephew
(and Lesley's lover), Paul Bauer, wonders while observing his fellow
countrymen in a Berlin café:

Did they differ essentially from their peers in Copenhagen, Edinburgh, Barcelona?
An attempt to rally Danes, Scots or Spaniards to war in the name of racial
superiority would surely fail. Almost anywhere else in the civilized world, such
an attempt would be met with anger, derision and, in extreme cases, even
revolution. Yet in Germany it was thinkable.[16]

As swastika-clad German toughs wander the streets of Berlin decrying the "international Jewish plot to discredit worldwide acceptance of German racial and cultural superiority," *Elleander Morning* strongly implies that, even without Hitler, history would have been no better than had he lived. It may even have been worse. For as Paul realizes, Seydlitz's war would be "even more catastrophic than that which was visualized in the *Time-Life* books. Millions would die . . . perhaps hundreds of millions."[17] Yet, by the end of the novel, individual human agency trumps structural constants in determining the course of events. In a somewhat farcical repetition of the failed assassination attempt against Hitler on July 20, 1944, Lesley and her German lover Paul succeed in killing Seydlitz and his entourage at the *Wolfsschanze* in Rastenburg with a hidden bomb. In amazement, a dazed Paul observes that Lesley has duplicated her grandmother's historic deed by preventing World War II from erupting a second time.[18] If only by a slim margin, history does ultimately turn out for the better without Adolf Hitler.

In offering this conclusion, Yulsman confirmed the Führer's reputation as the epitome of evil, while at the same time refusing to exonerate the German people, whom he portrayed as less than trustworthy. The author's critical portrayal of the Germans likely reflected his own personal background as an American (born in 1924) who had fought against Nazi Germany as a tail gunner in the U.S. Air Force in World War II.[19] Moreover, his portrait may have also reflected lingering Western suspicions of the Germans at a time, in the early 1980s, when the Federal Republic was taking a turn to the political right with the election of the conservative CDU government of Chancellor Helmut Kohl. Significantly, the Federal Republic at this time largely resembled the Germany that Yulsman depicted as having developed in the absence of Hitler – prosperous, democratic, and advanced in science and technology. And yet, lurking beneath the surface, Yulsman implied, was the specter of German national superiority. *Elleander Morning* can thus be seen as a cautionary tale reflecting the enduring suspicions towards Germany caused by the Nazi experience.

Around the same time as the appearance of *Elleander Morning*, German writer Hans Pleschinksi published a short story entitled "Ausflug" ("Excursion") that offered a somewhat different depiction of its basic premise.[20] Set in the author's present in the early 1980s, this simple tale focuses on a German student named Carl who, while traveling by train to visit his cousin Luise in Dresden, chats with fellow passengers and reads newspaper articles about the current political state of the world. Carl's world, the reader learns as the tale unfolds, is a very different one from that produced by real history. Scattered clues, such as an encounter with a drunken passenger from Silesia, a current copy of the *Middle German Newspaper*, and ruminations about a recent trip to Leipzig, reveal, first of all, that Germany is a united country without internal boundary divisions. The sight of a Polish train car bearing the emblem of a white eagle, moreover, informs the reader that communism has not spread to Eastern Europe. Communism *has* remained in power in Russia, as is indicated by ongoing arms reduction talks between the Soviet Union and the European Community. But the insistence of European governments that the continent has "had enough merely with one World War" makes it clear that superpower rivalry has erupted *despite* World War II never having occurred. Why the war never occurs emerges at the end of the tale. When Carl finally meets up with Luise, who works as a journalist, she tells him of her plan to write a piece of "horror fiction" for an illustrated magazine, entitled "Hitler in Power." After disagreeing about how bad history would have been had Hitler ever risen to power (Carl believes it would have been worse than Luise does), Carl declares his admiration for General Paul von Hindenburg's decision on January 30, 1933 to ban the Nazi party and throw Adolf Hitler in jail for "disturbing the peace." As a result of this fateful decision, Hitler is denied an impact upon history up until his death in a mental institution called Buchenwald on July 21, 1954.

Although a very subtle piece, "Ausflug" was a classic expression of the fantasy that eliminating Hitler would have improved history. By preventing Hitler from seizing power, Pleschinski spared Germany a multiplicity of tragedies that it suffered in real history. The existence of national unity as depicted in the story, for one thing, reflected the enduring traumatic impact of national division upon postwar West German consciousness. This impact was illustrated by the frequent references to inner-German contacts (especially in the realm of travel) and the story's simple conclusion, in which Carl, Luise, and her new boyfriend plan an excursion (or *Ausflug*, from which the tale gets its title) to the mountains of Bohemia in non-communist Czechoslovakia. These passages expressed a desire for access to lands barred to West Germans by the iron curtain and illustrated the pain of national division. Moreover, the tale's depiction of a healthy sense of German national identity reflected the negative impact of the Nazi experience upon postwar German national pride. As a chat on the train between Carl and a middle-aged Italian woman reveals, it is Italy (which has suffered the lengthy dictatorship of Mussolini's fascists) and not

Germany that has suffered a besmirched national reputation in this alternate world. As the Italian woman wistfully declares:

'Today ... I refuse to say "patria." The entire Italian dictionary is dirty. When someone says "we must," my heartbeat immediately quickens.'
   'In my gut, that generation ... is entirely suspect. You have to understand, I don't know who denounced whom, who approved what ...'
   'How different everything is here [in Germany], how unburdened by trauma ... You had more luck than we had ...'[21]

In projecting the negative historical experience of fascism onto the shoulders of the Italians, Pleschinski's tale allowed Germans to indulge the fantasy of evading historical guilt and embracing a much-desired sense of historical innocence.

   Pleschinski's actual aim in writing "Ausflug," however, was less to allow Germans to evade the Nazi past than to provide them with a new method for confronting it. As he has noted, the short story gave voice to his own morally rooted "revulsion against the Nazi contamination (*Verdreckung*) of [our] national history" while, at the same time, it also reflected an attempt to escape its shadow through the means of allohistorical fantasy. Pleschinski has observed how his "elimination of Hitler from our history" in "Ausflug" expressed his desire to "create an alternate Germany as a utopia" – a Germany that would have "existed in the continuity of its more distant history, as a pleasant (*lebenswertes*), multicultural, imaginative land in the middle of Europe (as was once true in the Habsburg era)." Pleschinski's desire for such a vibrant nation underscored his discontent with the contemporary reality of West Germany, a place he regarded at the time as "boring, unimaginative ... [and] provincial." The writer's downcast view of his nation no doubt partly stemmed from the restlessness of youth (born in 1956, Pleschinski was twenty-six when he wrote the tale). Yet his unease also reflected a profound sense of guilt for "the course of German history in the 20th century." Significantly, Pleschinski conceded that his fantasy was driven by "the dream of getting rid of 'guilt.'" It was indicative, then, of Pleschinski's desire for a cleansed national history that he depicted Hitler as the primary cause of Germany's modern catastrophe. For to produce his desired utopian vision of German history, he had to defend the reputation of the German people as a whole. Unlike Yulsman, then, his tale preserved much less of a structuralist focus upon the German people's culpability for the Third Reich. While Pleschinski was firmly committed to a moralistic view of Hitler – indeed, while he expressed signs of an emotional "pleasure ... in eliminating Hitler from ... history" – his tale reflected the difficulty faced by Germans attempting to come to terms with their own collective responsibility for the Nazi era.[22]

Around the same time as the appearance of Pleschinski's tale, German historian Alexander Demandt arrived at a similar conclusion about the world without Hitler. In a short section of his 1984 book *History That Never Happened* entitled "[What] If Hitler had Died in 1938?," Demandt agreed that history without the Nazi dictator would have been much improved. Demandt argued that, in light of "the resistance among the generals to Hitler's war plans," the elimination of the Führer would have made "the outbreak of the Second World War" unlikely. To be sure, he conceded, the structural reality of German nationalism would have persisted in the country; thus, "there would still have been a desire to regain the border territories of the German Empire ... lost through the Treaty of Versailles." Yet, Demandt insisted, there would have been few supporters of Hitler's maximalist expansion plans, since very few Germans adhered to Hitler's idiosyncratic "living-space theory." In the end, then, there not only would not have been a general European war without Hitler, but "the murder of the Jews" and "the division of Europe" would also have been easily consigned to the realm of "history that never happened." "When we remove Hitler ... from history," Demandt concluded on an upbeat note, "we are left with German unity."[23]

In submitting this wish-fulfillment fantasy, Demandt, like Pleschinski, registered an emphatic sense of dissatisfaction with the present – specifically with Germany's postwar division. This discontent was in keeping with his conservative political views, which he expressed through his support for reunification at a time in which it was still somewhat taboo to do so.[24] Demandt's narrative also had conservative political implications insofar as it assigned to Hitler most of the blame for the disastrous course of recent German history and exonerated the German people of any responsibility for it. In these ways, Demandt's essay expressed a desire for a normalized national past.

Following the accounts of Yulsman, Pleschinski, and Demandt, the next narrative to optimistically assess the historical consequences of Hitler's premature demise was historian Henry Turner's 1996 essay "Hitler's Impact on History."[25] Turner began his piece by speculating how a real episode in Hitler's life – a near-fatal automobile accident in 1930 – would have shaped subsequent historical events had it led to the future dictator's death. For Turner, Hitler's absence from history would have changed everything. And it would have done so in a positive fashion. Without Hitler, there would have been no Third Reich at all.[26] Only Hitler's iron will and stature kept the Nazi party's competing factions together and prevented the party from splitting entirely in the early 1930s. Without him, the party would have collapsed before ever rising to power in 1933. As Turner asserted:

Hitler's demise in ... 1930 would have unleashed the latent factionalism in National Socialism and produced an insuperable succession crisis. With rare exceptions his henchmen disliked and mistrusted each other. Only their shared allegiance to him kept them from each other's throats ... With its Führer removed by death, the ... NSDAP ... would have disintegrated ... just as it fell apart during Hitler's imprisonment following the abortive Munich beerhall putsch of 1923 ... The truncated story of the NSDAP's brief existence would today amount to no more than a curiosity, worthy at most of obscure doctoral dissertations.[27]

To be sure, Turner conceded that even without the Nazis in power, Germany would likely still have experienced the emergence of a military dictatorship that have would tried to revise the Treaty of Versailles. Germany would have thus risked war to regain its 1914 borders with Poland, including Danzig and the Polish Corridor, and likely would have succeeded, given the Western Allies' policy of appeasement and the Soviet Union's historical acquiescence in the face of the German aggression towards Poland. Still, despite its similarities to the policies of Nazi Germany, Turner noted, "a military dictatorship ... would not have left scars as deep ... as those inflicted ... on ... Europe by Hitler's Third Reich. Such a regime would have been fundamentally conservative, free of the fanatical radicalism unleashed by the Nazis. It would have been authoritarian, but not totalitarian; nationalistic, but not racist; distasteful, but not demonic."[28] Thus, Turner asserted that an authoritarian Germany would have differed from the Third Reich in refusing to pursue its expansionist agenda any further into Austria or the Sudetenland, given that its Prussian, Protestant military rulers would have frowned on reintegrating these regions' unwanted Catholic populations.[29] As a result, there would have been no World War II, no Auschwitz, and no Hiroshima. Without these twentieth-century catastrophes, the world would have been a much more innocent and optimistic place. Moreover, without World War II, the Soviet Union would never have become a superpower (indeed, it might have collapsed much earlier without its Eastern European sphere of influence), and the world would have been spared the cold war. To be sure, there also would have been costs to bear in this scenario, such as the absence of European integration, and a later and bloodier process of decolonization. Most profoundly for Americans, without the war (and the benefits that accrued from it, such as the import of European brain-power and the economic stimulus provided by increased defense spending), the United States would never have become the global superpower that it did. Yet, these "costs" notwithstanding, the world without Hitler would today be a much more forward-looking place, blissfully ignorant of the cataclysms it "never" experienced.[30]

In arriving at this upbeat assessment, Turner revealed himself to be a firm believer in the paramount importance of individuals in history. Like Alexander the Great, Napoleon, or Stalin, Hitler was one of those "great men" in history who shaped historical events by the force of their will and personality. Like any good professional historian, of course, Turner conceded a significant place to "impersonal forces" in his account as well.[31] Even without Hitler, he noted, the rampant nationalism and militarism that existed in Germany due to the resentment stemming from the outcome of World War I and the Treaty of Versailles would have led the nation to pursue an aggressive, expansionist foreign policy, similar to the Nazis'. And yet, in the end, while "great impersonal forces make events possible," it was "people [who] make events happen." As Turner concluded, "If Hitler's career demonstrates nothing else, it confirms beyond any doubt that individuals can have an enormous impact on the course of human affairs."[32] In submitting this conclusion, Turner exhibited his conservative tendencies as a historian. Not only was his "great man" approach to history methodologically quite traditional, his support for the conclusions of Pleschinski and Demandt could be seen as politically conservative by minimizing the historical responsibility of the German people for Nazism.[33] As an American, Turner had no personal reasons for going easy on the Germans. His generous evaluation of their historical role in the Third Reich largely derived from his larger body of historical scholarship, which stressed that the Nazi dictatorship was more of a historical accident than a logical outgrowth of German history.[34] Believing Hitler's rise to power to be the product of contingent – and thus avoidable – events, Turner had little trouble concluding that had Hitler only been eliminated from history, everything would have turned out much for the better.

This was also the conclusion of German science fiction writer Sabine Wedemeyer-Schwiersch in her 1999 short story, "Requiem für einen Stümper" ("Requiem for a Dilettante").[35] In this tale, Hitler's impact on history is altered by his decision to pursue a career in art instead of politics. The story unfolds in the form of a laudatory speech, given in the year 1975 by an unnamed narrator employed at the newly established Adolf-Hitler-Museum in Stuttgart, on the career of the recently deceased German painter, Adolf Hitler. The speaker explains how, after two failed attempts, Hitler's acceptance into the Vienna Art Academy in 1909 set the stage for his eventual meteoric rise within the German art world. Hitler's career is temporarily sidetracked by the eruption of World War I, the speaker notes, but he makes good use of his experiences on the Western Front by injecting a "heroic sensibility" into his postwar work, which he produces in a modest studio in Stuttgart.[36] The immediate postwar years are difficult for Hitler as he suffers, along with other Germans, in the tough economic climate, but he finally catches a break in 1930 when he meets his future patron, Albert Häberle, who is immediately taken by his work and resolves to support his career. Indeed, it is largely thanks to Häberle – a young and wealthy industrialist who presides over the mammoth Great German Georg-Häberle-Werke (named after his father) – that Hitler's artistic output increases exponentially during the 1930s. So prolific is he that he establishes an entire school of acolytes defined by their embrace of the "Hitler Style: plain portraits of working people, heroic landscapes, and scenes from German mythology and history."[37] Before long, Hitler's work becomes so popular that "an original Hitler painting soon hung on every German living room [wall]."[38] When Hitler finally dies at the ripe old age of 85, the narrator solemnly concludes, "His death leaves a hole that can never be filled."[39]

The allohistorical significance of Wedemeyer-Schwiersch's short story lies in its contention that German history would have turned out much better had Hitler never gone into politics but rather had become an artist. As the narrator's speech reveals, Hitler's failure to go into politics enables Germany to escape its real historical plunge into dictatorship and instead develop into a thriving economic powerhouse. The credit for this achievement goes to the Georg-Häberle-Werke, whose global economic influence enables it by the fateful year 1933 to wield political power in beneficent fashion in Germany.[40] Thanks to the firm's "uniquely fortuitous combination of economic and political vision," Germany becomes the envy of the world, prompting other nations' leaders – such as U.S. President Richard Nixon – to praise it for its prosperity and stability.[41] The narrator sums up the nation's result of such achievements by proudly declaring, "Today the entire world recognizes ... our greatness. 'German industriousness' has become a concept that is used all over the world and which no one dares to translate. German quality goods have long become indispensable across the globe."[42]

In portraying history as vastly improved without Hitler, Wedemeyer-Schwiersch expressed the same kind of fantasy embraced by her fellow

Germans, Pleschinski and Demandt. Like their tales, hers presumed a strong degree of faith in the German people who, in her estimation, would not have fallen into dictatorial behavior without Hitler. In the process, she implicitly exonerated her countrymen for the rise of the Nazis and saddled Hitler instead with most of the historical responsibility for the Third Reich. Yet her short story still exhibited a certain critical tone. Like the tales of Pleschinski and Demandt, hers imagined a superior alternate past in order to express a degree of disaffection with the present.

The three writers' respective political contexts, of course, were quite different. Whereas Pleschinski and Demandt were responding to what they saw as the bleak emptiness of pre-reunification West Germany, Wedemeyer-Schwiersch was reacting to post-reunification developments. Specifically, she was taking aim at what she has described as the adverse impact "of international corporations . . . upon human beings" in an age of globalization.[43] This agenda is indicated in the story by the narrator's habit of thinking much more critical thoughts to himself throughout his otherwise effusive speech. Even as he praises Hitler's art in his remarks, for example, he bemoans its insufferable mediocrity, thinking to himself, "It's a scandal! We should openly embrace . . . Beckmann, Dix, and all the truly great painters. But what do we have instead? Hitler, nothing but Hitler."[44] As shown by these and similar remarks, the narrator believes Germany to be a place dominated by an "unmistakably middlebrow" culture produced by its reliance on large-scale industrial patrons like Häberle. "If only money and taste could be found together in one person," the narrator sighs at one point, "that would be too good to be true."[45] Wedemeyer-Schwiersch's allohistorical portrait of Germany as a land of corporate-minded cultural philistines could easily be interpreted as being directed at the contemporary Federal Republic. But she has asserted that contemporary Germany is hardly the only country dominated by enormous corporations, being in good company with Japan, Great Britain, France, and Switzerland as well.[46] As a result, her story's relevance to the present was mostly universalistic in nature and less focused on Germany itself. Her exemption of Germany from specific criticism may be fitting, though, for her account ultimately ratified the optimistic belief that the German people would have been perfectly capable of leading their country in a healthy direction had it not been for Hitler's decision to go into politics.

Taken together, the accounts of Yulsman, Pleschinski, Demandt, Turner, and Wedemeyer-Schwiersch indulged in the fantasy that removing Hitler from history would have improved its course. These authors not only affirmed Hitler's centrality to history but revealed an enduring belief in his essential evil. This conclusion clearly illustrated the lingering trau-matic effect of the Nazi era on the postwar imagination. Many of the writers who fantasized about eliminating Hitler were driven by a sense of dissatisfaction with the present-day consequences of the Nazi experience: Yulsman expressed an enduring fear of resurgent German nationalism, while in a very different manner, Pleschinski and Demandt voiced a frustration with Germany's national division. Thanks to German reunifi-cation in 1990, such fears and yearnings largely disappeared as factors driving the fantasy of eliminating Hitler. For this reason, the tales of the 1990s expressed a less overt sense of discontent with the contemporary world – and where they did (as with Wedemeyer-Schwiersch's disaffection with globalization), its roots were more universal in nature. The idea of improving history by eliminating Hitler, therefore, may today have less to do with overcoming the traumatic legacy of the Nazi era in particular than it once did. Still, whatever their diverging motivations, the alternate histories that have depicted history as better without Hitler have retained a common function throughout the postwar years – namely, to blame the Nazi dictator rather than the German people for the establishment of the Third Reich. This fact, finally, helps explain why more than half of the accounts were written by Germans. Given the heavy historical burdens faced by Germans in the postwar era, it is no wonder that they in particular have been drawn to an allohistorical scenario that provides a sense of consolation for the past by unmaking it altogether.

THE WORLD NO BETTER WITHOUT HITLER

Since 1945, however, most alternate histories depicting Hitler's elimination from history have asserted that such an event would have done little to improve it. These narratives have appeared in two different forms. Some have explored the consequences of Hitler *never* becoming the Führer of Nazi Germany in the first place, while others have examined what would have happened had he been removed from the historical stage *after* having already become the Führer. Regardless of the means of Hitler's allohistorical elimin-ation – whether emigration or assassination – all of these works have asserted that Hitler's absence would have done little to make history turn out better. All have illustrated the declining fantasy of improving history through Hitler's elimination. Interestingly enough, this trend seems to have grown out of two very different views of the present. In certain cases, the fading fantasy of eliminating Hitler has reflected – as one would expect – an increased degree of satisfaction with the postwar world and a diminished sense of Hitler's evil. In short, it has reflected the organic normalization of the Nazi era through the passage of time. In other cases, the diminished concern with Hitler has reflected a heightened attention towards present-day turmoil and a sober belief that its deep structural causes would be little affected – and history little improved – by Hitler's elimination. Here, a different agent of normalization has been at work – namely, the desire to universalize the Nazi era's significance in order to shift attention towards contemporary problems. In both cases, however, it has been the overt diminution of Hitler's evil that exemplifies the normalization of the Nazi past.

THE DICTATOR WHO WASN'T: HITLER NEVER BECOMES THE FÜHRER

In his memoirs, Albert Speer wrote, "I sometimes ask myself whether Hitler would have forsaken his political career if in the early twenties he had met a wealthy client willing to employ him as an architect."[47] Like the hypothetical question whether Hitler ever would have gone into politics had he been accepted at the Vienna Academy of Fine Arts in 1907, Speer's rumination echoes what many people have long wondered: Would history have turned out better if Hitler had realized his original career ambitions and not gone into politics? Speer's opaque answer – "I think, his sense of political mission and his passion for architecture were always inseparable" – implies that if Hitler had become an architect, he still would have striven for a more tangible sense of power and may well have achieved it.[48] History may not have been very different. Significantly, many alternate histories have taken Speer's conclusion one step further. Not only would history not have been much different, it very possibly could have been worse.

One of the first such pessimistic narratives was well-known American science fiction writer Norman Spinrad's 1972 novel *The Iron Dream* (see Figure 23).[49] A novel within a novel, *The Iron Dream* is merely the exterior packaging for another story, *Lord of the Swastika* – a work touted as "a science fiction novel" written by Adolf Hitler in 1953. The Hitler of this alternate world has not become the dictator of Nazi Germany. Instead, as the reader learns in an introductory note to the book – as well as in a lengthy critical commentary by the (fictional) literary critic, Homer Whipple, of New York University – Adolf Hitler:

was born in Austria on April 20, 1889 ... and served in the German army during the Great War ... before finally emigrating to New York in 1919. While learning English, he eked out a precarious existence as a sidewalk artist and occasional

Figure 23 Cover of Norman Spinrad's 1972 novel *The Iron Dream*.

translator in ... Greenwich Village. After several years of this freewheeling life, he began to pick up odd jobs as a magazine and comic illustrator ... [By] 1935, he had enough confidence in his English to make his debut as a science fiction writer ... Although best known to present-day SF fans for his novels and stories, Hitler was a popular illustrator during the Golden Age of the thirties, edited several anthologies, wrote lively reviews, and published a popular fanzine, *Storm*, for nearly ten years.

He won a posthumous Hugo at the 1955 World Science Fiction Convention for *Lord of the Swastika*, which was completed just before his death in 1953. For many years, he had been a popular figure at SF conventions, widely known ... as a wit and nonstop raconteur ... Hitler died in 1953, but the stories and novels he left behind remain as a legacy to all science fiction enthusiasts.[50]

Following this clever introduction, readers are confronted with more than 200 pages of turgid prose that make up *Lord of the Swastika*'s futuristic narrative. Set in a postnuclear holocaust world, Hitler's novel depicts the heroic exploits of one Feric Jaggar, a human inhabitant of the republic of Heldon, who battles various inferior races and assorted mutants in neighboring lands in the struggle to preserve the genetic purity of his Helder people. As the discerning reader quickly recognizes, Jaggar is both a mouthpiece for the allohistorical Hitler's nationalistic fantasies and a thinly veiled, fictional version of the real historical Hitler himself. Just as Hitler emigrated from Austria to Germany (both in real history and in Spinrad's alternate history) as a way of escaping the multi-ethnic Habsburg Empire, so too does Jaggar gain entry into his rightful fatherland of Heldon as a human born outside its borders in the neighboring, mutant-filled land of Borgravia. Jaggar's mission of preserving Heldon's racial purity, moreover, also parallels Hitler's own sense of mission for Germany, down to the struggle against its primary enemies, the so-called "Dominators" (or "Doms") who, working for the Empire of Zind to the east, have infiltrated Heldon and are slowly subverting its racial purity. In short, as seen in the basic contours of *Lord of the Swastika* – as well as in the titles of Hitler's other published novels (including *The Master Race*, *The Thousand Year Rule*, and *The Triumph of the Will*) – Hitler's obsessions are consistent both in real history and alternate history.

These parallels are further developed through the plot of *Lord of the Swastika* which, while the product of the allohistorical Hitler's fantasies in American exile, portrays events that mirror his rise to power as the leader of the Nazi party in real history. Thus, as the novel unfolds, Hitler's protagonist, Jaggar, discovers his oratorical powers, establishes a movement known as the "Sons of the Swastika" to restore genetic purity to Heldon, finagles his way into power, holds histrionic mass rallies *à la* Nuremberg, and ultimately invades and conquers the Empire of Zind. In this portion of the novel, Hitler-the-novelist gives his pulpy prose full throttle as he depicts, in page after page of gory detail, the Heldons annihilating their subhuman enemies. To cite one representative example, Hitler writes:

Feric swung the Great Truncheon of Held in a steady rhythm before him ... without skipping a single beat ... At each swing, a score or more Warriors were clove in twain at the waist, erupting gore and slimy greenish intestines. In moments, the blood on the slick shaft of his mystic weapon was so thick that it ran down his arm and baptized the spotless black leather of his fresh uniform with the life juices of the enemy.[51]

While Hitler depicts the Heldons making mincemeat of their enemies, however, he does not make them invincible. Indeed, at the end of the novel, they suffer a frightening setback when the ruler of Zind detonates a final nuclear explosion contaminating the "germ plasm" of all humans, seemingly for eternity. Yet, in the end, Hitler portrays Jaggar using a new cloning technology to realize his utopian vision of spreading the "master race" across the globe and, at the novel's conclusion, throughout the universe. *Lord of the Swastika* thus concludes on a redemptive note.

The end of *Lord of the Swastika*'s narrative, however, is not the end of *The Iron Dream*. Spinrad's novel reaches its tour de force conclusion in the fictional afterword supplied by literary critic, Homer Whipple, who offers a trenchant analysis of *Lord of the Swastika*'s underlying agenda. As Whipple describes it, *Lord of the Swastika* is an anticommunist work of literature that reflects the widespread fears of communism in the West during the allohistorical 1950s. Hitler, Whipple informs the reader, had been a well-known opponent of communism ever since his days in the little-known National Socialist, or Nazi, party, which he describes as having faded into irrelevance after a communist-led coup in Germany in 1923. As communist power in Europe grew – especially after 1948 when the Greater Soviet Union took over Great Britain – Hitler's anticommunist stance became all the more strident. The time in which Hitler writes his novel in the 1950s, in short, is one of immense Soviet power. Significantly, Soviet power continues unabated in Whipple's own present. As he observes from his vantage point in the year 1959, the era is one in which "the Greater Soviet Union bestrides Eurasia like a drunken brute. Most of Africa is under its sway, and the South American republics are beginning to crumble. Only the great Japanese-American lake that is the Pacific stands as the final bastion of freedom in the world."[52] Against this backdrop, Whipple notes, "the fundamental political allegory of *Lord of the Swastika* is quite clear: Heldon, representing either Germany or the non-communist world, totally annihilates Zind, representing the Greater Soviet Union."[53] *Lord of the Swastika* is thus clearly a fictional expression of Hitler's deepest personal fantasy.

What the narratives of *Lord of the Swastika* and *The Iron Dream* reveal about Spinrad's own views of history, however, is less obvious. On one level, Spinrad evidently believed that Hitler's failure to become Führer would have done little to improve the course of history. In offering this conclusion, Spinrad embraced a structuralist model of historical causality that identified broader forces leading history to turn out for the worse in Hitler's absence. These forces included the political extremism of the German people who, lacking the option of Nazism, end up embracing communism (as is suggested by Whipple's reference to a communist coup in 1923).[54] The persisting power of communism is a second structural constant for Spinrad. As a result of the communists' rise to power in Germany (and the resulting formation of the Greater Soviet Union, or GSU), the cold war between the communist and capitalist worlds erupts at the same time in alternate history as it does in real history. Indeed, it manifests itself in even more extreme fashion. For Hitler's failure to become Führer and launch Operation Barbarossa against the Soviets actually allows them to extend their power to a much further extent than they did in real history. Moreover, the most obvious potential historical windfall from Hitler's absence from history – namely, the prevention of the Holocaust – is also not realized. As Whipple reports, the Soviet Union has become such a hotbed of antisemitism in recent years that "five million Jews have perished."[55] In other words, had Hitler not perpetrated the Holocaust, the Soviet Union under Stalin may well have done the same thing anyway. Hitler's absence from history, it is true, prevents 35 million Europeans from dying in World War II. Yet, since a much greater portion of the world is threatened by Soviet tyranny, since the world continues to live under the shadow of nuclear weapons (which have proliferated even without World War II), and since it has just recently witnessed genocide on a horrible scale, history has turned out just as bad, if not worse.

In submitting this pessimistic view of history, Spinrad expressed disaffection with his own historical present.[56] At first glance, Spinrad's assertions would seem to suggest that he harbored deep fears of communism at the time. Writing during the height of the American war against communism in Vietnam, this would be a reasonable assumption. Spinrad, however, was no conservative anticommunist, but rather belonged to the political left.[57] His intentions in writing *The Iron Dream* were thus part of a broader agenda of cultural and social criticism. As he put it, the novel was "a kind of exorcism ... an attempt to work through the heart of psychic Nazism by letting the spirit of Hitler himself express his inner reality through wishful-filling science fiction and by thus laying bare the prurient inner soul of the Nazi-sword-and-sorcery mentality, to destroy its unconscious power."[58] Or to put it differently, Spinrad believed that fascism's unconscious power had hardly disappeared with the collapse of the Third Reich. In part, he believed it had survived in the violent and racist subtexts of postwar science fiction, which he aimed to satirize through the narrative of *Lord of the Swastika*.[59] More importantly, though, Spinrad sought to expose fascism's survival in postwar society by revealing its links to anticommunism.[60] Spinrad made this connection by depicting how Homer Whipple's own anticommunism leads him to sympathize with Hitler's novel. Even though Whipple is partly repelled by Hitler's prose, he declares that the writer's "political wish-fulfillment fantasy strikes a chord in the heart of every American," "appeals to our deepest desires," and "represents our fondest hope." Speaking of Hitler's fascistic hero, Jaggar, Whipple goes as far as to write that "in these dark times, who in his heart of hearts does not secretly pray for the emergence of such a leader?" Whipple ultimately steps back from this wish, noting that "such a man could gain power only in the extravagant fancies of a pathological science fiction novel."[61] But, in denying the possibility of such a fascist leader taking power in the United States, Whipple articulated Spinrad's main cautionary point, which was to warn readers against complacently believing that fascism was impossible in the democratic United States. Just as few people ever thought the civilized nation of Germany could have embraced Nazism prior to 1933, Spinrad made the universalistic argument that fascism was possible anywhere. Writing at a time in which the United States was perceived to be committing war crimes in Vietnam, Spinrad took a similar position to that displayed in Brian Aldiss's short story "Swastika!" and Harry Mulisch's novel, *De toekomst van gisteren*, by polemically arguing that Nazism was hardly a unique German phenomenon and could indeed find a home in America.

In arriving at this larger conclusion, however, Spinrad exhibited a normalized view of the Nazi past. As was true of other writers who universalized the Third Reich's significance, his concerns about postwar political problems diminished the regime's aura of evil in his conscious-ness. The dynamic was most obvious in Spinrad's transformation of Hitler from the world's most notorious dictator into a hack science fiction writer – a transformation from ultimate evil to prosaic banality. Moreover, his depiction of history without Hitler as no better than history with him reduced his evil into something comparatively insignificant. Finally, in the process of trying to exorcise the demons of Nazism through the purple prose of *Lord of the Swastika*, Spinrad – like so many other writers in the 1970s – seemed to surrender to the fascination of fascism and partly aestheticized it.

More than twenty years after the publication of *The Iron Dream*, British-Israeli writer Simon Louvish's novel *The Resurrections* described the world without the Führer in similar fashion.[62] Published in 1994, *The Resurrections* was crafted in the form of a long series of diary entries written by various fictional and non-fictional characters – the central one being an American journalist named Rachel Levy – spanning the years 1961–70. The time is a chaotic one in the United States, in large part due to the blatantly racist campaign for the American presidency being waged by one Rudolph Hitler, the son of longtime U.S. Senator, Adolf Hitler, in 1961. Like Spinrad's *The Iron Dream*, the central allohistorical premise of Louvish's novel is that instead of leading the Nazi party to power in Germany in 1933, Hitler emigrated to the United States following the eruption of a successful communist revolution in Germany in 1923.[63] In this alternate world, Hitler and other leading Nazi party leaders such as Hermann Goering and Josef Goebbels flee to the United States in 1925, at which point they attempt to refound their movement and lead the American people in an Aryan crusade against communism. In this effort, Hitler continues his career as a politician. However, unlike in real history, his rise to power is ultimately thwarted. He is elected U.S. senator from the state of Illinois in 1946 and establishes the new "American party" in 1958, but his inability to shake his German accent and the legal prohibition against him running for president as a foreign-born American prevent him from making the most of his political potential. By the mid-1960s, Hitler has lost his sense of political ambition altogether.

The premise of Hitler as a failed politician might easily be seen in a positive light, yet *The Resurrections* depicted his failure to become the Führer of Germany as having extremely negative consequences for the course of history at large. American history, for one thing, is drastically worse. Even though the United States is never threatened by the Nazis (who never seize power), it still faces a direct threat from Germany, whose citizens support a leftwing coup in 1923 that brings a communist government to power. Barely a generation later, this communist government develops the atomic bomb and covertly supplies it to the United States' chief rival, Japan, which proceeds to devastate Los Angeles in the

"L.A. Holocaust" of 1952. (For good measure, the U.S. retaliates by nuking Tokyo.) In America, Hitler skillfully exploits the resulting upsurge in domestic anticommunist sentiment to promote his racist and antisemitic agenda. His demagoguery strikes a chord throughout the country, particularly in the American South, which witnesses a strong increase in racial violence, capped by the lynching of Jews in Florida and the assassination of Martin Luther King. Finally, in 1961, Hitler engineers the candidacy of his son, Rudolph, for president on the American party ticket and achieves a stunning success when he wins one-third of the national vote, sparking a constitutional crisis. Rudolph's assassination that same year, however, sets back Hitler's agenda and permanently sours the elder demagogue on radical politics. Yet, by the end of the 1960s, the indefatigable Josef Gable continues to promote Hitler's longstanding goal of a "Revived, Volkisch Germany, purified of the Red Scum and of International Jewry" by engineering the rise of Rudolph's younger brother, Frederick, to political prominence, which occurs when he becomes the vice-president to the newly elected President, Joseph Patrick Kennedy.[64] In a rather cumbersome plot twist, Gable intends to assassinate President Kennedy, thereby ensuring that Frederick will become president and provide American support for a planned coup in Poland, from which he will then launch an invasion of communist Germany in order to reclaim the nation for Nazism. In the end, however, Gable meets with defeat when Frederick Hitler refuses to play the puppet and has him killed. Frederick, however, is hardly an altruistic figure. In a highly cynical and opportunistic move, Frederick does nothing to prevent Gable's hired sniper from killing President Kennedy, thereby ensuring his own rise to the presidency. The downward spiral of American history is thus capped in 1970 with the rise of a criminal to the most powerful post of the nation. By the novel's epilogue, set in the year 1990, continuing Japanese aggression in the Pacific has raised the threat of a "Second Japanese–American War," if not the "Second World War" itself.[65] "The lights are going out all over America," Rachel Levy reports on the novel's last page. "It's a topsy turvy world."[66]

Underlying the overall allohistorical conclusions of *The Resurrections* was a model of historical causality that elevated structural forces over individual agency. To be sure, Louvish did not entirely dismiss Hitler's power as an individual to effect historical change. Hitler's failure to become the Führer, after all, has significant implications not only for Germany (which becomes communist instead of fascist) but for America as well, which is thrown into upheaval by his political activism. Yet Hitler's individual abilities as a political agitator reach their limits in America, whose political and social traditions emerge as Louvish's structural constants par excellence. It is largely due to America's historic embrace of democracy that Hitler is unable to sell his movement of Nazism to the American people. Moreover, America's ability to compel newcomers to assimilate and embrace its values prevents Hitler from passing on the Nazi torch to his children. Hitler's ultimate failure as a politician is confirmed at his funeral in 1970, when his son Frederick thinks to himself:

Well, old man, here we are, and your coffin ... trundling on its conveyor belt towards the discreet black curtains hiding the crematorium furnace ... [You] lived so deep in your world of makebelieve you almost ... made it real. There was certainly something titanic and marvellous about your awesome vision ... Your imagined victory over the dark forces of the 'Jewish Satan' and his minions. Instead ... you ... passed away in the ironic peace of your coma ...
There could have been no question, father, of mounting the grotesque [burial] display you had planned. In that, as in so much else, I have to disregard you. I fulfilled the central aim. I rode your plots to ascendancy. I am the President of the United States. But that is as far as it goes. I am no German exile yearning for a bloody revenge ... I am an American, pledged to my country's prosperity ... The old emblems and standards of the NSDAP stay under lock and key in your attic, to be ... quietly burned, as soon as possible, in the municipal dump.[67]

In the end, the Americanization of Hitler's children constitutes a silver lining of sorts for *The Resurrections'* otherwise gloomy narrative. Even if America proves temporarily vulnerable to the appeal of Nazism, its democratic traditions help resist it. By the end of the novel, however, the consignment of Hitler and Nazism to the ash can of history does not prevent the world from remaining a highly dangerous place. Alternate history without Hitler as the Führer of Nazi Germany is little better than real history with him.

In submitting this bleak conclusion, Louvish, like Spinrad, exhibited a tendency to view the Nazi era from a normalized perspective. This tendency was partly visible in Louvish's humanization of Hitler as a character. In America, Hitler is no longer a demon but merely a troublemaker with no hope of landing upon the world historical stage. By the 1960s, Hitler degenerates into a frail and pathetic figure who increasingly succumbs to hallucinatory and nostalgic visions of the past. So dottering is he near the end of his life that Josef Gable likens him to a "stricken dachshund."[68] Louvish's normalized view of the Nazi era was not merely visible in his reduction of Hitler's ability to wreak havoc, however, but in his emphasis on the ability of larger structural forces to spark conflict. One structural constant identified by the author is the extremist politics of the German people, whom Louvish depicted as just as capable of causing trouble in alternate history (as communists) as they did in real history (as Nazis). But Louvish focused even more on such universal forces as nationalism, imperialism, and economic competition, all of which he portrayed as more likely to disrupt the course of history than isolated individuals like Hitler. This structuralist bent to Louvish's philosophy of history is summed up by one of the main characters, a man by the name of Michael, who notes near the novel's end, "However the pieces move, the game remains the same."[69]

Louvish's focus upon the structural threats to peace reflected a strong sense of moral engagement with present-day political problems. Born in Scotland in 1939 and brought up in Israel, Louvish developed a strong leftwing political sensibility that expressed itself in a universal concern with injustice throughout the world.[70] His leftwing views may have influenced his downplaying of the ability of individuals to shape historical events. Preferring a structuralist model of historical causality typical of the Marxist left, Louvish no doubt wanted to challenge the complacent notion that history without Hitler would have somehow been better. Writing in the early 1990s, at a time when unexpected international crises were erupting in the wake of the cold war, Louvish may have wanted to admonish readers that enduring structural forces would continue to play havoc with history. Moreover, by showing how a world without Hitler would have been a very dangerous place — especially by showing how America nearly embraces fascism — Louvish likely hoped to debunk the triumphalistic notion, common in the West in the early 1990s, that liberalism's triumph was inevitable. In short, Louvish's goal in writing *The Resurrections* was to universalize the significance of Nazism in order to make a larger comment about the broader forces that continue to shape history.

Similar conclusions can be drawn about another work that appeared the same year as *The Resurrections*, American writer Barbara Delaplace's 1994 short story, "Painted Bridges."[71] Set in an indeterminate point in history (but probably some time in the 1920s), Delaplace's tale outlined what might have happened had Adolf Hitler never become the dictator of the Third Reich but instead had been diagnosed as insane and placed in a German mental institution. "Painted Bridges" focuses on the sudden improvement in the condition of a violent mental patient by the name of Adolf Schickelgruber when his Jewish doctor, Josef Goldstein, introduces him to an experimental form of art therapy. In short order, Goldstein's belief that Adolf might improve if allowed to "express [his] ... delusions and fantasies on canvas" seems to be borne out, as the patient's prodigious output of paintings is accompanied by a decrease in his "ranting out-bursts."[72] Yet Goldstein's "cautiously optimistic" perspective is soon clouded by a worrisome turn of events. All of the people who come into contact with Adolf's abstract images seem to be adversely affected by them. A janitor at the sanatorium smears antisemitic graffiti on Dr. Goldstein's door after viewing the canvases; the owner of a modern art gallery, Helmut Vos, who is interested in the work of the mentally ill, turns combative after Dr. Goldstein displays reluctance in allowing Adolf's work to be shown in public; and finally, when Dr. Vos prevails and prominently displays the works of "Patient S." in his gallery, pedestrians walking by become anti-semitic after gazing upon them. The transformative effect of Hitler's work is epitomized in a review of his work by the art critic of the *Berlin News* who writes:

Stand in front of one of 'Patient S''s paintings and you find you're drawn into a vision of a world where each man knows his place and takes pride in it. A world where each labors for the good of all, where joy brings strength. A place of pure air, clean water, and blond, healthy children running laughing in the grass.

Study another [painting by a different artist] and you discover a statement about our current condition: a place ... where Germans aren't permitted to stand proud and free. Where we are ground under the heel of the mongrel races of the world. Injustice rules us!

Another painting – a call to action. We must show our enemies our power and destroy them ... Nothing must stop us. Not plotting Jews. Not lazy Gypsies. Not Poles, not queers ... no one. We Germans are supreme! A superior race.

Any ... true German looking at these paintings *must* feel these things. 'Patient S' is a genius! A spokesman for the true German spirit![73]

Before long, Dr. Goldstein realizes that "It's the paintings ... [that are causing] people who view them to change radically," and he resolves to put an end to the burgeoning insanity by prohibiting his patient from further artistic production and by withdrawing his existing works from public display. Yet he is too late. Behind the scenes, Dr. Vos, various journalists, and the agitated masses themselves have mobilized to combat the "censorship" of the imprisoned patient–artist's work and increasingly embraced violence on behalf of their cause. As the tale ends, Dr. Vos writes to an editor of the *Berlin News* proposing a plan to liberate "Adolf Schickelgruber, who is being held against his will by a vicious Jewish doctor" and to "show these kikes who's in charge."[74]

Given the limited parameters of "Painted Bridges," it is difficult to know whether the story ultimately depicted history as turning out better, worse, or the same. On the one hand, Hitler's failure to become a politician does little to improve the course of history, for the German people remain intolerant, resentful, and prone to mischief. On the other hand, Hitler's absence from politics does not make the course of history worse, for while the story ends with the foreshadowing of incipient nastiness, it has not yet come to pass. In short, history is no better and no worse – in a word, the same. Not surprisingly, in arriving at this conclusion Delaplace asserted the importance of structural factors as well as individual agency in shaping history. While she affirmed the inherent antidemocratic proclivities of the German people, she credited Hitler with the unique ability to unleash them. Still, the primary responsibility for the tragedy-to-come lay with the German people. For by depicting them as willing to follow even a certifiably insane artist, she placed blame more on the irrational masses than on their demonstrably lunatic leader. Delaplace, to be sure, affirmed Hitler's demonic potential to a greater degree than did Spinrad or Louvish. Yet she refrained from drawing the optimistic conclusions of Hans Pleschinski or Alexander Demandt, both of whom argued that Hitler's removal from history would have made it much better. Delaplace followed both Spinrad and Louvish in assuming that the political extremism of the German people would probably have led history to turn out just as bad if not worse without Hitler as Führer as with him.

The most pessimistic portrayal of the historical consequences of Hitler never becoming Führer was the well-known British comic actor and writer Stephen Fry's 1996 novel, *Making History* (see Figure 24).[75] Set in the present, the novel focuses on a shleppy, if endearing, British graduate student in history at the University of Cambridge named Michael Young, who has just completed a doctoral dissertation on Adolf Hitler's early life. In preparing to deliver the final manuscript to his doctoral adviser one day, however, Michael's life quickly takes an unusual turn. While walking across campus, he drops his briefcase and looks with horror as the pages of his dissertation fly into the wind. As chance has it, however, another professor observes the scene and helps Michael retrieve his work, at which point the older man expresses great interest in reading it. Michael lends it to him, expecting little to come of it. However, when he invites Michael up to his laboratory to see his work, events quickly head in an unexpected direction. The older professor is a man named Leo Zuckerman, a German-born physicist at the university who has invented a "temporal imaging machine" (or TIM) that can gaze into the past, just like a video recorder looks into the present, and transmit images of it in the form of vivid abstract colors. Impressed by the concept, Michael becomes amazed when Leo sets the machine to focus upon Auschwitz on the date of

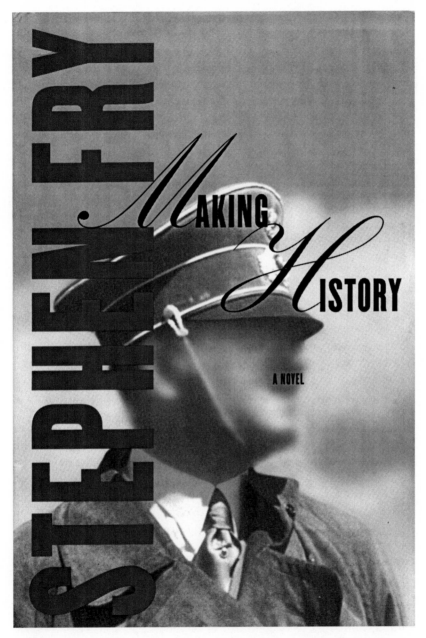

Figure 24 Cover of the American edition of Stephen Fry's 1996 novel *Making History*.

October 9, 1942 – the day after the arrival there of the scientist's father from Germany. After recovering from his initial shock, Michael begins to meditate upon the machine's implications and shortly thereafter seizes upon the idea that becomes the novel's central narrative conceit – using the machine as a transmitter that may somehow be able to "liquidate Hitler." In embarking upon the plan to eliminate the Führer, Michael expresses the classical motives driving most allohistorical accounts that rest on this premise. Without Hitler, he tells Leo, "Everything will be better. We're going to make a better world."[76] Things, however, are not so simple. Leo, for one, is initially opposed to the idea of killing Hitler, exclaiming:

> No. Absolutely not! ... You think the thought hasn't crossed my mind? You think the idea of being able to rid humanity of the curse of Adolf Hitler isn't something I think of every minute of my waking life? But listen to me Michael ... The day I was first told what happened to my father ... in Auschwitz ... I swore before God ... that never ... would I involve myself in war, in murder, in the harming of another human being. You understand me?[77]

Michael, however, is not bent on murder. Holding up an experimental male contraceptive pill that he has stolen from his girlfriend's chemistry lab, he responds, "We just make sure the motherfucker is never born."[78] Gradually, Michael's firm sense of conviction begins to sway Leo. But matters remain complicated. Although Michael assumes that Leo is obsessed with the past because of his father's time in Auschwitz, Leo eventually confesses that his father was not there as a Jewish prisoner but as an SS officer. It is historical guilt as the son of a German perpetrator that drives Leo's obsession with the past. Michael is taken aback by this news but voices his respect for Leo's honesty, and both men soon embark upon improving the course of history. Before long, Michael and Leo devise a plan to send several contraceptive pills back in time, to Hitler's birthplace, Braunau-am-Inn, in the summer of 1888, where they will land in the local well used by Hitler's mother, Klara, to fetch the family's water supply. Their hope is that Alois Hitler will drink from the drugged water, become infertile, and prevent Klara from ever conceiving baby Adolf. To their shock, the plan works. Once Michael and Leo send the pills back in time, a sudden shudder begins to shake their laboratory room, and both men are sucked back into the vortex of an alternate history in which everything is much different.

From this point on, *Making History* explores the world as it turns out without Hitler. As the second half of the novel opens, Michael awakens from an unconscious stupor in unfamiliar surroundings: Princeton University in the year 1996. His world, he soon learns, is quite different from the one he has just left. Initially unable to remember who he is, Michael gradually recalls his late-night attempt to change the world and, in eager anticipation, asks a fellow college student named Steve, "Tell me everything you know ... about Adolf Hitler." When Steve has no idea who the man is, Michael exclaims with joy, "We've done it!" and thinks to himself:

If only I could get to Europe now! Check out London, Berlin, Dresden, all the buildings standing there whole, firm, unblitzed and all because of me. My God, I was a greater man than Churchill, Roosevelt, Gandhi, Mother Teresa and Albert Schweitzer rolled into one ...
Auschwitz, Birkenau, Treblinka, Bergen-Belsen, Ravensbrück, Buchenwald, Sobibor. What were they now? Small towns in Poland and Germany. Happy silly little towns whose names were washed clear of sin and blame.[79]

Soon, however, Michael's euphoria vanishes. For as he gloats once again to Steve that he has never heard of Hitler or the Nazi party, Steve halts him and says, "What do you mean I've never heard of the Nazi party? ... Oh sure ... and I've never heard of Gloder and Göbbels and Himmler and Frick, right?"[80] Shocked, Michael races to the library and with great dismay reads an encyclopedia entry that describes one Rudolf Gloder as "Founder and leader of the Nazi party, Reich Chancellor and guiding spirit of the Greater German Reich from 1928 until his overthrow in 1963."[81]

As *Making History* makes clear, not only has the world without Hitler not turned out better, it has become far worse. Gloder's formation and leadership of the Nazi party are much more successful than Hitler's role in the same capacity. Although Gloder resembles Hitler in being a war veteran, ardent nationalist, and fierce anti-Semite, he is much more of a disciplined, rational, cold-hearted, real-politician than Hitler ever was. However, the most fateful difference, Michael learns from the encyclopedia and from other historical sources, is the fact that Gloder appreciated "the potential of science, engineering, and technological innovation."[82] For it enables him to swiftly develop the atomic bomb, which he uses to destroy Moscow and Leningrad in 1938. Thereafter, Gloder successfully invades and defeats most of Eastern Europe, at which point he also compels the surrender of France and England, seizing all of their overseas colonies. Worse still, Gloder's New Reich that same year evacuates all Jews to a new "'Jewish Free State' ... carved out between Montenegro and Herzegovina under control of Reichsminister Heydrich" and later murders them all.[83] This crime brings Germany and the United States (which has separately developed the bomb) to the brink of nuclear war, where the two great powers have remained ever since. All in all, the existence of German hegemony over

Europe, the completion of the "Final Solution," and enduring nuclear stalemate between the New Reich and the United States all vividly illustrate the disastrous effects of Michael and Leo's alteration of history.

At the personal level, moreover, life for Michael and Leo also takes a turn for the worse. For his part, Michael is reborn as a homosexual version of himself into an American society that has become so repressive that it has criminalized homosexuality. This is particularly painful for Michael, as he is unable to consummate his blooming relationship with Steve, who has long been infatuated with him. Leo, meanwhile, is unable to assuage his guilt about his father's historical misdeeds. While his father was a Nazi medical doctor at Auschwitz in real history, in alternate history he performs essentially the same function, helping Gloder to synthesize mass quantities of "Braunau Water" (which has since been discovered from the original, contaminated supply created by Leo and Michael in Braunau-am-Inn) in order to sterilize and eliminate Germany's racial enemies. At both the personal and geopolitical levels, then, Michael and Leo's attempt to improve the course of history backfires completely.

And yet, despite this terrible turn of events, *Making History* smuggles a happy ending through the back door. Through the help of Steve, Michael is able to track down Leo Zuckerman at Princeton where, as in "real" history, he has continued to work on a time machine. After convincing Leo about their misguided role in preventing Hitler's birth in real history, they attempt together to re-route history back onto its rightful course. Michael and Leo seize upon the idea of sending several maggot-infested rat carcasses back in time into Klara Hitler's village well so that she does not bring the contraceptive-laden water back to her home, thus ensuring that the (still virile) Alois Hitler will succeed in impregnating her with baby Adolf. Everything seems ready to proceed according to plan. Yet, just before pressing the button, Michael and Leo are suddenly interrupted by federal agents who are poised to foil their efforts. Finally, however, Leo and Michael are aided by Steve, who emerges from hiding, knocks down the agents, takes a bullet intended for Michael, and presses the button altering history once more for good before dying. In performing this heroic deed, Steve redeems Michael and Leo's misguided efforts to shape history and sets everything once more aright.

Like many of the accounts that preceded it, *Making History* was characterized by a deep-seated structuralist approach to historical causality. By rejecting the long-held premise that removing Hitler would have changed history in any way – indeed, by asserting that someone else would have most likely fulfilled Hitler's role in real history – Fry rejected the model of "great individuals" being able to shape the course of historical events. Fry's philosophy of history de-emphasized free will in favor of something akin to predestination. Or, as Michael declares:

> It was genes, genes and nothing but genes. I mean, look at Leo's father ... A son of a bitch who goes to Auschwitz to help wipe out the Jews in one world and a son of a bitch who goes to Auschwitz to help wipe out Jews in another. And his son, a decent man in both worlds ... This was predetermination either way you sliced it. The will of history or the will of DNA.[84]

For Fry, the world of history was one shaped by powerful forces that individuals are essentially powerless to resist. As in the works of Spinrad, Louvish, and Delaplace, the structural force of significance in *Making History* was the role of the German people – specifically, their willingness to support a charismatic authoritarian dictator and his war of world conquest. Fry may well have intended this skeptical view of the German people to be the chief message of his novel. As the son of an Austrian-Jewish mother whose family fled to England in the 1930s (and who lost many relatives in the Holocaust), his focus on the German people's role in supporting the Nazis was understandable.[85] Fry's endorsement of Daniel Goldhagen's scathing indictment of the German people, *Hitler's Willing Executioners* (which had appeared earlier in 1996), makes it especially likely that his novel's focus on the culpability of the German people was intentional.[86] Still, it would be a mistake to view *Making History* as primarily driven by a serious agenda. The novel's overwhelmingly comic tone strongly suggests that it was written with the lighthearted intent to entertain rather than instruct. Moreover, unlike the novels of Spinrad and Louvish, which fantasized about improving the past out of a sense of discontent with the present, Fry's ultimate decision to restore history to its rightful course and to allow the novel's protagonist Michael to blithely saunter away as if nothing had happened suggests that the writer was driven by a much more positive assessment of the contemporary world. While *Making History* indulged the fantasy of eliminating Hitler in order to improve history, it ultimately suggested the fantasy's fading appeal.

By contrast, the opposite was true of the last narrative of the 1990s to portray the world without Hitler – episode number 11 from the fourth season of the sci-fi television series *Sliders* entitled "California Reich."[87] First aired on August 24, 1998, this episode features the series' four main characters traveling in time to an alternate California in which the white majority, under the leadership of the state's new governor, Schick, has detained and imprisoned all ethnic minorities, especially blacks, in order to scientifically transform them into low-cost slave laborers. While the vagaries of the episode's plot do not merit detailed exposition (being mostly comprised of melodramatic clashes between good guys and bad guys), "California Reich" was notable for portraying America's turn to racist extremism as resulting from Hitler's absence from history. When the series' black character, Rembrandt, is imprisoned in a detention center and angrily compares Governor Schick to Hitler, another black inmate, Harold, looks blankly at him without recognizing the German dictator's name. As this scene reveals, the alternate world of "California Reich" is one in which Hitler and World War II have, for whatever reason, never come to be. The episode's main didactic point here was that even without Hitler, history could have easily turned out terribly. Like Simon Louvish's *The Resurrections*, "California Reich" implied that broader structural forces, such as racial intolerance, could well have caused mayhem all on their own.

In offering this bleak vision of an alternate world without Hitler, "California Reich" expressed discontent with the present. Specifically, writer Scott Smith Miller criticized the state of California's divisive racial politics in the mid-1990s. By portraying Governor Schick as having passed a bill called "proposition 286" decreeing the internment of all minorities, Miller obviously was referring to California Governor Pete Wilson's 1994 support for the controversial proposition 187, which aimed to deny medical aid to illegal immigrants. Beyond merely criticizing current politics, however, Miller's script, like Louvish's novel *The Resurrections*, aimed to provide a broader cautionary reminder to Americans in the 1990s that their history could easily have proceeded in a very different and unsavory manner had Hitler never existed. "California Reich" implied that it was precisely the negative example of Hitler's crimes in real history that led Americans after 1945 to reject racism and embrace the civil rights movement. Without the negative example of Hitler, American society is portrayed in the episode as suppressing the civil rights movement (the imprisoned black man, Harold, refers to the futility of having marched at Selma) and embracing racism instead.

In submitting this conclusion, Miller aimed to condemn contemporary racial intolerance. Yet in the process he expressed a normalized view of the Nazi past. This view was most visible in the episode's evaluation of Hitler himself. Instead of depicting him as irredeemably evil, the episode invested Hitler with redemptive significance. When one of the show's central characters observes that the alternate California "needs a harsh lesson to learn, since they never had a Hitler," the implication is that our real historical world should be grateful for possessing the Nazi dictator as an object lesson in the dangers of intolerance. Like Fry's *Making History,* "California Reich" implied that our real historical world as shaped by Hitler may have been better off than one in which he never existed. The episode thereby reflected the diminishing sense of Hitler's evil and the declining fantasy of eliminating him from history. The reason for this fantasy's decline, however, had little to do – as it did for Fry – with a growing sense of contentment with the present. Instead, as with Spinrad and Louvish, it reflected a preoccupation with present-day crises that served to displace attention from, and diminish the frightfulness of, the Nazi era. "California Reich" obeyed the broader dynamics of universalization insofar as it used Hitler and the Nazi past to direct attention to contemporary problems only to reduce the singularity of the former by comparing it with the latter.

After the turn of the millennium, a less politically charged affirmation of the pointlessness of killing Hitler appeared in the United States in the fall of 2002 with an episode of the UPN television network's revived *Twilight Zone* series entitled "Cradle of Darkness." In this episode (which originally aired on October 2) a woman by the name of Andrea Collins (played by Katherine Heigl) goes back in time in order to kill the infant Adolf Hitler and thereby improve the course of history. When she arrives, posing as a housekeeper, at the home of Alois and Klara Hitler in Braunau-am-Inn in Austria, however, she is struck by the young baby's innocence and finds herself unable to follow through with her task (see Figure 25). Yet as Andrea gradually gets to know Alois Hitler (played by James Remar), she comes to recognize the detrimental effect that his fierce nationalism and racial antisemitism will inevitably have on his son.[88] She therefore resolves to complete her mission and, at the end of the episode, jumps off a bridge into a river, drowning herself and the baby. History, though, is not so easily altered. Alois Hitler's other nanny, Christina, who is entrusted with the main duty of caring for the infant Adolf, witnesses the murder-suicide and, hoping to avert blame for his death, purchases another baby from a nearby destitute gypsy in the hope of passing him off as the genuine article. At the episode's conclusion, Alois seems not to notice the bait-and-switch and accepts a dinner guest's compliment that his son represents "a fine example of Aryan breeding." The conclusion is thus a bleak one. As the show's host, Forest Whitaker, intones ominously at the end, "A moment of silence for Andrea Collins. She sacrificed her life for the good of humanity. But she also created the very monster she sought to destroy. History can never be changed. Not even in the Twilight Zone."

The conclusion of "Cradle of Darkness" echoed the familiar notion that early twentieth-century German nationalism would have produced a

Figure 25 Time-traveling baby nurse Andrea Collins (Katherine Heigl) lifts up the infant
Adolf Hitler in the 2002 *Twilight Zone* episode "Cradle of Darkness."

vicious leader regardless of his identity. Even though Adolf Hitler is
eliminated from history, the episode suggests that nurture trumps nature.
The rabidly nationalistic and antisemitic environment of the Hitler household would have turned any child reared there into a future dictator – even,
the episode implies, a gypsy baby. History will turn out no better as a result
of Hitler's death. In offering this message, the episode's writer, Kamran
Pasha, shared the skeptical view of early twentieth-century German culture
common to most Anglo-American tales, while adding a philosophical
belief that little good can come of an evil act like murder.[89] At the same
time, "Cradle of Darkness" explained Hitler's evil as a product of his
environment, rather than a part of his very genetic code. However accurate
this explanation may be as a reading of human behavior, it served somewhat to exonerate the historical Hitler for his actions, blaming them upon
an irresponsible father and a racist upbringing. In this vision, Hitler
himself is transformed into something of a victim, being born into a
fanatical household and ultimately being murdered as an innocent infant.
In the end, "Cradle of Darkness" once more confirmed how blaming

structural forces at work in German society for Nazism could ironically serve to diminish Hitler's own share of culpability.

Finally, this point was confirmed by German alternate history writer Christian v. Ditfurth's 2003 novel, *Der Consul.*[90] Taking the form of a detective thriller, *Der Consul* explores what would have happened had Adolf Hitler been murdered in the fall of 1932 in the midst of his campaign to seize power in Germany. The novel opens with its protagonist, a grizzled Berlin policeman named Stefan Soetting, being sent to the city of Weimar to investigate the puzzling circumstances of Hitler's demise. While Soetting immediately deduces that the aspiring dictator has been bludgeoned to death in his upscale hotel room with a marble bust of the famed German poet, Johann Wolfgang von Goethe, he is initially at a loss as to who might be responsible. The local Weimar police accuse two communist hotel employees of the crime, but Soetting suspects that other parties are to blame. Many leading Nazis had been seen with Hitler the night before his murder and some in particular, he believes, stood to gain from it. It so happens that on the day before Hitler's murder, November 6, 1932, the NSDAP (Nazi party) had suffered a major setback in the national elections, losing some two million votes. For this reason, Soetting assumes that a power struggle to control the party is to blame, and he immediately focuses attention on Hitler's Nazi rivals, such as Gregor Strasser, with whom the Führer had disagreed about political strategy. Yet when Strasser is murdered in grisly fashion, and when SA chief Ernst Röhm and propaganda czar Josef Goebbels are knocked off as well, rumors begin to fly that a deranged ritual murderer is responsible for the killing spree, and Soetting becomes exasperated about the possibility of ever learning the truth.

Soon enough, however, he discovers that Hitler's death is part of a broader rightwing conspiracy. Through old-fashioned detective work, Soetting finds conclusive evidence that a shadowy extremist organization known as the Organisation Consul (OC) led by former Freikorps captain Arthur Ehrhardt has engineered the killings as part of a larger plot to topple the Weimar Republic and seize control of Germany. Ehrhardt's hope is that the killings will weaken the Nazi party and create a power vacuum that will, in turn, spark a communist coup and thereby provide the Reichswehr with a convenient pretext for crushing the left and restoring order once and for all. The OC rationalizes this plan by claiming that if the Nazis are able to seize power by themselves, they will be able to unite Germany's enemies against it, thus making it far more difficult for the nation to overturn the hated Treaty of Versailles and commence a crash program of rearmament. To this end, they win Hitler's not-so-loyal underling, Hermann Goering, over to their cause, and it is he who, Soetting realizes, has killed Hitler personally in a fit of rage at the Führer's refusal to accept President Paul von Hindenburg's offer of the vice-chancellorship.

Soetting's discovery of the truth about Hitler's murder, however, does not enable him to prevent the subsequent flow of historical events from unfolding in an ominous direction. As Ditfurth's narrative makes clear, Hitler's elimination from history does little to improve its course. Following the Führer's death, the OC conspirators, who include Goering, Kurt von Schleicher, and officers of the Reichswehr, spread the rumor that the murder is part of a communist plot organized by the Soviet secret police, the GPU, and they thereafter use this alleged plot as a pretext for launching a rightwing coup against the Weimar government. In short order, the conspirators succeed in dissolving the Reichstag, proclaim new emergency laws, and form a new secret police agency to combat the alleged communist threat. Soon thereafter the main democratic political parties, apart from the NSDAP and other rightwing parties, are banned, and concentration camps are established. Against the backdrop of this rightwing coup, Soetting stubbornly attempts to find evidence proving the OC's involvement in Hitler's murder. But he ultimately fails. At the novel's depressing climax, Soetting is forced to stand trial and defend himself from the charge that he abetted the escape of one of the communists (falsely) accused of killing Hitler. And while he valiantly makes his case – even compelling Hermann Goering to take the witness stand to account for his whereabouts on the night of Hitler's murder – he finally is found guilty and sentenced to death.

With this bleak ending, Ditfurth added his name to the long list of writers who have argued that Hitler's removal from history would have done little to improve its outcome. Like many of the writers who came before him, Ditfurth believed that the nationalistic and authoritarian tendencies of the German people would have ended up leading Germany down an antidemocratic path with or without Hitler. To be sure, unlike Stephen Fry, Ditfurth did not assert that history would have been worse without Hitler. After all, he himself has noted that while "there would have been a Second World War even without Hitler," there would not have been a "war of extermination and the Final Solution."[91] To a degree, then, Ditfurth implicitly conceded the unique contribution of Hitler to the uniquely criminal course of real history. Still, Ditfurth was unwilling to see history as improved without Hitler. Unlike Henry Turner, who much more dramatically emphasized the positive effects of a similar rightwing coup in the wake of Hitler's premature death (no World War II,

Holocaust, or Hiroshima), Ditfurth chose to dwell on the depressing reality of the German people's turn towards authoritarianism. In doing so, he distinguished himself as one of the few Germans writing on the subject to take a self-critical view of Germany's recent past. Unlike Hans Pleschinski, Alexander Demandt, and Sabine Wedemeyer-Schwiersch, who indulged the fantasy that eliminating Hitler would have made everything better, Ditfurth soberly argued that it would have done little good. In making this claim, Ditfurth gave expression to his longstanding leftwing political views.[92] At the same time, it was probably easier for any German writer to take this stance after the turn of the millennium than it would have been twenty years earlier, when the country's persisting national division made the open wounds of the Nazi era all the more visible. In short, a greater degree of satisfaction with the German present may have subtly led Ditfurth to forgo a fantasy that a generation earlier was much more appealing. In the process, he contributed to the ongoing diminution of Hitler's demonic aura.[93]

Overall, the allohistorical portrayals of Hitler's elimination from history shared common conclusions. All of them argued that history would have been no better, and may indeed have been worse, had Hitler never become the dictator of Nazi Germany. They did so out of a structuralist conviction that had Hitler never become Führer, broader forces – whether the extremist political tendencies of the German people or the latent racism of the American people – would have led to disaster anyway. In showing how history without Hitler would have been worse, these tales expressed concerns about the present by exposing the continued structural threats to peace, whether in the form of nationalism or racism. At the same time, however, they effectively ratified the course of real history as having produced a world that – while perhaps not the best of all possible ones – was certainly superior to the more dangerous world that might have been.

KILLING HITLER: THE FÜHRER'S PREMATURE DEATH

If the tales portraying Hitler's failure to become Führer before 1933 largely insisted that his absence would have done little to improve the course of history, other accounts depicting Hitler's assassination *after* he had already become the Führer largely agreed. These tales portrayed Hitler's removal from history at a later date as doing little to make the world any better. To a degree, this conclusion was easy to arrive at, since the longer Hitler had been in power *before* being killed, the less likely his elimination would have undone the damage he had already caused and thereby improve the course

of history. Had Claus Graf Schenck von Stauffenberg successfully assassinated Hitler in 1944 – at a point when the Nazis had already sown so much
destruction – for example, he would have had less of a chance of improving
history than Elleander Morning would have had, had she successfully killed
the Nazi dictator-to-be in 1913. This aspect of the scenario notwithstanding, it is still notable that most narratives portraying the Führer's assassination refused to credit his killers with performing any heroic function
whatsoever. In refusing to do so, these narratives favored a structuralist
view of historical change that also expressed an enduring suspicion of the
German people's antidemocratic political tendencies.

The first pessimistic depiction of the Führer's premature death appeared
in 1952 with American science fiction writer Robert Donald Locke's short
story, "Demotion."[94] Published in the popular magazine, *Astounding
Science Fiction*, "Demotion" opens with the seemingly unrelated and
admittedly outlandish (but for science fiction, rather tame) scenario of a
war between Earth and Mars. Against this backdrop, Locke focuses on the
attempt of military authorities in Earth's "Department of Planetary
Defense" to formulate a strategy to tip the conflict's outcome in their
favor. In this effort, the authorities attempt to prevent the war from
occurring by using the technological means of "time erasure" to eliminate
from the historical record the event responsible for the ill-fated "causal
warp" in the first place: the assassination of Adolf Hitler at his alpine retreat
at Berchtesgaden in 1943 by American air force bombs.

Hitler's death, they assert, "brought an early end to World [War] II,"
but it left in its wake a bitter legacy known as "Bismarck's disease."[95]
A nationalistic type of "war lust" originally generated by "the easy peace
terms fixed on leaderless Germany," Bismarck's disease soon begins to
spread beyond its German place of origin and infects other peoples. By
1960, it has "approached pandemic proportions" by spreading to the
Asiatic Entente, which proceeds to launch "the six-months-long World
War III" which, in turn, is only "ended by the atomic bombing of the
Asiatic Entente capital in 1960."[96] Hitler's death, in short, produces a
worsening spiral of virulent nationalism and war that finally climaxes
with the infection of the Martians with Bismarck's disease in 1985 and
the outbreak of interplanetary war. "Had it not been for World War III's
sudden termination," military authorities argue, they could have "isolated"
and discovered a vaccine for Bismarck's disease, inoculated the Martians,
and thus averted the present crisis.[97] Realizing that "[had] Hitler survived
the Berchtesgaden bombing of 1943, the war would have been fought to a
bitter climax," military leaders conclude that "for the good of mankind, we

suggest that World War II proceed to a violent conclusion [and] the Berchtesgaden bombing be erased."[98] At the tale's end, the American pilot responsible for originally killing Hitler, Charles Leslie, this time develops engine trouble above Dieppe and is forced to return to England, crash landing in Ipswich. Hitler is spared and, as the military authorities conclude with satisfaction, "the [Martian] crisis has passed its peak and is subsiding ... The system is at peace."[99]

As one of the admittedly more futuristic examples of alternate history to appear on the subject, Locke's account was the first to challenge the seductive belief that doing away with Hitler would have had positive consequences for the subsequent course of history. To a degree, Locke's pessimistic conclusion reflected a deeper structuralist belief that even in Hitler's absence other, broader forces would have caused history to turn out poorly. In Locke's case, the pivotal one was that of nationalism – or what he called "Bismarck's disease" – an aggressive force which, while German in origin, had since spread throughout the rest of the world. It is highly likely, however, that Locke was less concerned about the survival of German nationalism in the early 1950s than the threat posed by Soviet communism, and his tale can be seen as reflecting a general sense of disillusionment caused by the cold war in the early 1950s. In these years, Americans began to realize that their defeat of Nazism had not only saved the world for democracy but also helped save it for communism; rather than inaugurating a new era of peace, the defeat of the Nazis brought about the continuation of war. The profound disappointments of this disillusioned era were sounded in the narrative of "Demotion," in which an ostensibly heroic deed – the assassination of Hitler – unexpectedly perpetuates a new cycle of violence to such an extent that it needs to be erased from history altogether. "Demotion," therefore, expressed the impulse to universalize the historical significance of Nazism in order to direct attention to the contemporary threat of communism.

Over twenty years would pass before another work was published on the possible consequences of Hitler's assassination. But in a 1974 essay entitled "Wenn der Anschlag gelungen wäre" ("If the attack had succeeded"), the prominent German historian Eberhard Jäckel raised the question of how history would have turned out had the July 20, 1944 plot succeeded in killing Hitler.[100] Jäckel's laconic answer was that even "if the assassination attempt against Hitler had succeeded, the attack of July 20th may well have collapsed" anyway.[101] The Third Reich's power structure was so tightly organized, according to Jäckel, that the absence of the Führer would not have created that much of a crisis. With Goering, Himmler, Ribbentrop,

Jodl, Keitel, and others all still occupying their positions, the conspirators around Stauffenberg would have had little chance of seizing power. This was especially true because of the "horrible but unfortunately true" fact that the German people decried the assassination, rejected the conspirators, and remained loyal to the Nazi government.[102] Because of this unity between Volk and state, according to Jäckel, Hitler's absence after 1944 would have made very little difference in the course of history. Even if the conspirators could have seized power (and established a Beck–Goerdeler government), moreover, they would have suffered the same crushing defeat by the Allies, who were fully committed to Germany's unconditional surrender with or without Hitler in power.[103] Moreover, had the conspirators seized power, history might have actually turned out worse. For the successful assassination of the dictator would have "certainly given rise to a new stab in the back legend" that could easily "have impeded the re-establishment of German democracy."[104]

This conclusion was important coming from a German historian. As the earliest German account to question the fantasy that killing Hitler would have improved history, Jäckel emphasized the importance of structural factors in shaping history. Although Jäckel himself was a so-called intentionalist historian who focused on Hitler's decisive role in the Nazi state, his essay reserved a considerable portion of blame for the German people themselves.[105] Even without Hitler, he implied, the German people would have continued to make Germany a conservative, nationalistic place. This self-critical perspective identified Jäckel as a scholar on the liberal wing of the German political spectrum and appropriately echoed the liberal spirit of the era. In the early 1970s, West Germany had turned to the left under the SPD government of Chancellor Willy Brandt and had begun to abandon its strict postwar nationalistic position on the desirability of reunification, pursuing détente with Eastern European nations like East Germany and Poland under the policy of *Ostpolitik*.[106] Unlike the positions later taken by Germans like Pleschinski and Demandt (whose disaffection with German national division led them to embrace the self-congratulatory fantasy that the German people could have avoided all the problems that led to it if only Hitler had never risen to power), Jäckel's essay demonstrated a German capacity to adopt a more self-critical view of the nation's past. It also reflected a degree of contentment with the West German present. In a bold move, Jäckel was willing to consider the possibility that "it was better for German democracy that the assassination attempt [against Hitler] failed."[107] After all, Hitler's survival led to Germany's unconditional surrender, defeat, and reconstruction – all of which were crucial for laying the foundation for the nation's postwar success. Given the belief that everything worked out for the best anyway, fantasizing about Hitler's early death had little appeal for Jäckel.

After the scattered early tales of Locke and Jäckel, portrayals of the negative consequences of Hitler's assassination began to appear in greater number in the 1990s. In 1991, the well-known alternate history writer Harry Turtledove published a short story on the theme entitled "Ready for the Fatherland."[108] Turtledove's story opens in German-occupied Russia in the wake of the German defeat at Stalingrad in early 1943 and reaches its basic point of divergence from the real historical record when German Field Marshal Erich von Manstein, having just been upbraided by an irate Hitler over military strategy, pulls out a pistol and kills the Führer with three shots to the chest. Explaining to his fellow generals that the war against the Soviets cannot be won, he declares, "Let us make certain we do not lose it." At this point the story shifts to the city of Rijeka in "the independent nation of Croatia" in the year 1979. History has turned out very differently, as is made clear by the remarks of the story's protagonists, two British intelligence agents named Smith and Drinkwater, who are posing as Italian fishermen as part of an intelligence-gathering operation in Croatia. Bemoaning the continuing danger of nuclear war between "fascist Germany, the Soviet Union, the U.S.A., and Britain," they once more revisit the fateful killing of Hitler by Manstein, which has allowed the Nazis and the Soviets to forge a separate peace and thus continue as major world powers.[109] After this discussion, Smith and Drinkwater arrange to meet a Serbian agent, Bogdan, who is seeking weapons in support of the occupied Serbs' resistance effort against the Croats and Germans. As they are about to seal the deal, however, Croatian Ustasha agents surprise the threesome and shoot Bogdan in the stomach before taking him away for interrogation. The story concludes with the surprising declaration of thanks from the Ustasha agents to the British pair, who have actually betrayed Bogdan to the Croatians in accordance with higher orders from London. Because of sensitive negotiations between the British and Germans over North Sea oil rights (made all the more pressing by Russian machinations in the oil fields of Turkey, Iraq, and Persia), the London government has sold out its erstwhile Serbian allies. Realpolitik has trumped morality in the conduct of great power politics.

For Turtledove, Hitler's early death would have led history to turn out worse from both a geopolitical and moral perspective. While in real history, Hitler's survival ends up sealing Nazi Germany's doom, his early death allows the Nazis to emerge from the war with their power intact.

Despite Hitler's disappearance, Turtledove argued that Germany's leadership (and population) would have remained nationalistic and fascist. The survival of Nazi Germany, in addition to the presence of the Soviet Union, would have posed terribly awkward strategic dilemmas for the nations of Western Europe. "If this poor, bloody world held any justice at all," says Smith at one point, "the last war would have knocked out either the Nazis or the bloody Reds ... Dealing with one set of devils would be bad enough; dealing with both sets, the way we have the last thirty-odd years ... it's a miracle we haven't all gone up in flames."[110] Smith and Drinkwater are upset at the role they have to play in the shadowy world of postwar espionage. If it were not for the Russians, Drinkwater notes, "you and I wouldn't have to deal with the likes of the bloody Ustasha – and we'd not have to feel we needed a bath afterwards." "No," replies Smith, "we'd be dealing with the NKVD instead, selling out Ukrainian nationalists to Moscow ... Would you feel any cleaner after that?"[111] In short, with Hitler's early death preserving Germany as a great power, the world would have been a much more complicated, multipolar place of shifting alliances and moral compromises.

In all likelihood, "Ready for the Fatherland" was meant as a broader commentary on the unexpected resurgence of nationalism and the new political instability in Eastern Europe – specifically in the former Yugoslavia – in the wake of the revolutions of 1989.[112] The title of the short story itself hinted at this, as "Ready for the Fatherland" was the English translation of the Croatian Ustasha movement's slogan, "Za Dom Spremny."[113] The basic allohistorical premise of Turtledove's tale, moreover, revolved around nationalism by showing how, in the wake of Hitler's death and Nazism's survival, most European nations essentially turn inward and only look after their own national interests in amoral fashion. Finally, the allohistorical turn to nationalism in the story paralleled the real historical turn to nationalism after 1989 in its unexpected origins. Turtledove's depiction of a putatively positive event like Hitler's death bringing about the unforeseeable success of the Third Reich may have been a bitter commentary upon the fall of communism which, despite also being a positive event on the surface, ironically brought about the resurgence of destructive nationalism as well. Turtledove's tale, then, resembled Locke's insofar as both were written in periods of sober disillusionment with present-day politics. Like Locke, Turtledove stressed the role of chance, unpredictability, and unintended consequences in history and seemed to embrace the familiar adage, "Be careful what you wish for – you might get it." In the process, "Ready for the Fatherland" signaled the increasing willingness to view Hitler from a less demonized perspective. Writing in an era in which Europeans were demonstrating their capacity to kill each other just as readily as in World War II, Turtledove quite logically expressed the broader conviction that Hitler had no monopoly on destructiveness. By concluding that eliminating the Führer might not have made history any better, Turtledove's tale universalized the Nazi past in such a way as to direct attention to the persistence of contemporary political problems.

One year after the publication of Turtledove's short story, another brief tale, entitled "On the Death of Hitler's Assassin" and written by an anonymous Israeli writer using the pseudonym "Ivor H. Yarden," offered a similarly skeptical account of the consequences of Hitler's premature demise.[114] Published in 1992 in the prominent American Jewish journal *Midstream*, Yarden's first-person narrative is a (mock) obituary of his (fictional) friend and former client, Paul Aronsohn, a German Jew who, at the height of the Sudeten crisis in September 1938, goes down in history as the individual who killed the ruler of Nazi Germany, Adolf Hitler. As it unfolds, Yarden's narrative reveals the ambiguous historical significance of Aronsohn's deed. On the one hand, the deed has positive results. Yarden reports that Aronsohn himself spoke with great pride about how his act "removed the danger of war and had made it possible first for the Beck–Goering and then the Goerdeler Government to come to power in Berlin." Beyond claiming to have prevented World War II, Aronsohn claimed to have prevented the extermination of European Jewry. As reported by Yarden, Aronsohn believed his deed helped boost the immigration of European Jews to Palestine and was convinced that "If Hitler had lived ... there may not have been a million Jews left in Europe by the end of the war." And yet Aronsohn was totally alone in thinking he had helped avert a major catastrophe. In the story's unexpected twist, the rest of society – especially Jews – believes Aronsohn's murder of Hitler actually made history turn out *worse*. As Yarden recounts, Hitler's death unleashed a massive pogrom that took the lives of "almost 40,000 men and hundreds of women and children ... in the Nazi rampage that followed." "In comparison," Yarden notes, "the number of Hitler's victims between 1933 [and his death] ... was less than ten thousand." From the perspective of this alternate world that does not know it has averted World War II, Paul Aronsohn has gone down in history as a villain rather than a hero. As Yarden concludes, "Paul Aronsohn ... wanted to make things better and made them immeasurably worse." "Let his life ... be a warning. Nothing is solved by violence."

By virtue of this clever ending, "On the Death of Hitler's Assassin" provided important insights into the capriciousness of historical interpretation and the elusiveness of historical "truth." Only a society that actually experienced World War II could view Hitler's hypothetical assassination as having been a worthwhile undertaking. From the perspective of an alternate world that could not possibly know of the war's horrors, Hitler's murder was a disastrous mistake. All of the history of the 1930s, in turn, is reinterpreted against this allohistorical backdrop. Hitler's aggressive foreign policy, for example, is seen as far less threatening than it has come to be perceived in real history. Yarden sums up the consensus view of his alternate world by noting that "Hitler, with all of his rantings and threats, did not really mean aggression ... And we now know ... that, when Paul killed Hitler, it was only days before the action planned by the German army leadership that would have put an end to Nazi power anyway." In real history, of course, Hitler's historical triumph at Munich in 1938 exposed him as an uncompromising aggressor while also revealing the German generals and Western Allies to be hesitant cowards. Yet his allohistorical assassination provided a radically different context for Yarden's alternate world to interpret preceding events. The ultimate irony, the writer points out, is that Hitler's assassination turns him into a martyr, for, as he notes, he "had become to most Germans their second Bismarck." Indeed, the story confirmed Joachim Fest's famous assertion that, had Hitler been killed in 1938, he would have gone down in history as Germany's greatest leader of all time.[115] In the end, therefore, "On the Death of Hitler's Assassin" powerfully highlighted the contingency of historical truth.

Little is known about the pseudonymous "Ivor H. Yarden," an Israeli international lawyer whose real name is Pol Ribenfeld.[116] It is clear, though, that by challenging the intuitively appealing view that killing Hitler would have improved history, indeed in being able to conceive of a world in which Hitler's assassination is regarded as a horrible mistake, Ribenfeld vividly illustrated both the fading fantasy of eliminating Hitler from history and the declining tendency to view him as the embodiment of evil.

Following the brief tales of Locke, Jäckel, Turtledove, and Yarden, the first full-length exploration of the consequences of the Führer's assassination appeared in 2000 with Douglas Niles and Michael Dobson's novel, *Fox on the Rhine*.[117] This work, like many of the tales that preceded it, also argued that Hitler's assassination in Operation Valkyrie on July 20, 1944 would not have made history much better. In the initial sections of the novel, the authors lay out the guidelines of their historical divergence: Stauffenberg's group succeeds in killing Hitler, but strategic errors (most notably the decision to broadcast their results to co-plotters in code) create a temporary power vacuum that is swiftly filled by Heinrich Himmler's SS. In short order, Himmler dragoons the fence-sitting Wehrmacht leadership to agree to a bold plan called "Operation Carousel" to forge a separate peace with the Soviets, who, along with the Western Allies, are quickly approaching Germany's borders. Himmler promises to give the Soviets access to Germany's V-1 weapons technology along with dominance in Eastern Europe (including a warm-water port in Greece) if they bow out of the conflict, which they soon do. Thereafter, Himmler enlists Erwin Rommel to mount a spirited defense of the Western Front, while ordering the mass production of Me-262 jet fighters, which succeed in neutralizing Allied bombers (over seven hundred are shot down in November 1944). Before long, Rommel attempts a make-or-break military campaign, called "Fox on the Rhine," to destroy the Allied troops in the West. But it ultimately fails. At the novel's climax, in late December 1944, Rommel surrenders and the war in Europe is over.

Fox on the Rhine, in short, portrays Hitler's death as failing to improve the course of history. Even though the war comes to an earlier end, the novel concludes by describing the continuation of SS resistance to Allied troops as well as the incipient intrusion of the Soviet Union into Germany proper. Thus, much as in real history, Germany will be divided after it is conquered. And the cold war will thereafter erupt – sooner this time, however, owing to Allied anger towards Soviet duplicity. Most of the novel's allohistorical conclusions, to be sure, are merely implied instead of explored in elaborate fashion. *Fox on the Rhine* lacked the same literary pedigree as other works of allohistorical fiction, being more concerned with describing hypothetical military tactics (Patton versus Rommel) than developing believable characters or plot twists. This aspect of the book was predictable given the authors' backgrounds in the subculture of war-gaming.[118] Most of the novel is given over to describing in endless detail the full nature of the battles between American and German armies. Still, in the book's initial sections, which deal more closely with the assassination of Hitler itself, familiar views were outlined. Most importantly, *Fox on the Rhine* echoed the notion that eliminating Hitler would have done little to improve history owing to the persisting reality of fanatical German nationalism. Epitomizing the novel's main allohistorical point, the novel's narrator refers to Himmler's rise to power by declaring, "Hitler was dead, but it was looking as if Germany had simply swapped one sociopathic tyrant for another. Or worse: had they swapped a dictator sinking into dementia for one who was still dangerously sane?"[119] In short, by focusing on the capacity of other Germans to pursue criminal policies, the novel subtly relativized Hitler's reputation as the embodiment of evil.

Overall, *Fox on the Rhine* was most significant for its resemblance to a more literary exploration of the exact same theme that appeared the following year, German writer Christian v. Ditfurth's novel *Der 21. Juli* (*The Twenty-First of July*).[120] Published in 2001, *Der 21. Juli* also explored what would have happened had the conservative German resistance movement succeeded in assassinating Hitler on July 20, 1944. Ditfurth's novel is written in the form of a spy thriller that focuses on the exploits of its protagonist, a former Sturmbannführer and SD agent named Knut Werdin. As the novel opens, the year is 1953 and Werdin is living under an assumed name in a remote shack in the California desert near the Mexican border, when he is visited by two American CIA agents hoping to enlist him in a risky plan to assassinate Nazi Germany's de facto ruler, SS-chief Heinrich Himmler. In Ditfurth's alternate world, Himmler has risen to power in 1944 as a direct result of Hitler's assassination. Significantly, this transition of leadership occurs less through chance than intent, for Himmler is portrayed as having known about the planned putsch all along but done nothing to impede it. Ditfurth's Himmler allows the assassination to take place, since he believes Hitler has mismanaged the war and is convinced that by eliminating him it can still be brought to an early end with halfway decent terms for Germany.

Werdin's role in these events is central. Having infiltrated the circle of Wehrmacht figures associated with Stauffenberg (one of whose members he convinces to become a "V-Man," or informer, to the SD) he is an important conduit of information to the SS about the planned coup. But he is also a double agent, involved in notifying the Soviet government of the coup's impending occurrence. Werdin's work for the Russians derives from his lifelong communist sympathies, but he is no dogmatic Stalinist. Indeed, Werdin is a loose cannon with a fierce independent streak who owes allegiance to no one. This personality trait assumes pivotal significance in 1944 when he disregards the order of Soviet secret police chief, Lawrenti Beria, to *prevent* Hitler's assassination. By the summer of 1944, Stalin has concluded that if Hitler is killed, the successor government might simply lay down its weapons, thus denying the Soviets (who have not yet entered German territory) any pretext to keep fighting on to Berlin, which they hope to do in order to permanently exterminate fascism and boost their power on the continent.[121] For his part, Werdin is shocked at the Soviet order to let Hitler live, and exclaims with regret, "I was Moscow's henchman ... I believed that what Stalin wanted I did as well ... Yet Stalin was not interested in what was good for the German people [namely, Hitler's death] ... Stalin wanted to enlarge his enormous empire ... That ... was no better than the imperialistic policy of the tsars."[122] Being a German patriot first and foremost, then, Werdin declines to prevent the assassination. Yet, in meeting with Stauffenberg prior to the bomb attack, Werdin convinces him to spare the life of Heinrich Himmler, whose death, he fears, will unleash a civil war between the SS and Stauffenberg's supporters in the Wehrmacht.[123] Through his various machinations, in short, Werdin ends up playing an important role in the events leading up to and following Hitler's assassination.

Yet, while Werdin intends to improve the course of history, his actions ultimately fail. In the aftermath of the Führer's death, the SS rushes to assert its power over the German state. Knowing that the conspirators have little support among the German people, the SS forbids publicizing the real reason behind Hitler's death and claims the Führer was killed in a British air strike. They stylize Hitler into a martyr of sorts in order to prevent the formation of popular opposition to the new government of "national reconciliation." Headed by Carl Goerdeler as Chancellor and Ludwig Erhard as Minister of Economics, this government is merely a front for the SS, which quickly emerges as the real power behind the throne. Under Himmler's rule, Germany approves pragmatic reforms which quickly turn the tide of the war. To curry favor with the German population, Himmler works to suppress the ideological wing of the Nazi party, arresting leading Nazi radicals like Josef Goebbels and Julius Streicher and dissolving the feared Gestapo. On the military front, Himmler reorganizes the military leadership in the East (placing it under the capable rule of Generals Manstein, Witzleben, and Rommel), and most importantly, accelerates the development of new weapons, like the Me-262 jet fighter and, most fatefully, the atomic bomb. Finally, in May 1945, the ace German fighter pilot Helmut von Zacher is sent over Russia to drop the first atomic bomb on Minsk, whose ensuing nuclear devastation quickly demoralizes the Western Allies and brings the war to an end. The Germans thus escape defeat in World War II (even if they do not win it outright).

In the aftermath of the war, moreover, Germany quickly recovers its old might. Ruins still can be seen in the capital of Berlin, but the nation's economy is humming along by the early 1950s, thanks to the social market policies of Ludwig Erhard. Politically, the nation is stable as well, largely thanks to the SS, which is now credited with having brought the nation back from the brink of certain defeat. As part of the organization's postwar make-over, moreover, the new SD chief, Walter Schellenberg, convinces the civilian government that the crimes of the Final Solution were forced upon a reluctant Himmler by an adamant Hitler. The Führer, meanwhile, has gone down in the history textbooks as an imperfect leader who, despite having "led Germany back to national greatness," made the fatal errors of attacking all the great powers at once and perpetrating the murder of the Jews.[124] It is a sign of Germany's new self-conception that most Germans believe that "Hitler's death ... saved Germany from defeat."[125] Yet the new stability is deceptive. Nearly a decade after the end of the war, Germany's rulers, particularly Himmler, have again become eager for world conquest and begin to embark upon the ominous-sounding "Operation-Thor" to defeat the nation's enemies.[126] To advance this effort, Himmler proposes a risky initiative to forge an alliance with the Soviets in order to strike a blow at the United States and end the tripolar geopolitical reality of the postwar world. All the while, Himmler plans on turning against the Soviet Union as soon as the threat of the United States is eliminated as a means of securing total world domination.

The primary plot of *Der 21. Juli* revolves around the American attempt to prevent the impending alliance of Nazi Germany and Soviet Russia. The CIA initially requests that Werdin undertake the risky mission of assassinating Himmler for precisely this reason. With Himmler the prime supporter of a Soviet alliance, and with other German officials like Erhard and Goerdeler calling for an alliance with the United States, the CIA hopes that eliminating the Reichsführer can swing the balance of power in favor of the Americans. For his part, Werdin could not care less about geopolitics. But he accepts the mission. At first, he does so merely to get back to Germany and find his long-lost love, Irma, whose survival the CIA has notified him of. But he gradually embraces the mission more wholeheartedly out of a sense of guilt. As Werdin learns over the course of the novel, it was he who was largely responsible for the tragic outcome of the war in the first place. Much of the backstory of *Der 21. Juli* recounts how the SS uses Werdin to ferry disinformation about the German atomic bomb project to the West. Stationed at the atomic weapons production facility near Stuttgart in 1944, Werdin is informed that the Germans have developed thirteen bombs, where in reality they had only developed a single one. The SS, thereafter, intentionally chases Werdin out of Germany into the arms of the Americans (under the pretext that they have learned about his treasonous spying on behalf of the Soviets) so that he will spread the false information that the Germans have more bombs and are willing to use them against London. Thanks to this ruse, the Germans intimidate the Allies and secure an armistice from them. Werdin's realization of his role in bringing about Germany's triumph and cementing the power of Heinrich Himmler lead him to accept the dangerous mission asked of him.

As it climaxes, *Der 21. Juli* modifies its bleak portrayal of the consequences of Hitler's premature death by supplying a somewhat redemptive ending. Like any good storyteller, Ditfurth keeps the reader unsure of the outcome until the very end, planting numerous false leads that seem to promise a depressing conclusion. For one thing, Werdin fails to carry out his assassination mission against Himmler, being caught by the SS near the novel's end while seeking out his long-lost love, Irma, in the suburbs of Berlin. Meanwhile, Himmler and Beria convene at the SS headquarters at the Wewelsburg castle and sign a twenty-year alliance that seems to seal the defeat of the United States. Yet in a surprise conclusion, Himmler and the entire SS leadership (including Kaltenbrunner and Schellenberg) are killed by none other than ace German air pilot Helmut von Zacher, who, as a result of his profound guilt for dropping the atomic bomb over Minsk, and his hatred for Himmler who duped him into doing it, unburdens his conscience by crashing his airplane into the Wewelsburg castle, killing himself and all on the ground. With the SS leadership annihilated, Carl Goerdeler undertakes a total purge of the organization, placing it under the control of the Wehrmacht, and reasserts civilian leadership over the German state. At the novel's end, Werdin is released from prison and returns to his lonely desert existence in the American southwest. Germany, meanwhile, has begun to improve its relations with the United States and has embarked upon what the reader is left to assume will be a more moderate and Western path of geopolitical orientation. History, despite initially taking a negative turn because of Hitler's premature death, now seems to be pointed in the right direction again. In all likelihood it will be no worse (if also no better) than real history.

In its overall allohistorical conclusions, *Der 21. Juli* offered a somewhat ambiguous view of the historical consequences of Hitler's assassination. This ambiguity was visible primarily in Ditfurth's model of historical causality, which gave equal attention to the power of structural constraints and individual actions. Ditfurth shared the pessimistic estimation of other writers about the likely allohistorical role of the German people, whom he portrayed as hopelessly nationalistic and slavishly loyal to their authoritarian leaders (whether Himmler or Goerdeler) even after Hitler's death. Ditfurth's primary goal in painting this pessimistic portrait was his left-leaning desire to diminish the heroic reputation of the German resistance by exposing its members – like the German people in general – as antidemocratic conservatives who would have collaborated with the SS in the wake of Hitler's death out of a nationalistic desire to save the nation. [127] Yet Ditfurth softened his critical representation of the German people by creating protagonists like Werdin and Zacher, whose capacity for heroic, individualistic action served to redeem the nation and save it from its worst tendencies. In so doing, Ditfurth expressed a belief in the existence of "good Germans" during the Third Reich. In real history, of course, such Germans existed but were unable to achieve many notable historical accomplishments. In real history, moreover, Nazi Germany was defeated from without, while the democratic Federal Republic was only created thanks to the prolonged occupation of the nation by the victorious allies. Ditfurth's novel, like Alexander Demandt's 1995 essay "Wenn Hitler gewonnen hätte," by contrast, satisfied the fantasy of the Germans being able to rehabilitate their nation themselves with no outside assistance. The writer clearly aimed to debunk the fantasy that killing Hitler would have improved history, but he was less willing to condemn the German people than were Anglo-American writers. Like them, however, he produced a work whose conclusions had the effect of subtly normalizing Hitler's evil.

On balance, the tales of Locke, Jäckel, Turtledove, Yarden, Niles and Dobson, and Ditfurth shared a belief that the Führer's untimely death would have done little to improve the course of history and might have made it worse. The appeal of this pessimistic scenario suggests a decline in the fantasy of eliminating Hitler, a diminishing sense of him as the incarnation of evil. This trend is further borne out by the appearance, since the late 1980s, of a wide range of related narratives that have offered similar conclusions. Accounts of a Nazi victory in World War II (already discussed in chapters 1–5), such as David Dvorkin's *Budspy*, Newt Gingrich and William Forstchen's *1945*, A. Edward Cooper's *The Triumph of the Third Reich*, and Harry Mulisch's *De toekomst van gisteren*, as well as Steve Erickson's *Tours of the Black Clock*, were based on the premise that Hitler's elimination actually enables the Nazis to improve their military fortunes in the war. [128] Moreover, the skepticism that killing Hitler would make history any better has given rise to narratives depicting the *prevention* of his murder. Thus, issue Nr. 292 of the comic book *The Fantastic Four*, (from 1986) has the superhero quartet preventing the renegade Nick Fury from killing Hitler (see Figure 26); W. R. Thompson's 1993 short story "The Plot to Save Hitler" portrays a time-traveler going back to Linz in 1903 to prevent a rogue colleague from murdering the fourteen-year-old Führer-to-be; while the 1985 film *The Dirty Dozen: Next Mission* shows a ragtag team of American troops preventing Hitler from being assassinated

Figure 26 Questioning the value of killing Hitler in issue Nr. 292 of the comic book *The Fantastic Four* (1986).

by representatives of the German army.[129] In short, as these additional narratives make clear, the fantasy of eliminating Hitler from history has, of late, enjoyed only limited appeal.

THE BIFURCATION OF MEMORY

In surveying the many allohistorical depictions of the world without the Führer, it is striking that many more have portrayed it as no better than the world with him. Given the intuitive logic of the belief that eliminating Hitler – one of the twentieth century's worst criminals – would have improved history's course, it is puzzling that this outcome has been depicted so rarely in postwar alternate history. A mere quarter of the total number of narratives have expressed the view that history could be made better by somehow preventing Hitler from having a prominent role in it.[130] The infrequent projection of a superior world without Hitler is no doubt due to the relative absence of the fantasy of undoing the past in the first place. If the producers of alternate history have seldom imagined a world without Hitler to be a better place, might it not be owing to their relative degree of satisfaction with the very postwar world that he unwittingly helped to create? Might it not even reflect the grateful recognition that history could have turned out worse had Hitler never been in the first place?

These suppositions are partly supported by examining the different national origins of the allohistorical narratives themselves. The texts in this chapter reveal that German writers have tended to describe history as better without Hitler, while Anglo-American writers have leaned towards the opposite view, developing narratives that have depicted it as worse.[131] This fact suggests that Germans have been more likely than Britons or Americans to fantasize about changing the past for the better. Given the three nations' diverging historical experiences of World War II, it is no surprise that Germans would be less satisfied with the postwar world than their Anglo-American colleagues. The Germans' enduring awareness of the Third Reich's destructive legacy has, to this day, encouraged them to imagine ways in which the nation's real historical fate could have been avoided – a fact that was recently illustrated in the 2004 commemorations of the sixtieth anniversary of the failed assassination attempt against Hitler on July 20, 1944, where German observers pointed to its horrible consequences (the prolonging of the war, the death of 4 million of their fellow citizens, and the further destruction of their cities) as proof that Hitler's death would have made history considerably better.[132] Another reason Germans have embraced the premise of the world being better without

Hitler involves the model of historical causality underlying it. As we have seen, narratives positing the improvement of history via Hitler's removal have privileged human agency as the decisive factor, while narratives rejecting this view have asserted the ultimate influence of structural constants. Viewing Hitler as the crucial cause of Nazism might understandably appeal to many Germans, since it elides the role of structural factors – especially the role of the German people themselves – in the establishment of the Third Reich. The German tendency to see the world as a better place without Hitler thus may signal a reluctance to face up to the full scope of the nation's culpability for the recent past.

It is likely for this same reason that a higher proportion of Anglo-American writers have gravitated towards the structuralist historical perspective and have tended to see history as no better, or even worse, without Hitler.[133] This emphasis on structural forces may well reflect the endurance of longstanding Western suspicions of the German people. As far back as World War II itself, the existence of widespread distrust of the Germans prevented Anglo-American leaders from backing the attempts of the German resistance to assassinate Hitler.[134] The same distrust, moreover, kept them from being terribly disappointed when the July 20, 1944 assassination plot failed. As the British intelligence officer and later historian John Wheeler-Bennett noted in 1944, "We are better off with things as they are today than if the plot of 20th July had succeeded and Hitler been assassinated … The Gestapo and the SS have done us an appreciable service in removing a selection of those who would undoubtedly have posed as 'good' Germans after the war, while preparing for a Third World War."[135] Hitler, in the minds of Anglo-American leaders, was merely the most visible face of a larger "German problem," which would continue to pose a threat even without the dictator. Given this longstanding tendency to view Nazism in a broader political and cultural context, it is no wonder that Anglo-American alternate histories have shied away from portraying history without Hitler in positive terms. Indeed, seeing history as no better without Hitler may reflect an Anglo-American desire not to let the German people off the hook for the crimes of the Third Reich.

These conclusions notwithstanding, the notion that structural forces were primarily responsible for Nazism may also indicate a fading perception of Adolf Hitler as the embodiment of evil. This trend partly reflects a general sense of contentment among Americans and Britons with the postwar world. Best expressed in Stephen Fry's comic novel, *Making History*, the reluctance to indulge in the fantasy of eliminating Hitler has partly expressed a broader desire for history to remain as it is. Yet the diminished fantasy of eliminating Hitler may also stem from a more pessimistic view of the present. Many of the accounts that have transformed the scenario of Hitler's elimination from a fantasy into a nightmare have done so in order to universalize the Nazi past in such a way as to direct attention to the existence of contemporary problems. As seen in the early works of Locke and Spinrad, which respectively reflected cold-war concerns about communism and anticommunism, or later works by Louvish, Turtledove, and the television episode "California Reich" (all of which voiced worries about the unexpected resurgence of nationalism and racism after the end of the cold war), certain alternate histories have dismissed the fantasy of eliminating Hitler as an unrealistic panacea unlikely to improve a world whose historical trajectory continues to be guided by powerful structural forces. These works, by focusing on the persistence of nationalism and racism outside of Germany, reveal how various postwar problems have displaced and gradually marginalized the Nazi experience in the minds of many Americans and Britons. In either case, whether due to a sense of contentment with, or lingering concerns about, the present, Anglo-American alternate histories have demonstrated a diminished sense of Hitler as the epitome of evil.

RECEPTION

The divided reception of these accounts further confirms the divergence between Anglo-American and German memories of the Nazi era. Many of the works have been warmly received, but some have elicited sharp criticism and sparked controversy. Significantly, the polarized response has frequently fallen along national lines. Anglo-American reviews have praised the structuralist narratives depicting history as worse without Hitler and have been more critical of narratives describing it as better. German reviewers, on the other hand, have sharply criticized the structuralist narratives for seemingly normalizing Hitler in the process of blaming Germans for Nazism. Underlying this divergence of views is a disagreement about the historical origins of the Third Reich.

Overall, Anglo-American critics have been the most positively disposed towards narratives depicting the world without the Führer as no better than the world with him. These works have achieved an impressive degree of both critical and commercial success. Stephen Fry's *Making History* received extremely enthusiastic reviews and was a bestseller in England.[136] Norman Spinrad's *The Iron Dream* was nominated for the National Book Award and the Nebula in 1973, received France's Prix Apollo in 1974, and has long been recognized as one of the all-time classic works of alternate history.[137] The same can be said of Jerry Yulsman's well-regarded *Elleander Morning*, which for years has long enjoyed a cult following in America and Europe.[138] Simon Louvish's *The Resurrections* was also warmly reviewed by critics.[139] And the *Twilight Zone* episode "Cradle of Darkness" was widely hailed by American viewers, some 4 million of whom tuned in to what came to be regarded as one of the revived series' most popular episodes.[140] To be sure, in many cases, reviewers praised these works without specifically mentioning any support for their broader allohistorical conclusions. Thus, the novels of Louvish, Yulsman, and Spinrad were given kudos mostly for their ingenious premises (and occasionally also scolded for their mediocre literary quality). In other cases, however, critics specifically commended the novels' allohistorical conclusions. None other than Simon Louvish favorably reviewed Fry's *Making History*, noting: "This Adolf Hitler was a thoroughly bad egg, but can we pin the blame for it all on one man alone? Or are not the circumstances in which we all live, at any period, overwhelming enough to keep time's arrow on the selfsame, terrible path?"[141] Equally suggestive were the numerous American and British criticisms of Henry Turner's essay, which de-emphasized the German people's role in the rise of Nazism.[142] Overall, the Anglo-American reception of allohistorical narratives of the world without Hitler demonstrated a broader tendency to focus on the role of the German people, instead of merely Hitler, in the rise of Nazism and confirmed the larger belief that the world without Hitler would have been no better than the world with him.

By contrast, the critical German reaction to these structuralist alternate histories demonstrated a very different understanding of the Nazi past. The most extreme reaction was directed towards Norman Spinrad's *The Iron Dream*, which was officially banned in West Germany in 1982 for allegedly exhibiting Nazi sympathies.[143] The decision by the Federal German Agency for the Restriction of Texts Dangerous to Minors (*Bundesprüfstelle für jugendgefährdende Schriften*, or BPS) was based on the contention that the mock novel, *Lord of the Swastika*, was written at such a low literary level and was so overflowing with gory battle scenes that it advanced the "articulation of Nazi ideas."[144] Spinrad's defenders and his German publisher raced to the novel's defense, arguing that the court had ignored the book's clearly satirical dimensions, and in 1987 they eventually won an overturn of the ban.[145] But the flap over the book clearly demonstrated the endurance of strong German sensitivities about works that failed to portray Hitler from a non-judgmental perspective. Even since the lifting of the ban on the book, readers have maintained a cautious distance from it. Thus, one recent reader commented that the book "failed" as a satire and concluded, "We in Germany can only shake our heads at how the Americans handle Hitler. They have NO IDEA how hard it is to live with our history."[146]

The German reaction to Stephen Fry's *Making History* was equally critical. German reviewers attacked the book for embracing the controversial thesis of Daniel Goldhagen's *Hitler's Willing Executioners* that the German people had primarily been responsible for the Holocaust.[147] In particular, German reviewers argued that Fry's focus on the culpability of the German people exonerated Hitler of the crimes of Nazism. As one reviewer argued:

Fry has overlooked the dangerous ... logic [of his argument] that ... if history would have been even worse without Hitler ... [then] we are somehow supposed to be grateful that with Hitler we got off easy? With the same logic, could not incorrigible ignoramuses maintain that Hitler was the lesser evil?[148]

Other German readers shared the concern that *Making History* normalized Hitler. One wrote that Fry's portrayal of the "future [without Hitler as] ... hardly a paradise" implied that "Hitler [had] resulted in something decent."[149] German readers, to be sure, hardly regarded Fry as a Hitler apologist and were generally enthusiastic about his novel. But they confessed an inability as Germans to embrace such a normalized view of the Nazi dictator. As one noted, "In reading [the novel] I wondered whether a German writer could have produced it."[150] Or, as another insisted, "Only an Englishman could pull off the feat of discussing the Holocaust ... as a comedy ... without making it embarrassing."[151] Finally, one concluded that "When Germans and Austrians are also able one day to tell such stories, then they will finally be able to call themselves 'normal.'"[152]

In short, the critical German response to *The Iron Dream* and *Making History* revealed a strong German resistance to normalizing Hitler. Compared with the greater willingness of American and British reviewers to accept the novels' playful representation of Hitler, German reviewers maintained a more rigid commitment to depicting him in moralistic fashion.[153] This trend – which echoes the ethically grounded German allohistorical narratives of a Nazi wartime victory – is certainly praiseworthy for its condemnation of the Nazi dictator. Yet at the same time the opposition to such structuralist accounts may be hiding a reluctance to accept the German people's share of responsibility for Nazism. This possibility is suggested by German reviewers' praise for alternate histories that portrayed the heroism of individual Germans ultimately triumphing over the German people's nationalistic tendencies in shaping the course of history.

Two of the most important works to offer this redemptive conclusion were Jerry Yulsman's novel *Elleander Morning*, which was awarded the prestigious Kurd-Lasswitz Prize for best foreign science fiction tale after its publication in German in 1986, and Christian v. Ditfurth's novel *Der 21. Juli*, which received numerous positive reviews as well.[154] Although neither shied away from critical comments about the Germans, they shifted attention away from them by providing readers with happy endings enabled by individual acts of German heroism. Overall, the German reception of alternate histories of the world without Hitler seems to reflect a broader desire to blame Hitler and exonerate the German people of any responsibility for the Third Reich.

CONCLUSION

In the final analysis, both Anglo-American and German portrayals of the world without Hitler have normalized the Nazi past in different ways. By imagining history as better without Hitler, German alternate histories have continued to focus on Hitler's responsibility for Nazism and have thereby preserved a clear sense of his evil. At the same time, by criticizing structuralist alternate histories depicting history as no better without Hitler, they have continued to de-emphasize their own historical culpability for Nazism. Meanwhile, Americans and Britons have largely focused on the responsibility for Nazism as lying mostly with the Germans themselves and not just Hitler. But, in the process, they have normalized the image of the Nazi dictator. Judging the relative merits and flaws of these two perspectives is difficult. The Anglo-American perspective is undoubtedly superior to the German one in terms of historical comprehensiveness. It also enjoys a sort of moral superiority insofar as it refrains from restricting blame to one individual who has frequently been scapegoated in apologetic fashion. The unintended consequence of this Anglo-American position, however, has been its role in de-demonizing Hitler himself. Indeed, it has largely been Anglo-American, rather than German, alternate histories that have normalized the image of the Führer. For this reason, the enduring German focus on Hitler's culpability for the Third Reich has brought with it the salutary consequence of preserving the image of Hitler's historical evil intact. Paradoxically enough, then, although the motives of British and American writers may be more progressive than those of their German counterparts, they have been more responsible for the ongoing normalization of the Nazi past.

PART 3

Hypothetical Holocausts

CHAPTER 7

Hypothetical Holocausts and the mistrust of memory

'Don't say anything, Mr. Valentin," said Lohannon with a barely audible voice . . . ' Just listen. We only have this one opportunity . . . '

'Today a man has been delivered to the Institute [of reincarnation science named] . . . Sean Crawford . . . What's important is that Crawford is not his real name. In reality, he is . . . Karl von Hutten.'

Valentin looked at the old man speechless. Karl von Hutten. The director of VEB Electronics, the secret ruler of reunified Germany, was here in the institute . . .

Lu Lohannon looked at him urgently: 'We know, Mr. Valentin . . . that Karl von Hutten . . . has come to Los Angeles to save the lives of the six million Jews murdered by the Nazis through a time experiment . . . '

It became still.

Only the rain could be heard.

It's absurd, thought Valentin.

To alter the past . . . To save the lives of six million people who have been dead for over one hundred years . . . Absurd, senseless, and impossible.

But, he thought with a shiver, this is exactly the kind of plan that the crazy, monomaniacal Germans would love.[1]

German science fiction writer Thomas Ziegler's portrayal of the attempt to undo the Nazi genocide of European Jewry in his 1988 novella *Eine Kleinigkeit für uns Reinkarnauten* provides one of the most vivid depictions of a seldom-explored topic within the field of alternate history: the Holocaust. In contrast to the numerous counterfactual accounts of how the world would have been different had Hitler won World War II, fled into hiding, or been removed from history, there have been relatively few such accounts of the genocide of the Jews. This absence is especially striking, as it runs counter to the recent proliferation of historical, literary, and cinematic attention to the Holocaust in both the worlds of academic scholarship and popular culture. Still, in the last two decades, a scattered number of works have addressed a variety of allohistorical scenarios pertaining to the Nazis' extermination of the Jews: What if the Germans had been able to complete the "Final Solution" of the Jewish question? What if they had been punished more severely for perpetrating it? What if the Holocaust could be undone? How would history have been different?

In examining how allohistorical depictions of the Holocaust have answered these questions, several broad trends emerge. First, the vast majority of narratives have focused upon the perpetrators rather than the victims. Second, they have largely revolved around the themes of repentance and remembrance. Thus, there have been portrayals of the perpetrators (or their descendants) attempting to atone for the Holocaust long after its completion. There have also been accounts of the perpetrators being forcibly compelled to atone for the Holocaust. And there have even been depictions of rueful perpetrators attempting to undo the Nazi genocide altogether. Despite their diverse themes, however, these narratives have all been linked by a pessimistic belief in the impossibility of ever atoning for the crimes of the Holocaust. It is no surprise, then, that they have exhibited a skeptical stance towards the virtues of remembrance and have concluded that recalling the Nazis' crimes against the Jews is essentially counterproductive, if not entirely futile.

In arriving at this bleak conclusion, these works of alternate history have exhibited a normalized perspective towards the Nazi past. If one thing has united most of the countless academic and cultural explorations of the Holocaust that have appeared since 1945, it has been a shared belief in the virtues of memory. The injunction to "never forget" the Holocaust's horrors has been central in most postwar novels, films, and works of history – the vast majority of which have been set within firm moral frameworks that have clearly distinguished between loathsome perpetrators and sympathetic victims.[2] Recent allohistorical depictions of the Holocaust, however, have substantially loosened these morally grounded frameworks, blurring the lines between perpetrators and victims and questioning the utility of remembrance. In so doing, they have signaled a shift towards a more normalized view of the Nazi genocide. To be sure, this trend has not stood unopposed, as is indicated by these alternate histories' highly polarized reception. But on balance, recent allohistorical accounts of the Holocaust suggest that the longstanding commitment to representing the Nazi genocide in moralistic fashion has begun to break down.

THE HOLOCAUST IN ALTERNATE HISTORY

More than anything else, alternate histories of the Holocaust have been distinguished by their small number.[3] They are also noteworthy for their relatively recent vintage, most having appeared only since the late 1980s. To a degree, the late arrival of these narratives reflects the broader fact that Western interest in the Holocaust is a relatively recent phenomenon that dates only to the past generation.[4] And yet, while alternate histories on the Holocaust have increased in recent years, they have hardly kept pace with the proliferation of films, novels, plays, and other cultural works on the subject. Alternate history, while drawn to the topic of the Third Reich, seems puzzlingly averse to confronting the regime's worst crimes. There is no easy explanation for this trend, but the counterfactual reasoning that lies at the core of alternate history may be partly responsible. Ever since Theodor Adorno's famous dictum concerning the immorality of art after Auschwitz, there has reigned a general view among mainstream writers that the Holocaust should be "approached as a solemn event" and portrayed from an appropriate moral perspective.[5] Given this consensus, it is understandable why alternate scenarios that tinker with the facticity of the Holocaust might easily be misinterpreted as frivolous, if not dangerous. The allohistorical premise of the Holocaust's never having occurred, for example, smacks of Holocaust denial.[6] And the premise of the Nazis completing the Final Solution is simply too painful for many Jews to even consider. After all, while the Nazis did end up losing World War II, they themselves believed they had won their genocidal crusade against the Jewish people.[7] Given the lingering sensitivities surrounding the Holocaust, most writers have preferred to document its real historical dimensions than explore it in playful allohistorical fashion.

Nevertheless, counterfactual speculation is hardly alien to the subject of the Holocaust. "What if?" scenarios have frequently appeared in academic scholarship of the Nazi genocide. Historians have speculated, for example, about how Jewish history might have been different had the Holocaust never occurred. The size of the world's Jewish population, according to some scholars, would have been much larger today, close to 26 million instead of the current 12.8 million.[8] The location of world Jewry, other scholars maintain, would have been far different, with European Jewry outnumbering the communities in Israel and the Americas.[9] Indeed, the state of Israel, still others argue, might never have been established at all without the moral mandate provided by the Holocaust.[10] It is not just the scenario of the Holocaust's non-occurrence, moreover, that has attracted the attention of scholars. Some have also investigated the possibility that the Holocaust might have been interrupted or otherwise brought to an earlier end. For example, if Pope Pius XII had spoken out against Nazi atrocities or if the Allies had bombed the rail lines leading to Auschwitz, the Nazi government might have been compelled to abandon the Final Solution sooner than it actually did.[11] The mentioning of such allohistorical scenarios in the professional work of academic scholars is significant for highlighting the importance of counterfactual reasoning for mainstream historical and social science scholarship. It is noteworthy, therefore, that the scenarios of the Holocaust's never occurring or being interrupted have hardly ever been seriously explored in fictional alternate histories, whether novels, films, television programs, or plays.[12] Instead, most allohistorical narratives on the Holocaust have focused on a much darker scenario.

THE WORLD WITHOUT JEWS: COMPLETING THE FINAL SOLUTION

The most frequently portrayed allohistorical scenario pertaining to the Holocaust has been the Nazis' successful completion of the Final Solution. The premise of a world without Jews has most often been addressed in alternate histories depicting the Nazis winning World War II.[13] Most of these works, however, have depicted the completion of the Holocaust only in passing. Rather than make the extermination of the Jews the centerpiece of their narratives, alternate histories by such writers as C. M. Kornbluth, William Shirer, Philip K. Dick, Eric Norden, and J. N. Stroyar (discussed in chapters 1 and 2) relegated it to the background. Despite the marginal presence of the Holocaust in such accounts, however, the premise of its completion has long served an important function by affirming that a Nazi-ruled world would have been an utterly horrific place.

By contrast, recent works on the Holocaust's completion suggest that this sense of horror has begun to fade. This tendency was visible in the most prominent narrative of recent years to imagine a world without Jews, bestselling American writer Daniel Quinn's 2001 novel *After Dachau* (See Figure 27).[14] As it opens, *After Dachau* appears to be a quirky tale about reincarnation. The book's unconventional protagonist, Jason Tull, is the scion of one of New York City's wealthiest families, who turns his back on his privileged background to take a job as a low-level employee at an obscure, non-profit organization devoted to reincarnation research called *We Live Again.* Through his field-work for the organization, Jason one day

Figure 27 Cover of Daniel Quinn's 2001 novel *After Dachau*.

learns of the existence of a young woman named Mallory Hastings, who has reportedly exhibited erratic behavior in the wake of an automobile accident. Intrigued, Jason tracks Mallory down at a local hospital and there encounters a woman who, according to her distraught mother, bears no resemblance to her former self. Speaking only in sign language and openly hostile to those around her, Mallory exhibits behavior that Jason believes possesses all the signs of being the much sought-after "golden case" that proves the existence of reincarnation. When Mallory responds favorably to Jason's cryptic suggestion, "You're not Mallory Hastings at all," his suspicions appear to be confirmed.[15]

Through intense discussion, Jason helps Mallory realize that she is actually the reincarnated soul of someone else. In the face of Mallory's disbelief, Jason insists that:

> every human is animated by a soul which departs the body at death and subsequently migrates to another body, which it animates at conception sometime soon after. In this incarnation, the soul has no recollection of its previous incarnation . . . But once in a very great while someone will spontaneously begin to recollect details of a previous incarnation – name, family, place of residence, and so on . . . Sometimes . . . memories of the past incarnation overwhelm those of the present incarnation . . . [and] blot them out.[16]

Jason thus concludes that while Mallory's body remains the same, she has "lost all memory of *being* Mallory."[17] Instead, she has retained the memory of being someone else – a woman, she finally confesses to Jason, by the name of Gloria MacArthur. As the novel proceeds, Mallory reveals important details of Gloria's life – among others, that she was born in 1922 in New York City and was an aspiring artist who, in the 1940s, associated with such leading members of the abstract expressionist movement as Jackson Pollock and Mark Rothko. In confiding these and other details of her past life to Jason, Mallory grows closer to him, and their relationship slowly becomes romantic. Yet Mallory continues to display strange outbursts of hostility towards Jason, calling him a "murderer" and remaining haunted by distant phantoms. In response, Jason resolves to discover the reasons behind her continuing trauma.

Mallory's plight, the novel divulges in a major twist, is that she has been reincarnated not into our contemporary present, but two thousand years into the future (roughly the year 4000 A.D.), into a world in which the Nazis have exterminated all Jews and other "mongrelized races" in the wake of their victory in the "Great War." Mallory learns this shocking news through an impromptu history lesson organized by Jason at a local girls' high school. By means of a socratic dialogue, Jason gets the students to recite the (alternate) history of the Nazis' triumph. What emerges is a strongly mythologized view of the past, the centerpiece of which is the Germans' triumph over their 2000-year-old enemy, the Jews, at the famous "Battle of Dachau" in the year 1943. In the wake of this pivotal date in world history, Jason observes, "the Christian dating system was junked, and a new zero year was adopted worldwide," defined by the new designation "A.D.: years After Dachau."[18] Soon thereafter, in the year 11 A.D. (or 1954), an "Aryan Council of Nations" was formed by the "hero of Dachau," Adolf Hitler, in order to carry "the Spirit of Dachau ... across the entire face of the earth" and help "humanity ... purge itself of mongrel strains once and for all."[19] This process, the class's teacher, Miss Crenevant adds, "took at least eight hundred years," but in the end, she notes:

if you were to visit the bookstores and libraries of the world and assemble all the books you could locate showing photographs of people – movie stars, fashion models, musicians, workers, farmers, people at sporting events, school children, and so on – you wouldn't be able to find a single face in them that wasn't white. For more than a thousand years, there hasn't been such a face. For more than a thousand years, being human has meant being Aryan and nothing else.[20]

In hearing this broader narrative, Mallory is understandably shocked. But she is not surprised. For, as the novel reveals, Mallory herself was an eyewitness to the Nazis' original triumph. As she tells Jason, she was present in New York when the Nazis developed the atomic bomb and compelled the Americans to accept a cease-fire in the war. The cessation of hostilities, she says, soon led to a sinister turn of events. Deeply humiliated, the American people gradually fell prey to Nazi propaganda and lashed out at the Jews for their nation's plight. Specifically, they began to view the continuing "rumors about death camps" in Europe as being "manufactured by the Jews themselves" in an effort "to keep alive hatred of the Hun" and prolong the war.[21] Before long, America joined with its former German enemy to eliminate all Jews from the United States. Worse still, the United States thereafter moved to eliminate *all* ethnic and racial minorities who were non-white. Mallory tells Jason that she knows of these events from personal experience, because she herself was black in her former life. And like her fellow African-Americans, she too fell victim to the brutal wave of persecution, choosing to commit suicide instead of being deported to Africa for extermination.

In chronicling this shocking series of events, *After Dachau* arrived at its primary theme: the struggle of society to face the truth about its criminal past. Jason's world – inhabited by the heirs of the perpetrators – is utterly unrepentant about its historical foundations. "We're ninety-nine percent sure that what we have is truly a wonderful Aryan paradise," Jason notes.[22] "We live in a world that is *stable* – wonderfully stable, blessedly stable, as it *deserves* to be for the race that is the pinnacle of cosmic development."[23] Hearing such racist claptrap, Mallory attempts to demythologize Jason's whitewashed view of the past. In the classroom, she responds with indignation that Dachau was not a battle at all but a brutal "concentration camp" and that "the Jews of Dachau weren't soldiers ... [but] unarmed civilians, including women and children."[24] Yet her counter-narrative meets with general bemusement from both the class and teacher. Mallory's pursuit of truth is parried with the counter-thrust of historical relativism. To Mallory's incredulous remark, "You actually believe [Dachau] was a battle," the schoolteacher, Miss Crenevant, replies, "As much as I believe that Thermopylae or Hastings or Verdun were battles."[25] And to her attempt to make Jason feel some degree of responsibility for his nation's past, he replies:

The greatest library of the ancient world, full of unique and irreplaceable manuscripts, was in Alexandria. Near the end of the fourth century, the Roman emperor Theodosius had it burned so as to rid the world of all those horrid pagan works, most of which were lost to us forever ... Did you feel guilty about this act of barbarism when you were alive as Gloria MacArthur?[26]

In the face of such emphatic denials, Mallory gradually begins to see the futility of holding Jason morally responsible for his nation's crimes. Born long after his nation's commission of genocide, Jason has grown up in a world in which the murderous events of the past have long since become transfigured into hazy historical myths. As he observes, "The Great War is essentially the stuff of legend, as the Trojan War must have seemed in Gloria MacArthur's day. The Jews have hardly more reality for us than the dragons of the Middle Ages."[27] The reality of Jason's racially homogenous world has been fixed for centuries. As he asserts, "White is the color of people, the way yellow is the color of bananas. To see a red man in Santa Fe would be as startling as to see a lavender lion in Africa."[28] Jason's world, in short, is one in which a uniquely criminal past has become totally normalized and has receded into the distant sands of time. Mallory comes to accept this reality and resolves to forgive Jason of any culpability for the past. As she puts it, "I'm through calling you a murderer ... It doesn't do me any good, and it certainly doesn't do you any good. You might as well apologize for killing Julius Caesar."[29]

Yet, perhaps out of Mallory's de facto act of forgiveness, perhaps out of a desire to add some spice to his otherwise monotonous life, Jason, in *After Dachau*'s concluding section, experiences a change of heart and resolves to use his family's connections to publicize, and thereby help atone for, his nation's historical crimes. At first, Jason attempts to discuss his revelations by arranging a meeting with a journalist friend named Ward, as well as with a used-book dealer who collects unwanted titles (and who sells Jason several rare copies of Erich Maria Remarque's *All Quiet on the Western Front* and Sinclair Lewis's *It Can't Happen Here*). To his chagrin, however, Jason meets with profound indifference towards his quest. Only when his uncle, Harry Whitaker, a man who works in state intelligence, casually swings by and inquires as to the reasons about his activities, does it become clear that Jason has violated the norms of his society. Before long, Jason is drugged by one of his uncle's associates, whisked away to an undisclosed location, and kept in isolation until (in a fairly contrived twist) he is able to write three specific words on a nearby chalkboard. Jason's journalist friend, Ward, is enlisted to try to help him figure the words out, and through a videophone engages him in a long discussion about his new interest in his nation's past. In the ensuing discussion, Jason declares, "I want to wake people up to the pious lies they learned in school," to which Ward responds that the extermination of "billions of people" was "just one more piece of ancient history."[30] After further discussion, during which Jason becomes exasperated at his friend's impassive attitude towards "the most terrible [crime] in human history," Jason finally realizes the three words and writes them on the board: "*No one cares.*"[31] The crusade for repentance and remembrance falters in the face of widespread indifference.

Having learned this sobering lesson, Jason is freed and the novel ends with him abandoning his ambitious crusade for mass enlightenment and instead embracing a small-scale policy of public commemoration by opening up an art gallery and a publishing house dedicated to the art and literature of forgotten races. Near the novel's end, he is visited one last time by his Uncle Harry, who unaccountably drops off an ancient, dog-eared manuscript, thinking Jason might be interested in publishing it as part of his fledgling enterprise. As the novel concludes, Jason has resolved to undertake the daunting task of translating and publishing the manuscript – a long-extinct Dutch-language text chronicling the sufferings of a young Dutch-Jewish teenager by the name of Anne Frank.

After Dachau's overall narrative expressed a normalized portrait of the Holocaust's completion in a variety of ways. In depicting post-genocidal America as an "Aryan paradise," Quinn abandoned the morally grounded frameworks of prior allohistorical depictions of the Nazi genocide. Whereas earlier writers focused directly upon the horror of a Nazi-ruled world, Quinn focused on its humdrum normalcy. Most previous works, moreover, depicted the perpetrators as sadistic beasts, while *After Dachau* focused on their well-adjusted (if uninformed) descendants. Finally, whereas the stereotypically evil Nazi perpetrators in most prior accounts were intended to repel readers, the apparently normal characters of *After Dachau* — Jason Tull in particular — were much more sympathetic. In submitting this unconventional vision, in short, Quinn essentially vali-dated Saul Friedlander's theoretical contention that, had the Nazis won World War II and completed the Final Solution, they would have emplotted the Holocaust in comic terms as a "happy ending."[32] To be sure, Quinn hardly endorsed this alternate world, as was made clear by his sympathetic portrayal of Jason's rebellion against his society's historical amnesia. Yet, while Quinn clearly appreciated the capacity of memory to challenge history, he was highly pessimistic about its chances of success. In portraying the ultimate failure of Jason's crusade to enlighten his society about its historical crimes, and in depicting Mallory absolving him of any responsibility for them, Quinn affirmed the bitter reality that the passage of time effaces the memory of atrocity. In contrast to the more morally absolute narratives of earlier years, then, Quinn's disconcertingly normal-ized depiction of the Holocaust reflected a less optimistic view of the powers of remembrance.

At the same time, though, Quinn retained some degree of faith – however faint – in memory's ability to produce enlightenment. In many ways, *After Dachau* was a work that affirmed the subversive power of memory to challenge the tyranny of history. Quinn, it seems, wrote *After Dachau* partly to expose the inherently subjective nature of history itself. Having geared much of his literary work to exposing what he has called "the secret that nobody wants to hear about," Quinn suggested that all history is deceptive.[33] Indeed, he seemed to embrace the postmodern notion that all history is inseparable from relationships of power – that it is victors' history – a point he made explicit through Jason's frequent invocation of Napoleon's famous remark that "History is just an agreed-upon fiction."[34] Quinn's specific motives for endorsing this idea are unknown, but they were likely tied to his larger goal of critiquing what he believed to be contemporary American society's white-washed view of its own past. This goal was most clearly visible in the novel where Jason, intent on defending himself against Mallory's accusations, makes the observation that:

Mallory seemed to think that I should live in sackcloth and ashes because my ancestors exterminated the original inhabitants of Asia and Africa to make room for people like me. I made a mental note to ask her if Jackson Pollock lived in sackcloth and ashes because his ancestors exterminated the original inhabitants of North America to make room for people like him.

It isn't just *our* history that is an agreed-upon fiction.[35]

By depicting Mallory's view of history as no more truthful than Jason's, Quinn provocatively reminded present-day Americans of their nation's own historical crimes and challenged them to take responsibility for them. Instead of regarding the persecution of African slaves and Native Americans as crimes committed by distant ancestors, Americans, Quinn implied, should follow Jason's lead and realize the need for a moral awakening. Quinn's unorthodox portrait of the Holocaust's completion, therefore, was a provocative means of pursuing a larger didactic end.

In advancing his broader agenda, however, Quinn exhibited a distinctly normalized view of the Holocaust. By using the allohistorical premise of the Nazis' total extermination of the Jews to direct attention to the real historical persecution of African slaves and Native Americans, Quinn universalized the Holocaust's significance. His comparison of the Nazi genocide to the historical atrocities perpetrated in American history considerably overstated the similarities and elided the substantial differences between them. In doing so, Quinn was participating in (and may have been influenced by) the increasing tendency in American society to challenge the longstanding belief in the Holocaust's uniqueness. In recent years, the notion that the Jews suffered a singular fate at the hands of the Nazis during World War II has come under fire in the United States from a wide range of groups – most prominently, Native Americans and African Americans, but also Armenians, Gypsies, Poles, and others – who have blamed the concept of uniqueness for the lack of public attention to their own historical sufferings, which they have attempted to rectify by comparing them to the Nazi genocide.[36] This process of "historicization" via comparison is, in its best versions, perfectly legitimate and contributes to broader historical understanding. However, the process has also inevitably promoted (as indeed it has grown out of) a declining belief in the Holocaust's exceptionality. Quinn's narrative directly expressed this trend, for it was ultimately less concerned with exploring the (allo)historical fate of the Jews for its own sake than using it as a means of condemning the (allo)historical crimes of the United States.[37] However admirable the novel's larger goals might be, then, *After Dachau*'s instrumental usage of the Holocaust reflected the erosion of prior moral perspectives towards it.

THE HOLOCAUST AND THE FUTILITY OF RETRIBUTION

While *After Dachau* explored the consequences of the Holocaust's completion, other works of alternate history have examined what would have
happened had the Germans been punished more severely for having
perpetrated it. In these accounts, the Nazi genocide of the Jews happens
as it does in real history, but the Allies' ensuing treatment of the Germans
varies dramatically. All of the tales written on this subject have described
attempts to impose retribution from above in the hope of inspiring contrition, repentance, and atonement from below. All of them, however, have
portrayed such attempts as failing catastrophically. In so doing, these texts
have suggested the futility of remembrance.

The first such alternate history to appear was American writer Jesse
Bier's 1964 short story "Father and Son."[38] Set in the immediate aftermath
of World War II, "Father and Son" focuses on an exchange of letters
between Konrad Brendt, a German official in the newly installed provisional government in Berlin, and his son Joachim, a Wehrmacht soldier
and SS lieutenant, who is being detained at his last place of employment,
the (fictive) concentration camp of "Auchswald-am-Main." As in real
history, Germany has just lost World War II, and its major leaders have
either been caught or have committed suicide. But in an allohistorical
twist, the Germans themselves now decide to embrace an elaborate plan to
atone for their crimes. Instead of merely putting their "vice-führers" on
trial, the provisional government plans to subject them to forced employment on the kibbutzim of "those people" (the Jews) along the
Mediterranean coast in Palestine. More radical still, the new German
government decides not merely to punish its former leaders but the
German population at large. Three weeks after the cessation of hostilities,
on June 19, 1945, the provisional government mysteriously rounds up
exactly 6,408,793 randomly selected Germans and orders their deportation
on trucks to "temporary destinations unknown."

Here the exchange of letters between Joachim and Konrad begins. On
the same day that the deportations are announced, Joachim worriedly
writes to his father to explain their meaning, calling them "a little cruel
for everyone, all things considered."[39] Konrad, in response, refuses to
clarify the meaning of the deportations, noting "what you ask is now out
of the question."[40] As the tension builds, Joachim's fears lead him to
suspect a devilish plan of retribution for the Holocaust, writing, "in all
my nightmares . . . I never . . . conceived such a retaliation. A lottery! The
thing is indescribable. And that you have it figured to the six million, four

hundred and eight thousand, seven hundred and ninety-third person! The insane calculation in it is absolutely grotesque."[41] Joachim's fears are further stoked when his father replies dispassionately, "It is the only way, this: to be – clean. Not an eye for an eye, or tooth for tooth, but detergency for that other bloodbath. Talk of enormity!"[42] Finally, in reply to Joachim's panicked cry, "*Gott im Himmel,* stop it!!" Konrad replies out of sympathy, and in the strictest confidence, that:

[all] of it is a ruse, a joke. *Ja!* That is why you are not allowed on the other side of the doors. Everyone is whisked out the other side . . . to transfer to trucks to other camps. For a month or two like that, thinking, each place, this, *this* will be the time. Utterly reduced by the experience. Which they and their families and neighbors, guards, everyone will never forget, this way. We won't need to use the chambers.[43]

Hence, the apparent German plan for auto-genocide is revealed to be an elaborate and sadistic prank designed to promote the larger goal of educating the German masses about the horror of the Holocaust.

And yet, in the end, the attempt to punish the Germans for the Holocaust backfires. Konrad's moral lesson goes completely unnoticed by Joachim. Instead of generating empathy in Joachim for the Jewish victims of the Nazis, the plan produces classic signs of self-pity and victimization; as he groans, "Why *me?* . . . What a cross I have had to carry!"[44] Moreover, the fear of retribution gradually leads him to display his Nazi prejudices in open fashion. He defensively rationalizes the killing of the Jews, saying, "All right then, for argument's sake, though I do not personally believe it: it may have been wrong to kill the Jews. [But] . . . will it bring them back to do this thing?" Furthermore, he offers an antisemitic explanation for the new policy, saying, "Don't tell me there is not a Jew there behind [the policy of retribution]."[45] Finally, Joachim's fears of Jewish vengeance get the best of him. Although his father responds to his final desperate calls for help with the reassuring news that the deported members of his family have already arrived and are safe and sound, Joachim in the end goes insane. In his final letter, he is totally calm and inquires about the health of his long-dead mother, leading his now-panicked father to reply, in the very last line of the story, "Get hold. Come back to yourself. *Come back!* . . . *Joachim!*"[46] With this abrupt conclusion, "Father and Son" offers a pessimistic message about the possibility of atonement after the Holocaust. Most of the failure, of course, is due to the Germans' intransigence in the face of their nation's massive historical guilt. It is Joachim's unwillingness to abandon his Nazi views that is largely responsible for the inability to embark upon the cleansing process. Yet Bier does not blame "the Germans" collectively. The figure of Konrad demonstrates a German willingness to come to grips with the past. In the end, then, it is the tragic generational and political divisions between the "fathers" and the "sons" that have made genuine atonement and reconciliation impossible.

In presenting this sober conclusion, Bier was motivated by a mixture of personal and political concerns. As a writer of Jewish background, he wrote the tale in part to express the fantasy of allohistorically punishing the Germans for crimes they had largely gotten away with.[47] Bier had long sympathized with the punitive nature of the Allies' early postwar policies towards the Germans.[48] But he had extra motivation to punish them in his short story in the early 1960s, when the capture (and subsequent trial) of the fugitive Nazi, Adolf Eichmann, dramatically exposed the judicial shortcomings of the early postwar period. Overall, "Father and Son" used an allohistorical premise to present a critique of contemporary German history. By featuring a well-intentioned German effort to atone for the past as backfiring owing to traditional German stubbornness, the tale focused attention on the real historical shortcomings in Germans' attempts to confront the Nazi legacy. In the process, Bier hinted that the mandated attempt to face the past was destined to failure.

Echoing the same point a generation later were two German-language novels, Thomas Ziegler's *Die Stimmen der Nacht* (1984) and Christoph Ransmayr's *Morbus Kitahara* (1995). Both novels differed in important respects from Bier's short story, however. Whereas "Father and Son" depicted the Germans' failure to atone for the Holocaust as a result of their own intransigence, Ziegler and Ransmayr's books blamed the Germans' refusal to repent as the result of a clumsy Allied program of compulsory contrition. Moreover, while Bier depicted the punishment of the Germans as a fantasy, Ziegler and Ransmayr depicted it as a nightmare. As a result, while all three tales pessimistically highlighted the futility of atonement for the Holocaust, their differences in national origin possessed quite different implications for the memory of the Nazi era.

Thomas Ziegler's *Die Stimmen der Nacht* (*The Night Voices*) focuses on the world as it would have been in the 1980s had the Allies, after defeating Nazi Germany in World War II, imposed the draconian Morgenthau Plan upon the beaten nation (see Figure 28).[49] The novel's point of divergence from the real historical record occurs late in the war when Franklin Roosevelt (who does not die until 1947) allows himself to be persuaded by Secretary of the Treasury, Henry Morgenthau, to implement a hard peace upon the Germans. Having already suffered the dropping of an

Figure 28 Cover of Thomas Ziegler's 1984 novel, *Die Stimmen der Nacht.*

atomic bomb upon Berlin in February 1945, Germany becomes a shadow
of its former self with the imposition of the Morgenthau Plan. Its industry
dismantled, Germany is reduced to an agrarian land dotted with desolate,
ruin-filled cities. Most Germans in this alternate world have either fled to
the countryside or been transported by the Allies to South America to avoid
starvation in the economically destitute old Reich.[50] Once relocated, however, the new "Latino-Germans" proceed to turn the tables on the Allies
and begin rebuilding the Third Reich on Latin-American soil. Led by such
Nazi fugitives as Martin Bormann, Klaus Barbie, and Josef Mengele, the
Germans build up a new power base, establishing the capital city of
Germania in Brazil (replete with grand buildings designed by Albert
Speer and sculptures by Arno Breker) and rearming with advanced weapons
technology provided by Wernher von Braun. Within the span of two
generations, the Germans have once again become a formidable power.

It is against this backdrop that *Die Stimmen der Nacht*'s main narrative
unfolds. The novel opens with its protagonist, an American television
entertainment show host named Jacob Gulf, being flown into the old
Reich by American government officials. Gulf has been chosen for an
unspecified mission owing to the unusual fact that he has been continually
shadowed by the disembodied voice of his dead wife, Elizabeth, who had
committed suicide on his live television show four years earlier. Initially,
Gulf hears Elizabeth's voice through electronic "burrs" (*Kletten*) – motorized,
airborne devices the size of fruit flies, which contain data storage chips that the
Latino-Germans have invented in order to disseminate propagandistic
"audio-letters." Elizabeth had purchased one of these devices while visiting
Latin America and had programmed it with her voice to keep her husband
company while away on business. Yet, after Elizabeth's death, Gulf disman-
tles one of the devices and discovers its data chip is actually empty. He
thereupon realizes that Elizabeth has somehow succeeded in contacting him
from the dead.[51] Shortly thereafter, U.S. government officials become
alarmed when they receive reports from the city of Cologne that similar
voices of deceased Nazi leaders such as Hitler, Himmler, and Goebbels have
recently been heard pontificating from within the ruins of the city's famous
cathedral. With Gulf as the potential key to understanding the significance
of the voices, and with U.S. officials concerned about their ability to foment
a rebellion in the old Reich, he is swiftly dispatched to Germany to try to
provide some answers.

Once in Germany, however, Gulf becomes a strategic pawn in the
intensifying conflict between the Allies and the upstart Latino-Germans.
Soon after his arrival, he is kidnapped by German Werewolf units, which

have been supported with funds and weapons from the Latino-Germans' primary covert organization, ODESSA. The Latino-Germans have learned of Gulf's unique ability to attract the disembodied voices of the deceased Nazi leaders and hope to exploit him for their own purposes. In due course, Gulf is rescued by Allied forces, who destroy the rural Werewolf hideout with helicopter gunships, but he is eventually re-kidnapped by agents working for the Latino-Germans' political leader, Martin Bormann, who hopes Gulf can lure the disembodied Nazi voices to his mountain fortress in the Andes and thus inspire an overall Latino-German crusade against the Allies. Before long, Gulf is taken to Latin America, where he is powerless to stop the eighty-year-old Bormann's suicidal nuclear assault upon England. At the novel's apocalyptic end, he witnesses firsthand the devastation of the Latino-Germans' homeland by Allied missiles. As he gazes upon the fiery mushroom clouds spreading towards him, Gulf hallucinates being taken to the great beyond by Elizabeth, while fantasizing about an alternate world in which he converses with Reich President Claus Graf Schenk von Stauffenberg in Berlin about his successful assassination of Adolf Hitler on July 20, 1944.[52]

The bleak ending of *Die Stimmen der Nacht* underscored its author's skeptical views about memory. Ziegler's skepticism was clearest in his description of the genesis of, and reaction to, the Morgenthau Plan. Ziegler describes the Morgenthau Plan's origins as underpinned by a fanatical commitment to remembrance. Morgenthau (a Jew, and thus a representative of the proverbial "people of memory") is portrayed as having been driven "insane by grief and anger due to the murders in the concentration camps" – emotions that drive him to embrace a plan that will hold the Germans accountable for, and force them to recall, their crimes on a daily basis by preserving the ruins around them.[53] The German reaction to the Morgenthau Plan similarly illustrates the power of memory, but in a negative sense, since instead of teaching the Germans a lesson, the Morgenthau Plan only makes them thirst for revenge. The Latino-Germans remain obsessed with recollections of the Reich's bygone glory and yearn to restore it in the present. As Gulf notes:

In German America ... people often speak of the Reich. The exiled Nazis never abandoned Germany. When I was in Brazil ... [I was taken] to the German pubs in which politics was discussed as once before in the Hofbrauhaus ... The Latino-Germans ... sit there, ninety degrees in the shade, with their pigs knuckles and Sauerkraut, and recount the grand years in the Reich. Old, white-haired SS men, their hands still soiled with the blood of Treblinka and Bergen-Belsen, drinking large steins of Bavarian beer, brewed in Caracas, and tears well up in their eyes when they blather on about the Black Forest, the Eifel, the Kyffhäuser, or the blue waters of the Rhine ... 'The Führer,' they say, 'was right.' 'The Jew did in fact want to exterminate us and he almost succeeded. Screw Morgenthau, we're going back,' they say. 'We'll rebuild Berlin and hoist the flag over the Reichstag, the flag with the black-red-gold and the swastika.'[54]

As depicted by Ziegler, the Germans' thirst for revenge demonstrates the fundamental misguidedness of the Morgenthau Plan. As an American military official named Mr. Splitz exlaims to Gulf, the plan had only:

> strengthened the Germans in their insanity. Hitler now is more popular than before the war. The Germans no longer build tanks and airplanes, but rather ... tend to their meadows, but they are still Nazis, worse than ever before. Morgenthau achieved the precise opposite of what he wanted. Now the Nazis [in Latin America] are sitting at our front door ... And they have not given up their plans.
>   They hate us Americans ... from the depths of their souls, because of Morgenthau and what he did to the Reich, and they are preparing for ... a holy war against everything Jewish and American and Bolshevist, against the whole world, as once before, except this time they have the bomb ... and the only thing that's missing is a single spark and the world will explode.[55]

The Germans, in short, are consumed by the forces of memory. "Locked up within a cage in which time has ceased to flow ... in which there is no development or progress," they are condemned to live in a world in which time has lost the ability "to heal wounds" and where "the helpless thirsting for revenge and the yearning for old greatness remains unbroken."[56] In the end, as both the victims of the original Nazi barbarism (the Jews, represented by Morgenthau) and the perpetrators (in both the old Reich and German-America) remain unable to forget the past, history careens out of control towards disaster.

Implicit within this nightmare narrative was Ziegler's contention that, without the implementation of the Morgenthau Plan, history would have proceeded in a better direction. In Ziegler's novel, the Morgenthau Plan has absolutely no redeeming features. So misconceived is it that Americans as well as Germans clearly see its many serious flaws. As Gulf's escort, Splitz, complains as they arrive in the old Reich:

> I thought I could forget this ghostland, these thousand-year ruins ... These ruins are the main problem. Jesus, they could have at least rebuilt Berlin ... That was the main mistake, Jacob ... The Germans would have forgiven us everything else; the lost war, the dissolution of the Reich, the lost territories ... but not what we did with Berlin ... Berlin was Germany ... an idea, a century-old dream, and now ivy is growing in the cracks in the uninhabited, collapsing walls. God ... And Berlin was merely one of their many cities![57]

As Gulf reflects more and more throughout the novel about the plan's drawbacks, he starts to wonder how things might have been had it never been imposed, observing that because it *was* implemented:

even people who were against the Nazis began to hate America ... And very few of these emigrated to the USA after the war ... I wonder where we would be today if we had been able to utilize this potential. Von Braun, Heisenberg, Heidegger, Pinder, Sauerbruch, Hahn ... All that scientific potential that was lost to us.[58]

In raising the question of how history might have been different had the Morgenthau Plan never been implemented, Ziegler's novel justified the course of history as it really occurred. For in real history, of course, the Allies did not impose the Morgenthau Plan on Germany, but instead reconstructed the country into an industrial power. Many moral compromises were made, however, in the process of rebuilding Germany after World War II, ranging from the Allies' failure to purge ex-Nazis from German society, to their recruitment of war criminals to aid in the Western fight against communism.[59] Ziegler's novel, however, diverted attention from these moral shortcomings by showing how much *worse* history would have been if a more moralistic, punitive peace had been imposed on the Germans. Indeed, the novel largely accepted the conservative idea that the evasion of the Nazi past was a precondition for reconstructing West Germany on a democratic basis.[60] In the end, *Die Stimmen der Nacht* ratified the real historical evasion of the Nazi past by exposing the terrible consequences of imposed remembrance.

Ziegler's motives in writing the novel were varied, but they reflected important shifts that occurred in the German memory of the Nazi era during the early 1980s. As the Federal Republic took a conservative political turn with the election of Chancellor Helmut Kohl of the Christian Democratic Union (CDU) in 1982, many Germans began to voice the desire to "draw a line" under the Nazi era (*einen Schluβstrich ziehen*) and reclaim a normal sense of national identity. While they did not advocate forgetting the past in its entirety, events such as the Bitburg controversy and the Historians' Debate revealed that the advocates of normalcy attempted to diminish the Holocaust as an object of special attention.[61] Ziegler exhibited similar signs of the desire to both remember and move beyond the past. He openly embraced the cause of remembrance, citing his concern about the upsurge of neo-Nazism in West Germany in the early 1980s as a reason for his novel's critical depiction of surviving Nazis.[62] But he also asserted that "too much memory is as dangerous as forgetting the ... Holocaust."[63] This implicit support for measured amnesia was expressed in the novel's overall allohistorical conclusion that history would have turned out worse with the imposition of forced remembrance. This skepticism towards memory dovetailed with the attempt of conservatives to fashion a normal sense of national identity for the Federal Republic. By blaming memory for (the allohistorical) Germany's enduring commitment to Nazism, *Die Stimmen der Nacht* created a useful foil that vindicated (the real historical) Germany's early postwar evasion of its Nazi past. Overall, then, while *Die Stimmen der Nacht* was aware of the obligation to remember, it displayed a conservative desire for normalcy as well.

A similar message was conveyed a decade later by another important German-language novel focusing on the Morgenthau Plan, *Morbus Kitahara*, by the esteemed Austrian writer, Christoph Ransmayr.[64] Originally published in 1995, *Morbus Kitahara* is set in a fictional village called Moor, located on an alpine lake in an unnamed country (clearly Austria) that has just lost a major war (World War II). The novel's point of divergence from the real historical record appears within the first three pages, with the imposition of the draconian "Peace of Oranienburg" upon the inhabitants of the village by the American occupying forces. This punitive peace falls upon the entire German-speaking world, but falls particularly hard on Moor because of its wartime role as a notorious slave labor camp centered around a granite quarry.[65] Moor's punishment is epitomized by its complete de-industrialization and isolation from the outside world, as decreed by the American Supreme Court Justice, Lyndon Porter Stellamour. As the mastermind of Allied retribution, the ironically named Stellamour (his German-French last name translates roughly as 'bestow love') ensures that Moor quickly "slid[es] inexorably back through the years" to a pre-industrial state of existence.[66] As a message from Stellamour intones to the villagers:

Riffraff! ... work the fields ... haystacks, not bunkers ... no more factories, no turbines, no railroads, no steelworks ... armies of shepherds and farmers ... re-education and conversion: of warmongers into swineherds and asparagus diggers! And of generals into carters of cow manure ... back to the fields! ... with oats and barley among the ruins of industry ... cabbage heads, dunghills ... and steaming cow-pies in the lanes of your autobahn, where potatoes will grow next spring![67]

Beyond suffering economic punishment, the villagers of Moor are also subjected to didactic commemorative rituals organized by Stellamour's deputy on the ground, the American occupation official, Major Elliot. Shortly into the occupation, Elliot orders the erection of an immense stone monument, high on a mountainside above the feared quarries, that reads:

Here
Eleven Thousand Nine Hundred
Seventy-Three People Lie Dead
Slain by the Inhabitants of this Land
Welcome to Moor[68]

Although Elliot intends this monument to stand for eternity, he does not rest there. For "instead of . . . letting the horrors of the war years gradually grow pale and indistinct," he invents new "rituals of remembrance," such as the so-called "Stellamour Parties," where the people of Moor are forced to don wartime garb and act out the roles of perpetrators and victims against the backdrop of the town's fearsome quarries.[69]

It is in Moor, twenty-three years after the conclusion of the war (roughly 1968) that the reader is fully introduced to the novel's protagonist, Bering. Born at the very end of military hostilities (in real historical time, around April 1945), Bering grows up in a world of deprivation. Forced to be largely self-reliant owing to a traumatized family, he becomes gainfully employed as the town's only blacksmith. It is in this capacity that he is introduced to one of the novel's other central characters, Ambras. A non-Jewish survivor of Moor's slave labor camp, Ambras is given special privileges after the war by Major Elliot, who places him in control of the stone quarry and permits him to move into an abandoned villa patrolled by around a dozen vicious dogs – a fact that leads fearful local residents to refer to him as the "dog king." Ambras furthermore enjoys unlimited travel rights, as well as the use of the only functioning machine in town, Major Elliot's aging Studebaker. Ambras and Bering meet when the former crashes his automobile and takes it to the latter to be repaired. Shortly thereafter, Ambras invites Bering to live with him and serve as his personal chauffeur and bodyguard. It is through Ambras, finally, that Bering meets the novel's third major character, Lily. Like Bering and Ambras, she too suffers from a painful past (being the daughter of an SS war criminal) while struggling in the present to eke out an existence by smuggling black-market goods between Moor and locales beyond the mountains.

For the three figures, life proceeds in largely stagnant fashion, in keeping with their deprived surroundings. In a place where time moves backwards, all three struggle to cope with the aftermath of past traumas. Ambras remains haunted by his experience as a forced laborer in the quarries.[70] Plagued by chronic physical ailments stemming from wartime torture, he struggles to forget the past by busying himself collecting precious stones, "which for a moment let[s] him forget the horrors of his own history, and even his hate."[71] Bering, meanwhile, struggles to escape his own misfortune of having been born into a family incapacitated by the war and strives to cope with his own physical ailment – puzzling black spots in his field of vision – which convince him that he is going blind. Lily, finally, attempts to control her rage against the many "enemies" (mostly wild bandits and random skinheads) who harass her in her smuggling operations.

Life for the three continues in this grueling fashion until the day that Ambras notifies them that Moor and the surrounding lakefront villages are to be evacuated, on the orders of the American army, so that they can be utilized as military training grounds. From this moment, the three make the long journey from the mountains to the lowlands, to the bustling, modern town of Brand, home to an American military base replete with neon street lights, fully stocked stores, and trains linking up to the rest of the world. Ambras, Bering, and Lily arrive in Brand on the momentous evening when the United States finally concludes its ongoing twenty-year war against Japan by dropping an atomic bomb on the city of Nagoya on the island of Honshu.[72] With the war finally over, the American troops prepare to pull out of central Europe, which presents the three main characters with a final new challenge. The aged Stellamour's final decree is that all the machinery from Moor's quarry should be dismantled by the local inhabitants and shipped to Brazil, where it is to be re-erected under the supervision of Ambras, Bering, and Lily. Yet, while life initially seems to become easier for the three in the new, tropical climate of Brazil, it quickly takes a tragic turn. In the novel's dramatic ending, Ambras, Lily, Bering, and Bering's new Brazilian girlfriend, Muyra, go on an afternoon boat excursion to the nearby "dog island," a lush sanctuary dominated by the ruins of an abandoned prison fortress. There, Bering and Ambras's historically rooted psychological traumas lead them, as well as Muyra, to a grisly end. For unknown reasons (but most likely due to his increasingly painful unrequited love for Lily, whom the day before he has discovered making love with Ambras), Bering shoots at Lily, down on the beach, with a rifle from high up on the island's hillside, but ends up killing Muyra, to whom Lily has just given her signature rain poncho as a gift. Meanwhile, on the climb up the steep, rock-hewn stairs of the abandoned prison, Ambras – who is increasingly suffering flashbacks to his time in the forced labor camp – falls off the cliffside, dragging Bering (who is tethered to Ambras with a climbing rope) down with him to a violent death on the beach below. Before long, a nearby brush fire consumes the bodies, rendering them into contorted ashen heaps.

The tragic end of Ambras and Bering in *Morbus Kitahara* highlights the novel's central claim about the dangers inherent in memory. Tension characterizes the relationship between the two men throughout the novel, in no small part due to their inability to empathize with their respective past sufferings. Ambras and Bering represent different types of postwar Germans: the former, a victim by virtue of his suffering at the hands of the Nazis; the latter, a perpetrator by virtue of his inability to escape the inheritance of his father's violent character.[73] Complicating matters is the fact that Bering is also partly a victim, as someone innocent of wartime atrocities by virtue of his postwar birth, but whose bleak postwar surroundings turn him into a perpetrator. Either way, Bering and Ambras, consumed by their own resentments and suffering, coexist uneasily through the novel. This uneasy coexistence is epitomized by Bering's withdrawal from Ambras when the latter tells him his life story. After hearing his tales of torture in the quarries, Bering desperately tries to "to pull away from Ambras's memories" and forget them in the mindless labor of mechanical repair work.[74] For his part, Ambras is left with the stinging realization that "the first man, the only man among the men of Moor in whom Ambras had ever confided, still would rather listen to the pounding and hammering of engines than to the words of memory."[75] The growing distance between Ambras and Bering reflects the uneasy relationship between two very different generations of postwar Germans: those who cannot escape from memory and those who yearn to escape from it.

This uneasy relationship highlights one of the novel's central points, the profound inability of the Peace of Oranienburg's imposed culture of remembrance to bring about genuine contrition among the Germans. Over time, as the occupation wears on into its third decade, repentance becomes a stale ritual. The occupiers' methods of promoting memory become more and more artificial – like holding trivia contests where contestants could win "sticks of margarine, some powdered pudding ... a carton of unfiltered cigarettes ... or even trips to distant zones of occupation," by "scribbling the old answers" to familiar questions.[76] Especially for the first generation of Germans born after the war and coming into adulthood in the 1960s, the distant past is increasingly irrelevant:

Moor's children were bored by memories of a time before their time. What did they care about black flags at the docks and at the ruins of the gravel works? Or about the message of the Grand Inscription at the quarry? Veterans and men crippled in the war might be outraged by a Stellamour Party and protest the truth of the victors – for Bering and those like him, the rituals of remembrance ... were only gloomy shows.[77]

Worse than becoming irrelevant, the imposed culture of remembrance gradually begins to backfire against the occupiers by fostering deep resentments among the occupied. Although less dramatically than in Ziegler's *Die Stimmen der Nacht*, where the Germans plot a Third World War out of their hatred of the United States, the Germans in *Morbus Kitahara* slowly begin to sense that the culture of remembrance is a sham. Near the end of the novel, Bering witnesses the material abundance of the lowlands in Brand and brims over with anger at the needless deprivation and suffering imposed on Moor, exclaiming:

Cars, tracks, runways! High-tension lines, department stores! Garbage cans full of delicacies ... Was that the penitence, the punishment that the great Bringer of Peace had prescribed for the lowlands? ... Was it? Shit, goddamn bullshit ...
  Some justice – the lowlands sparkled ... like a huge amusement park, while ... under the cliffs of the Blind Shore ... banners were unrolled: *Never forget. Thou shalt not kill* ... The great penitential spectacle of Stellamour ... was surely staged only where there wasn't much else to stage ...
  Never forget.
  Forget it all.[78]

Soon after his disillusioning experience in Brand, Bering starts a self-destructive descent into amorality. It begins near the end of the novel, when the army orders the pullout from Moor and instructs Bering to oversee the enlistment of the local inhabitants as forced laborers to dismantle the army's installations. In this capacity, Bering soon is behaving with nearly the same brutality as the Nazi perpetrators did once before, striking a surly laborer with a steel rod to get him working.[79] When Bering finally kills Muyra, his descent into the moral abyss is complete.

  In its major thrust, *Morbus Kitahara* seems to endorse the cause of forgetting. The Allied refusal to let postwar Germans escape the past is a curse for all, since their policy of compulsory remembrance transforms the former perpetrators into unrepentant victims and the victors into dehumanized perpetrators. Out of an inability to forget the past, all end up being cursed by blindness. Indeed, the relationship between blindness and vision, darkness and light, is the novel's central motif. The book's very title, *Morbus Kitahara*, refers to Bering's eye condition – literally, the "blind spots" identified by (and later named after) a Japanese ophthalmologist who discovered their psychosomatic cause lying in feelings of fear, hatred, or misery on the part of the patients.[80] While Bering's partial blindness partly stems from the anger caused by his unrequited love for Lily, it is his unarticulated anger towards the Allied occupation for subjecting him and his fellow villagers to decades of needless deprivation that is ultimately responsible for his physical ailment. Like other members of his family, many of whom also suffer from different forms of blindness, Bering embodies the artificial handicaps imposed upon Germans by the postwar Allies.[81] Significantly, Bering's blind spots begin to fade as he prepares to leave Moor, and they finally disappear for good when he sails for Brazil, where he finds bliss in the forgetfulness afforded him by repair work in the ship's engine room as well as in the arms of Muyra, his non-European girlfriend. Distance from the past, *Morbus Kitahara* concludes, liberates the individual from the disabilities imposed by memory.

In challenging the merits of remembrance, Ransmayr expressed many of the ambiguities of contemporary German memory. Like Ziegler, Ransmayr has openly declared himself personally committed to preserving the lessons of the Holocaust.[82] Having grown up in a village not far from the notorious concentration camp of Mauthausen, he was long aware of the horrors of the Nazi era. Yet Ransmayr has demonstrated a palpable uneasiness with the legacy of the Holocaust, as well as with the ways in which Germans have attempted to come to grips with it.[83] *Morbus Kitahara* can thus easily be read as a conservative critique of the increasingly ritualized nature of German memory in the 1990s. As Germany marked the fiftieth anniversary of the end of World War II and began plans for a national Holocaust memorial in Berlin, both leftwing and rightwing critics assaulted the nation's official culture of remembrance, the former perceiving a lack of conviction in the state-sponsored commemorative ceremonies, the latter desiring to abolish them altogether as impediments to a "normal" sense of national identity.[84] One of the most vociferous conservative critics, Martin Walser, singled out the gap between private and public memory, criticizing the latter for its inherent tendency to be politicized and wielded as a "moral cudgel."[85] Like Walser, Ransmayr has openly opposed what might be called "organized memory" – that is, any state-imposed program of remembrance – declaring that "every attempt to facilitate comprehension ... for the suffering ... of people in the form of an organized ... program ... is destined to remain hopeless."[86] For him, as for Walser, all confrontations with the past have to take place on an individual level. As he put it, "insight, regret, [and] ... consciousness [are] ... highly individual ... Only at the individual level are we able to clearly see the horror, as well as the unfulfilled hope ... of being able to master it."[87] Ransmayr's preference for an individualistic, as opposed to an organized, form of remembrance dovetailed, moreover, with his general aversion to organized political engagement and placed him on the conservative side of the political spectrum.[88] His stance suggested that, in struggling to balance the competing demands of remembrance and normalcy, Ransmayr tended to favor the latter over the former.

Taken together, *Die Stimmen der Nacht* and *Morbus Kitahara* high-lighted the Germans' ongoing difficulty in coming to terms with the legacy of the Holocaust. This difficulty was partly indicated by Ziegler and Ransmayr's very decision to write their respective novels about the fictional imposition of the Morgenthau Plan. Ever since 1945, the plan has served as a *bête noire* for rightwing Germans, who have singled it out (along with Allied policies of de-nazification and re-education) as responsible for crippling the nation's self-esteem.[89] Even though it was never enacted, the Morgenthau Plan has become a symbol of Germany's unjust persecution and suffering – in short, it has served as an icon of German victimization. The functionality of this myth, of course, lies in its ability to distract attention from the real historical crimes perpetrated by the Germans during the Holocaust. It is probably no coincidence that increased German interest in the Holocaust since the early 1980s has been accompanied by increased attention to the Morgenthau Plan.[90] Within this context, *Die Stimmen der Nacht* and *Morbus Kitahara* reflected a lingering inability to deal with Germany's guilt for the Holocaust. Although their allohistorical portrayals of the Germans' unwillingness to repent for their crimes were critical in tone, their decision to blame it on the Allied policy of coerced remembrance expressed a tendency to evade any sense of guilt for the nation's mnemonic failures.

UNDOING THE HOLOCAUST

If the tales of Bier, Ziegler, and Ransmayr portrayed the unwillingness of allohistorical Germans to repent for the Holocaust, three other fictional works, Thomas Ziegler's novella *Eine Kleinigkeit für uns Reinkarnauten*, Martin Amis's novel *Time's Arrow*, and Stephen Fry's novel *Making History* imagined the Germans striving to repent for the Holocaust by trying to undo it altogether. In chronicling the failure of these attempts to undo the past, however, these texts affirmed the dangers inherent in remembering it.

Perhaps the most outlandish of these tales was Thomas Ziegler's 1988 novella *Eine Kleinigkeit für uns Reinkarnauten*. Loosely, if awkwardly, translated as *A Small Matter for Us Reincarnauts*, Ziegler's narrative is set in a dystopian Los Angeles in the middle of the twenty-first century.[91] At this point in time, roughly 100 years since the end of World War II, the United States has become a third-rate world power, having suffered a series of calamities ranging from a colossal west coast earthquake, an AIDS epidemic, and a horrific wave of rightwing, evangelical Christian terrorism. Replacing America as the dominant world superpower is "reunified

Germany," which has parlayed its scientific and technical might into near-global hegemony. Against this larger backdrop, *Eine Kleinigkeit für uns Reinkarnauten* unfolds as more of a "future history" than a full-fledged alternate history. At no point in the story is the established historical record (that is, our timeline) ever altered. Nevertheless, *Eine Kleinigkeit für uns Reinkarnauten* constantly skirts the edge of alternate history by featuring, as its plot's central focal point, the intention of its central characters to turn back the hands of time and alter history's course.

Eine Kleinigkeit für uns Reinkarnauten focuses on the fate of its protagonist, Valentin, an industrious but hard-luck employee at the Los Angeles-based Institute for Reincarnation Science (*Institut für Reinkarnautik*). By this point in history, humanity has learned the secrets of reincarnation, and private institutes have arisen offering another chance at life for individuals (largely a wealthy clientele) who are near death. Valentin is a "reincarnaut" at the institute, a job that entails traveling, like an astronaut, through the "regions on the other side of the grave" to escort reincarnation candidates to the wombs of expectant mothers-to-be.[92] Valentin's job is physically taxing (particularly owing to the effects of "retro-time," a freak condition in which all actions occur backwards), but it is generally uneventful. Besides facing the prosaic problems of workers everywhere, such as being evicted from his apartment and having domestic disputes with his girlfriend, Christine, Valentin's life is unremarkable.

His humdrum existence changes swiftly, however, when a mysterious client arrives one day from Germany. The individual in question is "the secret ruling power of ... Germany," the founder of VEB Electronics, Karl von Hutten.[93] Dying of an AIDS-related illness, Hutten arrives in Los Angeles hoping to have Valentin assist him in becoming reincarnated. But along with this wish he requests Valentin's assistance with a much more controversial plan – "to unmake the occurrence of the Holocaust of European Jewry in the 1940s."[94] Shocked, Valentin wonders how he can help in this unprecedented undertaking. From Hutten he learns that "chrono-physicists" working for his company in Heidelberg have developed a machine, known as a *Zeitsonde*, that can enable individuals to be reincarnated in the past, not merely the future. Hutten informs Valentin that he needs to be escorted back to a precise time and place – April 20, 1889, in the village of Braunau-am-Inn. The reason? So that he can be reincarnated as a newborn infant by the name of Adolf Hitler.

Valentin reacts incredulously to this plan, objecting that such a radical intervention into history will have incalculable consequences. Hutten, however, reassures him that very little will change: "I will be Adolf

Hitler. I will think like him, act like him, live like him, die like him. With one difference. There will be no gas chambers. Persecution of the Jews – yes. Concentration camps – yes. War – yes. But no gas chambers, no mass shootings, no Holocaust."[95] According to Hutten, the reason the Holocaust will not occur in this hypothesized alternate history is because a:

post-hypnotic decree ... will change Hitler's Jewish policy [after 1938 and give rise to] ... a Führer order that will lead the participants at the Wannsee conference to decide to spare the Jews' lives by using them as forced laborers for the German armaments industry. A rational decision, corresponding to the war situation, that will be acceptable even to Himmler, Rosenberg, and the other antisemitic Nazi ideologues.[96]

In short, Hutten hopes that by having Hitler slightly alter the course of history in early 1942, he can prevent total genocide while not throwing off the course of history too radically.

Yet the alteration of history never occurs. As the story culminates, Valentin agrees to the plan, citing his Jewish background as an important reason for his participation. Yet in a dramatic, if somewhat bizarre, ending, the plan is sabotaged by a conspiratorial cell of Palestinian Islamic fundamentalists who fear that unmaking the Holocaust will pave the way for a "second" Holocaust of the Palestinian nation. By this point in history, the Palestinians have successfully established an independent state next to Israel, against which it has fought new wars. The Jewish people, it turns out, are only able to defeat their Arab enemies in one war with the help of German military aid – a fact that demonstrates the amicable relations between the two nations. Yet, when the Palestinians get wind of Hutten's plan to unmake the Holocaust, they recognize the possible consequences for their own welfare. As one Palestinian radical named Mohammed exclaims:

We know that the success of this [reincarnation] plan will mean the end of the Palestinian nation ... Imagine, Mr. Valentin, an Israel with six million additional citizens, six million European Jews, many of whom are educated scientists, technical specialists, and engineers ... The Zionists stole the land from us Palestinians after the Second World War ... Our struggle for our own state lasted for over a century. And the Islamic Republic of Palestine only exists because they reluctantly had to accept that they are merely a puddle in an Arab sea ... But imagine how the Zionists would have behaved if they had been stronger and more numerous ... They would not have given in. Never! They would have stolen more land and killed more Palestinian mothers and children. The Holocaust of the European Jews prevented the Holocaust of the Palestinians. That is the truth.[97]

In order to prevent their renewed persecution, one of the Palestinian group's members, Lu Lohannon, infiltrates the reincarnation institute and helps thwart the plan. In the book's dramatic culmination, one of Lohannon's co-conspirators, one Dr. Janosz, pulls out a laser and kills Hutten as he prepares for reincarnation. With Valentin already catapulted into the past, the tale ends on the rather incongruous, if comic, note of him being reincarnated as the newborn twin brother of his estranged wife (now his infant sister). Since Hutten is not reincarnated as Hitler (whose real historical birth and death remain unaffected) *Eine Kleinigkeit für uns Reinkarnauten* stops short of changing the historical record and leaves the reader with the tantalizing and appropriately allohistorical question: What if Hutten's plan had succeeded?

Although it never becomes a full-fledged work of alternate history, *Eine Kleinigkeit für uns Reinkarnauten* was nevertheless a thoughtful, if flawed, discussion of the complex dynamics underlying contemporary German and Jewish memory of the Holocaust. Ziegler's depiction of the Germans' motives in attempting to unmake the Holocaust were particularly insightful in acknowledging their complexity. On the one hand, there exists the genuine desire of Germans to repent for the past. As Hutten declares to Valentin:

You must understand that we are acting out of the most honest motives, that this plan that we are pursuing is unique in world history, that it is of such existential significance, that all means are permitted in order to ensure its success. Six million lives are at stake and we will save ... [them].[98]

On the other hand, the German plan is driven by a desperate desire to cast off guilt for the past. As Valentin thinks to himself, "[The Germans] are the perpetrators, and for this deed there is no forgiveness. Because they cannot forgive themselves. Because there are crimes for which there is no repentance ... their sole hope for redemption is to unmake the deed. Thus this faustian plan, this intervention in time. To rid themselves of their guilt."[99] Finally, the German plan is rooted in the crass motives of image-management and self-interest. For all of Hutten's efforts to deplore the Holocaust as an "inhuman, unforgivable crime," he is especially concerned that it has "sullied Germany's name in the whole world for centuries" and "branded [it with] the mark of Cain."[100] This stigma is especially worrisome for Hutten in light of the fact that – in an ultra sci-fi twist – an alien spaceship is approaching earth and is sure to seek out allies among the earth's peoples. "But how will it be," Hutten asks, "when we Germans come to the space travelers? When they ask us who we are as a people, where we come from, and what we have done? When we have to tell them about what our grandfathers did ... about the mountains of corpses and the sweetish odor of the crematoria?"[101] Ultimately, the plan to unmake the Holocaust emerges as a German method of banishing unpleasant memories.

Yet for all of the Germans' difficulties in coping with the legacy of the Holocaust, the Jews have an equally difficult time with it. Ziegler's tale, while a commentary on German memory, was also a German commentary on the problems of Jewish memory. Ziegler made this point through the character of Valentin, himself of Jewish background, who represents the Jewish inability to forget the past. Illustrating Valentin's typically Jewish sense of the immediacy of the past is his belief that while:

[the] Holocaust lay one hundred years in the past ... the six million Jewish victims of Nazi Germany found no peace.

The concentration camps, the gas chambers, crematoria and mountains of corpses – they still existed.

Not in the material world, but in the world of archetypes, in the Jewish soul, where time obeyed different boundaries, and a century lasted no longer than the blink of an eye. When [his colleague] Bernstein spoke, then six million dead spoke through him, of their fear, their hate, and their determination to prevent a repetition of the Holocaust at any price. Fixated on the genocide in this manner, no Jew was able to see the world as it really was. For Jewish eyes, it was darkened by Hitler's shadow.[102]

This historical sensibility of Valentin, in turn, nurtures what the book clearly presents as his longstanding suspicion, if not hatred, of Germany. Believing that "the Germans will never change ... [not even] in ... one thousand years," Valentin argues that "[their] dream of world dominance is a part of their national character [and is] perhaps even genetically determined."[103] Thus, he is suspicious of participating in the plan to save the Jews killed in the Holocaust because of the fact that "its magnitude and megalomania [represented] Germanness in its most extreme incarnation."[104] And so, both Germans and Jews – equally traumatized by the crimes of the past – are unable to unmake history. Both remain cursed by the burdens of memory.

In offering this conclusion, *Eine Kleinigkeit für uns Reinkarnauten* exemplified changing German views of the Nazi past in the era of reunification. Interestingly enough, Ziegler first began writing the novella in 1987, at a time in which, as he has noted, "[Mikhail Gorbachev's policies of] glasnost and perestroika ... [made] German reunification seem ... not ... so far away."[105] In this new climate of expectation, which would be realized a few short years later, Germans showed both an increasing willingness to confront the Holocaust while also exhibiting desperate signs of the desire to finally be done with it. A commitment to memory coexisted with an increasing desire for normalcy. Ziegler's work illustrated the tension between both trends. If the novella's premise of undoing the Holocaust expressed the fantasy of many Germans for normalcy, its depiction of the plan's failure reflected an awareness of the danger of attempting to realize it. On the face of it, then, *Eine Kleinigkeit für uns Reinkarnauten* could easily be read as an eloquent plea to resist normalization. But as with much of German memory, the novel's ultimate message was more ambiguous. Although it seemed to critique the desire to flee from the past, Ziegler's narrative hardly endorsed the cause of memory. Indeed, the ultimate target of its critique was the same as Christoph Ransmayr's *Morbus Kitahara* – the German cult of remembrance and repentance. The text clearly shows that it is the Germans' constant brooding over the past and their desire to gain absolution for it that are ultimately responsible for the novella's disastrous conclusion. In the end, then, rather than standing as a clear critique of the desire for normalcy, *Eine Kleinigkeit für uns Reinkarnauten* seemed to recommend a healthy dose of amnesia in order to achieve it.

While *Eine Kleinigkeit für uns Reinkarnauten* stopped short of undoing the Holocaust, Martin Amis's 1991 novel *Time's Arrow* pursued this scenario to its logical conclusion.[106] Strictly speaking, *Time's Arrow* was far from being a traditional work of alternate history (and is thus best classified as on the margins of the genre), as it did not so much alter the historical record as completely reverse it.[107] Amis's novel is distinguished by its backwards narrative, beginning with the end and ending with the beginning of the life of its protagonist, Tod T. Friendly. The reader first encounters Friendly having just died, and yet "[moving] forward, out of the blackest sleep, to find [himself] ... surrounded by *doctors.*"[108] After being zapped by a heart revival machine and given mouth-to-mouth resuscitation, he begins to move backwards into the house and perform humdrum tasks in reverse order (like taking hair grease off of his head, bottling it, and "[taking] it to the drugstore for like $3.45.").[109] At this point, the text's narrator (apparently Friendly's disembodied soul, who somehow separates from his body at his death) wonders in confusion, "What ... is the sequence of the journey I'm on? What are its rules? ... Where am I heading?"[110] As it proceeds, *Time's Arrow* emerges as a voyage of discovery for the soul of Tod Friendly, who revisits his entire corporeal life on earth, as if for the first time, by watching it unfold in reverse order. Beginning with his bland suburban existence at the end of his life in the 1980s, Friendly's soul witnesses his physical self going back in time – past his career as an obstetrician-gynecologist in an American hospital (where he stuffs wailing newborns back into their mothers' wombs), through his love affairs in the 1960s, to his arrival in New York in 1948, where he is provided with an old/new identity and name, John Young, and returns to Europe. All the while, Tod's soul perceives a growing psychological torment in his physical self and recognizes that he is in the possession of a terrible secret.

Tod's secret, his soul soon discovers, is his former career as a Nazi SS doctor in Auschwitz during World War II. There, under his original name, Odilo Unverdorben, Tod has made good on his American namesake ("Tod" translates as "death" in German) by acting as an ideological killer. It is at this point in the narrative that *Time's Arrow* embarks upon the bizarre, if logically consistent, description of the Holocaust's unmaking. Thus, in short order, Tod "personally remove[s] ... the pellets of Zyklon B and entrust[s] ... them to the pharmacist in his white coat," observes Josef Mengele seemingly cure "a shockingly inflamed eyeball ... [with] a single injection," witnesses the Jews "being deconcentrated and ... channeled back into society," helps to "dismantle and disperse the ghettos," and assists in picking up a "batch [of Jews] from the mass grave in the woods ... and then [driving] ... them closer to town."[111] By the end of the novel, as Tod retreats to his teenage self in the 1930s, all the Holocaust's victims have come "back from Auschwitz-Birkenau-Monowitz, from Ravensbruck ... from Buchenwald and Belsen and Majdanek," to their original places of origin.[112] In short, from the perspective of Tod's soul – who experiences, and can only understand, the backward flow of time in a forward-looking, real-time sense – the passage of time from the 1940s to the 1930s logically improves the course of history. As he enters the 1930s, Tod's soul observes:

A parallel pleasure and comfort, for me at any rate, was to watch the Jews. The people I had helped to dream down from the heavens ... Wisely cautious at first ... German society duly broadened itself to let the newcomers in. Their brisk assimilation, and their steady success, caused some harsh words to be spoken ... [Yet] the racial-law repeals ... rallied me ...
   With step after step the Jews move blinking into the sunlight ...
   Jews allowed to keep pets ... puppies ... doled out at police stations ... Jews weeping with gratitude as they take their new playmates home ...
   Jews permitted to buy meat, cheese, and eggs ...
   Jews empowered to have friendly relations with Aryans ...
   Curfew for Jews lifted ...[113]

By the 1920s, all signs of the Holocaust have been erased from history. On a camping trip near the military barracks that would later be transformed into the camp of Auschwitz, Tod's soul observes, "Everything was ... innocent.

All the quiddity, all the power and wonder, had been washed away by time and weather."[114] By the time Tod "dies" in the process of returning to his mother's womb, the Holocaust is all but unknown.

Although a very different kind of tale from Thomas Ziegler's *Eine Kleinigkeit für uns Reinkarnauten*, *Time's Arrow* also indulged in the allohistorical fantasy of undoing the Holocaust. To be sure, the novel reversed the genocide of the Jews in a highly oblique, idiosyncratic, and ontologically indeterminate fashion. For one thing, it is never clear whether or not the Jews are really brought back to life. They do in fact seem to be resurrected from the perspective of a highly metaphysical subject – Tod's soul. Indeed, Amis's novel seems to endorse the highly theoretical possibility that if one person's life could be reversed, all of the historical events witnessed by that person would, by necessity, also have to be undone as well. No greater claim can be imagined for the power of the individual to effect historical change. Yet the tension between the subjective perception of history and its objective unfolding remains unresolved in the text. At the novel's end, at the moment when Tod "dies" (or more accurately, is unborn), Tod's soul witnesses with horror an arrow flying forward, point first.[115] Here, Amis seems to suggest that history is now resuming its regular – and tragic – course all over again. The Holocaust, in short, will occur as once before.

The ambiguous conclusion of *Time's Arrow* illustrates a deeper ambivalence towards one of its central themes: the possibility of atonement after the Holocaust. Amis strongly suggests the possibility of atonement by depicting Tod's soul journeying backwards in time at the moment of his body's death.[116] The author never clarifies *why* this reverse journey occurs.[117] But, as with the very similar journey undertaken by the title character in Jerry Yulsman's 1984 novel *Elleander Morning*, Tod Friendly most likely wills his life into reverse at his death in order to make amends for the past. Amis provides several indications of Tod's desire for atonement. For one thing, *Time's Arrow* leaves the reader with the impression that the soul of the evil man – Tod Friendly-John Young-Odilo Unverdorben – is essentially good. At the symbolic level, this is implied by three of Tod's last names: "Friendly" (connoting benevolence), "Young" (connoting innocence), and "Unverdorben" (which can be loosely translated as "unspoiled" or "pure"). Moreover, Amis's empathetic potrayal of the bewildered, morally upright soul who admonishes his physical self for his transgressions and openly rejoices (perhaps naively) at their apparent reversal suggests an authorial view of the soul's inherent goodness. This is a view of humanity that assumes all people are good inside and that evil is a contingent property. Even the evil of Tod's physical self is not absolute. As Tod's soul notes near the end of the novel, "I've come to the conclusion that Odilo Unverdorben, as a moral being, is absolutely unexceptional, liable to do what everybody else does, good or bad, with no limit, once under the cover of numbers."[118]

Were this the end of the novel, *Time's Arrow* could be seen as partaking in the larger trend of the 1990s of representing the Holocaust through the prism of a "happy ending." For like *Schindler's List*, the novel provided a redemptive conclusion not only for the victims (who are brought back to life) but also *for the perpetrators*, who are granted psychic relief by the reversal of history. Up until the novel's last line, its narrative seems to point to a redemptive conclusion. Yet, by depicting Tod's "death" as once more setting time's arrow moving forward at the end of the novel, Amis implies, however elusively, the ultimate futility of Tod's attempt at repentance. The moral awakening of Tod Friendly's soul on his body's deathbed may come too late to have any positive effect on history. This conclusion is supported by the novel's last line, in which Tod's soul declares, "And I within, who came at the wrong time – either too soon, or after it was all too late."[119] Despite this bleak ending, the tale refrains from rejecting a redemptive conclusion altogether. For even if Tod's soul realizes the futility of repentance, his successfully unborn body never witnesses the redirection of time and thus seems to succeed in reversing the past, thereby atoning for it.

Amis's ambiguous conclusion of *Time's Arrow* reflected the somewhat contradictory reasons for which he wrote the novel in the first place. By all accounts, Amis sincerely believed in the need to preserve the Holocaust's lessons in memory.[120] Yet his decision to write about the subject seems to have been made for somewhat superficial, if not opportunistic, reasons. There is considerable evidence that Amis stumbled upon the theme of the Holocaust more or less by accident. As one journalist who interviewed the author reported, "Amis is candid to say that he had already decided to write a backward-in-time story and was, so to speak, shopping for a suitable theme to go with it."[121] In selecting the Holocaust like any stock-in-trade scenario (whether a sword-and-sorcery tale, a western, or a romance), Amis treated it as an unexceptional event – one like any other. This normalized mindframe was further reflected by the novel's overtly comic tone. *Time's Arrow* was not only extremely clever, but in many places also jarringly funny. Aside from its motives and innovative literary features, however, it was the conclusions of *Time's Arrow* that seemed to reflect a normalized stance towards the Holocaust. For in stressing the futility of atoning for the Holocaust, the novel affirmed the potential pitfalls of remembering it in the first place.

The conclusions of Ziegler and Amis were echoed by Stephen Fry in his 1996 novel, *Making History*.[122] As discussed in chapter 6, *Making History* is a work that largely explores the premise of the world without Hitler. But it also shared with *Eine Kleinigkeit für uns Reinkarnauten* and *Time's Arrow* the premise of undoing the Holocaust. Like the characters of Karl von Hutten and Tod T. Friendly, the character of Leo Zuckerman fulfilled the role of the German perpetrator desperate to atone for his nation's historical crimes. In this effort, Zuckerman, as von Hutten before him, tries to prevent Hitler's birth as a method of preventing the genocide of the Jews. But like his two predecessors, he fails in his attempt to improve the course of historical events. The Germans, even without Hitler, succeed in wiping out the Jewish people – even more thoroughly than Hitler was himself able to do in real history.

As discussed in chapter 6, Fry's aims in writing the novel were partly to shift attention towards the German people's role in perpetrating the Holocaust and thereby broaden the popular understanding of the crime as one caused not only by Hitler. Fry's identity as the son of an Austrian-Jewish woman who fled to England in the 1930s no doubt helps explain part of his novel's focus upon the culpability of the German people. Yet it does not explain the novel's puzzling hostility towards memory. Whether he intended to or not, Fry, like Ziegler and Amis, strongly suggested the futility of remembrance. This point emerges near the end of the novel when Zuckerman's partner in historical revisionism, Michael, finally returns to Cambridge after having returned history to its proper course. Upon entering his apartment, Michael looks with disgust at his dissertation on Hitler and exclaims, "I'm sick of you. Sick of Gloder who never was. Sick of the lot of you. Sick of history. History sucks. It sucks."[123] At this juncture, Michael turns on his computer, locates the file containing his dissertation, and deletes it from his hard drive. With this ending, *Making History* advocated a stance of forgetting rather than remembering the past. Indeed, the novel's ending rejected one of the primary modern rationales of historical study – Santayana's dictum that those who forget the lessons of history are condemned to repeat it.[124] Fry, in fact, asserted the opposite, by depicting Michael as not only *causing* the repetition of history but the worsening of history *despite* having taken to heart what he believes are its lessons. Studying and remembering the past, in short, emerge as pointless undertakings for those hoping for a better world.

Whatever Fry's reasons, his skeptical views of memory reflected a normalized view of the Holocaust. By depicting the world without Hitler as worse than the world with him, Fry's narrative imagined real history as not so bad after all – despite the murder of six million Jews. To be sure, history might always have turned out worse. Yet the very idea that the world could be made "a better place by ensuring that Adolf Hitler lived and prospered," could itself only emerge at a time when the Third Reich's horrors had diminished in popular consciousness.[125] This dulling of horror, finally, was illustrated in the novel's comic tone. If it was anything, *Making History* was a raucously funny novel, full of sophomoric jokes, pratfalls, and comic turns of plot. The ability to insert a theme possessing the seriousness of the Holocaust into this kind of comedic packaging was the best reflection of a mindset unconcerned with the moral limits of representing the Nazi genocide.

RECEPTION

On balance, the conclusions offered by recent allohistorical depictions of the Holocaust have strongly challenged traditional conceptions of memory. Whereas most of the scholarly and fictional representations of the Holocaust have been animated by the mantra "Never forget," the works surveyed in this chapter appear to recommend the opposite. All of them have underscored the futility of repentance after the Holocaust and have raised questions about the utility of remembrance. In breaking with the tradition of portraying the Holocaust within morally grounded narrative frameworks, these alternate histories reveal an increasing tendency to view it from a normalized perspective. However, the highly polarized reception of such alternate histories suggests that the normalization of the Holocaust has not proceeded without resistance. Many of the narratives discussed in this chapter have received lavish praise, but they have also been subject to fierce criticism. It is far from clear, therefore, that the pessimistic views of memory's moral imperatives contained within these accounts have been shared by a broader audience.

It is true that many allohistorical depictions of the Holocaust have enjoyed significant critical and commercial success. This success is unsurprising given the high-profile reputations enjoyed by most of these works' authors.[126] Of all the texts, the most successful was probably Christoph Ransmayr's *Morbus Kitahara*, which shared Europe's coveted Aristeion prize with Salman Rushdie's novel *The Moor's Last Sigh* in 1996.[127] Not much further down the list, however, were Thomas Ziegler's *Die Stimmen der Nacht* and *Eine Kleinigkeit für uns Reinkarnauten*, both of which won the top prizes in the German science fiction world.[128] For its part, Martin Amis's *Time's Arrow* was nominated for (though did not receive) Britain's prestigious Booker prize.[129] Stephen Fry's *Making History* was a bestseller in England.[130] And Daniel Quinn's *After Dachau* had an impressive commercial showing as well.[131] Beyond winning or being nominated for prestigious literary prizes, the books in question received many favorable reviews. The most widely reviewed texts, *Morbus Kitahara* and *Time's Arrow*, earned accolades both for their innovative style and literary accomplishment.[132] Daniel Quinn's *After Dachau* was called "fascinating," "intelligent," and "provocative" and was favorably compared to the work of Ray Bradbury and Robert Heinlein.[133] Thomas Ziegler's novels *Die Stimmen der Nacht* and *Eine Kleinigkeit für uns Reinkarnauten* helped elevate him to being one of the "top acts" in German science fiction.[134] And the short story of Jesse Bier, though less widely reviewed, was also given substantial praise.[135] In light of such acclaim, it is reasonable to conclude that the books' underlying mnemonic conclusions enjoyed a considerable degree of support.

And yet it is notable that many reviewers arrived at contradictory conclusions about the books' specific positions on remembrance. Christoph Ransmayr's *Morbus Kitahara* is a case in point. Many reviewers praised the novel as a forthright confrontation with the evils of Nazism. One reader, for example, hailed the novel as a "condemnation of an officially sanctioned, 'let bygones be bygones' attitude with respect to the recent Nazi past," while another praised it as a "sensitive" and "careful" discussion of the Holocaust informed by the author's personal experiences.[136] Still other reviewers, however, saw the book as a much more hesitant confrontation with the legacy of Nazism. Many critics went so far as to charge Ransmayr with the "aestheticization of horror" in his novel.[137] More strident still were reviews that perceived *Morbus Kitahara*'s critique of memory as justifying the Germans' postwar evasion of the Nazi past.[138] One of the most emphatic was the critique of the novel by German journalist Thomas E. Schmidt, who argued:

After only a couple of chapters ... [the] depiction of moral re-education becomes ever more bitter and caricatured. Here the author expresses from the heart the resentment against the westernization (*Westbindung*) of that culture in which it was his 'fate' to grow up ...

[Ransmayr has submitted a] sarcastic verdict on the culture of remembrance and commemoration ... [He] ... exposes everything as a lie, the talk of peace and reconciliation between the peoples ... This exaggerated cultural criticism allows one to foresee whom this book will appeal to and why.[139]

As it turned out, the fact that conservative feuilletonists in Germany applauded Ransmayr's critique of remembrance as a broader indictment of the East German cult of antifascism showed that Schmidt's hypothesis was on the mark.[140] *Morbus Kitahara*'s reception in its totality, though, did not reveal any clear political trends; neither liberals nor conservatives were able to agree with themselves, let alone each other, about the novel's meaning.

Similar contradictions appeared in the reviews of other works. Thomas Ziegler's *Die Stimmen der Nacht* was praised by some as "an attempt to master the Nazi past" and a clear "warning ... against the mistakes caused by an insufficient working through of the past." Others, however, insisted that the "thorny issue of mastering the past ... is actually not the book's main theme."[141] Martin Amis's more widely read novel received equally contradictory reviews. Many critics celebrated *Time's Arrow* for its innovative literary representation of the Holocaust.[142] Leslie Epstein summed up this view, calling the novel "[p]erverse and brilliant, insightful and exasperating ... a true contribution to the literature of the Holocaust."[143] Many other critics, however, questioned the novel's subordination of its serious content to its overly "playful" or "mannered" form.[144] Certain critics went further still, attacking the novel's backwards narrative as a "nasty little game," while some went so far as to charge it with denying the Holocaust.[145] In the end, some questioned whether the book was really even about the Holocaust at all.[146]

Finally, the most heated criticism was directed towards Stephen Fry's *Making History*. While praised by many for its intricate plot (and while extremely popular with most readers), many critics were highly skeptical towards its overall approach to the Holocaust.[147] Certain reviewers pointed out that the comic narrative chosen by Fry to deliver his thoughts on history was highly unsuited to its sensitive subject. One wrote that Fry's novel was a "misconceived" effort that made "no effort to recognize the horror of [its] ... subject," which ended up merely becoming a "colourful backdrop for his jokes."[148] Another opined that "It is difficult to take seriously the fact [a] ... comic actor ... has written a serious novel about Nazism and the Holocaust ... This novel is serious but it's hard to take seriously."[149] Juxtaposing a "soppy love story" with the Holocaust, said another, "amounts to a frightful infraction of the rules of taste."[150] Michiko Kakutani, writing in the *New York Times*, called the novel "shockingly tasteless and deeply offensive" and concluded that by using the "same flippant, tongue-in-cheek tone ... used in his earlier comic novels," Fry came across as a writer eager to get his readers to realize "this is all a goof – can't you take a joke?" "The problem," she concluded, "is that this time Mr. Fry has tried to make the death of six million people part of the joke, and the joke isn't funny – it's repellent."[151] Fry was "out of his depth" in writing his "inept" work.[152] Even some readers, most of whom enjoyed the book, felt uncomfortable that "there was something funny about Auschwitz or Dachau."[153]

On the whole, while the novels in question received considerable praise, enough critical voices were heard as to raise questions about what made them so controversial. In all likelihood, the mixed reception of the books was due to their ambiguous positions on remembrance itself. Given the fact that most readers of Holocaust fiction expect such works to affirm moral certainties, it is no wonder that the reluctance of alternate histories to do so elicited consternation.[154] The lack of precision in their overall messages helps explain why so many contradictory interpretations appeared. In many cases, positively disposed readers wanted to identify a praiseworthy stance towards remembrance even when it was not there. In other cases, however, critics sensed the presence of a breezy apathy, if not hostility, towards remembrance. The vocal nature of the resulting criticism makes it difficult, if not impossible, to view the critical and commercial popularity of these novels as implying an endorsement of their conclusions about history and memory.

CONCLUSION

Overall, recent allohistorical works about the Holocaust reveal surprising conclusions about the event's evolving status in popular consciousness. The conventional wisdom among most scholars today is that the Nazi genocide has progressively gained a larger place within the broader Western memory of the Third Reich.[155] If the Holocaust was generally ignored as a historical event in the early decades of the postwar world, the years since the late 1970s have witnessed such a proliferation of Holocaust-related films, television programs, memorials, museums, and artworks, that the Nazi genocide has become regarded as *the* signature event of the entire Nazi experience.[156] Yet signs of a backlash against the enhanced status of the Holocaust have become apparent in recent years. Various scholars, intellectuals, and political activists in the United States, Europe, and Israel – the most notable include Peter Novick, Norman Finkelstein, David Stannard, Martin Walser, Stéfane Courtois, and Amos Elon – have argued that the growing attention to the Holocaust has become, among other things, an ersatz source of Jewish identity, a geopolitical tool for suppressing Palestinian rights, a crude method of financial blackmail, a politically correct moral cudgel, and a bad-faith excuse for ignoring other horrific cases of genocide.[157] Having diagnosed a surfeit of memory, these and other observers have preached the virtues of forgetting.[158]

Alternate histories of the Holocaust seem to dovetail with this growing opposition to what some regard as the hegemony of Holocaust memory. The appearance of such a small number of narratives on the Holocaust at a time in which alternate history has experienced a notable growth spurt as a genre suggests a basic resistance to the subject in and of itself. But, as this chapter has shown, the best evidence of an increasing backlash is the fact that alternate histories of the Holocaust have challenged the widely accepted belief in the basic necessity of remembrance. By depicting memory as a burden that leads to frustration, if not outright disaster, allohistorical accounts of the Holocaust have seemingly gone so far as to endorse the remedy of amnesia. No doubt one can draw other and more charitable interpretations of these texts' messages. They may plausibly be seen as *descriptive* accounts of the difficulty in coping with the Holocuast. Yet the impatience with memory that suffuses them more likely reflects a *prescriptive* desire to be done with the Holocaust once and for all. This supposition is supported by recalling that the authors in question have largely chosen to present their narratives from the perspective of the perpetrators (or their guilt-ridden descendants) instead of the victims. Moreover, the perpetrators in these accounts – whether Jason Tull, Karl von Hutten, the soul of Tod Friendly, or Leo Zuckerman – have been depicted in strikingly sympathetic fashion as engaged in the admirable struggle to atone for the crimes of the past. By contrast, the victims have seldom found mention in these accounts. And where they have appeared (as in Ransmayr's character of Ambras or Ziegler's character of Valentin), they have been depicted negatively as bitter slaves to memory. On balance, by rehabilitating the perpetrators and ignoring or criticizing the victims, recent alternate histories have challenged the truism that remembrance is the closest approximation of justice for the crimes of the Holocaust.

By failing to consider this ethical function of memory, these works have revealed a reluctance to explore the Holocaust's most profound moral implications and, instead, have displayed a tendency to subordinate it to separate agendas.[159] Quinn, Ransmayr, and Ziegler seem to have embraced the subject intentionally to launch moral-political critiques of their respective societies' cultures of remembrance. Amis embraced the subject more randomly to provide a thematic focus for a long-planned formalistic literary experiment. Fry, meanwhile, seemed to approach the subject from a devil-may-care stance of comic escapism. Whatever their underlying motives, the authors of the novels in question have shown an emotionally distanced relationship to the Holocaust, which they have treated with considerable superficiality. This was particularly true of the novels of Amis and Fry, whose comic tone and partially happy endings subverted the subject's historical seriousness. In the end, it is the instrumental use of, and the emotionally disengaged relationship to, the Holocaust that suggests an increasingly normalized view of the event.

Allohistorical accounts of the Holocaust indicate that we are at a transitional point in the broader evolution of Holocaust memory. We are living in an era in which the "authentic" memories of the survivors who personally experienced the Holocaust are being displaced by the "vicarious" memories of later generations who have merely imagined it.[160] It is revealing that the authors of allohistorical portrayals of the Holocaust largely belong to these postwar generations.[161] With little personal and emotional investment in the Holocaust, they have no doubt found it easy to consider unconventional approaches to it and to derive new conclusions about it. Their narratives admittedly constitute some of the more extreme vicarious memories of the event. But they are part of a broader trend that is shaping the future of Holocaust memory.

It is unclear to what degree the phenomenon of alternate history will influence future fictional representations of the Holocaust. Allohistorical narratives of the Holocaust still constitute only a very small portion of fictional representations of the event. Their authors are relative outsiders to the community of scholars, artists, and writers who have devoted their careers to contemplating the Nazi genocide's historical and cultural significance. The appearance of strong criticism of these works, moreover, suggests the existence of substantial resistance to their playful approach to the subject and a desire to remember the Nazi past in traditional, moralistic terms. The ultimate importance of alternate histories thus may well be limited to their function as foils that reveal the current norms of collective memory. At the same time, however, these works have earned sufficient praise to suggest widespread support for depicting the Holocaust without undue regard for traditional, moral, or aesthetic imperatives. In this regard, allohistorical representations of the Holocaust may well foreshadow the future shape of remembrance. And given the genre's hostility to remembrance itself, that memory may eventually be no memory at all.

Conclusion

NEWS ITEM: Northern Italy: September 19, 2003.

When German Justice Minister Brigitte Zypries recently called a line of Italian wines "tasteless," she wasn't referring to the grapes.

Since 1995, a winery in northern Italy called Azienda Vinicola Alessandro Lunardelli has produced a line of "historical" wines featuring images of important men of history on the label – among them ... Adolf Hitler.

The Hitler line – called "Fuehrerwein" and featuring pictures of Hitler and slogans from Nazi Germany on the label – made headlines worldwide this month after a family of Polish tourists found the wine in an Italian supermarket ... and handed it over to [a] Polish newspaper ... which ran a photo of the bottle on its front page. Since then vintner Alessandro Lunardelli has been under attack ...

Lunardelli ... said ... "I see no reason for such a fuss. People like these characters ... They make good table conversation. So I'm not about to stop selling."

The Hitler wine, Lunardelli told the newspaper, is his bestseller, moving more than 30,000 bottles a month.[1]

Wherever one looks, signs of the normalization of the Nazi past abound in contemporary culture. The recent flap over Italian wine bottles bearing Hitler's face is merely one of the more bizarre manifestations of a larger trend. In the last several years, numerous controversies have erupted over the growing exploitation of Nazi symbols, themes, and motifs in tasteless and morally insensitive fashion. Among others: a pub in Seoul, South Korea made headlines by featuring a Nazi-themed interior, replete with Swastika banners and jackbooted waitresses; avant-garde artists in the "Mirroring Evil" art exhibition in New York City drew protests by irreverently incorporating Nazi iconography into mock LEGO sets and perfume advertisements; a well-known German novelist raised hackles by publishing an exploitative novel on the lurid subject of Nazi pornography; recent feature films in the United States sparked objections by focusing on the "human" side of the young Hitler; a German company raised eyebrows by selling toilet-bowl scrubbers made of Hitler heads studded with plastic bristles; and a wide range of comic books and video games have drawn concerned comments for their use of Hitler and other Nazis as central characters.[2] What these diverse examples demonstrate is clear: over half a century since the collapse of the Third Reich, Hitler and the Nazis have ceased being viewed solely as the archetypal symbols of evil. To a degree that few would have dared predict in 1945, the Nazi era has become transformed into an all-purpose grab bag of symbols guaranteed to fascinate, titillate, garner attention, and – not surprisingly – sell.

Alternate histories of the Third Reich sell, too. And like some of the crasser products of Western commercialism, they also reflect the ongoing normalization of the Nazi past. Since they first began to appear during World War II, alternate histories of Nazism have developed from a minor curiosity into a noteworthy phenomenon. Well over 100 narratives have appeared in the form of novels, short stories, films, television broadcasts, plays, comic books, and historical essays. As the chapters of this book have shown, these diverse texts have focused largely on four specific allohistorical themes: the Nazis winning World War II; Hitler surviving the war and fleeing into postwar hiding; Hitler being eliminated from history at some point in his life; and the Holocaust occurring in different fashion. Over the course of the postwar era, the shifting allohistorical portrayal of these themes has illustrated the emergence of a distinct normalizing trend in the Western memory of the Nazi era. From 1945 up through the mid-1960s, during what I have called the *era of moralism*, alternate histories adhered to strict ethical conventions in representing the Third Reich. In the ensuing *era of normalization*, from the mid-1960s to the present day, such morally principled tales have continued to appear, but they have been challenged and dramatically outnumbered by those offering a more nuanced view of the Nazi years. This trend clearly reveals that the fears and fantasies which animated alternate histories of Nazism in the first place have begun to fade. In the process, the injunction to remember the past lest it be repeated in the future has diminished in urgency. Alternate histories of Nazism, in short, seem to indicate a growing apathy towards memory.

ALTERNATE HISTORIES OVER TIME

This trend is made evident by surveying the evolution of alternate histories of Nazism chronologically across the four phases of the postwar era in which they have appeared:

1. To begin with, from 1945 to the late 1950s, during the *era of moralism's* initial *cold-war phase*, relatively few narratives appeared.[3] The small

number of accounts reflected the diminished attention to the Nazi era caused by cold-war fears of the Soviet Union. Still, those narratives that did appear in these years consistently featured morally unambiguous conclusions. The nightmare scenario of a Nazi victory, for example, was always depicted in dystopian fashion. Similarly, the nightmare scenario of Hitler's survival was always represented in such a way as to satisfy the fantasy of bringing him to justice. Both scenarios underscored Nazism's historical evil. Both, moreover, served psychologically consoling functions. British accounts of a Nazi victory, for instance, validated the myth of the "finest hour" by confirming the importance of the nation's real historical defeat of the Third Reich and thereby ratified the present as the best of all possible worlds. American accounts of Hitler's postwar survival, meanwhile, satisfied the fantasy of bringing him to justice, and thus provided a measure of closure to World War II. Significantly, both scenarios offered a welcome distraction from the tensions of the cold war and provided some solace that, even if things were hardly ideal in the present, they could have been much worse.

2. From the late 1950s to the middle of the 1960s, during the *era of moralism's* ensuing *rediscovery phase*, alternate histories rapidly increased in number.[4] The reason for this heightened focus on a Nazi triumph in World War II was the worldwide growth of attention to Germany's Nazi past in the years 1958–61, caused by the capture and trial of Adolf Eichmann, the upsurge of neo-Nazi activity, and the eruption of the Berlin crisis. As with the accounts of the 1940s and 1950s, the narratives of these years offered strongly moralistic conclusions, only now they did so with extra urgency. During an era in which many Europeans and Americans were not yet convinced of Germany's commitment to democracy, fears of a neo-Nazi revival prompted the writers of alternate histories to remind their readers of the Third Reich's historical crimes. The scenario of a Nazi wartime victory, therefore, was depicted in more explicitly dystopian terms than before, most powerfully in the tales of C. M. Kornbluth, William Shirer, Philip K. Dick, and Comer Clarke. The intensified commitment to memory was also illustrated by the new depiction of Hitler *evading* justice in *The Twilight Zone* episode "He's Alive!" and the British television drama "The Night Conspirators," both of which aimed to underscore the enduring threat of Nazi ideas in the present. Finally, the first-time expression of the fantasy of punishing the Germans for the Holocaust, seen in Jesse Bier's short story "Father and Son," reflected a reawakened belief in the need for justice. These latter narratives were exceptional for their era, but, like the more numerous

accounts of a Nazi wartime victory, they shared a belief in Nazism's inherent evil and expressed a reinvigorated commitment to remembrance. On balance, the tales of these years reflected the enduring trauma of the Nazi experience. At the same time, by imagining a nightmarish vision of an alternate past, they validated the virtues of the present.

3. With the dawn of the *era of normalization* after the mid-1960s, however, the ethically conscientious mode of representing the Nazi era began to decline. This trend was especially visible during this era's *crisis phase*, from the mid-1960s to the early 1980s, when the growing number of alternate histories exhibited progressively more normalized conclusions.[5] The content of these tales reflected the new anxieties of the era. As Great Britain, the United States, and Germany entered periods of economic decline and political turbulence, alternate histories ceased representing the Nazi past in a self-congratulatory manner and began to do so more self-critically. Employing the varied techniques of *universalization, relativization,* and *aestheticization,* these tales advanced the process of normalization in emphatic fashion.

This trend was particularly visible in accounts of a Nazi victory in World War II. British narratives by such figures as Kevin Brownlow, Giles Cooper, and Len Deighton abandoned the traditional black-and-white portrait of demonic Nazi perpetrators and heroic British victims and instead depicted the latter as collaborators and the former as normal human beings. The goal of this new approach was to challenge the notion – central to the myth of the "finest hour" – of Britain's moral superiority to the rest of Europe and thereby to express dissatisfaction with the nation's fall from global dominance. In the process, however, these tales universalized the significance of the Nazi experience by suggesting that Nazism was far from being solely a German phenomenon and could have taken root just as easily in Britain. American accounts, meanwhile, diminished the horror of a Nazi victory in order to cast doubt upon the wisdom of the United States' decision to intervene against the Germans in World War II. In an era of increasing concerns about the Soviet Union, alternate histories by such disparate figures as John Lukacs, Brad Linaweaver, and Bruce Russett speculated about whether, by staying out of the war, America could have avoided the costly postwar struggle against communism. In the process, these writers relativized Nazism's evil by implying that communism was even worse. Present-day fears, in short, were instrumental in diminishing the memory of the Third Reich's horror. Finally, German accounts of a Nazi victory, which first began to appear in this era, adhered more closely to the reigning moralistic pattern. By depicting the scenario in frightening fashion, they ratified the German present, which, while also characterized by relative decline after the mid-1960s, was far superior to the nation's devastated reality in the early postwar years.

Alternate histories on other themes related to the Third Reich also reflected the era's broader normalizing trend. One of the most notable developments was the renewed appearance of accounts depicting Hitler's survival. Like the tales of the early 1960s, the narratives that appeared after 1970 also depicted Hitler evading justice. Now, however, their function was different. If the former had portrayed Hitler's survival in order to focus on the enduring danger of Nazism as a German phenomenon, the latter were more eager to universalize Hitler's significance into an all-purpose symbol of contemporary evil. This tendency, which was seen most prominently in the tales of Brian Aldiss, Gary Goss, and George Steiner, reflected the pessimism of an era that was profoundly shaped by the Vietnam War and other crises. The portrayals of Hitler's survival in the 1970s, however, normalized the Nazi past not only by universalizing it but also by aestheticizing it. Thus, the narratives of Pierre Boulle, Michel Choquette, and Richard Grayson fell victim to the era's intense fascination with the Führer by using various literary and visual methods to portray his human side – a trend that subtly served to neutralize his evil. In short, the tales depicting Hitler's evasion of justice displayed a growing apathy towards the injunction to remember the crimes of the Nazi era in their unique historic specificity.

The theme of the world without Hitler slowly came into its own during the latter part of this period. Tales on this subject strongly diverged in their conclusions, however. While some, such as those by Jerry Yulsman and Hans Pleschinski, affirmed Hitler's evil by representing his elimination as improving history, others, like those of Norman Spinrad, diminished his evil by portraying history without him as just as bad, if not worse. The small number of accounts and their competing conclusions in this era make it difficult to identify a single pattern of normalization. But most of the narratives reflected the pessimism of the era and expressed dissatisfaction with the present.

4. Finally, during the *post-cold-war phase* from the late 1980s up to the present day, the normalization of the Nazi past in alternate histories has intensified along with their growing number.[6] The narratives that appeared in Britain, the United States, and Germany during this period were quite diverse in nature and were not linked by a single trend. However, it is clear

that in both content and function, British, American, and German alternate histories varied in direct relation to their nations' divergent experiences of the defining event of the period – the end of the cold war. This epochal event exerted a very different effect upon Great Britain, the United States, and Germany. If all three nations experienced political and economic crises during the late 1960s and the 1970s, their paths separated after 1989. While the end of the cold war initially did little to shake Britain out of its doldrums, it boosted the status of the United States and Germany, enabling the reunification of the latter and the rise to unrivaled global influence of the former.

These divergent experiences were clearly visible in allohistorical accounts of a Nazi victory in World War II. Most British accounts of the period, like those by Adrian Gilbert, Craig Raine, Robert Harris, Madeleine Bunting, John Charmley, and Christopher Priest, remained self-critical and continued to challenge the myth of the "finest hour" by blurring the line between the British and the Germans. Only by the end of the decade, once Britain had begun to recover its self-confidence under Tony Blair, did a minority of alternate histories once more adopt a self-congratulatory tone and offer ethically grounded portrayals of a Nazi victory. Accounts in the United States, by contrast, were much more consistent in triumphalistically reverting back to the older, morally informed patterns of the early 1960s. Yet, although the novels of Leo Rutman, Arthur Rhodes, and Harry Turtledove, and films like *Clash of Eagles*, *The Philadelphia Experiment II*, and the HBO version of *Fatherland* once more portrayed a Nazi victory in negative terms, they were less dystopian than the accounts of the 1960s and far more prone to embrace redemptive endings. Both of these trends suggest that the end of the cold war contributed to the fading horror of the Nazi past in American memory. The cold war's end also had a major impact upon German narratives, which ceased offering judgmental, self-critical depictions of a Nazi victory and instead began to portray it in benign terms in the effort to create a revived sense of national identity. Although it did so in different ways and in differing degrees, the end of the cold war promoted the process of normalization in Britain, the United States, and Germany.

This trend was further confirmed by narratives on other themes related to the Nazi era that appeared during this phase. Accounts of Hitler's survival exhibited an aversion to moralism by portraying the fugitive Führer continuing to evade justice. These accounts, whether by Americans, such as Steve Erickson, Barry Hershey, and E. M. Nathanson, or Germans, such as Armin Mueller-Stahl and Walter Moers, humanized Hitler by representing him less as a threatening demon than as a debilitated, and at times even comic, human being who no longer posed a danger to the world. This de-demonization of Hitler was further echoed in the many narratives that removed Hitler from the course of history. Allohistorical narratives that portrayed history as no better in Hitler's absence by such figures as Stephen Fry, Simon Louvish, and Harry Turtledove reflected the role of contemporary events in diminishing the horror of the Third Reich and universalizing its overall significance. Finally, allohistorical tales of the Holocaust exhibited an impatience with the injunction to remember the Nazis' genocidal crimes by depicting the attempt to atone for them as doomed to failure.

FADING FEARS AND FANTASIES

The shifting conclusions of alternate histories since 1945 illustrate the fading intensity of the fears and fantasies that originally inspired them. This trend is quite visible in surveying postwar alternate histories thematically according to scenario. The most powerful nightmare scenario of all, that of a Nazi victory in World War II, has lost much of its power to frighten in the last generation. If the dystopian accounts of the early postwar years expressed both lingering memories of the Nazi era's brutality and ongoing uncertainty about postwar Germany's political reliability, the normalized narratives of later years (especially in Britain and the United States) revealed the displacement of these fears by new, present-day anxieties about national decline. A similar trend is visible in allohistorical accounts of Hitler's postwar survival. If early postwar narratives depicting Hitler being held accountable for his crimes expressed the enduring nightmare of Hitler's survival and the enduring fantasy of bringing him to justice, the narratives that portrayed him evading justice after the 1970s suggested that the underlying nightmares and fantasies had begun to fade. The same can be said about the fantasy of eliminating Hitler from the course of history, the diminishing intensity of which is demonstrated by the far greater number of accounts portraying history without him as worse rather than better. Finally, alternate accounts of the Holocaust have illustrated the fading fantasy of motivating the perpetrators to repent of the Nazi genocide by exposing the ultimate futility of atonement.

The waning of the fears and fantasies that have animated alternate histories suggests that Western society has largely recovered from the traumatic experience of the Nazi era. The declining intensity of the three primary fantasy scenarios, in particular, provides strong evidence of this process of recovery. At the most basic level, of course, fantasy scenarios testify to the existence of dissatisfaction with the world of today by imagining alternate history being superior to real history. Originally, the fantasies of bringing Hitler to justice, eliminating him from history, and engendering repentance after the Holocaust testified to the Nazi era's lingering traumatic effect on the present. The repudiation of these fantasies in recent alternate histories, however, suggests the diminution of Nazism's traumatic legacy. This process has occurred for two different reasons. In part, the declining tendency to fantasize about history turning out better reveals an increased sense of contentment with the contemporary world – a sentiment that has served to marginalize the Nazi legacy in Western consciousness. Yet the fading of postwar fantasies just as much reflects the emergence of new postwar anxieties. The declining fantasy of bringing Hitler to justice and eliminating him from history has expressed the increasing concern of many writers about contemporary political problems, to which they have tried to direct attention by comparing them to the crimes of the Nazi era – a practice that has ended up either universalizing or relativizing them. It is not only the fading of fantasies that demonstrates the recovery of the Western world from the experience of the Third Reich, however, but also the declining intensity of the major nightmare scenario – a Nazi victory in World War II. The diminishing tendency to portray a Nazi wartime victory as a nightmare provides evidence of the displacement of the Third Reich in Western consciousness by pessimistic concerns about new postwar problems as well as by an optimistic sense of contentment with postwar successes. Fifty years after the collapse of the Third Reich, it seems, the Western world has progressively liberated itself from the nightmares and fantasies related to the Nazi era.

The declining power of these nightmares and fantasies is perhaps best indicated by the increasing use of humor in alternate histories of Nazism. Whereas the total absence of humor in early postwar alternate histories testified to the seriousness of their underlying fears and fantasies, its growing presence over time reveals the dawn of a less earnest mindset. Indeed, it confirms the old adage that tragedy plus time equals comedy.[7] The satirical portrayal of a Nazi victory in World War II in John Lukacs's essay "What if Hitler Had Won the Second World War?", in the *Saturday Night Live* skit "What If: Überman," and in the *National Lampoon* cartoon "What if World War II Had Been Fought Like the War in Vietnam?"; the comic portrayal of Hitler in Armin Mueller-Stahl's film *Conversation with the Beast*, in Michel Choquette's satirical photoessay "Stranger in Paradise," and in Walter Moers's comic book series *Adolf die Nazi-Sau*; and the disarming application of humor to the subject of the Holocaust in Stephen Fry's *Making History* and Martin Amis's *Time's Arrow* all demonstrate the amenability of alternate history to the use of humor. This trend, of course, is not unique to alternate history, but confirms an increasing willingness within Western popular culture since the late 1960s to burlesque the Nazis, as seen in television shows like *Hogan's Heroes*, Mel Brooks's classic film (and recent play) *The Producers*, and Roberto Benigni's film *Life is Beautiful*. The use of humor is, in and of itself, an important index of normalization. But even more telling is the identity of those willing to utilize it. If, traditionally, most humorous accounts were produced by Americans and Britons, today the fact that Germans have overcome their traditional inability to laugh at the Nazi era reveals further evidence of normalization. Through their use of humor, alternate histories demonstrate that there really are no more limits to representing the Nazi past.

THE FADING OF MEMORY

Alternate histories also suggest a growing sense of apathy towards preserving the lessons of the Nazi past in memory. For the first two decades after 1945, allohistorical depictions of the Third Reich consistently endorsed the cause of remembrance. More recent narratives, however, have displayed less interest in pursuing this original mnemonic objective. Early postwar accounts of a Nazi wartime victory, for example, depicted the scenario in bleak terms in order to admonish society to remember the Third Reich's real historical crimes. By contrast, later narratives, in using the scenario mostly for the purpose of national self-critique, treated the Third Reich less as a topic of intrinsic historical importance – to be remembered for its own sake – than one that could be instrumentally used in the pursuit of other, unrelated agendas. Similarly, while early alternate histories on the topic of Hitler's survival endorsed the need to remember the Nazis' crimes by depicting the ex-dictator being brought to justice, later accounts that described Hitler's evasion of justice programmatically implied that the preservation of memory was either futile, dangerous, or otherwise counterproductive. The same pessimistic message was featured in narratives of the world without Hitler, most of which, by showing how history is not made any better – and sometimes is made worse – by the desperate attempt to eliminate him, highlighted the pointlessness of dwelling on the past and affirmed the virtues of amnesia. Finally, alternate accounts of the Holocaust have cast doubt on the common postwar maxim that memory is the path to salvation by portraying the perpetrators' attempted (or coerced) attempt to atone for the Nazi genocide as leading to frustration, if not disaster. All of these tales, by questioning the virtues of remembering the Nazi era, have affirmed that it should be regarded as no different from any other historical legacy and thus illustrate the ongoing phenomenon of normalization.

ALTERNATE HISTORIES IN COMPARATIVE NATIONAL CONTEXT

The phenomenon of normalization has hardly been monolithic, however, but has varied according to national context. Alternate histories of Nazism tell us less about the Nazi past than about the shifting concerns within the nations that have produced them. In the early years after World War II, British, American, and German alternate histories were strikingly similar. From 1945 until the mid-1960s, all three nations depicted the era's dominant theme – a Nazi victory in World War II – in self-congratulatory fashion in order to validate the present as the best of all possible worlds. Britain proudly affirmed the myth that the defeat of Nazi Germany constituted its "finest hour"; America confidently confirmed the wisdom of wartime intervention; and Germany smugly distanced its reformed postwar self from its deviant wartime predecessor. Yet this manner of representation functioned smoothly only as long as the postwar histories of all three nations were success stories. After the mid-1960s, all three slowly began to suffer phases of decline that led alternate histories to shift their conclusions, as well as function.

In Great Britain, most alternate histories that appeared after the mid-1960s continued to focus on the scenario of a Nazi triumph in World War II, but they now began to portray it in more normalized ways as part of the self-critical mission of challenging the myth of the "finest hour."[8] This penchant for self-criticism largely emanated from the political left, which was responding to Britain's fall from great-power status. Believing that Britain needed to abandon its traditional separatism from, and ultimately link its fate to, the European community, left-liberal Britons took aim at the presumption of moral exceptionalism which lay at the root of the "finest hour" myth by emphasizing the British people's penchant for collaboration in their accounts of a Nazi wartime victory. Conservatives, by contrast, tried to uphold the "finest hour" myth by continuing to underscore the serious threat posed to Britain by a hypothetical Nazi victory and by emphasizing the likelihood of British resistance to it. On balance, though, the liberal penchant for self-critique has been the predominant trend among British alternate histories. By universalizing the significance of Nazism and portraying how it could have easily been embraced in Britain, these accounts have advanced the normalization of the Nazi past in the process of normalizing British national identity.

In the United States, the alternate histories that appeared after the mid-1960s were much more diverse than those that appeared in Britain.[9] Many American alternate histories also focused on the scenario of a Nazi victory in World War II. Yet in doing so they never completely abandoned the self-congratulatory, moralistic approach of the early postwar years. Not only did this view survive during the self-critical era of the 1970s and 1980s, but it experienced a major revival after the end of the cold war. This allegiance to moralism reflects the United States' greater ability to stave off postwar decline than Britain and explains why it has enjoyed the luxury of a more optimistic and triumphalistic mindset. American narratives on other allo-historical topics, however, have been much less moralistic. Tales of Hitler's postwar survival and accounts of his elimination from history largely de-demonized the ex-dictator by showing him successfully evading justice and by imagining world history as no better as a result of his absence. These pessimistic conclusions reflect how concerns about new postwar problems (such as the Vietnam War) reduced the singularity of Nazism as the epitome of evil within American consciousness. Unlike the case in Britain, then, where alternate histories normalized the Nazi past for the sake of national self-critique, a broader range of motives, rooted both in triumphalism and pessimism, shaped the allohistorical representation of Nazism in the United States.

German tales demonstrate perhaps the most striking trajectory of normalization. German alternate histories did not appear on any subject whatsoever until the mid-1960s. At this point, they mostly focused on the subject of a Nazi wartime victory, consistently depicting it as a nightmare. Beginning in the 1980s and especially since re-unification in 1990, however, this ethically grounded perspective began to wane. It did so at the same time that German alternate histories began to swell in number.[10] Both trends expressed the emergence of a broader desire for a sanitized history and a normal national identity. These desires were visibly present in tales on a variety of counterfactual themes. German depictions of the Nazis winning World War II, for example, ceased depicting Hitler's triumph as a nightmare and relativized its horror to make it seem not such a terrible event. Accounts of the world without Hitler portrayed it as a better place in order to blame the Führer alone for the Third Reich and thus absolve the German people of the primary responsibility for the Nazi dictatorship. Narratives of the Germans being punished more severely for the Holocaust through the imposition of the Morgenthau Plan allowed Germans to play the role of innocent victims, while depictions of the attempt to undo the Holocaust reflected an enduring German discomfort with the memory of Nazi crimes. The most recent German accounts of all, on the subject of Hitler's survival, have dramatically humanized the Führer by depicting him as a comic figure who evades justice – a bold strategy of transforming the Nazi past into one like any other. In all of these ways, German alternate histories, like those in Britain and the United States, were involved in the process of refashioning their respective national identities to suit new postwar realities.

In short, British, American, and German alternate histories reveal distinct national differences in the normalization of the Nazi era. In all three nations, the process of normalization commenced at different times, emerged for different reasons, and developed varying degrees of intensity. In Britain, it emerged the earliest, in the mid-1960s, as part of a broader dynamic of national self-critique caused by the dawning awareness of national decline, and has been consistent in its thrust. In the United States, it began somewhat later, after the early 1970s, and was sparked by a growing concern about world problems, but faded in intensity with the end of the cold war. In Germany, normalization emerged the latest, only in the 1980s, as part of the desire to renationalize German national identity, and has further intensified with the passage of time.

THE CAUSES OF NORMALIZATION

Comparing British, American, and German alternate histories reveals insights into the specific dynamics of normalization and shows the phenomenon to be really the byproduct of separate, yet mutually reinforcing, trends. Common to all, at the most basic level, has been *organic normalization*. As the Nazi era has receded further into the past, the disappearance of the living witnesses and the emergence of new generations lacking firsthand knowledge of the Third Reich have promoted the emergence of a less judgmental and more flexible perspective towards it as a historical epoch. This trend has been partly visible, as noted above, in the fading intensity of the fantasies and nightmares that originally underpinned the various allohistorical scenarios in the first place. Yet it is important to stress that these fantasies and nightmares have not so much faded owing to the simple passing of time, but more specifically owing to the emergence of new postwar concerns that have increasingly placed the Nazi era in their shadow. As a result of this trend, the writers of alternate history have ceased viewing the Nazi past as a subject possessing historic value in and of itself.

Instead, they have regarded it more and more from a presentist perspective and have instrumentalized it in polemical fashion to serve other interests.

The two primary ways in which the Nazi legacy has been instrumentalized has been through its *universalization* and *relativization*. Many writers, typically possessing left-liberal political views, have universalized the experience of the Nazi era in order to draw lessons from it that might help direct attention to present-day problems. Some, such as Brian Aldiss, Norman Spinrad, Harry Mulisch, Ward Moore, and David Dvorkin, used alternate history to condemn cold-war anticommunism, whether during the Vietnam or Reagan eras. Others, like Gary Goss, George Steiner, Simon Louvish, and Harry Turtledove, used alternate history to condemn the persistence of nationalism, racism, and the recurrence of genocide in the present (or, in the case of Daniel Quinn, to condemn the contemporary ignorance of genocides of the past). Many left-leaning British writers, like Giles Cooper, Kevin Brownlow, Len Deighton, and Madeleine Bunting, universalized the Nazi era by claiming that it was not merely the Germans but rather all people (and especially the British) who possessed the capability to embrace fascism. And German writers, like Otto Basil and Helmut Heissenbüttel, used the Third Reich as a universal metaphor for the persistence of various and sundry contemporary evils. The relativization of the Nazi past, by contrast, typically has been promoted by writers on the conservative side of the political spectrum. In the United States during and after the cold war, anticommunist writers like John Lukacs, Brad Linaweaver, and Pat Buchanan portrayed a Nazi victory in World War II in benign terms in order to focus attention on the evils of the Soviet Union. In Britain, conservatives like John Charmley and Alan Clark dismissed the threat of a Nazi victory in order to condemn the legacy of Churchill. While in Germany, self-professed conservatives like Alexander Demandt and Michael Salewski, as well as less openly political writers like Christoph Ransmayr and Thomas Ziegler, have seemingly done the same in order to help clear the way for the creation of a normal sense of national identity for the newly reunified German nation.

Another factor involved in the process of normalization has been the *aestheticization* of the Nazi era. This phenomenon – which largely refers to the tendency of writers to approach the Nazi era less from a moral than an aesthetic perspective – has appeared in different forms. Writers such as Craig Raine, David Dvorkin, E. M. Nathanson, and Len Deighton portrayed their Nazi characters as complex human beings partly to reject the common literary stereotypes of Nazis as sadistic brutes.[11] In so doing, however, they abandoned the morally principled tradition of portraying

Nazism as absolute evil. Other writers aestheticized the Nazi past by producing narratives that dwelled excessively on the era's violence and horror. The utilization of sadistic imagery and gratuitous sex and violence by such writers as Norman Spinrad, Steve Erickson, Eric Norden, Joseph Heywood, Brad Linaweaver, David Dvorkin, Newt Gingrich, and Otto Basil, among others, shows an ongoing fascination with the deviant world of the perpetrators and a diminished concern with the suffering of the victims. Finally, the application of humor to the subject of the Third Reich in recent years provides clear evidence of the waning appeal of moralism.

The normalization of the Nazi past, in short, is not an undifferentiated process but should be seen as a complex phenomenon composed of parallel trends that are different in motivation but ultimately quite similar in their cultural consequences.

ALTERNATE HISTORY AND NORMALIZATION: HOW REPRESENTATIVE A TREND?

Having described how postwar works of alternate history have normalized the Nazi past, it remains unclear how representative this trend really is. Although a great many allohistorical narratives of the Third Reich have appeared in the years since 1945, they remained largely unnoticed and were regarded as quite marginal until the last decade or so. This relative neglect is partly due to the undeniable fact that many of these narratives are of uneven literary quality. For certain skeptics, this fact alone would suffice to reject alternate histories altogether as unworthy of serious study. It is true that, at their worst, alternate histories are poorly written, implausible works of low-brow literature produced by obscure, mediocre, and onetime writers.[12] Novels like Newt Gingrich's *1945* and films like David Bradley's *They Saved Hitler's Brain* have done little to boost alternate history's reputation. One might object that it is unfair to judge the entire genre by its least distinguished examples, yet even if they are tossed aside, the fact remains that alternate histories of Nazism have largely been produced by amateurs. Few of the figures who have produced such narratives have had significant prior experience writing in an allohistorical vein. Fewer still have devoted their careers to writing about the Third Reich.[13] Critics could be forgiven, therefore, for viewing these alternate histories with a healthy dose of skepticism.

Nevertheless, such accounts demand respectful consideration for several reasons. While most authors of alternate histories have been newcomers to

the genre, they have been able to draw upon unique experiences and
indisputable talents in crafting their tales. A significant number of writers
possessed direct firsthand experience of the Nazi era, either as soldiers who
fought against the Germans in World War II, as journalists who covered it
for the Allied press, or as propagandists who were deeply involved in the
effort to defeat the enemy. Brian Aldiss, Aaron Bank, Pierre Boulle, Ewan
Butler, David Charnay, Giles Cooper, Len Deighton, Edwin Fadiman,
H. L. Gold, Helmut Heissenbüttel, C. M. Kornbluth, Philip Mackie,
William Overgard, Rod Serling, and Jerry Yulsman all served in the war
as combat soldiers or intelligence officers. William Shirer worked as a
wartime journalist, and C. S. Forester, Noël Coward, and Hendrik
Willem van Loon pitched in as propagandists. Their postwar speculations
about how the past might have been different reflect valuable eyewitness
experiences of how it "really" was. Moreover, even if the producers of
alternate history have lacked experience in the genre and in-depth famil-
iarity with the subject of Nazism, a great many have been highly regarded
in their own fields of endeavor. These include prominent science fiction
writers like Brian Aldiss, Philip K. Dick, Harlan Ellison, H. L. Gold,
C. M. Kornbluth, Barry Malzberg, Ward Moore, Rod Serling, and
Norman Spinrad; mainstream novelists like Martin Amis, Pierre Boulle,
Len Deighton, Steve Erickson, C. S. Forester, Harry Mulisch, Christopher
Priest, Daniel Quinn, Christoph Ransmayr, Philip Roth, and George
Steiner; filmmakers like David Bradley, Kevin Brownlow, and Armin
Mueller-Stahl; playwrights like Noël Coward, Giles Cooper, and Philip
Mackie; journalists like William Shirer and Robert Harris; historians such
as Henry Turner, Niall Ferguson, and Eberhard Jäckel; poets like Craig
Raine; and comic book authors such as Len Wein and Walter Moers. As
producers of alternate histories, these figures have proved themselves to be
thoughtful, creative, and provocative individuals who have earned critical
acclaim in the general world of Western arts and letters.

   More importantly, these writers' prominent reputations have enabled
their works to reach an extremely large audience. Many alternate histories
of the Third Reich have attained impressive commercial success. A signi-
ficant number of allohistorical novels have become bestsellers, including
Norman Spinrad's *The Iron Dream*, Len Deighton's *SS-GB*, George
Steiner's *The Portage to San Cristóbal of A.H.*, Robert Harris's *Fatherland*,
Otto Basil's *Wenn das der Führer wüsste*, Philip K. Dick's *The Man in the
High Castle*, Joseph Heywood's *The Berkut*, Christoph Ransmayr's *Morbus
Kitahara*, Stephen Fry's *Making History*, and Martin Amis's *Time's
Arrow*.[14] Non-fiction works employing allohistorical reasoning have also

become bestsellers, such as Pat Buchanan's *A Republic, Not an Empire*, John Charmley's *Churchill: The End of Glory*, and Ralph Giordano's *Wenn Hitler den Krieg gewonnen hätte*. Television broadcasts like *The Other Man* and *An Englishman's Castle* were hailed as media events at the time of their initial showing, while *The City on the Edge of Forever* has gone down in history as among the most notable American television episodes ever. Even those narratives that were not bestsellers reached many millions of people simply owing to the mass-market nature of the cultural media in which they appeared. William Shirer's *Look Magazine* article "If Hitler Had Won World War II," the *Saturday Night Live* skit "What If: Überman," the *Twilight Zone* episodes "He's Alive!," and "Cradle of Darkness," as well as the satirical pieces published in *National Lampoon*, reached many millions of readers and viewers when they originally appeared.

With this kind of massive popularity, alternate histories of the Third Reich have arguably reflected as well as shaped Western views of the Nazi era to a greater extent than critics might care to admit. Of course, evaluating the extent to which the normalized conclusions of alternate histories have reflected and influenced the broader views of society is an extremely difficult task that can only be approached by surveying their postwar reception. Generally speaking, the response to alternate histories since 1945 can be divided into two distinct phases. From the time of World War II itself up through the early 1960s, alternate histories in Britain, the United States, and Germany largely received unanimous praise.[15] In these years, the general public accepted these accounts' adherence to the traditional moralistic mode of portraying Nazism as well as their affirmation of the virtues of remembrance. With the increasing normalization of alternate histories after the mid-1960s, however, the reaction to them became quite polarized. Hardly any works were given unanimous praise any longer, and quite a number sparked fierce controversy. In Germany, Norman Spinrad's *The Iron Dream* was banned by the courts for over a decade, while Robert Harris's *Fatherland* was seized by the police and partially confiscated after being rejected by numerous publishers and roundly criticized by the press. In Britain, Kevin Brownlow's film *It Happened Here* was censored for over a generation after being widely attacked in the media; John Charmley's book *Churchill: The End of Glory* was unanimously condemned; and novels such as George Steiner's *The Portage to San Cristóbal of A.H.*, Martin Amis's *Time's Arrow*, and Stephen Fry's *Making History* were subjected to vigorous condemnations as well. These latter works were also attacked in the United States, as was Pat Buchanan's book *A Republic,*

Not an Empire. Many works of alternate history escaped critical assault and met with respectful, if not admiring, reviews, but the strongly negative reactions towards the higher-profile examples clearly signify that they had struck a nerve. The negative reaction underscores the enduring opposition to depicting the Nazi era in anything but condemnatory terms. In short, as the conclusions of alternate histories have become more normalized, the resistance to them has grown increasingly strong.

What explains the divergence between the representation of the Nazi past in postwar alternate histories and the popular response towards them? In part, it is due to the conflicting priorities of the creators and consumers of popular culture.[16] As Herbert Gans has argued, the writers, filmmakers, and others who create works of popular culture typically come from educational and economic backgrounds that are quite different from those of their audiences.[17] As a result, the former bring a range of expectations to their work that are not necessarily shared by the latter. The creators of popular culture are typically driven by genuine artistic ambitions and strive to make their work as original and imaginatively compelling as possible.[18] They are therefore reluctant to remain confined by predictable and stereotypical conventions of character, plot, and setting, and frequently attempt to break with them in the effort to create something inventive and new. Audiences, by contrast, usually expect the familiar. In particular, Gans notes, they expect and prefer works of popular culture to affirm time-honored moral certainties.[19] The problem, of course, is that these expectations of moralism are frequently not met by authors who are eager, instead, for their work to subvert conventional expectations.

The diverging priorities of the producers and consumers of popular culture partly explain why postwar alternate histories of the Third Reich have met with such a stormy reception. Many of these narratives' creators have, in fact, been motivated by artistic ambitions to abandon ethically rooted stereotypes associated with the Nazi era and to portray it in more normalized fashion. Various political agendas, as noted above, have also driven the creators to universalize and relativize the Nazi past. But whatever the motives, the result has been the same – the abandonment of moralism. The consumers of these texts, by contrast, have persisted in desiring them to validate pre-existing moral certainties.[20] Audiences want to see Nazis portrayed as evil demons rather than as complex human beings and protest when their expectations are not satisfied. That being said, how readers have responded to the normalization of the Nazi past in works of alternate history is quite difficult to determine with any degree of certainty. While an enduring desire for moralism is strongly suggested by the critical reviews of many alternate histories, it is true that most reviews are produced by a professional class of critics, journalists, and scholars whose perspectives may not be representative of typical readers. Judging by the fact that many works of alternate history have become commercial successes *despite* negative reviews, it is possible that their depictions of the Nazi era have resonated with a greater portion of society than the negative reviews suggest. Indeed, the more that alternate history continues to prosper as a commercial enterprise, scholars will have to seriously consider the possibility that the genre is tapping into a popular willingness to accept unconventional methods of representing the real past.

Regardless of how alternate histories have been read and interpreted by a broader audience, their mass popularity reveals the need to acknowledge their importance in shaping the memory of the Nazi era. Until now, alternate history has been seen as a fringe phenomenon and basically discounted as culturally insignificant. Continuing to ignore it, however, would be a mistake. Popular culture, scholars have shown, possesses great subversive potential; its narratives, images, and messages can easily challenge and undermine those produced by the "official" or high-culture establishment.[21] This being the case, it is highly possible that allohistorical narratives on the Third Reich may be subverting the historical narratives disseminated by political, cultural, and academic elites. In recent years, such elites in Great Britain, the United States, Germany, and other Western nations have worked energetically to keep the Nazi past at the forefront of public attention. Whether in the form of official, state-sponsored commemorative sites, such as the United States Holocaust Memorial Museum in Washington D.C. and Germany's new national Holocaust memorial in Berlin, or high-brow works of individual creative expression – films such as *Schindler's List*, *The Pianist*, and *The Grey Zone* – not to mention the unending stream of scholarly monographs on the Third Reich, the representatives of high culture have consistently affirmed a message of Nazism's inherent evil and the need to remain vigilant against its recurrence by preserving its lessons in memory. Yet this impulse towards cultural moralism has hardly stood unopposed and, indeed, seems to have begun to spawn something of a backlash. This reaction has been most visible in the growing hostility towards Holocaust consciousness among polemically minded academic scholars, such as Norman Finkelstein and Peter Novick. It has further surfaced in recent complaints in Great Britain about the "Hitlerisation" of history courses in British schools, whose strong focus on the subject of Nazi Germany has allegedly led to the neglect of other historical eras.[22] And, as noted above, it

has manifested itself at the popular cultural level in the shameless exploitation of the Nazi past for commercial as well as artistic purposes, whether
in the form of Hitler wine bottles or toilet-bowl scrubbers. The impulse to
break taboos visible in all of these examples testifies to an increasing
exhaustion, if not outright boredom, with moralism and a desire for a
more uninhibited relationship with the Nazi past. Alternate histories have
strongly contributed to this trend by abandoning ethically oriented modes
of representation and by questioning the utility of remembrance. This
undercurrent of dissent may, as yet, still be exceptional within an otherwise
vigorous tradition of moralistic historical representation, but in the future
it may become normative. We need to be aware of its existence, therefore,
lest we become overly complacent about the task of educating future
generations about the past.

ALTERNATE HISTORY AND NORMALIZATION: HOW WORRISOME A TREND?

Given the subversive potential of alternate history, to what extent does its
normalized depiction of the Nazi past represent a worrisome trend? To be
sure, alternate history is merely one of many forms of culture through
which the representation – and, by extension, the eventual memory – of the
past is influenced. All the same, it is worth being aware of its potential
impact. The proliferation of allohistorical narratives of the Third Reich
presents grounds for concern for several reasons. First, alternate history can
easily be seen as *diverting* our attention away from real history.[23] While
studying history can enable us to understand the problems of the past (and
possibly discover new solutions for the present), reading works of alternate
history can easily be dismissed as escapist entertainment. At a time in which
educators are constantly bemoaning the lack of historical knowledge
within the population at large, alternate history may be worsening the
problem by siphoning off the attention that real history deserves, but
currently lacks. Moreover, alternate history risks *distorting* what little
people already know of the past. The more allohistorical tales one reads,
the blurrier the line can become between fact and fiction, between reality
and wishful thinking. The producers of alternate history, furthermore,
have frequently been guilty of *confusing* readers about their underlying
motivations or agendas for speculating about the past. Tales of a Nazi
victory in World War II, for example, have frequently been misunderstood
as fantasy scenarios produced by rightwingers (a suspicion bolstered by the
fact that neo-Nazis embraced – even as they overlooked the anti-Nazi

messages of – Norman Spinrad's *The Iron Dream* and Robert Harris's *Fatherland*).²⁴ So common have such cases become that the producers of alternate history now frequently take pains to stress the apolitical nature of their work so as to not be branded neo-Nazis.²⁵ Finally, the humorous depiction of the Nazi era in many works of alternate history risks *trivializing* the past and dulling people's sensitivity towards an era of great pain and suffering. Satirizing the Nazi era, after all, makes it harder for it to be taken seriously as a repository of important admonitory moral lessons. By distracting us from, by distorting our awareness about, and by discouraging us from remembering the reality of, the *actual past*, alternate history represents a phenomenon that bears watching.

Yet the situation is complicated. Although normalization presents certain dangers, it is not without its virtues. For it is precisely by counteracting and breaking down traditional moralistic views towards the past that normalization can be seen as providing a useful service. Historians, after all, have long recognized that an ethically oriented approach to history can easily lead to the subjective distortion of the past and ultimately block true historical understanding. As Leopold von Ranke asserted long ago, to truly understand the past, we have to adopt an objective and empathetic, rather than a judgmental, perspective towards the historical figures who determined its course. Without evaluating the past on its own terms and by its own moral standards, we impose our own values upon the historical record and thereby risk misjudging and distorting it. At the same time, an overly moralistic view runs the risk of mythologizing history and transforming it into a collection of ritualized ethical lessons that, over time, can easily become stale and cease to resonate within society at large. It was for this reason that German historian Martin Broszat in the 1980s called on Germans to "historicize" the Nazi era by abandoning their simplistic black-and-white image of the Third Reich as a story of demonic villains and virtuous heroes and replacing it with a grayer perspective that recognized the period's immense complexity. Normalizing the past thus can be greeted as a method of removing distortions, reinvigorating interest in the past, and advancing genuine historical understanding.

To a degree, the normalization of the Nazi past in postwar works of alternate history can be seen as advancing these praiseworthy goals. The normalized depiction of a Nazi victory in World War II in British alternate histories, for example, can be viewed as a helpful corrective to an overly mythologized view of the war in British memory. For even if the concept of the "finest hour" possessed obvious moral utility in reaffirming the evil of Nazism, it obscured how contingent Britain's decision to fight on against the Germans really was in 1940, sustained an unrealistic view of British power that ill served the nation in an era of European integration, and preserved jingoistic stereotypes of the Germans that had long since ceased to correspond to reality. A similar claim might be made for alternate histories that have portrayed Hitler's evasion of justice. Although such tales have frequently universalized the significance of the Nazi era, their portrayal of the dictator remaining at large can be seen as offering an ethically grounded reminder about the survival of evil in – and the difficulty of eradicating it from – the contemporary world. Alternate histories that have portrayed Hitler's elimination from history as making it worse can also be seen as providing a useful service. While such tales have clearly de-demonized the dictator, they have prevented us from blaming him alone for the rise of the Third Reich and have reminded us of the German people's contribution to it. Finally, allohistorical tales of well-intentioned Holocaust perpetrators seeking forgiveness for their crimes might be charitably viewed as restoring our awareness of the gray realities of human behavior. In view of such examples, alternate history's subversion of moralistic narratives can be seen as part of a healthy process of reassessing inherited historical views. Normalization need not, therefore, be seen as inevitably having a detrimental impact upon historical consciousness.

Yet normalization also has more problematic dimensions. A value-neutral approach towards history can easily shade into an apologetic kind of historical writing that excuses the immoral acts of the past as simply the result of different ethical standards. When seeking to explain acts of evil, a purely objective approach fails, for the attempt to understand such acts ends up condoning them.[26] This is particularly true of the Nazi era, for to insist that it be treated like any other historical period necessarily marginalizes its unique criminal features. It is too soon to expect the Nazi past to be treated like more distant eras of history. Indeed, the impatient call to normalize this particular era can often mask a desire to forget it altogether. Certain works of alternate history have clearly fallen into this category, most notably those produced by politically conservative American and German writers, who have consciously relativized Nazi crimes as part of the respective efforts to condemn communism or pave the way for a healthy German sense of national identity. These works embody the form of normalization that is the most troubling, and consequently they should be exposed to rigorous criticism.

To fully assess how worrisome alternate histories of Nazism really are, however, it is necessary to return to the important matter of their national origins. As this study has shown, the allohistorical representation of the Nazi past has largely been an Anglo-American phenomenon. German accounts have been comparatively small in number. This fact provides some reassurance, for even if recent German narratives have normalized the Nazi past for nationalistic reasons, they represent a minority trend within the broader movement. Were Germans today the chief producers of alternate histories, it would be another matter entirely, for it would suggest that the nation responsible for the Third Reich was failing to heed its lessons. As it is, however, German accounts have been far outnumbered by those produced in Great Britain and the United States. And however unfair it might seem to say it, it is less worrisome to see the normalization of the Nazi era being promoted by Britons and Americans than by Germans, for their nations' lack of responsibility for producing the Third Reich in the first place diminishes (though by no means eliminates) their historical obligation to learn its "proper" lessons. This being said, Anglo-American alternate histories of Nazism are hardly unproblematic. We have seen that they have contributed significantly to an increasingly normalized view of the Nazi period within British as well as American consciousness. Further still, their impact may not merely be confined to the domestic scene but may be international in scope. As Anglo-American alternate histories continue to attain worldwide reach through translation and foreign distribution, their unconventional depictions of the Nazi era may shape the contours of memory worldwide. In partaking of the increasing globalization of culture, in short, alternate histories of Nazism may be promoting the globalization of normalization.

THE FUTURE OF ALTERNATE HISTORY

It is far from certain how alternate histories of Nazism will evolve in the future. Our world today has become anything but predictable in the wake of the events of September 11, 2001. But if past trends provide any indication, future allohistorical narratives will directly reflect contemporary fears and fantasies. The rise of Islamic terrorism, in particular, may have a notable impact upon Western views of the Nazi past. The likely effect of this threat is anything but clear, but it is possible that fears of terrorism may help attenuate the memory of the Nazi era. Just as new crises after 1945 gradually came to overshadow the Third Reich in Western consciousness, the threat of new enemies today may serve to displace the memory of vanquished ones. At the same time, though, the specter of militant Islamism may serve to further anchor the place of Nazism in Western memory. For as this violent ideological movement and its notorious figurehead, Osama bin Laden, have emerged as the new symbols of contemporary evil, they have prompted numerous comparisons among Western observers to the established symbols of evil in the Western imagination – Nazism and Adolf Hitler.[27] As long as the latter evils are consistently invoked in order to understand the former, the Nazi past will remain solidly rooted in popular awareness as the West's benchmark of immorality.

Whatever the impact of our post-September 11 world on future works of alternate history, the ultimate significance of the latter may lie in their ability to help us understand the former. Throughout this study, we have seen that alternate history relies fundamentally upon the imagination to envision alternate outcomes for the past. At the deepest level, nothing has been altered as much since September 11, 2001 as the Western imagination. Deeds once thought impossible – planes toppling skyscrapers, biological weapons being mobilized against civilians – have now become part of our new everyday reality. Propitiously, alternate history may help us become more attuned to a world as yet unimagined. Eerily enough, some of the allohistorical works discussed in this study anticipated some of the events of September 11. For instance, Vita Sackville-West's novel *Grand Canyon* presaged the destruction of the World Trade Center by depicting the toppling of New York City's skyscrapers along Fifth Avenue in the wake of a Nazi attack, and Craig Raine's play *'1953'* anticipated the 2001 anthrax scare by depicting Vittorio Mussolini defeating Britain and "changing the face of war ... with the anthrax spore." Alternate history, of course, cannot predict the future. But it can stretch our ability to imagine how it might come about. At a time in which the United States military has consulted Hollywood screenwriters to conceive of still unimagined terror threats, at a time in which pundits everywhere are calling for the development of new paradigms for formulating foreign policy, collecting intelligence, and ensuring domestic security, any means of reshaping our imagination of what may one day come to pass are welcome.

By reminding us that history's course is not inevitable, that historical events are highly contingent, alternate history can help us rethink our ingrained assumptions not only about the past but also about the present. More than a few of the works discussed in this study suggest ways to protect against unforeseen perils in the new struggle against militant Islamism. The many accounts that have portrayed the Nazis using the threat of nuclear warfare to triumph in World War II, for example, such as Robert Harris's *Fatherland* or Daniel Quinn's *After Dachau*, reinforce the need for vigilance against weapons of mass destruction falling into the hands of Islamic terrorists. Alternate histories might also be able to help us avoid major foreign policy blunders in the struggle against terrorism. Had the Bush administration only consulted Stephen Fry's novel, *Making History*, and reflected on its underlying premise that pre-emptively eliminating evil villains like Hitler can actually make history turn out worse rather than better, it might have thought twice about invading Iraq in order to pre-empt Saddam Hussein's ability to use weapons of mass destruction – a decision that threatens to have a boomerang effect and worsen the course of history rather than improve it. Alternate histories may also caution us against certain unexpected risks in the fight against terrorism. In light of the unforeseen difficulties emerging out of the invasion of Iraq, we might do well to recall Len Deighton's novel *SS-GB* and Kevin Brownlow's film *It Happened Here*, whose portrayal of the British people turning against each other after being defeated by the Germans provides us with a sober lesson about the dangers of domestic divisiveness. And inasmuch as alternate histories prompt us to imagine not only nightmares but also fantasies, we might take solace in the fact that, just as various writers have imagined a world without Hitler being superior to our own, we too can imagine a better Middle East without Osama bin Laden or any number of other threatening figures associated with al-Qaeda and its allies.

In short, by imagining history turning out differently, alternate histories can help us cope with the unpredictability of our contemporary world. Many people have a sense today that the course of history has been dramatically altered by the attacks of 9/11. In attempting to understand where we are headed, we can profit by consulting alternate histories of worlds that never were. By familiarizing ourselves with them, and with the mode of counterfactual thinking underlying them, we may be better equipped to fashion the world as we would like it to be.

Notes

INTRODUCTION

1 Robert Harris, *Fatherland* (New York, 1992), pp. 82–84.
2 See, for example, Laura Miller, "It's Philip Dick's World, We Only Live in It," *The New York Times Book Review*, November 24 (2002), p. 39.
3 The scholarly literature on alternate history is small but growing. Historians as well as literary scholars have contributed important works. Among the pioneering studies by historians are: Alexander Demandt, *History That Never Happened: A Treatise on the Question, What Would Have Happened If ...?* (Jefferson, NC, 1993, German original 1984) and Niall Ferguson, ed., *Virtual History: Alternatives and Counter-Factuals* (New York, 1997). Studies by literary scholars include Jörg Helbig, *Der parahistorische Roman: Ein literarhistorischer und gattungstypologischer Beitrag zur Allotopieforschung* (Frankfurt, 1987); Christoph Rodiek, *Erfundene Vergangenheit: Kontrafaktische Geschichtsdarstellung (Uchronie) in der Literatur* (Frankfurt, 1997); Karen Hellekson, *The Alternate History: Refiguring Historical Time* (Kent, OH, 2001); William Joseph Collins, *Paths Not Taken: The Development, Structure, and Aesthetics of Alternative History* (Ph.D. Dissertation, University of California, Davis, 1990); Edgar V. McKnight Jr., *Alternative History: The Development of a Literary Genre* (Ph.D. Dissertation, University of North Carolina, Chapel Hill, 1994). See also Johannes Bulhof, "What If? Modality and History," *History and Theory*, Nr. 2, 1999, pp. 145–68. And finally, Gavriel D. Rosenfeld, "Why Do We Ask 'What If?' Reflections on the Function of Alternate History," *History and Theory*, December, 2002, pp. 90–103.
4 Helbig discusses the origins of alternate history (or what he calls "parahistorical" novels) in both history and science fiction. Helbig, pp. 108–09. David Pringle notes that science fiction and alternate history came of age around the same time in the 1950s: David Pringle, *The Ultimate Guide to Science Fiction: An A-Z of Science Fiction Books* (London, 1990), pp. ix–x. Alternate history's similarity to science fiction lies in both genres' proclivity to speculate about alternatives to our real historical present, the former setting them in the past, the latter in the future. For a detailed discussion of the relationship between science fiction and alternate history, see Collins, chapter 1.
5 The term "allohistorical" comes from the Greek root, "allo," for "other" or "altered." The term "uchronia" plays off of the Greek word "utopia"

("u-topos" = "no place") to imply a time that never was ("u-chronos"). For a helpful introduction to the concept, see Gordon Chamberlain, "Afterword: Allohistory in Science Fiction," in Charles G. Waugh and Martin H. Greenberg, *Alternative Histories: Eleven Stories of the World as It Might Have Been* (New York, 1986), pp. 281–300. In this book I use the term "alternate history," which has become the term of choice among most scholars. Over the years, however, some scholars have used other terms, such as "alternative history," "allohistory," "uchronia," "counterfactual," and "parahistory." Hellekson, p. 3.

6 Helbig refers to "discursive" and "narrative" alternate histories. Helbig, pp. 108–09.

7 There are numerous types of narrative that are closely related to alternate histories. *Secret histories* describe alternate pasts that are never discovered because they do not end up changing the historical record. *Future histories* describe the history of the future from the perspective of the present. These accounts become known as *retroactive alternate histories* once the time period they depict is no longer in the future. (For example, a future history written in 1940 that depicts the Nazis winning World War II in 1945 becomes a retroactive alternate history after 1946.) *Parallel world stories* describe changes of the historical record on an earth different from our own. *Time-travel tales* change the course of history through direct human intervention in the past. All of these narratives exhibit their own unique traits in speculating about the past. While I have attempted to retain an awareness of the distinctions between these different counterfactual narratives, I have chosen to group future histories and secret histories under the larger umbrella term "alternate histories" for reasons of analytical convenience. I explain my rationale for doing so on pp. 410–11, note 2, and p. 202. For a general overview of the typological differences between these narratives, see Chamberlain in Waugh and Greenberg. See also Helbig, pp. 118–19 and Hellekson, p. 5.

8 Hellekson distinguishes between most literature, which is rooted in realism, and "fantastic literature," which transfigures or estranges one from reality. Hellekson, p. 19. See also Collins, pp. 7–8, chapter 1.

9 Demandt, *History That Never Happened*, pp. 70, 122; Chamberlain, in Waugh and Greenberg, p. 284; McKnight, p. 10.

10 Demandt, *History That Never Happened*, chapters 3 and 4; Bulhof, pp. 145–68; Ferguson, *Virtual History*, pp. 79–90; Helbig, pp. 46–52.

11 Demandt, *History That Never Happened*, pp. 1–8; Helbig, pp. 37, 53–55. Edward Hallett Carr was one of the more critical historians of counterfactual thinking in history. As he put it, "One can always play a parlour game with the might-have-beens of history." E. H. Carr, *What Is History?* (New York, 1961), p. 127 and chapter 4 more broadly.

12 Charles Renouvier's *Uchronie* (1876) explored the possible consequences of Christianity's failure to take root in the West, which would have prevented the fall of the Roman empire and the birth of the Middle Ages. Renouvier wrote the novel as a liberal critique of Catholicism during the rule of Napoleon III. Charles Renouvier, *Uchronie (l'utopie dans l'histoire): esquisse historique apo-cryphe du développement de la civilisation européenne tel qu'il n'a pas été, tel qu'il*

aurait pu être (Paris, 1876); Ferguson, *Virtual History*, pp. 8–9. Preceding *Uchronie* was Louis-Napoléon Geoffroy-Château's 1836 novel, *Napoléon et la conquête du monde 1812–1832, Histoire de la monarchie universelle* (Paris, 1983), which was a fantasy written by an adoptive son of Napoléon Bonaparte that describes Napoléon's creation of a universal monarchy that brings peace and tranquility to the earth. Rodiek, pp. 68–70.

13 Overtly fictional alternate histories began to form a trend in science fiction in the 1930s, appearing most frequently as time travel tales in such magazines as *Amazing Stories.* Chamberlain, in Waugh and Greenberg, pp. 285–86; Hellekson, p. 18. Among academic alternate histories, the most influential early work was J. C. Squire's *If It Had Happened Otherwise: Lapses into Imaginary History* (London, 1931).

14 Patton writes that "It was not until the 1960s that the genre [of alternate history] gained real momentum." Phil Patton, "Lee Defeats Grant," *American Heritage*, September 1999, p. 41. Helbig dates the prominence of alternate history to the late 1960s and early 1970s; Helbig, pp. 79–84.

15 See, for example, "Historians Warming to Games of 'What If,'" *New York Times*, January 7, 1998; Martin Arnold, "The 'What Ifs' That Fascinate," *New York Times*, December 21 (2000), p. E3. *American Heritage* devoted several articles to the subject in its September 1999 issue, including Patton, pp. 39–45 and Frederic Smoler, "Past Tense," *American Heritage*, September 1999, pp. 45–49. The German media has covered the trend as well. See Sven Felix Kellerhoff, "Was wäre, wenn … Ein neuer Trend in der Geschichtswissenschaft: Historiker spekulieren. Was wäre geschehen, wenn Ereignisse gar nicht oder anders stattgefunden hätten?" *Die Berliner Zeitung*, January 30, 2000.

16 Among the anthologies are: Harry Turtledove and Martin H. Greenberg, eds., *The Best Alternate History Stories of the 20th Century* (New York, 2001); Charles G. Waugh and Martin H. Greenberg, *Alternative Histories: Eleven Stories of the World as It Might Have Been* (New York, 1986); Gardner Dozois and Stanley Schmidt, eds., *Roads Not Taken: Tales of Alternate History* (New York, 1998); Martin Greenberg, ed., *The Way It Wasn't: Great Science Fiction Stories of Alternate History* (Secaucus, NJ, 1996); Nelson W. Polsby, *What If? Explorations in Social Science Fiction* (Lexington, MA, 1982). In German, see Erik Simon, ed., *Alexanders langes Leben, Stalins früher Tod und andere abwe-gige Geschichten: Erzählungen und Berichte aus Parallelwelten* (Munich, 1999). See the web site, *Uchronia* at www.uchronia.net for a comprehensive list of novels and short stories (and see note 18 below).

17 Besides the recent example of Philip Roth, Michael Chabon is due to publish a new novel, entitled *The Yiddish Policeman's Union*, that focuses on a scheme to repatriate Jewish refugees from Europe to Alaska in the 1940s.

18 By far and away the leading web site is *Uchronia*, whose originator, Robert Schmunk, has compiled a vast bibliography of allohistorical works on a wide range of historical themes (www.uchronia.net). One of the leading publishing houses known for alternate history novels is Del Rey Books,

which has published the well-known work of the prolific alternate history writer, Harry Turtledove, the author of *The Guns of the South*, among many others. A quick internet search using the term "alternate history" turns up a multitude of individual web sites of varying degrees of quality devoted to the topic.

19 See "Historians Warming to Games of 'What If,'" *New York Times*, January 7, 1998. This article refers to the publication of a special issue of the *Quarterly Journal of Military History*, which includes some thirty-six allohistorical essays by leading military historians. An expanded, book-length version of this issue appeared in the fall of 1999, edited by Robert Cowley, entitled: *What If? The World's Foremost Military Historians Imagine What Might Have Been*, New York, (1999). See also Cowley's follow-up volumes, *What If? 2: Eminent Historians Imagine What Might Have Been* (New York, 2001) and *What Ifs? of American History: Eminent Historians Imagine What Might Have Been* (New York, 2003); see also the widely reviewed book, edited by Niall Ferguson, *Virtual History: Alternatives and Counter-Factuals* (London, 1997) and the new study by Andrew Roberts, ed., *What Might Have Been: Imaginary History from Twelve Leading Historians* (London, 2004). See also the exchange between Richard Evans and other scholars in the March 2004 issue of *Historically Speaking*.

20 This is not to say, however, that alternate history cannot arrive at deterministic conclusions. Helbig, p. 97. Whether or not the world would have been better had Hitler never lived, for example, can be answered in two ways: Hitler's absence can easily be seen as improving world history, but it is just as possible to deterministically cite structural factors (nationalism, imperialism, etc.) that would have led to global conflict even without him. See chapter 6. In short, alternate history's opposition to determinism manifests itself in its opposition to viewing the outcomes of real history as *necessarily* the only ones that were possible.

21 See Lutz Niethammer, *Posthistoire: Has History Come to an End?* (London, 1994). Niethammer's book discusses the contention of such rightwing intellectuals as Arnold Gehlen, Ernst Jünger, Hendrik de Man, Bertrand de Jouvenel, and Alexander Kojeve that postwar Europe had arrived at a point of stasis due to the elite's inability to any longer guide the unwieldy masses.

22 Herbert Marcuse's *One Dimensional Man* (1964) foreshadowed leftwing disillusionment with the possibility of future change. After the abortive revolutions of 1968, many European leftwing radicals abandoned the idea of struggling for global causes and began to support more limited, localized agendas. The French intellectual and pioneer of postmodernism, Michel Foucault, is a good example of this pattern.

23 The classic formulation of this notion was Francis Fukuyama's article, "The End of History?", which first appeared in *The National Interest*, summer, 1989, pp. 3–18.

24 Richard Overy's book *Why the Allies Won* (New York, 1995) frankly admits this reality. Mark Mazower's *Dark Continent: Europe's Twentieth Century*

(New York, 1999) also questions the notion that liberalism's triumph was preordained.

25 E. H. Carr alludes to this phenomenon in noting that "in a group or nation that is riding in the trough, not on the crest, of historical events, theories that stress the role of chance or accident in history will be found to prevail." Carr, p. 132.

26 Studies of postmodernism make no mention of alternate history, though studies of alternate history make ample reference to postmodernism. See especially the works of Helbig, Rodiek, Hellekson, McKnight, and Collins, *passim*.

27 Rodiek, p. 11; Helbig, p. 27.

28 See, among others, Linda Hutcheon, *A Poetics of Postmodernism: History, Theory, Fiction* (New York, 1988); Charles Jencks, *The Language of Post-Modern Architecture* (New York, 1984); Ada Louise Huxtable, *The Unreal America: Architecture and Illusion* (New York, 1997). Generally, see David Harvey, *The Condition of Postmodernity* (Cambridge, MA, 1992).

29 Steven Connor, *Postmodernist Culture: An Introduction to Theories of the Contemporary* (Cambridge, MA, 1991); McKnight, pp. 4, 211.

30 For a broader discussion, see Keith Jenkins, *Rethinking History* (London, 1991).

31 Ferguson, *Virtual History*, pp. 74–76.

32 Ibid., p. 79.

33 Ibid., pp. 86–87. Deciding what is a plausible alternative to the past, according to Ferguson, needs to be based upon alternatives "that contemporaries actually considered."

34 Mark Slouka, *War of the Worlds: Cyberspace and the High-Tech Assault on Reality* (New York, 1995); Ruth La Ferla, "Perfect Model: Gorgeous, No Complaints, Made of Pixels," *New York Times*, May 6, 2001, section 9, pp. 1, 8. A good example of a cinematic expression of this confusion about reality is the recent film *Simone* (2002), starring Al Pacino.

35 In a related development, the film *28 Days Later* (2002) made headlines by actually giving viewers the option to select from multiple different endings according to their personal preference.

36 Joshua Klein, "DVDs featuring directors' cuts and alternative endings prove a movie buff's power is all ... in the cut," *Chicago Tribune*, February 1, 2004.

37 As Thomas M. Disch notes, "In 1971 the overlapping categories of SF, horror, and fantasy accounted for only 5 percent of U.S. box office receipts; in 1982 that figure was approaching 50 percent ... [Moreover], more than half of the ten top-grossing films of all time have been SF." Thomas M. Disch, *The Dreams Our Stuff is Made Of: How Science Fiction Conquered the World* (New York, 1998), p. 208. The origins of the recent popularity of science fiction and fantasy can be located in its embrace by the counter-culture of the late 1960s, which was seeking alternatives to the real world as defined by the conservative "establishment." Edward James, *Science Fiction in the Twentieth Century* (Oxford, 1994), p. 180.

38 While there are numerous problems in defining and delimiting the genres of science fiction and fantasy, it is clear that both "deal with imaginative alternatives to the real world." James, p. 3. James argues that the difference between science

fiction and "mainstream fiction" lies in their respective subject matter, the latter focusing on "human personalities or human relationships," the former focusing on "the potentialities and possibilities of the human species ... in the universe." James, p. 96. For a further definitional treatment, see Rosemary Jackson, *Fantasy: The Literature of Subversion* (London, 1998), chapter 2.

39 Neal Gabler, *Life, the Movie: How Entertainment Conquered Reality* (New York, 1999).

40 Gabler traces the rise of entertainment back to the "graphic revolution" of the mid-nineteenth century, when the advent of photography allowed images to replace printed text as a primary source of information and cognition. Gabler goes on to show how this process was further accelerated by the rise of movies and television in the twentieth century, both of which transformed American values by diminishing the status of analytical reasoning and replaced aspiration with gratification. Gabler relies heavily on the work of Daniel Boorstin and Neil Postman in his historical analysis. See Daniel Boorstin, *The Image: A Guide to Pseudo-Events in America* (New York, 1987) and Neil Postman, *Amusing Ourselves to Death: Public Discourse in the Age of Show Business* (New York, 1986).

41 Among innumerable examples that could be cited: the enduring success of *People Magazine* and its many imitators; the rise of entertainment "news" shows, like *Entertainment Tonight*; the interminable fascination with trials of celebrities and ordinary Americans, whether O. J. Simpson or wife-murderer Scott Peterson; and the entire genre of reality television, some of whose examples, such as *Jackass* and *Fear Factor*, depend on the eagerness of human beings to degrade themselves for the sake of publicity.

42 See Robert Darnton, "It Happened One Night," *New York Review of Books*, June 24, 2004, pp. 60–64. In this essay, Darnton also describes this scholarly trend as "incident analysis."

43 Alessandro Portelli confirms this in his interesting essay, "Uchronic Dreams: Working-Class Memory and Possible Worlds," which discusses how disappointments about the present led Italian workers after 1945 to misremember the real past. Published in *The Death of Luigi Trastulli and Other Stories: Form and Meaning in Oral History* (Albany, 1991) pp. 99–116.

44 In using the term "presentism," I loosely refer to the application of present-day ethical standards to judge the events of the past. For a discussion of the controversy over moral judgments in history see Peter Novick, *That Noble Dream: The 'Objectivity Question' and the American Historical Profession* (Cambridge, 1988).

45 Demandt writes that alternate history is based upon "private conjecture, which reveals more about the character of the speculator than about the probable consequences [of a different historical scenario]." Demandt, *History That Never Happened*, p. 5.

46 This is a common point made by many scholars. See Rodiek, p. 30.

47 No one has yet provided decisive empirical backing for this assertion, though it is frequently asserted nevertheless. See, for example, Chamberlain, in Waugh and Greenberg, p. 288.

48 Some of the general surveys of alternate history make mention of selected texts. But hardly any have concentrated on the theme in and of itself. One exception is a brief survey of some of the literature by Klaus Geus, "Hitlers vergeblicher Kampf – Ein Beitrag zu [sic] Thema Nationalsozialismus und Science Fiction," *Kopfgeburten*, March, 1996, pp. 30–35. Relatedly, see chapter 5 of Paul A. Carter's book, *The Creation of Tomorrow: Fifty Years of Magazine Science Fiction* (New York, 1977), entitled "The Phantom Dictator, Science Fiction Discovers Hitler." On the margins is Harald Husemann, "When William Came; If Adolf Had Come. English Speculative Novels on the German Conquest of Britain," *Anglistik & Englischunterricht*, Vols. 29–30, 1986, pp. 57–83.

49 Ernestine Schlant, *The Language of Silence: West German Literature and the Holocaust* (New York, 1999); Anton Kaes, *From Hitler to Heimat: The Return of History as Film* (Cambridge, MA, 1989); Eric L. Santner, *Stranded Objects: Mourning, Memory and Film in Postwar Germany* (Ithaca, 1990); Andreas Huyssen, "Anselm Kiefer: The Terror of History, the Temptation of Myth," *October*, spring, 1989, pp. 22–45; Barbie Zelizer, *Remembering to Forget: The Holocaust Through the Camera Eye* (Chicago, 1998); Dagmar Barnouw, *Germany 1945: Views of War and Violence* (Bloomington, IN, 1996); Gavriel D. Rosenfeld, *Munich and Memory: Architecture, Monuments, and the Legacy of the Third Reich* (Berkeley, 2000); Brian Ladd, *The Ghosts of Berlin: Confronting German History in the Urban Landscape* (Chicago, 1997); James E. Young, *The Texture of Memory: Holocaust Memorials and Meaning* (New Haven, 1993); Rudy Koshar, *Germany's Transient Pasts: Preservation and National Memory in the Twentieth Century* (Chapel Hill, 1998).

50 Here I should stress that in invoking the term "memory" I recognize the ongoing scholarly debate about the best methods of conceptualizing a term that has often been utilized in vague and metaphorical fashion. While preferring to avoid an extended theoretical discussion of the subject, I would like to emphasize that I use the term "memory" generally in a cultural sense, following Jan Assmann's notion of "cultural memory," as distinct from "communicative memory." For definitions of these terms, see p. 17 of the current study. Jan Assmann, "Kollektives Gedächtnis und kulturelle Identität," in Jan Assmann and Tonio Holscher, eds., *Kultur und Gedächtnis* (Frankfurt am Main, 1988).

51 It is notable that even the historians who have attempted to legitimize alternate history as a field of historical analysis have dismissed its subjective dimensions rather than employ them as a vehicle for examining memory. Thus Niall Ferguson dismisses the essays in J. C. Squire's *If It Had Happened Otherwise* as largely "products of their authors' contemporary political or religious preoccupations." Ferguson, *Virtual History*, p. 11.

52 This is a very conservative estimate. Beyond the 116 accounts discussed in detail in this book, dozens of other works have appeared as well. They are easily located on www.uchronia.net (see also note 18 above). I have chosen not to discuss any of these accounts here, either because they deal with aspects of the

Nazi era not discussed in this study or because they are of marginal quality. The number increases still further when one includes alternate histories about World War II.

53 Thus the premise of Hitler surviving into the postwar era is a clear nightmare scenario, yet its corollary that Hitler is discovered, captured, and brought to justice, expresses an obvious fantasy. Similarly, while the completion of the Holocaust is a clear nightmare scenario, the notion that it could be undone expresses a common fantasy.

54 A note of caution for readers: I regret that in discussing the texts, I have had little choice but to spoil many of their surprise endings. For this I apologize!

55 As various scholars have noted, examining the representation of Nazism is not the same as studying the memory of it. Only by combining an analysis of representation with reception does a clear sense of a narrative's broader societal resonance emerge. Alon Confino has been one of the leading advocates of including the societal reception of cultural products in analyzing their significance as indices of memory. See Alon Confino, "Collective Memory and Cultural History: Problems of Method," *American Historical Review*, December, 1997, pp. 1386–1403. To this end, I have drawn upon the notion (taken from reception theory) that the way in which a given work confirms or violates a reader's "horizon of expectations" provides a useful gauge for examining, among other things, their knowledge of and views towards history. See Hans Robert Jauss's influential essay, "Literary History as a Challenge to Literary Theory," *New Literary History*, Vol. 2, Nr. 1, 1970–71, especially pp. 13–15.

56 In utilizing the term "popular culture," I follow the lead of sociologist Herbert Gans and view it as an ideal-typical concept whose differences from "high culture" (itself a construct) are numerous but hardly absolute. As Gans has pointed out, the class determinants of cultural taste have waned in recent years with the rise of incomes, education, and the phenomenon of "omnivorous" cultural consumption, in which people seek out products of culture from all realms, whether high, middle, or low. Herbert J. Gans, *Popular Culture and High Culture: An Analysis and Evaluation of Taste* (New York, 1999), pp. 5–13.

57 On the representation of Nazism in popular literature, see Alvin H. Rosenfeld, *Imagining Hitler* (Bloomington, IN, 1985). On comic books, see James Young's essay on Art Spiegelman in his recent book *At Memory's Edge: Afterimages of the Holocaust in Contemporary Art and Architecture* (New Haven, 2000). On television see Wulf Kansteiner, *Television and the Historicization of National Socialism in the Federal Republic of Germany: The Programs of the Zweite Deutsche Fernsehen Between 1963 and 1993* (Ph.D. Dissertation, University of California, Los Angeles, 1997). Georg Seeßlen's *Tanz den Adolf Hitler: Faschismus in der populären Kultur* (Berlin, 1994) deals less with the representation of Nazism than the persistence of what he sees to be fascist tendencies in postwar German popular culture. Generally speaking, scholars have devoted more effort to studying popular cultural representations of the Holocaust than the Nazi period in its overall sweep. See, for example, Alan Mintz, *Popular Culture and the Shaping of Holocaust Memory in America*

(Seattle, 2001) and Jeffrey Shandler, *While America Watches: Televising the Holocaust* (New York, 1999).

58 This is not to say that the producers of popular culture do not themselves have artistic ambitions, or that the producers of high culture are indifferent to economic considerations. In recent years, the priorities of both fields have converged. Gans, pp. 31–38.

59 The fact, for example, that the producers of the 2001 film *Pearl Harbor* reportedly tried "not to portray [the] Japanese in a bad light" in order to secure a place for the film in the lucrative Japanese market reveals the role of commercial interests in determining a film's portrayal of a key historical event: Paul Greenberg, "War Movie's 'Sensitivity' Helps Make It a Farce," *Greenwich Time*, June 5, 2001, p. A10. For a parody using the Third Reich as backdrop, see Bruce McCall, "'Blitzkrieg!,' The Movie," *New Yorker*, July 2, 2001, p. 35. On the subject of distortion, Michael C. C. Adams, in his book *The Best War Ever: America and World War II* (Baltimore, 1994), argues that Hollywood's depiction of World War II has glamorized and romanticized an era in American history that was much more fraught with tensions than is presently realized in American consciousness. Adams, chapter 1.

60 This is not to say that the work of professional historians does not influence the producers of popularized accounts. For example, the recent CBS mini-series on Hitler was based upon the scholarly work of British historian Ian Kershaw. This kind of explicit acknowledgment, however, is rare.

61 Most studies have understandably focused upon the memory of the Nazi past in Germany, the literature about which is too vast to list here. Other nations have naturally been studied as well. For France, see Henry Rousso, *The Vichy Syndrome: History and Memory in France since 1944* (Cambridge, MA, 1991) and Sarah Farmer, *Martyred Village: Commemorating the 1944 Massacre at Oradour-sur-Glane* (Berkeley, 1999). For Israel see Tom Segev, *The Seventh Million: The Israelis and the Holocaust* (New York, 1993). Some works have aspired to a more comparative approach. They include Caroline Alice Wiedmer, *The Claims of Memory: Representations of the Holocaust in Contemporary Germany and France* (Ithaca, 1999) and Ian Buruma, *The Wages of Guilt: Memories of War in Germany and Japan* (New York, 1994). The comparative approach has recently become embraced in memory studies, but these include works that cover far more topics than simply the Nazi era. See, for example, Martha Minow's book *Between Vengeance and Forgiveness: Facing History after Genocide and Mass Violence* (Boston, 1999) and Elazar Barkan's *The Guilt of Nations: Restitution and Negotiating Historical Injustices* (New York, 2000).

62 For purposes of analytical convenience, I have included within the category of German works several that were written by Austrians (two out of sixteen total works were Austrian in origin). Scattered accounts have appeared in France, Italy, Spain, the Netherlands, and Russia. See the *Uchronia* web site (www.uchronia.net), which permits searching for texts by national origin.

63 See Appendix.

64 To the best of my knowledge, there are next to no studies that have systematically examined cultural representations (high or low) of the Third Reich in
postwar British or American culture in order to draw broader conclusions
about these two nations' memories of the Nazi era.

65 In making this claim, I recognize the difficulty of using such a generalized term
as "Western memory," which, like such terms as Western society, consciousness, and culture, are problematic on account of their abstract, sweeping
character. Nonetheless, I have chosen to use the terms "Western" and "the
West" in this study in order to link together trends that have appeared in
various European countries as well as the United States, hoping that I will not
be seen as implying wholesale representativeness of these trends in all areas of
the Western world.

66 The term has most frequently appeared in studies of German memory and has
also been invoked to refer to national identity. Among the few that have made
efforts to discuss the term conceptually are Aleida Assmann and Ute Frevert,
*Geschichtsvergessenheit, Geschichtsversessenheit. Vom Umgang mit deutschen
Vergangenheiten nach 1945* (Stuttgart, 1999), pp. 59–63; Jeffrey K. Olick,
"What Does It Mean to Normalize the Past?", *Social Science History*, winter,
1998, pp. 547–71; Stefan Berger, *The Search for Normalcy: National Identity and
Historical Consciousness in Germany since 1800* (Providence, 1997); Siobhan
Kattago, *Ambiguous Memory: The Nazi Past and German National Identity*
(Westport, CT, 2001).

67 To avoid any misunderstanding, I use the terms "moralism" and "moralistic"
in this study in a purely descriptive sense, as terms denoting a genuine concern
with morality, rather than in a pejorative sense, as terms implying a narrow-
minded or somehow unfair variety of moral judgment.

68 The distinction between official and counter-memory is quite common in the
current literature on memory. The notion of "official" memory, understood as
one that predominates in a given society, is implied in Maurice Halbwachs's
undifferentiated notion of "collective memory" itself and finds elaboration in
Pierre Nora's discussion of the nation-state's role in crafting memory to suit
the needs of national identity: Maurice Halbwachs, *The Collective Memory*
(New York, 1980); Pierre Nora, "Between Memory and History: *Les lieux de
mémoire*," *Representations*, Vol. 26, spring, 1989, pp. 7–25; and Pierre Nora,
ed., *Realms of Memory: Rethinking the French Past*, Vols. I–III (New York,
1996–1998). The notion of counter-memory as an oppositional form of
remembrance can be traced back to Michel Foucault in *Language, Counter-
memory, Practice: Selected Essays and Interviews* (Ithaca, 1977).

69 Assmann, pp. 10–13. Assmann points out how the communicative memory of
events is finite in duration (lasting 80–100 years) and eventually gives way to the
cultural memory of them as the eyewitnesses to the past disappear from society.

70 This process would correspond to Assmann's idea that communicative memory gradually fades over time.

71 Saul Friedlander, ed., *Reflections of Nazism: An Essay on Kitsch and Death*
(New York, 1982), pp. 11–12.

72 Other films include Luchino Visconti's *The Damned* (1969) and Hans-Jürgen Syberberg's *Hitler, a Film from Germany* (1977). Other novels include William Styron's *Sophie's Choice*. On the work of Leon Krier, see Gavriel Rosenfeld, "The Architects' Debate: Architectural Discourse and the Memory of Nazism in the Federal Republic of Germany, 1977–1997," in Geulie Ne'eman Arad, ed., *Passing into History: Nazism and the Holocaust Beyond Memory*, special issue of *History and Memory*, Nr. 1–2, fall, 1997, pp. 189–225. On Anselm Kiefer, see Huyssen.

73 See Friedlander; Rosenfeld; Susan Sontag, "Fascinating Fascism," in *Under the Sign of Saturn* (New York, 1980), pp. 73–105, originally published in the *New York Review of Books* on February 6, 1975.

74 Comedic depictions of the Nazi era, of course, extend as far back as the war years, as shown by Charlie Chaplin's *The Great Dictator* (1940), but they became increasingly common after the 1960s, with such works as Mel Brooks's film *The Producers* and the television series *Hogan's Heroes*. Besides films, which also include Radu Mihaileanu's *Train of Life* (1999), the issue of Holocaust jokes by Jewish comics has emerged and raised the question of the appropriateness of applying humor to atrocity. See, for example, Cynthia Dettelbach, "Does Humor Have Role in Holocaust?" *Cleveland Jewish News*, March 26, 1999, p. 4; Michael Elkin, "Humor and the Holocaust ... Perfect Together?" *Jewish Exponent*, December 20, 2001, p. 45.

75 The strategy of relativization dates back to the early history of the Federal Republic (FRG), although it was not so openly pursued as it was to be in the 1980s. Both Theodor Adorno and Margarete Mitscherlich identified the embrace of this strategy in their scholarship of the late 1950s and 1960s: Theodor W. Adorno, "What does Coming to Terms with the Past Mean?" in Geoffrey H. Hartmann, ed., *Bitburg in Moral and Political Perspective* (Bloomington, IN, 1986), pp. 114–30; Alexander and Margarete Mitscherlich, *Die Unfähigkeit zu trauern* (Munich, 1977).

76 Wolfgang Gessenharter, *Kippt die Republik? Die neue Rechte und ihre Unterstützung durch Politik und Medien* (Munich, 1994); Jacob Heilbrunn, "Germany's New Right," *Foreign Affairs*, November–December, 1996, pp. 81–98. To be sure, not all the calls for a normal national identity in the 1990s have reflected a desire to relativize the Nazi past. Germans on the center and left of the political spectrum have claimed that Germany's normality now lies precisely in its admirable willingness to face its Nazi past. Chancellor Gerhard Schroeder recently described the creation of a central Holocaust memorial in Berlin as evidence that the Germans today are "ein normales Volk." Karl Wilds, "Identity Creation and the Culture of Contrition: Recasting 'Normality' in the Berlin Republic," *German Politics*, April, 2000, pp. 94–98.

77 As Salomon Korn has put it, "It is just as impossible to talk normalcy into existence as it is to decree spontaneity." Salomon Korn, *Geteilte Erinnerung* (Berlin, 1999).

78 Among the more influential works were: C. J. Friedrich, *Totalitarianism* (New York, 1954); Hannah Arendt, *The Origins of Totalitarianism* (San Diego, 1979); and Ernst Nolte, *Three Faces of Fascism* (New York, 1966).

79 Martin Broszat, "Plädoyer für eine Historisierung des Nationalsozialismus," in Hermann Graml and Klaus Dietmar Henke, eds., *Nach Hitler: Der schwierige Umgang mit unserer Geschichte: Beiträge von Martin Broszat* (Munich, 1987).

80 The literature on this subject is extensive. See, for example, Uwe Backes, Eckhard Jesse, and Rainer Zitelmann, eds., *Die Schatten der Vergangenheit: Impulse zur Historisierung des Nationalsozialismus* (Berlin, 1990); and Zygmunt Baumann, *Modernity and the Holocaust* (Ithaca, New York, 1989). For a general discussion, see the introductory essay in Michael Burleigh and Wolfgang Wippermann, *The Racial State: Nazi Germany, 1933–1945* (Cambridge, 1991).

PART ONE: THE NAZIS WIN WORLD WAR II

COMPARATIVE OVERVIEW

1 Eric Norden, *The Ultimate Solution* (New York, 1973), pp. 71–73.

2 Some 50 percent of all the tales surveyed in this study (53 out of 106 *postwar* narratives) are devoted to the theme. The second most commonly explored theme, Hitler's survival, comprises only 27 percent (29 of 106) of all postwar narratives. See Appendix.

3 See Robert Herzstein, *When Nazi Dreams Come True: The Horrifying Story of the Nazi Blueprint for Europe* (London, 1982), which discusses the Nazi notion of the "New Order" in their plans for a "unified Europe." Austrian historian Dirk Rupnow has examined the Nazis' own plans to write the history of their anticipated victory. Dirk Rupnow, *Vernichten und Erinnern: Spuren national-sozialistischer Gedächtnispolitik* (Ph.D. Dissertation, Klagenfurt, 2002).

4 Mark Walker writes that "many people ... have a macabre fascination with the dream or nightmare of National Socialist nuclear weapons winning World War II for Germany." Mark Walker, *Nazi Science: Myth, Truth, and the German Atomic Bomb* (New York, 1995), p. 262. Paul Lawrence Rose's book, *Heisenberg and the Nazi Atomic Bomb Project: A Study in German Culture* (Berkeley, 1998), emphasizes Heisenberg's conviction that a Nazi victory would have been in Europe's best interests. See especially, pp. 282–91. See also Robert C. Fried, "What If Hitler Got the Bomb? (1944)," in Nelson W. Polsby, ed., *What If? Explorations in Social Science Fiction* (Lexington, MA, 1982), pp. 81–93.

5 Bevin Alexander, *How Hitler Could Have Won World War II: The Ten Fatal Errors that Led to Nazi Defeat* (New York, 2000); Peter Tsouras, *Third Reich Victorious: Alternate Decisions of World War II* (London, 2002); Richard Overy, *Why the Allies Won* (New York, 1995). A recent book by Jane and Burt Boyar, *Hitler Stopped by Franco*, opens with a seven-page allohistorical description of a horrific, Nazi-ruled world in order to further enhance the significance of Spanish dictator, Generalissimo Francisco Franco's real histor-ical decision to remain neutral in World War II, which they argue was decisive in preventing Hitler from emerging triumphant. Jane and Burt Boyar, *Hitler Stopped by Franco* (Los Angeles, 2001), pp. 1–7.

6 See, for example, Richard C. Lukas, *The Forgotten Holocaust: The Poles under German Occupation, 1939–1944* (Lexington, KY, 1986). Götz Aly writes that if "Nazi Germany had lasted for twenty-four instead of twelve years, the extermination program would have been considerably expanded ... [and led] to the reduction of the Slavic peoples by some thirty million people." Götz Aly, "Das Unbewältigte Verbrechen: Die Ausrottung der europäischen Juden," *Der Spiegel*, Nr. 36, 1999.

7 The game *Mortyr* places the player in the role of the son of a Nazi officer who has to go back in time to kill the inventor of a time machine that enables the Nazis to win World War II. See http://firingsquad.gamers.com/games/mortyr.

8 In Mel Brooks's smash hit, *The Producers*, Max Bialystok sings to Leo Bloom about the necessity of making sure the "Nazis win" World War II in their planned musical, *Springtime for Hitler*.

9 See discussion threads on the subject of "what if?" on the web site www.thirdreichforum.com. More broadly, see www.thirdreich.net.

10 A British review of Mel Gibson's 2000 film *The Patriot* declared that "If the Nazis had won the war in Europe, and their propaganda ministry had decided to make a film about the American revolution, *The Patriot* is the sort of movie you could expect to see." Jonathan Foreman, "How Mel Gibson Helped to Turn Us into Nazis," *Guardian*, July 10, 2000, p. 10. At the United Nations World Conference against Racism held in Durban, South Africa in 2001, Israeli policies towards the Palestinians were singled out for special condemnation and pamphlets were distributed by unknown persons featuring a photo of Hitler and the sensationalistic headline "What if Hitler had won? There would be no Israel, and no Palestinian bloodshed." Michael J. Jordan, "Activists seek to place blame for U.N. forum," *Jewish News of Greater Phoenix*, September 7, 2001/Elul 19, 5761, Vol. 53, Nr. 48.

11 The premise of a Nazi victory is usually mentioned in the same breath as the premise of a Confederate victory in the American Civil War. A brief glance at the *Uchronia* web site (www.uchronia.net) reveals far more allohistorical works devoted to the subject of Nazism than the Civil War.

CHAPTER 1: GREAT BRITAIN DEFEATED: BETWEEN
RESISTANCE AND COLLABORATION

1 Len Deighton, *SS-GB: Nazi-occupied Britain 1941* (New York, 1978), p. 14.

2 Some might object to classifying such accounts as genuine alternate histories, since they were written *before* the historical events being depicted had either begun or had concluded. It is true that the authors who wrote tales of a hypothetical Nazi wartime victory prior to the outbreak of the war, and those who were writing such accounts while its outcome was still uncertain, were, strictly speaking, crafting alternate visions of the present or future rather than the past. As Robert Schmunk has argued, an account written in 1940 of Europe as it might have been under Nazi rule in 1944 represents a vision of the future

and should be classified as a "future history." (Schmunk's introductory essay, "What is Alternate History?" on his web site, *Uchronia* [www.uchronia.net], explains the misguided description of such accounts as alternate histories as a product of the fact that the passing of time has since relegated the future possibilities depicted within them to our past.) Further still, it is important to recognize that such accounts (which Schmunk also describes as "retroactive alternate histories") were produced under vastly different conditions from those that appeared after 1945. Those writing in the climate of security produced by the defeat of Nazism could not possibly have held the same fears as those writing in the climate of uncertainty prior to that point. Still, it is worth including such "future histories" within the broader category of alternate histories for several reasons. First, the images of Nazism contained within them by no means disappeared after 1945, but continued to appear in subsequent postwar allohistorical works. In this sense, prewar and wartime "future histories" shaped the evolution of postwar alternate histories, making it imperative to study the former in order to fully understand the latter. Secondly, and more significantly, given the influence of wartime works upon those that appeared after 1945, it is clear that the fears of Nazism that emerged before, and increased during, the war directly shaped the postwar *memory* of Nazism in its own right.

3 Katharine Burdekin (Murray Constantine), *Swastika Night* (London, 1937). *Swastika Night* was republished in 1985 with a new introduction by the feminist critic Daphne Patai.

4 The forms of knowledge include "all history, all psychology, all philosophy, [and] all art except music." Burdekin, p. 79.

5 Ibid., p. 5.

6 British leftists like Gollancz strongly believed in the notion of the "good German" during and after World War II. This belief led Gollancz after 1945 to oppose supporters of a hard peace on the Germans, such as Robert Vansittart.

7 In *Swastika Night*, women (and Christians) rank above Jews in the hierarchy of Hitler's victims. Indeed, Jews figured only marginally in the novel's narrative, being briefly described (with eerie prescience) as having all been "killed ... off" during the Twenty Years War. Burdekin, p. 72.

8 Douglas Brown and Christopher Serpell, *Loss of Eden: A Cautionary Tale* (London, 1940). The novel was republished in 1941 under the title, *If Hitler Comes*. Brown was a correspondent for the *Daily Telegraph*.

9 The main character of *Loss of Eden*, Charles Fenton, sullenly declares that it was the "Quislings ... who had been our downfall." Brown and Serpell, *Loss of Eden*, p. 182.

10 H. V. Morton, *I, James Blunt* (Toronto, 1942). Henry Canova Vollam Morton (1892–1979) was a well-known British travel writer who usually wrote non-fiction works. *I, James Blunt* was his only work of fiction.

11 Ibid., p. 61.

12 Ibid., p. 10.

13 Ibid., pp. 10, 5.

14 Blunt's arrest is only implied. See the novel's conclusion, ibid., p. 83.

15 Vita Sackville-West, *Grand Canyon* (Garden City, NY, 1942).

16 Morton, p. 5. This can be seen as a direct response to the view, common among many conservative supporters of appeasement in the 1930s, that the British would fare relatively well under Nazi rule.

17 Sackville-West, pp. 79–80. Although she had pacifist tendencies, Sackville-West was herself a strong opponent of appeasement. Phyllis Lassner, *British Women Writers of World War II: Battlegrounds of their Own* (Houndmills, 1998), p. 111.

18 Brown and Serpell, *Loss of Eden*, p. 9.

19 Roger Manvell, *Films and the Second World War* (New York, 1974), p. 161.

20 Anthony Armstrong and Bruce Graeme, *When the Bells Rang* (London, 1943); Martin Hawkin, *When Adolf Came* (London, 1943). Similar plots were featured in films of the period. Two of the earliest were *Miss Grant Goes to the Door* (released August 1940) and *Went the Day Well?* (released November 1942). Since both films stopped short of depicting the Nazis actually defeating the British following their invasion of the island nation (in both, the British repel the Germans), the films cannot be regarded as full-fledged alternate histories. For a detailed discussion, see Anthony Aldgate and Jeffrey Richards, *Britain Can Take It: The British Cinema in the Second World War* (Oxford, 1986), pp. 115–37.

21 J. S., "If We Made Peace With Hitler," *The Times*, August 17, 1940, p. 7.

22 "If England Fell," *Times Literary Supplement*, August 10, 1940, p. 385.

23 Quoted in query by L. J. Hurst, http://ds.dial.pipex.com/l.j.hurst/ifhitler.htm. A positive American review noted that the novel's "message ... is as inescapable here as in England." K. W., "Hitler in Britain," *New York Times Book Review*, June 21, 1942, p. 15.

24 Hawkin's novel, *When Adolf Came*, was praised in the *Times Literary Supplement* (*TLS*) in the following terms: "This portrayal of life as it might have been in England ... is one that can be read with something approaching relish while Allied aeroplanes stream out over the Continent, but within its fictional coating there is a pill calculated to preserve even the most optimistic reader from complacency." Review of *When Adolf Came* in *Times Literary Supplement*, September 25, 1943, p. 467.

25 The *TLS* reviewer wrote that while Sackville-West "has her moments ... she has not integrated the diverse elements of her fancy into an imaginative whole." "Cautionary Tale," *Times Literary Supplement*, November 7, 1942, p. 545. American reviewers were more critical of the novel, finding it preachy and condescending. See the review of *Grand Canyon* in *The Nation*, January 2, 1943, p. 31.

26 By way of comparison, seven accounts appeared in the eight-year period 1937–45, whereas five accounts appeared in the sixteen-year period 1945–61. See Appendix.

27 This declining interest was exemplified by the decreased production of films about World War II in Britain in the early postwar years. Manvell, p. 232.

28 The Beveridge Plan, first broached in 1942, provided the basis of the postwar system of comprehensive, cradle-to-grave social insurance, spanning disability, sickness, unemployment, and old age. Peter Clarke, *Hope and Glory: England, 1900–1990* (London, 1996), pp. 213–17. By 1950, Britons felt bold enough to declare that "poverty has been abolished." Clarke, *Hope and Glory*, p. 303.

29 John Darwin points out the relative ease with which British de-colonization proceeded. John Darwin, *The End of the British Empire: The Historical Debate* (London, 1991), p. 2. Britain left India (and Pakistan) in 1947, Jordan in 1947, and Palestine in 1948.

30 Winston Churchill immortalized this phrase in his famous speech to Parliament in June 1940. In it, he declared: "I expect the Battle of Britain is about to begin. Upon this battle depends the survival of Christian civilization ... Hitler knows that he will have to break us in this island or lose the war. If we can stand up to him, all Europe may be free and the life of the world may move forward into broad, sunlit uplands. But if we fail, then the whole world, including the United States ... will sink into the abyss of a new Dark Age ... Let us therefore brace ourselves to our duties and so bear ourselves that, if the British Empire and its Commonwealth last for a thousand years, men will say, 'This was their finest hour.'" Quoted in Winston Churchill, *Their Finest Hour: The Second World War* (Boston, 1949), pp. 225–26.

31 Andrew Roberts, "We May Have Won, But the War Goes On," *Sunday Telegraph*, March 5, 2000, p. 31.

32 Noël Coward, *Peace in Our Time* (New York, 1948). The play was first performed in Britain on July 22, 1947. Graham Payn and Sheridan Morley, eds., *The Noël Coward Diaries* (Boston, 1982), p. 87.

33 Coward, p. 122.

34 Ibid., pp. 46–47.

35 Ibid., pp. 76–77.

36 Ibid., pp. 149–53.

37 Robert F. Kiernan notes, "Coward's intention [in writing *Peace in Our Time*] was to stir his audience to patriotic fervor." Robert F. Kiernan, *Noël Coward* (New York, 1986), p. 114. As far as the play's origins are concerned, Coward first spoke about the idea for the play in his diary in November 1946, but he claimed in the foreword to *Peace in Our Time* that "the idea of it had lain in my mind ... since 1945, when I visited France soon after the liberation." Payn and Morley, p. 66; Coward, p. 13.

38 Manvell, pp. 107–09. Kiernan adds that *Peace in Our Time* "flatter[s] the national character [of the British]." Kiernan, p. 114.

39 Coward, p. 75.

40 Coward, p. 108.

41 Sarban (a.k.a. John W. Wall), *The Sound of His Horn* (New York, 1960).

42 Ibid., p. 48.

43 Ibid., p. 51.

44 Wall (1910–89) was stationed at a variety of locations in the Middle East and served as the British ambassador to Paraguay in the 1960s. Peter Nicholls, "Sarban," in E. F. Bleiler, ed., *Supernatural Fiction Writers: Fantasy and Horror. Vol. II* (New York, 1985), pp. 667–73. The pseudonym "Sarban" comes from a Persian term for the itinerant storytellers who traveled with caravans.

45 This was clearly illustrated by the sadistic character of Hackelnberg, whom Querdilion describes, upon first glimpsing him, as someone who "belonged to an age when violence and cruelty were more personal ... the time of the aurochs ... the wild bulls of that ancient German forest which the City had never subdued." Sarban, pp. 74–75.

46 Sarban, p. 101. Kit has been deported from Britain to Germany because of her membership of a patriotic British study group.

47 An indication of this was the increase in opposition among Britons to stationing nuclear weapons on German soil. *New York Times,* January 7, 1960, p. 3 and January 14, 1960, p. 4.

48 Comer Clarke, *England under Hitler* (New York, 1961). In 1962, the book was published in Great Britain as *If the Nazis Had Come* (London, 1962).

49 For *England under Hitler,* Clarke interviewed, among others, the head of the German navy, Karl Doenitz, Walter zu Christian (the compiler of the Black List), SS man Otto Begus (entrusted with kidnapping the royal family), and Franz Alfred Six (the designated chief of the Sicherheitsdienst or SD for England).

50 Clarke, *England under Hitler,* pp. 47, 49.

51 Ibid., pp. 48–50, 61–62.

52 Ibid., p. 94.

53 Ibid., p. 143.

54 Comer Clarke, *Eichmann: The Man and His Crimes* (New York, 1960). (See also Comer Clarke, *The Savage Truth* [London, 1960].) The dedication to Clarke's book on Eichmann reads as follows: "Dedicated to the millions of people of all races and religions who suffered death and the horrors of hell during the black years of the Nazi rule of Germany. And particularly dedicated, as a Gentile, to the Jewish people who bore the terrible worst of the crimes of the human apostles of Satan."

55 Ibid., p. 9.

56 Ibid., p. 143.

57 The essay was simultaneously published in the United States in the *Saturday Evening Post* in the spring of 1960. All quotations are taken from the American version. C. S. Forester, "If Hitler Had Invaded England," *Saturday Evening Post,* April 16, 23, and 30, 1960. The story is reprinted in Forester's posthumously published collection of stories, *Gold from Crete* (Boston, 1970), pp. 183–263. Forester's novels, which include *The African Queen* (1935) and ten titles featuring his best-known character, Horatio Hornblower, have sold over 8 million copies worldwide. Sanford Sternlicht, *C. S. Forester* (Boston, 1981), p. 159.

58 Other books around the same time further illustrated the enduring British interest in the Nazis' plans to invade Britain. See Peter Fleming, *Operation Sea*

Lion (New York, 1957) and Walter Ansel's *Hitler Confronts England* (Durham, NC, 1960).

59 This quotation comes from the April 30 issue, p. 80.

60 Sternlicht, p. 34.

61 Forester, "If Hitler Had Invaded England," April 30, p. 74.

62 C. S. Forester, *The Nightmare* (Boston, 1954), p. viii.

63 Anonymous, *The Occupation* (London, 1960).

64 Thomas's authorship is uncertain but likely. On the *Alibris* internet site, a copy of *The Occupation* was listed for sale with Thomas as the author. Upon inquiring further, I learned from the dealer selling the title that he had written to Thomas about his possible authorship and received the elusive reply from him, "I simply don't remember the answer to your question." While not an admission, this response was hardly a denial either, which leaves his authorship likely. E-mail message from Jodi at *Alibris*, Customer Service Department, May 23, 2002. For the record, Thomas did not reply to any of my direct inquiries.

65 Anonymous, *The Occupation*, pp. 122–32.

66 The communists are portrayed very critically. Their leader, Baratov (alias W. G. Grace), under the order of Stalin engineers the purge of non-communist leaders from the resistance by betraying them to the Gestapo, an act which leads to the death of many of them. Anonymous, *The Occupation*, pp. 211–12. This subtext to the novel reflected Thomas's own anticommunist tendencies, which were visible in his description of the self-destructive factionalism that plagued the Republican side during the Spanish Civil War in his well-known book, *The Spanish Civil War* (New York, 2001).

67 In one outlandish episode, British children eat the stewed corpse of a murdered German soldier in order to hide it from the Gestapo. Anonymous, *The Occupation*, pp. 24, 204–05.

68 Review of *Peace in Our Time*, *Daily Telegraph*, July 21, 1947, no page number. I am grateful to John Knowles for forwarding me an excerpt of this review. Coward himself noted that "The press reviews were mixed. Some critics ... were enthusiastic. Others ... didn't care for it at all. However, the play ran for over five months." Coward, p. 15. *The Times* found the play somewhat stale. Review of *Peace in Our Time*, *The Times*, July 23, 1947, p. 7.

69 Review of *The Sound of His Horn* in the *Yorkshire Evening Post*, June 18, 1952. See also the positive reviews by Richard Church in *John O' London's Weekly*, June 13, 1952 and in the *Daily Express*, May 29, 1952. I am grateful to Ray Russell of Tantalus Books for forwarding me excerpts of these reviews.

70 Kingsley Amis, *New Maps of Hell: A Survey of Science Fiction* (New York, 1960), p. 102. In the United States, Richard Plant described the book as "a stunning tour de force, a horror-thriller with depth," in the *New York Times*. "Nazis Rule the Nightmare," *New York Times*, April 3, 1960, p. 5. See also the positive review in the science fiction journal, *Analog*, August, 1960, pp. 168–69.

71 These comments appeared in a 1973 review of Forester's short story collection, *Gold from Crete,* in which his speculative essay was reproduced. "Paperback Shortlist," *The Sunday Times,* September 9, 1973, p. 40.

72 The *TLS* credited the author with "start[ing] ... off with a good idea," while concluding that its "melodramatic" character ultimately rendered the overall work somewhat "disappointing." "Heart and Head," *Times Literary Supplement,* November 25, 1960, p. 753.

73 Clarke, *Hope and Glory,* p. 319. In the late 1950s and early 1960s, Britain departed from Cyprus, Sudan, Ghana (then the "Gold Coast"), Nigeria, Sierra Leone, Gambia, Uganda, and Kenya, and others. See Darwin, pp. xiii–xvi.

74 One of the best examples of this movement was John Osborne's 1956 play (later made into a film) *Look Back in Anger* (New York, 1982).

75 Britain's share of world trade in manufactures dropped during this period from a total of 16 percent in the mid-1950s to less than 10 percent by 1966. Clarke, *Hope and Glory,* p. 279.

76 John Sutherland has observed that the loss of sovereignty implied in EEC membership led many Britons to claim that "we might as well have lost the [Second World] war" and explains the upsurge in allohistorical accounts in the 1970s. While certainly a part of the story, feelings of national decline were rooted in a wider array of causes. John Sutherland, *Bestsellers: Popular Fiction of the 1970s* (London, 1981), p. 244.

77 See Tom Nairn's *The Break-Up of Britain: Crisis and Neo-Nationalism* (London, 1977). Devolution referred to the desire of Scotland, Wales, and Northern Ireland in the 1970s and 1980s for increased political autonomy from Britain, a movement that bore fruit in the late 1990s with the creation of regional parliaments.

78 See Donald Watt, "Appeasement: The Rise of a Revisionist School?" *The Political Quarterly,* April, 1965, pp. 191–213. A. J. P. Taylor's 1961 book, *The Origins of the Second World War* (New York), offered the most famous and controversial challenge to reigning British views on the war at this time.

79 In France, the Algerian crisis and the revolutions of 1968 prompted historians to replace the dominant, black-and-white view of collaboration and resistance with a far more nuanced and self-critical portrait. See Henry Rousso, *The Vichy Syndrome: History and Memory in France since 1944* (Cambridge, MA, 1991), pp. 98–132. In Britain, it was the Suez Crisis in particular that "discredited argument by historical analogy," as the attempt to oppose Gamal Abdel Nasser as a latter-day Hitler ended in an embarrassing failure. Watt, p. 111. As a result, Peter Hitchens notes that in the mid-1960s, the British Left returned to its antipatriotic roots and led the "open mockery of the war years." Peter Hitchens, *The Abolition of Britain: From Winston Churchill to Princess Diana* (San Francisco, 2000), p. 11.

80 Gallup polls revealed that in 1962, 54 percent of Britons described their attitudes towards Germans positively; by the end of the decade, the figure had risen to 70 percent. Cited S. P. Mackenzie, "Nazis into Germans: *Went the*

Day Well? and *The Eagle Has Landed* – 1942–1976 – Critical Essay," *Journal of Popular Film and Television,* summer, 2003.

81 Ibid. According to Mackenzie, the hit film *The Battle of Britain* portrayed Luftwaffe pilots in the same admirable terms as RAF pilots. Jack Higgins's novel *The Eagle Has Landed* (later turned into a hit film) also portrayed German soldiers in respectful, rather than demonized, terms.

82 Giles Cooper, *The Other Man: A Novel Based on His Play for Television* (London, 1964).

83 Ibid., p. 152. A total of 3,254 men end up dying in the process of constructing the road.

84 At various junctures in the novel, George betrays fellow battalion members Percy Vale, Henry Potter, and Paddy Ryan to the Germans, sending them to certain deaths.

85 George begins to face his repressed feelings of guilt after betraying his longtime friend Paddy to the Germans. Ibid., p. 188.

86 The most extreme example is the Nazi doctor, Werner Klaus, who performs grisly medical experiments. Ibid., pp. 154, 172.

87 George displays strong antisemitism on numerous occasions, for example when he does away with his superior, a man named Vale, by publicly accusing him of being a Jew. Ibid., p. 59.

88 Giles Cooper (1918–66) served in the army 1939–46, being stationed in Burma for four years. *Dictionary of Literary Biography, Volume XIII: British Dramatists since World War II* (Detroit, 1982). Philip Purser wrote that Cooper intended to critique "the finest Army traditions of obedience and service" by pointing out how they "could all too easily be distorted to sinister ends." Philip Purser, "Hitler's Common Market," *London Review of Books,* August 6, 1992, p. 22.

89 Cooper's main literary focus has been described as "the routine existence dictated by a sterile society" and "the dark underbelly of everyday life." *Dictionary of Literary Biography, Volume XIII: British Dramatists since World War II* (Detroit, 1982), p. 127. See also *Contemporary Authors,* Vol. CLXXIX, pp. 257–60. Cooper's "favourite political myth" has been described as "the decline and fall of the British empire," a subject he explored in such radio plays as *Dangerous Word* and *The Return of General Forefinger.* Frances Gray, "Giles Cooper: The Medium as Moralist," in John Drakakis, *British Radio Drama* (Cambridge, 1981), p. 152.

90 Cooper, *The Other Man,* pp. 75, 197.

91 Two new British arrivals in India report to Henry Potter about "the new cars that were succeeding the Volkswagen, the satellite launching rockets that were being built on the Baltic coast, the monorail system from Bremen to Hamburg." Ibid., p. 134.

92 Ibid., p. 162.

93 Ibid., p. 90.

94 Ibid., p. 95.

95 The most the novel does is imply that by the early 1960s, there "is no really constructive enthusiasm for the [Nazi] New Order." Ibid., p. 201.

96 Ibid., p. 11.

97 Ibid.

98 The scholarly literature on fascism in the 1960s de-emphasized it as a German phenomenon and stressed its origins in the economic system of capitalism. See Ian Kershaw, *The Nazi Dictatorship: Problems and Perspectives of Interpretation* (London, 1985), chapter 2.

99 Kevin Brownlow, *How It Happened Here: The Making of a Film* (New York, 1968), pp. 58, 145.

100 Ibid., p. 43.

101 Brownlow was confident that the "unprejudiced" narrative of the film would lead audiences to take away the "right" antifascist lesson. The director confidently expected "the Nazis to ... condemn themselves out of their own mouths." Brownlow, pp. 138, 167–68.

102 After 1956 (the year in which superpower showdowns over the Suez Crisis and the Soviet invasion of Hungary grabbed the headlines), many Britons united to form the Campaign for Nuclear Disarmament (CND), which campaigned in highly public fashion on behalf of pacifism. Clarke, *Hope and Glory*, p. 276.

103 Brownlow's original intention was for "the film ... to demonstrate the inevitability of war ... [and] its utter futility." Brownlow, p. 27.

104 Ewan Butler, *Without Apology: The Autobiography of Sir George Maudesley, Bart.* (London, 1968).

105 Ibid., p. 3.

106 In one remark, Maudesley notes that "the Germans ... show[ed] signs of a virility which seemed to have been drained from our people." Ibid., p. 97.

107 Ibid., pp. 121, 166.

108 Ibid., pp. 195–96.

109 Ibid., p. 290.

110 Ibid., p. 277.

111 As the introductory summary blurb for the book declares, "This ... novel ... is the story of an Englishman who in mind and heart was a patriot but who was, nevertheless, branded a traitor." Ibid., no page number.

112 Ibid., p. 281.

113 Near the end of the novel, George's second wife, Grace, upbraids him for leaving Britain for America, saying, "I thought you were doing what you did because you honestly sympathized with the English people and wanted to help them ... But you do what you do because you think it will do George Maudesley a bit of good." Ibid., pp. 332–33.

114 Ibid., p. 335.

115 Obituary of Ewan Butler, *The Times*, October 5, 1974, p. 16. Butler (1911–74) held a commission in the supplementary reserve of officers and was a junior staff officer of the fiercely anti-Nazi British Lieutenant-General, Sir Noel Mason-MacFarlane. He was a member of the British Expeditionary Forces that were evacuated from Dunkirk in 1940, an event he documented in *Keep the Memory Green: The First of the Many, France, 1939–40* (London, 1950).

After World War II, Butler remained interested in German affairs, publishing *City Divided: Berlin, 1955* (London, 1955).

116 Butler expressed conservative political leanings in some of his other written works. For example, in his book *The Murder of the* News Chronicle *and the* Star: *Killed by Trade Union Restrictive Practices, October 17, 1960* (London, 1960), Butler blamed British labor unions for embracing "restrictive practices" that "[ate] away at the economic health of our nation," pp. 16–17.

117 George himself declares that "moralizing . . . is one of the defects . . . of American public life." Butler, *Without Apology*, p. 360. "America was inhibited by her own conscience from striking the blows which would quickly have destroyed the Reich and set Europe free. The American people had come to feel that Europe was a bore and that her peoples, starving and tormented though they might be, must achieve their own salvation with[out] . . . the help of American blood." Ibid., p. 376.

118 The war's turning point occurs (as in real history) with Hitler's assault on the USSR and Japan's sneak attack on Pearl Harbor. Unlike the real historical course of events, however, the United States remain satisfied with defeating Japan and never make an effort to invade Germany, which eventually is defeated and occupied (together with all of Eastern Europe) by the Soviets.

119 I thank Gary Kenneth Peatling for pointing out the link to Suez.

120 See Wm. Roger Louis, "The Dissolution of the British Empire in the Era of Vietnam," *The American Historical Review*, February, 2002, pp. 1–25.

121 Roberts's tale de-heroized the British by telling the tale of a collaborator who enjoys the perks of German patronage, only to experience firsthand the savage reality of German rule. Keith Roberts, "Weihnachtsabend," in Gregory Benford and Martin H. Greenberg, *Hitler Victorious: Eleven Stories of the German Victory in World War II* (New York, 1986), pp. 89–120. *If Britain Had Fallen* de-demonized the Germans by depicting their occupation as relatively mild. As Longmate put it, "[the] truth was . . . that most Germans . . . were not hateful" and behaved, for the most part, with "exemplary restraint" towards ordinary civilians (not including members of the resistance and Jews). Norman Longmate, *If Britain Had Fallen* (New York, 1974), pp. 77–78, 246.

122 See Dennis Potter, "A True Tartan Tragedy," *The Times*, June 11, 1978, p. 39. David Chamberlin, "An Englishman's Castle," in Richard P. Adler, *Understanding Television: Essays on Television as a Social Force* (New York, 1981), pp. 255–66.

123 For a brief biographical sketch of Mackie, see *Contemporary Authors Online*.

124 Deighton, *SS-GB*.

125 Ibid., p. 15.

126 Deighton later served in the Special Investigation Branch of the RAF. See the entry for Len Deighton in *Contemporary Literary Criticism*, Vol. XXII (Detroit, 1982), p. 113.

127 Deighton's father was a chauffeur and his mother a cook. His education as an adolescent was interrupted by the war and he never took his matriculation.

After his military service, he worked as a steward for BOAC and later as a designer and illustrator. See Edward Milward-Oliver, *The Len Deighton Companion* (London, 1987), pp. 108–09.

128 See the entry for Len Deighton in *Contemporary Authors, New Revision Series*, Vol. LXVIII (Detroit, 1998), pp. 141, 145.

129 Deighton has asserted, "I don't write books to give messages to anyone, I'd consider that arrogant. I'm an entertainer, not a politician ... Obeying any political party sounds rather like leaving others to do your thinking for you." Milward-Oliver, pp. 24–25.

130 Ibid., p. 17.

131 Deighton demonstrated his iconoclastic tendencies in his books *Fighter: The True Story of the Battle of Britain* (London, 1978) and *XPD* (Thorndike, ME, 1981). *Fighter* was a work of non-fiction that challenged the myths about the Battle of Britain, while *XPD* was a fictional "secret history" of a clandestine meeting between Churchill and Hitler in 1940, in which the former offered to surrender to the latter. One reviewer has referred to "Deighton's urge to demythologize" as well as to his "bolshy" (that is, leftwing) tendencies. See review of *XPD* by John Sutherland, quoted in *Contemporary Literary Criticism*, Vol. XXII (Detroit, 1982), p. 118.

132 In speaking about his novel *Winter* (London, 1987), Deighton asserted, "I didn't want the book to become an apologia for the Nazis, and yet I wanted to say that it could happen here. I have never been able to see Hitler as an extraordinary man ... Perhaps Germans are particularly vulnerable to such a tyranny [as created by Hitler], but it would be dangerous to think they are unique in this respect." Milward-Oliver, p. 24.

133 The notion that England was vulnerable to a fascist take-over was also expressed in works of popular culture at the time. See, for example, comic book writer Alan Moore's comic book *V for Vendetta* (1982), in which England is taken over by a fascist government after a nuclear holocaust.

134 "London Pavilion: It Happened Here," *The Times*, May 12, 1966, p. 6. See review of the film in the larger article, "Pasolini Makes the Cinema's most Serious Film about Christ," *The Times*, November 3, 1964, p. 14.

135 *Film Daily*, August 17, 1967. File on *It Happened Here*, The Academy Archive (AA) at the Academy of Motion Pictures' Center for Motion Picture Study in Beverly Hills, California.

136 Similarly, one BBC journalist wrote that the film's "hypothesis [was] inconceivable," while the *Daily Telegraph* called it "totteringly implausible." See Brownlow, pp. 163, 165, 167.

137 Ibid., pp. 138, 167–68.

138 The *Jewish Chronicle* denounced the film as "a foul outpouring." "British Nazis' Film to be Shown after 30-Year Ban," *Independent*, September 29, 1996. See also "Film about Fascists Revives Row over Cuts," *Sunday Telegraph*, September 29, 1996, p. 14.

139 See letter to the editor by members of the New Arts Theatre Club to *The Times*, February 25, 1966, p. 13. See also letter to the editor by Stanley Reed,

Director of the British Film Institute (BFI), *The Times*, March 3, 1966, p. 13. See the position taken by a representative of United Artists, *The Times*, March 1, 1966, p. 13.

140 See the *Yorkshire Post*, September 7, 1964, cited at: www.625.org.uk/frames.htm.

141 The *Yorkshire Post*, September 7, 1964. www.625.org.uk/frames.htm. L. Marsland-Gander, "Gloomy Play of 'Nazified Britain,'" *Daily Telegraph*, August 9, 1964. Courtesy of the BFI.

142 "If Winston Had Died," *Daily Mail*, August 9, 1964. Courtesy of the BFI.

143 "Questions of Value Much Too Close for Comfort," *The Times*, September 12, 1964, p. 12.

144 Sylvia Clayton, review of *An Englishman's Castle*, *Daily Telegraph*, June 20, 1978; Philip Purser, review of *An Englishman's Castle*, *Sunday Express*, June 25, 1978; Martin Jackson, "Soap Opera's Secret Weapon," *Daily Mail*, June 17, 1978. Courtesy of the BFI.

145 James Murphy, "The Horrors of Fascism in Britain," *Daily Express*, June 6, 1978. As another reviewer noted, "This is not a satire on what might have been, but what is." "Soap Opera's Secret Weapon," *Daily Mail*, June 17, 1978. Courtesy of the BFI.

146 Clive James, review of *An Englishman's Castle*, *Observer*, June 18, 1978; Auberon Waugh, "At Last, Mr. More's Finest Hour," *Daily Mail*, June 13, 1978. Courtesy of the BFI.

147 Richard Ingrams, review of *An Englishman's Castle*, *Spectator*, June 10, 1978. Courtesy of the BFI.

148 Len Deighton's *SS-GB* was published with an original print run of 110,000. Milward-Oliver, p. 318.

149 Anthony Burgess, "Britain under Hitler," *Observer*, August 27, 1978, p. 22.

150 Michael Howard, "In Occupied Britain," *Times Literary Supplement*, September 15, 1978, p. 1011.

151 David Williams praised Deighton's "sharp-eyed awareness of probabilities" in depicting Nazi-occupied Britain. David Williams, review of *SS-GB*, *Punch*, February 27, 1980, p. 360. The reviewer for the *Observer* described the book's plot as "credible," *Observer*, July 13, 1980, p. 29. See also H. R. F. Keating's review in *The Times*, August 31, 1978, p. 20.

152 James Cameron, "Damn Nearly Happened Here," *Guardian*, September 3, 1978, p. 22.

153 Ibid., p. 22.

154 Paul Ableman, "Programmed," *Spectator*, September 2, 1978, p. 22, cited in *Contemporary Literary Criticism*, Vol. XXII, p. 116. Another comparable observation was made by Marghanita Laski, who summed up her view of *SS-GB* by writing, "It won't do. For one thing, on grounds of taste which do not permit boyish fun with the Nazis." Marghanita Laski, "Dying Leaves," *Listener*, November 9, 1978, p. 622.

155 Britain's unemployment rate fell from 12 percent in 1983 to 6 percent in 1990. Clarke, *Hope and Glory*, p. 393. Moreover, economic growth was 3.7 percent in the years 1984–88, beating the previous records of the postwar years.

156 Ibid., p. 375.

157 Thatcher's approval ratings shot up during the Falklands conflict – a fact that, together with improving figures on unemployment, enabled her to win a second term in office. Ibid., p. 376.

158 In his article "Margaret Thatcher, the Foreign Office, and German Reunification," *Cercles* 5, 2002, Klaus Larres reports that 71 percent of those Britons who were polled declared their support for reunification. Larres, p. 177.

159 See Clive Ponting's books, *1940: Myth and Reality* (London, 1990), *Churchill* (London, 1994), and *The Reality behind the Distortions, Myths, Lies, and Illusions of World War II* (New York, 1995).

160 "The Finest Hour," *New Statesman and Society*, September 8, 1989, p. 4.

161 Peter Hitchens has praised the notion of the "finest hour" for "[holding] the national patriotic consensus together" and has expressed fear that Britons have become apathetic about sustaining it. Hitchens, *The Abolition of Britain*, pp. 42, 60–61.

162 Adrian Gilbert, *Britain Invaded: Hitler's Plans for Britain: A Documentary Reconstruction* (London, 1990).

163 Ibid., p. 100.

164 Ibid., p. 108.

165 Ibid., p. 103.

166 Ibid., p. 112.

167 Ibid., p. 124.

168 E-mail messages from Adrian Gilbert to author, July 6 and July 10, 2002.

169 Gilbert has described his politics as "broadly centre-left." Ibid.

170 Raine (born 1944) is considered to be "among the foremost British poets." *Contemporary Authors, New Revision Series*, Vol. XXIX (Detroit, 1990), p. 363.

171 The play was originally published in 1990. See Craig Raine, '*1953*': *A Version of Racine's* Andromaque (London, 1990).

172 To offer one example, a world in which the fascist powers of Germany and Italy had won World War II would certainly not have been one in which monarchs of any kind would have had any meaningful role.

173 Raine, p. 10.

174 Ibid., p. 28.

175 Ibid., p. 50.

176 As Raine has written, "It wasn't ... anything about attitudes to Germany in the 1980s which dictated what I wrote." E-mail message from Raine to author, March 26, 2002.

177 As Raine notes, "Jonathan Miller commissioned a 'clean, modern translation' of Racine's *Andromaque* ... I decided that Jonathan would anyway update my version since he had set *Tosca* in Fascist Rome and *Rigoletto* in gangster New York, so I might as well pre-empt him by updating the piece myself." Ibid.

178 When Raine needed an "equivalent of Racine's Pyrrhus," for example, he turned to Mussolini, who, having sons, provided a better modern equivalent

than Hitler for the marriage to Hermione (Annette LeSkye). E-mail message from Raine to author, March 27, 2002.

179 E-mail message from Craig Raine to author, March 26, 2002.

180 Ibid.

181 Ibid.

182 Robert Harris, *Fatherland* (New York, 1992).

183 Ibid., p. 162.

184 Harris burst on the British scene in the early 1980s with his bestselling exposé of the forgery of the Hitler Diaries, *Selling Hitler*. Harris has described himself as a supporter of the British Labour party. See the entry for Harris in *Contemporary Authors*, Vol. CXLIII (Detroit, 1994), p. 184.

185 "I'm only Accused of Insensitivity to Germans," *Baltimore Jewish Times*, June 26, 1992, p. 61.

186 Harris added, "It would have been a morally bankrupt system, with the ghastly ... secret of the Holocaust at its heart. Speer's monumental buildings would, in the end, have proved as fragile ... as Nicolae Ceausescu's. As one of the characters in my book says: 'Fifty years from now ... the society will fall apart. You can't build on a mass grave.'" Robert Harris, "Nightmare Landscape of Nazism Triumphant," *The Sunday Times*, May 10, 1992, Section 2, p. 1.

187 As Harris put it in a 1992 essay, "I spent four years writing [a] ... novel about a fictional German superpower and, as I wrote, it started turning into fact ... One does not have to share the views of ... Margaret Thatcher to note the similarity between what the Nazis planned for western Europe and what, in economic terms, has come to pass." Robert Harris, "Nightmare Landscape of Nazism Triumphant," *The Sunday Times*, May 10, 1992, Section 2, p. 1.

188 As he put it, "I don't mean to suggest that Europe now is as it would have been if the Nazis had won." Harris further denied that *Fatherland* was anti-German, adding, "I like Germany a lot." Craig R. Whitney, "Inventing a World in which Hitler Won," *New York Times*, June 3, 1992, p. C17. As a journalist, moreover, Harris has opposed anti-European Union sentiment in Britain and is a close friend of Prime Minister Tony Blair.

189 Responding to an interviewer who asked him, "How would Britain have behaved under Nazi occupation?" Harris responded, "There would have been a compliant regime in power, under someone like Halifax." "The Devil's Interview with Robert Harris," no date. www.thedevilmag.co.uk/harris.html.

190 Madeleine Bunting, *The Model Occupation: The Channel Islands under German Rule* (New York, 1995).

191 Ibid., pp. 6, 3.

192 Ibid., p. 316.

193 Ibid., pp. 81–83.

194 Bunting's precise date of birth is unavailable, but her photograph on the *Guardian* web site reveals her probably to be in her 40s (that is, born in the late 1950s or early 1960s).

195 Bunting, p. 336.

196 Ibid., p. 6.

197 John Charmley, *Churchill: The End of Glory: A Political Biography* (New York, 1993).

198 In making this claim, Charmley harked back to the prior scholarship of Maurice Cowling and Correlli Barnett. Cowling's *The Impact of Hitler* (Cambridge, 1975) suggested that Nazi Germany never posed a serious threat to Britain and should have been allowed to take eastern Europe. Barnett's *The Audit of War* (London, 1986) traced Britain's postwar decline to its economic mismanagement of World War II.

199 Charmley wrote disapprovingly, "The 'finest hour' myth has such a hold on the British national consciousness that even to suggest, fifty years later, that a compromise peace might have been had is enough to prompt letters to the press denouncing such an idea as 'shameful.'" Charmley, *Churchill*, p. 422. Charmley implied the possibility of bowing out of the war at the end of May 1940, writing "in the eyes of many sensible folk, the time had come to think about coming to terms with Herr Hitler." Ibid., p. 398.

200 As Charmley put it, "If the war was fought to save the freedom of Poland ... it was a failure ... If the war was fought to safeguard Europeans against totalitarianism, it was a failure ... If the war was fought to maintain Britain's position as a world power, it was a failure. We ended the war broke." "British Author in Fulton Blasted for WWII Views," *St. Louis Post Dispatch*, January 5, 1993, p. 4A.

201 Charmley, *Churchill*, p. 649.

202 Alan Clark, "A Reputation Ripe for Revision," *The Times*, January 2, 1993.

203 Ibid.

204 Alan Clark, "Historians Who Go to War with Hindsight," *The Times*, January 16, 1993.

205 As Charmley noted, "When my critics say I'm using arguments from hindsight, nobody in 1939 was saying we should go to war for the Jews. The real Holocaust only really got underway in 1943–4 when the Germans were losing." Valerie Grove, "The Man Who Rewrote History," *The Times*, January 8, 1993.

206 Alan Clark, "Historians Who Go to War with Hindsight," *The Times*, January 16, 1993; Stuart Jeffries, "Alan Clark's Peace in Our Time," *Guardian*, June 21, 1995, p. T13.

207 Valerie Grove, "The Man Who Rewrote History," *The Times*, January 8, 1993.

208 "British Author in Fulton Blasted for WWII Views," *St. Louis Post Dispatch*, January 5, 1993, p. 4A.

209 As Charmley wrote, "What grounds were there for supposing that Germany's [peace] terms would necessarily be so Carthaginian?" Charmley, *Churchill*, p. 403.

210 "British Author in Fulton Blasted for WWII Views," *St. Louis Post Dispatch*, January 5, 1993, p. 4A.

211 Ibid.

212 As Charmley put it, Churchill's "vision failed him ... in relation to domestic politics, as he neglected the Conservative Party and allowed the Socialists to secure a hold on power." Charmley, *Churchill*, p. 467. Clark agreed, criticizing "Churchill's neglect of the Tories' domestic image and policies," and blamed him for its "catastrophic electoral defeat" in 1945. Andrew Roberts also implicated Churchill in Britain's postwar decline in his 1995 book *Eminent Churchillians* (London, 1994).

213 John Charmley, *Chamberlain and the Lost Peace* (London, 1989). Charmley's 1995 companion book, *Churchill's Grand Alliance: The Anglo-American Special Relationship, 1940–57* (New York, 1995), portrayed America's subjugation of Britain in the sphere of foreign relations. Charmley's 1999 book, *Splendid Isolation? Britain and the Balance of Power, 1874–1914* (London, 1999), criticized Sir Edward Grey's abandonment of Britain's late nineteenth-century isolationism and his entanglement of Britain in the affairs of France and Russia for setting the stage for the nation's intervention in World War I. Other conservative scholars revolved in the same revisionist orbit as Charmley but were less strident and later distanced themselves from him. See, for example, Andrew Roberts, *The Holy Fox: A Biography of Lord Halifax* (London, 1991).

214 *Fatherland* has been translated into twenty-five languages. See the profile of Harris in *Contemporary Authors*. Christy Campbell, "The Shrinking of *Fatherland*," *Sunday Telegraph*, June 26, 1994, p. 5; Craig R. Whitney, "Inventing a World in Which Hitler Won," *New York Times*, June 3, 1992, p. C17.

215 As Philip Purser wrote, "*Fatherland* is a formidable thriller ... terse, involving, and expertly constructed." "Hitler's Common Market," *London Review of Books*, August 6, 1992, p. 22. Geoffrey Wheatcroft called *Fatherland* "very clever" and a "deserved best-seller." Geoffrey Wheatcroft, *Spectator*, November 21, 1992, p. 43. John Mortimer called it "very good" and "readable." John Mortimer, "The Reich's Progress," *The Sunday Times*, May 3, 1992, Book Review Section, p. 5. See also review by Woodrow Wyatt, *The Times*, May 7, 1992, p. 4.

216 The fact that *Fatherland* met with a hostile response in Germany, moreover, no doubt further endeared it to many British readers and boosted its sales. This pattern would be duplicated four years later with Daniel Goldhagen's *Hitler's Willing Executioners* (New York, 1996).

217 John Mortimer characterized Xavier March as a "decent ... chap." John Mortimer, "The Reich's Progress," *The Sunday Times*, May 3, 1992, Book Review Section, p. 5. Simon Louvish praised *Fatherland* as "an honourable contribution," but criticized Harris's formulaic use of the "stock hero" of the "Good German" as unoriginal. Simon Louvish, "If Hitler Lived," *New Statesman and Society*, May 22, 1992, p. 38.

218 See the reviews on www.amazon.com's Britain web site.

219 Michael Billington, "First Night: Tangled Passion with Lots of 'Ifs'," *Guardian*, February 15, 1996, p. 2; Paul Taylor, "A Year of Living

Dangerously," *Independent*, February 22, 1992, p. 30; Alistair Macaulay, "Molière and Racine Revisited," *The Financial Times*, February 16, 1996, p. 19. David Bryer praised the play's poetic dimensions, calling it "a linguistic feast." David Bryer, review of '*1953*,' *Observer*, March 18, 1990, p. 63. See also Joyce McMillan's review in the *Guardian*, February 24, 1992.

220 Alistair Macaulay, "Molière and Racine Revisited," *The Financial Times*, February 16, 1996, p. 19; John Gross, "Making Misanthropy Sparkle," *Sunday Telegraph*, February 18, 1996, p. 12. John Weightman was bothered by the play's "implausibilities." "The Tragedy That Gets Lost in Translation," *Independent*, March 18, 1990, p. 20. Paul Taylor quibbled with the premise that "any claimant to the English throne would have married a Jewess." "Theater 1953," *Independent*, February 16, 1996, p. 9.

221 In his book *Under the Shadow of the Swastika: The Moral Dilemmas of Resistance and Collaboration in Hitler's Europe* (New York, 1999), Rab Bennett cites Gilbert's book as exhibiting a "most fertile example of speculative imagination," Bennett, pp. 16–17.

222 E-mail message from Gilbert to author, July 10, 2002.

223 Hugh R. Trevor-Roper, "A Little Bit of Nazi Britain," *Sunday Telegraph*, January 29, 1995, Books Section, p. 11. The phrase "scrupulously fair" appears in the review of the book by Kirsty Milne, "Officers and Gentlemen," *New Statesman and Society*, January 13, 1995, p. 36. M. R. D. Foot, "Nowhere to Run Away," *Times Literary Supplement*, May 5, 1995, p. 32. Foot said that *The Model Occupation* was "much the best book ... on the German occupation of the Channel Islands."

224 "No Time for Heroics," *The Economist*, January 28, 1995, pp. 83–84.

225 Jonathan Keates, "The Shame History Hid," *Observer*, February 19, 1995, p. 17.

226 John Keegan, "We Would Have Fought Them on the Beaches," *Daily Telegraph*, November 27, 1996, p. 20. See also John Keegan, "Appeal of Sleeping with the Enemy," *Daily Telegraph*, January 21, 1995, Books Section, p. 4.

227 Linda Holt, "Our Dear Channel Islands," *London Review of Books*, May 25, 1995, pp. 9–11.

228 Various reviewers criticized Charmley's revisionism as part of a rightwing plot. Harrington called the vision of peace with Nazi Germany "a slightly tarted-up version of the old day-dream of the Tory Right." Michael Harrington, "Mr. Clark's Gothic View of Herr Hitler," *Sunday Telegraph*, June 25, 1995, p. 31. Some located Charmley's thesis within the "springs of anti-Americanism [that] have always run ... deep on the right-wing of the Conservative party." Anthony Howard, "No More Heroes," *The Sunday Times*, June 25, 1995.

229 Historians Alan Bullock and Donald Cameron Watt both accused Charmley of what they referred to in clearly derisive terms as "counterfactual thinking." R. Barry O'Brien, "Top Historians Join Row over Churchill Book," *Daily Telegraph*, January 4, 1993, p. 3. Michael Harrington dismissed Charmley's implausible scenario as "one of those

'alternate world' science fiction novels." Michael Harrington, "Mr. Clark's Gothic View of Herr Hitler," *Sunday Telegraph*, June 25, 1995, p. 31. For his part, Charmley defended the allohistorical method, arguing, "I'm an old-fashioned Cleopatra's nose historian: if her nose had been a different shape, Caesar and Mark Antony would not have fallen for her, and history would have been different." Valerie Grove, "The Man Who Rewrote History," *The Times*, January 8, 1993.

230 Quoted in Eugene Robinson, "A New Look at an Old Hero – Churchill – Sparks a Furor in Britain," *Washington Post*, January 18, 1993.

231 Ibid.

232 R. Barry O'Brien, "Top Historians Join Row over Churchill Book," *Daily Telegraph*, January 4, 1993, p. 3.

233 Winston S. Churchill, "Book Asserts That Churchill Could Have Made Peace with Hitler, Preserved Empire," *Jerusalem Post*, May 4, 1993.

234 British support for European integration began already under John Major, who ratified the Maastricht Treaty in 1992–93, and continued under the government of Tony Blair. Conservatives questioned the need for Britain to accept closer EU ties, especially by the mid-1990s, when the nation's improving economy seemed to suggest that Great Britain was perfectly fine without closer European ties.

235 Andrew Roberts and Niall Ferguson, "Hitler's England," in Niall Ferguson, ed., *Virtual History: Alternatives and Counter-Factuals* (New York, 1997), pp. 281–320.

236 The factors cited by Roberts ranged from the many men who volunteered to fight in the Local Defense Forces to the firm support of the British for their government (unlike the French before Vichy).

237 Roberts and Ferguson, in Ferguson, *Virtual History*, pp. 296–98.

238 Andrew Roberts, "Prime Minister Halifax," in Robert Cowley, *What If? 2: Eminent Historians Imagine What Might Have Been* (New York, 2001).

239 Roberts's novel *The Aachen Memorandum* (London, 1995), demonstrated this clearly.

240 See especially Niall Ferguson's recent book, *Empire: The Rise and Demise of the British World Order and the Lessons for Global Power* (New York, 2003), which points out the positive aspects of British imperialism.

241 Niall Ferguson, "The Kaiser's European Union," in Ferguson, ed., pp. 228–80; Niall Ferguson, *The Pity of War* (New York, 1998).

242 Recent mainstream works of history have done so as well. See, for example, Geoffrey Best's recent biography, *Churchill: A Study in Greatness* (London, 2001), in which the author reaffirmed Hitler's aggressive intentions towards Britain and rejected the notion of a separate peace. See also Paul Addison, "Churchill and the Price of Victory: 1939–1945," in Nick Tiratsoo, ed., *From Blitz to Blair: A New History of Britain since 1939* (London, 1997), pp. 53–76.

243 See Hugo Young, "Germano-phobia Still Grips Us as the British Refuse to Forget the War," *Guardian*, February 16, 1999, p. 16.

244 Christopher Priest, *The Separation* (London, 2002).

245 Ibid., pp. 214–15.
246 Ibid., p. 318.
247 Ibid., pp. 289, 13.
248 Ibid., p. 214.
249 "The Interrogation: An Interview with Christopher Priest by Nick Gevers," originally published in *Interzone*, October, 2002. Cited on: www. infinity-plus.co.uk/nonfiction/intcpriest.htm.
250 Ibid. Priest's pacifism may also explain why, in an era of growing world opposition to American foreign policy, he painted such an unflattering portrait of America as a corrupt, militaristic nation in decline.
251 See, for example, the glowing review by John Clute, "Trying to Find *The Separation* in This World," www.scifi.com/sfw/issue285/excess.html.
252 Reviews of *Peace in Our Time* were largely positive. See Sarah Hemming, "Peace in Our Time – Theatre," *The Financial Times*, March 14, 1995, p. 19; Paul Taylor, "Being Beastly to the Germans," *Independent*, March 11, 1995, p. 28; Charles Spencer, "If Adolf Hitler Had Won the War," *Daily Telegraph*, March 10, 1995, p. 21. *It Happened Here* was first re-released at the Jersey International Film Festival in September 1996. Thereafter it was re-released in the United States after thirty-six years without American distribution. VHS and DVD versions followed. Interestingly, resistance to the film's conclusions remained high on Jersey, where one audience member was quoted as saying, "There was never the kind of collaboration [there] that the film portrayed." "Islands Face the Nazi Facts," *The Times*, October 4, 1996. Regarding *Invasion: 1940*, the original document was entitled *Informationsheft Grossbritannien*, drafted by SS chief Walter Schellenberg, who received the order to do so in June 1940. This document had appended to it the so-called "Black List" of 2,820 people designated by the Gestapo for immediate arrest, as well as Walther von Brauchitsch's 1940 occupation orders. Some 20,000 copies of the handbook were published, though most were destroyed in an Allied bombing of a warehouse where they were being stored. British intelligence officials ordered them hidden after 1945 for fear of security leaks. Walter Schellenberg, John Keegan, and John Erickson, *Invasion 1940* (London, 2001). See Christopher Hudson, "What If They'd Won?" *Sunday Mail*, March 5, 2000, p. 61. James Dalrymple, "Fatherland UK," *Independent*, March 3, 2000.
253 Significantly, this trend fits into a larger tradition of British historians being "soft" on their longtime rival, the Germans, in the process of critiquing themselves. David Blackbourne and Geoff Eley's book *The Peculiarities of German History* (Oxford, 1984) dismissed the notion that Germany's path of historical development deviated from that of Britain and France in order to diminish a sense of British exceptionalism.
254 For a recent account of this trend, see "Gefangene der Geschichte," *Der Spiegel*, Nr. 51, 2002, p. 130.

CHAPTER 2: THE UNITED STATES AND THE DILEMMAS
OF MILITARY INTERVENTION

1 *Moon of Ice* was originally published as a novella in 1982 and was expanded into a full-length novel in 1988. All quotations in this chapter come from the novel. Brad Linaweaver, *Moon of Ice* (New York, 1988), pp. 4–10. The short story version is reproduced in Harry Turtledove and Martin H. Greenberg, eds., *The Best Alternate History Stories of the 20th Century* (New York, 2001), pp. 356–415.

2 Britain produced seven accounts between the years 1937–45, compared with three in the United States. See Appendix.

3 Isolationists regularly dismissed the threat of the Third Reich to the United States. Warren I. Cohen, *The American Revisionists: The Lessons of Intervention in World War I* (Chicago, 1967); Wayne Cole, *Roosevelt and the Isolationists: 1932–45* (Lincoln, NE, 1983), p. 343.

4 Hendrik Willem van Loon, *Invasion: Being an Eyewitness Account of the Nazi Invasion of America* (New York, 1940); Fred Allhoff, *Lightning in the Night* (Englewood Cliffs, NJ, 1979). Allhoff's novel was serialized in the magazine *Liberty* in thirteen installments between August 24 and November 16, 1940.

5 Van Loon wrote: "The facts of this book ... are the revaluation against an American background of what happened in those neutral European countries which were ... overthrown by the Nazis ... Up to the last moment, these poor victims ... had been writing me, 'don't worry ... the Germans will never do us any harm ... it can never happen here.' Alas ... a week later ... they had lost ... their old freedom ... America sometime very soon will have to decide what course it intends to follow. Hence this little book." Van Loon, pp. 201–02. Van Loon (1882–1944) moved to the United States in 1902 and made his reputation as a bestselling author of popular histories for juveniles – in particular, *The Story of Mankind* (1921). He was known for his short-wave broadcasts to the Netherlands as "Uncle Hank" during World War II. *Contemporary Authors Online*. The Gale Group, 2000.

6 This fanaticism is made clear when the narrator encounters a dying German soldier in Vermont whose last wish is to gaze at a photograph of his beloved Führer, Adolf Hitler.

7 Allhoff wrote the novel "with the advice and counsel of Lieutenant General Robert Lee Bullard, Rear Admiral Yates Sterling, and George E. Sokolsky." Terry Miller, "Introduction: A Basis in Fact," in Allhoff, p. 17.

8 Marion White, *If We Should Fail* (New York, 1942). White essentially transferred Nazi atrocities committed in Europe to American towns and cities.

9 See Thomas Doherty, *Projections of War: Hollywood, American Culture, and World War II* (New York, 1993), especially chapter 6; Bradford W. Wright, *Comic Book Nation: The Transformation of Youth Culture in America* (Baltimore, 2001), chapter 2, for a discussion of comic books' support for American intervention against the Nazis.

10 Yet fears of a Nazi revival persisted and were expressed in scattered "future histories." One of the most important was Erwin Christian Lessner's 1944 novel

Phantom Victory: The Fourth Reich, 1945–1960 (New York, 1944), which told the story of Germany emerging unrepentant from World War II and ultimately conquering the United States. Lessner's well-received book was a thinly veiled appeal for Germany to be subjected to a "hard peace" after 1945. For reviews, see *Book Review Digest*, 1944, pp. 453–54. See also Robert Abernathy, "Hostage of Tomorrow," *Planet Stories*, spring, 1949, pp. 86–117, which depicts the Germans overthrowing the Allied occupation in 1949 with "radioactive dust."

11 See F. T. Marsh, review of *Invasion* in *Books*, October 27, 1940, p. 3 and review of *Invasion* in *The Nation*, November 9, 1940. These and other positive reviews are listed in *Book Review Digest*, 1940, p. 939.

12 *Liberty*'s sales reached an all-time high when Allhoff's story appeared. Terry Miller, "Introduction: A Basis in Fact," *Lightning in the Night*, pp. 17–18.

13 Review of *If We Should Fail* in *Books*, November 22, 1942, p. 30. Cited in *Book Review Digest*, 1942, p. 828.

14 Kurt Piehler notes the relative lack of interest in erecting monuments to World War II after 1945, typified by the twenty-year delay in erecting the memorial to Pearl Harbor. G. Kurt Piehler, *Remembering War the American Way* (Washington, D.C., 1995), see chapter 4.

15 See Studs Terkel, '*The Good War': An Oral History of World War II* (New York, 1984).

16 Michael C. C. Adams writes that "of the major belligerents, the United States was alone in enjoying a higher standard of living as a result of the war." *The Best War Ever: America and World War II* (Baltimore, 1994), p. 6.

17 Such images were visible in films like *13 Rue Madeleine* (1946), *Battleground* (1949), and *The Colditz Story* (1954). See discussion in Manvell, *passim*. Most films about the war, however, did not focus directly on the Germans and were more interested in commenting on American wartime behavior, whether valorous or flawed. See, for example, *The Best Years of Our Lives* (1946) and *From Here to Eternity* (1953). This focus was also true of novels, such as Norman Mailer's *The Naked and the Dead* (1948).

18 See such works as Leonard Engel and Emmanuel S. Piller, *The World Aflame: The Russian–American War of 1950* (New York, 1947), Cyril M. Kornbluth, *Not This August* (New York, 1955), and Pat Frank, *Alas Babylon* (New York, 1959), all of which focused on a catastrophic Third World War.

19 It is notable that British alternate histories were republished in America at precisely this time. Thus, Sarban's 1952 novel *The Sound of His Horn* was reprinted by Ballantine books in 1960 for an American audience. Ballantine also brought out British journalist Comer Clarke's 1961 book *England under Hitler*.

20 Cyril M. Kornbluth, "Two Dooms," reprinted in Gregory Benford and Martin H. Greenberg, *Hitler Victorious: Eleven Stories of the German Victory in World War II* (New York, 1986), pp. 11–52. "Two Dooms" first appeared in *Venture* in July 1958. Timothy P. Szczesuil, ed., *His Share of Glory: The Complete Short Science Fiction of C. M. Kornbluth* (Framingham, MA, 1997), p. vi.

21 Kornbluth, "Two Dooms," p. 52.

22 See Kornbluth's obituary, "Cyril M. Kornbluth Dead at 35: Wrote Science-Fiction Stories," *New York Times,* Saturday, March 22, 1958, p. 17. http://members.tripod.com/~gwillick/obit/korno.htm/l. After 1945, Kornbluth was a member of a group of science fiction writers known as the Futurians (including Isaac Asimov and Frederik Pohl) who were known for their leftwing politics and opposition to fascism. Edward James, *Science Fiction in the Twentieth Century* (Oxford, 1994), p. 64.

23 Kornbluth, "Two Dooms," p. 41.

24 William L. Shirer, "If Hitler Had Won World War II," *Look,* December 19, 1961, pp. 28–43. For the controversy sparked by Shirer's history of Nazi Germany, see Gavriel D. Rosenfeld, "The Reception of William L. Shirer's *The Rise and Fall of the Third Reich* in the United States and West Germany, 1960–1962," *Journal of Contemporary History,* January, 1994, pp. 95–129.

25 Shirer, p. 28.

26 Ibid., p. 34.

27 Ibid., p. 42.

28 Ibid., p. 34.

29 Ibid., p. 42.

30 Ibid., p. 43.

31 Philip K. Dick, *The Man in the High Castle* (New York, 1992).

32 Ibid., p. 246.

33 Ibid., pp. 66–67.

34 This tolerant mentality is epitomized by Mr. Tagomi, who, late in the novel, refuses to approve a Nazi request to deport a Jewish antiques forger, Frank Frink, to the German zone for certain extermination.

35 As he puts it, "If Germany and Japan had lost the war, the Jews would be running the world today. Through Moscow and Wall Street." Dick, pp. 111–13.

36 Lawrence Sutin writes that the two "great themes" of Dick's work were "What is human? What is reality?" Lawrence Sutin, ed., *The Shifting Realities of Philip K. Dick: Selected Literary and Philosophical Writings* (New York, 1995), p. xiii.

37 Dick portrays Abendsen as having used the *I Ching* to write *The Grasshopper Lies Heavy.* Near the end of the novel a character named Juliana visits Abendsen and tells him to ask the oracle (which never lies) why it wrote the novel, to which the oracle replies, "Chung Fu," or "Inner Truth." Dick, p. 257. While the idea that the Nazis might have actually lost the war remained somewhat hazy in *The Man in the High Castle,* Dick planned on clarifying it in a never-completed sequel to *The Man in the High Castle,* begun in 1974, in which he explored the idea that the Nazis had lost the war in an alternate world (called the *Nebenwelt*). See Sutin, pp. 119–34.

38 Dick portrays Abendsen's reaction to Juliana's claim that his book is true as follows: "Hawthorne ... had an almost savage expression. 'It means ... that my book is true?' 'Yes,' she said ... Hawthorne said nothing. 'Even you don't face it,' Juliana said ... 'I'm not sure of anything,' he said. 'Believe,' Juliana said. He shook his head no." Dick, p. 257.

39 See Patricia S. Warrick, "The Encounter of Taoism and Fascism in *The Man in the High Castle*" and N. B. Hayles, "Metaphysics and Metafiction in *The Man in the High Castle*," in Martin Harry Greenberg and Joseph D. Olander, eds., *Philip K. Dick* (New York, 1983), pp. 27–72.

40 For background on Dick's interest in Nazism, see the June 26, 1976 radio interview with Dick on KPFK-FM. See www.geocities.com/pkdlw/dickivo4.html.

41 In acknowledging the individuals whose work influenced *The Man in the High Castle*, Dick openly wrote in the book's preface, "I have made much use of *The Rise and Fall of the Third Reich* ... by William L. Shirer." Dick, p. ix.

42 As he put it, "Fascism is very much with us today, boys and girls. And it's still the enemy." Interestingly, Dick differed from Shirer in de-emphasizing fascism's German dimensions, noting that "fascism and Germany are not that intimately linked. Fascism is a world wide phenomena [sic]." www.geocities.com/pkdlw/dickivo4.html.

43 Harlan Ellison, "The City on the Edge of Forever: An Original Teleplay," in Roger Ellwood, *Six Science Fiction Plays* (New York, 1976), pp. 5–138.

44 Ellison was famously irate about rewrites in the script for the television version, but none of the changes affected the episode's allohistorical dimensions. See Harlan Ellison, "Introduction to The City on the Edge of Forever," in Ellwood, pp. 5–14.

45 Harlan Ellison's original script was somewhat more vague in its formulation, consisting solely of Spock's observation, "in a few years this planet will have ... a great war. What if [Edith Keeler's] ... philosophy spread, and it kept America out of the war for a mere two years longer ... and in that time Germany perfected its atomic weapons? The outcome of the war would be reversed." Ellison, "The City on the Edge of Forever," p. 100.

46 Many *Star Trek* time-travel episodes featured such redemptive endings. See Jon Wagner and Jan Lundeen, *Deep Space and Sacred Time: Star Trek in the American Mythos* (Westport, CT, 1998), pp. 198–99.

47 Ellison has noted that his boyhood experience of antisemitism in Ohio helped him develop his sense of being an outsider. Thomas Dillingham, "Harlan Ellison," *Dictionary of Literary Biography, Volume VIII, Twentieth-Century American Science Fiction Writers* (Detroit, 1981), p. 163.

48 H. Bruce Franklin's "Star Trek in the Vietnam Era," *Science Fiction Studies*, March, 1994, pp. 24–34, cited in Ellen Weil and Gary K. Wolfe, *Harlan Ellison: The Edge of Forever* (Columbus, OH, 2002), pp. 111–15.

49 Eric Norden, *The Ultimate Solution* (New York, 1973).

50 Ibid., p. 18.

51 Ibid., p. 138

52 Ibid., p. 13.

53 Norden was the pseudonym of Eric Pelletier (1899–1979). www.locusmag.com/index/s574.html#A13582.

54 Tom Rosenstiel, "The Lost Art of Interviewing," *The Columbia Journalism Review*, January/February 1995. www.cjr.org/year/95/1/interviewing.asp.

55 This quotation comes from a longer one that serves as the epigraph to Norden's novel. Norden, p. 142.

56 "Crisis on Earth-X," *Justice League of America*, Nr. 107, October, 1973; "Thirteen Against the Earth," *Justice League of America*, Nr. 108, December, 1973.

57 Len Wein created such comic book series as Swamp Thing, X-Men, and many others.

58 In the tale, the Nazis win the war after developing the atomic bomb, which they use to cow the politically polarized United States into submission (the story vaguely refers to "the governmental balance of power [going] ... the wrong way" after the American president dies of a heart attack in 1944).

59 Wein has asserted that there was no "political agenda" behind the story. Wein's Jewish background no doubt sensitized him to the evils of Nazism. E-mail message from Len Wein to author.

60 The tales written between 1945 and the 1970s were composed by people generally born between the years 1905–35. The oldest, Eric Norden, was born in 1899; William Shirer was born in 1905; Kornbluth was born in 1925; Dick was born in 1928; and Ellison was born in 1934. The youngest, Len Wein, was born in 1948.

61 Review of *The Man in the High Castle* in *Amazing Stories*, June, 1964, p. 123. The Hugo is named after Hugo Gernsback, the pioneering founder of the first science fiction magazine, *Amazing Stories*, in 1926. Carter, *The Creation of Tomorrow*, p. 4.

62 *Entertainment Weekly* ranked "The City on the Edge of Forever" the number-one episode of all 303 that were ever produced. Fall, 1994, Special *Star Trek* issue. *TV Guide* in 1995 ranked the episode Nr. 68 in the top 100 "most memorable moments in TV history." *TV Guide*, July 1, 1975. Quoted in Harlan Ellison's *The City on the Edge of Forever* (Clarkston, GA, 1993), pp. 35, 277.

63 Review of *The Man in the High Castle* in *Amazing Stories*, June, 1964, p. 123. The novel was also called "a remarkable book" and a "veritable jewel." Avram Davidson, review of *The Man in the High Castle*, in *Fantasy and Science Fiction*, June, 1963, pp. 59–61; S. E. Cotts, review of *The Man in the High Castle* in *Amazing Stories*, February, 1963, pp. 119–20. The *New York Times* gave the novel a positive review, writing that the novel skillfully presented its basic "moral ... that things could always be worse." Review of *The Man in the High Castle* in the *New York Times Book Review*, October 28, 1962, p. 53.

64 Review of *The Ultimate Solution* in *Publishers Weekly*, March 19, 1973, p. 73.

65 This is suggested by its inclusion in Benford and Greenberg, *Hitler Victorious*.

66 "Hakenkreuz über New York," *Stern*, January 28, 1962, pp. 32–43, 85–89.

67 Ibid., pp. 37, 86. *Stern* described Shirer as "one of those who persecute us [Germans] with their hatred," p. 32.

68 Ibid., p. 38.

69 See Letters to the editor, *Look*, January, 1962, p. 9.

70 Ibid., p. 9.

71 This figure was cited in the *Stern* essay.

72 This sensibility was especially visible in both popular music and film. Notable examples include – to name merely a few – the music of the Beatles, Bob Dylan, and Joan Baez, and films like *M*A*S*H* (1970), *The Deer Hunter* (1978), and *Apocalypse Now* (1979). Doherty, pp. 282–86. While these works reflected the impact of the Vietnam War, fears of nuclear conflict found echo in the music of such rock groups as REM and films like *The Day After* (1983).

73 Bruce M. Russett, *No Clear and Present Danger: A Skeptical View of the U.S. Entry into World War II* (New York, 1972). Russett currently holds an endowed chair in political science at Yale University.

74 Ibid., pp. 20, 22.

75 As he wrote, "Germany probably would not have been defeated, though ... neither could it have won." Russett continued, "Probably World War II would have ended in some sort of draw ... or would have continued on for a decade or two with occasional truces ... [like] the Napoleonic Wars." Ibid., p. 30.

76 Ibid., p. 31.

77 As a result, "It would have been quite a while before Hitler could have marshalled the resources of Europe for any serious ... drive either east or west." Ibid., pp. 33–34.

78 Ibid., p. 40.

79 Ibid., p. 24.

80 Ibid., pp. 11–13.

81 Ibid., pp. 11–12.

82 Ibid., p. 42.

83 Ibid., pp. 41–42.

84 John Lukacs, "What if Hitler Had Won the Second World War?", in David Wallechinsky, ed., *The People's Almanac, #2* (New York, 1978), pp. 396–98.

85 *The People's Almanac* rose to number one on the trade-paperback bestseller list in early 1978. Review of *The People's Almanac, New York Times Book Review,* January 28, 1979, p. 16.

86 Other examples of Lukacs's humor include his depiction of Mussolini's son, Vittorio, marrying Betty Grable and Rudolf Hess petitioning to become an Englishman (and being renamed the Duke of Wessex). Lukacs, "What if Hitler Had Won?," p. 398.

87 Postcard from John Lukacs to author, February 21, 2002.

88 Lukacs's conservative credentials are documented in Patrick Allitt, *Catholic Intellectuals and Conservative Politics in America, 1950–1985* (Ithaca, 1993), especially pp. 64–66 and chapter 6. Lukacs is at heart a schismatic conservative who, as a result of disagreements with many American neoconservatives in particular, has preferred to call himself a "reactionary." Lukacs has long been associated with the "paleoconservative" journal, *Chronicles,* which has supported Patrick Buchanan for president.

89 Lukacs has been more critical of the Soviet/Russian domination of Europe than of communism as an ideology. In general, Lukacs argues that very few Eastern Europeans believed in communism after 1945, using it instead as a pretext for traditional imperialistic practices. For this reason, he has been critical of American

conservatives for harping on the communist menace during the cold war. For
the most recent articulation of this belief, see Lukacs's essay, "The Poverty of
Anti-Communism," *The National Interest*, spring, 1999.

90 Lukacs's book *The Hitler of History* took a fairly sympathetic view of
arch-conservative German historian Rainer Zitelmann's relativistic characterization of Hitler as a progressive revolutionary leader. Volker
Berghahn's review of the book in the *New York Times* expressed concerns
about this fact. "The Ultimate Modern," *New York Times*, November 9,
1997. Istvan Deak called the book "peculiar" in his review of it for the
New Republic, December 15, 1997, p. 37. At the same time, Lukacs has
been quite critical of Nazism. In his recent book, *Five Days in London:
May 1940* (New Haven, 1999), he criticized the revisionist claim of John
Charmley that Britain should have forged a separate peace with Germany
after the fall of France in 1940, declaring that "the greatest threat to
western civilization was not communism. It was National Socialism."
Lukacs, *Five Days in London*, pp. 217–18. As this statement directly contra-
dicts the entire thrust of Lukacs's *People's Almanac* essay, the best explanation is that his views on the relative dangers of communism and
Nazism changed with the end of the communist threat in 1989.

91 Linaweaver, *Moon of Ice* (New York, 1988).
92 Ibid., p. 100.
93 Ibid., p. 92.
94 Ibid., p. 196.
95 Ibid., pp. 246–48.
96 Linaweaver is quite open about his libertarian political beliefs. See "Brad
Linaweaver – Libertarian," www.self-gov.org/celebs/Linaweaver.html. Other
libertarian science fiction writers include Poul Anderson, James Hogan,
L. Neil Smith, Vernor Vinge, and F. Paul Wilson. See "LFS sponsors
convention," on the Libertarian party's web site, www.lp.org/lpnews/0104/
newsbriefs.html. The Libertarians sponsor a science fiction prize called the
Prometheus Award.

97 Linaweaver, pp. 90, 104.
98 Ibid., p. 15.
99 Ibid., p. 104.
100 Ibid., p. 18.
101 Ibid., p. 10.
102 Ibid., p. 116.
103 Linaweaver's turn towards conservative politics, as well as his interest in
Nazism, reflected the social and political tensions raging in America during
the Vietnam War. As he has put it, "In the early 1970s, I was in [the] Air Force
R. O. T. C. at Florida State University. Every Thursday we had to wear the
uniform all day. Every Thursday we were called Nazis all day. The shrillest
critics were members of the Young Socialist Alliance. One day I learned that the
full name of the Nazis was the National Socialist German Workers Party . . .
I couldn't stop noticing the word socialist. I became so confused that I began

researching the history of Nazi Germany." E-mail message from Brad Linaweaver to author, March 7, 2002.

104 Linaweaver, p. 8.

105 Ward Moore, "A Class with Dr. Chang," in Sandra Ley, ed., *Beyond Time* (New York, 1976).

106 Ibid., p. 135.

107 Ibid., p. 136.

108 Moore (1903–78) came to support leftwing politics early on in life. Expelled from his New York City high school for adhering to "Red" ideas, he assumed a variety of blue-collar jobs before settling on the career of a writer. He is best known for his classic alternate history of the South winning the Civil War, *Bring the Jubilee* (1953). See *Contemporary Authors*, Vol. CXIII (Detroit, 1985), p. 335; and also www.scifi.com/scifiction/classics/classics_archive/moore/moore_bio.html.

109 Ibid., p. 136. The phrase "America, love it or leave it" was popular among opponents of the antiwar movement, especially soldiers who painted it on their helmets in 1968. This phrase was a response to the leftwing motto, "Vietnam, love it or leave it." Richard Sennett, "A Nation's Narrative Written to an End," Index, July 27, 2003. www.indexonline.org/news/20030727_unitedstates.shtml

110 P. J. O'Rourke and Tod Carroll, "If World War II Had Been Fought Like the War in Vietnam," *National Lampoon*, October, 1980, pp. 54–57.

111 This panel reflects the common misperception that the famous photograph of people rushing to board an American helicopter in Saigon were themselves Americans. In fact, they were Vietnamese. "Getting It Wrong in a Photo," *New York Times*, April 23, 2000, cited at: www.mishalov.com/Vietnam_finalescape.html.

112 Born in 1947, O'Rourke was a baby-boomer who rejected his generation's embrace of leftwing politics. It is notable that the original idea for the essay was provided by a retired U.S. Marine, George S. Rickley. O'Rourke and Carroll, p. 54.

113 William Overgard, *The Divide* (New York, 1980).

114 Ibid., p. 64.

115 Ibid., p. 35.

116 Ibid., pp. 175, 209.

117 Ibid., p. 224.

118 Ibid., p. 161.

119 Ibid., p. 49.

120 Overgard (1926–90) was the author of several well-received novels, including *Shanghai Tango* (1987) and *A Few Good Men* (1988). See entry for Overgard in *Contemporary Authors Online*. The author seems to have distanced himself from *The Divide*, however, which is not listed among his works. One of the few clues that link the William Overgard of *The Divide* to the author of *Shanghai Tango* is the dedication of *The Divide* to Arthur Rankin, the producer of the 1980 film, *The Bushido Blade*, for which Overgard is listed as the screenwriter.

121 Overgard, p. 71

122 Ibid., p. 243.

123 David Dvorkin, *Budspy* (New York, 1987).

124 Ibid., p. 77.

125 Ibid., p. 63.

126 Ibid., p. 79.

127 As several newspaper headlines read, "Negro Districts in Atlanta Remain Calm" and "White Men are Still Unsafe in Parts of Oklahoma!" Ibid., p. 11.

128 When Chic first sees Germany's autobahns, he notes, "There was simply no comparison ... the American highways were only a poor, scaled-down imitation of the original." Ibid., p. 25.

129 Ibid., p. 79.

130 Ibid., p. 79.

131 Ibid., pp. 171, 130.

132 Ibid., p. 113.

133 Ibid., p. 182.

134 Dvorkin describes himself as "very liberal." Source: *Contemporary Authors Online*. The Gale Group, 1999.

135 E-mail message from Dvorkin to author, February 2, 2002.

136 Dvorkin, p. 190.

137 Dvorkin was born in 1943 in England, the son of Rabbi Israel Dvorkin. He spent time as a youth in South Africa and later emigrated to the United States, moving to Indiana, where he grew up and went to college. Source: *Contemporary Authors Online*. The Gale Group, 1999.

138 Dvorkin has openly described himself as an atheistic "ex-Jew" opposed to traditional Jewish religious and cultural practice. See his polemical essay "Why I am Not a Jew," a version of which was published in *Free Inquiry* magazine in 1990. www.csd.net/~dvorkin/yinotjew.htm.

139 As Dvorkin has noted, "I grew up hearing about the Holocaust [and] ... reached the point where I didn't want to hear about it again. I object to 'never forget.'" E-mail message from Dvorkin to author, February 2, 2002.

140 Dvorkin has written that, growing up, he found himself "responding with disturbing fascination to photographs of ranks of marching Nazi soldiers ... I felt the seductive pull of the Reich ... So I had a lot of demons of my own to exorcise." E-mail message from Dvorkin to author, February 2, 2002.

141 I am grateful to my colleague Harold Forsythe for alerting me to the existence of this episode.

142 E-mail message from Franken to author, May 1, 2002.

143 Review of *Budspy* in *Science Fiction Chronicle*, January, 1988, p. 48; Norman Spinrad, review of *Budspy* in *Isaac Asimov's Science Fiction*, November, 1988, p. 184. Another reviewer praised it as an "involving ... thriller." Review of *Budspy* in *Booklist*, October 15, 1987, p. 363. The reviewer for the *Denver Post* said he "enjoyed it." Don C. Thompson, review of *Budspy*, the *Denver Post*, November 15, 1987, Books, p. 21.

144 *The Encyclopedia of Science Fiction*, p. 24. Review of *Budspy* in Robert A. Collins and Robert Latham, eds., *Science Fiction and Fantasy Book Review Annual*, 1988 (Westport, 1989), pp. 160–61.

145 Norman Spinrad, review of *Budspy* in *Isaac Asimov's Science Fiction*, November, 1988, pp. 185–86.

146 Heinlein's blurb appears on the front cover of the paperback edition of the novel. Review of *Moon of Ice* in *Publishers Weekly*, December 25, 1987, p. 65. This reviewer noted, however, that "Linaweaver's relegating [of] the Holocaust to a small corner of his sometimes comic opera plot is sure to offend some." Review of *Moon of Ice* in *Science Fiction Chronicle*, January, 1988, p. 48.

147 Robert H. Ferrell, review of *No Clear and Present Danger*, *Political Science Quarterly*, September, 1973, p. 492; review of *No Clear and Present Danger*, *The Nation*, July 16, 1973, p. 60; Thomas Bailey, review of *No Clear and Present Danger*, *AHR*, April, 1974, p. 608.

148 Review of *Moon of Ice* in Robert A. Collins and Robert Latham, eds., *Science Fiction and Fantasy Book Review Annual*, 1988 (Westport, 1989), pp. 325–26. Bill Collins called the novel "a browbeating of the reader with political science lectures." Morton Tenzer, review of *No Clear and Present Danger*, *American Political Science Review*, March, 1976, pp. 293–94. See also the critical review by John Lewis Gaddis: review of *No Clear and Present Danger* in *Military Affairs*, December, 1973, p. 160. See the response by Russett in the March 1977 issue, p. 276. See also Thomas Bailey, review of *No Clear and Present Danger*, *AHR*, April, 1974, p. 608; Daniel Smith, review of *No Clear and Present Danger*, *Journal of American History*, September, 1973, pp. 503–04.

149 The co-writer of the sketch, Al Franken, has observed, "I think the complaints were specific to the headline in the sketch, which was something to the effect: 'Überman kills several thousand Jews – total now over 6 million.'" E-mail message from Franken to author, May 1, 2002. It is worth noting that this line in the skit got few laughs from the live audience.

150 This view was already beginning to emerge at the time of the fortieth anniversary celebrations of the war in the early to mid-1980s. See Jonathan Yardley, "The Way Things Weren't in WWII: Our National Delusions of the Last 'Good' War," *Washington Post*, June 11, 1984, p. B1.

151 Arthur M. Schlesinger, Jr., *The Disuniting of America: Reflections on a Multicultural Society* (New York, 1998).

152 Leo Rutman, *Clash of Eagles* (New York, 1990).

153 Ibid., p. 530.

154 E-mail message from Rutman to author, October 21, 2002.

155 Christy Campbell, "The Shrinking of *Fatherland*," *Sunday Telegraph*, June 26, 1994, p. 5. Harris also surmised that HBO might not have wanted to besmirch the reputation of the powerful Kennedy family. Cited in John Lyttle, "Hitler: Back on Screen," *Independent*, November 24, 1994, p. 31.

156 Newt Gingrich and William Forstchen, *1945* (Riverdale, NY, 1995).

157 Mayhew is depicted as falling into the clutches of a sexually ravenous German spy named Erica. Ibid., pp. 2–3, 129.

158 Ibid., p. 134.

159 Ibid., pp. 125, 336.

160 Why a politician like Gingrich undertook to write a science fiction book is explained by the fact that he is a big science fiction buff who has made frequent appearances at sci-fi conventions. See Maureen Dowd, "Newt's Potboiler," *New York Times*, December 4, 1994, Section 6, p. 44.

161 This astute point is made in Fred Smoler's review, "A Sci-Fi History of WWII Offers a New Take on an Old Story," *Los Angeles Times*, August 1, 1995, p. E4.

162 Gingrich and Forstchen, p. 125.

163 Ibid., p. 92.

164 Ibid., pp. 365–66.

165 See Tom Brokaw, *The Greatest Generation* (New York, 1998).

166 Arthur Rhodes, *The Last Reich* (Danbury, CT, 2001). Rhodes is the pen name of retired bond trader Clem Schaefer (born in 1935). In writing the book, Rhodes has declared his desire not to portray the Nazis as horrific demons, but rather as incompetent "buffoons." Phone interview with Clem Schaefer, April 7, 2003.

167 J. N. Stroyar, *The Children's War* (New York, 2001). Stroyar extended this plot line in her sequel to *The Children's War*, *A Change of Regime* (Authorhouse [online publisher], 2004).

168 Harry Turtledove, *In the Presence of Mine Enemies* (New York, 2003). This novel was a substantially lengthened version of an older short story by the same name. See Harry Turtledove, "In the Presence of Mine Enemies," in Harry Turtledove, *Departures* (New York, 1993), pp. 200–17.

169 Turtledove, *In the Presence of Mine Enemies*, pp. 182, 202.

170 Ibid., p. 353.

171 Ibid., pp. 439–40.

172 The distinction between Nazis and Germans is non-existent in Turtledove's account, as all Germans (save the few Jews who remain) identify with and support the Nazi system.

173 Ibid., p. 440.

174 Patrick J. Buchanan, *A Republic, Not an Empire: Reclaiming America's Destiny* (Washington, D.C., 1999).

175 Buchanan blamed American intervention in World War I for the rise of Nazism, writing, "The war to make the world safe for democracy made the world safe for Bolshevism, fascism, and Nazism." Buchanan, p. 219. Had the United States stayed out of the war and allowed Germany to escape without being defeated, he wrote, "a strong ... Germany would not have spawned a Hitler. There might have been no Holocaust, no quarter-century reign of Stalin, no Cold War." Buchanan, p. 218.

176 Ibid., p. 278.

177 Ibid., p. 266.

178 Ibid., p. 266.

179 Ibid., p. 297.

180 Buchanan specifically relied on William Henry Chamberlin's *America's Second Crusade* (Chicago, 1950).

181 Buchanan, p. 262.

182 Ibid., p. 276.

183 Stephan Courtois, et al., eds., *The Black Book of Communism: Crimes, Terror, Repression* (Cambridge, MA, 1999).

184 "By the late 1940s Americans had concluded that a Soviet invasion of western Europe ... could tilt the balance of power against us; and the communists had declared that their ultimate enemy in this struggle was the United States." Buchanan, p. 310.

185 A. Edward Cooper, *Triumph of the Third Reich* (Salt Lake City, 1999).

186 As Minister of Economics Walther Funk notes, "The simple fact is ... that we won the war ... but lost the peace." Cooper, *Triumph of the Third Reich*, p. 248.

187 That this scenario did not necessarily have to challenge the belief in interventionism was indicated by Harry Turtledove's *In the Presence of Mine Enemies*, which validated interventionism while portraying the Nazis reforming their regime from above.

188 http://utahbooks.com/Third_Reich_Alternate_History.htm. This is further suggested by a reader's observation on amazon.com, submitted on August 2, 1999.

189 Cooper, *Triumph of the Third Reich*, p. 211.

190 Philip Roth, *The Plot against America* (New York, 2004).

191 Roth, p. 325.

192 Roth's portrayal of Lindbergh attacking American Jews as warmongers eager to fight against Nazi Germany no doubt reflected the author's fear that American Jews could be seen as the primary lobbyists for war against Iraq and would be scapegoated if the war's outcome was worse than expected.

193 The novels by Leo Rutman, Arthur Rhodes, and A. Edward Cooper received little critical attention. Rutman's *Clash of Eagles* (New York, 1990), however, did sell over 100,000 copies in paperback. E-mail message from Rutman to author, October 21, 2002.

194 Dusty Saunders, review of *Fatherland*, *Denver Rocky Mountain News*, November 28, 1994, p. 10D. One of the more positive reviews was by Ray Loynd, "Provocative Journey into the 'Fatherland,'" *Los Angeles Times*, November 26, 1994, p. 21.

195 David Bianculli, review of *Fatherland*, in *Baltimore Sun*, November 26, 1994, p. 6D. See also Robert Bianco, "If Hitler Had Won," *Pittsburgh Post-Gazette*, November 25, 1994, p. 26.

196 Tom Shales, "HBO's *Fatherland*, A Pale Thriller," *Washington Post*, November 26, 1994, p. B1.

197 Matt Roush, "'Fatherland' falters," *USA Today*, November 25, 1994, p. 3D.

198 Joseph Gelmis, review of *The Philadelphia Experiment II*, *Newsday*, November 12, 1993, p. 73, in *Film Review Annual* (Englewood, NJ, 1994), p. 1117; Stephen Holden, "Back to a Big 'What If' in '43," *New York Times*,

November 13, 1993; Bill Hoffman, review of *The Philadelphia Experiment II*, *New York Post*, November 12, 1993, p. 36, in *Film Review Annual* (Englewood, NJ, 1994), pp. 1116–17. *Variety* criticized the film for its "humdrum action plot," while the *Hollywood Reporter* termed it "dark, murky, and slow." See reviews of the film in *Variety*, November 29, 1993 and the *Hollywood Reporter*, November 15, 1993.

199 Harry Levins, "Newt's Improbable Novel has Nazis Wage War in '46," *St. Louis Post-Dispatch*, July 30, 1995, p. 5C; Jonathan Yardley, "Stick to Politics, Mr. Speaker," *Washington Post*, July 12, 1995, p. D2.

200 Joan Didion called it a "primitive example of . . . 'alternate history.'" Joan Didion, "The Teachings of Speaker Gingrich," *New York Review of Books*, August 10, 1995, p. 7. Even conservative publications like the *National Review* offered tepid reviews of the book. James Bowman, review of *1945*, *National Review*, October 23, 1995, p. 62.

201 Sandra McElwaine, "Newt Romances the Reich," *Washington Monthly*, September, 1995, p. 45H; Bruce Franklin, "Only the Hardware is Erotic," *The Nation*, August 14/21, 1995, pp. 174–75.

202 David Streitfeld, "Pulp Fiction: Gingrich's Novel A Disastrous Flop," *Washington Post*, August 2, 1996, p. B1.

203 Jonathan Yardley, "Stick to Politics, Mr. Speaker," *Washington Post*, July 12, 1995, p. D2; Susan Larson, "Sex, Violence, and Newtity," *Times-Picayune*, July 2, 1995, p. E7.

204 An exception was the claim of one reviewer that Gingrich and Forstchen offered up a "sanitized view of Nazi Germany [that] might well be retitled Romancing the Reich." Sandra McElwaine, "Newt Romances the Reich," *Washington Monthly*, September, 1995, p. 45

205 Boyd Tonkin, "Newt Lays Down the Law," *New Statesman and Society*, August 11, 1995, p. 40. Tonkin added that "*1945* makes Robert Harris's *Fatherland* look like Tolstoy." Other British reviewers came up with highly creative methods of condemning the novel. Thus, one said that, "To call this bird a turkey would be to do grave injustice to a dignified . . . bird." John Naughton, "Newt's 15-Pound Turkey," *Observer*, August 13, 1995, p. 15.

206 John Judis, "The Buchanan Doctrine," *New York Times Book Review*, October 3, 1999, p. 16.

207 Adam Cohen, "Foreign Policy from the Fringe," *Time Magazine*, September 27, 1999, p. 46.

208 The work of historian Norm Goda was cited explicitly in Michael Kelly's review, "Republican Stunts," *Washington Post*, October 6, 1999, p. A33.

209 Michael Lind, "Minority of One," *Los Angeles Times Book Review*, October 3, 1999, p. 8.

210 Francis X. Clines, "Buchanan's Views on Hitler Create a Reform Party Stir," *New York Times*, September 21, 1999, p. 22.

211 Cited in Phil Brennan, "The Buchanan Factor," www.buchanan.org/no–99–1003-ezo-brennan.html. Accessed October 7, 2002.

212 The overwhelming majority of readers' reviews on amazon.com's web site were supportive of the book. A recent survey of the readers' reviews reveals 103 supportive reviews and 27 critical reviews (roughly a four-to-one ratio). See www.amazon.com.

213 Review of *In the Presence of Mine Enemies, Publishers Weekly,* October 20, 2003, p. 39.

214 Ibid.; Adam-Troy Castro, review of *In the Presence of Mine Enemies.* www. scifi.com/sfw/issue351/books.html.

215 Review by Patrick Devenny, January 28, 2004; www.amazon.com.

CHAPTER 3: GERMANY'S WARTIME TRIUMPH: FROM DYSTOPIA TO NORMALCY

1 *Wenn das der Führer wüsste* was published in the United States in 1968 under the title *The Twilight Men.* All quotes from the novel have been taken from this version. Otto Basil, *The Twilight Men* (New York, 1968), pp. 3, 5, 12, 18.

2 Altogether, this study examines twenty-seven British accounts, twenty-eight American accounts, and six German accounts. See Appendix.

3 During the Nazi era itself, scattered future histories appeared that portrayed the Nazis triumphing over their racial enemies through military conquest. For a discussion, see Jost Hermand, *Old Dreams of a New Reich: Volkisch Utopias and National Socialism* (Bloomington, IN, 1992), especially pp. 246–62, for a discussion of Nazi science fiction novels.

4 Basil, p. 204.

5 Ibid., p. 198.

6 Ibid., pp. 228–29.

7 For a detailed introduction to Basil, see Volker Kaukoreit und Wendelin Schmidt-Dengler, eds., *Otto Basil und die Literatur um 1945* (Vienna, 1998).

8 Joe Julius Heydecker and Johannes Leeb, *Der Nürnberger Prozess; Bilanz der tausend Jahre* (Cologne, 1958). Contained in Basil's papers in Vienna are several underlined newspaper articles digesting the latest revelations from the Nuremberg trials. See, for example, "Der Nürnberger Prozess: Ihr Endziel: Weltreich bis zum Ural," *Abendzeitung,* no date; "Der Nürnberger Prozess: Die Deutschen müssen ein Volk von Nichtrauchern und Vegetariern werden!" (no date), in Nachlass Otto Basil: Signatur ÖLA: 52/W1/2; Gruppe 1.1.1.1.

9 Basil was also very interested in scientific advances in such fields as laser technology, synthetic drug production, and radiation research. He collected numerous newspaper and magazine articles on all of these themes. See Nachlass Otto Basil: Signatur ÖLA: 52/W1/2; Gruppe 1.1.1.1.

10 Otto Basil, "Kleiner Idiotenführer durch den 'Führer,'" no date (but most likely 1967), pp. 1–2. Nachlass Otto Basil: Signatur ÖLA: 52/W1/4.

11 Some were reluctant to take on the work, which was originally entitled *Wagenburg Deutschland,* because of its controversial depiction of a character

called "the arch Jew of the Third Reich." Eckhard Mahovsky, "Den befreienden Schüssen entgegen," *Express*, October 15, 1966, p. 8.

12 Basil, "Kleiner Idiotenführer," p. 2.

13 Ibid., p. 2.

14 Basil, *The Twilight Men*, introductory blurb, no page number.

15 F. K., review of *Wenn das der Führer wüsste* in *Die Wiener Zeitung*, November 11, 1966. Basil notes that some reviewers mistook his preface as a sign that he was a "negative figure, that is, a bad guy." Basil, "Kleiner Idiotenführer," p. 2.

16 Otto Fuchs, "Wenn das der Führer wüßte!" *Deutsche Volkszeitung*, December 22/23, 1966, p. 19; Christian Ferber, "Chaos auf dem Marsch," *Die Welt der Literatur*, September 22, 1966, p. 16. Other favorable reviews include "Endsieg und braune Walpurgisnacht," *Die Arbeiterzeitung*, November 13, 1966. Today, *Wenn das der Führer wüsste* ranks as one of the few "examples of a critical attempt to master the Nazi past in German science fiction." Klaus W. Pietrek, "Otto Basil (1901–1983), *Wenn das der Führer wüßte*," in Franz Rottensteiner and Michael Koseler, eds., *Werkführer durch die phantastische Literatur* (Augsburg, 1989–2000), p. 3.

17 The figure of 25,000 copies is cited in Mahovsky, p. 8. Otto Fuchs, meanwhile, reported that the "book proved itself to be a bestseller at the Frankfurt Book Fair" of 1966. Otto Fuchs, p. 19. The reissuing of the novel as a paperback by the Moewig Verlag in 1981 further attests to its popularity.

18 Fuchs, p. 19. Another reviewer of the novel wrote that the premise of Hitler winning the war should be used "to cure incorrigibles." Hans Daiber, "Thema zu vergeben," *Frankfurter Allgemeine Zeitung*, February 18, 1967.

19 Ferber, "Chaos," p. 16.

20 Helmut Heissenbüttel, "Wenn Adolf Hitler den Krieg nicht gewonnen hätte: Eine Phantasie," in *Wenn Adolf Hitler den Krieg nicht gewonnen hätte: Historische Novellen und wahre Begebenheiten. Projekt 3/2* (Stuttgart, 1979), pp. 7–17.

21 Heissenbüttel, p. 16.

22 See Hayden White, "Historical Emplotment and the Problem of Truth," in Saul Friedlander, ed., *Probing the Limits of Representation: Nazism and the 'Final Solution'* (Cambridge, MA, 1992), p. 40.

23 Heissenbüttel, p. 7.

24 Ibid., p. 17.

25 Ernst Neff, "Immer dorthin wohin man nicht kommt," in Christina Weiss, ed., *Schrift, écriture, geschrieben, gelesen: Für Helmut Heissenbüttel zum siebzigsten Geburtstag* (Stuttgart, 1991), p. 59.

26 See the obituary for Heissenbüttel in the *Süddeutsche Zeitung*, September 21, 1996.

27 Heissenbüttel's widow, Ida, lists these concerns as having been important to him at the time. Letter from Ida Heissenbüttel to author, May 26, 2001.

28 Most of the reviews largely praised its literary ambitions and qualities. See, among others, "Ein pedantischer Anarchist," *Die Zeit*, February 22, 1980; Karl

Riha, "Fikten und Fakten," *Frankfurter Rundschau*, October 9, 1979; Jörg Drews, "Anbieten, was widerrufen wird," *Die Süddeutsche Zeitung*, November 7, 1979; Elisabeth Andres, "Leben ohne Leben," *Deutsche Zeitung*, November 20, 1979, p. 30.

29 "Zu den Wurzeln des Faschismus," *Die Arbeiterzeitung*, January 19, 1980; Veit Hase, "Vertrackter Titel, vertrackte These," *Playboy*, November, 1979.

30 Arno Lubos, *Schwiebus: Ein deutscher Roman* (Munich, 1980).

31 Ibid., p. 169.

32 Ibid., p. 43.

33 Ibid., p. 96.

34 Ibid., p. 241.

35 Ibid., p. 250.

36 Ibid., p. 250.

37 Ibid., p. 252.

38 Ibid., p. 261.

39 Ibid., p. 192.

40 Ibid., p. 171.

41 Ibid., pp. 248–49.

42 Ibid., p. 252.

43 Ibid., pp. 346–47.

44 Ibid., p. 456.

45 Ibid., pp. 601–02.

46 I am grateful to Arno Lubos for providing me with a detailed summary of his biography. Letter from Arno Lubos to author, August 23, 2002.

47 Letter from Arno Lubos to author, August 23, 2002.

48 Letter from Arno Lubos to author, July 20, 2002.

49 Letter from Arno Lubos to author, August 23, 2002.

50 K. H. Kramberg praised the novel as a "realistic" work that "frequently achieved the tension of a perfidiously conceived thriller." K. H. Kramberg, "Im 4. Jahrzehnt nach dem Endsieg," *Süddeutsche Zeitung*, June 6, 1981. Horst Köpke, "Der Einzelne hat eine Chance," *Frankfurter Rundschau*, January 10, 1981, literature supplement, p. 4; Hartmut Binder, "Im Netz der Sicherheitsorgane," *Stuttgarter Zeitung*, April 11, 1981, p. 50; Ingeborg Drewitz, "Ein deutscher Alptraum," *Tagesspiegel*, May 10, 1981, p. 63; Rudolf Bartsch, "Zum Glück gewannen wir ihn nicht," *Frankfurter Allgemeine Zeitung*, July 17, 1981, p. 26.

51 Hellmut Diwald, "In den Wäldern selig verschollen," *Nürnberger Zeitung*, November 22, 1980. Köpke, p. 4.

52 Drewitz, p. 63.

53 See reviews by Binder, Drewitz, Köpke, and Kramberg.

54 Ralph Giordano, *Wenn Hitler den Krieg gewonnen hätte: Die Pläne der Nazis nach dem Endsieg* (Hamburg, 1989).

55 Merely the monumental expansion of Munich and Nuremberg would have required four times the annual granite production of France, Italy, and the Scandinavian countries combined. Ibid., p. 111.

56 Ibid., p. 165.

57 Ibid., p. 176.

58 See Giordano's autobiographical novel *Die Bertinis* (Frankfurt, 1982) and his non-fiction work *Die zweite Schuld: Von der Last Deutscher zu sein* (Hamburg, 1987).

59 Giordano, *Wenn Hitler den Krieg gewonnen hätte*, p. 10.

60 It sold 80,000 copies in its first twenty weeks. Figure cited in *Time International*, Februrary 12, 1990.

61 Jochen Thies called the book a "singular annoyance" for drawing so heavily on the secondary research of previous scholars (such as himself) without contributing any of his own original spade-work. Jochen Thies, "Ein einziges Ärgernis," *Frankfurter Allgemeine Zeitung*, October 9, 1989, p. 14.

62 Volker Ullrich, " . . . und morgen die ganze Welt," *Die Zeit*, October 20, 1989, p. 63.

63 Arno Weckenbecker, "Erst Europa, dann die Welt . . . ," *Das Parlament*, December 22/29, 1989, p. 19.

64 Alexander Demandt, "Wenn Hitler gewonnen hätte?" *Tango*, Nr. 18, 1995, pp. 20–27.

65 Ibid., pp. 23–24.

66 Ibid.

67 Ibid., p. 24.

68 Ibid., pp. 24–25.

69 Ibid., p. 25.

70 Ibid., p. 26.

71 Ibid., pp. 26–27.

72 Ibid., p. 27.

73 Ibid.

74 Ibid.

75 Ibid., p. 22.

76 Ibid., pp. 25, 26.

77 Ibid., p. 22.

78 Ibid., p. 23.

79 Ibid., p. 27.

80 Demandt's support for reunification is visible in his 1993 book, *History That Never Happened*, in which he declared that "the German question remains open as long as the Brandenburg Gate remains closed." Demandt also wistfully noted that if Hitler had never come to power, "Germany might still be flourishing from the Maas to the Memel." Demandt, *History That Never Happened*, pp. 149, 109.

81 Demandt, "Wenn Hitler gewonnen hätte?" p. 27.

82 Ibid.

83 See Bill Niven, *Facing the Nazi Past: United Germany and the Legacy of the Third Reich* (New York, 2002), pp. 95–118.

84 Demandt, "Wenn Hitler gewonnen hätte?", p. 25.

85 Ibid., p. 26.

86 Ibid., p. 27.
87 Niven, chapter 2; Stefan Berger, *The Search for Normalcy: National Identity and Historical Consciousness in Germany since 1800* (Providence, 1997), chapter 7.
88 Demandt, "Wenn Hitler gewonnen hätte?" p. 23.
89 Ibid., p. 24.
90 Ibid.
91 Joachim Rohloff, "Neues vom Endsieg," *Konkret*, July, 1995. I would like to thank Matthias Seeberg for sending me a copy of this essay. See also Detlef Kuhlbrodt, "Ratlosigkeit, etc.," which linked Demandt to rightwing political circles. *Tageszeitung*, May 20, 1995, p. 14.
92 Rohloff, p. 50.
93 Michael Salewski, "N. N.: *Der großgermanische Seekrieg gegen Japan und die USA im Jahre 1949. The Near Miss:* Eine Buchbesprechung," in Michael Salewski, ed., *Was wäre, wenn: Alternativ- und Parallelgeschichte: Brücken zwischen Phantasie und Wirklichkeit* (Stuttgart, 1999).
94 Ibid., p. 158.
95 Ibid., p. 158.
96 Ibid., p. 153.
97 Berger, p. 188. Salewski is also a former member of the German navy, a subject to which he has devoted a good deal of scholarly research.
98 Of the more than 100 alternate histories on the Third Reich that have appeared since 1945, Germans have produced around 15 percent. See Appendix.
99 See www.maasmedia.net/bubizin/slayer.htm.
100 "Stimmen der Woche," *Die Woche*, June 16, 1994, p. 32.
101 The works include Katharine Burdekin's *Swastika Night*, translated as *Nacht der braunen Schatten* (Münster, 1995), Robert Harris's *Fatherland*, translated as *Vaterland* (Munich, 1994), Philip K. Dick's *The Man in the High Castle*, translated as *Das Orakel vom Berge* (Munich, 2000), Len Deighton's *SS-GB*, translated under the same title (Vienna, 1980), Fred Allhoff's *Lightning in the Night*, translated as *Blitzkrieg: Die Nazi-Invasion in Amerika* (Munich, 1984), Harry Mulisch's *De toekomst van gisteren*, translated as *Die Zukunft von gestern* (Berlin, 1995). Other works include Stephen Fry's *Making History*, translated as *Geschichte machen* (Munich, 1999), Jerry Yulsman's *Elleander Morning*, translated under the same title (Munich, 1986), and Norman Spinrad's *The Iron Dream*, translated as *Der stählerne Traum* (Munich, 1994).
102 The belief that *Fatherland* had done this even drove the German ambassador to England to complain to *The Sunday Times* (Harris's employer) for running a promotional article about the book. See "Holocaust für Horror-Freunde," *Der Spiegel*, September 21, 1992.
103 This was the assessment of the reviewer in *Die Zeit*, quoted in Josef Joffe, "Wenn Hitler den Krieg gewonnen hätte," *Süddeutsche Zeitung*, October 2, 1992, p. 132. For other remarks see Bardo Fassbender, "Welche Geschichten dürfen über Nazis erzählt werden? *Fatherland* – ein politisch unkorrekter Roman," in *Die Neue Rundschau* (Berlin, 1995), pp. 61–62.

104 Fassbender, p. 60; "Auf der Hakenkreuz-Jagd," *Süddeutsche Zeitung*, December 30, 1993.

105 Joffe, p. 132; Philip Sherwell, "The Churchill Controversy," *Sunday Telegraph*, January 10, 1993, p. 18. Harris's book sold well among rightwing Germans.

106 The book sold 60,000 copies. Fassbender, p. 65.

107 "Frank Castorf für Uraufführung von 'Vaterland' ausgebuht," *Deutsche Presse-Agentur (DPA) – Europadienst*, April 21, 2000; Joachim Rohloff, "Lachen mit Eichmann wie Frank Castorf aus Robert Harris' Roman »Vaterland« einen Witz auf Auschwitz machte," *Konkret*, June, 2000.

108 See review of *Fatherland* by hjreyer@kdvz-frechen.de, dated February 9, 2001 and review by "aus Köln; NRW" dated September 13, 1999 at www.amazon.de.

CHAPTER 4: OTHER NATIONS: A DISSENTING VIEW

1 Randolph Robban, *Wenn Deutschland gesiegt hätte* (Stuttgart, 1951).

2 For France, see, most notably, the work of Alain Paris, who produced a ten-volume series of science fiction books that invoke the premise of the Nazis winning World War II. Perhaps the most prominent contemporary Russian writer to utilize allohistorical scenarios in his "surrealistic science fiction" is Vladimir Sorokin, whose two novels *A Month in Dachau* (1994) and *Blue Lard* (1999) employ the premise of a world in which the Nazis won World War II. For a profile, see Jamey Gambrell, "Russia's New Vigilantes," *New York Review of Books*, January 16, 2003, pp. 40–43. See also Dmitry Oleinikov and Sergei Kudryashov, "What If Hitler Had Defeated Russia?" *History Today*, May, 1995, pp. 67–70. Israeli writer Uri Avnery has written several alternate history tales that utilize the theme of a Nazi triumph. Norwegian writer Sjur Hermansen has made use of the theme as well, as has Czech writer Frantisek Novotny and Polish writer Marek Pakcinski.

3 I have used the German translation of the book.

4 Ibid., p. 276.

5 Robban claimed throughout the novel that it "parodied the Allies as well as the Germans." Ibid., p. 5.

6 As the narrator says, "Doubtless ... inhuman deeds were perpetrated by both sides. Doubtless the Allied bombing raids caused the destruction of numerous open cities ... and killed hundreds of thousands of women, children, and elderly ... But did not the National Socialists do the same if not worse in their death camps? Nobody risks speaking of these things today." Ibid., p. 159. Robban further indicated his scorn for the trials by giving the main German prosecutor the surname "Hypocrite" (in German *Heuchler*).

7 This is made clear with the (ironic) remark by the narrator's French colleague, M. Tatillerand, that "if only Stalin had won [the war], he would never have violated the holy rights of human beings in such brutal a fashion." Ibid., p. 88.

8 In the novel, a significant minority of Americans are depicted as rallying to the cause of totalitarianism, while the majority "fall silent and subordinate themselves externally to Nazi rules ... in order to avoid worse dangers." Ibid., pp. 51–52.

9 Ibid., p. 194.

10 Ibid., chapter 16, pp. 191–220.

11 Robban vigorously guarded his true identity, declaring in the book's preface, "Why so many [false] suppositions about the author? ... I am a Sycambrian and have served my country in various forgeign delegations. I was a diplomatic observer in Vichy ... at the Sycambrian embassy. After the occupation of my country by an army of liberation I departed and became a political emigrant. That is all." Ibid., p. 6.

12 See, for example, the review by Robert Ingrim, who in *Christ und Welt* praised the novel as an antidote against Allied "self-satisfaction." Excerpt cited on book jacket of *Wenn Deutschland gesiegt hätte*.

13 All quotes from the novel come from the German translation, Harry Mulisch, *Die Zukunft von gestern: Betrachtungen über einen ungeschriebenen Roman* (Munich, 1995).

14 Mulisch, pp. 191–93.

15 Ibid., pp. 159–61.

16 Ibid., p. 155.

17 Ibid., p. 156.

18 Ibid., pp. 152, 162.

19 Ibid., p. 169.

20 That Mulisch's mother was Jewish helps explain his moral revulsion towards Nazism.

21 Ramaker tells Textor, "If Germany had lost the war ... the world would not be equivalent to that which exists today, it would not *be* in the same way that it is now different. Things would not be so much better for people – although doubtless also that, but above all different." Ibid., p. 166.

22 Mulisch wrote, "True to cannibalistic principles, America internally began to transform itself into ... Nazi Germany, while outside of its borders, it continued the Japanese war of conquest in Asia." Ibid., p. 42. Mulisch writes how he became "a-american" during the cold war. Ibid., p. 39.

23 Ibid., p. 145.

24 Ibid., p. 20.

25 Ibid., p. 156.

26 As he put it, the "fixation on the Second World War" was a "sickness" that blinded people to the crimes of today, whereas someone who has been "healed" or "never been made sick by Nazism" is able to "busy themselves with what is going on in the world today," "for example, the events in southeast Asia, which are comparable to Auschwitz." Ibid., pp. 121–22. Another reason for Mulisch's failure to complete the novel was his recognition of the limits of representing Nazism. As he put it, "the thousand-year Reich is an image of impossibility" that led to the "impossibility of depiction." Ibid., pp. 173–74.

CHAPTER 5: THE FUGITIVE FÜHRER AND THE SEARCH
FOR JUSTICE

1 Philippe van Rjndt, *The Trial of Adolf Hitler* (New York, 1978), pp. 30, 33–34.
2 Twenty of the twenty-nine works discussed in this chapter (68 percent) were produced by Americans. The next highest number is four, produced by British authors (14 percent). See Appendix.
3 Alternate histories have varied in the ways they have held Hitler accountable for his crimes. In some accounts, Hitler is formally brought to justice through legal means (i.e. the holding of an actual trial). In others, Hitler is subjected to more personal and brutal means of punishment or vengeance. In this chapter, I use "justice" and "vengeance" interchangeably while remaining aware of the conceptual distinctions between them.
4 Of the twenty-nine postwar accounts portraying Hitler's survival, sixteen have depicted him eluding justice, while thirteen have shown him being brought to justice. This might seem to be a comparable number at first glance, but such apparent equality is deceptive. First, the date of their appearance suggests a general pattern of normalization. In the 1950s, four works ("The Strange Fate of Adolph Hitler," "The Man Who Could Be Hitler," "The Wandering Gentile," and *The Master Plan of Fu Manchu*) depicted Hitler being brought to justice, while none depicted him eluding justice. In the 1960s, three works (*They Saved Hitler's Brain, Flesh Feast*, and *He Lives*) depicted him being brought to justice; while two works (*Night Conspirators* and "He's Alive") depicted him eluding justice. In the 1970s and 1980s, three works (by Van Rjndt, Marino, and Heywood) depicted Hitler being brought to justice, while seven (by Aldiss, Fadiman, Goss, Steiner, Boulle, Choquette, and Grayson) showed him eluding justice. Since 1989, seven works (by Erickson, Nathanson and Bank, Krakow, Hershey, Mueller-Stahl, Moers Vol. I, and Moers Vol. II) have depicted him eluding justice, while three (by Malzberg, Charnay, and Spiller) have depicted him being brought to justice. Secondly, throughout the postwar period, the works depicting Hitler eluding justice have been characterized by a much higher degree of overall quality and prominence than those depicting him being brought to justice. Of the thirteen accounts bringing Hitler to justice, four were substantial (i.e. full-length novels), four were much less substantial short stories or essays, three were universally panned films, and two were comic books. Of the authors of these accounts, moreover, few enjoyed high-profile reputations in the mainstream cultural realm. By contrast, of the sixteen accounts depicting Hitler's evasion of justice, eleven were substantial (i.e. full-length novels, films, plays, or comic books) and only four were brief short stories. Moreover, nearly all of the authors of these accounts enjoyed prominent reputations in the mainstream cultural realm. See Appendix.
5 Of course, the nightmare that Hitler's postwar survival might possibly lead history to turn out for the worse could also express a sense of contentment with the present as the best of all possible worlds. The ability of the scenario – as a

nightmare – to validate the present, however, was muted by its simultaneous status as a fantasy which expressed dissatisfaction with the present. Moreover, the scenario's nightmare status was diminished by the fact that most accounts (being secret histories) never actually depict the world taking a turn for the worse because of Hitler's survival.

6 Donald M. McKale's *Hitler: The Survival Myth* (New York, 1981) offers the most thorough survey of the survival myth. Historians have long strived to debunk the myth. One of the first to do so was Hugh R. Trevor-Roper, whose classic study from 1947, *The Last Days of Hitler*, unambiguously affirmed the dictator's death. Hugh R. Trevor-Roper, *The Last Days of Hitler* (New York, 1947). More recent efforts, such as Ada Petrova and Peter Watson's *The Death of Hitler: The Full Story, with New Evidence from Secret Russian Archives* (New York, 1996) have drawn upon long-hidden documentary evidence in Soviet archives to cast light upon the dictator's last days. Hugh Thomas's *The Murder of Adolf Hitler: The Truth about the Bodies in the Berlin Bunker* (New York, 1996) claims that Hitler was strangled and that Eva Braun escaped. See also Wolfgang Bihl, *Der Tod Adolf Hitlers: Fakten und Überlebenslegenden* (Vienna, 2000).

7 The Soviet Union promoted the myth of Hitler's survival for both internal and external political reasons. Internally, Stalin instructed Marshal Zhukov on June 9, 1945 to announce Hitler's possible escape in order to neutralize the general's burgeoning popularity in Russia by effectively blaming him for failing to capture the Führer. Externally, asserting Hitler's survival also helped the Soviets justify their continuing occupation of the eastern zone of Germany for reasons of security. McKale, pp. 49–58.

8 See McKale, chapter 8.

9 The *Simpsons* episode was entitled "Bart versus Australia" and originally aired on February 19, 1995 featured Hitler receiving phone calls in Chile. See www.snpp.com/guides/foreign.html. Hitler's encounter with Howard the Duck appeared in issue Nr. 4 of the magazine version of the comic book from March 1980. The Clash song "White Man in the Hammersmith Palais" includes the lines "All over people changing their votes/ Along with their overcoats/ If Adolf Hitler flew in today/ They'd send a limousine anyway." www.geocities.com/SunsetStrip/Palladium/1028/lyr_complete_lyrics_10.html. A recent issue of *All Hitler Comics* depicted Hitler surviving in cyberspace as a computer virus. See the issue entitled "Holocaust 2001" of *All Hitler Comics* (Longwood, Florida, 2001). One allohistorical depiction of the fugitive Führer that never got made was a film by Peter Sellers "in which the comic-strip hero, the Phantom, pursues the 90-year-old Hitler ... from the South American jungle to the stage of the Royal Albert Hall." J. Hoberman, "The Nazis as Nudniks," *New York Times*, April 15, 2001, p. 24.

10 *Weekly World News*, "Hitler's Nose Cloned," week of November 16, 2001. "Hitler Alive and Well in Experimental Disney Freeze-Pod," in Scott Dikkers, ed., *Our Dumb Century: The Onion Presents 100 Years of Headlines from America's Finest News Source* (New York, 1999), p. 75.

11 The most recent demonstration of this was the May 22, 2003 airing of a British-produced documentary, "Hitler of the Andes," on Channel 4 of British television, which documented the eleven-year FBI search for the allegedly escaped Führer in Latin America. http://media.guardian.co.uk/overnights/story/ 0,7965,962262,00.html.

12 See p. 399 note 7 for a definition.

13 For the record, twenty of the twenty-nine allohistorical texts discussed in this chapter (68 percent) appeared after 1970.

14 Max Radin, *The Day of Reckoning* (New York, 1943); Michael Young, *The Trial of Adolf Hitler* (New York, 1944). The idea of bringing Hitler to justice was also portrayed in the comic books of the era. *Futuro Kidnaps Hitler and Takes Him to Hades* (*Great Comics* Nr. 3, 1941). This issue is reproduced in *Anti-Hitler Comics*, Nr. 1 (Quincy, MA, 1992).

15 "The Strange Fate of Adolph Hitler," *Strange Adventures*, Nr. 3, 1950. I am extremely grateful to Mark Squirek for sending me a scan of this hard-to-find issue.

16 Horace Leonard Gold (1914–96) was the editor of the classic sci-fi magazine *Galaxy* and a Hugo award-winner. He was outspoken about the alleged presence of anti-Semitism in the science fiction publishing industry. See Eric Leif Davin, "SF and Anti-Semitism in the 1930s" at www.cs.cmu.edu/afs/cs/ user/roboman/www/sigma/Sigma900.html. Bradford Wright describes the liberal political goals of many postwar comic book writers. Bradford W. Wright, *Comic Book Nation: The Transformation of Youth Culture in America* (Baltimore, 2001), pp. 59–63.

17 *T-Man: World Wide Trouble-Shooter*, Nr. 6, July 1954 (Quality Comics). In quoting from this tale I have used a later reprint version of the issue, *T-Man*, Nr. 34, from April 1956. I am grateful to Bill Black of AC Comics for sending me a xerox copy of this issue.

18 In the early 1950s, press reports circulated on ex-Nazis (such as Alois Brunner and Otto Skorzeny) helping to train Nasser's special security forces and recruit rocket scientists to help in armaments development. See Christopher Simpson, *Blowback: The First Full Account of America's Recruitment of Nazis and Its Disastrous Effect on our Domestic and Foreign Policy* (New York, 1988), pp. 248–52.

19 Other comic books from the early 1950s offered similar messages. Issue Nr. 14 of *T-Man: World Wide Trouble-Shooter* (from 1954), entitled "Trouble in Bavaria," revived the premise of Hitler's survival – this time in southern Germany – only to reveal the alleged Führer to be an imposter. The desire for justice was also reflected in comic book stories that featured Hitler's survival in hell. In *Adventures into Weird Worlds*, issue Nr. 21 (from August, 1953), Hitler's ghost is unable to get other historical figures (Napoleon and Caesar, among others) to vouch for him and ends up condemned to eternal damnation. The same search for justice was seen in Bernard Krigstein's comic book tale from 1954–55, "Master Race." See Art Spiegelman, "Ballbuster," *New Yorker*, July 22, 2002.

20 Forester's tale was part of a collection of short stories that focused on the horrors of the Nazi concentration camp universe. C. S. Forester, "The Wandering Gentile," in C. S. Forester, *The Nightmare* (Los Angeles, 1979), pp. 225–37.

21 Ibid., p. 237.

22 Ibid., p. 234.

23 Ibid., p. viii. The full quotation is reproduced on p. 49 of the present study.

24 See Orloff's many writing credits on www.imdb.com.

25 For a fascinating discussion of the film's history, see Charles P. Mitchell, *The Hitler Filmography: Worldwide Feature Film and Television Miniseries Portrayals, 1940 through 2000* (Jefferson, NC, 2002), pp. 240–42.

26 *The Nation* magazine observed that while the book "may be diplomatically embarrassing" in an era in which "new world tensions make every effort to effect collective amnesia," it provided a "needed corrective" by "renew[ing] doubts as to whether [the] . . . minds [of the Germans] . . . have been entirely transformed into dependable allies in the present world." "Political Nightmare," *The Nation*, September 25, 1954, p. 265. The same point is made by Riley Hughes's review in *Catholic World*, October 1954, p. 74.

27 Review of *The Nightmare* by Frederic Morton, in *Saturday Review*, July 17, 1954, cited in *Book Review Digest*, 1954, p. 323.

28 The best estimate is that after 1945 and into the 1950s, some 70 million Americans (half the population) read comic books. Wright, p. 57.

29 *They Saved Hitler's Brain* was originally released under the title *Madmen of Mandoras*. The film was given new footage and re-released under its better-known title in 1968. See www.imdb.com. Other works have also explored Hitler's survival in transfigured form. Roland Puccetti's novel *The Death of the Führer* (New York, 1972) portrayed Hitler's survival through the implantation of his brain into the body of a voluptuous countess. In 1978, the British television series *The New Avengers* aired a broadcast entitled "The Eagle's Nest," in which a gang of Nazis on a Scottish island attempt to bring Hitler (who is in a state of suspended animation) back to life. See McKale, p. 205. Ira Levin's novel *The Boys from Brazil* (New York, 1976) focused on the potential threat to the world of a large number of youthful Hitler clones engineered by Josef Mengele. A 1977 episode of the television series *Wonder Woman* entitled "Anschluss 1977" featured the attempt of South American neo-Nazis to clone Hitler. Given Hitler's marginal presence in these works, I have excluded them from the present analysis.

30 In so doing, the surgeon avenges her mother, who died as a result of Nazi medical experiments. For a discussion of the film see Mitchell, pp. 69–72. *Flesh Feast* was completed in 1967 but not released until 1970.

31 Mitchell, pp. 86–89.

32 Review of *Madmen of Mandoras, Variety*, January 29, 1964. Reprinted in *Variety's Science Fiction Reviews* (New York, 1985), p. 176. Barely more charitable was *The Film Daily*, which wrote that "the idea [of Hitler's survival] was just too fantastic to jell," and *Box Office*, which noted that "the production effects are sufficiently novel to satisfy the undemanding audiences for whom

this modestly budgeted horror drama has obviously been designed." Review of *Madmen of Mandoras* in *The Film Daily*, February 6, 1964 and *Box Office*, March 9, 1964. See file for *Madmen of Mandoras* at the Academy Archive (AA) at the Academy of Motion Picture's Center for Motion Picture Study in Beverly Hills, California.

33 See the obituary for Bradley (1920–97) written by Roger Ebert, *Chicago Sun-Times*, December 31, 1997, p. 42. One indicator of Bradley's serious intent was his enlisting of award-winning cinematographer Stanley Cortez (of *The Magnificent Ambersons*) to shoot the footage.

34 See entry for Kane at www.imdb.com.

35 "Night Conspirators" was performed on the British stage in 1963. See review by T. C. Worsley, *The Times*, May 23, 1963, p. 6.

36 This summary is culled from the reviews of the television drama, copies of which are extremely scarce. Information provided to author by Sean Delaney of the British Film Institute.

37 See Don Presnell and Marty McGee, *A Critical History of Television's* The Twilight Zone, *1959–1964* (Jefferson, NC, 1998), pp. 141–42.

38 Muller was born in 1925. See "This Night May Be Evil," *TV Times*, no date, but most likely early May, 1962. British Film Institute, *Night Conspirators* file.

39 Serling (1924–75) fought in the Pacific theater. See *Dictionary of Literary Biography, Vol. XXVI: American Screenwriters* (Detroit, 1984), pp. 285–88. *Contemporary Literary Criticism*, Vol. XXX (Detroit, 1984). Another famous *Twilight Zone* episode, "Death's Head Revisited," about concentration camp ghosts exacting revenge upon a former guard (aired November 10, 1961) also reflected Serling's concern with justice for the Nazi past. Marc Scott Zicree, *The Twilight Zone Companion* (New York, 1982), pp. 228–30.

40 See Hal Erickson, "All the Little Hitlers," *The TZ Magazine Articles Archive, Taken from the Pages of the Twilight Zone Magazine.* www.thetzsite.com/pages/magazine/hitlers.html.

41 "If Hitler Came Back," *Daily Worker*, May 9, 1962; "Return of Hitler," *Daily Telegraph*, May 7, 1962. British Film Institute, *Night Conspirators* file.

42 Martin Jackson, "German Envoy Protests to ITV Chief," *Daily Express*, May 10, 1962. Some English reviewers were more critical of the drama. Thus, one called it a "shrill" and "vengeful assertion of German political original sin." "The Progress of Xenophobia," *The Times*, May 12, 1962. British Film Institute, *Night Conspirators* file.

43 Cited in Erickson, "All the Little Hitlers."

44 There are no studies of the Hitler Wave as a phenomenon, although Peter Wyden's recent book, *The Hitler Virus*, devotes a section to it. Peter Wyden, *The Hitler Virus: The Insidious Legacy of Adolf Hitler* (New York, 2001). See also McKale, especially chapter 9.

45 These included such works as Albert Speer's *Inside the Third Reich* (New York, 1970), Werner Maser's *Hitler* (New York, 1973), Joachim Fest's *Hitler* (New York, 1973), Hans-Jürgen Syberberg's film *Hitler: A Film from Germany* (1977), and the infamous scandal surrounding the publication of the (fabricated)

Hitler Diaries of 1983. Fest's cinematic dramatization of his Hitler book, entitled *Hitler: Eine Karriere* (1977), was also controversial for its bombastic potrayal of the dictator and minimal attention to Nazi crimes. The fact that Sebastian Haffner's short book *The Meaning of Hitler* (New York, 1978) rose to the top of the German bestseller list also confirmed the nation's fascination with the dictator. On the Hitler Diaries, see Robert Harris, *Selling Hitler: The Story of the Hitler Diaries* (New York, 1986). Other aspects of the Hitler Wave included the booming market for Nazi memorabilia and paraphernalia, including uniforms, furniture, flags, jewelry, daggers, and other pieces of assorted kitsch. Wyden, chapter 25.

46 See, for example, Robert Hughes, "The Hitler Revival: Myth v. Truth," *Time Magazine*, May 21, 1973, pp. 81–82. The wave was also a reaction against the structuralist, social-scientific analyses of fascism that de-emphasized the role of personality in history. See Ian Kershaw, *The Nazi Dictatorship: Problems and Perspectives of Interpretation* (London, 1985), chapter 2.

47 See Craig R. Whitney, "Papa Who was Hitler?" *New York Times Magazine*, October 28, 1973 p. 24. This generation was at liberty to explore the past in this way as it bore no direct responsibility for the Nazis' rise to power. See Karl-Heinz Janßen, "Bleibt uns Hitler nicht erspart?" *Die Zeit*, July 20, 1973, p. 1.

48 This is the argument of George Mosse's essay, "Hitler Redux," which surveys the growing interest of consumers in Nazi paraphernalia, memorabilia, pulpy novels, and melodramatic docu-dramas. George Mosse, "Hitler Redux," *New Republic*, June 16, 1979, pp. 21–24. See also Geoffrey Barraclough, "The Nazi Boom," *New York Review of Books*, May 17, 1979, pp. 18–21; "Springtime for Hitler," *Newsweek*, April 30, 1973, pp. 32–33; "Bidding for Adolf," *Time*, April 19, 1971, p. 29.

49 One of the most concerned was Saul Friedlander, who explored what he called the "new discourse" on Nazism in his book *Reflections of Nazism: An Essay on Kitsch and Death* (New York, 1982), p. 8.

50 Friedlander concluded that over time "attention has gradually shifted from the ... horror and pain [of Nazism] ... to voluptuous anguish and ravishing images." Friedlander, *Reflections of Nazism*, p. 21.

51 Between 1970 and 1987, seven tales portrayed Hitler evading justice, while three portrayed him being brought to justice. See Appendix.

52 Brian W. Aldiss, "Swastika!", reprinted in Harry Harrison, *Nova 1: An Anthology of Original Science Fiction* (New York, 1970), pp. 73–81.

53 Ibid., pp. 73–74.

54 Ibid., pp. 75–77.

55 Ibid., pp. 79–80.

56 Edward James, *Science Fiction in the Twentieth Century* (Oxford, 1994), pp. 168–72. Aldiss was born in 1925.

57 Aldiss, p. 75.

58 Ibid., p. 80.

59 Edwin Fadiman Jr., *Who Will Watch the Watchers?* (Boston, 1970), pp. 205–06.

60 Ibid., p. 260.

61 Ibid., p. 263.

62 Ibid., pp. 263–64.

63 Ibid., pp. 266–67.

64 Fadiman (1925–94) served in World War II and later became a novelist and popular journalist. See the profile of him in *Contemporary Authors, 29–32R* (Detroit, 1978), p. 196.

65 Gary Goss, *Hitler's Daughter* (Secaucus, NJ, 1973). Gary Goss affirms the novel was written in the years 1969–71 and was published in 1973. E-mail message from Goss to author, July 22, 2001.

66 Ibid., p. 146.

67 Ibid., p. 181.

68 Ibid., p. 244.

69 Goss affirms, "I was reacting to the Hitler phenomenon, and I was satirizing it, but I was feeling my way, not sure where the novel would take me." E-mail message from Goss to author, July 22, 2001.

70 Goss, pp. 23–24.

71 Richard Rose's novel *The Wolf* (New York, 1980) describes the rise of Hitler's son to the chancellorship of a Fourth Reich. Timothy B. Benford's *Hitler's Daughter* (New York, 1983) portrayed the dictator's offspring up to no good in the American White House. *Hitler's Daughter* was also made into a film. See www.imdb.com.

72 Goss, p. 250. This line echoed the thesis of Max Picard's famous work, *Hitler in Ourselves* (Hinsdale, IL, 1947).

73 Goss, p. 273.

74 Goss has confirmed this point in noting that "Tejedor's statement does represent a late 1960s comment on the destruction of the environment." E-mail message from Goss to author, July 19, 2001.

75 Goss, p. 266.

76 Goss has noted, "At any given time in the history of the human species, there are several genocides going on. European Americans committed genocide against the Native Americans, and certain Native Tribes committed genocide against other Native Tribes. And so on." E-mail message from Goss to author, July 24, 2001.

77 Goss, p. 264. Goss has written, "I'm as horrified by the Holocaust as most are … But obsessing about it doesn't help. Somewhere on earth there is a genocide in progress at this moment, as I write this. It is desirable to keep Hitler in mind, but it's wrong to think of him as unique. He's an example of a phenomenon that is all too common." E-mail message from Goss to author, July 24, 2001.

78 The novel was first published in the *Kenyon Review* and *Granta* in 1979. The British edition first appeared in 1979. The American edition followed in 1981. George Steiner, *The Portage to San Cristóbal of A.H.* (New York, 1981).

79 Ibid., p. 179.

80 Ibid., pp. 182–86.

81 Ibid., pp. 187–88.

82 Ibid., p. 189.

83 The danger of remembrance is a broader theme of Steiner's fiction. As Bryan Cheyette has pointed out, some of Steiner's stories, like "Return No More" and "Sweet Mars" (published in the volume *Anno Domini* [London, 1964]) depict individuals who choose to confront horrific memories of their pasts with suicidal consequences. Bryan Cheyette, "Between Repulsion and Attraction: George Steiner's Post-Holocaust Fiction," *Jewish Social Studies*, Vol. 5, Nr. 3, spring/summer, 1999, pp. 72–74.

84 Steiner, pp. 47–49.

85 Ibid., pp. 105, 71.

86 Ibid., p. 19.

87 Steiner moreover stressed that the book's ending was completely open-ended. "What is absolutely key is the name of the Indian [who exclaims "Proved!"] ... which is spelled T-e-k-u. That is the Hebrew word used in the Talmud to say that there are issues here beyond our wisdom to answer or decide." D. J. R. Bruckner, "Talk with George Steiner," *New York Times Book Review*, May 2, 1982, p. 20.

88 Alvin Rosenfeld suggests that Steiner, acting in the capacity of a creative novelist rather than a more analytically rigorous critic, was "seduced as well as inspired by the zeal of fictional invention." Alvin H. Rosenfeld, *Imagining Hitler* (Bloomington, IN, 1985), pp. 100–01.

89 D. J. R. Bruckner, "Talk with George Steiner," *New York Times Book Review*, May 2, 1982, p. 20. Steiner reiterated this universalistic point in the most recent edition of *The Portage to San Cristóbal of A.H.* (New York, 1999), saying that the novel was "a parable about pain. About the abyss of pain endured by the victims of Nazism. Endured by those being 'ethnically cleansed' in a ravaged habitat in Amazonia." See the afterword to *The Portage to San Cristóbal of A.H.*, p. 174.

90 That Steiner opposed any notion of the Holocaust's uniqueness is shown by his comment, located in the afterword to the new edition of *The Portage to San Cristóbal of A.H.*, that "the Shoah belongs to a more general phenomenology of the inhuman which extends, unbroken, from the slaughter of millions in the Belgian Congo at the turn of the century to the hecatombs of the First World War and the mass murdering now upon us in East Africa and the Balkans." Steiner, p. 174.

91 Pierre Boulle, "His Last Battle," in Pierre Boulle, *Because it is Absurd (On Earth as in Heaven)* (New York, 1971), pp. 9–38.

92 Ibid., pp. 26–28.

93 Ibid., p. 31.

94 Ibid., p. 33.

95 Ibid., p. 34.

96 Ibid., p. 38.

97 Lucille Frackman Becker, *Pierre Boulle* (New York, 1996), p. vii.

98 Michel Choquette, "Stranger in Paradise," *National Lampoon*, March, 1972, pp. 61–66.

99 Ibid., p. 66.

100 The photo credit provides lavish detail about the parrot on Hitler's shoulder but no mention of Hitler himself. It reads: "Cover: The colorful personage featured on our cover is not stuffed or made of wax but very much alive. His name is Loro, which is Spanish for parrot ... Also shown in the photograph is Swiss-born ex-acrobat Billy Frick ... "

101 Choquette's aesthetic proclivities were also illustrated by his comment "I wanted to create something reminiscent of an old *Holiday Magazine* article – easy on the eyes, textually fluffy – focusing on the classic postcard sunsets, beaches and verdant landscapes where one individual has found paradise." E-mail message from Choquette to author, February 15, 2003.

102 Richard Grayson, "With Hitler in New York," in Richard Grayson, *With Hitler in New York and Other Stories* (New York, 1979).

103 Ibid., p. 20.

104 Ibid., p. 22.

105 Ibid., p. 19.

106 Ibid., p. 12.

107 As Grayson has noted, "[I] was indeed aware of the Hitler Wave ... and I believe I did wonder where this could all lead to ... [This] was one of my motives in writing the story." E-mail message from Grayson to author, July 15, 2001.

108 Grayson noted in an interview that one of his aims was "to show just how much is lost when the name 'Hitler' gives up its force and no longer evolves anything of consequence from the past." *Dictionary of Literary Biography*, Vol. CCXXXIV, *American Short Story Writers since World War II* (Farmington Hills, MI, 2001), p. 98.

109 Philippe van Rjndt, *The Trial of Adolf Hitler* (New York, 1978).

110 Ibid., p. 151.

111 Ibid., p. 126.

112 Ibid., p. 108.

113 Ibid., p. 133.

114 Ibid., p. 144.

115 Ibid., p. 248.

116 Ibid., p. 253.

117 Ibid., p. 255.

118 Ibid., p. 269.

119 Ibid., p. 272.

120 Ibid., p. 191.

121 Ibid., p. 275.

122 Ibid., p. 278.

123 Ibid., p. 287.

124 Ibid., p. 317.

125 Ibid., p. 318.

126 Ibid., p. 331.

127 Ibid., p. 333.

128 An indication of the writer's penchant for privacy was his liberal usage of pseudonyms. He chose "Philippe van Rjndt" in 1974 and has also used the

name "Philip Michaels." Van Rjndt has also cryptically claimed to have worked in the intelligence field while living in Switzerland in the 1970s. *Contemporary Authors*, Vols. LXV–LXVIII (Detroit, 1977), p. 602; *Contemporary Authors, New Revision Series*, Vol. XIV (Detroit, 1985), p. 491.

129 Van Rjndt is the son of Ukrainian immigrants to the United States, Pieter and Helena Trubetskoy. *Contemporary Authors, Vols. LXV–LXVIII* (Detroit, 1977), p. 602.

130 James Marino, *The Asgard Solution* (New York, 1983).

131 Ibid., p. 24.

132 Ibid., p. 357.

133 Ibid.

134 Ibid.

135 Joseph Heywood, *The Berkut* (New York, 1987). I am grateful to E. M. Nathanson for alerting me to the existence of the novel.

136 Hitler is also depicted as somewhat mentally unhinged, as demonstrated by his insistence that a liberated Jewish female concentration camp prisoner is really his niece, Geli Raubal. Heywood, p. 272.

137 Ibid., p. 561.

138 See interview with Joseph Heywood by Jean W. Ross in *Contemporary Authors*, Vol. CXXXIV (Detroit, 1989), pp. 226–27.

139 Heywood, p. 558.

140 E-mail message from Heywood to author, September 30, 2002.

141 *New Yorker*, December 18, 1971, p. 135.

142 Stuart Schoffman, "A Parade of Jewish Relations," *Los Angeles Times*, July 17, 1979, Section V, p. 6. Another reviewer described Grayson's work with the terms "fiction as joke, word play, vehicle for whimsy." *Choice*, November, 1979, p. 1172. *Publishers Weekly* described Grayson's stories as "amusing if somewhat contrived satires." April 23, 1979, p. 70.

143 Martin Levin, review of *Hitler's Daughter, New York Times Book Review*, January 12, 1975, p. 16.

144 See review of *Who Will Watch the Watchers?* in *Library Journal*, April 1, 1970, p. 1390; the reviewer called it "pedestrian" but "engrossing for male espionage fans." The *New York Times* also gave the book a mixed review, noting that the book "contains some good ideas ... but [is] ... padded out with so many dollops of erotica that the author's valid titular point seems hardly worth the effort." Review of *Who Will Watch the Watchers?* in the *New York Times Book Review*, May 10, 1970, p. 37.

145 Choquette writes, "Shortly after we ran the article in *Lampoon*, it was picked up by *Pardon*, a Frankfurt-based satirical magazine ... The French equivalent of *Playboy* magazine, *Lui*, also ran the photos in 1972, but with no text. And in 1973, [they appeared in London in] ... *The Daily Mirror* ... Also flattering to my ego is the fact that Andy Warhol liked the piece, and that when I was in Barcelona someone showed the photos to Salvador Dali, who then invited me to drink pink champagne with him by his swimming pool." E-mail message from Choquette to author, February 13, 2003.

146 "*With Hitler in New York*," Rosenfeld concluded, is "the furthest extension to date of the neutralization of the historical Hitler and the normalization of a new image of the man." Rosenfeld, *Imagining Hitler*, pp. 72–73. Others criticized Grayson for aesthetic shortcomings. One critic wrote, "As a storytelling crafts-man, Grayson has a long, long way to go." Review of *With Hitler in New York*, *Kirkus Reviews*, May 1, 1979, p.535. Another wrote, "The mere title [of the story] creates expectations which the story itself fails to satisfy ... Grayson's deadpan treatment of Hitler comes across as, at best, cute." David Lionel Smith, review of *With Hitler in New York* in *Fiction International*, Nr. 12, 1984, pp. 284–85.

147 Rosenfeld, *Imagining Hitler*, p. 70.

148 Melvyn Bragg, "Fun with Adolph," *Punch*, June 17, 1981, p. 981; Edmund Fuller, "A Stunning Novel of the Fuehrer in the Jungle," *Wall Street Journal*, April 26, 1982, p. 26; Joseph Harrison, "If Hitler Were Found Alive," *Christian Science Monitor*, May 14, 1982, p. B2; Bernard Bergonzi, "The Return of the Führer," *Times Literary Supplement*, June 12, 1981, p. 660; Otto Friedrich, "Teaching the Grammar of Hell," *Time*, March 29, 1982, p. 68.

149 Otto Friedrich, "Teaching the Grammar of Hell," *Time*, March 29, 1982, p. 68.

150 Peter S. Prescott, "Hitler Defends Himself," *Newsweek*, April 26, 1982, p. 76.

151 Bernard Bergonzi, "The Return of the Führer," *Times Literary Supplement*, June 12, 1981, p. 660.

152 See Rosenfeld, *Imagining Hitler*, pp. 97–102; Friedlander, *Reflections on Nazism*, pp. 61, 111–15.

153 Peter Conrad, "Like the Ark," *New Statesman*, June 27, 1980, p. 968.

154 Morris Dickstein, "Alive and 90 in the Jungles of Brazil," *New York Times Book Review*, May 2, 1982, p. 21.

155 Martin Gilbert, "Steiner's Hitler: A Travesty," *Jewish Chronicle*, February 26, 1982, p. 20.

156 Quoted in Rosenfeld, *Imagining Hitler*, p. 100.

157 Stefan Kanfer, "The Perversity of G.S.," *New Republic*, April 21, 1982, pp. 35–36; Hyam Maccoby, in *Encounter*, May, 1982, quoted in *Book Review Digest*, 1982, p. 1287.

158 Hans Keller, "Hitler à la Dr. Steiner," *Spectator*, July 19, 1980, pp. 22–23. Still other critics assaulted the book's political implications. Thus, Stefan Kanfer argued that "to elevate Hitler to the role of Lucifer [meant taking] ... Germany off the hook." Stefan Kanfer, "The Perversity of G.S.," *New Republic*, April 21, 1982, pp. 35–36.

159 Review of *The Berkut* in *Booklist*, June 15, 1987, p. 1538; Michael Bandler, "Hitler's Escape Lets Thriller Really Take Off," *Chicago Tribune*, September 13, 1987, p. 10; review of *The Berkut* in *Publishers Weekly*, July 10, 1987, p. 57.

160 Review of *The Berkut* in *Publishers Weekly*, July 10, 1987, p. 57; review of *The Berkut* in *Kirkus Reviews*, July 15, 1987, p. 1015. *Playboy* agreed, noting that the novel ended with a "satisfyingly nasty come-uppance." Review of *The Berkut* in *Playboy*, cited in blurb on back cover of the novel. Some reviewers dissented, arguing that Heywood had depicted Hitler as a "sniveling twit [instead of] ... a monster." Stewart Kellerman, review

of *The Berkut* in the *New York Times*, November 29, 1987, section 7, p. 20.

161 James McLellan, "Evils of Hitler and the World," *Washington Post*, January 30, 1979, p. B4; Anthony Burgess, "An Eloquent Voice for Evil," *Observer*, May 24, 1981, p. 29. Other reviews called the novel "gripping" and commended van Rjndt for having skillfully explored one of "the ifs of history . . . [that] still [has] the power to excite and challenge the imagination." Review of *The Trial of Adolf Hitler* by L. W. Griffin, *Library Journal*, January 15, 1979, p. 212; A. E. I., review of *The Trial of Adolf Hitler*, *Kliatt*, spring, 1980, p. 12. *Publishers Weekly* called it "dramatic" and "imaginative." Quoted in full-page advertisement for the novel in the *New York Times Book Review*, January 28, 1979, p. 19.

162 Kristiana Gregory, review of *The Asgard Solution* in the *Los Angeles Times*, November 27, 1983 (Book Review section).

163 Between 1989 and 2001, seven tales portrayed Hitler evading justice, while three portrayed him being brought to justice. See Appendix.

164 See pp. 19–20 of the present study.

165 Steve Erickson, *Tours of the Black Clock* (New York, 1989).

166 Ibid., p. 185.

167 Ibid., p. 256.

168 Ibid., pp. 262–63.

169 Ibid., p. 257.

170 Ibid., p. 297.

171 Interview with Yoshiaki Koshikawa and Steve Erickson, "Imagination and Invention." www.isc.meiji.ac.jp/~yoshiaki/Imagination_and_ Invention.htm.

172 E. M. Nathanson and Aaron Bank, *Knight's Cross* (New York, 1993). Nathanson was the author of the bestselling novel *The Dirty Dozen*, which has sold over 4 million copies worldwide. See the jacket cover for *Knight's Cross*.

173 Interestingly, *Knight's Cross* depicts the hunt for Hitler as having little to do with the quest to bring him to justice. Early on, one of Brooks's German OSS recruits proclaims that "the Americans . . . want [Hitler] alive and secretly, for whatever reasons of their own. Perhaps even they would not know what to do with him." Nathanson and Bank, p. 76.

174 Ibid., p. 287.

175 In part, Brooks is skeptical of the legality of putting Hitler on trial. As he puts it, "Could the head of state of an enemy nation, as monstrous as this one was, be executed under international law?" Ibid., pp. 254–55.

176 Ibid., p. 287.

177 Ibid., p. 255.

178 Ibid., p. 287.

179 As Nathanson has put it, "We were writing an *action* story, a suspenseful *drama*, with real and imagined characters as fully fleshed out . . . as we could make them . . . We weren't writing a social, political or historical treatise – or trying to send a message." E-mail message from Nathanson to author, September 13, 2002.

180 *The Dirty Dozen* was made into a celebrated film in 1967. See James Berardinelli, review of *The Dirty Dozen*, at http://movie-reviews.colossus.net/movies/d/dirty_dozen.html.

181 Bank later became a colonel and distinguished himself as the founding father of American Special Forces, the famous Green Berets. Dennis McLellan, "Mission Accomplished: South County Team of Veteran and Novelist Picks Up the 'Get Hitler' Story Where History Left Off," *Los Angeles Times, Orange County Edition*, April 29, 1993, Part E, page 1.

182 E-mail message from Nathanson to author, August 12, 2002.

183 When Hitler declares to Reiter, "Have no fear ... ! We will rise from the ashes of today's Germany!" the latter regards Hitler's agenda as "the futile fantasy of a madman" and thinks to himself, "Couldn't he fathom that it was the very policies ... of the Nazi tyranny that had brought Germany to utter ruin?" Nathanson and Bank, pp. 170, 250.

184 Nathanson has noted that the novel was largely complete before reunification which, as an event, "had ... nothing to do with the tenor or direction of the novel." E-mail message from Nathanson to author, August 12, 2002. It is likely, however, that Germany's stability in the years leading up to reunification may have subtly led the writers to dismiss the likelihood that Nazism might one day resurface.

185 Robert Krakow, *The False Witness* (Unpublished play, Boca Raton, FL, 2000). The textual citations from the play are from a March, 2000 performance of it in Boca Raton, Florida. I am grateful to Robert Krakow for sending me a transcript of the play, along with a videorecording.

186 As the film's web site described it: "THE FALSE WITNESS is a morality play which questions our right to assign the blame for the HOLOCAUST only to Hitler and his THIRD REICH. This play challenges the conventional wisdom and seeks to lift the curtain on the subject of WHO IS REALLY TO BLAME." See the web address: www.falsewitness.com.

187 Krakow, p. 41.

188 www.falsewitness.com.

189 Krakow, p. 44.

190 At one point, the prosecutor, Joan of Arc, gets Hitler to admit he would have sent Jesus himself to the gas chambers, at which point she concludes passionately, "You are the Christ-killer!" *The False Witness*, p. 43.

191 It is unclear whether Hitler has survived in any real historical sense in the film, or if the events on screen are merely happening in his mind. As director Barry Hershey put it, "The sense is that Hitler is trapped – perhaps in an inner prison. The space is more like a 'mind space' – which metamorphoses throughout the film." www.emptymirror.com.

192 As listed on the film's web site: www.emptymirror.com.

193 At one point, moreover, Hitler basks in the glory of its destructiveness, declaring, "If someone kills another human being, he is hanged. But if someone kills 50 million people, he is immortal ... I am immortal."

194 At times, this lighthearted depiction of the Führer even produces a sense of empathy for the ex-dictator, as when he tells of his disappointment in being rejected for the part of the Nazi leader after auditioning for it in an American-produced film after the war (the director dismisses him as not being "funny enough" to be able to play the Führer).

195 "Der Bestien-Beschwörer," *Focus Magazin*, February 24, 1997, p. 170.

196 Ibid.

197 "Teufelsaustreibung in der Kantstrasse," *Die Süddeutsche Zeitung*, February 20, 1997.

198 Report by Edward Lifson on National Public Radio (NPR), February 17, 1997. www.npr.org/ramarchives/nc7f1701-5.ram. Mueller-Stahl was quoted as saying that the film "was a way to exorcise the demons ... since my father died at the hands of the Nazis." "Monster Man," *Hollywood Reporter*, October 8, 1996.

199 And indeed, Mueller-Stahl's own admission that Hitler "had to be funny in order for me to be able to keep him at a distance" illustrates the director's removal from his protagonist. "Der Magier mit den blauen Augen," *Die Süddeutsche Zeitung*, Febuary 7, 1997.

200 Interview with Armin Mueller-Stahl. http://sydney.citysearch.com.au/E/F/ SYDNE/0000/00/30.

201 Walter Moers, *Adolf die Nazi-Sau* (Vol. I) (Frankfurt am Main, 1998); Walter Moers, *Adolf die Nazi-Sau* (Vol. II) (Frankfurt am Main, 1999). Moers rose to prominence with his animated series "Käpt'n Blaubär" and his comic strip "Das kleine Arschloch," which sold in the hundreds of thousands. Oliver Fiechter, "Adolf, die Nazi-Sau," *Facts*, September 24, 1998. Following the publication of the two *Adolf* volumes, Moers produced an *Adolf-Kalender für das Jahr 2001*, complete with birthday entries marked for Mussolini and Arno Breker.

202 Moers, *Adolf die Nazi-Sau*, Vol. I, p. 9. (Note: There are no page numbers in the volume. I have begun counting pages from the very first page in the hardback version of the text.)

203 Ibid., pp. 29–30.

204 Ibid., pp. 49–50.

205 Moers, *Adolf die Nazi-Sau*, Vol. II, p. 17.

206 Ibid., p. 20.

207 Moers in fact was taken aback by the stormy reaction to the book's first volume. As he put it, "It was a completely new experience to stand in the spotlight in this way ... For a long time I couldn't understand how so much intellectualized blabber could be written and spoken about this stupid *Adolf* [book]." Quoted in "Aufklärerisch oder geschmacklos?" *Die Berliner Morgenpost*, November 10, 2000.

208 www.dap.nl/Adolf/Chronologie.html.

209 When Moers saw the Japanese comic (most likely, Osamu Tezuka's *Adolf* series), Moers thought to himself, "If they can do it, so can I." See Osamu Tezuka, *Adolf: Days of Infamy* (San Francisco, 1996), *Adolf: 1945 and All That*

Remains (San Francisco, 1996), and *Adolf: The Half-Aryan* (San Francisco, 1996), among others.

210 Barry Malzberg, "Hitler at Nuremberg," in Mike Resnick and Martin H. Greenberg, eds., *By Any Other Fame* (New York, 1994), pp. 296–302.

211 Ibid., p. 297. Hitler continues: "I did not want anything more to do with the Jews. Let Eichmann take care of it, I said to Himmler. Poof! I clean my hands of this."

212 David Charnay, *Operation Lucifer: The Chase, Capture, and Trial of Adolf Hitler* (Calabasas, CA, 2001). The book is divided into two volumes (pp. 1–617 and 1–347).

213 An unbelievably long series of events has to pass before Hitler is even brought to trial. Hitler is identified by American intelligence officers as early as page 177 of the novel, but he does not take the witness stand until page 922.

214 Charnay, Vol. II, p. 335.

215 One would expect a more leisurely execution of Hitler, given the hundreds of pages of suspense leading up to his capture and trial. But, in fact, the execution takes place with next to no literary drama. Hitler is led to the gallows along with six other concentration camp guards and has a noose placed around his neck; and then, in the climactic sentence, "The seven men fell to their deaths." Charnay, Vol. II, p. 337.

216 Obituary for David Charnay, *New York Times*, October 9, 2002, p. A25.

217 Charnay, Vol. I, p. 12.

218 Roger Spiller, "The Führer in the Dock: A Speculation on the Banality of Evil," in Robert Cowley, *What If? 2: Eminent Historians Imagine What Might Have Been* (New York, 2001), pp. 344–65.

219 Spiller, p. 365.

220 John Buckley, "Traveling through the Labyrinth of Evil," *Wall Street Journal*, March 13, 1989, p. A13. Also calling the book "remarkable" was Paul Kincaid, "Removing the Referents," *Times Literary Supplement*, July 28, 1989, p. 830. The book was called "powerful" in *Publishers Weekly*, November 11, 1988, p. 40. Kathy Acker called the book a "gorgeous" work of a fabulous mythmaker ... " but focused largely on its literary rather than historical dimensions. *New York Times Book Review*, March 5, 1989, p. 5.

221 Caryn James, "The Missing Conscience of the 20th Century," *New York Times*, January 7, 1989, p. 17.

222 Joe Collins, review of *Knight's Cross*, *Booklist*, May 1, 1993, pp. 1571–72.

223 As one reviewer put it, "even sophisticated readers may be confused by the [author's] kaleidoscopic vision of our century." *Library Journal*, January, 1989, p. 101. Another called it a "preposterous reinvention of the twentieth century" marred by "clumsy diction" and a "monotonous tone." *Booklist*, January 1, 1989, p. 751. One reviewer called the book "maddeningly flawed" and concluded that it too often slid "off the deep end into the bathetic and ridiculous." Tom Clark, *Los Angeles Times Book Review*, January 29, 1989, p. 3.

224 E. M. Nathanson and Aaron Bank's *Knight's Cross* was criticized as a "disappointingly unimaginative and ... actionless novel." Review of *Knight's Cross* in *Publishers Weekly*, March 29, 1993, p. 36.

225 Released only in selected cities in 1998, it finished its week-long run ahead of schedule in certain locales. Since being shown on HBO in 2000, its audience in the United States has been a limited one.

226 The *Houston Chronicle* called the film "insufferable" and "stultifying." "Stultifying 'Mirror' Makes Hitler Boring," *Houston Chronicle*, May 21, 1999, p. 14. Lawrence Van Gelder, "Hitler Meets Freud on a Blood-Red Couch," *New York Times*, May 7, 1999, p. E23; "'Empty Mirror' Reflects Sere Face of Hitler's Soul," *San Diego Union-Tribune*, May 15, 1999, p. E6; "'Mirror' Gives Back a Dull Reflection of Hitler," *Boston Globe*, May 7, 1999, p. D4.

227 Hershey's quotation appeared in the article, "Hitler Viewed in an 'Empty Mirror,'" *Jewish Journal*, May 7, 1999, p. 31. Bob Kurson, "Führer Furor Gets Old; Reflections Are Obvious in 'Mirror,'" *Chicago Sun-Times*, May 14, 1999, p. 34.

228 Kevin Thomas, "'Empty Mirror' Struggles to Find Insight on Hitler," *Los Angeles Times*, May 7, 1999, p. F8.

229 Although debuting at the prestigious Berlin Film Festival, Mueller-Stahl's film was never released in the United States and to this day has not appeared on videocassette or DVD. For these reasons, the number of people that have seen it is undoubtedly quite small.

230 Many reviewers used the term *befremdlich* ("strange") to describe the film and cited the director's "indecisiveness" about how he wanted to portray the Führer. "Teufelsaustreibung in der Kantstrasse," *Die Süddeutsche Zeitung*, February 20, 1997. "Der Magier mit den blauen Augen," *Die Süddeutsche Zeitung*, February 7, 1997. One reviewer called it "an unfinished ... and indecisive film." "Der Deutsche Untoter," *Die Woche*, February 21, 1997. Some argued the film did not make the most out of the premise of Hitler's survival. "Ein Interview mit Adolf Hitler aus dem Jahre 1996," www.artechock.de/arte/programm/f/kritik/cowith.htm. Others complained about the wooden dialogue and poor casting. Thilo Wydra, review of "Gespräch mit dem Biest," www.bs-net.de/kino/film-dienst/fd97-4/GESPRAECH_MIT_DEM_BIEST.html.

231 As one put it, "The elements of comedy and slapstick in the film do not convince. The viewer does not so much notice the comic form of the aged dictator as the sympathetic-amusing persona of the actor Mueller-Stahl." Axel Bieber, "Abrechnung mit einem Ekelpaket," *Die Rhein-Zeitung* online: http://rhein-zeitung.de/magazin/kino/galerie/gespraechmitdembiest. As another put it, "Hitler is only for a few moments horrifyingly funny or humorously demonic." "Teufelsaustreibung in der Kantstrasse," *Die Süddeutsche Zeitung*, February 20, 1997.

232 "Kein Praedikat für Armin Mueller-Stahl," *Die Frankfurter Allgemeine Zeitung*, February 28, 1997.

233 Calling it "the most human Hitler ... ever to be seen on the movie screen," one writer praised the "nuanced interpretation" as one of the "few positive things about the whole film." Thilo Wydra, review of "Gespräch mit dem Biest," www.bs-net.de/kino/film-dienst/fd97-4/GESPRAECH_MIT_DEM_BIEST.html.

234 After the book's initial print run of 10,000 copies sold out within a week, Moers's publisher, the Frankfurt-based Eichborn-Verlag, quickly accelerated the production of additional print runs. So popular was the book that it sold over 260,000 copies in the first three years. The second volume, meanwhile, also sold extremely well, coming in at over 150,000 copies. The figures of 260,000 and 150,000 are courtesy of Dr. Esther-Beatrice von Bruchhausen, Eichborn.Presse. E-mail message to author, July 3, 2001. The 10,000 figure can be found in "Hitler als Comic-Figur," *haGalil onLine*, March 30, 2000. "Hi Hitler!" *Die Woche*, July 17, 1998. See also the Eichborn-Verlag's web site for sales figures of the book: www.eichborn.de/autoren/default.asp?pos=145&key=8139&x=y.

235 Quoted in "Aufklärerisch oder geschmacklos?" *Die Berliner Morgenpost*, November 10, 2000.

236 Peter Finn, "Some Germans Start to Laugh at Hitler," *Washington Post*, September 17, 2000.

237 Oliver Fiechter, "Adolf, die Nazi-Sau," *Facts*, September 24, 1998.

238 See, for example, Chaplin's classic film *The Great Dictator* and Ernst Lubitsch's film *To Be or Not to Be* (which was remade by Mel Brooks in 1983).

239 Ursula Sautter, "Can Der Führer be Funny?" *Time International*, August 17, 1989, p. 48; Peter Finn, "Some Germans Start to Laugh at Hitler," *Washington Post*, September 17, 2000.

240 Alan Cowell, "Hogan! Germans Need You," *New York Times*, July 20, 1997. *Goebbels und Geduldig* portrays a Jewish look-alike to Josef Goebbels who ends up assuming the latter's identity. See Mark Landler, "German Comedy Lances the Nazis, but 'The Producers' Is Safe," *New York Times*, November 25, 2002, p. A9. Achim Greser, *Der Führer privat* (Berlin, 2000). Other examples of a German readiness to embrace humor have been visible in Christoph Schlingensief's 2002 play *Quiz 3000* (in which a fictional game show features contestants answering factual questions about the Holocaust). "Ordnen Sie diese KZ von Nord nach Süd," *Die Süddeutsche Zeitung*, March 18, 2002.

241 Letter to the editor from Michael Kramer, *Tageszeitung*, August 7, 1998. Mark Landler, "German Comedy Lances the Nazis, but 'The Producers' Is Safe," *New York Times*, November 25, 2002, p. A9.

242 McKale, p. 208.

243 Robert Hughes, "The Hitler Revival: Myth v. Truth," *Time Magazine*, May 21, 1973, p. 82.

CHAPTER 6: THE WORLD WITHOUT HITLER: BETTER
OR WORSE?

1 Simon Louvish, *The Resurrections* (New York, 1994), p. 102.

2 More than twice as many accounts have depicted history as being the same or worse without Hitler as opposed to being better. In this chapter, I have analyzed thirteen separate narratives in the former category and five in the latter.

Moreover, the proportion of substantial works (i.e. full-length novels, films, or television shows, as opposed to short stories or essays) is higher among narratives depicting history as worse without Hitler. Exactly 20 percent (one of five) of the narratives depicting history as better without Hitler were novels. By contrast, just over 60 percent (eight of thirteen) of the narratives depicting history as worse without Hitler were substantial in nature. Finally, analyzing the appearance of such narratives over time indicates a growing trend towards normalization. Most accounts portraying Hitler's removal as improving the course of history appeared in the 1980s and have since been displaced in the last decade by accounts portraying his removal as having little positive effect at all. The works of Yulsman (1984), Pleschinski (1983), and Demandt (1993) all viewed Hitler's removal as improving history, as did that of Turner's 1996 essay and Wedemeyer-Schwiersch (1999). Those depicting Hitler's absence as making history no better date back to Locke (1952), Spinrad (1972 [see the 1974 edition in the Bibliography]), and Jäckel (1974 ["Wenn der Anschlag gelungen wäre," 1989]), but have been concentrated in the years since 1989, as seen in the works of Koning (1990), Turtledove (1991), Yarden (1992), Louvish (1994), Delaplace (1994), Fry (1996), "California Reich" (1998), Niles and Dobson (2000), Ditfurth (2001), Ditfurth (2003), and "Cradle of Darkness" (2002). This is further supported by including works discussed in earlier chapters that also portray history as no better without Hitler, such as those of Mulisch (1972), Dvorkin (1987), Erickson (1989), Gingrich and Forstchen (1995), and Cooper (1999). In adding these works to the overall total, we arrive at a figure of eighteen accounts portraying history as worse without Hitler as opposed to five depicting history as better, nearly a 4–1 ratio. See Appendix.

3 W. Berthold has tabulated some forty-two assassination attempts. See W. Berthold's book, *Die 42 Attentate auf Adolf Hitler* (Munich, 1981). Joachim Fest lists the much smaller number of fifteen. See Joachim Fest, *Plotting Hitler's Death: The Story of the German Resistance* (New York, 1994), p. 1. See Ian Kershaw and Mark Seaman, *Operation Foxley: The British Plan to Kill Hitler* (London, 1998).

4 "I Killed Hitler" was reprinted in Ralph Milne Farley, *The Omnibus of Time* (Los Angeles, 1950), pp. 187–96. Farley was the pseudonym of Roger Sherman Hoar. Milne's tale features the attempt of an American painter angry about having just been called up to serve in World War II to go back in time to kill Hitler and prevent the war from occurring in the first place. For its part, the novel *The Man Who Killed Hitler* did not examine the impact of Hitler's assassination on the subsequent course of history and thus remained more of a curiosity than anything else. Anonymous, *The Man Who Killed Hitler* (Hollywood, 1939). In the film *Hitler: Dead or Alive* (1942), Hitler is ultimately killed, but the German military establishment fights on without him. On the film, see Thomas Doherty, *Projections of War: Hollywood, American Culture, and World War II* (New York, 1993), p. 126. See also Mitchell, *The Hitler Filmography: Worldwide Feature Film and Television Miniseries Portrayals, 1940 through 2000* (Jefferson, NC, 2002), pp. 96–100.

5 Writing on the July 20, 1944 assassination plot (Operation Valkyrie) against Hitler, historian Klemens von Klemperer asserted that if the plot had succeeded, it would have been instrumental in "shortening the war ... saving ... hundreds of thousands of lives ... [and] preventing the domination of Soviet Russia over Central Europe." See Klemens von Klemperer, *German Resistance against Hitler: The Search for Allies Abroad, 1938–1945* (Oxford, 1992). See also Joachim Fest, *Hitler* (New York, 1973), p. 4. For a British defense of this position, see Daniel Johnson, "Why Did We Hesitate to Kill Hitler?" *The Times*, July 24, 1998.

6 In an online chat on Hollywood Spotlight on April 28, 1998, Los Angeles prosecutor Marcia Clark responded to the question "If you could change one part of history, what would it be?" by noting "I would make Hitler never be born." www.universalstudios.com/unichat.30/newchat/transcripts/marciaclark.html.
Harvard law professor Alan Dershowitz also expressed the fantasy of doing away with Hitler, claiming in 2000 that "If Hitler had asked me to represent him during the Holocaust, I would have agreed in order to get close enough to him to strangle him with my bare hands." Quoted in letter to the editor, *Esquire*, March, 2000, p. 40. Kris Rusch's 1998 novel *Hitler's Angel* features the story of a German police investigator, Fritz Stecher, who discovers evidence of Hitler's personal responsibility for the murder of his lover and niece, Geli Raubal, in 1931, but decides not to publicize it, thus allowing the dictator-to-be to continue on his path to power. Stecher, in short, is "the man who could have stopped Hitler" and altered the course of history, but who did not. Kris Rusch, *Hitler's Angel* (New York, 1998), p. 206. Stacy Title's 1995 film *The Last Supper* features a group of young graduate students mulling over the morality of killing Hitler before he has had a chance to commit his crimes. For internet chats, see www.greenspun.com/bboard/q-and-a-fetch-msg.tcl%3Dmsg_id%3D002ix5+%22kill++hitler%22&hl=en.

7 The April 11, 2002 issue of the *Boston Herald* reported that the lawyer for "accused mass killer Michael 'Mucko' McDermott said his intoxicated client blasted seven co-workers because he thought they were Hitler and six Nazi generals who needed to be stopped to prevent the Holocaust." David Wedge, "Lawyer Presents Stunning Defense: Mucko Driven to Kill Hitler," *Boston Herald*, April 11, 2002.

8 Jerry Yulsman, *Elleander Morning* (New York, 1984).

9 Ibid., p. 55.

10 Ibid., pp. 112–14.

11 Ibid., pp. 145–46.

12 Ibid., p. 151.

13 Ibid., p. 92.

14 Ibid., pp. 95, 101.

15 Ibid., 150–51, 192.

16 Ibid., p. 194.

17 Ibid., p. 258.

18 Ibid., p. 270.

19 See obituary for Jerry Yulsman, *New York Times*, August 9, 1999, p. B7.
20 Hans Pleschinski, "Ausflug," in *Der Rabe: Magazin für jede Art von Literatur* (Stuttgart, 1983), pp. 24–38.
21 Ibid., p. 33.
22 All the quotations are taken from two e-mail messages from Pleschinski to the author, dated September 26 and September 28, 2002.
23 Alexander Demandt, *History That Never Happened: A Treatise on the Question, What Would Have Happened If . . . ?* (Jefferson, NC, 1993), pp. 107–08.
24 See p. 179 of the present study.
25 Henry Turner, "Hitler's Impact on History," in David Wetzel, ed., *From the Berlin Museum to the Berlin Wall: Essays on the Cultural and Political History of Modern Germany* (Westport, CT, 1996), pp. 109–26. Many of the ideas in this essay, in turn, were incorporated into the final chapter of Turner's book *Hitler's Thirty Days to Power: January 1933* (Reading, MA, 1996).
26 Turner, p. 110.
27 Ibid.
28 Ibid., pp. 111–12.
29 Ibid., p. 112.
30 Ibid., pp. 115–23.
31 Ibid., p. 126.
32 Ibid.
33 Turner has long been seen as conservative for his defense of German big business in his famous study, *German Big Business and the Rise of Hitler* (New York, 1985), and his criticism of Marxist scholar David Abraham in the controversy over the latter's use of historical source material. It is worth clarifying, moreover, that Turner wrote his essay in the same political and cultural climate of the late cold-war years that influenced the accounts of Pleschinski and Demandt. Even though his essay was published in 1996, it was actually based on his German-language book, *Geissel des Jahrhunderts: Hitler und seine Hinterlassenschaft*, which was originally published in Berlin in 1989. E-mail message from Turner to author, May 4, 2004.
34 This position was not only visible in Turner's *Hitler's Thirty Days to Power* but also in comments on Eberhard Kolb's essay, *Was Hitler's Seizure of Power on January 30, 1933, Inevitable?* (Washington, D.C., 1996).
35 Sabine Wedemeyer-Schwiersch, "Requiem für einen Stümper," in Erik Simon, ed., *Alexanders langes Leben, Stalins früher Tod und andere abwegige Geschichten: Erzählungen und Berichte aus Parallelwelten* (Munich, 1999), pp. 243–50.
36 Ibid., p. 244.
37 Ibid., p. 247.
38 Ibid.
39 Ibid., pp. 249–50.
40 The industrial behemoth has developed a massive chain of department stores from New York to Tokyo to satisfy the world's craving for German products.
41 Ibid., p. 246.

42 Ibid., p. 248.

43 E-mail message to author from Wedemeyer-Schwiersch, February 15, 2004.

44 Wedemeyer-Schwiersch, p. 244.

45 Ibid., p. 245.

46 E-mail message to author from Wedemeyer-Schwiersch, February 15, 2004.

47 Albert Speer, *Inside the Third Reich* (New York, 1970), p. 123.

48 Ibid.

49 Norman Spinrad, *The Iron Dream* (Frogmore, 1974). (Originally published 1972.)

50 Ibid., p. 9.

51 Ibid., p. 217.

52 Ibid., p. 255

53 Ibid., p. 253.

54 Ibid., pp. 252–53.

55 Ibid., p. 253.

56 Spinrad's bleak belief in inevitable disaster was a hallmark of all of his literary work. See the entry for "Norman Spinrad" in the *Dictionary of Literary Biography, Vol. VIII, Twentieth-Century American Science Fiction Writers*, p. 145.

57 Spinrad was a member of science fiction's left-leaning New Wave movement and an adherent of the 1960s counter-culture. Spinrad reports that the idea for *The Iron Dream* "emerged as a concept from a conversation in London with [British science fiction writer Michael] Moorcock." http://ourworld.compuserve.com/homepages/normanspinrad/bio.htm.

58 Norman Spinrad, "A Prince from Another Land," in Martin H. Greenberg, ed., *Fantastic Lives: Autobiographical Essays by Notable Science Fiction Writers* (Carbondale, IL, 1981), p. 159.

59 Ibid., p. 160.

60 E-mail message from Spinrad to author, October 10, 2002.

61 Spinrad, *The Iron Dream*, pp. 253–55.

62 See note 1. The novel was originally published in England in 1992 under the title *Resurrections from the Dustbin of History*.

63 In Louvish's vision, the alteration of history begins with the failure of the Freikorps to catch and kill Rosa Luxemburg and Karl Liebknecht in 1919, leaving Germany's leftwing coalition government in place. In 1923, the communists seize upon the Nazi party's assassination of Gustav Stresemann in the Reichstag as a pretext for launching a coup and establishing a Berlin commune, based on workers' and soldiers' councils. While Goebbels escapes to Munich and joins up with Hitler to form the Munich Völkisch Republic, it lasts for only fifteen days as Red forces suppress it, driving Hitler and his Nazi associates into Austria, from which they ultimately have to flee in 1925. Louvish, pp. 114–17.

64 Ibid., p. 48.

65 Ibid., pp. 214–15.

66 Ibid., p. 215.

67 Ibid., p. 206

68 Ibid., p. 34.

69 Louvish, p. 204. The quotation continues, "The basic choices and elements are unchanged: compassion or malice, generosity or greed, wisdom or stupidity, these are the human options, which are what the human race is about."

70 Louvish describes his politics as "left." One example of his leftwing credentials is his gradual disillusionment with Zionism, which he developed in part due to his tenure as a cameraman for the Israeli army in the West Bank during the 1967 war. His universalistic concerns manifested themselves in, among other subjects, the injustices of modern South Africa, a topic to which he devoted several documentary films. See the entry for Louvish in *Contemporary Authors, New Revision Series, Vol. XCVIII* (Detroit, 2001), pp. 259–61. See also "Sacred and Profane on the Fulham Palace Road," *Scotland on Sunday*, April 20, 1997.

71 Barbara Delaplace, "Painted Bridges," in Mike Resnick, ed., *Alternate Outlaws* (New York, 1994), pp. 390–402.

72 Ibid., pp. 390–91.

73 Ibid., pp. 396–97.

74 Ibid., p. 402.

75 Stephen Fry, *Making History* (London, 1996). The novel appeared in England in 1996 and in the United States in 1998.

76 Ibid., p. 158.

77 Ibid., p. 147.

78 Ibid., p. 149.

79 Ibid., pp. 312–13.

80 Ibid., p. 328.

81 Ibid., p. 345.

82 Ibid., p. 349.

83 Ibid., p. 372.

84 Ibid., p. 439.

85 Matthew Kalman, "Born to Be Wilde: The Many Faces of Stephen Fry," *The Forward*, April 24, 1998. www.forward.com/issues/1998/98.04.24/arts.html. Though Fry is not an affiliated Jew (and was born of a Gentile father), he identifies in certain ways with a Jewish identity. As he puts it, "I often wonder about my Jewishness ... I love being an outsider, having elements to me that are different." See also Fry's discussion of his Jewishness and of British antisemitism in his autobiography, *Moab is My Washpot* (New York, 1999), pp. 137–39.

86 Fry called Goldhagen's study "brilliant" in the postscript to *Making History*.

87 See the plot synopses at www.earthprime.com/archive/capsule.asp? season=4& episode=11 and at www.slidersweb.net/sarah/calireich.html.

88 At one point Alois asserts, "It is a tragedy that the Aryan people are divided, but one day Germany and Austria will be reunited." When Andrea questions the wisdom of this, Alois replies, "You sound like one of them ... The Jews have plotted for hundreds of years to divide our people."

89 Pasha has noted, "I think it is too simplistic to dismiss the Nazi era as the product of one man," adding, "In her effort to save the world, Andrea Collins became a monster herself. The karma of murdering an innocent could not lead to anything

good, so the universe balanced out her act by fulfilling history." E-mail message from Pasha to author, May 19, 2003.

90 Christian v. Ditfurth, *Der Consul* (Munich, 2003).

91 E-mail message from Ditfurth to author, February 25, 2004.

92 Ditfurth is the son of noted German journalist Hoimar von Ditfurth and the brother of Green politician Jutta Ditfurth. He was active in the West German communist party (DKP) in the early 1980s and later affiliated with the SPD. See interview with Ditfurth in *Capital*, Nr. 18/2001, August 23, 2001. www.cditfurth.de/21rezens.htm.

93 As he openly noted, "Of course one must de-demonize Hitler, for otherwise one cannot understand him." E-mail message from Ditfurth to author, February 25, 2004.

94 Robert Donald Locke, "Demotion," *Astounding Science Fiction*, September, 1952, pp. 71–81.

95 Ibid., pp. 72–73.

96 Ibid., p. 73.

97 Ibid., p. 75.

98 Ibid., p. 78.

99 Ibid., p. 80.

100 Eberhard Jäckel, "Wenn der Anschlag gelungen wäre," in *Umgang mit Vergangenheit: Beiträge zur Geschichte* (Stuttgart, 1989), pp. 195–206.

101 Ibid., p. 199.

102 Ibid., p. 198.

103 Ibid., pp. 204–05.

104 Ibid., p. 205. A similar conclusion was offered in a brief 1993 essay in *Harper's* by Hans Koning entitled "Ifs," which reiterated the view that if Hitler had been killed by Stauffenberg's bomb in 1944, history would have turned out worse. Hans Koning, "Ifs: Destiny and the Archduke's Chauffeur," *Harper's Magazine*, May, 1990, pp. 74–76.

105 Jäckel is perhaps best known for his book, *Hitler's World View: A Blueprint for Power* (Cambridge, MA, 1981), which argued that Hitler possessed a coherent ideology and acted on the basis of it guiding the policies of the Nazi regime.

106 Most notably, Brandt abandoned the Hallstein Doctrine, which forbade diplomatic relations with nations that recognized the existence of the communist German Democratic Republic.

107 He did not fully embrace this possibility owing to the "unseemliness" of praising the bravery of the plotters on the one hand and greeting their failure on the other. Jäckel, "Wenn der Anschlag gelungen wäre," p. 205.

108 Harry Turtledove, "Ready for the Fatherland," in Gregory Benford and Martin H. Greenberg, eds., *Alternate Wars* (New York, 1991), pp. 113–27.

109 Ibid., p. 118.

110 Ibid., p. 119.

111 Ibid., p. 127.

112 At the 1992 comedcon convention, Turtledove said that "Ready for the Fatherland" had rapidly become "more topical than he had expected" because

of the Balkan conflict and stressed its morally relativistic dimensions, saying, "The only reason the Serbs are the villains now is that they have more guns – if the Croats had more guns, they'd be just as bad." http://fanac.org/worldcon/MagiCon/w92-ecl.html.

113 Sam Vaknin, "The Insurgents and the Swastika," *Central Europe Review*, May 15, 2000. www.ce-review.org/00/19/vaknin19.html.

114 Ivor H. Yarden, "On the Death of Hitler's Assassin," *Midstream*, January, 1992, pp. 34–36.

115 In his celebrated biography, *Hitler*, from 1973, Fest wrote that "If Hitler had succumbed to an assassination or an accident at the end of 1938, few would hesitate to call him one of the greatest of German statesmen, the consummator of Germany's history." Fest, *Hitler*, p. 9.

116 According to the Uchronia web site, Ribenfeld is the author of the original Hebrew language version of the story, also published in 1992. Ribenfeld's choice of pseudonym may provide a hint as to his motives in writing the tale. "Ivor H. Yarden" is a clear reference to the biblical Hebrew phrase, "Ever ha Yarden," literally, "on the other side of the Jordan," referring to the Israelites living on the other side of the Jordan river. In a general sense, Ribenfeld may have been intending to allude to the alternate possibilities of history by referring to the alternate side of the Jordan river. The fact that Ribenfeld chairs a political organization called "Jordan is Palestine," however, suggests that a conservative political agenda may lie not only behind his choice of pseudonyms but also his esssay's conclusions. I am grateful to Eli Eshed for this reference. E-mail message from Eshed to author, February 6, 2002.

117 Douglas Niles and Michael Dobson, *Fox on the Rhine* (New York, 2000).

118 Both authors are described as "award-winning game designer[s]" on the book's back jacket flap.

119 Niles and Dobson, p. 69.

120 Christian v. Ditfurth, *Der 21. Juli* (Munich, 2001).

121 Ibid., pp. 151–52.

122 Ibid., p. 167.

123 Ibid., pp. 128, 173–74.

124 Ibid., p. 63.

125 Ibid., p. 63.

126 Ibid., p. 399.

127 Ditfurth noted, "I wanted to demystify the legend of the democratic conspirators. In reality, they were conservative patriots who wanted to prevent Germany's unconditional surrender." Interview with Christian v. Ditfurth, "Die Legende entzaubern," in *Capital*, Nr. 18, August 23, 2001. See www.cditfurth.de/21rezens.htm.

128 *Budspy*, *1945*, and *The Third Reich Victorious* are discussed in chapter 2; *Tours of the Black Clock* is discussed in chapter 5. Newt Gingrich's *1945* and Steve Erickson's *Tours of the Black Clock* are exceptions insofar as Hitler's elimination is only temporary (in the former, he is put in a coma as a result of a plane crash;

in the latter, he simply goes insane and ceases to be a factor in the military conduct of the war). Still, the point remains that his removal from history (if not necessarily through death) improves Germany's wartime performance.

129 See "The Man Who Dreamed the World," *The Fantastic Four*, Issue 292, 1986. In Thompson's short story, a time-traveler prevents Hitler's murder and provides Hitler with the monetary means to pursue his fantasy of being an artist. The tale never reveals whether the plan succeeds or not. W. R. Thompson, "The Plot to Save Hitler," 1993. On *The Dirty Dozen: Next Mission* (1985), see Mitchell, pp. 47–49. Relatedly, a story entitled "Killing Time" in issue 114 of the DC comic books series *Mystery Planet* from 1980 portrays a time-traveler going back in time to prevent Hitler's assassination (which in an alternate timeline had enabled the Nazis to win World War II and dominate the earth).

130 Around 28 percent (5 of 18) of the accounts have portrayed history as better with Hitler's elimination. This figure drops to 22 percent (5 of 23) upon including the tales of Mulisch, Dvorkin, Erickson, Gingrich and Forstchen, and Peterson.

131 Of the five writers who depicted history as better without Hitler, three were Germans (Pleschinski, Demandt, and Wedemeyer-Schwiersch), while a fourth (Turner) was a veteran German historian known for rejecting the view that Nazism had deep roots in German history. In short, four out of the five narratives (80 percent) were written by Germans or persons sympathetic to them. By way of comparison, only three of the thirteen texts (23 percent) depicting history as no better without Hitler were by Germans (Jäckel and the two works by Ditfurth). Ditfurth's *Der 21. Juli*, it should be noted, was by far and away the *least* pessimistic in depicting the negative course taken by history after Hitler's death. Indeed, by the novel's conclusion, history is again headed in a positive direction (the result, it should be recalled, of heroic German individuals who, in setting history aright once more, strike a blow for human agency against structural constants).

132 See "Helden und Mörder," *Der Spiegel*, Nr. 29, 2004, pp 32–48.

133 Anglo-American writers who have embraced this model include the Britons Louvish and Fry and the Americans Locke, Spinrad, Turtledove, Gingrich, Koning, and Delaplace. "Ivo Yarden" is an Israeli.

134 Klemens von Klemperer's book (see note 5 above) is full of allohistorical questions on the larger issue of whether the resistance could have succeeded had the Allies supported it. See pp. 10–12.

135 Quoted in Theodore Hamerow, *On the Road to the Wolf's Lair: German Resistance to Hitler* (Cambridge, MA, 1997), p. 356.

136 Many critics were captivated by the novel's clever premise and Fry's imaginative writing. Carolyn See called the novel "terrific" in her review of *Making History* in the *Washington Post*, April 3, 1998, p. F2. *Making History* ranked among the top 20 paperbacks sold in England in the fall of 1997. "Top 20 Paperbacks," *Observer*, November 23, 1997. Not all critics were enthusiastic about the book, a topic which is discussed in chapter 7 of this study.

137 Review of *The Iron Dream* from *SF Reviews.* www.sfreviews.net/irondream.html. When *The Iron Dream* was first released in the United States in 1972, American critics were strongly divided on its merits. Many agreed with one critic's description of it as "a remarkable tour de force, a dazzling display of ingenuity and originality." Bruce Franklin, review of *The Iron Dream* in *Book World*, July 25, 1972, p. 11. See also Ursula K. Le Guin, "On Norman Spinrad's *The Iron Dream*," *Science Fiction Studies*, September, 1973, p. 42. But others questioned the point of reading over 200 pages of "third-rate prose" and faulted the novel for its literary deficiencies. David Redd, review of *The Iron Dream* in *Speculation* (Birmingham), September, 1973, pp. 29–30. Still others praised the novel precisely for being such a bad book. As Theodore Sturgeon, one of America's leading science fiction writers, observed, "It's a really rotten book. And brilliant. And certainly unique. By all means get it." Theodore Sturgeon, "Peaks and Beacons," *National Review*, January 19, 1973, p. 103. See also Joanna Russ, review of *The Iron Dream* in *The Magazine of Fantasy and Science Fiction*, July, 1973, p. 69.

138 Yulsman's novel has been translated into German, Swedish, and Japanese. When published in the United States it was widely praised by reviewers, one paying it the ultimate compliment of calling it "an extraordinarily well-conceived" and "first-class book," on a par with Philip K. Dick's *The Man in the High Castle*. "Yulsman Scores with First Shot," *Fantasy Review*, April, 1985, p. 30. See also review of *Elleander Morning*, *Kirkus Reviews*, December 1, 1983, p. 1226.

139 Sympathetic reviewers of *The Resurrections* called it a "tart, challenging journey into many might-have-been worlds" and a "silly but fun" work that possessed enough "fortissimo successes to make up for the occasional bum note." Mary Carroll, review of *The Resurrections* in *Booklist*, December 1, 1994, p. 654. Review of *Resurrections from the Dustbin of History* in the *Guardian*, July 12, 1992, p. 27. Frederic Smoler called it one of the "best" works of recent alternate history. Frederic Smoler, "Past Tense," *American Heritage*, September, 1999, p. 46. Other reviewers faulted the novel for its literary deficiencies but still admired its clever premise. See review of *Resurrections from the Dustbin of History* in the *Herald* (Glasgow), July 4, 1992, p. 7; and Gerald Jonas, review of *The Resurrections* in the *New York Times Book Review*, January 1, 1995, Section 7, p. 22.

140 As the episode's writer, Kamran Pasha, has noted, "There was unanimous positive reaction from the viewer base. Almost 4 million people tuned in, which were some of the highest ratings we ever got on the show, and the Internet chat boards lit up with praise for my episode." E-mail from Pasha to author, May 19, 2003.

141 Simon Louvish, review of *Making History* in the *New Statesman*, Sept 27, 1996, p. 62. Whether or not other fans of the novel shared Louvish's structuralist perspective is unknown. But American and British reviewers' silence towards it at least indicates a lack of opposition to it.

142 In discussing the response to Turner's ideas, I have used the reviews of his book *Hitler's Thirty Days to Power: January 1933*, which was a broader

exposition of the same views contained in his essay "Hitler's Role in History" (and which was much more widely reviewed). Academic scholars were the most prone to criticize Turner's conclusions. Gordon Craig said he was "skeptical" about Turner's claim that, without Hitler, Germany would have avoided World War II. Gordon Craig, *New York Review of Books*, May 29, 1997, p. 8. Stanley Hoffmann rejected the notion that a mere cabal of conspirators close to Hitler had toppled the Weimar Republic in 1933, quoting Montesquieu's observation that "When states seem to collapse from one blow, there are deep reasons why that blow was sufficient." Stanley Hoffmann, review of *Hitler's Thirty Days to Power: January 1933* in *Foreign Affairs*, May–June, 1997, p. 135. Richard Bessel, likewise, critiqued Turner's rejection of "impersonal, long-term factors" for the Third Reich and argued that his emphasis on contingency was unsatisfactory without being augmented by a "general explanation." Richard Bessel, review of *Hitler's Thirty Days to Power: January 1933* in *The Journal of Modern History*, March, 1999, p. 242.

143 After being published by the well-known Heyne Verlag in 1982, the German version of the novel, *Der stählerne Traum*, was banned by the Federal German Agency for the Restriction of Texts Dangerous to Minors, or BPS, since it allegedly "glorified Nazism." See Rudolf Stefen, "Indizierungskriterien der Bundesprüfstelle für jugendgefährdende Schriften," originally published in *Dritter Kongress der Phantasie*, cited at: www.edfc.de/esr14a.htm. Stefen was the head of the BPS who presided over the decision to place *The Iron Dream* on the index.

144 Ibid.

145 Many observers defended the novel as a clear satire and argued that the court had largely ignored the book's crucial prefatory note and epilogue, which provided the context for appreciating the larger narrative. One German critic wrote that "Whoever understands the book [as Nazi propaganda] has either exchanged his brain for a [Deutsch]mark or has simply stopped thirty pages before the conclusion." www.bubis.com/muaddib/sf/rezi/sfrez_s.htm

146 Reader review by bungaooo@mail.uni-mainz.de in reviews of *The Iron Dream* at www.amazon.com.

147 As one put it, Fry "based his parable on Goldhagen's thesis of 'eliminationist' antisemitism." "Vom Risiko, Geschichte zu machen," *Die Neue Zürcher Zeitung*, January 13, 1998, p. 43. In fact, Fry openly admitted that *Hitler's Willing Executioners* had informed his novel. Beyond citing Goldhagen's book in the epilogue to *Making History*, Fry said that "the historical foundation of massive antisemitism was present . . . One cannot assume that the pure existence of [Hitler] caused the whole atrocity." Quoted in Helmut Ziegler, "Heil Hitl* aeh, Gloder!" *Die Woche*, October 24, 1997, p. 55.

148 "Vom Risiko, Geschichte zu machen," *Die Neue Zürcher Zeitung*, January 13, 1998, p. 43.

149 Review of *Making History* by Micha Dalok, no date, www.dalock.de/artikel/fry.htm. Another reader observed that "The book is so grippingly written that

one could nearly believe that we had 'luck' with Hitler." Reader review by JacobMarley@t-online.de (Nina Dralle), "'Geschichte machen' ist eine Chance, die nie geschehen ist," 22. März 1999, www.amazon.de.

150 Reader review by Thomas Kerstens, "Ein bemerkenswert kluges und witziges Werk," 9. August 1999, www.amazon.de.

151 Reader review by olafwe@yahoo.de, "Eine vollkommen unpeinliche Comedy über den Holocaust," 3. August 1999, www.amazon.de.

152 Reader review by Mats Valentin, "Geschichte als Thriller und rasante Lovestory," 5. November 1999, www.amazon.de.

153 This pattern is supported by further anecdotal evidence. Thus, when a recent *Spiegel* survey on German attitudes towards Nazism asked respondents the allohistorical question whether Hitler would have gone down in history as one of Germany's greatest statesmen had he not persecuted the Jews and waged World War II, nearly two-thirds answered no. Some 65 percent to 28 percent said Hitler would not have been one of Germany's greatest statesmen. "Die Kraft des Grauens," *Der Spiegel*, Nr. 19, May 7, 2001, p. 58.

154 According to Friedel Wahren of the Heyne Verlag, which published *Elleander Morning* in German, all 10,000 copies of the novel were sold. E-mail message from Wahren to author, July 12, 2001. On the Kurd-Lasswitz Prize, see www.epilog.de/Dokumente/Preise/SF/Lasswitz/Index.html. Ditfurth has said he expected a "terrible thrashing" for his book's provocative depiction of the resistance, but none ever came. Interview with Christian v. Ditfurth, *Facts*, Nr. 40, October 4, 2001. www.cditfurth.de/21rezens.htm. One of the more positive reviews praised it precisely for violating prevailing taboos about the political convictions of the conspirators. As Michael Wuliger noted, "This novel comes closer to the historical truth than many official commemorative speeches for the 20th of July [movement]." Michael Wuliger, "Ein Volk, ein Reich, kein Führer," *Allgemeine Jüdische Wochenzeitung*, November 22, 2001.

CHAPTER 7: HYPOTHETICAL HOLOCAUSTS AND
THE MISTRUST OF MEMORY

1 Thomas Ziegler, "Eine Kleinigkeit für uns Reinkarnauten," in *Eine Kleinigkeit für uns Reinkarnauten* (Windeck, 1997), pp. 129–31.

2 Holocaust survivors, for example, have long been sympathetically portrayed in American Jewish fiction. In such novels as Isaac Bashevis Singer's *Enemies* (1972), Saul Bellow's *Mr. Sammler's Planet* (1974), and Arthur Cohen's *In the Days of Simon Stern* (1973), "the immigrant survivor of the Holocaust is ... imbued with the moral power and will to preserve and transmit in the ... diaspora that Jewish heritage that was tragically destroyed in Europe." Dorothy Seidman Bilik, *Immigrant-Survivors: Post-Holocaust Consciousness in Recent Jewish-American Fiction* (Middletown, CT, 1981), p. 5. Nazi perpetrators, meanwhile, have typically been depicted as the embodiments of evil.

3 Only around 5 percent of the alternate histories discussed in this study focus on the Holocaust. See Appendix.

4 Peter Novick's *The Holocaust in American Life* (Boston, 1999) points out the paradox that the Holocaust has gained in attention the more the event has faded into the past. Alan Mintz, *Popular Culture and the Shaping of Holocaust Memory in America* (Seattle, 2001); Deborah Lipstadt, "America and the Memory of the Holocaust," *Modern Judaism*, Vol. 16, Nr. 3, 1996, pp. 195–214. For a dissenting view, see Lawrence Baron, "The Holocaust and American Public Memory, 1945–1960," *Holocaust and Genocide Studies*, Vol. 17, Issue 1, 2003, pp. 62–88.

5 Adorno famously wrote that "to write poetry after Auschwitz is barbaric." In addition to noting that the Holocaust should be viewed as "solemn," Terrence Des Pres adds that it should be approached "with a seriousness admitting no response that might obscure its enormity or dishonor its dead." Terrence Des Pres, "Holocaust Laughter?" in Berel Lang, *Writing and the Holocaust* (New York, 1988), p. 217. Other scholars, such as Michael Wyschogrod, have echoed this point, arguing "It is forbidden to make fiction of the holocaust." Quoted in Ernestine Schlant, *The Language of Silence: West German Literature and the Holocaust* (New York, 1999), p. 8.

6 This is confirmed by doing random key word searches on internet search engines. When entering "no holocaust" or "holocaust never happenened" one frequently ends up at neo-Nazi revisionist web sites. More broadly, certain scholars have argued that holocaust fiction, in general, "add[s] nothing substantial to our understanding of those events but instead gives fodder to the historical revisionists." Sara R. Horowitz, *Voicing the Void: Muteness and Memory in Holocaust Fiction* (Albany, New York, 1992), p. 20.

7 As one SS militiaman infamously insisted in Simon Wiesenthal's memoirs, "However this war may end, we have won the war against you; none of you will be left to bear witness, but even if someone were to survive, the world will not believe him . . . We will destroy the evidence together with you . . . We will be the ones to dictate the history of the Lagers." Quoted in Primo Levi, *The Drowned and the Saved* (New York, 1988), pp. 11–12.

8 Sander Diamond, "Had the Holocaust Not Happened, How Many Jews Would Be Alive Today? A Survey of Jewish Demography, 1890–2000," *Journal of Holocaust Education*, Vol. 6, winter, 1997, Nr. 3, pp. 21–54. The figure cited by Diamond is 25,894,000.

9 See, for example, Lesley Pearl, "U.S. Jewry Shaped by More Than Holocaust," *Jewish Bulletin of Northern California*, July 12, 1996.

10 For example, Henry Turner asserted, "Without the Holocaust . . . there would be no state of Israel . . . [for only] the profound shock produced by the Holocaust could have surmounted the many obstacles that had previously blocked . . . the Zionist dream of a Jewish state." Henry Turner, "Hitler's Impact on History," in David Wetzel, ed., *From the Berlin Museum to the Berlin Wall: Essays on the Cultural and Political History of Modern Germany* (Westport, CT, 1996), pp. 118–19. For a critique of this argument, see Michael Wolfssohn's chapter entitled "Ohne Hitler kein Israel?" in his book *Ewige*

Schuld? 40 Jahre Deutsch-Jüdisch-Israelische Beziehungen (Munich, 1988), pp. 10–21.

11 The literature on the subject of Pius XII's silence during the Holocaust is immense. But for a specifically allohistorical perspective, see Robert Katz, "Pius XII Protests the Holocaust," in Robert Cowley, ed., *What If? 2: Eminent Historians Imagine What Might Have Been* (New york, 2001), pp 317–33. On the bombing of Auschwitz, see the recent film, *They Looked Away* (2003).

12 Exceptions include Janet Berliner and George Guthridge's trilogy of historical novels, *The Madagascar Manifesto*, which is loosely based on (but never really fully explores the implications of) the scenario of the Nazis actually implementing the Madagascar Plan to ship Europe's Jews to the remote African island instead of gassing them. See Janet Berliner and George Guthridge, *Child of the Light: Book One of the Madagascar Manifesto* (Clarkston, GA, 1995); Janet Berliner and George Guthridge, *Child of the Journey: Book Two of the Madagascar Manifesto* (Clarkston, GA, 1997); Janet Berliner and George Guthridge, *Children of the Dusk: Book Three of the Madagascar Manifesto* (Clarkston, GA, 1997). In Christopher Priest's novel, *The Separation* (London, 2002), the British execute the Madagascar Plan and the Holocaust never occurs, but this is merely a footnote to the novel's main story line. The non-occurrence of the Holocaust is also mentioned in passing by Simon Louvish in his novel *The Resurrections* (New york, 1994). Michael Chabon's forthcoming novel, *The Jewish Policeman's Union*, is scheduled to describe the resettlement of Europe's Jews in Alaska.

13 For a full description, see chapter 1.

14 Daniel Quinn, *After Dachau* (New York, 2001).

15 Ibid., p. 47.

16 Ibid., pp. 55–56.

17 Ibid., p. 56.

18 Ibid., p. 118.

19 Ibid., pp. 124, 126.

20 Ibid., pp. 125–26.

21 Ibid., p. 167.

22 Ibid., p. 133.

23 Ibid., pp. 137–38.

24 Ibid., p. 120.

25 Ibid.

26 Ibid., p. 131.

27 Ibid., p. 137.

28 Ibid.

29 Ibid., p. 175.

30 Ibid., p. 215.

31 Ibid., p. 217.

32 Friedlander made this point in response to Hayden White who, when discussing the "limits" of representing the Holocaust in the early 1990s, conceded that "in the case of an emplotment of the events of the Third Reich in a 'comic' or 'pastoral'

mode, we would be eminently justified in appealing to 'the facts' in order to dismiss it from the lists of 'competing narratives' of the Third Reich." To this statement, Friedlander replied, "White's theses ... appear untenable ... [for] what would have happened if the Nazis had won the war? No doubt there would have been a plethora of pastoral emplotments of life in the Third Reich and of comic emplotments of the disappearance of its victims, mainly the Jews." Quoted in Saul Friedlander, *Probing the Limits of Representation: Nazism and the 'Final Solution'* (Cambridge, MA, 1992), pp. 40, 10.

33 "Quinn is Back with a Buzz," *Publishers Weekly*, February 19, 2001, p. 26.

34 Ibid., p. 126.

35 Ibid., pp. 137–38.

36 For a discussion, see Gavriel D. Rosenfeld, "The Politics of Uniqueness: Reflections on the Recent Polemical Turn in Holocaust and Genocide Scholarship," *Holocaust and Genocide Studies*, Nr. 1, spring, 1999, pp. 28–61.

37 The same can be said of Noam Chomsky's use of allohistorical reasoning in comparing the genocidal persecution of Native Americans to the Holocaust. In pointing out how, as a result of an American "war of extermination," the Seminole nation of Florida has survived today "in the national consciousness as the mascot of Florida State University," Chomsky concluded that "[if] the Nazis had been victorious, perhaps Jews and Gypsies would survive as mascots of the Universities of Munich and Freiburg." Quoted in Noam Chomsky, *Rethinking Camelot*, at www.zmag.org/chomsky/rc/rc-intro-s03.html#FN6.

38 Jesse Bier, "Father and Son," in *A Hole in the Lead Apron and Six Other Stories* (New York, 1964), pp. 186–99.

39 Ibid., p. 188.

40 Ibid., p. 189.

41 Ibid., p. 190.

42 Ibid., p. 192.

43 Ibid., p. 194.

44 Ibid., p. 193.

45 Ibid., p. 190.

46 Ibid., p. 199.

47 Bier has noted, "I suppose that as an ethnic Jew, I was at long last – 20 years after WWII – constructing a piece of wish-fulfillment nearest my heart ... As I recall, I didn't need the Eichmann trial – but maybe it played its part ... the matter of of generic German punishment had always plagued me, simmering, simmering." Letter from Bier to author, August 10, 2001.

48 As Bier has noted, "I would never have cared if [the Germans] ... felt injured ... by strong Allied treatment." Letter from Bier to author, August 10, 2001.

49 Thomas Ziegler, *Die Stimmen der Nacht* (Frankfurt, 1984).

50 Ibid., p. 23.

51 Ibid., p. 15.

52 Ibid., p. 175.

53 Ibid., p. 22. This strong Jewish adherence to memory is further amplified elsewhere in the novel where Gulf chats with his television show producer, Goldberg, about the political tensions with the Latino-Germans. Gulf thinks to himself, "One should never speak with a Jew about German-America ... The Jews are the same as the Latino-Germans: They cannot forget. For them, Auschwitz, Buchenwald, Dachau and Riga don't lie forty years, even forty days, in the past; for the Jews mere hours have passed by since then. Their hatred is unbroken and their memory undiminished. And who should be surprised about it? Six million people exterminated like vermin ... " Ziegler, *Die Stimmen der Nacht*, p. 71.

54 Ibid., p. 22.

55 Ibid., p. 23.

56 Ibid., p. 51.

57 Ibid., pp. 19–20.

58 Ibid., pp. 23–24.

59 Wernher von Braun has often been seen as the classic example of a German who closely affiliated himself with the Nazi regime, yet who was recruited by the Americans to aid in the cold-war fight against communism. See, among other works, Christopher Simpson, *Blowback: The First Full Account of America's Recruitment of Nazis and Its Disastrous Effect on our Domestic and Foreign Policy* (New York, 1988). To be sure, the failure to purge Nazis from German society was also the responsibility of the Germans themselves, as was made clear by Konrad Adenauer's policy of giving amnesty to, and reintegrating, ex-Nazis into German society after 1949.

60 This idea was most famously articulated by Hermann Lübbe, "Der Nationalsozialismus im politischen Bewusstsein der Gegenwart," in Martin Broszat, ed., *Deutschlands Weg in die Diktatur* (Berlin, 1983).

61 See, among other discussions of this subject, Geoffrey H. Hartmann, ed., *Bitburg in Moral and Political Perspective* (Bloomington, IN, 1986); Charles Maier, *The Unmasterable Past: History, Holocaust and German National Identity* (Cambridge, MA, 1988); Peter Baldwin, *Reworking the Past, Hitler, the Holocaust, and the Historians' Debate* (Boston, 1990).

62 Ziegler has asserted, "*Die Stimmen der Nacht* ... was a product of my lifelong preoccupation with the Nazi ... phenomenon and my occasional ... confrontation with old and neo-Nazis over the years ... Nazi-Skins were in Germany in the early '80s ... and they disturbed and annoyed me deeply." Ziegler, e-mail message to author, December 10, 2001.

63 Ziegler continues, "Sticking to the past can make you blind for the future; it distorts ... perception and lets you see [only] shadows instead of ... light." Ziegler, e-mail message to author, December 10, 2001.

64 *Morbus Kitahara* appeared in English as *The Dog King* (New York, 1997). All quotations in this chapter come from the English edition.

65 Moor's quarry was modeled on the Austrian concentration camp of Ebensee, a satellite camp, or *Aussenlager*, of Mauthausen, near Linz.

66 Ibid., p. 33.

67 Ibid., p. 32.

68 Ibid., p. 24.

69 Ibid., p. 35.

70 Having been arrested on the charge of "race defilement" for being romantically involved with a Jewish woman, Ambras is sent to the quarries, where he suffers brutal tortures (such as being hung on the infamous "swing" with his arms behind his back until they became dislocated from their sockets). Ibid., pp. 139–40, 170–74.

71 Ibid., p. 87.

72 Ibid., pp. 257–58.

73 By the end of the novel, Bering has committed three killings.

74 Ibid., p. 77.

75 Ibid., pp. 176, 178.

76 Ibid., p. 171.

77 Ibid., p. 142.

78 Ibid., pp. 267–68.

79 Ibid., pp. 307–08.

80 Ibid., p. 280.

81 Bering's father is physically blinded by metal shards at work and then sinks into a kind of psychological blindness, convinced he is still fighting on the front in the sands of North Africa; meanwhile, his fanatically religious mother physically descends into the pitch-black darkness of the family home's cellar in a penitential attempt to achieve salvation for what she believes is her son's lost soul.

82 See the essay "'... das Thema hat mich bedroht': Gespräch mit Sigrid Löffler über *Morbus Kitahara* (Dublin, 1995)," in Uwe Wittstock, ed., *Die Erfindung der Welt: Zum Werk von Christoph Ransmayr* (Frankfurt, 1997), in which Ransmayr describes his feelings about having grown up in a small village on Lake Traun, not far from Mauthausen.

83 Ransmayr's remark that the subject of the Holocaust has "threatened" him testifies to the ambiguity of his views towards it. See the title of the essay, "'... das Thema hat mich bedroht'" ("The Theme Threatened Me").

84 Most broadly, see Bill Niven, *Facing the Nazi Past: United Germany and the Legacy of the Third Reich* (New York, 2002), especially chapters 4 and 8.

85 Ibid., pp. 175–93, especially pp. 188–89. Alexander Mathäs, "The Presence of the Past: Martin Walser on Memoirs and Memorials," *German Studies Review*, Nr. 1, February, 2002, p. 3.

86 "'... das Thema hat mich bedroht,'" p. 218. The cumbersome original German sentence reads: "Jeder Versuch, diesen Prozeß der ... Einsicht in das Leiden ... der Menschen in ein Programm zu kleiden, das man nur organisieren müßte ... bleibt eine heillose Hoffnung."

87 Ibid.

88 As André Spoor notes, Ransmayr "does not take part in the initiatives or demonstrations of [his fellow Austrian] writers," declining, for example, to join the 1992 action against Jörg Haider's anti-foreigner campaign. André

Spoor, "Der kosmopolitische Dörfler," in Uwe Wittstock, ed., *Die Erfindung der Welt: Zum Werk von Christoph Ransmayr* (Frankfurt, 1997), p. 184.

89 Otto Köhler, "Der Morgenthau Plan – Legende und Wirklichkeit," in Reinhard Kühnl and Eckart Spoo, eds., *Was aus Deutschland werden sollte: Konzepte des Widerstands, des Exils und der Allierten* (Heilbronn, 1995), pp. 164–72. See also Wolfgang Benz, "Der Morgenthau Plan," in Wolfgang Benz, ed., *Legenden, Lügen, Vorurteile: Ein Lexicon zur Zeitgeschichte* (Munich, 1990), pp. 145–47.

90 Beyond the works of Ziegler and Ransmayr, other fictional works have incorporated the Morgenthau Plan's realization into their narratives. See, for example, Günter Herburger's *Die Augen der Kämpfer* (Darmstadt, 1980 and 1983), Martin Meyer's *Auge um Auge, Zahn um Zahn* (Frankfurt, 1992), and Ernst-Wilhelm Haendler's "Morgenthau" in his collection of short stories, *City with Houses* (Evanston, 2002), pp. 21–64. The German original is from 1995.

91 Thomas Ziegler, "Eine Kleinigkeit für uns Reinkarnauten," pp. 83–173. Originally written in the winter of 1987, this story was first published in 1988 and thereafter in English in the 1991 anthology, edited by Uwe Anton, entitled *Welcome to Reality: The Nightmares of Philip K. Dick* (Cambridge, MA, 1991), pp. 125–75. All quotations are my own translations from the 1997 German edition.

92 Ibid., p. 95.

93 Ibid., p. 129.

94 Ibid., p. 130.

95 Ibid., p. 159.

96 Ibid.

97 Ibid., pp. 148–49.

98 Ibid., p. 157.

99 Ibid., pp. 156–57.

100 Ibid., p. 161.

101 Ibid., pp. 160–61.

102 Ibid., pp. 155–56.

103 Ibid., p. 91

104 Ibid., p. 144.

105 Ziegler, e-mail message to author, December 10, 2001.

106 Martin Amis, *Time's Arrow* (New York, 1991).

107 It is interesting to note that the origins of the book developed with a classic, allohistorical "what if?" question. As recounted by Amis in a 1991 interview, he had wondered to himself during the summer of 1989, "What if a man were dying, and his life flashed before him? What if that life were so inverted, so perverted, that instead of flashing forward in time, as we always like to think, his life flashed backwards?" Todd Kliman, "What if?" *St. Petersburg Times*, December 15, 1991, p. 6D. For the record, Amis had been exposed to alternate history as a child through the work of his father, Kingsley Amis, himself the author of the much respected allohistorical novel, *The Alteration*.

108 Amis, *Time's Arrow*, p. 3.

109 Ibid., p. 10.

110 Ibid., p. 6.

111 Ibid., pp. 121, 134, 140, 141.

112 Ibid., p. 153.

113 Ibid., pp. 155–56.

114 Ibid., p. 162.

115 Ibid., p. 165. The text reads: "When Odilo closes his eyes, I see an arrow fly – but wrongly. Point first. Oh no ... "

116 Nor is there any clear literary or historical reason for telling a holocaust story backwards. Some have pointed out that a backwards narrative illustrates the upside-down world of holocaust morality. Michiko Kakutani, "Time Runs Backward To Point Up a Moral," *New York Times*, October 22, 1991, p. C17. Yet, given that two-thirds of the book does not even deal with the Holocaust, this seems an exaggerated point.

117 In splitting the two, Amis was most likely influenced by Robert Jay Lifton's psychological model of "doubling," which explained how Nazi perpetrators were able to commit heinous crimes during World War II while apparently remaining "normal" human beings. See Greg Harris, "Men Giving Birth to New World Orders: Martin Amis's *Time's Arrow*," *Studies in the Novel*, Nr. 4, winter, 1999. According to Lifton's model, perpetrators created their concentration camp "selves" and "normal" selves. The latter shifts all blame for crimes onto the former, who in turn justifies his criminal behavior through all means of rationalizations.

118 Amis, *Time's Arrow*, p. 157.

119 Ibid., p. 165.

120 Amis's commitment to memory was clearly shown in the novel's afterword, which (possibly intended to deflect expected criticism) explained his decision to write *Time's Arrow* as having been influenced by his readings of Primo Levi and Robert Jay Lifton. The fact that Amis's wife is Jewish has, no doubt, also contributed to a certain interest in the Holocaust.

121 Charles Trueheart, "Through a Mirror, Darkly," *Washington Post*, November 26, 1991, p. B1. Amis is quoted as having said, "I'd always been very interested in the Holocaust ... but it never occurred to me I would write about it." Todd Kliman, "What if?" *St. Petersburg Times*, December 15, 1991, p. 6D. One outspoken critic was novelist Simon Louvish, who criticized Amis's use of the Holocaust as modish, opportunistic, and commercially motivated. See Sue Vice, *Holocaust Fiction* (London, 2000), p. 13.

122 The novel appeared in England in 1996 and in the United States in 1998.

123 Stephen Fry, *Making History* (London, 1996), pp. 544–45.

124 The novel furthermore rejected the classical Marxian dictum that "the point of studying the history of the world is not to understand it but to change it." If it is anything, *Making History* is a cautionary tale about the hubris of attempting to bring about substantive historical change.

125 Fry, *Making History*, p. 528.

126 All of the writers in question have garnered substantial critical acclaim in the course of their careers. Christoph Ransmayr has won many literary prizes, including the Elais-Canetti-Stipendium der Stadt Wien, 1986–88; the Anton-Wildgans-Preis, 1988; the Grosser Literaturpreis, Bayerischen Akademie der Schönen Künste, 1992; the Franz-Kafka-Literaturpreis, 1995; the Europäischer Literaturpreis, 1995; the Solothurner Literaturpreis, 1997; and the Franz-Nabl-Preis der Stadt Graz, 1996. *Contemporary Authors Online.* The Gale Group 2000; "Kleiner Versuch über Denkmäler; Christoph Ransmayr als Dichter einer offenen Welt," *Neue Zürcher Zeitung,* April 20, 1996. Thomas Ziegler (born Rainer Zubeil) has been called "Germany's number one science fiction writer." www.google.com/search?q=cache:AlqOvgGEi2o:www.werner-saumweber.de/tbvkl/Blitz-KT.html+ziegler+reinkarnauten&hl=en. Having written for the famous Perry Rhodan series, Ziegler has distinguished himself by multiple prize-winning publications in the fields of science fiction and other popular contemporary genres. Ziegler won the prestigious Kurd Lasswitz prize for fantasy literature (bestowed by German-language creators of science fiction for German-language works of science fiction) in 1980 as well. http://ourworld.compuserve.com/homepages/KARR_WEHNER/ziegler.htm. Daniel Quinn established his reputation after winning the Turner Tomorrow Fellowship (a half-million-dollar prize created by the media mogul Ted Turner) in 1991 for his phenomenally popular novel, *Ishmael.* For the record, *Ishmael* ranks as one of the bestselling books on amazon.com and still sells around 80,000 paperback copies a year. "Quinn is Back with a Buzz," *Publishers Weekly,* February 19, 2001, p. 26. Martin Amis is one of England's most acclaimed novelists, having garnered substantial critical and commercial success for such works as *Money: A Suicide Note* (New York, 1986) and *Success* (New York, 1991).

127 *Morbus Kitahara* appeared on a variety of "must-read" and bestseller lists as well. "Die Schimmel- und Grass-Messe," *Bunte,* September 28, 1995, p. 96. "Die SWF-Bestenliste im Oktober," *Süddeutsche Zeitung,* September 30, 1995. Among the many positive reviews were those by Ursula K. Le Guin, "The Beasts in the Jungle," *Washington Post,* August 10, 1997, p. X5, Gilbert Taylor, *Booklist,* April 1, 1997, and *Kirkus Reviews,* March 1, 1997.

128 *Die Stimmen der Nacht* bagged the prestigious Kurd Lasswitz prize in 1984 (for its original version) as well as in 1994 (for a slightly updated version). *Die Stimmen der Nacht* enjoyed respectable commercial success, selling over 6,000 copies in its 1994 version published by the Heyne Verlag. Letter from Martina Geissler of the Heyne Verlag to author, November 14, 2001. Ziegler won the prize in 1990 for "best short story" for *Eine Kleinigkeit für uns Reinkarnauten.* www.epilog.de/Dokumente/Preise/SF/Lasswitz/Index.html.

129 www.utc.edu/~engldept/booker/booker.htm#1991.

130 See chapter 3.

131 The initial print run of *After Dachau* was 15,000 copies and quickly was increased to 35,000. In addition, the publishers organized a twenty-city book tour to promote the book. "A Buoyed Beau," *Publishers Weekly,* March 12, 2001, p. 20.

132 Many reviewers hailed *Morbus Kitahara* as an important postmodern novel. As Jutta Landa put it, "The book is grounded in . . . a postmodern tradition, in which sign leads to sign, but never to exhaustive signification." Jutta Landa, "Fractured Vision in Christoph Ransmayr's *Morbus Kitahara*," *German Quarterly*, spring, 1998, p. 137. Alberto Mangruel concluded that the book "cannot be reduced to any simplistic caution about the pervasiveness of evil or the infections of revenge." *Sunday Times*, April 6, 1997. Nearly all reviewers of *Time's Arrow* praised Amis's literary wizardry. Echoing the view of many, Dan Chow wrote, "*Time's Arrow* reveals . . . Amis . . . in absolute control of his materials, using them to overwhelming effect." Dan Chow, review of *Time's Arrow* in *Locus*, January, 1992, p. 25.

133 See Dolores Derrickson, "Quinn Draws Eerie, Fascinating World," *Rocky Mountain News*, March 18, 2001, p. 2E; review of *After Dachau* in *Publishers Weekly*, January 15, 2001, p. 54; Heather Lee Schroeder, "Hitler as Victor Will Make You Think," *Capital Times* (Madison, WI), March 23, 2001; Elizabeth Hand, review of *After Dachau* in *Voice Literary Supplement*, April, 2001; Scott Brown, review of *After Dachau* in *Entertainment Weekly*, April 2, 2002. Some critics dissented. Patrick Sullivan described the book as "disappointing" and "poorly conceived." Review of *After Dachau* in *Booklist*, February 15, p. 1117.

134 The phrase "top act" appears in a review of *Die Stimmen der Nacht* at www.sf-rezension.de/htmlversion/stimmen.html. Elsewhere, Jörg Weigand points out that *Die Stimmen der Nacht* "solidified" Ziegler's strong "position in the new German science fiction." Jörg Weigand, "In erster Linie unterhaltend," *Börsenblatt*, February 19, 1985, p. 407.

135 Judith Merril wrote of "Father and Son" that its "proposition is different and terrifying; its resolution somewhat disappointing – maybe necessarily so?" She also praised Bier as a "writer of intense awareness." Judith Merril, "Books," *The Magazine of Fantasy and Science Fiction*, October, 1965, p. 97. Malcolm Bradbury described Bier's volume of stories as "a strong [collection]" and Bier himself as "an important writer." Malcolm Bradbury, "New Short Stories," *Punch*, May 26, 1965, p. 790.

136 Jutta Landa, "Fractured Vision in Christoph Ransmayr's *Morbus Kitahara*," *German Quarterly*, spring, 1998, p. 137; Amir Eshel, "Der Wortlaut der Erinnerung: Christoph Ransmayr's *Morbus Kitahara*," in Stephan Braese, *In der Sprache der Täter: Neue Lektüren deutschsprächiger Nachkriegs- und Gegenwartsliteratur* (Opladen, 1998), pp. 254–55.

137 Armin Ayren, "Die Welt nach Morgenthau," in *Die Stuttgarter Zeitung*, October 10, 1995. Ayren wrote that while the novel in no way "glorified or even diminished the horror [of the Nazi past]," its cold and distanced tone made "evil easily consumable [and] left the reader completely untouched" at the emotional level. Another critic wrote that *Morbus Kitahara's* highly aestheticized language "distorted the unspeakable" and "did not so much serve the cause of memory as some false idea of beauty." See "Das Glück der Bernsteinfliege: Christoph Ransmayrs postapokalyptischer Roman *Morbus*

Kitahara," *Neue Zürcher Zeitung,* October 10, 1995. Another reviewer also questioned whether Ransmayr's "metaphorical language" was suitable for representing Auschwitz. Gustav Seibt, "Christoph Ransmayrs Roman vom Totenreich," *Die Frankfurter Allgemeine Zeitung,* September 16, 1995, p. B5.

138 According to André Spoor, many Dutch critics believed *Morbus Kitahara* was "dangerous" for justifying the postwar Austrian approach after 1945 of evading any direct confrontation with the Nazi experience. Spoor, pp. 186–87.

139 Thomas E. Schmidt, "Dunkelgrüner Granit, brüchig, beinahe schon zu Schotter zerbröselt," *Die Frankfurter Rundschau,* October 11, 1995, p. B3.

140 Thomas Neumann points out how many conservative German literary critics went out of their way to see the punitive plan of Stellamour/Morgenthau as rooted in a wrongheaded, leftwing strategy of dealing with the past. Thomas Neumann, "Mythenspur des Nationalsozialismus: Der Morgenthau Plan und die deutsche Literaturkritik," in *Die Erfindung der Welt,* p. 190.

141 Ulrike Gottwald, review of *Die Stimmen der Nacht* in *Grundwerk,* February, 1989, pp. 1–2. Review of *Die Stimmen der Nacht* in www.sf-rezension.de/htmlversion/stimmen.html.

142 Leslie Epstein, "Ceaselessly into the Past," *Washington Post,* October 27, 1991, p. X1. Other critics credited the book's backwards flow with helping to shed new light on the Holocaust. As David Chute noted, "The book's playfulness, its teasing quality, actually amplifies the emotional impact . . . [in the way it] 'makes strange' historical events that have been recited often." David Chute, "When the Clock Runs Backwards," *Los Angeles Times Book Review,* November 10, 1991, p. 3. See also Dan Cryer, "Backward Reeled the Crime," *Newsday,* November 10, 1991, p. 35. Frank Kermode, "In Reverse," *London Review of Books,* September 12, 1991, p. 11.

143 Leslie Epstein, "Ceaselessly into the Past," *Washington Post,* Books Section, October 27, 1991, p. 1.

144 Charles Trueheart, "Through a Mirror, Darkly," *Washington Post,* November 26, 1991, p. B1; Kakutani, p. C17; Claire Tham, "This Arrow is Amis," *Straits Times,* June 27, 1992, p. 17. Tham concluded that *Time's Arrow* was ultimately a "brilliant but . . . hollow book." As another reviewer concluded, "*Time's Arrow* falls as hideously flat as any novel I have read in the last decade." Stephen Goodwin, "Backwards, Imitating Forward," *USA Today,* November 15, 1991, p. 4D.

145 "Scream First, Pain Later," *The Economist,* October 5, 1991, p. 101. Frances Gertler, "Black Comedy Genre," *Jerusalem Post,* December 27, 1991; the charge of denial is cited in Claire Tham, "This Arrow is Amis," *Straits Times,* June 27, 1992, p. 17. Tham concluded, "Even as one marvels at Amis's bag of tricks, there is a lingering reservation about any literary response which manages to suggest, even ironically, that the Nazis were 'helping' the Jews."

146 As one reviewer for *The Economist* wrote, "Mr Amis's narrator has nothing of interest to say about the real Holocaust." "Scream First, Pain Later," *The Economist,* October 5, 1991, p. 101. As one commentator on amazon.com

noted, "I wish I could give [a] 10 for technique and 1 for morality where this strange book ... is concerned ... Amis appears to reduce the horror of this genocide to an ironic literary technique." Review by "a shopper," dated August 6, 1997. This led others to conclude that the novel was not really even "about Auschwitz ... [but] about Amis's technical wizardry." Judith Dunford, "Repeat Offender," *Tikkun*, May, 1992, p. 77. Dunford concluded, "*Time's Arrow* is ... breathtakingly worked. But how dare he?"

147 See the many reader responses on amazon.com.

148 "This book is low on irony and low on intelligence," she summed up. Natasha Walter, review of *Making History*, *Guardian*, October 17, 1996, p. T10.

149 "Comics should write comic novels if they want their writing to be taken seriously ... Overall the book does not quite work. Perhaps ... if [Fry] ... had written it under another name." Peter Guttridge, "How Can You Take a Holocaust Novel Seriously When It's Written by the Chap from Jeeves and Wooster?" *Observer*, September 22, 1996, p. 17. Another critic agreed, noting an "uneasy disparity between subject matter and style as the novel progresses." Helen Dunmore, "History's Lessons Are No Joke," *The Times*, September 21, 1996.

150 "Something Nasty in the Cistern," *Independent*, September 14, 1996, Books, p. 5.

151 Michiko Kakutani, "Plotting to Erase Hitler from History," *New York Times*, April 21, 1998.

152 Max Davidson, "History without Hitler," *Sunday Telegraph*, September 8, 1996, Books, p. 14.

153 Reader response by Gregg from Como, Mississippi at www.amazon.com. A German reviewer noted, "One wonders if ... this epochal subject [of the Holocaust] did not deserve some other narrative tone other than the brash one of the movie, [hip] hop, and drug generation." "Eine Kunst-Geschichte," *Die Süddeutsche Zeitung*, December 31, 1997.

154 This is the main argument of Sue Vice in her recent book, *Holocaust Fiction* (London, 2000), p. 9. Examples of texts that have received a polarized reception include Bernhard Schlink's *The Reader*, which was controversial for failing to deliver a moral judgment on the novel's female protagonist, an illiterate German concentration camp guard. See Julia M. Klein, "Schlink Evokes Certain Realities but Eludes Moral Certainties," *Chronicle of Higher Education*, December 7, 2001, p. B18.

155 This trend has held true across national lines. Peter Novick has pointed to the paradox of the Holocaust gaining in attention the more the event has faded into the past. See Novick, *The Holocaust in American Life*; Y. Michael Bodemann, *In den Wogen der Erinnerung: Jüdische Existenz in Deutschland* (Berlin, 2002); Norber Frei, "Vom Alter der jüngsten Vergangenheit. Die deutsche Reaktion: leider 'aus dem Ruder gelaufen,'" *Die Süddeutsche Zeitung*, January 30, 2003, p. 17.

156 See, for example, Annette Insdorf, *Indelible Shadows: Film and the Holocaust* (Cambridge, 2003); Jeffrey Shandler, *While America Watches: Televising the Holocaust* (New York, 1999); James E. Young, *The Texture of*

Memory: Holocaust Memorials and Meaning (New Haven, 1993); Dora Apel, *Memory Effects: The Holocaust and the Art of Secondary Witnessing* (New Brunswick, NJ, 2002).

157 See Novick, *The Holocaust in American Life*; Norman Finkelstein, *The Holocaust Industry: Reflections on the Exploitation of Jewish Suffering* (London, 2000); and David Stannard, "Uniqueness as Denial: The Politics of Genocide Scholarship," in Alan Rosenbaum, *Is the Holocaust Unique? Perspectives in Comparative Genocide* (Boulder, CO, 1996), pp. 163–208. Many of these critical voices have focused their attacks on the concept of the Holocaust's uniqueness. See Rosenfeld, "The Politics of Uniqueness," pp. 28–61. See also the introduction of Stéphane Courtois's edited work, *The Black Book of Communism: Crimes, Terror, Repression* (Cambridge, MA, 1999), p. 23; and Amos Elon, "The Politics of Memory," *New York Review of Books*, October 7, 1993, pp. 3–5.

158 Charles Maier's essay "A Surfeit of Memory? Reflections on History, Melancholy and Denial." *History and Memory*, winter, 1993, pp. 136–51 takes issue with the general memory boom of the 1990s but pays special attention to the subject of the Holocaust. A convincing retort can be found in John Torpey, "'Making Whole What Has Been Smashed': Reflections on Reparations," *Journal of Modern History*, June, 2001, pp. 333–58, who argues that it is precisely the increasing attention to the Holocaust in the last decade that explains the world's greater sensitivity to contemporary atrocities. For a general discussion of memory and forgetting, see Avishai Margalit, *The Ethics of Memory* (Cambridge, MA, 2002).

159 A similar point is made by Haviva Krasner-Davidson, who writes that "Holocaust fiction that reduces its subject to a mere device of the author ... does an injustice to those who did not survive to speak for themselves." Haviva Krasner-Davidson, "Whose History is it Anyway?" *Baltimore Jewish Times*, January 31, 1992, p. 56.

160 On the concept of vicarious memory, see James E. Young's recent book, *At Memory's Edge: After-Images of the Holocaust in Contemporary Art and Architecture* (New Haven, 2000). See also Efraim Sicher, "The Future of the Past: Countermemory and Postmemory in Contemporary American Post-Holocaust Narratives," *History and Memory*, fall/winter, 2000, pp. 56–83.

161 Fry was born in 1957, Ziegler in 1956, Ransmayr in 1954, and Amis in 1949. Daniel Quinn, born in 1935, is the exception to this trend.

CONCLUSION

1 "'Tasteless' Hitler Wine Causing Headaches Throughout Europe," *Forward*, September 19, 2003, p. 2. See also Ruth E. Gruber, "Jews Do Not Cheer Wine Bearing Faces of Dictators," *Jewish Telegraphic Agency*, May 1, 1995, p. 10.

2 David Cohen, "The Rise and Fall of the Third Reich Café," *Jerusalem Report*, May 22, 2000, p. 42. The "Mirroring Evil" exhibition took place in 2002 at

New York's Jewish Museum. See, among many others, Edward Rothstein, "Artists Seeking Their Inner Nazi," *New York Times*, February 2, 2002, p. B9. The novel in question is Thor Kunkel's *Final Stage*. Andrew Berg, "Novel about Nazi Pornography Scandalizes German Literati," *New York Times*, March 2, 2004, p. E5. Menno Meyjes's 2002 film *Max*, starring John Cusack and Noah Taylor, is a fictionalized account of the young Hitler's relationship with a Jewish artist in Munich after World War I. See "Portrait of the Führer as a Young Man," *Forward*, December 20, 2002. On the Hitler toilet brush, see "Brush with the Past," *Glasgow Herald*, January 17, 1992, p. 7. Grant Morrison's 1991 comic book series *The New Adventures of Hitler* portrayed Hitler as a disgruntled young man living in Liverpool in 1912. See Rob Rodi, "Cruel Britannia," *Comics Journal*, June 1991, pp. 41–47. Jonathan Kay, "Defying a Taboo, Nazi Protagonists Invade Video Games," *New York Times*, January 3, 2002, p. G6.

3 Only 7 percent of all postwar accounts appeared in these years. Eight accounts appeared out of a total of 106 postwar works (and out of 116 works surveyed in this study). Several British tales appeared of a Nazi wartime victory, but none were produced in the United States or Germany. A few scattered accounts of Hitler's survival in hiding, meanwhile, appeared in the United States, as did one tale of the world without Hitler. See Appendix.

4 Compared with the prior *cold-war phase*, nearly one-and-a-half times more accounts appeared in nearly half the time. Within a span of nine years (1958–67), thirteen moralistic alternate histories appeared, as compared with eight such accounts that appeared in the thirteen-year period 1945–58. Moreover, factoring in two normalized works that appeared in 1964 (*The Other Man* and *It Happened Here*) increases the number to fifteen works, which nearly doubles the number of accounts from the cold-war phase and further underscores the importance of the late 1950s and early 1960s in increasing popular attention to the Nazi past. See Appendix.

5 The number of alternate histories nearly tripled in a little more than twice the time in the preceding *rediscovery phase*. Thirty-eight works appeared in twenty years, compared with thirteen works in eight years. See Appendix.

6 This period has witnessed the most notable increase of allohistorical accounts, the total number exceeding that of the *crisis phase* in nearly half the time. Forty-seven works appeared in fifteen years, compared with thirty-eight works in twenty years. See Appendix.

7 This quotation has been attributed to a wide number of comedians, including Steve Allen, Woody Allen, Lenny Bruce, and Carol Burnett. www.citypaper.com/2001–10–24/funny.html.

8 Roughly 80 percent of all British alternate histories have focused on a Nazi wartime victory, the highest proportion of any nation. Only 47 percent of American accounts have focused on this theme, while 33 percent of German accounts have done so. See Appendix.

9 See Appendix.

10 Fifteen of eighteen German accounts (around 83 percent) appeared after 1981. See Appendix.

11 This trend confirms Susan Sontag's observation about writers rejecting realism as insufficient for simulating atrocity because of its "reinforcing [of] witless stereotypes." Cited in Saul Friedlander, ed., *Reflections of Nazism: An Essay on Kitsch and Death* (New York, 1982), p. 96.

12 Awful writing abounds in many novels. To cite one particular howler from the novel *Fox on the Rhine*, the figure of Claus Graf Schenck von Stauffenberg at one point remarks to Alfred Jodl: "You have sold out your people to kiss Hitler's rosy red rectum." Niles and Dobson, p. 62.

13 This is made embarrassingly clear by the flawed German in innumerable texts.

14 In calling these books bestsellers I do not adhere to a numerical standard of any kind (which, in any case, would vary according to national context) and instead rely upon the description of them as such in the mass media.

15 Exceptions existed, such as the politically charged criticisms by conservative cold-war warriors of William Shirer's essay "If Hitler Had Won World War II" and *The Twilight Zone* episode "He's Alive!" for distracting attention away from communism.

16 Herbert J. Gans, *Popular Culture and High Culture: An Analysis and Evaluation of Taste* (New York, 1999) p. 76.

17 Ibid., pp. 33–38.

18 Gans notes that this priority is no less true for the producers of middle- and low-brow works of culture than it is for those who produce the more high-brow variety. Ibid., p. 34.

19 Ibid., pp. 112–15.

20 The reason for this trend may or may not have to do with differences in the consumers' educational and economic backgrounds. Hard evidence is lacking about the identity of most alternate history readers, but in all likelihood they possess some degree of higher education in history, otherwise they would not be drawn to, let alone be able to make much sense of, the genre in the first place. After all, appreciating how history might have been different requires knowing how it really was to begin with. Moreover, if the typical alternate history reader resembles the average reader of science fiction and fantasy literature, they are most likely male, young, and middle-class – the profile, in a word, of the frequently cited but rarely analyzed "history buff." A. O. Scott, "A Hunger for Fantasy, an Empire to Feed It," *New York Times*, June 16, 2002, Section 2, pp. 1, 26. Scott's article describes the audience of sci fi and fantasy as young adolescents hungering for community through narratives that provide certain meaning for an age of transition.

21 See, for example, Robert Darnton's well-known study, *The Literary Underground of the Old Regime* (Cambridge, MA, 1982), which examines how the low-brow literature of Grub-Street writers in French society challenged the existing aristocratic establishment. Similarly, John Bodnar writes that "mass cultural forms undermine disciplinary institutions (such as governments or churches) in ... managing the public expression of human wants."

John Bodnar, "*Saving Private Ryan* and Postwar Memory in America," *American Historical Review*, June, 2001, p. 809.

22 Sarah Cassidy, "'Hitlerisation' is Damaging Pupils' Historical Knowledge," *Independent*, February 17, 2003. Quoted in the article was Simon Schama, who went so far as to say that he would prefer history teaching to be abolished altogether rather than continue with the current situation in which lessons are restricted to "Hitler and the Henrys."

23 This is similar to the observation made by scholars of the information revolution who warn that our obsession with the virtual reality of cyberspace is threatening to divert our attention away from the problems of reality itself. See Mark Slouka, *War of the Worlds: Cyberspace and the High-Tech Assault on Reality* (New York, 1995).

24 This confusion echoes the famous example of American artist Robert Crumb's ironically minded cartoon strip "When the Niggers Take Over America" (1993), which satirized racism but was instead embraced by white supremacists. See the posting of the comic at the rightwing web page www.tightrope.cc/rcrumbnig.htm.

25 See, for example, Kim Newman and Eugene Byrney's Alternate History Pages, which contain the remark: "PATENTLY BLOODY OBVIOUS DISCLAIMER TO ANYONE WHO DOESN'T GET IT: We believe that Nazis are bad people and if there is a hell, all Nazis go there." www.angelfire.com/ak2/newmanbyrne/index2.html.

26 As Saul Friedlander has noted, it is impossible to empathize with, or put ourselves in the shoes of, Hitler or Himmler, because of their deviant criminal personalities. Saul Friedlander, "'The Final Solution': On the Unease in Historical Interpretation," *History and Memory*, Vol. 2, fall, winter, 1989, pp. 66–68.

27 See, for example, Andrew Sullivan, "This *is* a Religious War," *New York Times Magazine*, October 7, 2001, pp. 44–47, 52–53. President George W. Bush's phrase, the "Axis of Evil," is another example of this form of historical analogy.

Bibliography

PUBLISHED SOURCES

Abernathy, Robert, "Hostage of Tomorrow," *Planet Stories*, spring, 1949, pp. 86–117.

Adams, Michael C. C., *The Best War Ever: America and World War II* (Baltimore, 1994).

Addison, Paul, "Churchill and the Price of Victory: 1939–1945," in Nick Tiratsoo, ed., *From Blitz to Blair: A New History of Britain since 1939* (London, 1997), pp. 53–76.

Aldgate, Anthony, and Jeffrey Richards, *Britain Can Take It: The British Cinema in the Second World War* (Oxford, 1986).

Aldiss, Brian W., "Swastika!", reprinted in Harry Harrison, *Nova 1: An Anthology of Original Science Fiction* (New York, 1970), pp. 73–81.

Alexander, Bevin, *How Hitler Could Have Won World War II: The Ten Fatal Errors that Led to Nazi Defeat* (New York, 2000).

Allhoff, Fred, *Lightning in the Night* (Englewood Cliffs, NJ, 1979).

Allitt, Patrick, *Catholic Intellectuals and Conservative Politics in America, 1950–1985* (Ithaca, 1993).

Amis, Kingsley, *New Maps of Hell: A Survey of Science Fiction* (New York, 1960).

Amis, Martin, *Time's Arrow* (New York, 1991).

Anonymous, *The Man Who Killed Hitler* (Hollywood, 1939).

The Occupation (London, 1960).

Ansel, Walter, *Hitler Confronts England* (Durham, NC, 1960).

Anton, Uwe, *Welcome to Reality: The Nightmares of Philip K. Dick* (Cambridge, MA, 1991).

Apel, Dora, *Memory Effects: The Holocaust and the Art of Secondary Witnessing* (New Brunswick, NJ, 2002).

Arad, Geulie Ne'eman, ed., *Passing into History: Nazism and the Holocaust beyond Memory*, special issue of *History and Memory*, Nr. 1–2, fall, 1997.

Arendt, Hannah, *The Origins of Totalitarianism* (San Diego, 1979).

Armstrong, Anthony and Bruce Graeme, *When the Bells Rang* (London, 1943).

Assmann, Aleida and Ute Frevert, *Geschichtsvergessenheit, Geschichtsversessenheit. Vom Umgang mit deutschen Vergangenheiten nach 1945* (Stuttgart, 1999).

Assmann, Jan, "Kollektives Gedächtnis und kulturelle Identität," in Jan Assmann and Tonio Holscher, eds., *Kultur und Gedächtnis* (Frankfurt am Main, 1988).

Assmann, Jan and Tonio Holscher, eds., *Kultur und Gedächtnis* (Frankfurt am Main, 1988).

Backes, Uwe, Eckhard Jesse, and Rainer Zitelmann, eds., *Die Schatten der Vergangenheit: Impulse zur Historisierung des Nationalsozialismus* (Berlin, 1990).

Baldwin, Peter, *Reworking the Past, Hitler, the Holocaust, and the Historians' Debate* (Boston, 1990).

Barkan, Elazar, *The Guilt of Nations: Restitution and Negotiating Historical Injustices* (New York, 2000).

Barnett, Correlli, *The Audit of War* (London, 1986).

Barnouw, Dagmar, *Germany 1945: Views of War and Violence* (Bloomington, IN, 1996).

Baron, Lawrence, "The Holocaust and American Public Memory, 1945–1960," *Holocaust and Genocide Studies*, Vol. 17, Issue 1, 2003, pp. 62–88.

Barron, Neil, *Anatomy of Wonder: A Critical Guide to Science Fiction* (New York, 1981).

Basil, Otto, *Wenn das der Führer wüsste* (Vienna, 1966).

The Twilight Men (New York, 1968).

Nachlass Otto Basil: Signatur ÖLA: 52/W1/2, 4 (private papers).

Baumann, Zygmunt, *Modernity and the Holocaust* (Ithica, New York, 1989).

Becker, Lucille Frackman, *Pierre Boulle* (New York, 1996).

Benford, Gregory and Martin H. Greenberg, *Hitler Victorious: Eleven Stories of the German Victory in World War II* (New York, 1986).

eds., *Alternate Wars* (New York, 1991).

Benford, Timothy B., *Hitler's Daughter* (New York, 1983).

Bennett, Rab, *Under the Shadow of the Swastika: The Moral Dilemmas of Resistance and Collaboration in Hitler's Europe* (New York, 1999).

Benz, Wolfgang, ed., *Legenden, Lügen, Vorurteile: Ein Lexicon zur Zeitgeschichte* (Munich, 1990), pp. 145–47.

Berger, Stefan, *The Search for Normalcy: National Identity and Historical Consciousness in Germany since 1800* (Providence, 1997).

Berliner, Janet and George Guthridge, *Child of the Light: Book One of the Madagascar Manifesto* (Clarkston, GA, 1995).

Child of the Journey: Book Two of the Madagascar Manifesto (Clarkston, GA, 1997).

Children of the Dusk: Book Three of the Madagascar Manifesto (Clarkston, GA, 1997).

Berthold, W., *Die 42 Attentate auf Adolf Hitler* (Munich, 1981).

Best, Geoffrey, *Churchill: A Study in Greatness* (London, 2001).

Bier, Jesse, "Father and Son," in Jesse Bier, *A Hole in the Lead Apron and Six Other Stories* (New York, 1964), pp. 186–99.

A Hole in the Lead Apron and Six other Stories (New York, 1964).

Bihl, Wolfgang, *Der Tod Adolf Hitlers: Fakten und Überlebenslegenden* (Vienna, 2000).

Bilik, Dorothy Seidman, *Immigrant-Survivors: Post-Holocaust Consciousness in Recent Jewish-American Fiction* (Middletown, CT, 1981).

Blackbourne, David and Geoff Eley, *The Peculiarities of German History* (Oxford, 1984).

Bleiler, E. F., ed., *Supernatural Fiction Writers: Fantasy and Horror*. Vol. II (New York, 1985).

Bodemann, Y. Michael, *In den Wogen der Erinnerung: Jüdische Existenz in Deutschland* (Berlin, 2002).

Boorstin, Daniel, *The Image: A Guide to Pseudo-Events in America* (New York, 1987).

Boulle, Pierre, *Because it is Absurd (On Earth as in Heaven)* (New York, 1971).

"His Last Battle," in Pierre Boulle, *Because it is Absurd (On Earth as in Heaven)* (New York, 1971), pp. 9–38.

Boyar, Jane and Burt, *Hitler Stopped by Franco* (Los Angeles, 2001).

Braese, Stephan, *In der Sprache der Täter: Neue Lektüren deutschsprächiger Nachkriegs- und Gegenwartsliteratur* (Opladen, 1998).

Brokaw, Tom, *The Greatest Generation* (New York, 1998).

Broszat, Martin, ed., *Deutschlands Weg in die Diktatur* (Berlin, 1983).

Brown, Douglas and Christopher Serpell, *Loss of Eden: A Cautionary Tale* (London, 1940).

If Hitler Comes (London, 1941).

Brownlow, Kevin, *How It Happened Here: The Making of a Film* (New York, 1968).

Buchanan, Patrick J., *A Republic, Not an Empire: Reclaiming America's Destiny* (Washington, D.C., 1999).

Bulhof, Johannes, "What If? Modality and History," *History and Theory*, Nr. 2, 1999, pp. 145–68.

Bunting, Madeleine, *The Model Occupation: The Channel Islands under German Rule* (New York, 1995).

Burdekin, Katharine, *Swastika Night* (London, 1937).

Burleigh, Michael and Wolfgang Wippermann, *The Racial State: Nazi Germany, 1933–1945* (Cambridge, 1991).

Buruma, Ian, *The Wages of Guilt: Memories of War in Germany and Japan* (New York, 1994).

Butler, Ewan, *Keep the Memory Green: The First of the Many, France, 1939–40* (London, 1950).

City Divided: Berlin, 1955 (London, 1955).

The Murder of the News Chronicle *and the* Star: *Killed by Trade Union Restrictive Practices, October 17, 1960* (London, 1960).

Loyalty is My Honour (London, 1964).

Without Apology: The Autobiography of Sir George Maudesley, Bart. (London, 1968).

Mason-Mac: The Life of Lieutenant-General Sir Noel Mason-MacFarlane (London, 1972).

Carr, E. H., *What Is History?* (New York, 1961).

Carter, Paul A., *The Creation of Tomorrow: Fifty Years of Magazine Science Fiction* (New York, 1977).

"The Phantom Dictator: Science Fiction Discovers Hitler," in Paul A. Carter, *The Creation of Tomorrow: Fifty Years of Magazine Science Fiction* (New York, 1977).

Chamberlain, Gordon, "Afterword: Allohistory in Science Fiction," in Charles G. Waugh and Martin H. Greenberg, *Alternative Histories: Eleven Stories of the World as It Might Have Been* (New York, 1986).

Chamberlin, David, "An Englishman's Castle," in Richard P. Adler, *Understanding Television: Essays on Television as a Social Force* (New York, 1981), pp. 255–66.

Chamberlin, William Henry, *America's Second Crusade* (Chicago, 1950).

Charmley, John, *Chamberlain and the Lost Peace* (London, 1989).

Churchill: The End of Glory: A Political Biography (New York, 1993).

Churchill's Grand Alliance: The Anglo-American Special Relationship, 1940–57 (New York, 1995).

Splendid Isolation? Britain and the Balance of Power, 1874–1914 (London, 1999).

Charnay, David, *Operation Lucifer: The Chase, Capture, and Trial of Adolf Hitler* (Calabasas, CA, 2001).

Cheyette, Bryan, "Between Repulsion and Attraction: George Steiner's Post-Holocaust Fiction," *Jewish Social Studies*, Vol. 5, Nr. 3, spring/summer, 1999, pp. 67–81.

Choquette, Michel, "Stranger in Paradise," *National Lampoon*, March, 1972, pp. 61–66.

Churchill, Winston, *Their Finest Hour: The Second World War* (Boston, 1949).

Clarke, Comer, *Eichmann: The Man and His Crimes* (New York, 1960).

The Savage Truth (London, 1960).

England under Hitler (New York, 1961).

If the Nazis Had Come (London, 1962).

Clarke, Peter, *Hope and Glory: England, 1900–1990* (London, 1996).

Cohen, Warren I., *The American Revisionists: The Lessons of Intervention in World War I* (Chicago, 1967).

Cole, Wayne, *Roosevelt and the Isolationists: 1932–45* (Lincoln, NE, 1983).

Collins, William Joseph, *Paths Not Taken: The Development, Structure, and Aesthetics of Alternative History* (Ph.D. Dissertation, University of California, Davis, 1990).

Confino, Alon, "Collective Memory and Cultural History: Problems of Method," *American Historical Review*, December, 1997, pp. 1386–1403.

Connor, Steven, *Postmodernist Culture: An Introduction to Theories of the Contemporary* (Cambridge, MA, 1991).

Cooper, A. Edward, *Triumph of the Third Reich* (Salt Lake City, 1999).

Cooper, Giles, *The Other Man: A Novel Based on His Play for Television* (London, 1964).

Courtois, Stéphane, et al., eds., *The Black Book of Communism: Crimes, Terror, Repression* (Cambridge, MA, 1999).

Coward, Noël, *Peace in Our Time* (New York, 1948).

Cowley, Robert, ed., *What If? The World's Foremost Military Historians Imagine What Might Have Been* (New York, 1999).

What If? 2: *Eminent Historians Imagine What Might Have Been* (New York, 2001).

What Ifs? of American History: Eminent Historians Imagine What Might Have Been (New York, 2003).

Cowling, Maurice, *The Impact of Hitler* (Cambridge, 1975).

"Crisis on Earth-X," *Justice League of America*, Nr. 107, October, 1973.

Darwin, John, *The End of the British Empire: The Historical Debate* (London, 1991).

"'. . . das Thema hat mich bedroht': Gespräch mit Sigrid Löffler über *Morbus Kitahara* (Dublin, 1995)," in Uwe Wittstock, *Die Erfindung der Welt: Zum Werk von Christoph Ransmayr* (Frankfurt, 1997), pp. 213–19.

Deighton, Len, *Fighter: The True Story of the Battle of Britain* (London, 1978).

SS-GB: Nazi-occupied Britain, 1941 (New York, 1978).

XPD (Thorndike, ME, 1981).

Winter (London, 1987).

Delaplace, Barbara, "Painted Bridges," in Mike Resnick, ed., *Alternate Outlaws* (New York, 1994), pp. 390–402.

Demandt, Alexander, "If Hitler had Died in 1938?" in Alexander Demandt, *History That Never Happened: A Treatise on the Question, What Would Have Happened If. . . ?* (Jefferson, NC, 1993).

History That Never Happened: A Treatise on the Question, What Would Have Happened If. . . ? (Jefferson, NC, 1993).

"Wenn Hitler gewonnen hätte?", *Tango*, Nr. 18, 1995, pp. 20–27.

Des Pres, Terrence, "Holocaust Laughter?", in Berel Lang, *Writing and the Holocaust* (New York, 1988), pp. 216–33.

Diamond, Sander, "Had the Holocaust Not Happened, How Many Jews Would Be Alive Today? A Survey of Jewish Demography, 1890–2000," *Journal of Holocaust Education*, Vol. 6, winter, 1997, Nr. 3, pp. 21–54.

Dick, Philip K., *The Man in the High Castle* (New York, 1992).

Dikkers, Scott, ed., *Our Dumb Century: The Onion Presents 100 Years of Headlines from America's Finest News Source* (New York, 1999).

Dillingham, Thomas, "Harlan Ellison," *Dictionary of Literary Biography, Volume VIII, Twentieth-Century American Science Fiction Writers* (Detroit, 1981), p. 163.

Disch, Thomas M., *The Dreams Our Stuff is Made Of: How Science Fiction Conquered the World* (New York, 1998).

Ditfurth, Christian v., *Der 21. Juli* (Munich, 2001).

Der Consul (Munich, 2003).

Doherty, Thomas, *Projections of War: Hollywood, American Culture, and World War II* (New York, 1993).

Dozois, Gardner and Stanley Schmidt, eds., *Roads Not Taken: Tales of Alternate History* (New York, 1998).

Drakakis, John, *British Radio Drama* (Cambridge, 1981).

Dvorkin, David, *Budspy* (New York, 1987).

Ellison, Harlan, "The City on the Edge of Forever: An Original Teleplay," in Roger Ellwood, *Six Science Fiction Plays* (New York, 1976), pp. 5–138.

The City on the Edge of Forever (Clarkston, GA, 1993).

Ellwood, Roger, *Six Science Fiction Plays* (New York, 1976).

Elon, Amos, "The Politics of Memory," *New York Review of Books*, October 7, 1993, pp. 3–5.

Engel, Leonard and Emmanuel S. Piller, *The World Aflame: The Russian–American War of 1950* (New York, 1947).

Erickson, Steve, *Tours of the Black Clock* (New York, 1989).

Eshel, Amir, "Der Wortlaut der Erinnerung: Christoph Ransmayrs *Morbus Kitahara*," in Stephan Braese, *In der Sprache der Täter: Neue Lektüren deutschsprächiger Nachkriegs- und Gegenwartsliteratur* (Opladen, 1998), pp. 227–55.

Fadiman, Edwin, Jr., *Who Will Watch the Watchers?* (Boston, 1970).

Farley, Ralph Milne, "I Killed Hitler," in Ralph Milne Farley, *The Omnibus of Time* (Los Angeles, 1950).

The Omnibus of Time (Los Angeles, 1950).

Farmer, Sarah, *Martyred Village: Commemorating the 1944 Massacre at Oradour-sur-Glane* (Berkeley, 1999).

Ferguson, Niall, ed., *Virtual History: Alternatives and Counter-Factuals* (New York, 1997).

"The Kaiser's European Union," in Niall Ferguson, ed., *Virtual History: Alternatives and Counter-Factuals* (New York, 1997), pp. 228–80.

The Pity of War (New York, 1998).

Empire: The Rise and Demise of the British World Order and the Lessons for Global Power (New York, 2003).

Fest, Joachim, *Hitler* (New York, 1973).

Plotting Hitler's Death: The Story of the German Resistance (New York, 1994).

Finkelstein, Norman, *The Holocaust Industry: Reflections on the Exploitation of Jewish Suffering* (London, 2000).

Fleming, Peter, *Operation Sea Lion* (New York, 1957).

Forester, C. S., *The Nightmare* (Boston, 1954 [first edition]).

"If Hitler Had Invaded England," *Saturday Evening Post*, April 16, 23, and 30, 1960.

Gold from Crete (Boston, 1970).

"The Wandering Gentile," in C. S. Forester, *The Nightmare* (Los Angeles, 1979), pp. 225–37.

Foucault, Michel, *Language, Counter-memory, Practice: Selected Essays and Interviews* (Ithaca, 1977).

Frank, Pat, *Alas Babylon* (New York, 1959).

Franklin, Bruce H., "*Star Trek* in the Vietnam Era," *Science Fiction Studies*, March, 1994, pp. 24–34.

Fried, Robert C., "What If Hitler Got the Bomb? (1944)," in Nelson W. Polsby, ed., *What If? Explorations in Social Science Fiction* (Lexington, MA, 1982), pp. 81–93.

Friedlander, Saul, ed., *Reflections of Nazism: An Essay on Kitsch and Death* (New York, 1982).

"'The Final Solution': On the Unease in Historical Interpretation," *History and Memory*, Vol. 2, fall, winter, 1989, pp. 66–68.

Probing the Limits of Representation: Nazism and the 'Final Solution' (Cambridge, MA, 1992).

Friedrich C. J., *Totalitarianism* (New York, 1954).

Fry, Stephen, *Making History* (London, 1996).

Moab is My Washpot (New York, 1999).

Fukuyama, Francis, "The End of History?," *The National Interest*, summer, 1989, pp. 3–18.

Gabler, Neal, *Life, the Movie: How Entertainment Conquered Reality* (New York, 1999).

Gans, Herbert J., *Popular Culture and High Culture: An Analysis and Evaluation of Taste* (New York, 1999).

Geoffroy-Château, Louis-Napoléon, *Napoléon et la conquête du monde 1812–1832, Histoire de la monarchie universelle* (Paris, 1983).

Gessenharter, Wolfgang, *Kippt die Republik? Die neue Rechte und ihre Unterstützung durch Politik und Medien* (Munich, 1994).

Geus, Klaus, "Hitlers vergeblicher Kampf – Ein Beitrag zu [sic] Thema Nationalsozialismus und Science Fiction," *Kopfgeburten*, March, 1996, pp. 30–35.

Gilbert, Adrian, *Britain Invaded: Hitler's Plans for Britain: A Documentary Reconstruction* (London, 1990).

Gingrich, Newt and William Forstchen, *1945* (Riverdale, NY, 1995).

Giordano, Ralph, *Die Bertinis* (Frankfurt, 1982).

Die zweite Schuld: Von der Last Deutscher zu sein (Hamburg, 1987).

Wenn Hitler den Krieg gewonnen hätte: Die Pläne der Nazis nach dem Endsieg (Hamburg, 1989).

Goldhagen, Daniel, *Hitler's Willing Executioners* (New York, 1996).

Goss, Gary, *Hitler's Daughter* (Secaucus, NJ, 1973).

Graml, Hermann and Klaus Dietmar Henke, eds., *Nach Hitler: Der schwierige Umgang mit unserer Geschichte: Beiträge von Martin Broszat* (Munich, 1987).

Gray, Frances, "Giles Cooper: The Medium as Moralist," in John Drakakis, *British Radio Drama* (Cambridge, 1981).

Grayson, Richard, "With Hitler in New York," in Richard Grayson, *With Hitler in New York and Other Stories* (New York, 1979).

With Hitler in New York and Other Stories (New York, 1979).

Greenberg, Martin, ed., *Fantastic Lives: Autobiographical Essays by Notable Science Fiction Writers* (Carbondale, IL, 1981).

The Way It Wasn't: Great Science Fiction Stories of Alternate History (Secaucus, NJ, 1996).

Greenberg, Martin H. and Joseph D. Olander, eds., *Philip K. Dick* (New York, 1983).

Greser, Achim, *Der Führer privat* (Berlin, 2000).

Haendler, Ernst-Wilhelm, *City with Houses* (Evanston, 2002).

"Morgenthau," in Ernst-Wilhelm Haendler, *City with Houses* (Evanston, 2002), pp. 21–64.

Haffner, Sebastian, *The Meaning of Hitler* (New York, 1978).

Halbwachs, Maurice, *The Collective Memory* (New York, 1980).

Hamerow, Theodore, *On the Road to the Wolf's Lair: German Resistance to Hitler* (Cambridge, MA, 1997).

Harris, Greg, "Men Giving Birth to New World Orders: Martin Amis's *Time's Arrow*," *Studies in the Novel*, Nr. 4, winter, 1999, pp. 489–505.

Harris, Robert, *Selling Hitler: The Story of the Hitler Diaries* (New York, 1986).

Fatherland (New York, 1992).

Harrison, Harry, *Nova 1: An Anthology of Original Science Fiction* (New York, 1970).

Hartmann, Geoffrey H., ed., *Bitburg in Moral and Political Perspective* (Bloomington, IN, 1986).

Harvey, David, *The Condition of Postmodernity* (Cambridge, MA, 1992).

Hawkin, Martin, *When Adolf Came* (London, 1943).

Hayles, N. B., "Metaphysics and Metafiction in *The Man in the High Castle*," in Martin Harry Greenberg and Joseph D. Olander, eds., *Philip K. Dick* (New York, 1983), pp. 53–71.

Heilbrunn, Jacob, "Germany's New Right," *Foreign Affairs*, November–December, 1996, pp. 80–99.

Heissenbüttel, Helmut, "Wenn Adolf Hitler den Krieg nicht gewonnen hätte: Eine Phantasie," in Helmut Heissenbüttel, *Wenn Adolf Hitler den Krieg nicht gewonnen hätte: Historische Novellen und wahre Begebenheiten. Projekt 3/2* (Stuttgart, 1979), pp. 7–17.

Helbig, Jörg, *Der parahistorische Roman: Ein literarhistorischer und gattungstypologischer Beitrag zur Allotopieforschung* (Frankfurt, 1987).

Hellekson, Karen, *The Alternate History: Refiguring Historical Time* (Kent, OH, 2001).

Herburger, Günter, *Die Augen der Kämpfer* (Darmstadt, 1980 and 1983).

Hermand, Jost, *Old Dreams of a New Reich: Volkisch Utopias and National Socialism* (Bloomington, IN, 1992).

Herzstein, Robert, *When Nazi Dreams Come True: The Horrifying Story of the Nazi Blueprint for Europe* (London, 1982).

Heydecker, Joe Julius and Johannes Leeb, *Der Nürnberger Prozess; Bilanz der tausend Jahre* (Cologne, 1958).

Heywood, Joseph, *The Berkut* (New York, 1987).

Hitchens, Peter, *The Abolition of Britain: From Winston Churchill to Princess Diana* (San Francisco, 2000).

Horowitz, Sara R., *Voicing the Void: Muteness and Memory in Holocaust Fiction* (Albany, New York, 1992).

Husemann, Harald, "When William Came; If Adolf Had Come. English Speculative Novels on the German Conquest of Britain," *Anglistik & Englischunterricht*, Vols. 29–30, 1986, pp. 57–83.

Hutcheon, Linda, *A Poetics of Postmodernism: History, Theory, Fiction* (New York, 1988).

Huxtable, Ada Louise, *The Unreal America: Architecture and Illusion* (New York, 1997).

Huyssen, Andreas, "Anselm Kiefer: The Terror of History, the Temptation of Myth," *October*, spring, 1989, pp. 22–45.

Insdorf, Annette, *Indelible Shadows: Film and the Holocaust* (Cambridge, 2003).

Jäckel, Eberhard, *Hitler's World View: A Blueprint for Power* (Cambridge, MA, 1981).

Umgang mit Vergangenheit: Beiträge zur Geschichte (Stuttgart, 1989).

"Wenn der Anschlag gelungen wäre," in Eberhard Jäckel, *Umgang mit Vergangenheit: Beiträge zur Geschichte* (Stuttgart, 1989), pp. 195–206.

Jackson, Rosemary, *Fantasy: The Literature of Subversion* (London, 1998).

James, Edward, *Science Fiction in the Twentieth Century* (Oxford, 1994).

Jauss, Hans Robert, "Literary History as a Challenge to Literary Theory," *New Literary History*, Vol. 2, Nr. 1, 1970–71, pp. 13–15.

Jencks, Charles, *The Language of Post-Modern Architecture* (New York, 1984).

Jenkins, Keith, *Rethinking History* (London, 1991).

Kaes, Anton, *From Hitler to* Heimat: *The Return of History as Film* (Cambridge, MA, 1989).

Kansteiner, Wulf, *Television and the Historicization of National Socialism in the Federal Republic of Germany: The Programs of the Zweite Deutsche Fernsehen Between 1963 and 1993* (Ph.D. Dissertation, University of California, Los Angeles, 1997).

Kattago, Siobhan, *Ambiguous Memory: The Nazi Past and German National Identity* (Westport, CT, 2001).

Katz, Robert, "Pius XII Protests the Holocaust," in Robert Cowley, *What If?* 2: *Eminent Historians Imagine What Might Have Been* (New York, 2001), pp. 317–32.

Kaukoreit, Volker und Wendelin Schmidt-Dengler, eds., *Otto Basil und die Literatur um 1945* (Vienna, 1998).

Kershaw, Ian, *The Nazi Dictatorship: Problems and Perspectives of Interpretation* (London, 1985).

Kershaw, Ian and Mark Seaman, *Operation Foxley: The British Plan to Kill Hitler* (London, 1998).

Kiernan, Robert F., *Noël Coward* (New York, 1986).

Kleeblatt, Norman, ed., *Mirroring Evil: Nazi Imagery/Recent Art* (New Brunswick, NJ, 2001).

Köhler, Otto, "Die Morgenthau Plan – Legende und Wirklichkeit," in Reinhard Kühnl und Eckart Spoo, eds., *Was aus Deutschland Werden Sollte: Konzepte des Widerstands, des Exils und der Allierten* (Heilbronn, 1995).

Kolb, Eberhard, *Was Hitler's Seizure of Power on January 30, 1933, Inevitable?* (Washington, D.C., 1996).

Koning, Hans, "Ifs: Destiny and the Archduke's Chauffeur," *Harper's Magazine*, May, 1990, pp. 74–76.

Korn, Salomon, *Geteilte Erinnerung* (Berlin, 1999).

Kornbluth, Cyril M., *Not This August* (New York, 1955).

"Two Dooms," in Gregory Benford and Martin H. Greenberg, *Hitler Victorious: Eleven Stories of the German Victory in World War II* (New York, 1986), pp. 11–52.

Koshar, Rudy, *Germany's Transient Pasts: Preservation and National Memory in the Twentieth Century* (Chapel Hill, 1998).

Krakow, Robert, *The False Witness* (Unpublished play, Boca Raton, FL, 2000).

Kühnl, Reinhard and Eckart Spoo, eds., *Was aus Deutschland Werden Sollte: Konzepte des Widerstands, des Exils und der Allierten* (Heilbronn, 1995).

Ladd, Brian, *The Ghosts of Berlin: Confronting German History in the Urban Landscape* (Chicago, 1997).

Lang, Berel, *Writing and the Holocaust* (New York, 1988).

Larres, Klaus, "Margaret Thatcher, The Foreign Office, and German Reunification," *Cercles* 5, 2002, pp. 175–82.

Lassner, Phyllis, *British Women Writers of World War II: Battlegrounds of their Own* (Houndmills, 1998).

Lessner, Erwin Christian, *Phantom Victory: The Fourth Reich, 1945–1960* (New York, 1944).

Levi, Primo, *The Drowned and the Saved* (New York, 1988).

Levin, Ira, *The Boys from Brazil* (New York, 1976).

Ley, Sandra, ed., *Beyond Time* (New York, 1976).

Linaweaver, Brad, *Moon of Ice* (New York, 1988).

Lipstadt, Deborah, "America and the Memory of the Holocaust," *Modern Judaism*, Vol. 16, Nr. 3, 1996, pp. 195–214.

Locke, Robert Donald, "Demotion," *Astounding Science Fiction*, September, 1952, pp. 71–81.

Longmate, Norman, *If Britain Had Fallen* (New York, 1974).

Louis, Wm. Roger, "The Dissolution of the British Empire in the Era of Vietnam," *The American Historical Review*, February, 2002, pp. 1–25.

Louvish, Simon, *The Resurrections* (New York, 1994).

Lübbe, Hermann, "Der Nationalsozialismus im politischen Bewusstsein der Gegenwart," in Martin Broszat, ed., *Deutschlands Weg in die Diktatur* (Berlin, 1983), pp. 329–49.

Lubos, Arno, *Schwiebus: Ein deutscher Roman* (Munich, 1980).

Lukacs, John, "What if Hitler Had Won the Second World War?", in David Wallechinsky, ed., *The People's Almanac, #2* (New York, 1978), pp. 396–98.

Five Days in London: May 1940 (New Haven, 1999).

Lukas, Richard C., *The Forgotten Holocaust: The Poles under German Occupation, 1939–1944* (Lexington, KY, 1986).

Mackenzie, S. P., "Nazis into Germans: *Went the Day Well?* and *The Eagle Has Landed* – 1942–1976 – Critical Essay," *Journal of Popular Film and Television*, summer, 2003.

Maier, Charles, *The Unmasterable Past: History, Holocaust and German National Identity* (Cambridge, MA, 1988).

"A Surfeit of Memory? Reflections on History, Melancholy and Denial," *History and Memory*, winter, 1993, pp. 136–51.

Malzberg, Barry, "Hitler at Nuremberg," in Mike Resnick and Martin H. Greenberg, eds., *By Any Other Fame* (New York, 1994), pp. 296–302.

Manvell, Roger, *Films and the Second World War* (New York, 1974).

Margalit, Avishai, *The Ethics of Memory* (Cambridge, MA, 2002).

Marino, James, *The Asgard Solution* (New York, 1983).

Maser, Werner, *Hitler* (New York, 1973).

Mathäs, Alexander, "The Presence of the Past: Martin Walser on Memoirs and Memorials," *German Studies Review*, Nr. 1, February, 2002, p. 3.

Mazower, Mark, *Dark Continent: Europe's Twentieth Century* (New York, 1999).

McKale, Donald M., *Hitler: The Survival Myth* (New York, 1981).

McKnight, Edgar V. Jr., *Alternative History: The Development of a Literary Genre* (Ph.D. Dissertation, University of North Carolina, Chapel Hill, 1994).

Meyer, Martin, *Auge um Auge, Zahn um Zahn* (Frankfurt, 1992).

Milward-Oliver, Edward, *The Len Deighton Companion* (London, 1987).

Minow, Martha, *Between Vengeance and Forgiveness: Facing History after Genocide and Mass Violence* (Boston, 1999).

Mintz, Alan, *Popular Culture and the Shaping of Holocaust Memory in America* (Seattle, 2001).

Mitchell, Charles P., *The Hitler Filmography: Worldwide Feature Film and Television Miniseries Portrayals, 1940 through 2000* (Jefferson, NC, 2002).

Mitscherlich, Alexander and Margarete, *Die Unfähigkeit zn trauern* (Munich, 1977).

Moers, Walter, *Adolf die Nazi-Sau* (Vol. I) (Frankfurt am Main, 1998).

Adolf die Nazi-Sau (Vol. II) (Frankfurt am Main, 1999).

Moore, Ward, "A Class with Dr. Chang," in Sandra Ley, ed., *Beyond Time* (New York, 1976).

Morton, H. V., *I, James Blunt* (Toronto, 1942).

Mulisch, Harry, *De toekomst van gisteren* (Amsterdam, 1972).

Die Zukunft von gestern (Berlin, 1995).

Nairn, Tom, *The Break-Up of Britain: Crisis and Neo-Nationalism* (London, 1977).

Nathanson, E. M. and Aaron Bank, *Knight's Cross* (New York, 1993).

Neumann, Thomas, "Mythenspur des Nationalsozialismus: Der Morgenthau Plan und die deutsche Literaturkritik," in Uwe Wittstock, ed., *Die Erfindung der Welt: Zum Werk von Christoph Ransmayr* (Frankfurt, 1997), pp. 188–93.

Nicholls, Peter, "Sarban," in E. F. Bleiler, ed., *Supernatural Fiction Writers: Fantasy and Horror.* Vol. II (New York, 1985), pp. 667–73.

Niekerk, Carl, "Vom Kreislauf der Geschichte," in Uwe Wittstock, ed., *Die Erfindung der Welt: Zum Werk von Christoph Ransmayr* (Frankfurt, 1997), pp. 158–80.

Niethammer, Lutz, *Posthistoire: Has History Come to an End?* (London, 1994).

Niles, Douglas and Michael Dobson, *Fox on the Rhine* (New York, 2000).

Niven, Bill, *Facing the Nazi Past: United Germany and the Legacy of the Third Reich* (New York, 2002).

Nolte, Ernst, *Three Faces of Fascism* (New York, 1966).
Nora, Pierre, "Between Memory and History: *Les lieux de mémoire*," *Representations*, Vol. 26, spring, 1989, pp. 7–25.
  ed., *Realms of Memory: Rethinking the French Past*, Vols. I–III (New York, 1996–1998).
Norden, Eric, *The Ultimate Solution* (New York, 1973).
Novick, Peter, *That Noble Dream: The 'Objectivity Question' and the American Historical Profession* (Cambridge, 1988).
  The Holocaust in American Life (Boston, 1999).
Olick, Jeffrey K., "What Does It Mean to Normalize the Past?", *Social Science History*, winter, 1998, pp. 547–71.
O'Rourke, P. J. and Tod Carroll, "If World War II Had Been Fought Like the War in Vietnam," *National Lampoon*, October, 1980, pp. 54–57.
Overgard, William, *The Divide* (New York, 1980).
Overy, Richard, *Why the Allies Won* (New York, 1995).
Patton, Phil, "Lee Defeats Grant," *American Heritage*, September 1999, pp. 39–45.
Payn, Graham and Sheridan Morley, eds., *The Noël Coward Diaries* (Boston, 1982).
Petrova, Ada and Peter Watson, *The Death of Hitler: The Full Story, with New Evidence from Secret Russian Archives* (New York, 1996).
Picard, Max, *Hitler in Ourselves* (Hinsdale, IL, 1947).
Piehler, Kurt, G. *Remembering War the American Way* (Washington, D.C., 1995).
Pleschinski, Hans, "Ausflug," in *Der Rabe: Magazin für jede Art von Literatur* (Stuttgart, 1983), pp. 24–38.
Polsby, Nelson W., *What If? Explorations in Social Science Fiction* (Lexington, MA, 1982).
Ponting, Clive, *1940: Myth and Reality* (London, 1990).
  Churchill (London, 1994).
  The Reality behind the Distortions, Myths, Lies, and Illusions of World War II (New York, 1995).
Portelli, Alessandro, "Uchronic Dreams: Working-Class Memory and Possible Worlds," in Alessandro Portelli, *The Death of Luigi Trastulli and Other Stories: Form and Meaning in Oral History* (Albany, 1991), pp. 99–116.
Postman, Neil, *Amusing Ourselves to Death: Public Discourse in the Age of Show Business* (New York, 1986).
Presnell, Don and Marty McGee, *A Critical History of Television's* The Twilight Zone, *1959–1964* (Jefferson, NC, 1998).
Priest, Christopher, *The Separation* (London, 2002).
Pringle, David, *The Ultimate Guide to Science Fiction: An A-Z of Science Fiction Books* (London, 1990).
Puccetti, Roland, *The Death of the Führer* (New York, 1972).
Quinn, Daniel, *After Dachau* (New York, 2001).
Radin, Max, *The Day of Reckoning* (New York, 1943).
Raine, Craig, *'1953': A Version of Racine's* Andromaque (London, 1990).
Ransmayr, Christoph, *The Dog King* (New York, 1997).

Renouvier, Charles, *Uchronie (l'utopie dans l'histoire): esquisse historique apocryphe du développement de la civilisation européenne tel qu'il n'a pas été, tel qu'il aurait pu être* (Paris, 1876).

Resnick, Mike, ed., *Alternate Outlaws* (New York, 1994).

Resnick, Mike, and Martin H. Greenberg, eds., *By Any Other Fame* (New York, 1994).

Rhodes, Arthur, *The Last Reich* (Danbury, CT, 2001).

Robban, Randolph, *Si l'Allemagne avait vaincu* (Paris, 1950).

Wenn Deutschland gesiegt hätte (Stuttgart, 1951).

Roberts, Andrew, *The Holy Fox: A Biography of Lord Halifax* (London, 1991).

Eminent Churchillians (London, 1994).

The Aachen Memorandum (London, 1995).

"Prime Minister Halifax," in Robert Cowley, *What If? 2: Eminent Historians Imagine What Might Have Been* (New York, 2001), pp. 279–90.

ed., *What Might Have Been: Imaginary History from Twelve Leading Historians* (London, 2004).

Roberts, Andrew and Niall Ferguson, "Hitler's England," in Niall Ferguson, *Virtual History: Alternatives and Counter-Factuals* (New York, 1997), pp. 281–320.

Roberts, Keith, "Weihnachtsabend," in Gregory Benford and Martin H. Greenberg, *Hitler Victorious: Eleven Stories of the German Victory in World War II* (New York, 1986), pp. 89–120.

Rodiek, Christoph, *Erfundene Vergangenheit: Kontrafaktische Geschichtsdarstellung (Uchronie) in der Literatur* (Frankfurt, 1997).

Rose, Paul Lawrence, *Heisenberg and the Nazi Atomic Bomb Project: A Study in German Culture* (Berkeley, 1998).

Rose, Richard, *The Wolf* (New York, 1980).

Rosenbaum, Alan, *Is the Holocaust Unique? Perspectives in Comparative Genocide* (Boulder, CO, 1996).

Rosenfeld, Alvin H., *Imagining Hitler* (Bloomington, IN, 1985).

"The Americanization of the Holocaust," (Ann Arbor, MI, 1995), pp. 1–45.

Rosenfeld, Gavriel D., "The Reception of William L. Shirer's *The Rise and Fall of the Third Reich* in the United States and West Germany, 1960–1962," *Journal of Contemporary History*, January, 1994, pp. 95–129.

"The Architects' Debate: Architectural Discourse and the Memory of Nazism in the Federal Republic of Germany, 1977–1997," in Geulie Ne'eman Arad, ed., *Passing into History: Nazism and the Holocaust Beyond Memory*, special issue of *History and Memory*, Nr. 1–2, fall, 1997, pp. 189–225.

"The Politics of Uniqueness: Reflections on the Recent Polemical Turn in Holocaust and Genocide Scholarship," *Holocaust and Genocide Studies*, Nr. 1, spring, 1999, pp. 28–61.

Munich and Memory: Architecture, Monuments, and the Legacy of the Third Reich (Berkeley, 2000).

"Why Do We Ask 'What If?'? Reflections on the Function of Alternate History," *History and Theory*, December, 2002, pp. 90–103.

Roth, Philip, *The Plot against America* (New York, 2004).

Rousso, Henry, *The Vichy Syndrome: History and Memory in France since 1944* (Cambridge, MA, 1991).

Rupnow, Dirk, *Vernichten und Erinnern: Spuren nationalsozialistischer Gedächtnispolitik* (Ph.D. Dissertation, Klagenfurt, 2002).

Rusch, Kris, *Hitler's Angel* (New York, 1998).

Russett, Bruce M., *No Clear and Present Danger: A Skeptical View of the U.S. Entry into World War II* (New York, 1972).

Rutman, Leo, *Clash of Eagles* (New York, 1990).

Sackville-West, Vita, *Grand Canyon* (Garden City, NY, 1942).

Salewski, Michael, "N.N.: *Der großgermanische Seekrieg gegen Japan und die USA im Jahre 1949. The Near Miss*: Eine Buchbesprechung," in Michael Salewski, ed., *Was wäre, wenn: Alternativ- und Parallelgeschichte: Brücken zwischen Phantasie und Wirklichkeit* (Stuttgart, 1999).

ed., *Was wäre, wenn: Alternativ- und Parallelgeschichte: Brücken zwischen Phantasie und Wirklichkeit* (Stuttgart, 1999).

Santner, Eric L., *Stranded Objects: Mourning, Memory and Film in Postwar Germany* (Ithaca, 1990).

Sarban (a.k.a. John W. Wall), *The Sound of His Horn* (New York, 1960 [first edition 1952]).

Schellenberg, Walter, John Keegan, and John Erickson, *Invasion 1940* (London, 2001).

Schlant, Ernestine, *The Language of Silence: West German Literature and the Holocaust* (New York, 1999).

Schlesinger, Arthur M., Jr., *The Disuniting of America: Reflections on a Multicultural Society* (New York, 1998).

Seeßlen, Georg, *Tanz den Adolf Hitler: Faschismus in der populären Kultur* (Berlin, 1994).

Segev, Tom, *The Seventh Million: The Israelis and the Holocaust* (New York, 1993).

Shandler, Jeffrey, *While America Watches: Televising the Holocaust* (New York, 1999).

Shirer, William L., "If Hitler Had Won World War II," *Look*, December 19, 1961, pp. 28–43.

Sicher, Efraim, "The Future of the Past: Countermemory and Postmemory in Contemporary American Post-Holocaust Narratives," *History and Memory*, fall/winter, 2000, pp. 56–83.

Simon, Erik, ed., *Alexanders langes Leben, Stalins früher Tod und andere abwegige Geschichten: Erzählungen und Berichte aus Parallelwelten* (Munich, 1999).

Simpson, Christopher, *Blowback: The First Full Account of America's Recruitment of Nazis and Its Disastrous Effect on our Domestic and Foreign Policy* (New York, 1988).

Slouka, Mark, *War of the Worlds: Cyberspace and the High-Tech Assault on Reality* (New York, 1995).

Smoler, Frederic, "Past Tense," *American Heritage*, September 1999, pp. 45–49.

Sontag, Susan, "Fascinating Fascism," in *Under the Sign of Saturn* (New York, 1980), pp. 73–105.

Speer, Albert, *Inside the Third Reich* (New York, 1970).

Spiller, Roger, "The Führer in the Dock: A Speculation on the Banality of Evil," in Robert Cowley, *What If? 2: Eminent Hitorians Imagine What Might Have Been* (New York, 2001), pp. 344–65.

Spinrad, Norman, *The Iron Dream* (Frogmore, 1974).

"A Prince from Another Land," in Martin H. Greenberg, ed., *Fantastic Lives: Autobiographical Essays by Notable Science Fiction Writers* (Carbondale, IL, 1981), p. 159.

Spoor, André, "Der kosmopolitische Dörfler," in Uwe Wittstock, ed., *Die Erfindung der Welt: Zum Werk von Christoph Ransmayr* (Frankfurt, 1997), pp. 181–87.

Squire, J. C., *If It Had Happened Otherwise: Lapses into Imaginary History* (London, 1931).

Stannard, David, "Uniqueness as Denial: The Politics of Genocide Scholarship," in Alan Rosenbaum, *Is the Holocaust Unique? Perspectives in Comparative Genocide* (Boulder, CO, 1996), pp. 163–208.

Steiner, George, *The Portage to San Cristóbal of A.H.* (New York, 1981).

Sternlicht, Sanford, *C. S. Forester* (Boston, 1981).

Stroyar, J. N., *The Children's War* (New York, 2001).

Sutherland, John, *Bestsellers: Popular Fiction of the 1970s* (London, 1981).

Sutin, Lawrence, ed., *The Shifting Realities of Philip K. Dick: Selected Literary and Philosophical Writings* (New York, 1995).

Szczesuil, Timothy P., ed., *His Share of Glory: The Complete Short Science Fiction of C. M. Kornbluth* (Framingham, MA, 1997).

Taylor, A. J. P., *The Origins of the Second World War* (New York, 1961).

Terkel, Studs, *The Good War: An Oral History of World War II* (New York, 1984).

Tezuka, Osamu, *Adolf: The Half-Aryan* (San Francisco, 1996).

 Adolf: 1945 and All That Remains (San Francisco, 1996).

 Adolf: Days of Infamy (San Francisco, 1996).

"The Man Who Could Be Hitler," *T-Man: World Wide Trouble-Shooter*, Nr. 34, April 1956.

"The Strange Fate of Adolf Hitler," *Strange Adventures*. Nr. 3, 1950.

"Thirteen against the Earth," *Justice League of America*, Nr. 107, December, 1973.

Thomas, D. M., *The White Hotel* (Phoenix, 1981).

Thomas, Hugh, *The Murder of Adolf Hitler: The Truth about the Bodies in the Berlin Bunker* (New York, 1996).

 The Spanish Civil War (New York, 2001).

Tiratsoo, Nick, ed., *From Blitz to Blair: A New History of Britain since 1939* (London, 1997).

Torpey, John, "'Making Whole What Has Been Smashed': Reflections on Reparations," *Journal of Modern History*, June, 2001, pp. 333–58.

Trevor-Roper, Hugh R., *The Last Days of Hitler* (New York, 1947).

Tsouras, Peter, *Third Reich Victorious: Alternate Decisions of World War II* (London, 2002).

Turner, Henry, *German Big Business and the Rise of Hitler* (New York, 1985).

"Hitler's Impact on History," in David Wetzel, ed., *From the Berlin Museum to the Berlin Wall: Essays on the Cultural and Political History of Modern Germany* (Westport, CT, 1996), pp. 109–26.

Hitler's Thirty Days to Power: January 1933 (Reading, MA, 1996).

Turtledove, Harry, "Ready for the Fatherland," in Gregory Benford and Martin H. Greenberg, eds., *Alternate Wars* (New York, 1991), pp. 113–27.

Departures (New York, 1993).

"In the Presence of Mine Enemies," in Harry Turtledove, *Departures* (New York, 1993), pp. 200–17.

In the Presence of Mine Enemies (New York, 2003).

Turtledove, Harry, and Martin H. Greenberg, eds., *The Best Alternate History Stories of the 20th Century* (New York, 2001).

Van Loon, Hendrik Willem, *Invasion: Being an Eyewitness Account of the Nazi Invasion of America* (New York, 1940).

Van Rjndt, Philippe, *The Trial of Adolf Hitler* (New York, 1978).

Variety's Science Fiction Reviews (New York, 1985).

Vice, Sue, *Holocaust Fiction* (London, 2000).

Von Klemperer, Klemens, *German Resistance against Hitler: The Search for Allies Abroad, 1938–1945* (Oxford, 1992).

Wagner, Jon and Jan Lundeen, *Deep Space and Sacred Time:* Star Trek *in the American Mythos* (Westport, CT, 1998).

Walker, Mark, *Nazi Science: Myth, Truth, and the German Atomic Bomb* (New York, 1995).

Wallechinsky, David, ed., *The People's Almanac, #2* (New York, 1978).

Warrick, Patricia S., "The Encounter of Taoism and Fascism in *The Man in the High Castle*," in Martin Greenberg and Joseph D. Olander, eds., *Philip K. Dick* (New York, 1983), pp. 27–52.

Mind in Motion: The Fiction of Philip K. Dick (Carbondale, IL, 1987).

Watt, Donald, "Appeasement: The Rise of a Revisionist School?", *The Political Quarterly*, April, 1965, pp. 191–213.

Waugh, Charles G. and Martin H. Greenberg, *Alternative Histories: Eleven Stories of the World as It Might Have Been* (New York, 1986).

Wedemeyer-Schwiersch, Sabine, "Requiem für einen Stümper," in Erik Simon, ed., *Alexanders langes Leben, Stalins früher Tod und andere abwegige Geschichten: Erzählungen und Berichte aus Parallelwelten* (Munich, 1999), pp. 243–50.

Weil, Ellen and Gary K. Wolfe, *Harlan Ellison: The Edge of Forever* (Columbus, OH, 2002).

Weiss, Christina, ed., *Schrift, écriture, geschrieben, gelesen: Für Helmut Heissenbüttel zum siebzigsten Geburtstag* (Stuttgart, 1991).

Wetzel, David, ed., *From the Berlin Museum to the Berlin Wall: Essays on the Cultural and Political History of Modern Germany* (Westport, CT, 1996).

White, Hayden, *The Content of the Form: Narrative Discourse and Historical Representation* (Baltimore, 1987).

"Historical Emplotment and the Problem of Truth," in Saul Friedlander, ed., *Probing the Limits of Representation: Nazism and the 'Final Solution'* (Cambridge, MA, 1992), pp. 37–53.

White, Marion, *If We Should Fail* (New York, 1942).

Wiedmer, Caroline Alice, *The Claims of Memory: Representations of the Holocaust in Contemporary Germany and France* (Ithaca, 1999).

Wilds, Karl, "Identity Creation and the Culture of Contrition: Recasting 'Normality' in the Berlin Republic," *German Politics*, April, 2000, pp. 83–102.

Wittstock, Uwe, ed., *Die Erfindung der Welt: Zum Werk von Christoph Ransmayr* (Frankfurt, 1997).

Wolfssohn, Michael, *Ewige Schuld? 40 Jahre Deutsch-Jüdisch-Israelische Beziehungen* (Munich, 1988).

Wright, Bradford W., *Comic Book Nation: The Transformation of Youth Culture in America* (Baltimore, 2001).

Wyden, Peter, *The Hitler Virus: The Insidious Legacy of Adolf Hitler* (New York, 2001).

Yarden, Ivo H., "On the Death of Hitler's Assassin," *Midstream*, January, 1992, pp. 34–36.

Young, James E., *The Texture of Memory: Holocaust Memorials and Meaning* (New Haven, 1993).

At Memory's Edge: After-images of the Holocaust in Contemporary Art and Architecture (New Haven, 2000).

Young, Michael, *The Trial of Adolf Hitler* (New York, 1944).

Yulsman, Jerry, *Elleander Morning* (New York, 1984).

Zelizer, Barbie, *Remembering to Forget: The Holocaust Through the Camera Eye* (Chicago, 1998).

Zicree, Marc Scott, *The Twilight Zone Companion* (New York, 1982).

Ziegler, Thomas, *Die Stimmen der Nacht* (Frankfurt, 1984).

"Eine Kleinigkeit für uns Reinkarnauten," in Thomas Ziegler, *Eine Kleinigkeit für uns Reinkarnauten* (Windeck, 1997), pp. 83–173.

FILMS AND TELEVISION PROGRAMS

An Englishman's Castle (1978)
The Battle of Britain (1969)
"California Reich" (1998)
The City on the Edge of Forever (1967)
Conversation with the Beast (1996)
"Cradle of Darkness" (2002)
The Dirty Dozen: Next Mission (1985)
The Empty Mirror (1996)
Fatherland (1994)
Flesh Feast (1967)

He Lives (1967)
"He's Alive!" (1963)
Hitler: Dead or Alive (1942)
If Britain Had Fallen (1972)
It Happened Here (1964)
The Last Supper (1995)
The Man He Found (1951)
"The Master Plan of Dr. Fu Manchu" (1956)
Miss Grant Goes to the Door (1940)
Night Conspirators (1962)
The Other Man (1964)
The Philadelphia Experiment II (1993)
The Silent Village (1943)
They Saved Hitler's Brain (1963)
Went the Day Well? (1942)

Appendix:
Alternate histories by theme, era, nation, and medium

KEY:

N	=	Novel
SS	=	Short story
F	=	Film
TV	=	Television broadcast
P	=	Play
C	=	Comic book
AAH	=	Analytical alternate history (book or essay)
UK	=	British
US	=	American
G	=	German
O	=	Other

Please note that the dates given for these works are those of the *original* publication, release or broadcast. The dates in the Bibliography are those of the edition used by the author.

CHAPTER 1: GREAT BRITAIN DEFEATED: BETWEEN RESISTANCE AND COLLABORATION

1. Katharine Burdekin, *Swastika Night* (1937) N
2. Douglas Brown and Christopher Serpell, *Loss of Eden: A Cautionary Tale* (1940) N
3. H. V. Morton, *I, James Blunt* (1942) N
4. Vita Sackville-West, *Grand Canyon* (1942) N
5. Anthony Armstrong and Bruce Graeme, *When the Bells Rang* (1943) N
6. Martin Hawkin, *When Adolf Came* (1943) N
7. *The Silent Village* (1943) F
8. Noël Coward, *Peace in Our Time* (1948) P
9. Sarban (a.k.a. John W. Wall), *The Sound of His Horn* (1952) N

10. C. S. Forester, "If Hitler Had Invaded England" (1960) N
11. Comer Clarke, *England under Hitler* (1961) AAH
12. Anonymous, *The Occupation* (1960) N
13. Giles Cooper, *The Other Man: A Novel Based on His Play for Television* (1964) TV, N
14. *It Happened Here* (1964) F
15. Ewan Butler, *Without Apology: The Autobiography of Sir George Maudesley, Bart.* (1968) N
16. Keith Roberts, "Weihnachtsabend" (1972) SS
17. Norman Longmate, *If Britain Had Fallen* (1972) TV, (1974) AAH
18. *An Englishman's Castle* (1978) TV
19. Len Deighton, *SS-GB: Nazi-occupied Britain, 1941* (1978) N
20. Adrian Gilbert, *Britain Invaded: Hitler's Plans for Britain: A Documentary Reconstruction* (1990) AAH
21. Craig Raine, *'1953': A Version of Racine's* Andromaque (1990) P
22. Robert Harris, *Fatherland* (1992) N
23. Madeleine Bunting, *The Model Occupation: The Channel Islands under German Rule* (1995) AAH
24. John Charmley, *Churchill: The End of Glory: A Political Biography* (1993) AAH
25. Andrew Roberts and Niall Ferguson, "Hitler's England" (1997) AAH
26. Andrew Roberts, "Prime Minister Halifax" (2001) AAH
27. Christopher Priest, *The Separation* (2002) N

Total

Number of works	27	
Prewar/wartime phase: 1937–45	7	(26%)
Cold war phase: 1945–late 1950s	2	(7%)
Rediscovery phase: late 1950s–mid-1960s	3	(11%)
Crisis phase: mid-1960s–early 1980s	7	(26%)
Post-cold war phase: late 1980s–present	8	(30%)
Novels	13	(49%)
Short stories	1	(4%)
Films	2	(7%)
Television programs	3	(11%)
Plays	2	(7%)
Comic books	0	(0%)
Analytical alternate histories	6	(22%)

CHAPTER 2: THE UNITED STATES AND THE DILEMMAS
OF MILITARY INTERVENTION

 1. Hendrik Willem van Loon, *Invasion: Being an Eyewitness Account of the Nazi Invasion of America* (1940) N
 2. Fred Allhoff, *Lightning in the Night* (1940) N
 3. Marion White, *If We Should Fail* (1942) N
 4. C. M. Kornbluth, "Two Dooms" (1958) SS
 5. William L. Shirer, "If Hitler Had Won World War II" (1961) AAH
 6. Philip K. Dick, *The Man in the High Castle* (1962) N
 7. "The City on the Edge of Forever" (1967) TV
 8. Eric Norden, *The Ultimate Solution* (1973) N
 9. "Crisis on Earth-X," *Justice League of America*, Nr. 107 (October, 1973) C
10. "Thirteen against the Earth," *Justice League of America*, Nr. 107 (December, 1973) C
11. Bruce M. Russett, *No Clear and Present Danger: A Skeptical View of the U.S. Entry into World War II* (1972) AAH
12. John Lukacs, "What if Hitler Had Won the Second World War?" (1978) AAH
13. Brad Linaweaver, *Moon of Ice* (1982) N
14. Ward Moore, "A Class with Dr. Chang" (1975) SS
15. P. J. O'Rourke, "If World War II Had Been Fought Like the War in Vietnam" (1980) C
16. William Overgard, *The Divide* (1980) N
17. David Dvorkin, *Budspy* (1987) N
18. "What If: Überman" (1979) TV
19. Leo Rutman, *Clash of Eagles* (1990) N
20. *The Philadelphia Experiment II* (1993) F
21. *Fatherland* (HBO version, 1994) TV
22. Newt Gingrich and William Forstchen, *1945* (1995) N
23. Arthur Rhodes, *The Last Reich* (2001) N
24. J. N. Stroyar, *The Children's War* (2001) N
25. Harry Turtledove, *In the Presence of Mine Enemies* (2003) N
26. Pat Buchanan, *A Republic, not an Empire: Reclaiming America's Destiny* (1999) AAH
27. A. Edward Cooper, *Triumph of the Third Reich* (1999) N
28. Philip Roth, *The Plot against America* (2004) N

Total

Number of works	28	
Prewar/wartime phase: 1937–45	3	(16%)
Cold war phase: 1945–late 1950s	0	(5%)
Rediscovery phase: late 1950s–mid-1960s	4	(11%)
Crisis phase: mid-1960s–early 1980s	11	(35%)
Post-cold war phase: late 1980s–present	10	(33%)
Novels	15	(53%)
Short stories	2	(7%)
Films	3	(11%)
Television programs	3	(11%)
Plays	0	(0%)
Comic books	2	(7%)
Analytical alternate histories	3	(11%)

CHAPTER 3: GERMANY'S WARTIME TRIUMPH: FROM DYSTOPIA TO NORMALCY

1. Otto Basil, *Wenn das der Führer wüsste* (1966) N
2. Helmut Heissenbüttel, "Wenn Adolf Hitler den Krieg nicht gewonnen hätte" (1979) SS
3. Arno Lubos, *Schwiebus: Ein deutscher Roman* (1980) N
4. Ralph Giordano, *Wenn Hitler den Krieg gewonnen hätte: Die Pläne der Nazis nach dem Endsieg* (1989) AAH
5. Alexander Demandt, "Wenn Hitler gewonnen hätte?" (1995) AAH
6. Michael Salewski, "N.N.: *Der großgermanische Seekrieg gegen Japan und die USA im Jahre 1949. The Near Miss:* Eine Buchbesprechung" (1999) AAH

Total

Number of works	6	
Prewar/wartime phase: 1937–45	0	(0%)
Cold war phase: 1945–late 1950s	0	(0%)
Rediscovery phase: late 1950s–mid-1960s	1	(17%)
Crisis phase: mid-1960s–early 1980s	2	(33%)
Post-cold war phase: late 1980s–present	3	(50%)
Novels	2	(33%)

Short stories	1	(17%)
Films	0	(0%)
Television programs	0	(0%)
Plays	0	(0%)
Comic books	0	(0%)
Analytical alternate histories	3	(50%)

CHAPTER 4: OTHER NATIONS: A DISSENTING VIEW

1. Randolph Robban, *Si l'Allemagne avait vaincu* (1951) N
2. Harry Mulisch, *De toekomst van gisteren* (1972) N

Total

Number of works	2	
Prewar/wartime phase: 1937–45	0	(0%)
Cold war phase: 1945–late 1950s	1	(50%)
Rediscovery phase: late 1950s–mid-1960s	0	(0%)
Crisis phase: mid-1960s–early 1980s	1	(50%)
Post-cold war phase: late 1980s–present	0	(0%)
Novels	2	(100%)
Short stories	0	(0%)
Films	0	(0%)
Television programs	0	(0%)
Plays	0	(0%)
Comic Books	0	(0%)
Analytical alternate histories	0	(0%)

Grand Total for Part One: the Nazis win World War II

Number of works	63	
Prewar/wartime phase: 1937–45	10	(16%)
Cold war phase: 1945–late 1950s	3	(5%)
Rediscovery phase: late 1950s–mid-1960s	7	(11%)
Crisis phase: mid-1960s–early 1980s	22	(35%)
Post-cold war phase: late 1980s–present	21	(33%)
British	27	(43%)
American	28	(44%)
German	6	(10%)
Other	2	(3%)
Novels	33	(52%)

Short stories	4	(6%)
Films	3	(5%)
Television programs	6	(10%)
Plays	2	(3%)
Comic books	3	(5%)
Analytical alternate histories	12	(19%)

CHAPTER 5: THE FUGITIVE FÜHRER AND THE SEARCH FOR JUSTICE

1. "The Strange Fate of Adolph Hitler" (1950) C, US
2. "The Man Who Could Be Hitler" (1952) C, US
3. C. S. Forester, "The Wandering Gentile" (1954) SS, UK
4. "The Master Plan of Dr. Fu Manchu" (1956) TV, US
5. *They Saved Hitler's Brain* (1963) F, US
6. *Flesh Feast* (1967) F, US
7. *He Lives* (1967) F, US
8. *Night Conspirators* (1962) TV, UK
9. "He's Alive!" (1963) TV, US
10. Brian Aldiss, "Swastika!" (1970) SS, UK
11. Edwin Fadiman Jr., *Who Will Watch the Watchers?* (1970) N, US
12. Pierre Boulle, "His Last Battle" (1971) SS, O
13. Michel Choquette, "Stranger in Paradise" (1972) SS, US
14. Gary Goss, *Hitler's Daughter* (1973) N, US
15. George Steiner, *The Portage to San Cristóbal of A.H.* (1981) N, UK
16. Richard Grayson, "With Hitler in New York" (1979) SS, US
17. Philippe van Rjndt, *The Trial of Adolf Hitler* (1978) N, O
18. James Marino, *The Asgard Solution* (1983) N, US
19. Joseph Heywood, *The Berkut* (1987) N, US
20. Steve Erickson, *Tours of the Black Clock* (1989) N, US
21. E. M. Nathanson and Aaron Bank, *Knight's Cross* (1993) N, US
22. Robert Krakow, *The False Witness* (1996) P, US
23. *The Empty Mirror* (1996) F, US
24. *Conversation with the Beast* (1996) F, G
25. Walter Moers, *Adolf die Nazi-Sau* (Volume 1) (1998) C, G
26. Walter Moers, *Adolf die Nazi-Sau* (Volume 2) (1999) C, G
27. Barry Malzberg, "Hitler at Nuremberg" (1994) SS, US
28. David Charnay, *Operation Lucifer: The Chase, Capture, and Trial of Adolf Hitler* (2001) N, US
29. Roger Spiller, "The Führer in the Dock" (2001) AAH, US

Total

Number of works	29	
Cold war phase: 1945–late 1950s	4	(14%)
Rediscovery phase: late 1950s–mid-1960s	5	(18%)
Crisis phase: mid-1960s–early 1980s	10	(34%)
Post-cold war phase: late 1980s–present	10	(34%)
British	4	(14%)
American	20	(68%)
German	3	(10%)
Other	2	(8%)
Novels	9	(31%)
Short stories	6	(21%)
Films	5	(18%)
Television programs	3	(10%)
Plays	1	(3%)
Comic books	4	(14%)
Analytical alternate histories	1	(3%)

CHAPTER 6: THE WORLD WITHOUT HITLER: BETTER OR WORSE?

Accounts depicting history as better

1. Jerry Yulsman, *Elleander Morning* (1984) N, US
2. Hans Pleschinski, "Ausflug" (1983) SS, G
3. Alexander Demandt, "If Hitler had Died in 1938?" (1984) AAH, G
4. Henry Turner, "Hitler's Impact on History" (1996) AAH, US
5. Sabine Wedemeyer-Schwiersch, "Requiem für einen Stümper" (1999) SS, G

Accounts depicting history as no better or worse

1. Norman Spinrad, *The Iron Dream* (1972) N, US
2. Simon Louvish, *The Resurrections* (1994) N, UK
3. Barbara Delaplace, "Painted Bridges" (1994) SS, US
4. Stephen Fry, *Making History* (1996) N, UK
5. "California Reich" (1998) TV, US
6. "Cradle of Darkness" (2002) TV, US

7. Christian v. Ditfurth, *Der Consul* (2003) N, G
8. Robert Donald Locke, "Demotion" (1952) SS, US
9. Eberhard Jäckel, "Wenn der Anschlag gelungen wäre" (1974) AAH, G
10. Harry Turtledove, "Ready for the Fatherland" (1991) SS, US
11. Ivo Yarden, "On the Death of Hitler's Assassin" (1992) SS, O
12. Douglas Niles and Michael Dobson, *Fox on the Rhine* (2000) N, US
13. Christian v. Ditfurth, *Der 21. Juli* (2001) N, G

Total

Number of works	18	
Cold war phase: 1945–late 1950s	1	(5%)
Rediscovery phase: late 1950s–mid-1960s	0	(0%)
Crisis phase: mid-1960s–early 1980s	5	(28%)
Post-cold war phase: late 1980s–present	12	(67%)
British	2	(11%)
American	9	(50%)
German	6	(34%)
Other	1	(5%)
Novels	7	(39%)
Short stories	6	(33%)
Films	0	(0%)
Television programs	2	(11%)
Plays	0	(0%)
Comic books	0	(0%)
Analytical alternate histories	3	(17%)

CHAPTER 7: HYPOTHETICAL HOLOCAUSTS AND THE MISTRUST OF MEMORY

1. Daniel Quinn, *After Dachau* (2001) N, US
2. Jesse Bier, "Father and Son" (1964) SS, US
3. Thomas Ziegler, *Die Stimmen der Nacht* (1984) N, G
4. Christoph Ransmayr, *Morbus Kitahara* (1995) N, G
5. Thomas Ziegler, *Eine Kleinigkeit für uns Reinkarnauten* (1988) N, G
6. Martin Amis, *Time's Arrow* (1991) N, UK

Total

Number of works	6	
Cold war phase: 1945–late 1950s	0	
Rediscovery phase: late 1950s–mid-1960s	1	(17%)
Crisis phase: mid-1960s–early 1980s	1	(17%)
Post-cold war phase: late 1980s–present	4	(66%)
British	1	(17%)
American	2	(33%)
German	3	(50%)
Novels	5	(83%)
Short stories	1	(17%)
Films	0	(0%)
Television programs	0	(0%)
Plays	0	(0%)
Comic books	0	(0%)
Analytical alternate histories	0	(0%)

Final Total

Number of works	116	
Theme		
The Nazis Win World War II	63	(54%)
The Fugitive Führer	29	(25%)
The World without Hitler	18	(16%)
Hypothetical Holocausts	6	(5%)
Era		
Prewar/wartime phase: 1937–1945	10	(9%)
Cold war phase: 1945–late 1950s	8	(7%)
Rediscovery phase: late 1950s–mid-1960s	13	(12%)
Crisis phase: mid-1960s–early 1980s	38	(32%)
Post-cold war phase: late 1980s–present	47	(40%)
Nation		
British	34	(29%)
American	59	(51%)
German	18	(16%)
Other	5	(4%)
Medium		
Novels	54	(46%)
Short stories	17	(14%)
Films	8	(7%)
Television programs	11	(10%)
Plays	3	(3%)
Comic books	7	(6%)
Analytical alternate histories	16	(14%)

Index